P9-BVM-745

ENCYCLOPEDIA OF

DRUGS, ALCOHOL & ADDICTIVE BEHAVIOR

EDITORIAL BOARD

ENCYCLOPEDIA OF
DRUGS, ALCOHOL & ADDICTIVE BEHAVIOR

THIRD EDITION

Volume 4

S–Z; Index

Pamela Korsmeyer and Henry R. Kranzler

EDITORS IN CHIEF

MACMILLAN REFERENCE USA
A part of Gale, Cengage Learning

GALE
CENGAGE Learning

Detroit • New York • San Francisco • New Haven, Conn • Waterville, Maine • London

GALE
CENGAGE Learning™

Encyclopedia of Drugs, Alcohol, & Addictive Behavior, 3rd edition

Pamela Korsmeyer and Henry R. Kranzler, Editors in Chief

© 2009 Macmillan Reference USA, a part of Gale, Cengage Learning

For product information and technology assistance, contact us at
Gale Customer Support, 1-800-877-4253.
For permission to use material from this text or product,
submit all requests online at **www.cengage.com/permissions.**
Further permissions questions can be emailed to
permissionrequest@cengage.com

While every effort has been made to ensure the reliability of the information presented in this publication, Gale, a part of Cengage Learning, does not guarantee the accuracy of the data contained herein. Gale accepts no payment for listing; and inclusion in the publication of any organization, agency, institution, publication, service, or individual does not imply endorsement of the editors or publisher. Errors brought to the attention of the publisher and verified to the satisfaction of the publisher will be corrected in future editions.

Library of Congress Cataloging-in-Publication Data

Encyclopedia of drugs, alcohol & addictive behavior / Pamela Korsmeyer and Henry R. Kranzler. -- 3rd ed.
    p. cm.
    Includes bibliographical references and index.
    ISBN 978-0-02-866064-6 (set) -- ISBN 978-0-02-866065-3 (vol. 1) -- ISBN 978-0-02-866066-0 (vol. 2) -- ISBN 978-0-02-866067-7 (vol. 3) -- ISBN 978-0-02-866068-4 (vol. 4)
    1. Drug abuse--Encyclopedias. 2. Substance abuse--Encyclopedias. 3. Alcoholism--Encyclopedias. 4. Drinking of alcoholic beverages--Encyclopedias. I. Korsmeyer, Pamela, 1945- II. Kranzler, Henry R., 1950-

HV5804.E53 2009
362.2903--dc22   2008012719

Gale
27500 Drake Rd.
Farmington Hills, MI 48331-3535

ISBN-13: 978-0-02-866064-6 (set)   ISBN-10: 0-02-866064-1 (set)
ISBN-13: 978-0-02-866065-3 (vol. 1)   ISBN-10: 0-02-866065-X (vol. 1)
ISBN-13: 978-0-02-866066-0 (vol. 2)   ISBN-10: 0-02-866066-8 (vol. 2)
ISBN-13: 978-0-02-866067-7 (vol. 3)   ISBN-10: 0-02-866067-6 (vol. 3)
ISBN-13: 978-0-02-866068-4 (vol. 4)   ISBN-10: 0-02-866068-4 (vol. 4)

This title is also available as an e-book.
ISBN-13: 978-0-02-866114-8; ISBN-10: 0-02-866114-1
Contact your Gale sales representative for ordering information.

Printed in the United States of America
1 2 3 4 5 6 7 12 11 10 09 08

CONTENTS

SADD. *See* **Students Against Destructive Decisions (SADD).**

SCANDINAVIAN COUNTRIES. *See* **Nordic Countries (Denmark, Finland, Iceland, Norway, and Sweden).**

SCHIZOPHRENIA. Schizophrenia is a psychiatric illness that can be profoundly disabling and is usually chronic in nature. The cause is not known, but there appears to be a genetic predisposition. The etiology has been conceptualized in a stress/diathesis (vulnerability) model: Biological and environmental factors (e.g., drug abuse, psychosocial stresses) interact with a genetic vulnerability to precipitate the illness. Several theories have been proposed to explain the observed biological abnormalities of the disorder, including overactivity of the dopamine neurotransmitter systems in the central nervous system, changes in brain structure (e.g., enlargement of the lateral cerebral ventricles) and brain function (e.g., decreased frontal lobe function [hypofrontality], as evidenced by diminished blood flow, and deficits in attention and sensory filtering). Psychological and social factors are considered important in the expression and course of the disorder. It is likely that schizophrenia constitutes a group of disorders rather than a single entity; these disorders present with similar clinical signs and symptoms, but the etiologies, treatment responsiveness, and course of illness in each vary.

Detailed descriptions of the illness date back to the nineteenth century. Emil Kraepelin (1856–1926) used the term *dementia praecox* to describe psychiatric states with an early onset and deteriorating course. Eugen Bleuler (1857–1939) coined the term *schizophrenia* for a "splitting of the mind," in his belief that the illness was a result of the disharmony of psychological functions. The diagnosis of schizophrenia requires observation and clinical interviewing. No sign or symptom is specific for the illness, nor do any laboratory tests exist to establish the diagnosis. The *Diagnostic and Statistical Manual of Mental Disorders, fourth edition* (2000) contains the diagnostic guidelines of the American Psychiatric Association for schizophrenia. These include the presence of characteristic psychotic symptoms (delusions, hallucinations, a thought disorder, inappropriate emotion); impaired ability to work, social functioning, and self-care; and continuous signs of the illness for at least six months. The symptoms of an affected individual can change with time, therefore longitudinal follow-up is important. It should be noted that certain of these symptoms can be indicative of other conditions (including drug abuse [cocaine, crack, PCB, amphetamines], head injury, brain tumors, as well as other psychiatric disorders). Furthermore, it is important to take into account the educational level, intellectual ability, and cultural affiliation of the individual when making a diagnosis. The onset of illness is usually in late adolescence or early adulthood and is generally insidious. The typical course of schizophrenia is characterized by exacerbations and remissions. A gradual deterioration in functioning generally occurs that eventually reaches a plateau. However, a small proportion of persons may recover. It is estimated that 20 percent to 30 percent of affected individuals can lead somewhat normal lives whereas another 20 to 30 percent continue to experience moderate symptoms.

The prevalence rates of schizophrenia vary to a limited degree worldwide, but in the United States the lifetime prevalence is estimated to be between 0.5 and 1.5 percent (about one in 50 to one in 150 people). In industrialized countries, there is a disproportionate number of schizophrenic patients in the lower socioeconomic classes. Some experts think this is due to the schizophrenic's loss of education and social opportunity, while others maintain this is more a direct result of the stresses of poverty.

The management of affected individuals involves hospitalization when there is an exacerbation of the illness, plus the use of medication. The mainstay of pharmacologic treatment is the class of drugs known as antipsychotics. Many antipsychotics are available and they act to control the psychotic symptoms; most of them do so by blocking the actions of the neurotransmitter dopamine. About 75 percent of patients respond to these drugs; however, there are side effects, including muscle stiffness, tremors, and weight gain. The drugs may also cause tardive dyskinesia (TD), a disorder that causes involuntary repetitive movements of the body, mouth, and tongue.

Some of the more commonly prescribed antipsychotics include: chlorpromazine, fluphenazine, haloperidol, olanzapine, and risperidone. The atypical antipsychotic clozapine has been identified as the best choice for managing resistant schizophrenia; however, up to 73 percent of patients treated with clozapine report clinically relevant side effects. These can be quite severe, and include potentially fatal neuroleptic malignant syndrome (NMS), myocarditis, cardiomyopathy, and dangerous lowering of the white blood cell count (for the latter, regular and frequent blood testing is required during the treatment period). In a study following 8,000 patients in Australia who started clozapine treatment between January 1993 and March 1999, fifteen developed myocarditis, and eight developed cardiomyopathy; a total of six patients died within the six years.

After a person has recovered from an acute episode of schizophrenia, the emphasis is on practical aspects of management: living arrangements, self-care, employment, and social relationships. Education of and support made available to family members are important and can have an impact on relapse rates in the patient. Many schizophrenic patients have to remain on antipsychotic medication for prolonged periods, since the rate of relapse is high after drug discontinuation. Side effects, primarily of a neurologic nature (e.g., TD), are a source of concern, but in most cases the benefits of symptom control outweigh the risks of pharmacotherapy. Making sure that the patient complies with medication use is often a problem.

See also **Amphetamine; Cannabis Sativa; Complications: Mental Disorders.**

BIBLIOGRAPHY

Andreasen, N. C. (1986). Schizophrenia. In A. J. Frances & R. E. Hales (Eds.), *Psychiatry update: The American Psychiatric Association annual review* (Vol. 5). Washington, D.C.: American Psychiatric Press.

Apgar, B. (1999). Antipsychotic drugs for treatment of schizophrenia. *American Family Physician, 60,* 1220.

Berkow, R., Ed. (1997). *The Merck manual of medical information—home edition.* Whitehouse Station, NJ: Merck Research Laboratories. (2004, 2nd. Ed.)

Green, M. F. (2003). *Schizophrenia revealed: From neurons to social interactions.* New York: W. W. Norton & Company.

Karno, M., et al. (1989). Schizophrenia. In H. I. Kaplan & B. J. Sadock (Eds.). *Comprehensive textbook of psychiatry,* 5th ed. Baltimore, MD: Lippincott Williams & Wilkins. (2004, 8th ed.)

Kilian, J. G., et al. (1999). Myocarditis and cardiomyopathy associated with clozapine. *The Lancet, 354,* 1841.

Nasrallah, H. A., & Smeltzer, D. J. (2003). *Contemporary diagnosis and management of the patient with schizophrenia.* Newton, PA: Handbooks in Health Care Company.

Oldham, J. M. (1995). Schizophrenia and psychosis. In G. J. Subak-Sharpe (Ed.), *The Columbia university college of physicians & surgeons complete home medical guide,* 3rd ed. New York: Crown Publishers, Inc.

MYROSLAVA ROMACH
KAREN PARKER
REVISED BY PUBLISHER (2001)

SCOPOLAMINE AND ATROPINE.

Scopolamine (*d*-hyoscine) and atropine (*dl*-hyoscyamine) is a tropane alkaloid found in the leaves and seeds of several plant species of the family Solanaceae, including deadly nightshade (*Atropa belladonna*) and henbane (*Hyoscyamus niger*). Atropine, a major alkaloid in deadly nightshade, is also found in jimsonweed (*Datura stramonium*). In Europe, in centuries past, henbane was a component of socalled witches' brews or was applied as an ointment to mucous membranes. According to some folk tales, the idea that witches fly on broomsticks was derived from the sensation of a flying experience after the use of such ointments.

Scopolamine and atropine have very similar actions. They act as competitive antagonists at both peripheral and central muscarinic cholinergic receptors. Scopolamine is still sometimes used clinically for the treatment of motion sickness. The compound also causes central nervous system depression, leading to drowsiness, amnesia, and fatigue. It also has some euphoric effects and abuse liability, but these are not considered to be of such magnitude to require control of the drug under the Controlled Substances Act. Atropine has fewer actions on the central nervous system than scopolamine. It is used to reduce actions at peripheral cholinergic structures—it produces decreased gastric and intestinal secretions as well as spasms and also results in pupillary dilation. It blocks the action of the vagus nerve that results in slowing of the heart. It is often used before operations to prevent unwanted reflex slowing of the heartbeat.

High doses of either of these tropane alkaloids can cause confusion and delirium accompanied by decreased sweating, dry mouth, and dilated pupils.

See also **Alkaloids; Jimsonweed.**

BIBLIOGRAPHY

Brown, J. H., & Taylor, P. (1996). Muscarinic receptor agonists and antagonists. In A. G. Gilman et al. (Eds.), *The pharmacological basis of therapeutics*, 9th ed. New York: McGraw-Hill Medical. (2005, 11th ed.)

Hesse, M. (2002). *Alkaloids.* Weinheim, Germany: Wiley-VCH.

Houghton, P. J., & Bisset, N. G. (1985). Drugs of ethno-origin. In D. C. Howell (Ed.), *Drugs in central nervous system disorders.* New York: Marcel Dekker.

ROBERT ZACZEK

SECOBARBITAL.

Secobarbital, prescribed and sold as Seconal, is a short-acting barbiturate used principally as a sedative-hypnotic drug but occasionally as a preanesthetic agent. It is a nonspecific central nervous system (CNS) depressant and greatly impairs the mental and/or physical abilities necessary for the safe operation of automobiles and complex machinery.

Before the introduction of the benzodiazepines, secobarbital was the drug most commonly used to treat insomnia. Prolonged or inappropriate use of secobarbital can produce tolerance and physical dependence. If high doses have been used, abrupt cessation can result in severe withdrawal symptoms that include convulsions. Secobarbital is more likely to be abused than benzodiazepines and appears to produce greater euphoria in certain individuals than would a comparable sedative dose of a benzodiazepine. Consequently, it is classified as a Schedule II class drug in the Controlled Substances Act, which indicates that although it is acceptable for clinical use, it is considered to have a high abuse potential. As with other barbiturates, secobarbital should never be combined with another CNS depressant because respiratory depression can occur.

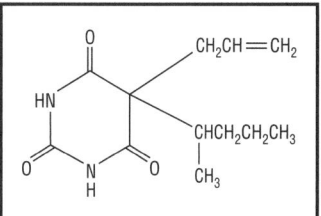

Figure 1. Chemical structure of secobarbital. ILLUSTRATION BY GGS INFORMATION SERVICES. GALE, CENGAGE LEARNING

See also **Abuse Liability of Drugs: Testing in Humans; Drug Interaction and the Brain; Drug Interactions and Alcohol.**

BIBLIOGRAPHY

Hobbs, W. R., Rall, T. W., & Verdoorn, T. A. (1996). Hypnotics and sedatives. In A. G. Gilman et al. (Eds.), *The pharmacological basis of therapeutics*, 9th ed. (361–396). New York: McGraw-Hill Medical. (2005, 11th ed.

Karch, S. B. (2006). *Drug abuse handbook*, 2nd ed. Boca Raton, FL: CRC Press.

SCOTT E. LUKAS

SECULAR ORGANIZATIONS FOR SOBRIETY (SOS).

Secular Organizations for Sobriety is a self-help organization for alcohol and drug users, founded as an alternative to Alcoholics Anonymous (AA) and other groups based on AA. It was intended to offer help to people who are uncomfortable with the emphasis on spirituality that is a central tenet of the AA Twelve-Step Programs. Founded by James Christopher, SOS began with a 1985 article. "Sobriety without Superstition," describing Christopher's own path to sobriety. SOS claimed in 1991 to have an international membership of 20,000, making it the largest of the alternative groups. In 1987, it was recognized by the State of California as an alternative to AA in sentencing offenders to mandatory participation in drug rehabilitation. Members of SOS are not necessarily nonreligious; however, many do not believe in an intervening higher power who takes responsibility for their individual problems.

Unlike AA—which emphasizes that the individual is powerless over alcoholism and must look to a "higher power" for help in achieving and maintaining sobriety—SOS and other alternative organizations assert the capacity of individuals to control their own behavior. SOS stresses total abstinence, personal responsibility, and self-reliance as the means to achieve and maintain sobriety (recovery), but the organization recognizes the importance of participating in a mutually supportive group as an adjunct to recovery. Members learn that open and honest communication aids in making the appropriate life choices that are essential to recovery. SOS shares with other self-help groups the importance of anonymity and the abstention from all drugs and alcohol.

SOS consists of a nonprofit network of autonomous nonprofessional local groups dedicated solely to helping individuals with alcohol and other drug addictions. It encourages and is supportive of continued scientific inquiry into the understanding of alcoholism and drug addiction.

Among other self-help organizations that see themselves as alternatives to AA are Rational Recovery (RR) and Women for Sobriety (WFS).

See also **Coerced Treatment for Substance Offenders; Models of Alcoholism and Drug Abuse; Treatment: An Overview; Treatment: An Overview of Alcohol Abuse/Dependence; Treatment: An Overview of Drug Abuse/Dependence.**

BIBLIOGRAPHY

Humphreys, K. (2004). Self-help organizations for alcohol and drug problems: Toward evidence-based practice and policy. *Journal of Substance Abuse Treatment, 26,* 3, 151–158.

Secular Organizations for Sobriety (SOS). Available from http://www. secularsobriety.org.

JEROME H. JAFFE

SEDATIVE.

Sedative is a general term used to describe a number of drugs that decrease activity, moderate excitement, and have a calming effect. The primary use for these drugs is to reduce anxiety, but higher doses will usually cause sleep (a drug used primarily to cause sleep is called a *hypnotic*). Although the term *sedative* is still used, the drugs usually prescribed to produce this calming effect are benzodiazepines, which are more commonly known as antianxiety agents or minor tranquilizers.

See also **Barbiturates; Drug Types; Sedative-Hypnotic.**

BIBLIOGRAPHY

Hobbs, W. R., Rall, T. W., & Verdoorn, T. A. (1996). Hypnotics and sedatives. In A. G. Gilman et al. (Eds.), *The pharmacological basis of therapeutics*, 9th ed. (361–396). New York: McGraw-Hill Medical. (2005, 11th ed.)

Meyer, J. S., &amp: Quenzer, L. F. (2004). *Psychopharmacology: Drugs, the brain and behavior.* Sunderland, MA: Sinauer Associates.

SCOTT E. LUKAS

SEDATIVE-HYPNOTIC.

Sedative-hypnotic drugs are used to reduce motor activity and promote relaxation, drowsiness, and sleep. The term is hyphenated because by adjusting the dose, the same group of drugs can be used to produce mild sedation (calming, relaxation) or sleepiness. Thus the distinction between a sedative and a hypnotic (sleeping pill) is often a matter of dose—lower doses act as sedatives and higher doses promote sleep.

In some people, sedative-hypnotics can produce a paradoxical state of excitement and confusion. This response tends to occur more frequently in the very young and older populations. Some of these drugs have the potential to be abused. Very high doses of most sedative-hypnotic drugs will produce general anesthesia and can depress respiration so much that breathing must be maintained artificially or death will occur. The benzodiazepines are an exception to this general rule in that higher doses typically produce sleep and are far less likely to severely depress respiration.

One of the first agents to be added to the list of the classic sedatives (alcohol and opiates) was bromide, introduced in 1857 as a treatment for epilepsy. Chloral hydrate was introduced in 1869 and paraldehyde was first used in 1882. The barbiturates were introduced in the early 1900s and remained the dominant drugs for inducing sleep and sedation until the bezodiazepines were developed in the late 1950s and early 1960s. A number of miscellaneous non-barbiturate sedatives (ethchlorvynol, glutethimide, carbromal, methylparafynol, methyprylon, methaqualone) were introduced in the 1940s and 1950s, and for a brief period rivaled the barbiturates in popularity, but their used declined rapidly along with the use of barbiturates. The bromides were recognized to have toxic properties, but they were still in use until the mid-twentieth century; chloral hydrate and paraldehyde were used well into the late 1970s and are still used in some places. Some drugs with other medical uses are prescribed as hypnotics, but the effectiveness of these substances remains to be proven in well-controlled clinical trials.

An advance in the development of sedative-hypnotics occurred with the discovery of non-benzodiazepine drugs that also act on the bensodiazepine receptor. Zolpidem and zaleplon are short-acting hypnotics that demonstrate fewer side-effects and less tendency for rebound insomnia when they are discontinued, a common problem with the benzodiazepines. These drugs also demonstrate less abuse potential than many of the other sedative-hypnotics and little respiratory depression.

See also **Abuse Liability of Drugs: Testing in Humans; Drug Interactions and Alcohol; Drug Types; Suicide and Substance Abuse.**

BIBLIOGRAPHY

Hobbs, W. R., Rall, T. W., & Verdoorn, T. A. (1996). Hypnotics and sedatives. In A. G. Gilman et al. (Eds.), *The pharmacological basis of therapeutics*, 9th ed. (361–396). New York: McGraw-Hill Medical. (2005, 11th ed.)

Katzung, B. G. (2006). *Basic & clinical pharmacology.* New York: McGraw-Hill Medical.

Nemeroff, C. B. & Schatsberg, A. F. (Eds.) (1998). *The American psychiatric press textbook of psychopharmacology.* Washington, D.C.: American Psychiatric Press.

Parker, J. N., & Parker, P. M. (2002). *The official patient' sourcebook on prescription CNS depressants dependence.* Boulder, CO: NetLibrary.

SCOTT E. LUKAS
REVISED BY NICHOLAS DEMARTINIS (2001)

SEDATIVES: ADVERSE CONSEQUENCES OF CHRONIC USE.

Sedative drugs are also called hypnotics or sedative-hypnotics. They are sometimes referred to as minor tranquilizers or anxiolytics (antianxiety medications). Technically, a *sedative* decreases activity and has a calming effect whereas a *hypnotic* produces drowsiness, allowing for the onset and maintenance of sleep. Ideally, a hypnotic produces a state of sleep similar to natural sleep and from which the sleeper may be easily awakened. The same drug used for sedation, pharmacologically induced sleep, and general systemic anesthesia may be seen to induce a continuum of central nervous system (CNS) depression. Such drugs are usually referred to, therefore, as sedative-hypnotics, and they are widely prescribed in the treatment of insomnia (sleep problems). Although some people take these drugs only occasionally and for specific sleep problems (e.g., secondary to grief, time-limited stress, long-distance flights), many more take them over prolonged periods (months, and even years) as a presumed aid to nightly sleep. They do this despite medical advice that restricts the use of such drugs to approximately two weeks.

All the sedatives are available in tablets or capsules for oral dosage, and some are also available for intravenous or intramuscular administration.

Almost all sedatives have the same behavioral effects as alcohol (ethanol). Many individuals who abuse sedatives, are, or have been, problem drinkers. According to guidelines published by the American Psychiatric Association (1990), patients with a history of alcoholism or other drug abuse problems should not be treated with benzodiazepine sedatives on a chronic basis because they are at a high risk of developing benzodiazepine abuse. This, however, remains a controversial issue (Ciraulo & Nace, 2000).

USE OF HYPNOTICS

Sleep problems in adults are of three main types:

1. Problems of falling asleep (sleep initiation);
2. Problems staying asleep (sleep maintenance);
3. Early-morning wakening.

Sleep-onset problems vary little with age; early-morning wakening is often secondary to depression, and sleep-maintenance problems show a clear and marked increase with aging. Whereas approximately 10 percent of young adults complain of serious sleep problems, this increases to 30 to 50 percent of those aged 70 or older (Morgan, 1990). This age-related pattern for complaints of insomnia is reflected in the pattern of use of sedative-hypnotic drugs. The results of one survey indicate that 4 percent of people older than 65 used a hypnotic agent continuously for more than a decade (Morgan et al., 1988). According to a 2002 poll conducted by the National Sleep Foundation, 15 percent of the subjects polled reported using a sleep aid (either prescription or over-the-counter) at least a few nights per month. Across all age groups, roughly twice as many women as men take sedative-hypnotic drugs.

COMMONLY USED HYPNOTICS

The most commonly prescribed hypnotics include the benzodiazepines temazepam (Restoril) and triazolam (Halcion). Some sedative benzodiazepines are also used to induce sleep including alprazolam (Xanax), lorazepam (Ativan), and diazepam (Valium). Newer agents include the non-benzodiazepines zolpidem (Ambien), zaleplon (Sonata), and eszopiclone (Lunesta). Although these drugs differ chemically from the benzodiazepines, their mode of action is similar in that they target the same receptors in the brain. The newest sedative, ramelteon (Rozerem), is a melatonin agonist. It differs both chemically and pharmacologically from the benzodiazepines. Other, older hypnotics are chloral hydrate (Noctec), a chloral derivative, and hydroxyzine (Vistaril), an antihistamine.

BENZODIAZEPINES

Although the use of benzodiazepines as sedative-hypnotic drugs is decreasing in favor of newer agents, they are still prescribed with great frequency. The key concerns in the use of the benzodiazepines as a hypnotic are:

1. Adverse effects experienced while the patient is taking the drug;
2. Possible physical and psychological dependence;
3. Rebound insomnia and withdrawal symptoms when the patient stops taking the drug.

Classification. Benzodiazepines can be classified on pharmacokinetic grounds into three groups: long-acting (e.g., flurazepam [Dalmane], diazepam, chlordiazepoxide [Librium]), medium-acting (temazepam), and short-acting (triazolam, oxazepam [Serax], lorazepam) sedative-hypnotics. Their efficacy, at least in short-term use, has been well documented. The pattern of improvement in sleep corresponds fairly closely with the pharmacokinetic properties of each drug, providing that factors of absorption and elimination are taken into account. For example, temazepam is absorbed relatively slowly and has little effect on sleep-initiation time whereas triazolam is absorbed relatively rapidly, which brings sleep on more quickly.

Each sedative-hypnotic has a minimally effective dose but the dose that is usually effective may be twice as high as the minimum. Further increases may, however, cause side effects and rebound insomnia without substantially improving sleep. In sleep-laboratory studies many benzodiazepines lose their efficacy after about two weeks of nightly use. Subjectively, however, patients often feel that their sleep is improved for longer periods than this.

Adverse Effects. Benzodiazepine sedatives have three major adverse effects:

1. Cumulative effects with repeated dosage, particularly if the patient has not yet metabolized the previous dose;

2. Additive effects when given with other classes of sedatives or with alcohol;

3. Residual effects after the medication is discontinued.

Patients taking benzodiazepines may feel drowsy, have reduced psychomotor speed, and impaired concentration. These in turn can adversely affect their ability to function, so they should be cautioned about driving and operating machinery while taking these drugs. The longer-acting the drug, the more pronounced these effects. Tolerance to these sedative effects builds up to some extent with repeated use of the drug.

All benzodiazepines can impair the user's ability to learn and remember new information. This memory impairment is most pronounced a few hours after taking the drug, so when taken as a sleep aid such effects may be much reduced by the time the person wakes the next morning. As with other adverse effects, higher doses cause greater problems. Rarer adverse effects include disinhibition and aggressive behavior. These effects have been reported for some benzodiazepines (e.g., triazolam, flunitrazepam [Rohypnol, not marketed in the United States]) more than others.

Rebound insomnia refers to the heightened insomnia that may occur when the patient stops taking the drug, such that the sleep pattern is actually worse than it was before the medication. Studies have established that rebound insomnia is generally at its worst following the use of shorter-acting benzodiazepines and at its least following the use of longer-acting benzodiazepines (Roehrs et al., 1986). Rebound is clearly dose-related, and the patient should be prescribed the lowest effective dose, with rebound effects described to warn the patient about overdosing for faster or better drug-induced sleep.

Age-related changes in the way that drugs are metabolized and excreted mean that benzodiazepines accumulate more in older patients and, therefore, adverse effects are more pronounced in the elderly, who are particularly susceptible to the effects of these drugs on their psychomotor performance (e.g., balance and gait). Consequently, older patients taking benzodiazepine sedatives are especially at risk of falls resulting in hip or femur fractures and are at an increased risk of being involved in a motor vehicle accident. In elderly patients with cognitive deterioration or dementia, use of a benzodiazepine may intensify these symptoms.

Abuse, Dependence, and Withdrawal. Some argue that rebound insomnia is itself a sign of physiological dependence on benzodiazepine hypnotics (e.g., Morgan, 1990). Others insist that dependence is shown only when withdrawal from a drug leads to symptoms other than a rebound of the original problems. In general, psychological dependence on benzodiazepines can develop rather rapidly. After only a few weeks, patients who attempt to discontinue the medication may experience restlessness, disturbing dreams, paranoid ideas and delusions, and feelings of tension or anxiety in the early morning. Withdrawal following the use of a moderate dose of a benzodiazepine may include dizziness, increased sensitivity to light and sound, and muscle cramps. Abrupt withdrawal following high-dose usage may result in seizures and delirium.

The syndrome of withdrawal from benzodiazepines may be slow in onset because these drugs remain in the body for relatively long periods. Withdrawal appears to be most severe in patients who used benzodiazepines that are absorbed rapidly and have a rapid decline in blood serum levels (e.g., alprazolam, lorazepam, and triazolam). In patients who abuse both benzodiazepines and alcohol, a delayed benzodiazepine withdrawal syndrome may complicate withdrawal from alcohol. Patients who are high-dose abusers of benzodiazepines usually require inpatient detoxification.

Abuse. Animal studies indicate that benzodiazepines, like cocaine and opioids, activate a reward pathway in the brains of most mammals. In humans the benzodiazepines have reinforcing effects that appear to be more pronounced in frequent users of other recreational drugs. For example, alcoholics and heroin addicts will at times use benzodiazepines to extend the supply of their most-preferred drug because alcohol and heroin are also depressants.

Abuse of benzodiazepines by themselves is relatively unusual but sometimes occurs among users who seek a high from massive amounts of these drugs. Street drug dealers sell benzodiazepines at a relatively low cost in most major cities. Some abusers combine benzodiazepines with other drugs to enhance the effects; for example, some believe that taking diazepam half an hour after an oral dose of methadone will produce a high that is more intense than can be obtained from taking either drug by itself.

Overdose. Benzodiazepine overdose is a serious though rarely fatal event unless accompanied by the concomitant ingestion of alcohol or other CNS depressants. Symptoms of benzodiazepine overdose include sleepiness, incoordination, and diminished mental facilities. In more serious cases, low blood pressure, respiratory depression, and coma can occur. In a conscious patient, treatment usually begins with the inducement of emesis (vomiting). In an unconscious patient, the contents of the stomach are removed by gastric lavage (stomach pumping). In addition to supportive care, a benzodiazepine antagonist, flumazenil (Romazicon) can be used to improve the level of consciousness.

NON-BENZODIAZEPINE HYPNOTICS

Newer compounds include such non-benzodiazepine hypnotics as eszopiclone (Lunesta), zolpidem (Ambien), and zaleplon (Sonata), which act either atypically or selectively on benzodiazepine receptors. They are also known as benzodiazepine receptor agonists though they are chemically distinct from benzodiazepines (and from each other). They are short-acting drugs and at normal clinical doses cause little residual sedation (hangover). The risk of rebound insomnia or dependence with these compounds is much lower than with benzodiazepines, but not absent (Lader, 1992). Memory problems have been reported with these agents. A phenomenon called *sleep driving* in which an individual operates a motor vehicle without memory of the event has been associated with zolpidem. Retrograde amnesia, a condition in which the patient cannot recall events immediately prior to taking the drug, has been reported in patients who have taken zalepon.

OTHER SEDATIVE/HYPNOTIC DRUGS

Barbiturates. Barbiturates were used until the 1950s as sleeping pills but were superseded by the benzodiazepines. With the exception of phenobarbital (Luminal), which is still used as a sedative and as an anticonvulsant, the barbiturates are rarely prescribed.

Chloral Derivatives. These compounds, which include chloral hydrate, are sometimes used with elderly patients because they are less likely to cause restlessness in confused or demented patients. Chloral derivatives are also relatively safe to give to children for sedation before or after surgery. They can, however, cause gastric irritation and rashes.

Antihistamines. Antihistamines, commonly used for the treatment of allergies, often cause drowsiness, leading to their use as sedatives. Diphenhydramine (Benadryl, Nytol, Sominex) and hydroxyzine (Atarax, Vistaril) are two antihistamines often prescribed for patients who need only a mild sedative. They are safe and do not produce dependency. They should not, however, be used together with alcohol. The most common side effect of these medications is dry mouth.

Buspirone. Buspirone (BuSpar) is the only anti-anxiety medication that is not a sedative. Because it does not produce depressant effects or dependence, it is used in the treatment of depression as well as anxiety. Unlike the sedatives, buspirone does not affect the patient's alertness or motor skills, it does not intensify the effects of alcohol, and it does not produce a withdrawal syndrome. Because it has no potential to be abused or to produce dependence in patients with a history of drug or alcohol dependence, buspirone may be the anxiolytic of choice for these patients.

Melatonin Agonists. Melatonin is a natural sleep-inducing hormone produced by the pineal gland in the brain. Natural melatonin has been used to induce sleep. Ramelteon, a prescription drug that works on melatonin receptors in the brain, is the most recently approved sedative and is believed to lack the potential to cause dependence or abuse.

See also **Accidents and Injuries from Drugs; Addiction: Concepts and Definitions; Aging, Drugs, and Alcohol; Barbiturates; Barbiturates: Complications; Benzodiazepines: Complications; Drug Interaction and the Brain; Drug Interactions and Alcohol; Memory, Effects of Drugs on.**

BIBLIOGRAPHY

American Psychiatric Association. (1990). *Benzodiazepine dependence, toxicity, and abuse: A task force report of the American Psychiatric Association.* Arlington, VA: American Psychiatric Publishing.

Beers, M. H., & Berkow, R. (Eds.). (1999). *The Merck manual of diagnosis and therapy* (17th ed.). Whitehouse Station, NJ: Merck Research Laboratories.

Ciraulo, D. A., & Nace, E. P. (2000). Benzodiazepine treatment of anxiety or insomnia in substance abuse patients. *American Journal on Addictions, 9,* 276–279; discussion 280–284.

Eisendrath, S. J. (1998). Psychiatric disorders. In L. M. Tierney et al. (Eds.), *Current Medical Diagnosis & Treatment* (37th ed.). Stamford, CT: Appleton & Lange.

Hardman, J. G., & Limbird, L. E. (Eds.) (1996). *Goodman and Gilman's: The pharmacological basis of therapeutics* (9th ed.). New York: McGraw-Hill.

Lader, M. H. (1992). Rebound insomnia and newer hypnotics. *Psychopharmacology, 108,* 248–252.

Leary, A., & MacDonald, T. (2000). *Interactions between alcohol and drugs.* Edinburgh, UK: Royal College of Physicians of Edinburgh.

Lieberman, J. A. (2007). Update on the safety considerations in the management of insomnia with hypnotics: Incorporating modified-release formulations into primary care. *Primary Care Companion Journal of Clinical Psychiatry, 9,* 25–31.

Longo, L. P., & Johnson, B. (2000). Addiction: Part I. benzodiazepines—side effects, abuse risk and alternatives. *American Family Physician, 61,* 2121–2128.

McEvoy, G. K. (Ed.) (2003). *American Hospital Formulary Service (AHFS) drug information.* Bethesda, MD: American Society of Health-System Pharmacists.

Medical Economics Company. (1999). *Physicians' desk reference,* (*PDR*) (53rd ed.). Montvale, NJ: PDR Staff.

Mellinger, G. D., Balter, M. B., & Uhlenhuth, E. H. (1985). Insomnia and its treatment. *Archives of General Psychiatry, 42,* 225–232.

Morgan, K. (1990). Hypnotics in the elderly: What cause for concern? *Drugs, 10,* 688–696.

Morgan, K., Dallosso, H., Ebrahim, S., Arie, T., & Fentem, P. H. (1988). Prevalence, frequency and duration of hypnotic drug use among the elderly living at home. *British Medical Journal, 296,* 601–602.

Oswald, I. (1983). Benzodiazepines and sleep. In M. R. Trimble, (Ed.), *Benzodiazepines divided: A multidisciplinary review.* New York: John Wiley.

Roehrs, T. A., Zorick, F. J., Wittig, R. M., & Roth, T. (1986). Dose-determinants of rebound insomnia. *British Journal of Clinical Pharmacology, 22,* 143–s147.

Wilson, B. A., Shannon, M. T., & Stang, C. L. (Eds.) (1995). *Nurses drug guide* (3rd ed.). Norwalk, CT: Appleton & Lange.

VALERIE CURRAN
REVISED BY REBECCA J. FREY (2001)
LEAH R. ZINDEL (2009)

SEIZURES OF DRUGS.

The seizure of drugs in the United States is a salient consequence of a variety of enforcement programs, particularly interdiction programs. These seizures provide evidence that the U.S. criminal justice system is imposing a cost on individuals involved in drug distribution. A large seizure, in particular, offers the most vivid evidence that those at the upper echelon of the illicit drug trade are subject to serious risks.

Seizures from smugglers have often been used as a measure of the effectiveness of interdiction efforts. One argument suggests that the larger the quantity of drugs seized, the more smugglers have been hurt by interdiction. Others view seizures as an indicator of the quantity smuggled. This view assumes that the percentage of imports seized is effectively a constant. These are clearly extreme assumptions. In fact, the quantity seized is a function of at least three factors: (1) the quantity shipped, (2) the relative skill of the interdictors, and (3) the care taken by smugglers. The last element—which is generally given the least attention in discussions of seizures—probably depends on the replacement cost of the drugs. In other words, if that cost goes down (e.g., because of good growing conditions in the producer country), smugglers will invest less in the concealment and protection of shipments. As a result the seizure rate (i.e., the percentage of shipments seized) is likely to rise.

Seizures of cocaine rose throughout the 1980s, reflecting both the rapid increase in total shipments and the declining replacement cost of the drug. Between 1989 and 2003, annual federal cocaine seizures fluctuated around 250,000 pounds and only exceeded 300,000 pounds twice (1992 and 1994). In 2004 and 2005, federal seizures for cocaine exceeded 380,000 pounds each year, and they remained above 330,000 pounds in 2006. Marijuana seizures grew dramatically during the same period. Federal authorities seized about 1.1 million pounds in 1989, and by 2006 this figure had exceeded 2.5 million pounds. This was largely a result of increased cultivation and production of marijuana within the United States itself. Between 1989 and 1999, federal heroin seizures ranged between 1,700 and 3,500 pounds with no clear trend. There was a large jump in 2000 and in 2002 over 6,000 pounds of heroin were seized by federal officials. Federal heroin seizures declined from 2002 to 2005, and there was a slight increase in 2006 to more than 3,900 pounds.

Methamphetamine seizures nearly doubled between 2002 and 2006, increasing from 5,500 pounds to over 10,000 in that time. Mexico is the main source of methamphetamine for the U.S. market, and many of these seizures occurred on the Southwest border. MDMA ("Ecstasy") seizures increased dramatically in the 1990s, with the Drug Enforcement Administration reporting that it seized less than 200 tablets in 1993 and more than 3 million tablets in 2000. This estimate is probably low, however, because the DEA is not the only federal agency that seizes drugs (the Federal Bureau of Investigation and U.S. Coast Guard also do so, for example).

Drugs are also seized by state and local enforcement agencies, but estimates are difficult to calculate at these levels. The growth of domestically grown marijuana has placed state and local police closer to the criminal activity. The number of domestic cannabis plants seized more than doubled between 2000 and 2007—from 2.8 million plants to 7 million plants, respectively. In addition, the proliferation of domestic methamphetamine labs made such facilities targets for federal, state, and local law enforcement agencies. Lab seizures increased from 6,777 in 1999 to over 10,000 in 2003, but they decreased dramatically between 2005 and 2007 (5,935 labs were seized in 2005; 4,002 were seized in 2006; and only 1,802 labs were seized from January to October 2007).

See also **Cocaine; Drug Interdiction; Heroin; International Drug Supply Systems; Marijuana (Cannabis); MDMA; Methamphetamine; Operation Intercept; U.S. Government: Agencies in Drug Law Enforcement and Supply Control; U.S Government Agencies: U.S. Customs and Border Protection (CBP).**

BIBLIOGRAPHY

Godshaw, J., Koppel, R., & Pancoast, R. (1987). *Anti-drug law enforcement efforts and their impact.* Bala Cynwyd, PA: Wharton Econometrics.

Maguire, K., Pastore, A. L., et al. (Eds.) (2005). *Sourcebook of criminal justice statistics 2003.* Washington, DC: U.S. Government Printing Office.

National Drug Intelligence Center (2005). *National Drug Threat Assessment 2005.* Washington, DC: U.S. Department of Justice.

National Drug Intelligence Center (2007). *National Drug Threat Assessment 2008.* Washington, DC: U.S. Department of Justice.

U.S. Drug Enforcement Administration (2008). Domestic Cannabis Eradication/Suppression Program. Available from http://www.usdoj.gov/.

U.S. Drug Enforcement Administration (2008). Stats & Facts: DEA drug seizures. Available from http://www.usdoj.gov/.

White House Office of National Drug Control Policy. (2000). *National drug control strategy: 2000 annual report.* Washington, DC: U.S. Government Printing Office.

White House Office of National Drug Control Policy. (2002). ONDCP fact sheet: MDMA (ecstasy). Washington, DC: U.S. Government Printing Office. Available from http://www.crsassociates.com/.

PETER REUTER
REVISED BY FREDERICK K. GRITTNER (2001)
BEAU KILMER (2009)

SELF MANAGEMENT AND RECOVERY TRAINING. *See* **SMART Recovery and Rational Recovery.**

SEMI-STRUCTURED ASSESSMENT FOR DRUG DEPENDENCE AND ALCOHOLISM (SSADDA).

The Semi-Structured Assessment for Drug Dependence and Alcoholism (SSADDA) is a diagnostic instrument that was developed for studies of the genetics of substance use and psychiatric disorders. The SSADDA was based on the Semi-Structured Assessment for the Genetics of Alcoholism (SSAGA), a comprehensive psychiatric interview schedule developed for use in the Collaborative Study on the Genetics of Alcoholism (Bucholz et al., 1994).

The SSADDA was developed to provide detailed coverage of drug dependence and other DSM-IV diagnoses (American Psychiatric Association, 1994) that commonly co-occur with these disorders. It is available in a computer-assisted format that allows the interviewer to enter subjects' responses directly. The computerized format includes such features as automatic "skip-outs," a cross-checking function to identify inconsistent responses, a running tabulation of diagnostic criteria, and a check for out-of-range values. These features streamline the interview process and aid in the collection of accurate information. The computerized SSADDA also permits direct uploading of data to a database. This eliminates the time-consuming steps of data entry and verification (with their potential for errors) and permits the ready generation of DSM-IV diagnoses using scoring algorithms.

The SSADDA allows a trained (non-clinician) interviewer to identify a variety of substance use and psychiatric disorders by collecting information about the onset of symptoms and about their severity and duration. The interview includes detailed questions about the onset of symptoms for the major drugs of abuse, including cocaine and opioids. In addition, the SSADDA contains sections covering attention deficit hyperactivity disorder and pathological gambling, which are theoretically and clinically relevant to substance dependence. Finally, the SSADDA includes a section on environmental factors, including adverse childhood experiences, which are considered likely to have an impact on the risk of drug and alcohol dependence.

A useful feature of the SSADDA that was retained from the SSAGA is the assessment of the relationship between alcohol and drug dependence clusters and the occurrence of other psychiatric disorders (Bucholz et al., 1994). The dates of occurrence of alcohol and drug use, clustering of problems, periods of abstinence from alcohol and drug use, and dates of psychiatric disorders are correlated. This makes it possible to categorize the respondent's history of psychiatric disorders as being either completely independent of substance problems or including at least some symptoms occurring in temporal association with substance use.

The SSADDA has been shown to yield reliable diagnoses for alcohol and drug dependence disorders, as well as a variety of psychiatric disorders (Pierucci-Lagha et al., 2005). The reliability for individual diagnostic items was also generally good, with minimal impact of any individual criterion on diagnostic reliability(Pierucci-Lagha et al., 2007). This is consistent with the idea that the DSM-IV diagnosis of substance dependence measures an underlying construct that is relatively consistent across specific substance categories. Although the SSADDA was developed for use in genetic studies,

its broad and detailed coverage of disorders and its computer-assisted format allow it to be used in a variety of applications requiring careful diagnostic assessment.

See also **Diagnostic and Statistical Manual (DSM); Semi-Structured Assessment for the Genetics of Alcoholism (SSAGA); Structured Clinical Interview for DSM-IV (SCID).**

BIBLIOGRAPHY

American Psychiatric Association. (1994). Diagnostic and statistical manual of mental disorders (4th ed.). Washington, DC: Author.

Bucholz, K. K., Cadoret, R., Cloninger, C. R., Dinwiddie, S. H., Hesselbrock, V. M., Nurnberger, J. I., Jr., et al. (1994). A new, semi-structured psychiatric interview for use in genetic linkage studies: A report on the reliability of the SSAGA. *Journal of Studies on Alcohol, 55,* 149–158.

Pierucci-Lagha, A., Gelernter, J., Chan, G., Arias, A., Cubells, J. F., Farrer, L., et al. (2007). Reliability of DSM-IV diagnostic criteria using the Semi-Structured Assessment for Drug Dependence and Alcoholism (SSADDA). *Drug and Alcohol Dependence, 91,* 85–90.

Pierucci-Lagha, A., Gelernter, J., Feinn, R., Cubells, J., Pearson, D., Farrer, L., et al. (2005). Diagnostic reliability of the Semi-Structured Assessment for Drug Dependence and Alcoholism (SSADDA). *Drug and Alcohol Dependence, 80,* 303–312.

HENRY R. KRANZLER

SEMI-STRUCTURED ASSESSMENT FOR THE GENETICS OF ALCO-HOLISM (SSAGA). The Semi-Structured Assessment for the Genetics of Alcoholism (SSAGA) is a research diagnostic interview designed to obtain a detailed psychiatric history of current and past mental health problems among adults, ages 18 and older (Bucholz et al., 1994). Developed by the Collaborative Study on the Genetics of Alcoholism (COGA) for use in its large-scale, multisite extended family study of the genetics of alcohol dependence, this research diagnostic interview covers the major Axis I psychiatric disorders defined in the American Psychiatric Association's *Diagnostic and Statistical Manual of Mental Disorders,* third edition, revised (DSM-III-R) and fourth edition (DSM-IV). The SSAGA also covers antisocial personality disorder (ASPD). Psychiatric diagnoses for many of the disorders covered can also be made using the Feighner,

DSM-III-R, and ICD-10 criteria sets. Special attention has been given to assessing comorbid psychiatric conditions, identifying the ages of onset and recency of different diagnoses, and distinguishing symptoms due to alcohol and drug use from symptoms typically seen in affective disorders or antisocial personality disorder.

In addition to the different diagnoses covered, the SSAGA contains sections that assess demographics, medical history, suicidality, and the home environment in which the person was raised. The SSAGA-II is an excellent instrument for assessing current and past psychiatric problems in clinical samples as well as in samples from the general population. Designed for use by lay interviewers, the SSAGA has been used in more than 200 studies in the United States and abroad and has been translated into nine foreign languages.

The Alcohol section of the SSAGA is comprehensive and was designed to assess alcohol use and the physical, psychological, social, and psychiatric manifestations of acute and chronic alcohol use in adults. The SSAGA differs from many other research diagnostic interviews in that it includes an assessment of alcohol abuse and dependence, the alcohol dependence syndrome, the alcohol withdrawal syndrome, the flushing response, periods of abstinence, and treatment history. This section also includes questions that are not used in diagnostic schemes but may be useful for characterizing alcohol use and problems (i.e., developing alcohol-related phenotypes that may be useful in studies of the genetics of alcoholism).

Considerable care has been taken to establish the reliability and validity of the SSAGA, which been shown to have good intra- and interrater reliability among raters from the COGA project trained to use it (Bucholz et al., 1994). A second study documented the reliability of the individual criterion items for psychoactive substance dependence and their impact on diagnosis (Bucholz et al., 1995). A third study compared the diagnoses of subjects interviewed twice: once by the SSAGA and again by the Schedule for Clinical Assessment in Neuropsychiatry (SCAN). The findings from the two interviews were highly similar, which supports the validity of the SSAGA (Hesselbrock et al., 1999).

The SSAGA is part of a suite of interviews developed by COGA for use in family studies. In addition to the SSAGA, COGA also developed companion instruments to assess children ages 6–12 (C-SSAGA-C),

adolescents ages 13–17 (C-SSAGA-A), and parents regarding their children's mental health status (C-SSAGA-P). The reliability of the adolescent interview, the C-SSAGA-A was examined and confirmed by Kuperman et al. (2001). A separate Family History Assessment Module (FHAM; Rice et al., 1995) was designed to obtain psychiatric history information on unavailable or deceased family members. The FHAM first screens "classes" of relatives of family members for a history of mental health problems using the family history/family story method. Individuals who are suspected of having a history of mental health problems can then be queried using the Individual Assessment Module. Family history diagnoses can be made using *DSM-III-R* or *DSM-IV*.

See also **Diagnostic and Statistical Manual (DSM); Semi-Structured Assessment for Drug Dependence and Alcoholism (SSADDA); Structured Clinical Interview for DSM-IV (SCID).**

BIBLIOGRAPHY

Each of these instruments is in the public domain. Copies of the versions of the SSAGA and associated documentation can be obtained at no charge via the Internet by accessing the Washington University (St. Louis, Mo.) COGA Web site at http://zork.wustl. edu/niaaa.

American Psychiatric Association. (1987). *Diagnostic and statistical manual of mental disorders* (3rd ed., rev.). Washington, DC: Author.

American Psychiatric Association. (1994). *Diagnostic and statistical manual of mental disorders* (4th ed.). Washington, DC: Author.

Bucholz, K. K., Cadoret, R., Cloninger, C. R., Dinwiddie, S., Hesselbrock, V. M., Nurnberger, J. I., et al. (1994). A new, semi-structured psychiatric interview for use in genetic linkage studies: A report of the reliability of the SSAGA. *Journal of Studies on Alcohol, 55,* 149–158.

Bucholz, K. K., Hesselbrock, V. M., Shayka, J. J., Nurnberger, J. I., Schuckit, M. A., & Reich, T.R. (1995). Reliability of individual diagnostic criterion items for psychoactive substance dependence and impact on diagnosis. *Journal of Studies on Alcohol, 56*(5), 500–505.

Feighner, J. P., Robins, E., Guze, S. B., Woodruff, R. A., Winokur, G., & Munoz, R. (1972). Diagnostic criteria for use in psychiatric research. *Archives of General Psychiatry, 26,* 57–63.

Hesselbrock, M., Easton, C., Bucholz, K. K., Schuckit, M. A., & Hesselbrock, V. M. (1999). A validity study of the SSAGA: A comparison with the SCAN. *Addiction, 94*(9), 1361–1370.

Kuperman, S., Schlosser, S. S., Kramer, J. R., Bucholz, K. K., Hesselbrock, V. M., Reich, W., et al. (2001). Risk domains of an adolescent alcohol diagnosis. *Addiction, 96*(4), 629–636.

Rice, J. P., Reich, T. R., Bucholz, K. K., Neuman, R. J., Fishman, R., Rochberg, N., et al. (1995). Comparison of direct interview and family history diagnoses of alcohol dependence. *Alcoholism: Clinical and Experimental Research, 19*(4), 1018–1023.

World Health Organization. (1992). *The ICD-10 Classification of Mental and Behavioural Disorders: Clinical descriptions and diagnostic guidelines.* World Health Organization. Geneva, Switzerland: Author.

VICTOR HESSELBROCK

SENSATION AND PERCEPTION AND EFFECTS OF DRUGS.

Every behavior in which an organism engages involves information from the primary senses, such as vision, hearing (audition), and touch. A number of drugs of abuse alter sensory information. Mind-altering drugs can also influence perception of time, thinking, behavior, and mood. Often abusers of these drugs experience severe depression, anxiety, paranoia, confusion, and terror.

Naturally occurring drugs, such as mescaline from the peyote cactus, increase awareness of visual and auditory sensations and also produce visual illusions and hallucinations. The psilocybin mushroom (Mexican or magic mushroom) produces similar effects. Because of these sensory changes, mescaline and psilocybin have been used since pre-Columbian times in religious ceremonies by the peoples of Mexico and the American Southwest.

Lysergic acid diethylamide (LSD), an artificially produced drug that was first synthesized in the late 1930s by the Swiss chemist Albert Hoffmann, has become well known for producing intense and colorful visual sensations. People also report changes in sensory behavior with drugs that are related to LSD (such as DMT, DOM, and MDMA, also known as Ecstasy or the "love drug"). DMT is a short-acting (cycle takes less than one hour) crystalline powder that produces visual hallucinations. DOM, also known as STP, is more than 50 times as potent as mescaline. MDMA produces "out-of-body" sensations and acts as a stimulant. Phencyclidine (PCP) is another synthesized drug that is sometimes added to the list of drugs that alter sensory behavior; however, its sensory effects are limited to numbness in the hands and feet. Ketamine, also known as Special K, is a veterinary medicine that is chemically similar to PCP; its effects range from delirium to inability to move.

The active constituent of marijuana, tetrahydrocannabinol (THC), also produces alterations in sensory behavior; however, hallucinations—such as those produced by mescaline or LSD—are less common with THC, although there is an increased risk of psychotic symptoms among users with a family or personal history of psychosis. Cocaine and amphetamine sometimes produce hallucinations and other sensory distortions, but only when they are taken for long periods of time.

Various names are used to describe drugs that alter sensory behavior. One term is *psychedelic*, which refers to mind-expansion or to experiencing events that go beyond normal boundaries; this word was coined in 1956 by Humphrey Osmond, a British psychiatrist. Another term is *psychotomimetic*, which refers to the similarities of hallucinations that occur in psychotic disorders, such as schizophrenia, and those produced by mescaline and LSD. The term *hallucinogenic* is slightly misleading, since not all drugs that alter sensory behavior produce hallucinations.

OBSERVATIONS IN HUMAN SUBJECTS

Most of our information about drugs and the ways in which they alter sensory behavior in people comes from individual reports (called anecdotal) rather than from well-controlled laboratory studies. People have reported vivid images, changes in perception, and hallucinations after they have taken mescaline or LSD. Synesthesias—a mixing of the senses, such as "the hearing of colors" or "the seeing of sounds"—may also occur. One of the first descriptions of LSD's effects is recounted as follows:

> I was seized by a peculiar sensation. . . . Objects, as well as the shape of my associates in the laboratory, appeared to undergo optical changes. . . . With my eyes closed, fantastic pictures of extraordinary plasticity and intensive color seemed to surge toward me. After two hours this state gradually wore off (Julien 1988, p. 180).

Although these sensory disturbances stop within a few hours, some people experience confusion, sensory distortions, or poor concentration for longer periods of time. For some people, drug effects recur long after the drugs have left their systems—these brief episodes are called *flashbacks*.

STUDIES IN THE LABORATORY

Since alterations in sensory behavior, such as hallucinations, cannot be observed directly, it is very difficult to examine these effects in laboratory animals. One way to investigate a drug's effect on sensory behavior is to train animals to behave differently in the presence of different types of visual or auditory stimuli. If a drug changes the animal's behavior, it is possible that these changes in behavior are due to a change in how well the animal hears or sees the stimuli. Another type of procedure examines how intense (e.g., how loud or how bright) a stimulus has to be for an organism to hear or see it. In these procedures, the intensity required to hear or see a stimulus is determined before a drug is given and then it is compared to the intensity required to hear or see the stimulus after the drug is given.

In general, drugs such as mescaline, LSD, and THC do not alter an animal's ability to tell the difference between visual or auditory stimuli—nor do they alter visual or auditory thresholds. This lack of effect in animals suggests one of two explanations: either drugs such as LSD produce different effects in animals than they do in people, or, more likely, the procedures that are used to study alterations in sensory behavior in animals do not measure the unique ways in which drugs such as LSD alter sensory behavior.

Conversely, MDMA testing has found comparable results in both animals and humans. A late 1990s study (conducted on red squirrel monkeys) at Johns Hopkins University showed that MDMA has damaging effects on memory. Published in 2000, a British study of both current and previous MDMA users has discovered both immediate and delayed memory deficits.

See also **Inhalants; Opiates/Opioids; Research, Animal Model: An Overview.**

BIBLIOGRAPHY

Earleywine, M. (2005). *Mind-altering drugs: The science of subjective experience.* New York: Oxford University Press USA.

Harrigan, P. (1999). Are cannabis and psychosis linked? *The Lancet, 353,* 730.

Jaffe, J. H. (1990). Drug addiction and drug abuse. In A. G. Gilman et al. (Eds.), *Goodman and Gilman's the pharmacological basis of therapeutics,* 8th ed. New York: Pergamon. (2005, 11th ed.) New York: McGraw-Hill Medical.

Julien, R. M. (1988). *A primer of drug action.* New York: W. H. Freeman. (2007, 11th ed.)

Kawasaki, A., & Purvin, V. (1996). Persistent palinopsia following ingestion of lysergic acid diethylamide (LSD). *JAMA, The Journal of the American Medical Association, 276,* 432.

Kowalski, K. M. (2000). What hallucinogens can do to your brain. *Current Health 2, 26,* 6.

Monroe, J. (1998). The LSD story. *Current Health 2, 24,* 24.

Seymour, R. B. (1999). The lunch-hour psychedelic: A 30-minute trip. *Psychopharmacology Update, 10,* 6.

Taylor, E. (1996). Psychedelics: the second coming. *Psychology Today, 29,* 56.

Wareing, M., et al. (2000). Working memory deficits in current and previous users of MDMA ('ecstasy'). *British Journal of Psychology, 91,* 181.

LINDA DYKSTRA
REVISED BY PUBLISHER (2001)

SEROTONIN. Chemically named 5-hydroxytryptamine (5-HT), serotonin is a monoamine transmitter found in neurons that project widely throughout the brain and spinal cord. The actions of 5-HT are mediated by at least fourteen genes that encode subtypes of 5-HT receptors (5-HTXR) that are as of 2008 grouped into seven families (5-HT1R – 5-HT7R) according to structural and functional characteristics. A ligand-gated ion channel (the 5-HT3R) and thirteen distinct receptors coupled to various effector systems influence the concentration within the neuron of ions such as K+ (potassium) and Ca+ (calcium) and thereby the activity of the cell. Permissive (5-HT1AR, 5-HT1BR, 5-HT2AR, 5-HT3R, 5-HT4R) and inhibitory (5-HT2CR) roles for 5-HT receptors localized within brain reward pathways appear to underlie 5-HT-elicited control over the abuse liability of several classes of abused drugs, including cannabinoids, ethanol, opiates, and psychostimulants (e.g., cocaine, nicotine). Cocaine, the best studied in this regard, results in the accumulation of 5-HT in the synapse consequent to reuptake inhibition, and this elevated synaptic 5-HT plays a fundamental and complex role in the processes that underlie the progression of cocaine addiction. Once the 5-HT1R and 5-HT2R subtypes are distinguished pharmacologically from one another, an excitatory role for the 5-HT1BR and 5-HT2AR and an inhibitory role for the 5-HT1AR and 5-HT2CR are evident in the control of cocaine-induced behaviors. In particular, the 5-HT2AR and the 5-HT2CR are known to control the neurochemical and behavioral effects of cocaine. Preclinical studies indicate that 5-HT2AR antagonists and/or 5-HT2CR agonists may effectively reduce craving and/or relapse and, likewise, enhance abstinence, whereas 5-HT2CR agonists may also effectively reduce cocaine intake in active cocaine users. Thus, serotonergic systems present great promise in the quest to define susceptibility to the behavioral effects of abused drugs, addictive processes, and/or relapse after recovery, and open the door to the development of new medications for the management of abuse and addiction.

See also **Lysergic Acid Diethylamide (LSD) and Psychedelics; Monoamine; Neurotransmitters; Receptor, Drug.**

BIBLIOGRAPHY

Bockaert, J., Claeysen, S., Becamel, C., Dumuis, A., & Marin, P. (2006). Neuronal 5-HT metabotropic receptors: Fine-tuning of their structure, signaling, and roles in synaptic modulation. *Cell and Tissue Research, 326,* 553–572.

Bubar, M. J., & Cunningham, K. A. (2006). Serotonin 5-HT2A and 5-HT2C receptors as targets for modulation of psychostimulant use and dependence. *Current Topics in Medicinal Chemistry, 18,* 1971–1985.

KATHRYN A. CUNNINGHAM

SEXUALITY AND SUBSTANCE ABUSE.

The interplay of sexuality and the use of alcohol and drugs is manifest in images as old as Bacchus, allusions to "wine, women, and song," and its modern transformation "sex, drugs, and rock-and-roll." The impact of alcohol on sexuality most commonly evokes images of Bacchanalian toga parties. Fears of "reefer madness" included alarms of unleashed licentiousness. The popular belief is that psychoactive substances loosen sexual inhibitions leading to increased sexual activity.

The purpose of this discussion is to explain the complex interaction between human sexual expression and the nonmedical social uses of intoxicating substances. Topics to be broached will include the specific effects of psychoactive substances on sexual function, the use of drugs to facilitate sexual behavior, and the association of drug use with high-risk sexual behavior. Peugh and Belenko (2001) provided a critical review of the research on the impact on human sexual function of acute and chronic substance use. The literature included controlled laboratory studies as well as survey and interview techniques.

DIFFICULTIES IN RESEARCH

Research typically characterizes sexual function as a physiological event by distinguishing between libido and sexual interest, arousal (erection in males; lubrication in females), ability to orgasm, and intensity of and emotional sense of satisfaction from the orgasm. In humans this complex biologic event is shaped by the individual's genetics, psychology, and previous history, as imbedded in an environmental and cultural milieu. Consequently, from a research point of view, the difficulty in controlling for these factors with sample sizes of sufficient number makes drawing conclusions a daunting task. In the face of the limitations in research methodology, Peugh and Belenko found sufficient evidence for harmful effects on sexual functioning. A 2007 study published in the United Kingdom (Sumnall, Beynon, Conchie, Riley, & Cole, 2007) suggested that sexual activity after drug use was most frequently circumstantial and associated with cannabis and MDMA (Ecstasy). When used intentionally to facilitate a sexual encounter, the effects of these drugs were to lower inhibitions, raise self-confidence, and give a greater perception of interpersonal contact with the partner.

ALCOHOL AND SEXUAL RESPONSE

Beckman and Ackerman (1995) noted that while many women acknowledge a subjective increase in sexual desire and pleasure with alcohol, it lowers physiological arousal and leads to a change in sexual behavior in few women. In 2007 Schacht and colleagues reported a fascinating study comparing the effects of alcohol intoxication on psychophysiological measures of sexual responding. Two groups of women, distinguished by the presence or absence of a history of having been sexually abused, were monitored in their response to erotic films. Women who had suffered sexual abuse reported more sexual arousal in the intoxicated state than when sober. They had higher mood ratings when intoxicated and were not able to suppress their sexual response to erotic films when given this instruction. Women without an abuse history demonstrated a decrease in sexual arousal and maintained their ability to suppress their sexual response when given this instruction while intoxicated. These findings are particularly germane to the association of heightened risk of sexual dysfunction in women with alcohol problems who have experienced childhood incest or sexual assault. It raises the possibility that early abuse resets the nervous system to experience alcohol hedonically as a mood enhancer and sexual disinhibitor. This could increase a woman's risk for both alcohol problems and high-risk sexual behavior.

Abbey and colleagues explored the acute effects of alcohol on sexual decision-making in men and women. The researchers used a laboratory paradigm of instructing subjects to read or listen to a vignette while sober and while intoxicated. When reviewing the dating vignette while intoxicated, both genders misread active attention as sexual interest and exaggerated dating availability cues as being sexually provocative. Extending the paradigm to date rape vignettes gave results in which, while intoxicated but not while sober, both genders failed to identify the inappropriateness of the man's sexual behavior and consistently overrated the level of the woman's sexual arousal. In a further experiment, the paradigm was used to demonstrate that intoxicated subjects were more likely than their sober cohort (matched study group) to expect unprotected sexual intercourse in a vignette of a couple contemplating sex without condoms.

DRUGS AND SEXUAL RESPONSE

The literature on opioids, notably, has minimal reference to opioids as enhancing sexual arousal or functioning. In a 2008 study from Australia (Hallinan et al., 2008), men on methadone had a high prevalence of erectile dysfunction related to hypogonadism compared to men on buprenorphine. A large study from Taiwan in 2007 (Bang-Ping, 2007) reported 46.7 percent of heroin users had diminished libido and erectile dysfunction. A study in Michigan in 2005 (Brown et al., 2005) also noted erectile and orgasmic dysfunction in a group of methadone patients.

In 2003 El-Bassel and colleagues reported on 38 women in methadone treatment who were interviewed because they acknowledged abuse by their drug-involved partners. Of note was the frequent report that male and female partners experienced the opposite sexual response to the same shared drug, which led to sexual coercion and violence. For example, many of these women experienced a decrease in sexual arousal with cocaine, whereas their male partner experienced increased sexual and aggressive arousal.

The malignant dynamics of sexual expression and drug use came to the fore during the crack cocaine epidemic in the 1980s and 1990s. In 1991 Marx reviewed sixteen epidemiological studies that examined drug use, sexual behavior, and sexually transmitted disease (STD). The exchange of sex for money or drugs was associated with STDs in seven studies. Eight studies found an association between crack and STDs. The exchange of sex for crack cocaine was both a rural and urban problem. Dramatic increases in juvenile delinquency and STDs among inner city teenagers were reported (Fullilove et al., 1993). Teenagers using crack were more likely to have sexual intercourse under the influence of drugs and alcohol, to engage in sex in exchange for money or drugs, and to have more sexual partners. These findings were true for both males and females.

A comparison of crack-abusing to opioid-abusing women revealed higher rates of high-risk sexual behavior including prostitution, infrequency of condom use, and a greater number of sexual partners in the crack-abusing women. The opioid-abusing group had a much greater proportion of high-risk behavior associated with needle use (Cohen et al., 1994).

Despite the consistent findings of high rates of risky sexual behavior in crack-abusing women, Henderson and colleagues (1995) found no evidence that these women found crack to be an aphrodisiac. To the contrary, they found high rates of sexual dysfunction. Recent studies have corroborated this finding, identifying the need to acquire money for drugs to avoid withdrawal, rather than increased libido, as the impetus to sexual behavior. DeBeck and colleagues reported in 2007 that 62 percent of women engaged in the sex trade would give up the illegal services if they did not need money for drugs. The need for drug money frequently overpowers the determination to insist on condom use as well. The phenomenon of sex-for-crack is most rampant in the crack house itself (Inciardi, 1995). Some studies report 30 percent of the men and 90 percent of the women had one hundred or more sexual partners within thirty days of being interviewed for the study. As might be expected, individuals described as crack-smoking drug injectors carried the highest risks of STD and HIV seropositive states. They also had the highest frequency of having a drug-injecting sex partner, multiple sex partners, low rates of condom use, and high rates of alcohol consumption and were more likely to exchange sex for drugs.

The health consequences of injection drug use and cocaine smoking show little signs of abating. HIV seropositive rates in 3,555 urban and rural Florida drug users and controls as reported by McCoy in 2004 were 7.3 percent of those in the control group, 20 percent of crack smokers, 30 percent of crack-smoking injectors, and 45 percent of injection-only drug users. In 2006 the emergence of injecting crack cocaine was described in Connecticut and Massachusetts, revealing even higher rates of risky sexual behavior and health consequences reported than with "speedball" (powder cocaine and heroin) injections or powder cocaine injections alone (Buchanan et al., 2006).

EFFECTS OF CLUB DRUGS

The burgeoning use of the group of drugs labeled by the National Institute on Drug Abuse [NIDA] as *club drugs* has raised widespread concern. The following drugs are included: methamphetamine, MDMA, amyl nitrate, LSD, GHB, rohypnol or flunitrazepam, and ketamine (Wu et al., 2006). These compounds are named for the context of their use, rather than for any chemical composition or biological activity. They are used recreationally at social events, like music festivals, nightclubs, circuit parties, and raves to enhance energy, endurance, sociability, sexual arousal, or to create an altered state of consciousness with heightened sensory stimulation. These compounds are generally low cost, conveniently distributed as small pills, powders, or liquids, and are perceived as safe by users.

The association between sexual activity and club drug use was initially described in the homosexual community in the 1990s. Most studies of club drug use have focused on adult sub-populations, for example, gay, bisexual, substance abusers, club/party participants who acknowledge drug use. In all studies, regardless of sample characteristics, the recurrent findings are of polydrug use, excessive high-risk sexual behavior, high frequency of substance abuse disorders, and STD and HIV transmission (Colfax et al., 2005; Halkitis et al., 2005; Rawstorne et al., 2007).

METHAMPHETAMINE USE

Studies of methamphetamine use in male gay populations frequently noted the pattern of methamphetamine, Viagra, and either amyl nitrate, GBH, or ketamine (Crosby and DiClemente, 2004; Spindler et al., 2007; Carey et al., 2008). Some users acknowledged wishing for "better, longer, harder sex." Unfortunately, the association of the use of such cocktails with the prevalence of HIV-positive sero-status and unprotected oral, anal, and anonymous sex is consistently high. Users acknowledge the yearning to combat loneliness, fears about the loss of physical attractiveness due to aging and illness, the psychological stress about HIV status, and the physical discomfort of the sexual act as predominant reasons for using these drugs (Kurtz, 2005).

Methamphetamine and MDMA are related in their chemistry to amphetamine. The subtle molecular differences of MDMA confer pharmacologic properties similar to the hallucinogen mescaline. This may be responsible for the differences reported in the subjective experiences of *crystal* and *Ecstasy* (Kalant, 2001). Both promote alertness and energy, but Ecstasy confers a euphoria, increased sensory awareness, enhanced emotional closeness, and intimacy. Zemishlany and colleagues (2001) reported on the subjective evaluation of sexual functioning in 35 recreational Ecstasy users. Desire and satisfaction were moderately to profoundly increased in 90 percent of subjects. Orgasm was delayed, but perceived as more intense. However, physiological arousal was impaired in 40 percent of the men.

There has been speculation that methamphetamine differs from other club drugs in relation to risky sexual behavior and the pattern of sexual arousal (Schilder et al., 2005). Studies have shown crystal users, whether homosexual or heterosexual, male or female, are consistently and significantly more likely to engage in high-risk sexual behaviors. Studies from Australia (Rawstorne et al., 2007), New York (Halkitis et al., 2005), and San Francisco (Colfax et al., 2005) suggest a more nuanced notion that different molecules may carry different risks to different groups. It is certainly conceivable that methamphetamine may separate itself in its capacity to precipitate devastating addiction cycles with consequent unsafe behaviors as a by-product, as seen in the crack-for-sex epidemic.

MDMA is by no means benign, as serious acute and chronic toxicities have been demonstrated. Adverse medical events and fatalities consistent with syndromes of excess neurotransmitter levels are being observed with increasing frequency (Kalant, 2001). There is increasing concern that long-term MDMA neurotoxicity leads to persistent neuropsychiatric difficulty, even after accounting for polydrug use and preexisting neuropsychological state (Gouzoulis-Mayfrank et al., 2006; Thomasius et al., 2006).

LSD is the most widely used hallucinogen among adolescents and is associated with risky sexual behavior and heavy alcohol use (Golub et al., 2001). Ketamine is an anesthetic agent with effects similar to phencyclidine, though of a much shorter duration. Flunitrazepam (rohypnol, "ruffies") and GHB ("liquid X") are both potent sedative-hypnotics. Ketamine, rohypnol, and GHB have been implicated with alcohol in the increasingly prevalent problem of drug-facilitated sexual assault.

Wu's (2006) published results from the National Survey of Drug Use and Health revealed 20 percent of the participants acknowledged using one or more club drugs. Eighty percent of the children studied used three or more drug classes. Club drug use was highly associated with criminal behavior and recent alcohol abuse or dependence.

Of fundamental importance in stressing and assessing the danger of club drugs is the consistent pattern of polydrug use in venues of extreme crowds, excess physical activity, and elevated temperatures with molecules of unknown purity whose toxic dose range and recreational dose range merge precariously (Parrott, 2006).

DRUGS AND SEXUAL DEVELOPMENT
The 1993 Massachusetts Youth Risk Behavior Survey of 3,000 students found a significant association between early onset of sexual intercourse and higher number of sexual partners with the early onset use of marijuana, cocaine, crack, and alcohol (Shrier et al., 1997). Staton and colleagues (1999), in a study of 952 young adults in Lexington, Kentucky, replicated the finding of earlier initiation of sexual activity being related to the early use of drugs. A 2001 survey reported that California youth in substance abuse treatment had an earlier age of onset of sexual activity, more partners, less use of condoms, more STD, more HIV-positive results, and more pregnancies (Tapert et al., 2001). Studies published in 2002 of 808 Seattle children, surveyed at age 10 in 1985 and followed to age 21 in 1996, found that binge drinkers and marijuana users had more sex partners and were less likely to use condoms consistently, as compared to their abstinent peers (Guo et al., 2002). In 1993 Fullilove and colleagues, reporting on crack-abusing inner city adolescents, found that almost 50 percent had sexual intercourse while intoxicated, and that 29 percent of boys and 25 percent of girls engaged in sex for drugs or money.

G. La Pera has authored a series of papers describing the increased incidence of sexual dysfunction and the impact this sexual dysfunction had on the original decision to use drugs in young Italian men who later developed substance abuse disorders. This raises the consideration that sexual dysfunction can be both a precipitant and a consequence of substance abuse disorders

In 2000 M. A. Bellis published the results of a survey of 1,340 16 to 35-year-olds from nine European cities. He explored the strategic roles for which young people utilize substances to facilitate sex. He found that 29 percent of alcohol users hoped to facilitate encounters, and 26 percent of cocaine users hoped to prolong sex. Substance abuse before 16 years of age consistently was associated with sex before 16 years of age. Previous studies by Bellis revealed that young adults traveling on holiday to European hot spots increased their drug use and at-risk sexual behaviors significantly. He also reported on the significant recruitment of new users of drugs during these vacations.

The catastrophic synergy between substance abuse and high-risk sexual behavior and the epidemic of sexually transmitted diseases has absorbed the energies of health care providers, researchers, and policymakers for decades. It has become evident that the use of psychoactive substances plays a significant role in the emergence of sexual victimization and violence. Nonetheless, it is the increasingly frequent early initiation of drug and alcohol use by youth and the concomitant emergence of high-risk sexual activity that is most troubling. M. A. Bellis described the problem as follows:

> An epidemic of recreational drug use and binge drinking exposes millions of young ... to routine consumption of substances which alter their sexual decisions and increases their chances of unsafe and regretted sex. For many, substance use has become an integral part of their strategic approach to sex, locking them into continued use. Tackling substances with both physiological and psychological links to sex requires approaching substance abuse and sexual behavior in the same way that individuals experience them; as part of the same social process (Bellis et al., 2008).

See also **Alcohol: Chemistry and Pharmacology; Childhood Behavior and Later Substance Use; Club Drugs; Complications; Epidemics of Drug Abuse in the United States; Gender and Complications of Substance Abuse; Injecting Drug Users and HIV; Intimate Partner Violence and Alcohol/Substance Use; National Survey on Drug Use and Health (NSDUH); Neurotransmitters; Opiates/Opioids; Polydrug Abuse; Psychoactive; Rave; Research: Measuring Effects of Drugs on Behavior; Risk Factors for Substance Use, Abuse, and Dependence: Sexual and Physical Abuse; Sensation and Perception and Effects of Drugs; Substance Abuse and AIDS.**

BIBLIOGRAPHY

Abbey, A., Zawacki, T., & McAusian, P. (2000). Alcohol's effects on sexual perception. *Journal of Studies on Alcohol, 61*(5), 688–697.

Abbey, A., Buck, P. O., Zawacki, T., & Saenz, C. (2003). Alcohol's effects on perceptions of a potential date rape. *Journal of Studies on Alcohol, 64*(5), 669–677.

Abbey, A., Saenz, C., & Buck, P. O. (2005). The cumulative effects of acute alcohol consumption, individual differences, and situational perceptions on sexual decision-making. *Journal of Studies on Alcohol, 66*(1), 82–90.

Bang-Ping, J. (2007). Sexual dysfunction in men who abuse illicit drugs. *Journal of Sexual Medicine.* Available from http: //www.ncbi.nlm.nih.gov.

Beckman, L. J., & Ackerman, K. T. (1995). Women, alcohol and sexuality. *Recent Developments in Alcoholism, 12,* 267–285.

Bellis, M. A., Hale, G., Bennett, A., Chaudrey, M., & Kilfoyle, M. (2000). Ibiza uncovered: Changes in substance abuse and sexual behavior amongst young people visiting an international night-life resort. *International Journal of Drug Policy, 11*(3), 235–244.

Bellis, M. A., Hughes, K., Bennett, A., & Thomson, R. (2003). The role of an international nightlife resort in the proliferation of recreational drugs. *Addiction, 98*(12), 1713–1721.

Bellis, M. A., Hughes, K., Thomson, R., & Bennet, A. (2004). Sexual behavior of young people in international tourist resorts. *Sexually Transmitted Infections, 80*(1), 43–47.

Bellis, M. A., Hughes, K., Calafat, A., Juan, M., Ramon, A., Rodriguez, J. A., et al. (2008). Sexual uses of alcohol and drugs and the associated health risks: A cross-sectional study of young people in nine European cities. *BMC Public Health, 8,*155.

Brown, R., Balousek, S., Mundt, M., & Fleming, M. (2005). Methadone maintenance and male sexual dysfunction. *Journal of Addictive Diseases, 24*(2), 91–106.

Buchanan, D., Tooze, J. A., Shaw, S., Kinzly, M., Heimer, R., & Singer, M. (2006). Demographic, HIV risk behavior and health status characteristics of "crack" cocaine injectors compared to other injection drug users in three New England cities. *Drug and Alcohol Dependence, 81*(3), 221–229.

Carey, J. W., Mejia, R., Bingham, T., Ciesielski, C., Gelaude, D., Herbst, J. H., et al. (2008, May 23). Drug use, high-risk sex behaviors, and increased risk for recent HIV infection among men who have sex with men in Chicago and Los Angeles. *AIDS and Behavior.* Available from http://www.ncbi.nlm.nih.

Cohen, E., Navaline, H., & Metzger, D. (1994). High-risk behaviors for HIV: A comparison between crack-abusing and opioid-abusing African-American women. *Journal of Psychoactive Drugs, 26*(3), 233–241.

Colfax, G., Coates, T. J., Husnik, M. J., Huang, Y., Buchbinder, S., Koblin, B., et al. (2005). Longitudinal patterns of methamphetamine, popper (amyl nitrite), and cocaine use and high-risk sexual behavior among a cohort of San Francisco men who have sex with men. *Journal of Urban Health, 82*(1 Suppl 1), i62–70.

Crosby, R., & DiClemente, R. J. (2004). Use of recreational Viagra among men having sex with men. *Sexually Transmitted Infections, 80*(6), 466–468.

DeBeck, K., Shannon, K., Wood, E., Li, K., Montaner, J., & Kerr, T. (2007). Income generating activities of people who inject drugs. *Drug and Alcohol Dependence, 91*(1), 50–56.

El-Bassel, N., Gilbert, L., & Rajah, V. (2003). The relationship between drug abuse and sexual performance among women on methadone. *Addictive Behavior 28*(8), 1385–1403.

Fullilove, M. T., Golden, E., Fullilove, R. E., III, Lennon, R., Porterfield, D., Schwarcz, S., et al. (1993). Crack cocaine use and high-risk behaviors among sexually active black adolescents. *The Journal of Adolescent Health, 14*(4), 295–300.

Golub, A., Johnson, B. D., Sifaneck, S. J., Chesluk, B., & Parker, H. (2001). Is the US experiencing an incipient epidemic of hallucinogen use? *Substance Use & Misuse, 36*, 1699–1729.

Gouzoulis-Mayfrank, E., & Daumann, J. (2006a). Neurotoxicity of MDMA in humans: How strong is the evidence for persistent brain damage? *Addiction, 101*(3), 348–361.

Gouzoulis-Mayfrank, E., & Daumann, J. (2006b). The confounding problem of polydrug use in recreational Ecstasy/MDMA users: A brief overview. *Journal of Psychopharmacology, 20*(2), 188–193.

Guo, J., Chung, I. J., Hill, K. G., Hawkins, J. D., Catalano, R. F., & Abbott, R. D. (2002). Developmental relationships between adolescent substance abuse and risky sexual behavior in young adulthood. *Journal of Urban Health, 31*(4), 354–362.

Halkitis, P. N., Shrem, M. T., & Martin, F. W. (2005). Sexual behavior patterns of methamphetamine-using gay and bisexual men. *Substance Use & Misuse, 40*(5), 703–719.

Hallinan, R., Byrne, A., Agho, K., McMahon, C., Tynan, P., & Attia, J. (2008). Erectile dysfunction in men receiving methadone and buprenorphine maintenance treatment. *Journal of Sexual Medicine, 5*(3), 684–692.

Henderson, D. J., Boyd, C. J., & Whitmarsh, J. (1995). Women and illicit drugs: Sexuality and crack cocaine. *Health Care for Women International, 16*(2), 113–124.

Inciardi, J. A. (1995). Crack, crack house sex, and HIV risk. *Archives of Sexual Behavior, 24*(3), 249–269.

Kalant, H. (2001). The pharmacology and toxicology of "Ecstasy" (MDMA) and related drugs. *Canadian Medical Association Journal, 165*(7), 917–928.

Kurtz, S. P. (2005). Post-circuit blues: Motivation and consequences of crystal meth use among gay men in Miami. *AIDS and Behavior, 9*(1), 63–72.

La Pera, G., Franco Giannotti, C., Taggi, F., & Macchia, T. (2003). Prevalence of sexual disorders in those young males who later become drug abusers. *Journal of Sex & Marital Therapy, 29*(2), 149–156.

La Pera, G., Carderi, A., Marianantoni, Z., Lentini, M., & Taggi, F. (2006). The role of sexual dysfunction in inducing the use of drugs in young males. *Archivio Italiano di Urologia Andrologia, 78*(3), 101–106.

La Pera, G., Carderi, A., Marianantoni, Z., Peris, F., Lentini M., & Taggi F. (2008). Sexual dysfunction prior to first drug use among former drug addicts and its

possible causal meaning on drug addiction: Preliminary results. *Journal of Sexual Medicine, 5*(1), 164–172.

Marx, R., Aral, S. O., Rolfs, R. T., Sterk, C. E., & Kahn, J. G. (1991). Crack, sex, and STD. *Sexually Transmitted Diseases, 18*(2), 92–101.

McCoy, C. B., Lai, S., Metsch, L. R., Messiah, S. E., & Zhao, W. (2004). Injection drug use and crack cocaine smoking: Independent and dual risk behaviors for HIV infection. *Annals of Epidemiology 14*(8), 535–542

Parrott, A. C. (2006). MDMA in humans: Factors which affect the neuropsychobiological profiles of recreational Ecstasy users, the integrative role of bioenergetic stress. *Journal of Psychopharmacology, 20*(2), 147–163.

Peugh, J., & Belenko, S. (2001). Alcohol, drugs and sexual function: A review. *Journal of Psychoactive Drugs, 33*(3), 223–232.

Rawstorne, P., Digiusto, E., Worth, H., & Zabiotska, I. (2007). Associations between crystal methamphetamine use and potentially unsafe sexual activity among gay men in Australia. *Archives of Sexual Behavior, 36*(5), 646–654.

Schacht, R. L., George, W. H., Heiman, J. R., Davis, K. C., Norris, J., Stoner, S. A., et al. (2007, March 16). Effects of alcohol intoxication and instructional set on women's sexual arousal vary based on sexual abuse history. *Archives of Sexual Behavior, 36*(5), 655–665.

Schilder, A. J., Lampinen, T. M., Miller, M. L., & Hogg, R. S. (2005). Crystal methamphetamine and Ecstasy differ in relation to unsafe sex among young gay men. *Canada Journal of Public Health, 96*(5), 340–343.

Shrier, L. A., Emans, S. J., Woods, E. R., & DuRant, R. H. (1997). The association of sexual risk behaviors and problem drug behaviors in high school students. *Journal of Urban Health, 20*(5), 377–383.

Spindler, H. H., Scheer, S., Chen, S. Y., Klausner, J. D., Katz, M. H., Valeroy, L. A., et al. (2007). Viagra, methamphetamine, and HIV risk: Results from a probability sample of MSM, San Francisco. *Sexually Transmitted Diseases, 34*(8), 586–591.

Staton, M., Leukefeld, C., Logan, T. K., Zimmerman, R., Lynam, D., Milich, R., et al. (1999). Risky sex behavior and substance use among young adults. *Health and Social Work, 24*(2), 147–154.

Sumnall, H. R., Beynon, C. M., Conchie, S. M., Riley, S. C., & Cole, J. C. (2007). An investigation of the subjective experiences of sex after alcohol or drug intoxication. *Journal of Psychopharmacology, 21*(5), 525–537.

Tapert, S. F., Aarons, G. A., Sedlar, G. R., & Brown, S. A. (2001). Adolescent substance use and sexual risk-taking behavior. *Journal of Urban Health, 28*(3), 181–189.

Thomasius, R., Zapletalova, P., Peterson, K., Buchert, R., Andresen, B., & Wartberg, L., et al. (2006). Mood, cognition, and serotonin transporter availability in current and former ecstasy (MDMA) users. *Journal of Psychopharmacology, 20*(2), 211–225.

Wu, L. T., Schlenger, W. E., & Galvin, D. M. (2006). Concurrent use of methamphetamine, MDMA, LSD, Ketamine, GHB, and Flunitrazepam among American youths. *Drug and Alcohol Dependence, 84*(1), 102–113.

Zemishlany, Z., Aizenberg, D., & Weizman, A. (2001) Subjective effects of MDMA on human sexual function. *European Psychiatry 16*(2), 127–213.

GERSON M. STERNSTEIN

SHISHA. *See* **Hookah.**

SHOCK INCARCERATION AND BOOT-CAMP PRISONS.

Shock incarceration programs, or boot-camp prisons, are short-term prison programs for young offenders that are modeled on military basic training programs. Since they were first established in 1983, all the U.S. states and many U.S. counties have adopted this type of program. Boot-camp prisons have proved to be controversial, however, and critics argue that this type of regimen does not reduce recidivism (the tendency to return to crime after release). In the late 1990s, allegations of misconduct and abuse by boot-camp prison staff members against their juvenile inmates led to criminal investigations and the closing of facilities. Nevertheless, this type of "tough love" approach remains a popular option for some correctional officials.

Those sentenced to boot-camp prisons are required to arise early each day to participate in a rigorous schedule of physical training, military drill and ceremony, and hard labor. While they are in the boot camp, participants are separated from other prisoners. They are allowed few personal possessions, no televisions, and infrequent visits from relatives on the outside.

The correctional officers in the programs are referred to as drill instructors and are responsible for seeing that the inmates obey the rules and participate in all activities. When speaking to staff, inmates must refer to themselves as "this inmate" and they must proceed and follow each sentence with "sir" or "madam," as in the familiar military response, "Sir, yes, sir." Disobedience is punished immediately using summary punishments, frequently in the form of some additional physical activity, such as push-ups or sit-ups. More serious rule violations may result in dismissal from the program.

BOOT-CAMP PRISONS AS INTERMEDIATE SANCTIONS

The boot-camp prisons were developed during the 1980s, partly in response to the phenomenal growth in the number of convicted young offenders. There were only two options in managing this population—either they were sent to prison or they were supervised in the community on probation. Neither option was entirely satisfactory for the large number of young offenders, however. Correctional jurisdictions faced severe prison overcrowding, and probation caseloads grew so large that many offenders received only nominal supervision during their time in the community. Alternative sanctions or intermediate punishments were proposed, such as intensive community supervision, house arrest, or residential-community corrections centers. These options provided more control than a sentence to probation but less than a sentence to prison. Boot-camp prisons were one relatively inexpensive alternative sanction that became particularly popular.

The first boot-camp prisons were begun in 1983 in Oklahoma and Georgia. These two programs attracted a great deal of attention, and other jurisdictions soon began developing similar programs. By 1999, more than 50 boot camps housed about 4,500 juveniles. Although the majority of the camps have male participants, some programs admit women as well, and some states developed completely separate boot-camp prisons for women. The Federal Bureau of Prisons developed one boot camp for males and a separate program for females. Despite this initial popularity, by 2000 various problems and doubts had led several states to either end their programs or drastically scale back the size of the programs.

ENTERING AND EXITING

Because most boot camps have strict requirements about who is eligible, inmates are carefully evaluated prior to being sent there. Most programs require participants to sign an agreement saying

Prisoners entering "Boot Camp" in Sumter County Correctional Institution. © BETTMANN/CORBIS.

they have volunteered. They are given information about the program and the difference between a boot-camp prison and a traditional prison. The major incentive for entering the boot camp is that the inmate serves a shorter term than under a traditional prison sentence.

The first day of the boot camp involves a difficult in-take process, during which the drill instructors confront the inmates. Inmates are given rapid orders about the rules of the camp, including when they can speak, how they are to address the drill instructors, and how to stand at attention. The men have their heads shaved, and the women receive short haircuts. This early period in the camp is physically and mentally stressful for most inmates.

The programs last from 90 to 180 days. Those dismissed prior to graduation are considered program failures, and they are either sent immediately to a traditional prison to serve a longer term of incarceration or they are returned to court for re-

sentencing. Offenders who successfully complete the boot camp are released. After graduating, they are supervised in the community for the rest of their sentence. There is usually an elaborate graduation ceremony during which inmates demonstrate the military drills they have practiced. Many programs encourage family members to attend the graduation ceremony.

A DAY IN BOOT CAMP

On a typical day, the participants arise before dawn, dress rapidly, clean their living quarters, and march in cadence to an exercise area, where they will spend an hour or more doing calisthenics and running. They then march back to their quarters for a quick cleanup before breakfast. As they do at every meal, they march to breakfast and stand at parade rest while waiting to be served. They stand at attention until ordered to sit and eat without conversation. Following breakfast they may work for up to six or eight hours. This is usually hard physical labor, such as cleaning state parks or public roads. They return in the late afternoon for additional physical exercise or practice in drill and ceremony. After a quick dinner, they attend rehabilitation programs until 9 p.m., when they return to their dormitories. In the short period before bedtime, they have time to be sure their shoes are shined and their clothes are clean and ready for the morning.

DRUG TREATMENT IN THE BOOT CAMP

The earliest boot camps focused on discipline and hard work. More recently, they have begun to emphasize treatment and education. It became clear that many of the entrants were involved with drugs. Realizing that punishment alone would not effectively reduce the drug use of these offenders, corrections officials introduced drug treatment or education into the daily schedule of boot-camp activities. By the late 1980s, all the camps had some type of substance abuse treatment or education (MacKenzie, 1994).

As with other aspects of the programs, the type of treatment and the amount of time devoted to substance abuse treatment varies greatly among programs. The 90-day Florida program includes only 15 days of treatment and education, while the New York program provides 180 days of treatment.

Most programs have reported that drug use is monitored during community supervision, the schedule and frequency of this monitoring varies greatly.

SIMILARITIES AND DIFFERENCES

All the boot-camp prisons incorporate the core components of military basic training, such as physical training and hard labor. Most target young offenders convicted of nonviolent crimes such as drug, burglary, or theft. Participation is limited to those who do not have an extensive past history of criminal activity. Other than these similarities, the programs differ dramatically. Some focus only on work, military drill, and exercise. In other boot camps, offenders spend a great deal of time each day in rehabilitation programs. The camps also differ in the type of the therapeutic programming provided. Some emphasize academic education, while others focus on group counseling or treatment for substance abuse.

The boot camps also differ in the ways offenders are managed after release. Some programs intensively supervise all the offenders who successfully complete the boot camp; others are supervised as they would be in traditional probation caseloads. Program officials worry about the difficulty the graduates have in making the transition from the rigid structure of the boot camps to the community environment. For this reason, some boot camps developed aftercare programs to help them make the change. These aftercare programs do more than increase the surveillance of the activities of the graduates. They are designed to provide drug treatment, vocational counseling, academic education, and short-term housing.

New York's Therapeutic Community Boot Camps. Among the boot camps that include substance abuse treatment as a component of the in-prison phase of the program, there are large differences in the way this treatment is delivered. The boot-camp programs developed by the New York Department of Correctional Services use a therapeutic community (TC) model. All offenders are given a similar regimen of drug treatment while they are incarcerated. Each platoon in the camp forms a small community, and they meet daily to solve problems and discuss their progress in the shock program. They spend over 200 hours during the six-month program in a substance-abuse treatment program based on the Alcoholics Anonymous

(AA) and Narcotic Anonymous (NA) models of abstinence and recovery. All the inmates participate in the treatment, regardless of their history of use and abuse.

Illinois's Boot Camp with Levels of Treatment. Like New York, the Illinois boot camp also targets substance abusers. However, the delivery of treatment services is very different. In Illinois, counselors evaluate offenders and match the education and treatment level to the identified severity level of the offender. Three different levels of treatment are provided. Inmates identified as level one have no substance abuse history, and therefore they receive only two weeks of education. Level-two inmates are identified as probable substance abusers. They receive four weeks of treatment in addition to the drug education. The treatment consists of group therapy focusing predominately on denial and family-support issues. Inmates identified as level three are considered to have serious drug addictions, and they receive ten weeks of education and treatment. In addition to the drug education and group therapy, they receive group sessions on relapse, codependency, behavioral differences, family addiction, and roles within the family.

Texas's Voluntary Participation Model. A third model is represented by the Texas program (MacKenzie, 1994). In the boot camp, all participants receive five weeks of drug education. During this phase, inmates may also receive individual counseling and attend twelve-step fellowship meetings. More drug treatment is available for those who volunteer (the substance abuse counselors in this program believe that treatment should be voluntary). These volunteers receive approximately four hours per week of treatment in the form of group therapy. The meetings are held during free time, so inmates are not released from work to attend. The group sessions focus on social values, self-worth, communication skills, self-awareness, family systems, self-esteem, and goal setting. Some inmates also receive individual counseling.

DISMISSAL RATES

As occurs in many drug-treatment programs, boot camps may have high dismissal rates. Depending upon the program, rates vary from 8 percent (Georgia in 1989) to as much as 80 percent (Wisconsin in

1993). Offenders can be dismissed from the boot camp because of misbehavior, and in some boot camps they can voluntarily ask to leave. Those who are dismissed will either be sent to a traditional prison, where they will serve a longer sentence than they would have in the boot camp, or they will be returned to the court for re-sentencing. Thus, in both cases, there is the threat of a longer term in prison for those who do not complete the boot-camp program.

There is very little information about how drug-involved offenders do in boot-camp prisons. One study of the Louisiana boot camp compared the dismissal rates of drug-involved offenders with the rates of offenders who were not identified as drug-involved (Shaw & MacKenzie, 1992). Two groups of drug-involved offenders were examined: those who had a legal history of drug-involvement (an arrest or conviction for a drug offense), and those who were identified as drug abusers on the basis of self-report. In this program, offenders were permitted to drop out voluntarily or they could be dismissed for misbehavior. Surprisingly, in comparison to other offenders, the drug-involved offenders were less likely to drop out of the program.

In another study of the Louisiana boot camp, 20 percent of the participants were identified as problem drinkers on the basis of their self-reported alcohol use and problems associated with use (Shaw & MacKenzie, 1989). The problem drinkers were no more likely to drop out of the boot-camp prison than were other inmates.

In interviews, offenders who are near graduation from boot camp report that they are drug free and physically healthy (MacKenzie & Souryal, 1994). Unlike offenders incarcerated in conventional prisons, boot-camp participants tend to believe that their experience was positive and that they have changed for the better. They also report that the reason they entered the boot camp was because they believed they would spend less time in prison—not because of the treatment or therapy offered.

PERFORMANCE DURING COMMUNITY SUPERVISION

Studies have compared the performance of boot-camp graduates during community supervision with those who served a longer time in prison or were sentenced to probation. In most cases, there were no significant differences between these offenders in recidivism rates or in positive social activities (MacKenzie & Souryal, 1994). One study used a statistical technique called meta-analysis to examine the results from 43 different studies of correctional boot camps. All these studies compared the recidivism of boot-camp participants with those who served other sentences (MacKenzie, 2007; Wilson et al., 2008). Overall, the findings were that the recidivism rate of boot-camp participants was almost identical to the recidivism rate of similar offenders who served different sentences. The researchers concluded, therefore, that boot camps are not effective in reducing recidivism. However, there was some suggestion in the studies that boot camps with more treatment and therapy in the daily schedule of activities may reduce recidivism. For example, boot-camp graduates in Illinois and Louisiana had fewer revocations for new crimes. Research examining New York offenders found mixed results. Graduates had fewer new crime revocations in one study (New York State Department of Correctional Services, 1994) and fewer technical violations in another study (MacKenzie & Souryal, 1994).

If the military atmosphere alone changed offenders, all the graduates would be expected to have lower recidivism rates and a better positive adjustment. The inconsistency of the results suggests that the boot-camp atmosphere alone will not successfully reduce recidivism or positively change offenders. Some other aspects of the Illinois, New York, and Louisiana programs, either with or without the boot-camp atmosphere, led to the positive impact on these offenders. After an examination of these programs, the researchers concluded that: (1) all three programs devoted a great deal of time to therapeutic activities, (2) a large number of entrants were dismissed, (3) the length of time in the boot camp was longer than other boot camps, (4) participation was voluntary, and (5) the in-prison phase was followed by six months of intensive supervision in the community. However, it was not possible to separate the effect of these components from the impact of the military atmosphere. Most likely, the therapy provided during the program and the transition and aftercare treatment provided during community supervision are critical components of the program for drug-involved offenders. It is not known if a drug treatment program without a boot-camp atmosphere would be more or less effective than drug treatment within a boot camp.

PERFORMANCE OF DRUG-INVOLVED OFFENDERS

Shaw and MacKenzie (1992) studied the performance of drug-involved offenders during community supervision in Louisiana. In comparison to offenders who were not drug-involved, these individuals did not do as well during community supervision. This was true of those on probation, parolees from traditional prisons, and parolees from the boot camp. Thus, the boot-camp parolees did not do better than those from other settings. During the first year of supervision, the drug-involved offenders were more likely to have a positive drug screen.

Problem drinkers who graduated from the Louisiana program were found to perform better, as measured by positive activities during community supervision (Shaw & MacKenzie, 1989). Their performance was, however, more varied, indicating that they may need more support and aftercare than other offenders. In contrast to the Louisiana findings, research in New York indicated that those who were returned to prison were more apt to be alcoholics (New York Department of Correctional Services, 1994). In both Louisiana and New York, offenders who were convicted of drug offenses did better than self-confessed alcoholics during community supervision.

THE FUTURE OF BOOT-CAMP PRISONS

Boot-camp prisons are still controversial. By the late 1990s, skepticism had risen about the effectiveness of this approach. Studies conducted for the U.S. Justice Department found that the national recidivism rate for boot camps ranged from 64 to 75 percent. This compared to recidivism rates from 63 to 71 percent for those who served their time in traditional detention centers. Although juveniles often responded well while in the camps, they returned to the same neighborhoods where they first got into trouble. Furthermore, news reports of abuse, injuries, and deaths in the camps led many correctional administrators to be wary of initiating new shock incarceration programs. Colorado, North Dakota, and Arizona ended their programs, and Georgia, where boot-camp prisons started, is phasing out its camps.

People are concerned that inmates' rights will not be observed in boot-camp prisons, and that inmates are being coerced to do something that is not good for them (Morash & Rucker, 1990). These critics argue that the summary punishments and the staff yelling at offenders may be abusive for inmates; that participants may leave the boot-camp prison angry and damaged by the experience; and that the military atmosphere, which is designed to create a cohesive fighting unit, may not be appropriate for young offenders. These concerns became public in the late 1990s, as state and federal prosecutors investigated allegations of abuse and misconduct by prison camp staff. Maryland fired its top five juvenile-justice officials in 1999 after officials investigated reports of systematic assaults at three boot-camp prisons.

Advocates of boot camps say that these programs have many benefits. In their opinion, these offenders lack the discipline and accountability that are provided by the program. Furthermore, they argue, the strong relationship between the offenders and the drill instructors may be helpful to the inmates, and that there may be some aspects of the boot camps that are particularly beneficial for drug-involved offenders. Thus, although controversy exists about the boot-camp prisons, they remain a popular alternative sanction.

See also **Civil Commitment; Coerced Treatment for Substance Offenders; Criminal Justice System, Treatment in the; Narcotic Addict Rehabilitation Act (NARA); Prisons and Jails; Treatment: An Overview.**

BIBLIOGRAPHY

Anglin, M. D., & Hser, Y-I. (1990). Treatment of drug abuse. In M. Tonry & J. Q. Wilson (Eds.), *Drugs and crime: Vol. 13. Crime and justice.* Chicago: University of Chicago Press.

Illinois Department of Corrections. (1991). *Overview of the Illinois Department of Corrections Impact Incarceration Program.* Springfield, IL: Author.

MacKenzie, D. L. (1994). Shock incarceration as an alternative for drug offenders. In D. L. MacKenzie & C. D. Uchida (Eds.), *Drugs and crime: Evaluating public policy initiatives.* Thousand Oaks, CA: Sage.

MacKenzie, D. L., Bierie, D., & Mitchell, O. (2007). An experimental study of a therapeutic boot camp: Impact on impulses, attitudes and recidivism. *Journal of Experimental Criminology, 3*(3), 221–246. Dordrecht, Netherlands: Springer.

MacKenzie, D. L., & Parent, D. G. (1992). Boot camp prisons for young offenders. In J. M. Byrne, A. J. Lurigio, & J. Petersilia (Eds.), *Smart sentencing: The emergence of intermediate sanctions*, 103–119. London: Sage Publications.

MacKenzie, D. L., & Souryal, C. (1994). *Multi-site evaluation of shock incarceration: Executive summary*. Report to the National Institute of Justice. Washington, DC: National Institute of Justice.

Marks, A. (1999, December 27). States fall out of (tough) love with boot camps. *The Christian Science Monitor*.

Morash, M., & Rucker, L. (1990). A critical look at the ideal of boot camp as a correctional reform. *Crime and Delinquency, 36*(2), 204–222.

New York State Department of Correctional Services, & New York Division of Parole. (1993). *The fifth annual shock legislative report*. Albany, NY: Unpublished report by the Division of Program Planning, Research and Evaluation and the Office of Policy Analysis and Information.

Shaw, J. W., & MacKenzie, D. L. (1992). The one-year community supervision performance of drug offenders and Louisiana DOC-identified substance abusers graduating from shock incarceration. *Journal of Criminal Justice, 20*(6), 501–516.

Shaw, J. W., & MacKenzie, D. L. (1989). Shock incarceration and its impact on the lives of problem drinkers. *American Journal of Criminal Justice, 16*(1), 63–97.

Souryal, C., & MacKenzie, D. L. (1994). Shock therapy: Can boot camps provide effective drug treatment? *Corrections Today, 56*(1), 48–54.

West, W. (2000). Civilian boot camps lack intended kick. *Insight on the News, 16*(13), 48.

Wilson, D. B., MacKenzie D. L. & Mitchell F. N. (2008) *Effects of correctional boot camps on offending*. Campbell Collaboration Review. Available from http://www.campbellcollaboration.org/.

DORIS LAYTON MACKENZIE
REVISED BY FREDERICK K. GRITTNER (2009)

SLANG TERMS IN U.S. DRUG CULTURES.

Because illicit drugs (and prescription drugs used in ways other than intended) are illegal, those who use them, and those who live within the drug culture, develop their own communication system—both for self-protection and as a means of identifying others within the group. This is the case for several marginalized underworld subcultures, such as street gangs, prison gangs, and incarcerated individuals. The argot, or slang, of drug users is this specialized vocabulary or the collection of words and phrases used by one drug user to communicate with another—often to the exclusion of non-users. In some instances, this argot extends to the intonation or pitch used to speak words and phrases.

Argot fascinates sociologists, anthropologists, and others who study human behavior because its use is an example of learned behavior that helps identify members of a particular social or cultural group. Alfred Lindesmith did substantial field research to create and verify his lexicon, recorded in his well-known 1938 essay "Argot of the Underworld Drug Addict."

A. M. Smith and colleagues studied more than 2,000 drug users in Baltimore, Maryland, in 1992. Subjects were shown a photograph of someone injecting a drug into his vein and asked, "What do you call this?" More than 50 percent identified the photo as an image of someone *firing up*; the others called it *shooting*. Most other people in Baltimore speak of *firing up* their furnaces or *shooting* baskets on a basketball court, but they do not think about drug use when these terms are used.

The argot of drug users also varies from place to place and from time to time. A very small minority of drug users in Smith's study spoke of *mainlining* the drug, *spiking*, or *oiling* when they looked at a photo of drug injection into a vein. These are older terms for the same injecting behavior called *firing up* and *shooting* by younger drug users.

In some ways, argot reflects the social structure of groups: In-group members use the argot, whereas others do not. However, if argot serves as a badge of membership in an in-group, then one might expect to hear it in general conversations, no matter who is present. Nonetheless, sociologists studying the use of argot often have been surprised to find that it is spoken mainly among group members but not as frequently when nonmembers are present.

Arguing from evidence of this type, some observers claim that argot serves more to convey and reinforce identities within groups than to distinguish one group from another. That is, the process of learning and using drug-related argot reinforces the experience of joining in with others who use drugs. In some ways, this process might

Term	Definition
a	amphetamines, a stimulant
a-bomb, bomb	LSD, a hallucinogen
acid	[a shortening of *d*-lysergic acid diethylamide; since about 1960] LSD
Adam	[originally named to connote a primordial man in a state of innocence] MDMA, a mild hallucinogen. *See* Ecstasy below.
amp	[from *ampoule*; the drug is sold in small glass ampoules, which are broken open and the contents inhaled] amyl nitrite, a dilator of small blood vessels and used in medicine for angina pains; used illicitly to intensify orgasm or for a stimulation effect
amps	amphetamines
angel dust	[since the 1970s] phencyclidine (brand-name Sernyl), an anesthetic used on animals but originally on humans; discontinued because of bizarre mental effects. *See* PCP below.
Are you anywhere?	"Do you use marijuana?"
author	medical professional who writes illegal prescriptions
bagging	taking an inhalant by breathing it from a bag
base	The pure alkaloid of cocaine that has been extracted from the salt (cocaine hydrochloride), in the form of a hard white crust or rock. *See* crack and rock below.
batu	crystalline methamphetamine
beamed up	[from "Beam me up, Scotty," an expression used in the television series *Star Trek*] intoxicated by crack
beamer	a crack addict
beans	dextroamphetamines
beast	LSD
beat	[from the idea of beating or cheating someone] a bogus or mislabeled drug or substance resembling a certain drug and sold as that drug (soap chips as crack; methamphetamine or baking soda as cocaine; catnip as marijuana; PCP as LSD, mescaline, or tetrahydrocannabinol (THC, the active principle of marijuana); procaine as cocaine)
big C	cocaine
big H	heroin
black beauties	amphetamines
black tar	heroin
blank	nonpsychoactive powder sold as a drug
blast	a drag of crack smoke from a pipe
blotter	[doses of the drug are dripped on a sheet of blotter paper for sale] LSD
blow	(1) to sniff a drug. (2) cocaine. (3) to smoke marijuana (*to blow a stick*).
blue heavens	methaqualone (a sedative) pills
blue lips	use of MDMA
bone	a marijuana cigarette; a joint
boom	marijuana
boomers	hallucinogenic mushrooms containing psilocybin
booze	alcohol
bottles	vials or small containers for selling crack
boy	heroin
breakfast cereal	ketamine. *See* K below.
brown	heroin from Mexico diluted with brown milk sugar (lactose), which is less pure than China white. Also called Mexican mud
brown sugar	heroin
buds	[from its appearance] marijuana or sinsemilla (a hybrid variety of marijuana); a quantity for sale consisting mainly of the more potent flowering tops of the marijuana plant (Cannabis sativa). *See* sinse below.
bump	(1) cocaine. (2) crack. (3) fake crack. (4) hit of ketamine. *See* K below.
bush	[from *righteous bush*] marijuana
bust	[from 1930s Harlem slang for a police raid, perhaps a shortened form of *busting in*] arrest
button	[from the shape of the appendages to the peyote cactus containing mescaline] peyote or San Pedro cactus
buzz, buzzed	[from *buzz*, onomatopoeic equivalent of subjective feeling; the onset of the drug sometimes causes buzzing in the ears] (1) high on marijuana. (2) an inferior high from heroin.
C	cocaine
candy	cocaine
caps	hallucinogenic mushrooms
chalk	[from its appearance] crystal methamphetamine or cocaine
Charlie	cocaine
chasing the dragon	[from a Chinese expression for inhaling the fumes of heroin after heating it; the melting drug resembles a wriggling snake or dragon] (1) inhaling heroin fumes after the substance is heated on a piece of tinfoil. (2) smoking a mixture of crack and heroin.
cheba	marijuana
China white	[from China (Indochina) white or white stuff = heroin; since the 1970s] (1) relatively pure heroin from Southeast Asia. (2) analogues of fentanyl (Sublimaze), an opioid more potent than heroin and sold on the street as China white.
chipping, to chippy	using heroin occasionally, avoiding addiction
chronic	marijuana
cocoa puff	[pun on the name of a chocolate-flavored breakfast cereal] a joint, to which cocaine has been added
coke	cocaine
cola	[a word play on *coke*, *cocaine*, and *Coca-Cola*, cocaine is derived from the coca (not the kola) plant] cocaine
cold turkey	[from the gooseflesh that is part of abrupt withdrawal] by extension, ending a drug habit without medicinal or professional help, *going cold turkey*
coming down	[from a *high*] losing the effects of a drug, all the way down to crashing
connect	[from the *connection*, a drug pusher] cocaine importer or wholesaler, who fronts (consigns) cocaine to a supplier, who in turn distributes to a street retailer. *See* dealing, mule, runner, steerer, touting.
cop	[from British slang of the 1700s; to obtain, to steal, to buy; since the 1890s] to get or purchase illicit drugs
cop a buzz	get high

[CONTINUED]

Table 1. Slang terms. ILLUSTRATION BY GGS INFORMATION SERVICES. GALE, CENGAGE LEARNING

Term	Definition
copping zone	an area where drugs are sold
crack	[from the crackling sound when smoked in a pipe] pebbles of cocaine base that are smoked
crack house	house or apartment (sometimes, an abandoned building) where crack cocaine is sold and smoked on the premises 24/7— twenty-four hours a day, seven days a week
crank	crystal methamphetamine
crank lite	[from *crank*, because of the amphetaminelike stimulant effect, + *lite*, meaning "lighter," as in low-alcohol beer] ephedrine, a stimulant used in nonprescription medicines such as a decongestant, which is lighter than amphetamines
crash, crashing	to come all the way down from a drug high
cross roads	[from the scored cross on the tablets] amphetamines
crystal	[in powder form] methamphetamine or cocaine
crystal supergrass	marijuana with PCP
cut	to add adulterants to a drug, extending it to make more money on its sale (some adulterants are relatively harmless, some toxic)
date rape drug	Rohypnol, called roofies. At a party this tasteless, odorless drug may be slipped into a woman's drink. After she loses consciousness, she may be raped and later have no memory of the incident.
deadeye	blank stare produced by an overdose of phencyclidine (PCP) or another drug
dealing	[from *dealer*, a person who sells drugs; since the 1920s] selling drugs of all kinds
designer drugs	synthetic compounds or drug analogues that produce the effects of certain regulated drugs but have slight differences in chemical composition to evade regulatory law, e.g., analogues of fentanyl (China white); analogues of amphetamine and methamphetamine, such as MDA, MDMA (Ecstasy), TMA, MMDA, MDE (Eve), MBDB; toxic by-products of the synthetic opiate meperidine (Demerol), such as MPTP and MPPP dexies: dextroamphetamines
devil's dandruff	crack or powder cocaine
ditch	veins on the inside of the arm at the elbow, a site for injecting heroin. *See* tracks below.
do drugs	take or use illicit drugs
doobie	a marijuana cigarette; a joint
dope	[from Dutch *doop*, meaning "sauce" (from *dopen*, "to dip"). In the late19th century the term came to be applied to opium, a black gum shaped into pellets and smoked in a pipe] (1) drugs. (2) marijuana. (3) heroin and other illicit drugs. (4) intoxicating fumes of airplane fuel or glue. (5) Coca-Cola.
dope fiend	[opprobrious term for users of narcotics and illicit drugs since the early 1900s; the term is used ironically by drug users to defy the social stigma] drug user, drug abuser, drug addict
dosing	slipping a hallucinogenic drug into punch, brownies, etc., so that it will be consumed unwittingly by others
downer	barbiturates
drag	to draw or pull on smoke from a cigarette, pipe, or other item (*to take a drag*); to convey that smoke into one's throat and lungs *See* toke below.
drop	to swallow LSD or a pill
dugie, doojee	[phonetic] heroin
dust	PCP
dusting	(1) mixing either cocaine with tobacco in a cigarette, or heroin or opium with marijuana or hashish in a joint. (2) smoking PCP.
Ecstasy, Extacy	[from the euphoria, heightened sensuality, intensified sexual desire attributed to the drug experience] methylenedioxymethamphetamine (MDMA), a mildly hallucinogenic drug synthesized from methamphetamine and resembling mescaline and LSD in chemical structure
eightball	an eighth of an ounce of cocaine
elephant tranquilizer	PCP
Emilio	[as in Emilio and Maria (Mary), from Mary Jane] marijuana
energize me	give me some crack
equalizer	pebbles of crack cocaine
Eve	[variant of Adam, MDMA, or Ecstasy] MDE, a mild hallucinogen derived from amphetamine. Adam and Eve is a compound of MDMA + MDE = MDEA (*n*-ethyl-MDA or 3, 4, methylene + dioxy-*N*-ethylamphetamine)
Exctasy	Esctasy used with Viragra
Exing	taking Ecstasy
fix	(1) a drug dose needed to hold off withdrawal. (2) a shot of heroin. *See* shoot below.
flake	[from its appearance] (1) cocaine hydrochloride. (2) the sediment of a rock or chunk of cocaine.
Flying Saucers	[tradename] hallucinogenic seeds of a variety of morning glory
forget pill	Rohypnol. *See* roofies below.
freebase	[the psychoactive alkaloid, the base, has been freed or extracted from the cocaine hydrochloride] (1) crystals of pure cocaine. (2) to prepare the base; to smoke it.
frost freak	one who inhales the fumes of Freon, a coolant gas, to get high
funky green luggage	A supply of marijuana in one's baggage
G, GHB	gamma-hydroxybutyrate: clear liquid, white powder, tablet, or capsule often combined with alcohol; used mainly by adolescents and young adults, often at nightclubs and raves. GHB is usually abused either for its intoxicating/sedative/euphoriant effects or for its growth hormone-releasing effects which can build muscles.
gangster	marijuana
ganja	[from *gaja*, Hindi word for India's potent marijuana, consisting of the flowering tops and leaves of the hemp plant, where most of the psychoactive resin is concentrated] marijuana
garbage can	drug user who takes anything, everything, combinations
Georgia gamma -hydroxybutyrate	*See* GHB above.
ghost	LSD
girl	cocaine
glass	crystalline methamphetamine
gluey	one who inhales glue forms

[CONTINUED]

Table 1 (continued). Slang terms. ILLUSTRATION BY GGS INFORMATION SERVICES. GALE, CENGAGE LEARNING

Term	Definition
goofing	[from goofballs = barbiturates, and from goof, meaning "to act silly, stupidly, heedlessly"] under the influence of barbiturates
grass	marijuana as chopped up for smoking, looks like dried grass
green	[harvested hemp leaves that are not properly cured; also, the lower leaves of the hemp plant, which contain a smaller proportion of the psychoactive resin] (1) marijuana of low potency, e.g., Chicago green. (2) ketamine, an anesthetic similar to phencyclidine (PCP) but milder in its effects, which is sprinkled on parsley or marijuana and smoked.
grievous bodily harm	gamma-hydroxybutyrate. See GHB above.
H	heroin; also Big H
hash, hashish	the concentrated resin of the marijuana plant, containing a high percentage of the active principle, tetrahydrocannabinol (THC)
hash oil	liquid extracted from hashish, providing a more potent dose of the active principle and more easily transported in vials. It produces more sedation and deeper states of reverie than hashish,
Henry, Harry	heroin
herb	[used to connote a benign natural substance] marijuana
herbal Ecstasy	herbal combinations marketed as a natural high that can be legally purchased over the counter in drug stores, music stores, and other shops. The active ingredients include caffeine and ephedrine.
high	[from the sense of euphoria, being above it all, detached from unpleasant reality] intoxicated by a drug
hip	[from lying on the hip to smoke opium— the addict lay on his side on a pad in an opium den; the term was then extended to illicit drug users. In the alienated subculture of the jazz scene of the 1930s and 1940s, using drugs was expected and made one keenly informed or hip (originally hep) until squares adopted the word] sophisticated, knowing, in; possessing taste, knowledge, awareness of the newest trends, and a lifestyle superior to that of conventional people
hit	(1) an injection of a narcotic. (2) a snort of cocaine. (3) a drag from a crack pipe. (4) a toke of marijuana. (5) to adulterate (cut) a drug. (6) a dose of LSD.
hitters	those who inject others who have hard-to-find veins
hog	[from its original use as a veterinary anesthetic] phencyclidine (PCP)
home boy	gamma-hydroxybutyrate. See GHB above.
hooch	alcohol
horse	heroin
hot shot	a potent dose of heroin sufficient to kill; heroin laced with cyanide
How do you like me now?	crack cocaine
huff	to inhale ordinary household products to get high. Users huff directly from the container or from inhalant-soaked rags, socks, or rolls of toilet paper. Inhalants include model airplane glue, nail polish remover, cleaning fluids, hair spray, gasoline, the propellant in aerosol whipped cream, spray paint, fabric protector, air conditioner fluid (Freon), cooking spray, and correction fluid.
ice	extremely pure and addictive smokable form of crystalline methamphetamine
J, jay	[from joint] a marijuana cigarette
jelly babies, jelly beans	amphetamine pills
joint	[from joint as part of the paraphernalia for injecting narcotics, particularly the needle; since the 1920s] a marijuana cigarette
jonesing	[after John Jones, the British physician who first described opiate withdrawal in 1700] withdrawal from addiction; by extension, craving of any drug
juice	steroids
Julio	marijuana. See Emilio and Mary Jane.
junk	[from junker, a pusher or peddler; since the 1920s. Also possibly from a word for opium—a play on junk, a Chinese boat—which was later extended to all narcotics] heroin (which is derived from opium)
K, Super K, Special K, Vitamin K	ketamine, an anesthetic similar in structure to PCP. First synthesized by a pharmaceutical company in the early 1960s, powdered ketamine emerged as a recreational drug in the 1970s. It became Vitamin K in the underground club scene in the 1980s and Special K in the 1990s rave scene.
keester plant	[from keester, "rump," and plant, "to place"] drugs in a rubber container or condom concealed in the rectum
Ketaject, Ketalar, ketamine	See K above.
kick the gong (around)	to smoke opium (especially in a Chinese opium den)
kick the habit	[related to kick it out, to suffer withdrawal symptoms, which include muscle spasms in the legs and kicking movements from hyperactive reflexes in the spinal cord] (1) abrupt withdrawal from a drug to which one is addicted. (2) to conquer drug dependence.
kif	marijuana
killer joints	marijuana with PCP
kind buds	potent marijuana. See buds above.
LA coke	ketamine. See K above.
la roche	Rohypnol. See roofies below.
lady	cocaine
laughing gas	nitrous oxide
lid	[from the now obsolete practice of selling a measure of marijuana in a pipe tobacco tin] an ounce of marijuana, usually sold in a plastic bag
line	(1) a thin stream of cocaine on a mirror or other smooth surface, which is sniffed through a quill—a rolled matchbook cover, tube, straw, tightly rolled dollar bill, etc. (2) a measure of cocaine for sale.
liquid Ecstasy	gamma-hydroxybutyrate. See GHB above.
luding out	[from ludes, short for Quaaludes (brand-name for methaqualone, an addictive sedative)] taking methaqualone
Lyle	[from lysergic acid] LSD
magic mushrooms	hallucinogenic mushrooms
mainline	[from main line, a major rail route; since the 1920s] (1) the large vein in the arm; the most accessible vein. (2) to inject morphine, heroin, or cocaine into any vein.
Mary Jane, MJ, Aunt Mary	marijuana

[CONTINUED]

Table 1 (continued). Slang terms. ILLUSTRATION BY GGS INFORMATION SERVICES. GALE, CENGAGE LEARNING

Term	Definition
MDMA	Ecstasy
meth	methamphetamine
Mexican brown	marijuana from Mexico
Mexican mud	brown heroin from Mexico. *See* brown above.
microdot	acid
mind-altering	the claimed mental effects of hallucinogenic drugs—altered or intensified states of perception
mind expansion	[related to psychedelic mind-manifesting; a descriptive term for hallucinogenic drugs coined in the 1960s] the claimed mind-altering effects of hallucinogenic drugs, including greater spirituality, enhanced self-awareness, and increased sensitivity to music, art, and nature; also synesthesia & cross-sensations, such as *seeing* music or *hearing* colors
Miss Emma	morphine
monkey on one's back	desperate desire for drugs; addiction; craving
moon	[from the shape of slices of the bud of the peyote cactus] peyote
moonrock	heroin mixed with crack for smoking
Moroccan candy	[*majoun* (Arabic) is candy laced with hashish, sold in Morocco and Afghanistan] hashish. *See* hash above.
mud	heroin
mule	(1) a low-level drug smuggler from Latin America; mules often swallow a condom filled with cocaine to be delivered at a destination—a dangerous practice called bodypacking. (2) heroin.
new Ecstasy	ketamine. *See* K above.
night train	PCP
nose candy	cocaine
on a mission	looking for crack
opium den	[from *den*, an animal's lair. The term was coined by Westerners in 19th-century China, to have lurid connotations] a place where opium is smoked. Chinese laborers brought the practice of smoking opium to America during the gold rush of 1849 and the 1850s. and the building of the transcontinental railroad.
ozone	PCP
pad	[from the mats in opium dens on which the smokers reclined and slept. In the 1930s Harlem apartments where marijuana was sold and smoked while reclining on couches or mattresses were called tea pads] (1) private place for taking drugs; a variant is crashpad, a place for recovering from the effects of a methamphetamine run (period of extended use); the user collapses (crashes) into an exhausted sleep. (2) by extension, since the 1950s, any dwelling place, room, or apartment.
paper bag	a container for drugs
PCP	[from PeaCe Pill] phencyclidine (brand-name Sernyl), a veterinary anesthetic that induces bizarre mental states in humans
peace pill	PCP
pearls	[medical nickname] amyl nitrite ampoules
Persian white	fentanyl. *See* China white above.
p-funk, p-dope	[*p* stands for pure] fentanyl. *See* China white above.
PG	paregoric, a traditional diarrhea remedy containing opium
pharming	the consumption of a mixture of drugs
piece	hashish, a form of marijuana. *See* hash above.
piggybacking	either the simultaneous injection of two drugs or the use of more than one tablet of MDMA
pill ladies	female elders who sell OxyContin (Oxycodone)
pill popping	[from popping something into one's mouth] promiscuous use of amphetamine and barbiturate pills or capsules. Drug user who does this is a *popper* and may be a *garbage can.*
pit	veins on the inside of the arm at the elbow, a main site for injecting heroin and the place to look for tracks. *See* ditch above.
pop	to inject. *See* shoot below.
poppers	[the glass ampoule is popped open and the contents inhaled] amyl nitrite ampoules
pot	[from *potaguaya*, a Mexican–Indian word for marijuana] marijuana
psychedelic heroin	ketamine. *See* K above.
pusher	[extension of this definition of *pusher*: a person who circulates counterfeit money; since the 1920s] drug seller, drug dealer. See dealing above.
quas, quacks	[from Quaalude, brand-name of methaqualone] methaqualone pills, an addictive sedative
Raoul	cocaine
rave	an all-night underground party, usually frequented by teens and college students. Raves are characterized by techno music and often designer drugs, especially Ecstasy.
reds, red birds	[also called *red devils*, *red jackets*, *red caps* because of the color of the capsules] Seconal (a brand of secobarbital) capsules
reefer	[from *grifa*, a Mexican–Spanish word for marijuana] (1) a marijuana cigarette. (2) marijuana.
rhoids	steroids
rib	Rohypnol. *See* roofies below.
righteous bush	marijuana plant
ringer	[from the idea of *hearing bells*; bells is a term for crack] powerful effect from a hit of crack
roach	[from its resemblance to a cockroach] the butt (end) of a marijuana cigarette
rock	[from its appearance] (1) large crystals or a chunk of pure cocaine hydrochloride. (2) crack. *See* base above.
rocket fuel	PCP
roofies, rophies, ruffies, R2, roofenol	Rohypnol, brand-name for the powerful sedative flunitrazepam. The pills are often used in combination with alcohol and other drugs.
rope	Rohypnol. *See* roofies above.
runner	a messenger (often a juvenile) who delivers drugs from the seller to the buyer (not to be confused with a drug runner, a smuggler)
rush	the quick initial onset of orgasmic sensations—of warmth, euphoria, and relaxation after injecting or inhaling heroin, cocaine, or methamphetamine
SAM	a federal narcotics agent
scag	heroin

[CONTINUED]

Table 1 (continued). Slang terms. ILLUSTRATION BY GGS INFORMATION SERVICES. GALE, CENGAGE LEARNING

Term	Definition
schoolboy	(1) codeine, a derivative of opium with relatively low potency, used as a cough suppressant and analgesic. (2) morphine.
Scotty	crack cocaine. *See* beamed up above.
script	prescription for a drug, often forged by addicts
script doctor	a physician who will provide a drug prescription for a price, or one who is deceived into providing one
shabu	crystalline methamphetamine
shake	[the mixture is made by shaking the drug and the adulterant] (1) cocaine adulterated (cut) with a harmless substance such as mannitol. (2) loose marijuana left at the bottom of a bag that held a pressed block of marijuana.
sheet	[from decorated blotter paper containing doses of the drug] acid or LSD
shit	heroin
shoot	inject a drug; also shoot up a fix or a shot (usually of heroin)
shooting gallery	place where heroin addicts shoot up and share needles and other drug paraphernalia (*works*)
shoot the breeze	inhale nitrous oxide (called laughing gas).
shrooming	high on hallucinogenic mushrooms
shrooms	hallucinogenic mushrooms
Sid	A play on the *s-d* sound of LSD
sinse	[from sinsemilla, without seeds] a hybrid variety of marijuana; also called *ses*
skin popping	[from *pop*, to inject] injecting heroin or any psychoactive drug subcutaneously (rather than into a vein), a practice of casual (*chippy*) users
skunk	marijuana
smack	[perhaps from *shmek*, Yiddish word for *sniff, whiff, pinch of snuff*; since the 1910s, when heroin users sniffed the drug; in the 1920s and 1930s some Jewish mobsters were involved in heroin trafficking] heroin
smoke	marijuana
snappers	[the ampoule containing the drug is snapped open] amyl nitrite capsules
snob	[from the idea of an elite or expensive drug] cocaine
snop	marijuana
snort	to sniff a drug
snow	[from its appearance; also, the drug is a topical anesthetic and numbs the mucous membranes] cocaine hydrochloride
snowbirds	cocaine
soapers	[from Sopor, brand-name of a sedative now off the market] methaqualone pills
space basing, space blasting	smoking a mixture of crack and phencyclidine (PCP) speed: (1) amphetamines, (2) caffeine pills, (3) diet pills.
speedball	[first used by GIs during the Korean War] injected mixture of heroin and cocaine
splif	a fat marijuana cigarette
spook	heroin
squirrel	a mixture of PCP and marijuana sprinkled with cocaine and smoked
stash	extension of hobo argot for hiding place; since the 1800s (1) hiding place for drugs. (2) a supply of drugs. (3) to hide drugs.
steerer	member of a cocaine or heroin crew who directs people to the seller
stepped on	adulterated or cut
stick	A marijuana cigarette
street drugs	drugs purchased from sellers on the street; hence, of dubious quality
strung out	severely addicted
sugar cubes	LSD
sunshine	[from the type sold as an orange-colored tablet] LSD
super grass	[the powder is sometimes mixed with parsley or marijuana and smoked] ketamine. *See* green.
tabs	[from *tablet*, a form in which the drug is sold] LSD
tea	marijuana
Thai stick	potent marijuana from Thailand
thing	(1) heroin. (2) an addict's works or hypodermic needle (needle and syringe).
tic	[from THC] fake tetrahydrocannabinol
toke	A drag on a marijuana cigarette
tooies	[from Tuinal, brand-name for a preparation containing amobarbital and secobarbital] sedative capsules
toot	(1) to sniff cocaine. (2) cocaine. (3) a binge, especially a drinking bout or spree (since the late 1700s).
touting	(1) purchasing drugs for someone else. (2) advertising or hawking drugs for sale.
tracks	a line of scabs and scars from frequent intravenous injections. *See* pit and ditch above.
tripping	[from *trip*, in the sense of a psychic journey] taking LSD
trips	(1) LSD tablets. (2) periods under the influence of various drugs, usually hallucinogens.
turkey	[from *turkey*, meaning a "jerk" or "theatrical failure or flop"] (1) a nonpsychoactive substance sold as a drug. (2) the seller of phony substances.
turn on	take drugs, especially hallucinogens
tweak mission	A mission to find crack
ups, uppers	amphetamines
V, Vs	Valium (brand-name for diazepam, a tranquilizer) tablets
wasted	[from *waste*, a street-gang term since the 1950s, meaning "to kill, beat up, destroy"] (1) severely addicted to the point of mental and physical depletion. (2) extremely intoxicated & out of it, beyond caring
weed	marijuana
whack	(1) to adulterate heroin, cocaine, or other drugs. (2) an adulterant. (3) phencyclidine (PCP). (4) to kill
whiff	[from the notion of smelling or sniffing] cocaine
white, white stuff	heroin
white beanies	amphetamines
white lady, white	[from the color] cocaine
window pane	[the drug is sometimes sold in a clear plastic square; also of a greater potency, providing a more intense experience and nonstructured sensations & *opening a window on reality*] LSD

[CONTINUED]

Table 1 (continued). Slang terms. ILLUSTRATION BY GGS INFORMATION SERVICES. GALE, CENGAGE LEARNING

Term	Definition
wired	(1) extremely intoxicated by cocaine. (2) anxious and jittery from stimulants (may be related to *amped*, a play on amphetamines and amperes).
woola	[phonetic spelling] a joint containing a mixture of marijuana and crack
works	equipment or paraphernalia for injecting drugs
X, the X, XTC	[from Ecstasy] MDMA
yellow jackets	[from the color of the capsules] Nembutal brand of pentobarbital
yen	[from English slang *yen-yen*, the opium habit, based on Cantonese *in-yan* (*in* meaning "opium" + *yan* meaning "craving"); since the 1800s] any strong craving
zenes	[short for Thorazine, brand-name for chlorpromazine] tranquilizer pills
zombie	(1) crack cocaine. (2) phencyclidine (PCP)
zooted up	high on crack cocaine

Table 1 (continued). Slang terms. ILLUSTRATION BY GGS INFORMATION SERVICES. GALE, CENGAGE LEARNING

serve to supplement the reinforcing functions of drug use, making continued drug use more rather than less likely.

According to historical data, the drug trade became popularized in the United States shortly after the end of the Civil War, during the time of national expansion and railroad building, subsequent to the large influx of Chinese laborers, who brought opium with them. With the passage of the Harrison Narcotics Act of 1914, the drug culture was forced to move underground, and addict argot was born. Persons who were opium-dependent were initially called *pipe fiends*; when smoking opium was banned, the term evolved to *dope fiend*. *Yen* came from the Cantonese word used for drug craving, and the phrase *to get one's yen off* referred to doing whatever was necessary to eliminate the symptoms of withdrawal among those who suddenly found themselves without ready access to drugs. *Yen-hock* was a large needle used to prepare opium for smoking, and *yenshee* was the residue left in the bowl after opium was smoked. Opium caused intestinal difficulties and often resulted in constipation, and a *yenshee baby* was a slang term for a particularly painful bowel movement subsequent to the smoking of opium.

Other general slang terms were *hop-head, gowster, user, gow-head, smacker, cookie, user, yenshee quay,* and *dope-hop.* In the 1920s *junker* became a universal term for a drug abuser. As the use of intravenously injected drugs grew in popularity, the side effects of this (local skin irritation) became well-known, and the term *laughing and scratching* became jargon for intravenous (IV) drug use. Those who continued to smoke opium were said to be *kicking the gong around* or *laying on the hip.*

In the 1930s the term *high* was coined to describe a state of intoxication brought on by the excessive use of drugs. Synonymous with high were *geed up, polluted, full of poison, loaded,* and *leaping.* The needle and syringe used in IV drug administration were referred to as a *harpoon,* a *nail,* a *spike,* or a *point.* Illicit drugs, in general, were referred to as *smack, junk, stuff,* and *hocus,* among others. By the mid-1930s specific slang developed for various drugs: Heroin was referred to as *H* and morphine as *M,* and very pure drugs, particularly with reference to heroin, were called *the real McCoys.* Individuals who used drugs very frequently were said to be *mainliners,* which came to specifically describe those who used drugs intravenously. Occasional drug users were said to have a *weekend habit, chippy-habit,* or *ice-cream habit.* People experiencing drug withdrawal without any assistance or intervention were said to be *going cold turkey,* apparently as a result of their pale bumpy skin brought on by the chills of withdrawal, or *kicking the habit.* The *iron cure* was forced withdrawal in a jail or prison setting.

Slang terms in the drug subculture are constantly changing, as its ethnic, social, and demographic composition changes and as new illicit drugs roll in and roll out with the tides of fashion, including geographical variations. Certain terms nevertheless show a remarkable durability, such as some of those used for heroin (first marketed by the German pharmaceutical concern, Bayer, in 1898), a narcotic that has been a staple street anodyne since the early 1900s. Drug-related terms that originated within the drug culture of the early twentieth century have come into the mainstream, remaining a permanent part of the English language, for example, *yen, hooked, pad, spaced out, high,* and *hip. Dope* has become a general-purpose term, widely used in relation to numerous types of drug; many people know that *weed* or *reefer* refers to marijuana, whereas *acid* is lysergic acid diethylamide or LSD.

Table 1 lists many words that came into common use during much of the twentieth century (a few antiques of sociological or historical interest are included, too). Some terms are the product of the 1980s and 1990s. Origins, if known, are given.

See also **Cocaine; Epidemics of Drug Abuse in the United States; Heroin; Marijuana (Cannabis); Opium: U.S. Overview.**

BIBLIOGRAPHY

De Lannoy, W. C., & Masterson, E. (1952, February). Teen-age hophead jargon. *American Speech*, *27*(1), 23–31.

Eisner, B. (1989). *Ecstasy: The MDMA story.* Berkeley, CA: Ronin.

Hurst, G., & Hurst, H. (1988). *The international drug scene.* Wurzburg, Germany: Harfst Verlag.

Indiana Prevention Resource Center. (2000). *On-line dictionary of street drug slang.* Available from http://www.drugs.indiana.edu/drug-slang.aspx.

JargonDatabase.com. *Drug references.* Available from http://www.jargondatabase.com/.

Julien, R. M. (1992). *A primer of drug action* (6th ed.). New York: W. H. Freeman.

Leinwand, D. (June 12, 2006). "Pharm parties" reflect problems. *USA Today.*

Lindesmith, A. R. (1938, July–August). The argot of the underworld drug addict. *Journal of Criminal Law and Criminology*, *29*(2), 261–278.

Lingeman, R. (1974). *Drugs from A to Z* (2nd ed.). New York: McGraw-Hill.

Maurer, D. W., & Vogel, V. H. (1973). Argot in narcotic addicts. In L. M. Snyder, et al. (Eds.), *Narcotics and narcotic addiction* (4th ed., pp. 364–455). Springfield, IL: Charles C. Thomas.

Mencken, H. L. (1967). *The American language*, abridged with new material by R. I. McDavid Jr. New York: Knopf.

National Clearinghouse for Alcohol and Drug Information (NCADI), U.S. Department of Health and Human Services. (2000). Available from http://www.health.org/.

National Institute on Drug Abuse (NIDA), U.S. National Institutes of Health (NIH). (2000). Available from http://www.nida.nih.gov/.

Partnership for a Drug-Free America. (2000). *Drug-free resource net.* Available from http://www.drugfreeamerica.org/.

Porter, R., & Teich, M. (Eds.). (1995). *Drugs and narcotics in history.* Cambridge, UK: Cambridge University Press.

Seymour, R. B., & Smith, D. E. (1987). *Guide to psychoactive drugs: An up-to-the minute reference to mind-altering substances.* New York: Harrington Park Press.

Smith, A. M., et al. (1992). Terminology for drug injection practices among intravenous drug users in Baltimore. *International Journal of Addictions*, *27*, 435–453.

Spears, R. A. (1986). *The slang and jargon of drugs and drink.* Metuchen, NJ: Scarecrow Press.

Street drugs: Drug slang. (2008). Available from http://argot.com/.

Street terms: Drugs and the drug trade. (2008). Available from http://www.whitehousedrugpolicy.gov/.

Tracy, S. W., & Acker, C. J. (Eds.). (2000). *Altering American consciousness: The history of alcohol and drug use in the United States, 1800–2000.* Amherst: University of Massachusetts Press.

U.S. Office of National Drug Control Policy. (2000). Available from http://www.whitehousedrugpolicy.gov/.

Wentworth, H., & Flexner, S. B. (1968). *The pocket dictionary of American slang.* New York: Pocket Books.

White House Office of National Drug Control Policy's Street Terms Database. (2008). Available from http://www.family.samhsa.gov/.

Williams, T. (1989). *The cocaine kids.* New York: Addison-Wesley.

RICHARD LINGEMAN
REVISED BY MARY CARVLIN (2001)
REVISED BY PAMELA V. MICHAELS (2009)

SLEEP, DREAMING, AND DRUGS.

The use of psychoactive drugs and alcohol to hasten the onset of sleep and to enhance the experience of dreaming is a phenomenon that dates to prehistory. The ancient Greeks used hallucinatory substances for religious purposes. The priestesses at Delphi, for example, chewed certain leaves while sitting in a smoke-filled chamber and going into a trance. On returning to consciousness, they would bring forth a divine prophecy. The various Dionysian cults encouraged their celebrants to enter ecstatic dream-like states through the use of wine and perhaps other drugs. The ancient Hindus imbibed a sacred drink called *soma*, and marijuana was used in practices of meditation. For the Arabs, hashish (a form of marijuana) was the substance of choice, while the Incas chewed the leaves of the coca plant (from which cocaine may be made). The opium poppy was used in Asia, and the ancient Mexicans used a variety of powerful psychoactive substances, including peyote, sacred mushrooms, and seeds from the Mexican morning glory plant, to enter the realm of dreams. The Australian aboriginals used the *pituri*, a psychoactive substance, to take them into "dream time," as they referred to it.

ALCOHOL

The effects of ethanol (alcohol) on sleep are complex and somewhat paradoxical. The acute bedtime administration of ethanol to healthy, nonalcoholic volunteers shortens the latency to sleep onset and, depending on dose, may initially increase the amount of relaxed, deep slow-wave (delta-wave) sleep. Additionally, ethanol reduces the amount of REM sleep, usually affecting the second REM period. An ethanol concentration in the blood of 50-milligram percent (mg%) or greater (80 mg% is legal intoxication in all states) is necessary to observe these sleep effects. The sleep effects of ethanol are observed primarily during the first half of an eight-hour sleep period. Ethanol is metabolized at a constant rate, and consequently the usual dose of ethanol (resulting in a blood alcohol concentration of 50–90 mg%) given in these studies is almost completely eliminated from the body after four or five hours.

Following elimination of ethanol, an apparent compensatory effect on sleep occurs. During the latter half of sleep, increased amounts of REM sleep and increased wakefulness or light sleep are found. Within three to four nights of repeated administration of the same dose of ethanol, tolerance occurs, and the initial effects on sleep are lost, while the secondary disruption of sleep during the latter half of the night persists. REM sleep time and sleep latency return to their basal levels, and the effects on slow-wave sleep, when initially present, do not persist. When nightly administration of ethanol is discontinued, a REM rebound is seen. But the REM rebound after repeated nightly ethanol administration in healthy, nonalcoholic subjects is neither consistent nor predictable. In alcoholics, however, the REM rebound has been demonstrated to be both intense and persistent. Some believe the presence of a REM rebound is characteristic of drugs with a high addictive potential.

OPIATES

Belladonna and opiates have historically been used for the specific purpose of producing vivid dreams. The most famous illustration is the story of the English poet Samuel Taylor Coleridge (1772–1834), who allegedly wrote his most celebrated work, "Kubla Khan," during a drug-induced dream. Lysergic acid diethylamide (LSD) became popular in the United States and Europe during the 1960s for allegedly facilitating higher states of consciousness and creativity. The writer John Lilley used a sensory-deprivation tank to emulate the state of sleep while taking LSD to induce creative dreaming.

Reference to the effects of drugs and alcohol on sleep and dreaming are also found in popular literature. It was a mixture made from poppies that caused Dorothy and her companions to fall into deep sleep in the *Wizard of Oz*. After ingesting a series of pills and liquids, in *Through the Looking Glass*, Alice finds herself in "Wonderland," where she has a conversation with an opium-smoking caterpillar who is sitting on a magic mushroom that alters the state of one who eats of it. After returning to the reality of her home in England, Alice realizes that she had, of course, fallen asleep and been dreaming.

Modern study of the effects of drugs and alcohol on sleep and dreams dates to the mid-1950s. With the use of electrophysiological machines, including electroencephalograms (EEGs), electrooculograms, and electromyograms, the state of sleep most closely associated with dreaming was discovered, studied, and named REM, for the rapid eye movements unique to that sleep state. In humans, REM sleep recurs in approximately 90-minute cycles throughout the sleep period, resulting in four or five REM episodes per night, each lasting from 10 to 30 minutes. Adults spend about 20 to 25 percent of their sleep period in REM sleep. Abrupt awakening from REM sleep is consistently associated with the recall of vivid dreaming. While the function of REM sleep is not completely understood, it appears to serve a necessary function. Deprivation of REM sleep by awakenings or by the administration of REM-suppressing drugs leads to a compensatory or rebound effect, specifically, a more rapid onset and a greater amount and intensity of REM sleep, when the sleep pattern is able to return to normal. This indicates that there is a physiological need for REM sleep, as deprivation of it causes an accumulation of need that must be satisfied for baseline sleep patterns to resume.

Many psychoactive substances have meaningful effects on sleep and particularly on REM sleep. While the effects of drugs on REM sleep are known, their effects on dreaming continue to be studied. Given the association of REM sleep and dreaming, one might think that REM-enhancing drugs would increase dreaming, while REM-suppressing drugs would decrease dreaming. The existing data as of 2008 suggest that the relationship is not that simple. After the discontinuation of REM-suppressing drugs, a REM rebound occurs, which is reported to be associated with increased and unpleasant dreams, as well as nightmares. Some have hypothesized that the visual hallucinations experienced during discontinuation of some drugs (e.g., alcohol) is a REM rebound intruding into wakefulness. While it is reductive to think of dreaming and REM in a one-to-one correspondence, it is reasonable to assume that drugs affecting REM will also affect the frequency and nature of dreams.

Morphine and Heroin. Morphine, an opiate analgesic (derived from the opium poppy), decreases the number and the duration of REM sleep episodes and delays the onset of the first REM period. It also increases awakenings and light sleep and suppresses slow-wave sleep. Heroin, a semi-synthetic opiate, also suppresses REM sleep and slow-wave sleep and increases wakefulness and light sleep, producing a disruption of the usual continuity of sleep. Heroin appears to be more potent than morphine in its sleep effects. The synthetic opiate, methadone, has similar effects on sleep and wakefulness, with a potency more comparable to that of morphine. When an opiate is administered just before the onset of sleep, the EEG pattern shows isolated bursts of delta waves on the background of a waking pattern. Animal studies have correlated these delta bursts with the behavior of head nodding (a possible physiological correlate to the street term *being on the nod*). Repeated administration of the opiates at the same dose leads to tolerance to the sleep effects of these drugs, particularly the REM sleep effects. The

cessation of opiate use leads to a protracted REM rebound, increased REM sleep, and a shortened latency to the first REM episode.

STIMULANTS

Stimulants, including amphetamines, when administered before sleep, delay sleep onset, increase wakefulness during the sleep period, and specifically suppress REM sleep. Cessation of chronic amphetamine use is associated with an increase in slow-wave sleep on the first recovery night and, on subsequent nights, with increased amounts of REM sleep and a reduced latency to the first episode of REM sleep, i.e., REM rebound.

Caffeine interferes with sleep in most nontolerant individuals. Once tolerance has developed, people are much less likely to report sleep disturbances, or they may sense that their inability to sleep because of caffeine intake has completely disappeared. To illustrate, 53 percent of those consuming less than 250 mg per day (about 2 to 3 cups of coffee) agreed that caffeine before bedtime would prevent sleep, compared to 43 percent of those consuming 250 to 749 mg per day, and only 22 percent of those consuming 750 mg per day or more. Even though the higher level caffeine consumers denied that caffeine interferes with their sleep, studies done in sleep laboratories confirm that caffeine consumers do have greater sleep latency, more frequent awakenings, and altered sleep architecture, and that these effects are dose-related. One study that investigated the effects of day-long consumption of coffee and tea on sleep onset and sleep quality demonstrated that caffeinated beverages had a dose-dependent negative effect on sleep onset, sleep time, and sleep quality.

Nicotine. Nicotine has varying effects on sleep. In a study conducted in rats, the higher the dose of nicotine that was administered, the lower the tota sleep time. In a study of the effects of nicotine transdermal patches on depressed patients, nicotine increased REM sleep time and alleviated some symptoms of depression. But another study that assessed the effects on sleep of four different doses of 24-hour transdermal nicotine showed no changes in sleep efficiency from baseline for any of the doses used. When a person is attempting to withdraw from nicotine addiction, sleep and concentration difficulties are often reported. Research has demonstrated that such withdrawal symptoms are lessened by maintaining an adequate blood level of nicotine, as can be supplied by transdermal patches. In that setting, sleep can appear to be enhanced by the use of 24-hour nicotine patches.

Cocaine. Cocaine also has stimulant effects on the central nervous system. Cocaine's effects on electroencephalogram readings were first studied in 1931 by Hans Berger (1873–1941), the Swiss researcher who developed the EEG. Cocaine was found to increase fast-frequency EEG activity, suggesting an alerting effect. The self-reported use of cocaine during the late afternoon and early evening is associated with reduced nocturnal sleep time. Electrophysiological studies show a reduction of REM sleep following cocaine administration. Cessation of chronic cocaine abuse is followed by increased sleep time and a REM rebound.

HALLUCINOGENS

The three classic hallucinogens are LSD, mescaline, and psilocybin. The state experienced following use of hallucinogens is somewhat similar to dreaming. Since REM sleep is highly correlated with dreaming, it would be expected that the hallucinogens facilitate REM sleep, but LSD is the only hallucinogen as of 2008 that has been systematically studied for its effects on sleep. One study done in humans showed that LSD enhanced REM sleep early in the night, although it did not alter the total amount of REM sleep for the night. However, studies in animals all indicate that LSD increases wakefulness and decreases the first episode of REM sleep for the night. The brain wave frequency changes seen in the waking EEG of animals (similar among all three hallucinogens) suggest an arousing effect. Thus the REM suppression seen with hallucinogen administration in animals may not be a specific REM effect but rather a sleep-suppressing effect.

Marijuana. Another drug with some hallucinogenic effects is marijuana, its active ingredient being tetrahydrocannabinol (THC). The effects of THC on the waking EEG pattern are significantly different than the effects of the classic hallucinogens cited above. THC has sedating effects at lower doses and hallucinatory effects at higher doses. The acute administration of marijuana or THC to

humans is associated with an increase in slow-wave sleep and a reduction in REM sleep. When THC is administered chronically (long-term), the effects on slow-wave and REM sleep diminish, indicating the presence of tolerance. Discontinuing the use of marijuana is associated with temporarily increased wakefulness and increased REM sleep time.

Most of these drugs, which are also drugs of abuse, have some effects on sleep, particularly on the amount and timing of REM sleep. Each affects chemicals in the brain that control sleep and wakefulness and, with chronic use, some adaptation is typically reported to occur. A characteristic REM rebound is seen on discontinuation of protracted drug use. (It may be that the ancients' experience of enhanced dreaming was the REM rebound that is typically associated with protracted drug use.) Some studies indicate that, in the formerly drug dependent individuals in recovery, the occurrence and intensity of the REM rebound has been predictive of relapse to drug use. How the sleep-wake pattern changes—and specifically the REM changes associated with these drugs— contribute to their excessive use need further study.

See also **Addiction: Concepts and Definitions; Benzodiazepines: Complications; Sedative-Hypnotic; Sedatives: Adverse Consequences of Chronic Use; Tolerance and Physical Dependence.**

BIBLIOGRAPHY

Greden, J. F., & Walters, A. (1997). Caffeine. In J. H. Lowinson, P. Ruiz, R. B. Millman, & J. G. Langrod (Eds.), *Substance abuse: A comprehensive textbook* (pp. 294–307). Baltimore: Williams & Wilkins.

Hindmarch, I., Rigney, U., Stanley, N., Quinlan, P., Rycroft, J., & Lane, J. (2000). A naturalistic investigation of the effects of day-long consumption of tea, coffee and water on alertness, sleep onset and sleep quality. *Psychopharmacology (Berl), 149*, 203–216.

Johnston, L. D., O'Malley, P. M., & Bachman, J. G. (2005). *Monitoring the Future: National survey results and drug use, Overview of key Findings 2004.* Bethesda, MD: National Institute on Drug Abuse, National Institutes of Health, Department of Health and Human Services.

Salin-Pascual, R. J., & Drucker-Colin, R. (1998). A novel effect of nicotine on mood and sleep in major depression. *Neuroreport, 9*, 57–60.

Substance Abuse and Mental Health Services Administration, Office of Applied Studies. (2004). *Results from the 2003 National Survey on Drug Use and Health: National Findings.* DHHS Pub. No. (SMA) 04–3964.

Turnheim, K. (2003). When drug therapy gets old: Pharmacokinetics and pharmacodynamics in the elderly. *Experimental Gerontology, 38*(8), 843–853, 2003.

Vogel G.W., Buffenstein, A., Minter, K., & Hennessey, A. (1900). Drug effects on REM sleep and on endogenous depression. *Neuroscience and Biobehavioral Reviews, 14,* 49–63.

Watson, R., Bakos, L., Compton, P., & Gawin, F. (1989). Cocaine use and withdrawal: The effect on sleep and mood. *Sleep Research, 18,* 83.

Williams, H., & Salamy, A. (1972). Alcohol and sleep. In B. Kissin & H. Begleiter (Eds.), *The biology of alcoholism* (Vol. 2, pp. 435–483). New York: Plenum.

Wolter, T. D., Hauri, P. D., Schroeder, D. R., Wisbey, J. A., Croghan, I. T., Offord, K. P., et al. (1996). Effects of 24-hour nicotine replacement on sleep and daytime activity during smoking cessation. *Preventive Medicine, 25,* 601–610.

TIMOTHY A. ROEHRS
THOMAS ROTH
REVISED BY RON GASBARRO (2001)
PAMELA V. MICHAELS (2009)

SLEEPING PILLS. This is a general term applied to a number of different drugs in pill form that help induce sleep, i.e. sedative-hypnotic agents. There is a wide range of such medications. Many require a doctor's prescription, but some can be purchased as over-the-counter drugs at a pharmacy. These latter preparations generally contain an antihistamine such as chlorpheniramine maleate, which produces drowsiness.

The prescription medications are much stronger. They include barbiturates, benzodiazepines, and a number of other compounds. However, due to the risk for fatal overdose, especially in combination with alcohol or other CNS depressants, the barbiturates are no longer widely prescribed for this indication. In general, the shorter-acting sleeping pills are used to help one relax enough to get to sleep, while the longer-acting ones are used to help prevent frequent awakenings during the night. Long-term or inappropriate use can lead to tolerance and physical dependence.

See also **Sedative-Hypnotic; Sedatives: Adverse Consequences of Chronic Use.**

BIBLIOGRAPHY

Hobbs, W. R., Rall, T. W., & Verdoorn, T. A. (1996). Hypnotics and sedatives. In A. G. Gilman et al. (Eds.), *The pharmacological basis of therapeutics,* 9th ed. New York: McGraw-Hill Medical (2005, 11th ed.

Pandi-Perumal, S. R., & Monti, J. M. (2006). *Clinical pharmacology of sleep* New York: Springer.

SCOTT E. LUKAS

SMART RECOVERY AND RATIONAL RECOVERY. Self-Management and Response Training (SMART) Recovery was formerly named the Rational Recovery Self-Help Network, and it was affiliated with the Rational Recovery (RR) program founded by Jack and Lois Trimpey. After a series of disagreements between Mr. Trimpey and the board of directors overseeing the Self-Help Network concerning the programs to be offered by the self-help groups, there was a mutual parting of the ways. In 1994, the Self-Help Network changed its name to SMART Recovery and severed its affiliation with RR.

The main difference between the two programs has to do with governance. A board of directors oversees SMART, a not-for-profit corporation (501c3), and RR, a for-profit corporation, is owned exclusively by the Trimpeys. There are some philosophical differences as well. RR appears to focus primarily on coping with urges, whereas SMART includes attention to motivation, controlling urges, problem-solving, and leading a balanced life. It is based on scientific knowledge and good practice as interpreted by the board of directors and the program committee. The conceptual framework for SMART Recovery is based on the principles of Rational Emotive Behavior Theory, as espoused by Albert Ellis and E. Velten (1992).

SMART Recovery is an evidence-based program utilizing groups, online meetings, online chat, and face-to-face meetings to assist people in recovery from the continuum of addictive behaviors, including (but not limited to) alcoholism, illicit drug abuse in general, general abuse of prescription medications, gambling and sex addiction, cocaine addiction, eating disorders, and addiction to other unwanted behaviors or substances. All programs are offered free of charge, although donations are accepted. SMART Recovery is offered as an alternative to the more traditional, spiritually based twelve-step groups. In an average week, SMART sponsors more than 300 face-to-face meetings worldwide, as well as nearly 20 online meetings. There is also an extensive interactive Web site and a message board.

SMART Recovery's stated mission is to assist and support individuals who are striving to achieve and sustain abstinence by offering a variety of educational opportunities, tools, and techniques as mechanisms for behavior change to help them shift from self-defeating thinking, emotions, and actions and achieve a lifestyle that brings both internal satisfaction and an improved quality of life.

SMART Recovery is based on a four-point program:

1. Enhancing and maintaining motivation to abstain.
2. Coping with urges.
3. Problem-solving: managing thoughts, feelings and behaviors.
4. Lifestyle balance: balancing momentary and enduring satisfactions.

The SMART Recovery program focuses on empowering individuals to free themselves from addictions and unwanted behaviors. There are myriad tools and techniques incorporated into the four-point program, with the understanding that they need repetition and practice to attain mastery. Skill building is progressive over time and across the four points.

RATIONAL RECOVERY
Jack and Lois Trimpey started Rational Recovery in 1986. It is focused on addiction recovery through abstinence and states that it is the "antithesis and irreconcilable arch-rival of Alcoholics Anonymous." RR purports that addiction is a choice, not a disease manifestation; co-dependency does not exist; and that group meetings can lead to substitute addiction and are, at best, counterproductive. RR holds that recovery from addiction is a highly personal journey that can best occur without external sources of support (groups, sponsors, family, friends, medical personnel, etc.). It also holds that people become addicts not because of genetic predisposition, cultural factors, poverty, stress, self-medication, or low self-esteem but simply because it feels good to be high.

A cornerstone of RR is Addictive Voice Recognition Technique (AVRT). This technique is based on the belief that the urge to use addicting substances arises from the primitive brain, which is based on instinctive, irrational, animal urges to seek pleasure. By recognizing this and giving it a name, the Addictive Voice (AV), it is possible to overcome it and conquer addictions. The AV becomes separated from the rest of the self through the use of the RR principles, and "*I* want to get high" becomes "*It* wants to get high." By shifting to thoughts of power and control to overcome the AV, recovery becomes automatic and, in RR parlance, effortless. *Never* is the operative word for abstinence, and living in the moment is key, so "I will never use drugs again" shifts to "I never use drugs now." The *Crash Course on AVRT*, which teaches abstinence techniques, is available on the Rational Recovery Web site.

Because neither program is able to collect complete outcome data, the overall effectiveness of SMART Recovery and of Rational Recovery is unknown. There are no reliable or valid outcome data for *any* self-help program, because of both the policy of anonymity that is a cornerstone of self-help programs and the relative scientific informality of such groups.

See also **Alcoholics Anonymous (AA); Sobriety; Treatment, Behavioral Approaches to: Self-Help and Anonymous Groups.**

BIBLIOGRAPHY

Bishop, F. M. (2001). *Managing addictions: Cognitive, emotive and behavioral techniques.* Lanham, MD: Jason Aronson.

Ellis, A., & Velten, E. (1992). *When AA doesn't work for you: Rational steps to quitting alcohol.* New York: Barricade Books.

Peele, S., Brodsky, A., & Arnold, A. (1991). *The truth about addiction and recovery.* New York: Fireside Books.

Peele, S., Bufe, C, Brodsky, A., & Horvath, T. (2000). *Resisting 12-Step coercion: How to fight forced participation in AA, NA or 12-Step treatment.* Tucson, AZ: See Sharp Press.

Schaler, J. A. (2000). *Addiction is a choice.* Peru, IL: Carus Publishing.

Solomon, M. (2005). *AA: Not the only way. Your one stop resource guide to 12-Step alternatives.* Venice, CA: Melanie Solomon.

Steinberger, H. (Ed). (2004). *The SMART Recovery Handbook.* Mentor, OH: SMART Recovery.

Tate, P. (1997). *Alcohol: How to give it up and be glad you did.* Tucson, AZ: See Sharp Press.

Trimpey, J. (1994). *The small book (Rational Recovery systems)*. New York: Dell.

Trimpey, J. (1996). *Rational Recovery: The new cure for substance addiction*. New York: Simon & Schuster.

PAMELA V. MICHAELS

SOBRIETY. The term *sobriety* is not defined in current medical or psychiatric literature. The term *abstinence* is found more often and is generally agreed upon as the treatment goal for severe alcoholics. Abstinence is defined as nonuse of the substance to which a person was addicted.

SOBRIETY AND SUBSTANCE ABUSE

The term *sobriety* is used by members of Alcoholics Anonymous (AA) and Narcotics Anonymous (NA), and also by members of other Twelve-Step groups and recovery groups not affiliated with AA. In AA and NA, sobriety is often preceded by the adjectives "stable" or "serene." Abstinence—the condition of being sober—is a necessary but insufficient condition for sobriety. Sobriety means something different from the *initial* abstinence so often achieved by alcoholics and other drug addicts. This initial abstinence is recognized as a time of vulnerability to RELAPSE, often referred to as a "dry drunk" or "white-knuckle sobriety."

Sobriety in NA and AA. According to AA beliefs, recovery from alcoholism and other addictions calls for more than just abstinence. The addict's central nervous system must undergo a substantial readaptation. This requirement means that the craving, drug-seeking, dysphoria (unhappiness), and negative cognitions that characterize early abstinence must not only diminish but must also be replaced by more normal positive behavior. This readaptation requires time and substitute activities. The activities most associated with successful readaptation are found in treatment programs and in AA or NA.

Sobriety, as used by most recovering people in AA and NA, refers to abstinence plus a program of activity designed to make the abstinence comfortable and to improve functioning in relationships and in other aspects of life. The program of recovery that leads to stable sobriety usually includes: (1) attending AA and/or NA meetings; (2) "working"

the Twelve Steps and continuing to use steps 10, 11, and 12 for the maintenance of sobriety; (3) working with a sponsor who acts as a mentor in maintaining sobriety; (4) belonging to a home group and engaging in service activities that help others with their sobriety; and (5) other activities that enhance or support sobriety (e.g., exercise, hobbies, and psychotherapy). A program of recovery recognizes that any activity has potential to either enhance or interfere with the recovering individual's sobriety. In addition, Twelve-Step programs emphasize the importance of basing sobriety on positive beliefs and ideals. "Shotgun sobriety" is defined in AA as a type of sobriety based only on fear of drinking.

Sobriety in Non-AA Recovery Groups. Secular Organization for Sobriety (SOS), Women for Sobriety (WFS), LifeRing Secular Recovery (LSR), and similar recovery groups for substance abusers also define sobriety in terms of abstinence from drugs and alcohol. A LifeRing pamphlet states, "Please look elsewhere for support if your intention is to keep drinking or using, but not so much, or to stop drinking but continue using, or stop using but continue drinking. The successful LifeRing participant practices the Sobriety Priority, meaning that nothing is allowed to interfere with staying abstinent from alcohol and drugs."

SOBRIETY AND BEHAVIORAL ADDICTIONS

One complication of the term *sobriety* has been the difficulty of defining it in the context of the so-called "process addictions" or "behavioral addictions," terms that have been used to distinguish addictions to such activities or behaviors as gambling, shopping, overeating, sexual acting-out, etc. from substance addictions in the strict sense. Unlike alcoholics and drug abusers, people with behavioral addictions cannot always define sobriety as simple abstinence. A compulsive overeater, for example, must learn to consume food in moderation, not avoid it. Persons addicted to compulsive spending or shopping cannot simply abstain from making purchases. Members of Sex Addicts Anonymous (SAA) rarely define sexual sobriety as complete abstinence from sex, although at times recovering persons may practice complete abstinence (celibacy) for a period of time in order to gain perspective on their life. In this Twelve-Step group, sexual sobriety is most often defined as "a contract that the sexual addict makes between him/herself and their 12-step recovery support and/or their therapist/clergy. These contracts . . . are always written and involve clearly defined concrete behaviors from which the sexual addict has committed to abstain in order to define their sobriety." Comparable abstinence contracts are used by recovering binge eaters, compulsive spenders, relationship addicts, etc.

One benefit of attempts to redefine sobriety in the context of behavioral addictions is that they have called attention to the problem of substitute addictions, which are addictions that develop when a recovering alcoholic or drug abuser substitutes food, tobacco, or certain activities (including exercise) for their drug of choice. Many members of Twelve-Step groups have found that sobriety requires a reexamination of addictive beliefs and attitudes in general as well as abstinence from alcohol or specific drugs.

SPONTANEOUS RECOVERY

One question that has arisen in recent years is whether some alcoholics can achieve sobriety through spontaneous recovery. G. G. May (1988) uses the term *deliverance* for this phenomenon and defines it as "healing [that] takes the form of empowerment that enables people to modify addictive behavior." Some researchers suggest that spontaneous remission and recovery is more common among alcoholics than was once believed, and that it is connected to growth and maturity in the course of the adult life cycle. G. E. Vaillant (1983) found that most alcoholics in his study outgrew their drinking problem, more often than not without going into treatment or joining AA. Stanton Peele (1992) is perhaps the best-known proponent of the view that ". . . some people who appear completely out of control of their actions at one point significantly change their outlooks and ability to regulate their behavior later in life." He likens spontaneous recovery of sobriety to the ability of some smokers to suddenly quit using tobacco.

SOBRIETY: SUMMARY

Despite these problems of precise definition, the concept of sobriety (abstinence or its equivalent for nonchemical addictions, plus a program of activity designed to make abstinence comfortable) is a useful one for health care professionals.

See also **Addiction: Concepts and Definitions; Treatment, Behavioral Approaches to: Minnesota Model; Treatment, Behavioral Approaches to: Self-Help and Anonymous Groups.**

BIBLIOGRAPHY

Alcoholics Anonymous World Services. (1976). *Alcoholics anonymous.* New York: Author.

American Psychiatric Association. (1989). *A.P.A. task force: treatment of psychiatric disorders.* Washington, D.C.: Author.

Augustine Fellowship, Sex and Love Addicts Anonymous. (1986). *Sex and Love Addicts Anonymous.* Boston: Fellowship-Wide Services, Inc.

Helgoe, R. (2002). *Hierarchy of recovery: From abstinence to self-actualization,* 2nd ed. Center City, MN: Hazelden.

Landry, M. J. (2004). *Understanding drugs of abuse: The processes of addiction, treatment and recovery.* Washington, D.C.: American Psychiatric Publishing.

LifeRing Secular Recovery. (2000). *Sobriety is our priority.* New York: LifeRing Secular Recovery Service Center.

Ludwig, A. M. (1986). Cognitive Processes Associated with "Spontaneous" Recovery from Alcoholism. *Journal of Studies on Alcohol, 47,* 53–58.

May, G. G. (1988). *Addiction & grace: love and spirituality in the healing of addictions.* New York: HarperCollins.

Peele, S. (1992). Why is everybody always pickin' on me? A response to comments. *Addictive Behaviors, 17,* (1) 83–93.

Stone, E. M., Ed. (1988). *American psychiatric glossary.* Washington, D.C.: American Psychiatric Press.

Vaillant, G. E. (1983). *The natural history of alcoholism.* Cambridge, MA: Harvard University Press.

Wilford, B. B., Ed. (1990). *Syllabus for the review course in addiction medicine.* Washington, DC: American Society of Addiction Medicine.

JOHN N. CHAPPEL
REVISED BY REBECCA J. FREY (2001)

SOCIAL COSTS OF ALCOHOL AND DRUG ABUSE.
Drinking, smoking, and the use of psychotropic drugs have a variety of consequences for those who use them, for their families and associates, and for society at large. A number of these consequences are negative. Smokers can die

young from heart or lung disease, drinkers can get into traffic accidents and fights, drug injectors can spread the HIV virus. In the context of public policymaking, when priorities must be set for the use of scarce resources, it seems important to have a measure of the overall magnitude of the social burden engendered by such consequences. One familiar approach is to express the magnitude of the problem in terms of the number of people who die each year. When one learns that there are over 50,000 deaths per year in the United States from alcohol abuse (National Highway Transportation Safety Administration, 2006), almost 20,000 from drug abuse other than alcohol (Centers for Disease Control, 2007), and that between 1.2 and 1.6 million Americans visited emergency rooms for situations associated with drug misuse or abuse (Substance Abuse and Mental Health Services Administration, 2007), it becomes clear that the stakes are very high in devising sound policies for controlling drinking and drugging. Such statistics, compelling as they are, tell only part of the story. In addition to causing early death, substance abuse makes for a variety of consequences that reduce the quality of life both for users and for other people.

To capture this broad array of consequences in a single number, analysts have estimated various measures of social cost. The estimates are important because they figure in the political process by which federal funds are allocated to the National Institutes of Health (NIH), the Substance Abuse and Mental Health Services Administration (SAMHSA) and to other agencies that play a role in combating substance abuse. A conceptual apparatus developed by a task force of the U.S. Public Health Service chaired by Dorothy Rice (Hodgson & Meiners, 1979) has been used to derive the most prominent estimates of social costs for substance abuse. In 1994 the International Symposium on the Economic and Social Costs of Substance Abuse issued guidelines recommending the use of this cost-of-illness (COI) method in an attempt to establish a common foundation and enhance the comparability of cost studies conducted in different countries (International Center for Alcohol Policies [ICAP], 1999).

Although prominent in policy debate, the cost-of-illness (COI) method has been faulted for its emphasis on production as the measure of social welfare. Economists favor a quite different approach that measures social welfare from the perspective of the consumer. The economists' preferred accounting framework is referred to in this entry as the *external social-cost* approach.

THE TWO FRAMEWORKS APPLIED TO SUBSTANCE ABUSE

A coherent assessment of the social costs of substance abuse requires an accounting framework that specifies criteria for judging which of the myriad effects are deemed to be of public concern. For example, in the case of drinking, on any one drinking occasion there may be harmful consequences: social embarrassment, loss of reputation or affection, failure to discharge some responsibility at work or home, physical injury from an accident, victimization by a mugger or rapist, and nausea or hangover. Chronic heavy drinking may result in still other consequences including rejection by family and friends, loss of a job or of an opportunity for promotion, progressive deterioration in physical health, and an early death. To capture these and other negative consequences in a single number, the list of consequences must be reviewed to determine which should be considered in establishing priorities for substance abuse policy. The consequences deemed relevant must then be quantified, translated into a standard unit of account (dollars), and summed.

The Cost-of-Illness Framework. The COI approach is concerned with measuring the loss or diversion of productive resources resulting from an illness or activity. In the case of alcohol abuse, human capital resources are lost and the gross national product reduced by the morbidity and early death of some drinkers, whether because of injuries sustained in alcohol-related traffic accidents or violent crime or because of organ damage and other diseases stemming from chronic heavy drinking. The loss to society in these cases is equal to the loss of the marginal product of the victims' labor, valued at the market wage. Unpaid work at home, including housework and child care, is included in the computation with values being assigned according to how much households pay for such services when paid employees are hired to do the work.

The COI approach also takes account of the diversion of resources from other productive uses necessitated by alcohol abuse. Thus the costs of medical care for alcohol-related illness and drug-related illness, treatment for alcoholism and drug abuse, and research on prevention and treatment are incorporated in the social-cost estimate. Similarly, the value of law-enforcement and justice resources devoted to alcohol-related crimes are included as are the costs of replacing property damaged in traffic accidents and fires caused by drinking.

Several prominent estimates of the total costs of alcohol abuse for the United States have used the COI framework (Berry & Boland, 1977; Harwood et al., 1998). In 1998 H. J. Harwood et al. published the most complete COI study to date, and using figures from 1992, the most recent year for which complete data were available, they found that the economic costs to society of alcohol abuse totaled $148 billion, broken down as follows:

About three quarters ($107 billion) of the total cost in this tabulation is the value of labor productivity lost because of illness, injury, or early death. The human capital lost because of alcohol-related mortality was computed for all those who died in 1992 from causes in which intoxication or chronic heavy drinking played a role. These include traffic fatalities and deaths from liver cirrhosis among other causes. The lost human capital was valued by estimating how much the deceased would have earned if they had lived and worked until retirement age;

The human capital lost because of morbidity was calculated by estimating the reduction in the productivity of the labor force resulting from alcohol dependence or abuse. Harwood et al. combined two sets of estimates to arrive at this number: (a) the percentage of the labor force in 1992 that was or had ever been subject to a diagnosis of alcohol dependence or abuse, and (b) an estimate of the loss in earnings associated with such a diagnosis.

Estimates of this sort have been challenged for two reasons. The first challenge is to the statistical methods used to generate the estimates of morbidity, mortality, and lost earnings (Cook, 1991). The second challenge is more fundamental because it concerns the basic principles that inform the COI accounting framework.

The COI procedure estimates the costs of morbidity and mortality in terms of lost productivity, but this emphasis on production as the measure of social welfare seems misplaced. A more liberal perspective, favored by economists among others, shifts the emphasis to consumption and interprets the task of measuring social welfare in terms of aggregating individual preferences. People are the best judges of their own welfare. It should not be considered problematic if sometimes they make choices that fail to maximize their productivity. In this view the choices that people make concerning how hard to work and when to retire are of little public concern. The same goes for choices that place someone's own health and safety at risk. Thus in economics there is a strong presumption in favor of consumer sovereignty, the principle that the individual person is in the best position to define what is best for him or her, and that social welfare is enhanced by free choice within certain limits. A negative consequence is deemed to be of *public* concern only when the actions of one individual impinge negatively on the welfare of others. The basic distinction, then, is between *internal* and *external* consequences of individual decisions, where the latter impose an involuntary cost on other people.

In the case of alcohol abuse, the internal costs include those suffered by drinkers and are foreseeable as a natural consequence of their choices. A small example explains the reasoning here. Suppose a woman decides to drink heavily despite knowing that she may be tired and unproductive the next day. By making this decision she is indicating that for her the pleasure of drinking outweighs the morning-after costs. The external costs are zero if no one else is harmed by this decision. If she were to drive after drinking, however, the accounting would change. She would be risking serious injury to herself and to others on the highway. Her injury would have external costs to the extent that a third party (group insurance or Medicaid) paid her medical expenses, and the risk that she might injure other people while driving is to be valued at the expected loss to them. That cost is not limited to their lost earnings but also includes their pain and suffering and the suffering of those who care about them.

The most fundamental challenge to the COI framework relates to its presumption that social welfare is synonymous with national product. Economists argue instead that the preferences of individuals are the proper measure of their well-being and that social welfare is the sum total of individual welfare. Some of the major costs in the COI framework, especially lost earnings, are less important in the external social-cost view, whereas a number of costs that are ignored in COI become important when the focus is on external costs.

The External Social-Cost Framework. In a study at the Rand Corporation, economists applied the external social-cost (ESC) framework to alcohol abuse and other poor health habits (Manning et al., 1989, 1991). Their estimate for alcohol abuse amounted to about $30 billion in 1985, less than half the COI estimate presented above for the same year. The accounting procedures used to generate this estimate of the ESC can be briefly summarized:

Heavy drinkers might have earned less than they otherwise would have during their careers and might have had their careers cut short by poor health and early death. Although the most obvious effect was a reduced standard of living, which was considered a private cost, a number of programs created a collective interest in the productivity of each individual. For example, those who died young saved their fellow citizens the expense of years of pension payments and medical costs. Those who retired early (perhaps because of poor health) imposed financial costs on others because their contributions to the Social Security system were reduced. Thus these collective financing arrangements had the effect of creating both external costs and external benefits in relation to heavy drinking. The net effect, according to W. G. Manning et al. (1991), was negative and equaled about 22 percent of the total external cost;

Heien (1996) reported that about 3,765 of the 13,984 people who died in alcohol-related traffic accidents in 1993 were innocent because they had not been drinking at the time. Their lives had value not because their work increased the size of the national product but because they enjoyed life. People are willing to pay to reduce the risk of a fatal accident, and the social cost of these innocent

deaths is in principle equal to the total amount the public would be willing to pay to eliminate the threat of being killed by a drunk driver. Manning et al. (1991) employed this willingness-to-pay approach and found that nearly half of the social cost of alcohol abuse stemmed from traffic fatalities;

The remaining $7.2 billion in the Manning et al. (1991) social-cost estimate stemmed primarily from the burden of alcohol-related cases on the criminal justice system and the share of collision insurance costs accounted for by the property damage caused by drunk drivers.

It appears that in several respects these estimates are incomplete. The costs of alcohol-related injuries to innocent victims are far higher than indicated by Manning et al. because they omitted the financial and personal costs of nonfatal injuries in traffic accidents (Miller & Blincoe, 1993) and the costs of both fatal and nonfatal injuries from violent crimes perpetrated by drunks. In addition, recent research has suggested that moderate alcohol consumption carries measurable health benefits, which must also be figured into any equation attempting to assess social costs (ICAP, 1999).

An even more interesting controversy has surfaced over the basic perspective that informs these external social-cost estimates. Some critics reject outright the liberal doctrine that individual preferences are to be accorded primacy in the definition of social welfare and social cost. They postulate a collective interest that can somehow be defined without reference to the choices made by individuals (Beauchamp, 1980). The COI approach reflects one such definition. Other critics accept the liberal doctrine but argue about its application. A particularly difficult set of philosophical and practical issues arises in setting the boundary between internal and external costs in the context of the family. Manning et al. (1991) view the family as a unit and accept the presumption that each member of the family will internalize the concerns of the others and act accordingly. In 1992 Harwood et al. found that abusers and their households bore $66.8 billion of the total cost of alcohol abuse. If the father is a heavy drinker or smoker it is not because he is unaware or unconcerned about the consequences for his wife and children, but because his enjoyment of these activities outweighs the costs to them. That presumption may seem particularly problematic in the case where the mother's substance abuse causes her baby to have birth defects.

COSTS OF DRUG USE AND ALCOHOL ABUSE

In calculating the current estimated social costs of alcohol abuse and drug use, analysts are forced to rely on data that may or may not have been developed consistent with one of the two approaches described above. Cost attributions for illegal drug use include but are not limited to: treatment and rehabilitation; emergency room consequences; lost productivity; increased demand for social services provided to dysfunctional families because of such use including the consequences of family violence, deaths from drug-related vehicle accidents (drugged driving), and drug-related illnesses; and law enforcement costs that are shifted from traditional activities to responding to the rise of local clandestine methamphetamine labs, drug use in schools, and related activities.

The most recent comprehensive assessment of the social costs of illegal drug use occurred in 2001 when the White House Office of National Drug Control Policy published a study on the social costs of drug abuse that indicated overall costs in excess of $160 billion a year (Office of National Drug Control Policy, 2001).

As the introduction in the 2001 study notes:

The most recent previous estimates of drug abuse related costs are for 1995 as developed by Harwood et al. (1998). In addition to providing new estimates of the societal cost of drug abuse, this report provides annual estimates for 1992 through 1998 and projections for 1999 and 2000 that are consistently developed so that trends in the overall societal cost and in component costs of drug abuse can be evaluated. Projections are only provided for 1999 and 2000 because there is a significant lag in the availability of the base data for estimating the component values. For the majority of components the most recent data available is from 1998. The estimates have followed guidelines developed by the U.S. Public Health Service for cost-of-illness studies. These guidelines have been applied in earlier studies of drug abuse in the U.S. (e.g., for 1992, 1985, 1980, and 1977), and to cost-of-illness studies for virtually all of the major medical problems. Accordingly, these estimates can be compared meaningfully to estimates

for diseases, such as cancer, stroke, heart disease, diabetes, alcohol abuse and mental illness.

The report noted that between 1992 and 1998 the overall cost of drug abuse to society increased at a rate of 5.9 percent annually and that the rate of increase in costs was in excess of the combined increase of 3.5 percent for the adult population and consumer price index for all services for this period.

The following tables reflect the cost categories and estimates for each estimate segment.

The report noted that the societal cost related to the three major categories of costs and that related to crime remained relatively constant between 1992 and 1998. However, it did not include the estimated $98 billion a year (Drug Enforcement Administration, 2008) that Americans spend on illegal drugs and did not account for the drug use impact on learning among elementary, secondary, and college students.

Although critics may shudder, applying a reasonable 5 percent a year increase to costs, it is likely that the 2008 estimates, if developed by the same methodology as used in 2001, would project social costs of illegal drug abuse in the United States to approximately $230 billion a year.

Costs attributed to alcohol abuse parallel those for illegal drug use. The most recent comprehensive assessment of the social costs of illegal drug use occurred in 2000 from the National Institute on Alcohol Abuse and Alcoholism (NIAAA) that estimated the economic costs for alcohol abuse to be almost $185 billion a year (Harwood et al., 1998).

Similar to the estimates for illegal drug use, the largest component was for loss productivity (72.7 percent), with health-related costs contributing 14.3 percent and other costs (crashes, fires, criminal justice etc.) contributing 13 percent.

Again, applying a reasonable 5 percent a year increase in costs, it is likely that the 2008 estimates, if developed by the same methodology as used in 2000, would project social costs of illegal drug abuse in the United States to approximately $300 billion a year.

The efforts to produce useful results have included controversy surrounding the issue of what is to be counted and how. The task of estimating the social costs of substance abuse requires a broad calculus, and the choice of a framework is not only a technical, scientific issue but also a matter of political philosophy. The conclusions reached through this extrapolation suggest that current estimates of the social and economic costs of illegal drug use and alcohol abuse could reach $500 billion a year.

See also **Accidents and Injuries from Alcohol; Accidents and Injuries from Drugs; Driving, Alcohol, and Drugs; Economic Costs of Alcohol and Drug Abuse; Industry and Workplace, Drug Use in; Productivity: Effects of Alcohol on.**

BIBLIOGRAPHY

Beauchamp, D. E. (1980). *Beyond alcoholism: Alcohol and public health policy.* Philadelphia: Temple University Press.

Berry, R. E., & Boland, J. P. (1977). *The economic cost of alcohol abuse.* New York: Free Press.

Centers for Disease Control. (February 9, 2007). Unintentional poisoning deaths—United States, 1999–2004, *MMWR Weekly.* 56 (05). 93-96.

Cook, P. J. (1991). The social costs of drinking. In *Expert meeting on the negative social consequences of alcohol abuse.* Oslo: Norwegian Ministry of Health and Social Affairs.

Drug Enforcement Administration. (2008). *Fact 5: Drug control spending is a minor portion of the U.S. budget. Compared to the social costs of drug abuse and addiction, government spending on drug control is minimal.* Available from http://www.usdoj.gov/dea/.

Harwood, H. J., Fountain, D., & Livermore, G. (1998). *The economic costs of alcohol and drug abuse in the United States: 1992.* Rockville, MD: The National Institute on Drug Abuse and the National Institute on Alcohol Abuse and Alcoholism.

Heien, D. M. (1996). Are higher alcohol taxes justified? *The Cato Journal, 15*(2–3).

Hodgson, T., & Meiners, M. (1979). *Guidelines for cost-of-illness studies in the public health service.* Bethesda, MD: Public Health Service Task Force on Cost-of-Illness Studies.

International Center for Alcohol Policies. (1999). Estimating costs associated with alcohol abuse: Towards a patterns approach. *ICAP Reports, 7.*

Kleiman, M. A. R. (1992). *Against excess: Drug policy for results.* New York: Basic Books.

Manning, W. G., et al. (1991). *The costs of poor health habits.* Cambridge, MA: Harvard University Press.

Manning, W. G., et al. (1989). The taxes of sin: Do smokers and drinkers pay their way? *Journal of the American Medical Association, 261*, 1604–1609.

Miller, T. R., & Blincoe, L. J. (1993). *Incidence and cost of alcohol-involved crashes.* Unpublished manuscript.

National Highway Transportation Safety Administration. (2007). *Traffic safety facts 2006.* (Research Note, DOT HS 810 821). Traffic Safety Annual Assessment—Alcohol-Related Fatalities. Washington, DC: Author.

Kung, H. C., Hoyer, D. L., Xu, J. Q., & Murphy, S. L. (2008). Deaths: Final data for 2005. *National Vital Statistics Reports, 56*(10). Hyattsville, MD: National Center for Health Statistics. Centers for Disease Control and Prevention. Available from http://www.cdc.gov/.

Office of National Drug Control Policy. (2001). *The economic costs of drug abuse in the United States, 1992–1998.* (Publication No. NCJ-190636). Washington, DC: Executive Office of the President. Office of National Drug Control Policy.

Rice, D. P., et al. (1990). *The economic costs of alcohol and drug abuse and mental illness: 1985* (Report submitted to the Office of Financing and Coverage Policy of the Alcohol, Drug Abuse, and Mental Health Administration, U.S. Department of Health and Human Services). San Francisco: University of California, Institute for Health and Aging.

Substance Abuse and Mental Health Services Administration, Office of Applied Studies. (2007). 2005: National estimates of drug-related emergency department visits. *DAWN Series D-29,* (DHHS Publication No. [SMA] 07-4256), Rockville, MD. Author.

PHILIP J. COOK
REVISED BY SARAH KNOX (2001)
RICHARD H. BUCHER (2009)

SOUTH AFRICA. The use of alcohol and other drugs in southern Africa stretches back more than a millennium. It is likely that the agricultural revolution that involved the domestication of grains was closely associated with the fermentation of those plants to produce alcohol. Even before the development of settled agriculture, in areas dominated by hunting and gathering peoples, substances such as wild fruits and honey provided the basis for making alcoholic drinks of various kinds. In addition, within every region, people exploited rich botanical resources that included many plants believed to possess various pharmaceutical properties and, in some cases, psychoactive powers. Cannabis certainly has a long history in the region, although very little is known about the history of cannabis or other local drug substances on the continent. Early reports regarding the native peoples of the Cape region indicated their taste for various kinds of alcohol as well as cannabis and other local narcotic plants.

THE COLONIAL PERIOD

Soon after the founding of the Cape of Good Hope Colony in the mid-seventeenth century, European officials and employers began to use liquor, tobacco, and cannabis as payment for work, and these kinds of labor arrangements were commonplace by 1800. A local desert root plant, known as *dagga,* was gathered, traded widely, and chewed. It apparently faded in importance during the 1700s, however, and was replaced by *canna*, a plant that was made into a drink reputed to induce a "frenzy most horrible to behold" (Gordon, 1996, p. 69). The use of these mild narcotics persisted well into the nineteenth century, and they spread among neighboring African peoples. Stronger alcoholic drinks, imported from Europe and produced in the expanding colonial economy, steadily pushed the indigenous drugs to the margins, however. Records indicate that local societies easily incorporated alcohol consumption, but that they were unfamiliar with smoking.

Cape Town was initially established as a provisioning station for the Dutch trade with the East Indies, but the port town quickly gained the nickname, "Tavern of the Seas." Some of the early white settlers established vineyards, and winemaking developed into a major industry. Cape wines were generally low quality, but they became an important element in the local and regional economies, which was based, for the most, part on the utilization of slave labor. Vineyard owners were soon converting their wines into cheap brandy known as "Cape Smoke." Labor patterns that rewarded work with brandy rations became a key element in the wine production system.

After the transfer to British rule around 1800 and the abolition of slavery several decades later, the *dop* system, by which brandy allotments were part of workers' wages, helped keep workers in semi-bondage. During the nineteenth century, the provision of these liquor payments, coupled with the cheap and easy availability of Cape Smoke, sustained a culture of excessive alcohol consumption and alcohol abuse among Colored (mixed-race) workers. Well into the twentieth century, the white vineyard owners continued to hold the kind of political clout that thwarted any efforts to reform the system. Thus, when employers in much of the rest of the country pressed for regulation to ensure a sober and disciplined workforce, the vineyard owners and their allies essentially saw sobriety as an enemy of discipline and control. Moreover, they were concerned with maintaining the large market for their products that the black population of the region represented. This system was created within a white-dominated society for which alcohol consumption was a critical element of social and economic life. Whites did not, therefore, regard the cheap brandy that they produced as dangerous, but South African whites did develop persistent stereotypes of the black and Colored population as innately attracted to alcohol.

BEER PRODUCTION IN THE NINETEENTH CENTURY

As Dutch-speaking white settlers and traders pushed into the interior of South Africa during the nineteenth century, they confronted and came into conflict with large populations of settled agriculturalists, such as the Xhosa, Zulu, Sotho, and Tswana. These peoples all had well-established traditions of producing grain-based beers, mostly produced through female labor. These beers were typically very thick, fermented drinks with a very limited shelf life, and their production was closely tied to the agricultural cycle. "Beer drinks" were almost always communal affairs held to mark important events, such as weddings and funerals. Beer was also used as a reward for help in accomplishing tasks that exceeded the capacity of family units to manage. And while they were primarily social affairs, beer drinks could also be highly ritualized reproductions of hierarchy. As such, they were typically dominated by adult men, although women were sometimes provided with drinks as well.

Grain beer was also a form of tribute, and it was commonplace during the harvest season for lines of people to offer calabashes of these beverages to local chiefs and rulers, such as the Zulu and Sotho kings, who played critical roles in nineteenth-century South African history. These leaders were themselves among the relatively small number of men who could command the labor resources to produce very large quantities of beer, and they had stores of grain adequate to produce alcohol throughout the year. This helped them to maintain their courts and attract followers.

The use of beer as tribute payment also accentuated sharp differences in wealth and status. The production of beer in rural agricultural societies represented a diversion of a critical food resource to the production of alcohol. Local grain beers certainly had food value, but beer production nevertheless shifted food supplies away from peripheral family members and dependents. This practice could therefore have dire impact during times when grain stocks ran low or disappeared.

CHRISTIANITY AND EARLY TEMPERANCE MOVEMENTS

By the middle of the nineteenth century, substantial areas of African settlement had been under white control for decades, and growing numbers of Africans had converted to Christianity. Many of these people settled into Christian communities that valued hard work, commerce, education, and devotion. Among these people, temperance gained substantial support, and the temperance organizations that formed represented not only efforts to reduce or eliminate drinking but nascent political movements as well. As Christianity spread, temperance spread with it, and South Africa evolved into a society in which a substantial portion of the population abstained, or claimed to abstain, from drink. Abstinence also found support among the sizeable Colored Muslim population based in Cape Town and surrounding areas.

The spread of commerce into the South African interior also involved the expansion of the liquor trade, notably brandy and other spirits. African leaders, such as Moshoeshoe in Lesotho and, later, Khama in Bechuanaland, attempted to resist the liquor trade, seeing these drinks as dangerous and fundamentally different from the traditional grain beers, which had a low alcoholic content and were regarded as foods. Cannabis smoking was also apparently quite widespread in African farming communities, but the evidence does not really make clear how common it was or in what circumstances smoking took place.

INDUSTRIALIZATION AND ALCOHOL AND DRUG CONTROL

The discovery of diamonds and gold in the interior of South Africa during the last part of the nineteenth century transformed the political economy of the region. Capital poured into the area and modern mining operations were established. These new industrial enterprises attracted migrants from across southern Africa, Europe, and Asia—especially to the new urban complex surrounding Johannesburg. During the early twentieth century, the area known as Witwatersrand became the hub of a huge migrant labor network that brought in young male contract workers from their rural homes, often hundreds of miles away to the north. Industrialization also set off a contest for territory that resulted in the defeat of the last independent African polities and the triumph of British imperial power, which culminated in the formation of the white-dominated Union of South Africa in 1910.

The urbanization and industrialization of South Africa resulted in two distinct approaches to the control of African drinking. Africans who migrated into the cities, whether permanently or temporarily, carried with them their existing drinking practices—although the young men who made up the bulk of the new migrants did not typically drink a great deal in their rural homes. In the cities, however, they found themselves within an industrial regime that often confined them to male-only residential hostels or compounds. In the late nineteenth century, a distillery was established in Johannesburg to supply African drinkers, who typically had little if any experience with distilled drinks. This successful enterprise soon provoked a backlash from white civic leaders and employers, who feared that excessive drinking would lead to crime and undermine worker discipline.

As part of a broader process of establishing progressively closer control over urban Africans, prohibition was imposed on Africans in 1897, and this ban remained in place until the 1930s. This measure probably succeeded in limiting drinking, especially of spirits, but it also led to the emergence of a network of criminal gangs that profited from distributing illicit alcohol. It also led to the development of a *shebeen* subculture in urban neighborhoods. These illegal drinking establishments—which were sometimes quite elaborate, but often little more than backrooms—became important centers of social life and focal points in the development of distinctive urban styles and tastes. Shebeen proprietors were almost always women, and they were the targets of continual police harassment. Indeed, by the 1950s more than 200,000 black South Africans were being convicted annually for liquor offenses. In 1959 the anger of Durban's women brewers exploded in riots in the working-class neighborhood of Cato Manor, and this was just one of a series of such protests across the region.

In the South African city of Durban, a different model of liquor control developed, one that eventually was adopted across the country and throughout much of eastern and central Africa. The "Durban system" involved restricting African drinking to municipally owned beer halls and using the substantial profits from these enterprises to fund the creation of segregated African residential areas and services. Illicit producers and sellers challenged this system, and the beer halls became for many one more symbol of white domination under apartheid. In the Cape region, the power of the wine growers prevented prohibition or even serious state restriction on the distribution and consumption of alcohol.

South Africa, following trends in Europe, the United States, and British colonial Africa, also imposed prohibitions on drugs such as cocaine and cannabis. In the postwar era, as South Africa evolved into a moralistic police state, drug use was pushed further under cover, but cannabis smoking was certainly an element of the vibrant urban youth culture that developed in black communities in the 1950s. When the drug revolution hit Europe and the United States in the 1960s, cannabis use also spread to white youths in South Africa. The repression and stress associated with life under the racially stratified white regime encouraged alcohol abuse among both Africans and whites, and mood-altering pharmaceuticals also grew in popularity.

From the 1960s on, the regime made efforts to liberalize alcohol regulations to give African consumers access to spirits, and eventually it legalized some shebeens. Nevertheless, until the apartheid system began to break down in the 1980s, the distribution and consumption of alcohol and illegal drugs (and indeed the customs of consumption) continued to be structured along racial lines. When youths in the massive Johannesburg ghetto of Soweto launched their revolt against the authorities in 1976, among the very first targets of their attacks were the state-owned liquor stores.

THE TRANSFORMATION OF THE ALCOHOL INDUSTRY

In South Africa in the early twenty-first century, the consumption of alcohol continues to be an important leisure activity. Adult alcohol consumption per capita was estimated in 2000 to be 12.4 liters per year (incorporating unrecorded consumption), which was considerably less than in many other countries. However, the amount consumed per drinker approached 20 liters, which was among the highest levels in the world at the time. In addition, a 1998 survey found that one-third of adult drinkers engaged in risky weekend binging (Parry, 2005, p. 426). Excessive consumption is facilitated by many customary drinking practices in South Africa, including public drinking, communal drinking, and the provision of large amounts of alcohol at weddings, funerals, and other ceremonies. Overall alcohol consumption appears to be stable, although there are trends away from "traditional" sorghum beer and toward spirit coolers and alcoholic fruit drinks. An increase in the proportion of younger men and women who are drinking has also been reported, suggesting that the percentage of abstainers in the population may be declining (Parry, 2005, p. 426).

In South Africa, as elsewhere, there is a close connection between the consumption of alcohol and illegal drugs and risky sexual behavior. This linkage is particularly ominous in South Africa, given the high levels of HIV infection among the nation's youth. South Africa has also recorded some of the highest rates of fetal alcohol syndrome ever observed. Alcohol abuse and associated social and health problems reflect a history of racial stratification and extreme inequality. Since the end of apartheid and the institution of democratic rule in the mid-1990s, notwithstanding robust economic growth, the state has lacked the resources to provide adequate, or even basic, health services to the substantial proportion of the population living in poverty. Alcohol and drug treatment programs are even more difficult to find. Moreover, as they have historically, alcohol sales continue to provide substantial revenues to official budgets. Since the late 1990s, the government has raised alcohol taxes, however, with the combined goals of increasing revenue, limiting drinking, and encouraging the consumption of drinks with lower alcohol content.

These efforts must contend with an aggressive corporate sector that actively promotes an array of alcoholic drinks through sophisticated promotional strategies. A small number of large companies have long held control over the production, importation, and distribution of spirits and European-type beer. The end of apartheid, meanwhile, along the concomitant elimination of international restrictions on trade with South Africa, has provided great opportunities for these companies to consolidate their positions and increase their sales, in particular in other African countries where they were largely forbidden to operate during the apartheid era. The South African Breweries Ltd. (SAB) experienced an especially dramatic period of growth, and by 2000 it had captured 98 percent of the South African market for bottled beer. The company was a pioneer in providing job and professional advancement opportunities for employees of color, and as a result it was able to build a strong working relationship with the African National Congress when it came to power in 1994. Building on its African base, the SAB repositioned itself as a global corporation. In 2002 the company acquired the U.S.-based Miller Brewing Company and shifted its headquarters to London, and it has become one of the four largest brewing companies in the world. On a smaller scale, winemaking concerns have systematically improved the quality of their products and aggressively pursued the international market.

Since the 1980s, the reduction and/or elimination of race-based restrictions on the sale of alcohol have combined with privatization to make this an attractive area for small businesses. Not surprisingly, the legalization of shebeens has encouraged small-scale businessmen to move into an area that was largely controlled by women when these establishments were illegal.

SOUTH AFRICA AND THE DRUGS TRADE

The international boycott of Apartheid-era South Africa, the country's ongoing confrontation with its neighbors to the north, and the related close scrutiny by the South African regime of its own borders have all had the effect of limiting the drug trade in South Africa. The transition to majority rule in the early 1990s had the ironic impact of not only removing barriers to legal commerce, but also to trade in illegal substances. By the mid-1990s, however, reports had begun to appear in the international media that South Africa was emerging as an important trans-shipment point for heroin and cocaine. Thus, the recent history of South Africa's drug use and engagement with international drug

trafficking, to a substantial extent, fits within the broader pattern of Africa as a whole. However, it also reflects South Africa's distinctive history of racial stratification, in particular in the popularity of the depressant methaqualone (Mandrax), hallucinogenics, and drugs such as Ecstasy that have been much more popular in Europe and North America than in Africa. As major South African cities have been drawn into the international heroin commerce, local use has apparently also increased dramatically (although estimates vary widely). Until recently, at least, heroin use remained confined largely to the whites and to the Colored (or mixed-race) population. In contrast to other parts of the world, smoking remains the most prevalent use of heroin consumption in South Africa.

Since 2000 South Africa has become an important methamphetamine center, particularly as the production and distribution of the synthesized drug has become increasingly globalized. Between 2004 and 2005 the importation into South Africa of pseudoephedrine, a key ingredient in the drug, grew by 1,300 percent. Much of South Africa's methamphetamine production is exported regionally and internationally, but the cost has been so low that a great deal has also spilled over into the local drug market. Although evidence is sparse, it appears that drug trafficking in South Africa is linked to networks of immigrants from other African countries, notably Nigeria. The number of migrants in the country increased sharply after the end of white rule, and whether fairly or unfairly, immigrants are often blamed for criminal activities and drug trading.

The most common drug used in Cape Town, and elsewhere in South Africa, remains cannabis. It is widely grown, but remote rural areas such as Lesotho dominate the trade. Little is known about the organization of the traffic, but the product tends to be carried along existing commercial and migrant labor routes into South Africa's cities. There have been substantial confiscations of sacks of cannabis in raids on migrant labor hostels.

The dismantling of the elaborate and repressive system of population controls associated with apartheid created a much more liberal social and cultural environment. However, the optimism associated with majority rule was soon dampened by the realities of unemployment, persistent poverty, and urban decay, which have created breeding grounds for alcohol and drug abuse. Popular concerns, particularly among the urban masses, were increasingly focused on economic and security issues. Beginning in the mid-1990s, these trends spawned a number of populist antidrug and anticrime crusades. In perhaps the most notorious example, in 1996 a Cape Town Muslim organization, People Against Gangsterism and Drugs (PAGAD), confronted a suspected drug dealer named Rashaad Staggie, who headed the Hard Livings gang. A motorcade of some 500 vehicles converged on his headquarters, and PAGAD members captured Staggie, set him on fire, and eventually shot him dead. No one was convicted of the murder, although organization leaders were ultimately found guilty of public violence. In the aftermath of these events, claims were made that the attack had been staged by rival drug dealers, illustrating both the growing pervasiveness of drug-trading gangs and the growing public alarm about drug use and the drug trade.

By the mid-1990s, the growing alarm about the rising consumption of illegal drugs had caused the new South African regime to enlist in the U.S.-sponsored "global war on drugs" and seek American government assistance in combating local drug use and drug trading. Nonetheless, drugs such as cocaine, crack cocaine, and cannabis continue to be easily available in the urban areas of South Africa.

In 1999 the Youth League of the ruling African National Congress prepared a policy on substance abuse that denounced the abuse of alcohol and drugs as deeply destructive of community and family life, reflecting the ANC's established moralistic tradition. Not surprisingly, most attention focused on alcohol. But given the close relationship between corporate and state interests in South Africa, the policy did not advocate abstinence and prohibition strategies, but rather the promotion of responsible drinking.

See also **Africa; Foreign Policy and Drugs, United States; International Drug Supply Systems; Kenya; Nigeria.**

BIBLIOGRAPHY

Cobley, A. (1990). Liquor and leadership: Temperance, drunkenness and the African petty bourgeoisie in South Africa. *South African Historical Journal, 31,* 128–148.

Crush, J., & Ambler, C. (Eds.). (1992). *Liquor and labor in southern Africa.* Athens: Ohio University Press.

Du Toit, B. M. (1975). Dagga: The history and ethnographic setting of cannabis sativa in Southern Africa. In V. Rubin (Ed.), *Cannabis and Culture* (pp. 81–116). The Hague: Mouton.

Gordon, D. (1996). From rituals of rapture to dependence: The political economy of Khoikhoi narcotic consumption, c. 1487–1870. *South African Historical Journal, 35,* 62–88.

Leggett, T. (2002). *Rainbow vice: The drugs and sex industries in the new South Africa.* London: Zed Books.

Mager, A. (2004). "White liquor hits black livers": Meanings of excessive liquor consumption in South Africa in the second half of the twentieth century. *Social Science & Medicine, 59*(4), 735–751.

McAllister, P.A. (1993). Indigenous beer in southern Africa: Functions and fluctuations. *African Studies, 52*(1), 71–88.

Mills, W. (1985). Cape smoke: Alcohol issues in the Cape Colony in the nineteenth century. *Contemporary Drug Problems, 12*(2), 221–247.

Parry, C. (2005). South Africa: Alcohol today. *Addiction, 100,* 426–429.

Van Onselen, C. (1982). *Studies in the social and economic history of the Witwatersrand, 1886–1914.* 2 vols. New York: Longman.

CHARLES AMBLER

SPAIN

SPAIN. Spain is a Mediterranean European Union (EU) country with about 46,063,000 inhabitants as of 2008. Its administration is divided into 17 regions (Autonomous Communities), each with a high degree of legislative and executive autonomy. This entry presents information relating to Spain as a whole; however, differences among regions exist because of the country's decentralized political structure.

HISTORY OF SUBSTANCE USE IN SPAIN

Before the mid-1960s, alcohol and tobacco were practically the only drugs consumed in Spain. Both were (and remained into the early twenty-first century) legal and widely accepted, but risks associated with their consumption were underestimated. Until the mid-1970s, the use of illicit drugs was rare. Spanish people did not begin to see drugs as a problem until the end of the 1970s. In fact, in 1979, the

Ministry of Health created the first drug abuse treatment centers. However, between the end of the 1970s and the mid-1980s, the consumption of drugs, and in particular heroin injected intravenously, increased sharply, along with an increased frequency of HIV/AIDS cases among these drug users. The use of drugs also became associated with delinquency and marginalization, causing alarm.

The alarm was so great, in fact, that the government created the 1985 National Plan on Drugs to coordinate and enforce regional governmental policies and various social entities. Regional Plans on Drugs were also created, and centers to treat drug dependent patients were established. These services were available to everyone since Spain has universal health care.

From the mid-1980s until the early twenty-first century, the situation changed radically, especially regarding illicit drug use, which became widespread. In fact, as of 2008, Spain had one of the highest levels of consumption of cannabis and cocaine in the world, although heroin use and its associated diseases have decreased. In contrast with the 1980s, consumption of cannabis, synthetic drugs, and cocaine is more often connected to the culture of leisure rather than with delinquency.

TRENDS AND PATTERNS OF SUBSTANCE USE
The main sources of information in Spain on the patterns of drug use are those obtained through the *Home Survey on Drug Abuse in Spain* (EDADES) (DGPND, 2006) and the *State Survey on Drug Use in Secondary Education Students* (ESTUDES) (DGPND, 2007). The questionnaires and methodology used in these surveys are similar to those used in other EU countries.

> *Home Survey on Drug Abuse in Spain* (EDADES): This survey has been carried out every other year since 1995 among the population from 14 to 65 years of age, except for 1995, in which no upper age limit was established. As of 2008, the data from 1995 to 2003 were available, whereas only the preliminary data of the studies from 2005 to 2007 were available (see Table 1).
>
> *State Survey on Drug Use in Secondary Education Students* (ESTUDES): This survey has been carried out every other year since 1994. It gathers information concerning illicit drug

use among students between 14 and 18 years of age.

Alcohol was the most frequently consumed drug in Spain, though between 1975 and 2005 there was an important change in the consumption pattern. The daily consumption of alcohol decreased, and the consumption of wine (typical in the Mediterranean diet) decreased. By contrast, the consumption of beer increased and the consumption of alcohol used only on weekends increased. Among students (aged 14 to 18) *binge drinking* (defined by the Ministry of Health as the intake of at least 60 g of alcohol in men or 40 g in women in a single drinking session and in which the person becomes intoxicated with a blood alcohol concentration of 0.8 percent or higher) increased. One statistic showed that the frequency of drunkenness in a test group in the 30 days prior to the survey rose from 20.7 percent in 1994 to 34.8 percent in 2004. Alcohol consumption was responsible for 2.08 percent of all deaths. Alcohol consumption per capita decreased in the early twenty-first century as Spanish people began to see the associated health problems.

The consumption of tobacco is responsible for 6 percent of all deaths according to several studies (González Enríquez et al., 1997; Banegas et al., 2005). Since the year 2000, a decrease in the daily consumption of tobacco has been noted, although this decrease can be seen mostly in men, where the decrease among women is much less. In fact, among young people, smoking is more common among women than among men. In the 1970s and 1980s most people smoked French-type tobacco known as *black* tobacco, whereas in the early twenty-first century the great majority smoked American-type *blond* tobacco. But people are increasingly aware of the health consequences of tobacco use. In the early twenty-first century, antismoking advice was provided at the primary-care service level, by physicians and other health-care professionals who have direct contact with patients, and several units specializing in tobacco addiction were created. Whereas the Public Health Service pays for the pharmacological treatment of various illnesses, as of 2008 pharmacological treatment to combat tobacco addiction was not reimbursed (it was paid for by the patient in contrast to medication for other diseases, which was free).

	1995	1997	1999	2001	2003	2005
Prevalence of consuming at some time during life						
Tobacco	—	69.7	64.9	68.4	68.9	69.5
Alcohol	—	90.6	87.3	89.0	88.6	93.7
Cannabis	14.5	22.9	19.6	23.8	29.0	28.6
Ecstasy	2.0	2.5	2.4	4.0	4.6	4.4
Hallucinogenics	2.1	2.9	1.9	2.8	3.0	3.4
Amphetamines/Speed	2.3	2.7	2.2	2.9	3.2	3.4
Cocaine powder	3.4	3.4	3.1	4.8	5.9	7.0
Cocaine base	0.3	0.4	0.4	0.5	0.5	0.6
Heroin	0.8	0.6	0.5	0.6	0.9	0.7
Other opiates	0.2	0.5	0.3	0.6	0.4	0.5
Inhalable volatiles	0.7	0.8	0.6	0.8	1.0	0.8
Prevalence of consuming in the previous 12 months						
Tobacco	—	46.8	44.7	46.0	47.8	42.4
Alcohol	68.5	78.5	75.2	78.1	76.6	76.7
Hypno-sedatives without medical prescription	12.3	2.3	2.3	2.8	3.1	—
Cannabis	7.5	7.7	7.0	9.2	11.3	11.2
Ecstasy	1.3	0.9	0.8	1.8	1.4	1.2
Hallucinogenics	0.8	0.9	0.6	0.7	0.6	0.7
Amphetamines/Speed	1.0	0.9	0.7	1.1	0.8	1.0
Cocaine powder	1.8	1.6	1.6	2.5	2.7	3.0
Cocaine base	0.1	0.1	0.2	0.1	0.1	0.2
Heroin	0.5	0.2	0.1	0.1	0.1	0.1
Other opiates	0.1	0.1	0.1	0.2	0.1	0.1
Inhalable volatiles	0.1	0.2	0.1	0.1	0.1	0.1
Prevalence of consuming in the last 30 days						
Tobacco	—	42.9	40.1	41.4	42.9	38.4
Alcohol	—	64.0	61.8	63.7	64.1	64.6
Cannabis	—	4.6	4.5	6.4	7.6	8.7
Ecstasy	—	0.3	0.2	0.8	0.4	0.6
Hallucinogenics	—	0.2	0.2	0.2	0.2	0.2
Amphetamines/Speed	—	0.2	0.3	0.6	0.2	0.4
Cocaine powder	—	0.9	0.9	1.3	1.1	1.6
Cocaine base	—	0.0	0.1	0.0	0.0	0.1
Heroin	—	0.1	0.0	0.0	0.0	0.1
Other opiates	—	0.1	0.1	0.1	0.1	0.1
Inhalable volatiles	—	0.1	0.0	0.1	0.0	0.1
Prevalence of daily consumption in the last 30 days						
Tobacco	—	34.9	33.6	35.7	36.7	32.8
Alcohol	—	12.7	13.7	15.7	14.1	14.9
Cannabis	—	0.7	0.8	1.5	1.5	2.0

Table 1. Evolution of the prevalences in the consumption of psychoactive substances among the population aged 15–64. Results of the Home Surveys on Drug Abuse (EDADES). Spain 1995–2003 (DGPND, 2006). Illustration by GGS Information Services. Gale, Cengage Learning

Heroin use was particularly high at the end of the 1970s and during the 1980s. For many years, Spain had one of the highest rates of AIDS in the world: In 2002, according to the Euro HIV Web site, the number of HIV/AIDS cases among intravenous drugs users was 30 per million inhabitants. The number of new cases of AIDS diagnosed among intravenous drug users increased in 1994 (5,082) and declined after that (1995: 4,733; 1997: 3,153; 1999: 1,811, 2001: 1,305; 2003: 1,102; 2005: 811; DGPND, 2008). Heroin consumption continued thereafter to decrease, and as of 2008 it was ever more difficult to find young heroin addicts. As of 2008, the great majority of heroin users consume other substances, especially cocaine. Injected heroin and needle sharing has become rare. Harm reduction approaches, including use of prescribed methadone, has contributed to controlling the medico-social problems of these patients, in particular AIDS and Hepatitis C. The consumption of other opiates is rare. Buprenorphine and naloxone were introduced in therapeutic treatment, but the cost is not covered by the Public Health Service.

In the early twentieth century, cannabis was the most popular illicit drug in Spain and was being

	1994	1996	1998	2000	2002	2004	2006
Prevalence of consuming at some time during life							
Tobacco	60.6	64.4	63.4	61.8	59.8	60.4	46.1
Alcohol	84.1	84.2	86.0	78.0	76.6	82.0	79.6
Hypno-sedatives	6.1	6.1	6.4	6.9	6.5	7.0	7.6
Cannabis	20.9	26.4	29.5	33.2	37.5	42.7	36.2
Ecstasy	3.6	5.5	3.6	6.2	6.4	5.0	3.3
Hallucinogenics	5.1	6.8	5.5	5.8	4.4	4.7	4.1
Amphetamines/Speed	4.2	5.3	4.3	4.5	5.5	4.8	3.4
Cocaine	2.5	3.4	5.4	6.5	7.7	9.0	5.7
Heroin	0.5	0.5	0.9	0.6	0.5	0.7	1.0
Inhalable volatiles	3.1	3.3	4.2	4.3	3.7	4.1	3.0
Prevalence of consuming in the previous 12 months							
Alcohol	82.7	82.4	83.8	77.3	75.6	81.0	74.9
Hypno-sedatives	4.4	4.5	4.7	5.0	4.5	4.7	4.8
Cannabis	18.2	23.4	25.7	28.8	32.8	36.6	29.8
Ecstasy	3.2	4.1	2.5	5.2	4.3	2.6	2.4
Hallucinogenics	4.4	5.6	4.0	4.2	3.2	3.1	2.8
Amphetamines/Speed	3.5	4.4	3.4	3.5	4.1	3.3	2.6
Cocaine powder	1.8	2.7	4.5	4.8	6.2	7.2	4.1
Heroin	0.3	0.4	0.6	0.4	0.3	0.4	0.8
Inhalable volatiles	1.9	2.0	2.6	2.5	2.2	2.2	1.8
Prevalence of consuming in the last 30 days							
Tobacco	31.1	32.5	31.9	32.1	29.4	37.4	27.9
Alcohol	75.1	66.7	68.1	60.2	56.0	65.6	58.0
Hypno-sedatives	2.6	2.2	2.3	2.5	2.4	2.4	2.4
Cannabis	12.4	15.7	17.2	20.8	22.5	25.1	20.1
Ecstasy	2.1	2.3	1.6	2.8	1.9	1.5	1.4
Hallucinogenics	2.6	2.8	2.0	2.0	1.2	1.5	1.3
Amphetamines/Speed	2.3	2.6	2.0	2.0	2.0	1.8	1.4
Cocaine	1.1	1.6	2.5	2.5	3.2	3.8	2.3
Heroin	0.2	0.3	0.4	0.3	0.2	0.4	0.5
Inhalable volatiles	1.1	1.2	1.8	1.5	1.1	1.1	1.1

Table 2. Evolution of the prevalence of the consumption of psychoactive substances among secondary education students 14–18 years of age. Results of the State Surveys on Drug Use in Secondary Education (ESTUDES). Spain 1994–2006 (DGPND, 2007). ILLUSTRATION BY GGS INFORMATION SERVICES. GALE, CENGAGE LEARNING

consumed at ever earlier ages. Although usually sporadic, consumption has increased considerably (Tables 1 and 2). There is a low perception of risks associated with cannabis and an increase in related hospital-treated emergencies.

Cocaine is the second most consumed drug in Spain, and its consumption has been rising. However, a student survey of 2006 (Table 2) showed a decrease in the prevalence of cocaine consumption, which must be confirmed in later studies. The information available showed an increase in requests for treatment, mortality, and hospital-treated emergencies related to cocaine use.

The use of amphetamines and other synthetic drugs began to increase in the mid-1990s. For a long time they enjoyed great popularity and a low perception of health risks. It is frequently difficult to ascertain exactly which group of substances is being consumed, as people sometimes consume amphetamines

believing that it is Ecstasy. Ecstasy, the street name for methylenedioxymethamphetamine or MDMA, is a semisynthetic drug in a subclass within the larger class of amphetamines. The consumption of LSD and other hallucinogenic drugs is infrequent.

REGULATIONS FOR LEGAL AND ILLEGAL SUBSTANCES

Because of Spain's decentralized political structure and the high degree of autonomy of its 17 regions, legislation concerning alcohol, tobacco, and illegal drugs can be either national, covering the whole of Spanish territory, or regional. In some cases, the national government makes the general rules, while the regional government has to make specific legislation within the general framework; thus differences among regions exist.

Regulations on alcohol are similar to those of other EU countries. For instance, it is illegal to drive with a blood alcohol concentration over 0.5 grams of alcohol per liter of blood (or 0.25mg of alcohol per liter of air in the lungs), 0.3 grams per liter of blood (0.15mg of alcohol per liter of air in the lungs) for professional or newly licensed drivers. The sale of alcohol to those under 18 years of age is prohibited, and restrictions apply to advertising. Given the growth in binge drinking among young people, there have been two attempts to pass a national law to regulate the consumption of alcohol by those under age 18. In both cases, the proposal was scrapped due to strong public and industry opposition.

An anti-tobacco law (Ley 28/2005) went into effect on January 1, 2006, prohibiting smoking in public places (e.g., the workplace, cultural centers). The law differentiates between areas in which smoking is totally forbidden and areas in which it is permitted (e.g., restaurants) if a special area for smokers is created.

The private consumption of drugs is not a chargeable offense in Spain. However, "consumption in public places, streets, establishments or public transport, as well as the illicit possession, even though it is not for trafficking, and the abandonment in the aforementioned places of instruments used for consumption" is considered an offense that carries a fine. Spain's penal code distinguishes between drugs that cause serious harm to a person's health and those that do not. All street drugs are considered harmful except for cannabis and benzodiazepines. The law punishes drug production (cultivation, elaboration, manufacture), as well as acts of drug trafficking (sale or exchange), prior acts (such as possession or the transport of drugs for the purposes of trafficking), and acts to encourage consumption (promoting, favoring, facilitating). In addition, driving a motor vehicle under the influence of any kind of drug is a chargeable offense. Efforts to control the supply of drugs and various other criminal activities such as drug trafficking, money laundering, and other related crimes were being developed in the early twenty-first century.

POLICIES ON ALCOHOL, SMOKING, AND ILLEGAL DRUGS

The Ministry of Heath and the regional health administrations are responsible for policy development. Illegal drugs policies are the responsibility of the National Plan on Drugs and Regional Plans on Drugs, whereas policies regarding alcohol and tobacco belong to either of these bodies or the Public Health Services.

In 2000, the National Drugs Strategy 2000–2008 (DGPND, 2000) defined its course of action and goals. Its strategy was based on the following:

Coordination of all those working in the drug field

Social prevention and awareness building through education and personal development

Integration of drug user care

Improvement in knowledge of drugs

Reduction in the supply through increased police and customs effectiveness in handling drug trafficking

International cooperation

Trends in alcohol, smoking, and illicit drug use in Spain in the last decades of the twentieth century show marked changes. Alcohol consumption patterns have changed noticeably, with beer drinking on the weekends increased. Alcohol consumption per capita decreased, and awareness regarding the consequences of alcohol consumption improved. Underage drinking remained a concern. Alcohol use has health, legal, and social consequences, but the government failed twice to introduce new regulations due to public resistance and industry lobbies. Smoking has started to decline, particularly among males, and the general population is concerned about the health consequences of smoking. Regarding illicit drugs, Spain has some of the highest rates of use in the world. Cannabis is the favorite drug, followed by cocaine, and synthetic amphetamines. Drug use moved from marginalization and delinquency (heroin use epidemic in late 1980s) to the culture of leisure (cannabis, cocaine, synthetic drugs). Cannabis, and to some extent synthetic drugs, are seen as harmless. However, illicit drugs use still generates a lot of health, legal, and social consequences, while the efforts carried out by the national and regional policies to some extent failed to decrease drug use and its consequences. Drug treatment has become increasingly integrated in the public health system. At the same time, smoking and alcohol treatment counseling (e.g., brief intervention) are more and more frequently offered at primary care services.

See also European Union; Foreign Policy and Drugs, United States; France; International Drug Supply Systems; Italy.

BIBLIOGRAPHY

Information on survey data, as well as information from other key indicators for illegal drugs (e.g., treatment, mortality, hospital treated emergencies related to drug use, infectious diseases), can be found at the Web site of the Ministry of Health (some are also available in English at http://www.pnsd.msc.es: for alcohol, http://www.msc.es/ciudadanos/proteccionSalud/adultos/alcohol/, and for smoking, http://www.msc.es/ciudadanos/proteccion-Salud/tabaco/.).

Banegas, J. R., Díez Gañán, L., González Enríquez, J., Villar Alvarez, F., & Rodríguez-Artalejo, F. (2005). Recent decrease in smoking-attributable mortality in Spain. *Medicina Clínica (Barcelona), 124*(20), 769–771.

Delegación del Gobierno para el Plan Nacional sobre Drogas (DGPND). (2000). National Drugs Strategy 2000–2008. Madrid: Author. Available from http://www.pnsd.msc.es/.

Delegación del Gobierno para el Plan Nacional sobre Drogas (DGPND). (2006). Encuesta Domiciliaria sobre Alcohol y Drogas en España 2005–2006. Madrid: Author. Observatorio Español Sobre Drogas. Plan Nacional sobre Drogas. Available from http://www.pnsd.msc.es/.

Delegación del Gobierno para el Plan Nacional sobre Drogas (DGPND). (2007). Encuesta Estatal sobre Uso de Drogas en Estudiantes de Enseñanzas Secundarias 2006–2007. Madrid: Author. Observatorio Español Sobre Drogas. Plan Nacional sobre Drogas. Available from http://www.pnsd.msc.es/.

Delegación del Gobierno para el Plan Nacional sobre Drogas (DGPND). (2008). Informe 2007. Madrid: Author. Observatorio Español Sobre Drogas. Plan Nacional sobre Drogas. Available from http://www.pnsd.msc.es/.

Euro HIV. *HIV/AIDS surveillance in Europe.* Available from http://www.eurohiv.org.

González Enríquez, J., Villar Alvarez, F., Banegas, J. R., Rodríguez Artalejo, F., & Martín Moreno, J. M. (1997). Trends in the mortality attributable to tobacco use in Spain, 1978–1992: 600,000 deaths in 15 years. *Medicina Clínica (Barcelona), 109*(15), 577–582.

F. JAVIER ALVAREZ

SPORT, DRUGS IN INTERNATIONAL.

There are extensive social, cultural, historical, and economic connections between drugs and sport. Although a great deal of international attention is given to performance enhancing drugs, the weight of harm associated with drug use as it relates to sport, lies with alcohol. In addition to exploring the issues related to performance enhancing drugs, this section focuses on the relationships between alcohol and sport.

DEVELOPMENT OF DRUG USE IN SPORT

Ancient Greek athletes were known to use special diets and potions in the ancient games, and in modern sports (professional and amateur) the use of artificial stimulants (performance enhancing drugs) may have been in widespread use since the nineteenth century (Yaselis et al., 2001). The emergence of modern pharmaceuticals in the early twentieth century was perhaps influential in the development of drug use in sport (Wilson & Derse, 2001). The World Anti-Doping Agency (WADA) asserts that in 1928 the International Amateur Athletic Federation (IAAF) became the first international athletics organization to ban the use of stimulating substances.

Stokvis (2003) suggests that in 1933 a member of the French National Olympic Committee lodged the first official complaint about the use of stimulant substances among amateur athletes. The nature of the complaint was that the use of injections among athletes at the 1932 Olympic Games was a sign of dishonesty. Stokvis also asserts that in 1938 the International Olympics Committee (IOC) decided to disallow drug-using athletes to compete in the games; however, it was not until the 1960s that doping became a subject of formal regulation. In 1963 the Council of Europe agreed on a draft convention against the use of performance enhancing drugs in sport, which was later ratified in 1989 (Council of Europe, 1989).

Increased appreciation of the extent and complexity of doping following a drug-doping incident in cycling in 1998 resulted in the Lausanne Declaration on Doping in Sport. The World Anti-Doping Agency, established in 1999, formed out of the Lausanne Declaration, with a mandate to promote and coordinate strategies to prevent doping in sport internationally. The formation of WADA effected a series of consultations to develop an international anti-doping code. Starting from the International Drugs in Sport Summit in Sydney 1999, the International Intergovernmental Consultative Group on Anti-Doping (IICGAD) in Sport met annually until

Adverse test results (detected drug)	Number of adverse results	Percent of total adverse test results
Anabolic agents	1,966	45.4%
Beta-2 agonists	631	14.6%
Cannabinoids	553	12.8%
Stimulants	490	11.3%
Diuretics and other masking agents	290	6.7%
Glucocorticosteroids	282	6.5%
Hormones and related substances	42	1.0%
Beta-blockers	28	0.6%
Agents with anti-estrogenic activity	30	0.7%
Narcotics	16	0.4%
Chemical and physical manipulation	4	0.1%

SOURCE: World Anti-Doping Agency, http://www.wada-ama.org/rtecontent/document/LABSTATS_2006.pdf (downloaded 10-06-2008).

Table 1. Adverse drug testing results reported by the World Anti-Doping Agency for 2006. ILLUSTRATION BY GGS INFORMATION SERVICES. GALE, CENGAGE LEARNING

2003 to develop a series of governance and funding arrangements to support WADA.

For example, it was agreed in 2001 that the five Olympic Regions of the world would contribute differentially to the WADA budget: Africa (0.50%), Americas (29%), Asia (20.46%), Europe (47.5%), and Oceania (2.54%). The regional share percentages were reconfirmed in the 2003 Copenhagen Declaration on Anti-Doping in Sport. The code was the first international agreement harmonizing anti-doping rules across all sports and all nations.

The WADA Foundation Board is now jointly composed of representatives of the Olympic Movement (the IOC, National Olympic Committees, International Sports Federations, and athletes) and representatives of governments from five continents.

DRUGS IN USE, HOW, AND THE EFFECTS
According to statistics from WADA the following drugs (Table 1) are most widely detected in international sport.

Anabolic Agents. Anabolic agents are clearly the most popular drugs used in conjunction with sport internationally (Table 1). Anabolic steroids accelerate the growth of muscle and bone and can subsequently improve the body's capacity for training and competition by reducing fatigue and recovery time. Both naturally produced and synthetically manufactured sources can create anabolic androgenic steroids. Beta-2 agonists are also considered

anabolic substances because they can also stimulate tissue growth.

Cannabinoids. Cannabinoids are substances derived from the cannabis plant and are commonly referred to as marijuana. Widely used in the general community, this illicit substance has a variety of depressant effects. Cannabinoids are not considered performance enhancing drugs, but they are prohibited by the WADA code in competition because they pose a risk to the health of athletes.

Stimulants. Stimulants such as amphetamine, cocaine, and ephedrine act directly on the central nervous system to increase alertness, reduce fatigue, and increase competitiveness and aggression. There are mental health, cardiovascular, and dependence risks associated with abuse of stimulants. Stimulants are prohibited in competition under the World Anti-Doping Code 2007 Prohibited List.

The World Anti-Doping Code accepts a range of mild stimulants used for therapeutic purposes; however, it is possible that they are banned in regional or local codes. These stimulants include bupropion, pseudoephedrine, caffeine, phenylephrine, penylpropanolamine, pipradrol, and synephrine.

Diuretics and Other Masking Agents. Diuretics and other masking agents are used to either cause rapid weight loss or to mask the presence of anabolic drugs in urine The health risks associated with diuretics include dehydration, dizziness, headaches, nausea, loss of coordination and balance, cramps, and kidney and heart failure. Diuretics are on the prohibited list, both in and out of competition in all sports as masking agents.

Glucocorticosteroids. Glucocorticosteroids are anti-inflammatory agents used and administered in a variety of ways to treat chronic inflammatory conditions such as arthritis, asthma, inflamed joints, and allergic reactions. Systemically administered glucocorticosteroids are prohibited in competition, whereas glucocorticosteroid use is permitted when applied topically (e.g., with a cream).

Hormones and Related Substances. Hormones and related substances are prohibited in and out of competition under the World Anti-Doping Code. Some hormones are used to stimulate tissue growth, enhance muscle strength, improve oxygen carrying capacity, and reduce recovery time. The following hormones and related substances are prohibited: corticotrophin (ACTH), erythropoietin (EPO), gonadotrophins, human growth hormone (hGH), insulin and insulin-like growth factor (IGF-1), and mechano growth factors (MGF).

Beta-Blockers. Beta-blockers are drugs that reduce the work of the heart through slowing heart rate and reducing blood pressure. They have been used by athletes competing in sports that require fine motor control such as archery, shooting, curling, and nine-pin bowling or in sports involving control of a vehicle as they can reduce shaking and produce a mild reduction in anxiety without sedation. Beta-blockers are prohibited in competition.

Agents with Anti-Estrogenic Activity. Anti-estrogenic substances serve as masking agents because they may reduce the negative physical side effects of using prohibited anabolic steroids. These include aromatase inhibitors, selective estrogen receptor modulators, and other anti-estrogenic substances.

Narcotics. Narcotic painkillers reduce pain and produce euphoric sensations. This class of drugs includes diamorphine (heroin), morphine, methadone, and pethidine. Because narcotics reduce pain, they can also mask physical damage by reducing the signs of damage. In this respect they are seen as a risk to the health of athletes. Prolonged use may also produce dependence. The use of narcotics is prohibited in competition.

Chemical and Physical Manipulation. The code prohibits tampering or physically manipulating the body or sample collection methods to alter the integrity and validity of biofluid collection. Manipulation can include catheterization or urine substitution.

Alcohol. Alcohol is prohibited in competition only, in selected sports: aeronautic, archery, automobile billiards, boules, karate, modern pentathlon, shooting, motorcycling, and powerboating. A doping violation threshold is established for each sport.

Historically, alcohol has been associated with both sporting participation and with sport spectatorship. Sport has become a significant marketing interest for the alcohol industry. Culturally associated with sociability and sporting celebration, alcohol has occupied an ambivalent place alongside sport, yet there are some troubling dimensions to the alcohol-sport connection that should be explored.

Participation Intensity and Alcohol Consumption. There is a debate in academic literature about the degree to which participating in sport can protect individuals from harmful alcohol consumption or if the participation can actually cause harmful alcohol consumption. It has been generally accepted in the community that participation in sport reduces the likelihood of excessive alcohol consumption. There is, however, a complex relationship between participation in sport and alcohol consumption. In the academic literature there is believed to be a U-shaped curve that relates alcohol consumption to the intensity of sport participation. Both low levels and high levels of sport participation are associated with higher levels of alcohol consumption among adolescents. The association between low levels of sport participation and alcohol use is well documented. Less discussed is the association between high intensity sport participation and high levels of alcohol consumption (Peretti-Watel et al., 2002). Although the U-curve is not uniform for all sports and varies across gender and drug type, the relationship still holds for alcohol consumption among adolescent men (Peretti-Watel et al., 2002).

The social bonding associated with team sports is thought to be an important factor in increasing alcohol consumption among participants above individual performance sports (Garry & Morrissey, 2000; Peretti-Watel et al., 2002).

Although the research is preliminary, alcohol sponsorship may well have a role to play in creating unsafe drinking environments. In a study of the impact of alcohol sponsorship on alcohol consumption among New Zealand amateur sportspeople, Kerry O'Brien and colleagues (2005; 2007) suggest that sponsorship and drink subsidies enhances hazardous drinking among sportspeople.

It is well documented that North American college athletes are a high-risk group for alcohol abuse. The level of alcohol abuse is associated with the level of competition. It has been reported that up to 34 percent of college athletes reported

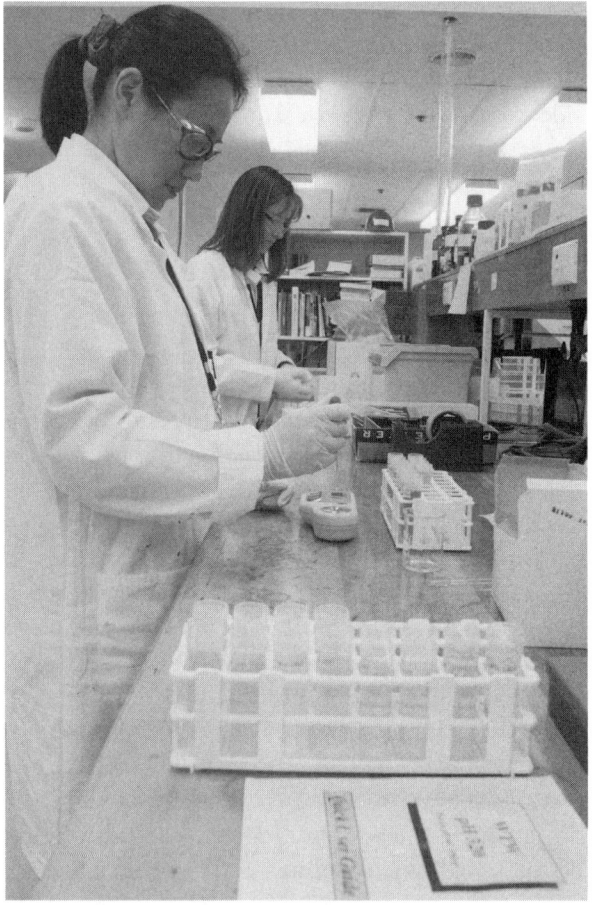

Performing a density test from urine samples at the Australian Sports Drug Testing Laboratory. AP IMAGES.

The social life associated with adolescent sport can be an important factor in non-competitive sporting environments. In a report on the effects of extracurricular activities on schoolchildren's alcohol consumption, Darling, Caldwell, and Smith (2005) suggest that participation in sporting extracurricular activities increases the likelihood of alcohol consumption above that of non-sporting extracurricular activities. It was suggested that sporting activities provide opportunities for adolescents to mix with adults and to learn from adult drinking behavior. When sporting events involve adult drinking, adolescents can more effectively model adult behaviors.

According to a large-scale North American college survey of hazing (humiliation associated with initiation into clubs, teams or other social grouping) (Allan & Madden, 2008), alcohol plays a major role in hazing behaviors. The most prevalent form of hazing behavior across nearly all student organizations and teams is *participation in drinking games*. Up to 54 percent of varsity sports students reported drinking games as part of hazing behavior. This overshadowed student fraternity clubs where only 20 percent of students reported drinking games as a hazing behavior. The hazardous consumption of alcohol occupies a socially institutionalized role within college sport to a greater extent in North American colleges than other social institutions.

In a study of alcohol consumption among team college sports, Jason Ford (2007) reports that male hockey players in the United States are twice as likely to binge drink, and women soccer players 48 percent more likely to binge drink than other female athletes. It was suggested that rather than the differences emerging from the characteristics of individual athletes, the differential application of social norms in different teams can profoundly shape why participants in teams tend to drink more alcohol than participants in individual sport.

Among specific football codes, results vary. Using a pre-season survey of non-professional rugby players in New Zealand, K. L. Quarrie and colleagues (1996) reported that 78 percent of male players were drinking at hazardous levels. R. J. Maughan (1997) reported an average intake of about 10–12 grams of alcohol per day in the first team squads of two Scottish Premier League teams.

consuming at short-term hazardous consumption levels (i.e., bingeing on 11 or more drinks in the past month). Division I athletes are more likely to binge than division III American college athletes (Nelson & Wechsler, 2001). It seems also that alcohol consumption among this group is related to the seasonality of competitive sport as college athletes drink demonstrably less in non-competition times (Martin, 1998).

Sport, Team Bonding, and Alcohol. The playing season can structure an athlete's life by controlling the nature and types of relationships formed, peer networks, and access to alcohol. Data suggest that alcohol consumption varies according to the time of season in competitive sports (Martin, 1998). Heavier drinking in non-competition periods is caused by a number of factors, some of which are individually oriented, whereas others are related to the social nature of sport (Ford, 2007).

Sport and the Alcohol Industry. The alcohol beverage industry provides a variety of sporting promotions, advertising, and sponsorships through football, motor sports, soccer, and basketball. Global sporting events in particular provide unique opportunities for alcohol producers to connect to large global audiences (Colin & Mackenzie, 2006). There are continuing policy calls to restrict alcohol advertising and sponsorships associated with sport (Klein & Jones-Webb, 2007).

According to WHO (2004a) few countries restrict alcohol industry sponsorship of sporting events, with only about 24 percent of countries having any statutory controls. A majority of countries (68%) do not have restrictions on alcohol sponsorship of sport. Twelve countries have complete bans on sponsorships. Sports sponsorship is banned in Jordan; in Croatia and Turkey sponsorship by the wine and spirits industries is banned, in Bosnia, Herzegovina, Finland, Gambia, Poland and Switzerland the spirits industry is banned.

Drinking at sporting events is the third least restricted drinking environment, with only 26 percent of countries having bans on drinking in sport contexts (WHO, 2004b).

Sports are the perfect vehicle for alcohol marketers to target a young male audience (Howard & Crompton, 1995). Entertainers and athletes are significant role models in shaping purchasing behavior (Martin & Bush, 2000). Athletes are reported to be stronger role models than entertainers in influencing purchasing intentions, especially for young adult male African Americans. It is, however, unclear the precise impact of athletic role models (who promote alcohol beverages) on alcohol consumption among young adults. There is some data suggesting that television beer advertisements in North America are aired most frequently during professional football and basketball games (Madden & Grube, 1994; Snyder et al., 2000; Ellickson et al., 2005).

In 2003 the alcohol industry in the United States spent more than $540 million to place approximately 90,000 ads in sports programs on television. It is estimated that 60 percent of all alcohol advertising on television occurs during sporting events (Center on Alcohol Marketing and Youth, 2003).

In summary, there are significant cultural and market pressures to maintain a strong association between sport and the consumption of alcohol. Although the outcomes from these associations are hotly debated, there is evidence that the saturation of sport can have deleterious effects on athlete performance. It is unclear whether the strong association between alcohol and sport can explain broader trends in hazardous alcohol consumption. It is also unclear whether reducing alcohol advertising on television will have demonstrable effects on binge drinking, as econometric analysis estimates that a 27 percent reduction in television alcohol advertising may result in a 1 percent drop in binge drinking (Saffer & Dave, 2006).

MODES OF CONTROL AND INTERNATIONAL REGULATION

The World Anti-Doping Program is the central mechanism for the international regulation of anti-doping. The program consists of three elements:

Level 1: The World Anti-Doping Code
Level 2: International Standards
Level 3: Models of Best Practice

Underpinning the program is the International Convention against Doping in Sport (2005) and the Copenhagen Declaration on Anti-Doping in Sport (2003).

The 33rd UNESCO General Conference unanimously adopted the International Convention against Doping in Sport in 2005. The convention outlines the conditions through which signatories should prevent, with the view to eliminate doping in sport. The convention under the auspices of UNESCO enables governments to align their domestic legislation with the Code and thereby harmonize sport and public legislation.

The Copenhagen Declaration on Anti-Doping in Sport (2003) is the mechanism through which governments signal their intention to formally recognize and implement the World Anti-Doping Code. At the end of 2007, 192 governments had signed the declaration.

The World Anti-Doping Agency (WADA) administers the World Anti-Doping Program and implements the World Anti-Doping Code. There are seven areas of activity in WADA: code acceptance

	2003	2004	2005	2006
Number of tests	151,210	169,187	183,337	198,143
Adverse results	2,447	2,909	3,909	3,887
Adverse results as a percentage of number of tests	1.6%	1.7%	2.1%	2.0%

SOURCE: World Anti-Doping Agency, http://www.wada-ama.org/rtecontent/document/LABSTATS_2006.pdf (downloaded 10-06-2008)

Table 2. Testing trends in the World Anti-Doping Program (WADP). ILLUSTRATION BY GGS INFORMATION SERVICES. GALE, CENGAGE LEARNING

and compliance, science and medicine, out of competition testing, athlete outreach, coordination through the anti-doping management system, anti-doping development, and education. Individual national sporting associations are not bound by the code; however, sovereign countries can introduce regulations that bind national associations to the WADA code.

LIKELY FUTURE DEVELOPMENTS
The level of testing for performance enhancing drugs among professional elite sportspeople through the World Anti-Drug Program has reached a plateau (Table 2). Data from the International Association of Athletics Federations testing program also suggests that testing is widespread and the production of positive tests remains low. Adverse testing rates have also reached a plateau at around 2 percent of total tests.

Unless there are some major advances in the illicit use of performance enhancing drugs, it would seem unlikely that there will be increased rates of adverse test results in the future.

It is likely, however, that national sporting codes will increasingly advocate the beginning of testing regimes for local sports, as they become integrated into the WADA code through national regulatory mechanisms. This will increase the rate of testing in non-elite sporting contexts and no doubt will increase the rate of adverse testing results among players. It is unclear what social and sporting impacts this will have. The desired effect of course will be to reduce drug use among sporting populations. It is, however, unclear whether the testing regimes in non-elite athletes will produce

the same preventative effects as it does in elite athletes.

See also **Accidents and Injuries from Alcohol; Accidents and Injuries from Drugs; Advertising and the Alcohol Industry; Cannabinoids; Fashion Industry, International; Foreign Policy and Drugs, United States; International Control Policies; Risk Factors for Substance Use, Abuse, and Dependence: An Overview.**

BIBLIOGRAPHY

Allan, E. J., & Madden, M. (2008). *Hazing in view: College students at risk. Initial Findings from the National Study of Student Hazing.* Orono: College of Education and Human Development, University of Maine. Available from http://www.hazingstudy.org/.

Center on Alcohol Marketing and Youth. (2003). *Alcohol advertising on sports television 2001 to 2003.* Washington, DC: Center on Alcohol Marketing and Youth, Georgetown University. Available from http://camy.org/.

Colin, J., & Mackenzie, R. (2006). The World Cup, sport sponsorship, and health. *Lancet, 367,* 1964–1966.

Council of Europe. (1963, 1989). *Anti-doping convention* (CETS No.: 135). Strassbourg: Author. Available from http://conventions.coe.int/.

Darling, N., Caldwell, L. L., & Smith, R. (2005). Participation in school-based extracurricular activities and adolescent adjustment. *Journal of Leisure Research, 37*(1), 51–76.

Ellickson, P. L., Collins, R. L., Hambarsoomians, K., & McCaffrey, D. F. (2005). Does alcohol advertising promote adolescent drinking? [Results from a longitudinal assessment] *Addiction, 100,* 235–246.

Ford, J. A. (2007). Substance use among college athletes: A comparison based on sport/team affiliation. *American Journal of College Health, 55*(6), 367–373.

Garry, J. P., & Morrissey, S. L. (2000). Team sports participation and risk-taking behaviors among a biracial middle school population. *Clinical Journal of Sport Medicine, 10*(3), 185–190.

Howard, D. R., & Crompton, J. L. (1995). *Financing sport.* Morgantown, WV: Fitness Information Technology.

International Intergovernmental Consultative Group on Anti-Doping (IICGAD). Available from http://www.dbcde.gov.au/.

Klein, E., & Jones-Webb, R. J. (2007). Tobacco and advertising in televised sports: Time to focus on policy change. *American Journal of Public Health, 97*(2), 198.

Madden, P. A., & Grube, J. W. (1994). The frequency and nature of alcohol and tobacco advertising in televised sports, 1990 through 1992. *American Journal of Public Health, 84,* 297–299.

Martin, M. (1998). The use of alcohol among NCAA division I female college basketball, softball and volleyball athletes. *Journal of Athletic Training, 33,*163–167.

Martin, C. A., & Bush, A. J. (2000). Do role models influence purchase intentions and behaviour. *Journal of Consumer Marketing, 17*(5), 441–454.

Maughan, R. J. (1997). Energy and macronutrient intakes of professional football (soccer) players. *British Journal of Sports Medicine, 31,* 45–47.

Nelson, T. F., & Wechsler, H. (2001). Alcohol and college athletes. *Medicine and Science in Sports and Exercise, 33,* 43–47.

O'Brien, K. S., Ali, A., Cotter, J. D., O'Shea, R. P., & Stannard, S. (2007). Hazardous drinking in New Zealand sportspeople: Level of sporting participation and drinking motives. *Alcohol, 42*(4), 376–382.

O'Brien, K. S., Blackie, J. M., & Hunter, J. A. (2005). Hazardous drinking in elite New Zealand sportspeople. *Alcohol and Alcoholism, 40*(3), 239–241.

Peretti-Watel, P., Beck, F., & Legleye, S. (2002). Beyond the U-curve: The relationship between sport and alcohol, cigarette and cannabis use in adolescents. *Addiction, 97*(6), 707–716.

Quarrie, K. L., Feehan, M., Waller, A. E., Cooke, K. R., Williams, S., & McGee, R. (1996). The New Zealand rugby injury and performance project: Alcohol use patterns within a cohort of rugby players. *Addiction, 91*(12), 1865–1868.

Saffer, H., & Dave, D. (2006). Alcohol advertising and alcohol consumption by adolescents. *Health Economics, 15*(6), 617–637.

Snyder, L. B., Milici, F. F., Mitchell, E. W., & Proctor, D. C. B. (2000). Media, product differences and seasonality in alcohol advertising in 1997. *Journal of Studies on Alcohol, 61,* 896–906.

Stokvis, R. (2003). *Moral entrepreneurship and doping cultures in sport.* [ASSR working paper 03/04]. Amsterdam: Amsterdam School for Social Science Research. Available from http://www2.fmg.uva.nl/.

Wilson, W., & Derse, E. (2001). *Doping in elite sport: The politics of drugs in the Olympic Movement.* Champaign, IL: Human Kinetics Publishers

World Anti-Doping Agency (WADA) Web site. Available from http://www.wada-ama.org/.

World Anti-Doping Code and the Australian Sports Anti-Doping Agency (ASADA) Web site. Available from http://www.asada.gov.au/.

World Health Organization (WHO). (2004a). Global Status Report on Alcohol 2004. World Health Organization Geneva. Available from http://www.who.int/.

World Health Organization (WHO). (2004b). Global Status Report: Alcohol Policy, 2004. World Health Organization Geneva. Available from http://www.who.int/.

Yesalis, C. E., Kopstein, A. N., & Bahrke, M. S. Difficulties in estimating the prevalence of use among athletes. (2001). In W. Wilson & E. Derse (Eds.), *Doping in elite sport: The politics of drugs in the Olympic Movement* (pp. 43–62). Champaign, IL: Human Kinetics Publishers.

JOHN FITZGERALD

SSADDA. *See* **Semi-Structured Assessment for Drug Dependence and Alcoholism (SSADDA).**

SSAGA. *See* **Semi-Structured Assessment for the Genetics of Alcoholism (SSAGA).**

STILL. Still is the colloquial term for distillery, a device used for distillation—to extract ethyl alcohol (ethanol) from various plants and food products. The simplest ones contain a cooking pot and a tightly fitted cap from which a long arm extends in a downward direction. A mash is boiled, the ethyl alcohol rises to the top and is deposited as a vapor which then condenses as it cools and passes through the arm.

See also **Alcohol: History of Drinking (International); Alcohol: History of Drinking in the United States.**

BIBLIOGRAPHY

Bryce, J. H., & Stewart, G. G. (2004). *Distilled spirits: Tradition and innovation.* Nottingham, U.K.: Nottingham University Press.

SCOTT E. LUKAS

STREET VALUE. When drugs are seized by a police or interdiction agency, the significance of the seizure is often measured in terms of its street value; that is, the revenues that would be fetched if each gram were sold at the current retail price.

Such measures are routine among police and customs service agents in the United States and in most other nations, although large price fluctuations can occur from one area to another and within short time frames.

The use of the term *street value* is potentially misleading when it is intended to convey the significance of the seizure as a loss to the traffickers. The price of drugs rises steeply as they move down the distribution chain from point of importation. In mid-2000s, for example, a gram of cocaine could sell on the streets of a U.S. city for about $77. That gram (1,000 milligrams) contained approximately 700 milligrams (mg) of pure cocaine—so that the "pure gram" price was about $109. Yet when sold in 100-kilogram (kg) units at the point of import, the cocaine could have sold for a pure-gram price of about $20. Thus it would cost drug traders $2 million to replace the 100 kilograms. That figure is the total value of payments that would have to be made to growers, refiners, and smugglers in order to obtain another 100 kilograms and bring the drug to the same point in the distribution system.

Valuing a 100-kg seizure at street value would then imply that the government had inflicted a $10.6 million blow to the drug industry, more than five times as much as the true value of the loss. The extent of overstatement increases with the size of the seizure, since the price of drugs goes down as the volume increases in a given transaction.

See also **Drug Interdiction; Drug Laws, Prosecution of; Seizures of Drugs.**

BIBLIOGRAPHY

Kopp, P. (2003). *Economics of illegal drugs.* New York: Routledge.

Mares, D. (2005). *Drug wars and coffee houses: The political economy of the international drug trade.* Washington, D. C.: CQ Press.

PETER REUTER
REVISED BY MARY CARVLIN (2001)

STRUCTURED CLINICAL INTERVIEW FOR DSM-IV (SCID). Structured Clinical Interview for *DSM-IV-TR* (SCID) is a diagnostic interview designed for use by mental health professionals. It assesses 33 of the more commonly occurring psychiatric disorders defined in the fourth edition text revision of the *Diagnostic and Statistical Manual* (*DSM-IV-TR*) of the American Psychiatric Association (2000). The SCID is a semi-structured interview that allows the experienced clinician to tailor questions to fit the patient's understanding; to ask additional questions that clarify ambiguities; to challenge inconsistencies; and to make clinical judgments about the seriousness of symptoms. The main uses of the SCID are for diagnostic evaluation, research, and the training of mental-health professionals.

The SCID is modeled on the standard clinical interview. It begins with an overview section that includes questions about basic demographic information (e.g., age, marital status), educational history, and work history, followed by questions about the chief complaint, past episodes of psychiatric disturbance, treatment history, and current functioning. The remainder of the interview is organized into the following sections: mood episodes, psychotic symptoms, differential diagnosis of psychotic disorders, differential diagnosis of mood disorders, substance-use disorders, anxiety disorders, somatoform disorders, eating disorders, and adjustment disorder. Although the substance use disorders (i.e., dependence and abuse) are assessed in a single section, the substance-induced disorders (i.e., substance-induced mood disorder, substance-induced psychotic disorder, and substance-induced anxiety disorder) are assessed in the mood, psychotic and anxiety disorder sections, respectively. Two optional modules, one for assessing suicidal thoughts and behavior (adapted from the Columbia Suicide-Severity Rating Scale) and one for assessing impulse control disorders, are also available. A separate interview, the Structured Clinical Interview for *DSM-IV* Axis II Personality Disorders (SCID-II) is available for the assessment of personality disorders.

The SCID comes in three basic versions: the research version (known as the SCID-I-RV), the clinician version (SCID-CV), and a clinical trials version (SCID-CT). The research version contains the full complement of disorders, subtypes, and specifiers that are of interest to researchers. It is provided by the Biometrics Research Department at Columbia University as an unbound packet of pages so that the investigator has the ability to leave out pages covering disorders or subtypes that are not relevant to a particular study. The bound clinician version (published by American Psychiatric Press) includes only those disorders and specifiers that are the most clinically relevant. The SCID-CT, designed specifically for clinical trials, provides customizable indication-specific configurations of the modules (e.g., for schizophrenia trials). A computer-assisted version of the SCID-CV is available from http://www.mhs.com, and a beta version of a computer-assisted SCID-RV is also available.

Training materials (e.g., didactic DVDs, DVDs of SCID interviews) can be ordered, and optional on-site training can be arranged. Additional detailed information about the SCID (including differences between the research and clinician versions, ordering information, training materials, reliability and validity references) is available on the SCID Web site (http://www.scid4.org).

Diagnostic criteria for substance dependence and abuse are assessed for eight classes of substances: Alcohol (ethanol), Sedative-Hypnotic-Anxiolytics, Cannabis (marijuana), Stimulants, Opioids, Cocaine, Hallucinogens/PCP, and Other (e.g., inhalants, atropine). For each class of substance, the interviewer determines whether the symptoms of dependence or abuse have ever been present during the subject's lifetime; whether they have been present during the last month; and the age when the first symptoms appeared. If dependence is current, the interviewer rates the current severity as mild, moderate, or severe. If dependence is in partial or full remission, the appropriate *DSM-IV-TR* remission specifier is noted (e.g., early partial remission, sustained full remission). Because alcohol use is so much more common than other substance use, the assessment for alcohol dependence and abuse is conducted first, followed by an assessment of dependence or abuse on the remaining categories of substances.

ALCOHOL SECTION

The alcohol section of the SCID begins with some overview questions about the subject's drinking history (e.g., "Has there ever been a period when you had five or more drinks on one occasion?" and "Has anyone ever objected to your drinking?"). The subject's answers to these initial questions

allow the interviewer to sequence the assessment questions to match the subject's drinking history as follows: If a history of dependence seems likely (e.g., the subject reports a history of detoxification from alcohol or attendance at AA), the interviewer begins with the assessment of the individual *DSM-IV-TR* dependence criteria. (If criteria are met for dependence, the assessment of abuse is skipped since a *DSM-IV-TR* diagnosis of dependence preempts a diagnosis of abuse). If the history is not suggestive of dependence but is indicative of excessive drinking or problematic use, the interviewer commences with the individual *DSM-IV-TR* criteria for abuse. (If the criteria are met for abuse, the interviewer must then continue the assessment to see if the problematic drinking is sufficiently severe to qualify for dependence). Only if there have never been any episodes of excessive drinking and there is no evidence of alcohol-related problems can the interviewer skip the alcohol section and move on to the assessment of other substances.

DRUG SECTION

The drug section of the SCID is similarly structured to tailor the sequence of questions to the subject's drug-taking history. If, for any class of substance, the subject reports having used the substance on at least ten occasions in any one-month period, the interviewer starts with the assessment for dependence. If the subject reports using a substance at least twice, but less than ten times in any month, the assessment focuses on abuse. (As with the assessment for alcohol, if criteria are met for abuse, the interviewer follows up with the assessment for dependence). The interviewer checks for dependence on prescribed medications if the subject reports having been "hooked" on the medication or often taking more of it than was prescribed.

Two versions of the drug section are available: a standard version that assesses whether dependence or abuse has ever been met for any class of drug, and an alternate, more comprehensive version that assesses lifetime dependence and abuse for every class of drug ever used by the subject. In the standard version, the interviewer first determines which drug class has either caused the most problems or been used the most and then proceeds with assessing the criteria for lifetime dependence and/or abuse for

Reference (See Below)	Skre et al., 1991	Zanarini et al., 2000	Zanarini et al., 2000	Segal et al., 1995	Wiliams et al., 1992	Zanarini et al., 2001	Zanarini et al., 2001
Population Studied	N554	N527	N552	N540	N5592; Mixed Inpt, Outpt, Non-Pt.	N545	N530
Version of SCID	DSM-III-R	DSM-IV	DSM-IV	DSM-III-R	DSM-III-R	DSM-III-R	DSM-III-R
Design of Reliability Study	Joint; Audio-Tape	Joint; 84 Rater-Pairs from 4 sites	7–10 Day Interval Test-Retest	Joint; Audio-Tape	1–3 Week Interval Test-Retest	Joint; Observed Live	7–10 Day Interval Test-Retest
Major Depressive Disorder	.93	.80	.61	.90	.64	.90	.73
Dysthymic Disorder	.88	.76	.35	.53	.40	.91	.60
Bipolar Disorder	.79				.84		
Schizophrenia	.94				.65		
Alcohol Dependence/ Abuse	.96	1.0	.77		.75	1.0	
Other Substance Dependence/ Abuse	.85	1.0	.76		.84	.95	.77
Panic Disorder	.88	.65	.65	.80	.58	.88	.82
Social Phobia	.72	.63	.59		.47	.86	.53
OCD	.40	.57	.60		.59	.70	.42
GAD	.95	.63	.44		.56	.73	.63
PTSD	.77	.88	.78			1.0	1.0
Any Somatoform Disorder	2.03			.84			
Any Eating Disorder		.77	.64				

Notes: Values shown are for kappa, a measure of chance-corrected agreement.

SOURCE: (1) Segal DL, Kabacoff RI, Hersen M, Van Hasselt VB, Ryan CF. Update on the Reliability of Diagnosis in Older Psychiatric Outpatients Using the Structured Clinical Interview for DSM-III-R. *J of Clinical Geropsychology* 1995; 1:313–321 (2) Skre I, Onstad S, Torgersen S, Kringlen E. High interrater reliability for the Structured Clinical Interview for DSM-III-R Axis I (SCID-I). *Acta Psychiatr Scand* 1991 Aug; 84(2):167–73 (3) Williams JBW, Gibbon M, First MB, Spitzer RL, Davis M, Borus J, Howes MJ, Kane J, Pope HG, Rounsaville B, Wittchen H. The Structured Clinical Interview for DSM-III-R (SCID) II. Multi-site test-retest reliability. *Arch Gen Psychiatry*,1992; 49:630– 636 (4) Zanarini MC, Frankenburg FR. Attainment and maintenance of reliability of axis I and axis II disorders over the course of a longitudinal study. *Comprehensive Psych* 2001 Sep–Oct 42(5):369–374 (5) Zanarini MC, Skodol AE, Bender D, Dolan R, Sanislow C, Schaefer E, Morey LC, Grilo CM, Shea MT, McGlashan TH, Gunderson JG. The Collaborative Longitudinal Personality Disorders Study: reliability of axis I and II diagnoses. *J Personal Disord* 2000 Winter; 14(4):291–9.

Table 1. Summary of selected SCID-I reliability studies. ILLUSTRATION BY GGS INFORMATION SERVICES. GALE, CENGAGE LEARNING

that class only. If criteria are not met for dependence or abuse on that class and there is evidence for problematic use of another class of drug, the interviewer next assesses dependence and abuse for that class of drug, continuing this process until the interviewer is satisfied that all relevant drug classes have been covered. In the alternate version, the interviewer makes ratings for every dependence and abuse item for each relevant drug class in parallel.

Table 1 summarizes the most comprehensive reliability studies of the SCID-I. Reliability for categorical constructs, such as the *DSM-IV* diagnoses being assessed by the SCID, is reported in terms of kappa, a statistic that corrects for chance agreement. Kappa values above 0.70 are considered to reflect good agreement; values from .50 to .70, fair agreement, and those below .50, poor agreement. As can be seen immediately in the table, the range of values of kappa from different studies and for different diagnoses is enormous. Many factors influence the reliability of an interview instrument

such as the SCID, including study design (i.e., whether the reliability is joint interrater, in which the agreement is between raters observing the same interview versus the more stringent test-retest design in which two raters independently interview the same subject); interviewer training, subject population (i.e., better reliability is typically achieved using subjects with severe psychopathology as compared to subjects with milder psychopathology whose symptoms are more likely to be at the level of the diagnostic threshold), and disorder base rates (i.e., it is harder to obtain good reliability for rare disorders).

The validity of a diagnostic assessment technique is generally measured by determining the agreement between the diagnoses made by the assessment technique and some hypothetical "gold standard." Unfortunately, a gold standard for psychiatric diagnoses remains elusive. Perhaps the most accepted (albeit flawed) standard used in psychiatric diagnostic studies is known as a *best estimate diagnosis* in which the subject is diagnosed by a committee of experts using all available data.

Several studies (e.g., Ramirez Basco et al., 2000; Fennig et al., 1996; Kranzler et al., 1996) compared the SCID to best estimate diagnoses and demonstrated superior validity of the SCID over standard clinical interviews at intake episode.

See also **Addiction: Concepts and Definitions; Complications: Mental Disorders; Epidemiology of Drug Abuse; International Classification of Diseases (ICD); Models of Alcoholism and Drug Abuse.**

BIBLIOGRAPHY

Fennig, S., Naisberg-Fennig, S., Craig, T. J., Tanenberg-Karant, M., & Bromet, E. J. (1996). Comparison of clinical and research diagnoses of substance use disorders in a first-admission psychotic sample. *American Journal on Addictions, 5,* 40–48.

First, M. B., Spitzer, R. L., Gibbon, M., & Williams, J. B. W. (1997). Structured clinical interview for *DSM-IV—clinical version (SCID-CV)* (User's guide and interview). Washington, DC: American Psychiatric Press.

Kranzler, H. R., Kadden, R. M., Babor, T. F., Tennen, H., & Rousaville, B. J. (1996) Validity of the SCID in substance abuse patients. *Addiction, 91,* 859–868.

Ramirez Basco, M. R., Bostic, J. Q., Davies, D. Rush, A. J., Witte, B., Hendrickse, B., et al. (2000). Methods to improve diagnostic accuracy in a community mental health setting. *American Journal of Psychiatry, 157,* 1599–1605.

Segal, D. L., Kabacoff, R. I., Hersen, M., Van Hasselt, V. B., & Ryan, C. F. (1995). Update on the reliability of diagnosis in older psychiatric outpatients using the Structured Clinical Interview for *DSM-III-R*. *Journal of Clinical Geropsychology, 1,* 313–321.

Skre, I., Onstad, S., Torgersen, S., & Kringlen, E. (1991.) High interrater reliability for the Structured Clinical Interview for *DSM-III-R* Axis I (SCID-I). *Acta Psychiatrica Scandinavica, 84*(2), 167–173.

Spitzer, R. L., Williams, J. B., Gibbon, M., First, M. B. (1992). The structured clinical interview for *DSM-III-R* (SCID). I. History, rationale and description. *Archives of General Psychiatry, 49,* 624–629.

Williams, J. B. W., Gibbon, M., First, M. B., Spitzer, R. L., Davis, M., Borus, J., et al. (1992). The Structured Clinical Interview for *DSM-III-R* (SCID) II. Multi-site test-retest reliability. *Archives of General Psychiatry, 49,* 630–636.

Zanarini, M. C., & Frankenburg, F. R. (2001). Attainment and maintenance of reliability of axis I and axis II disorders over the course of a longitudinal study. *Comprehensive Psychiatry, 42*(5), 369–374.

Zanarini, M. C., Skodol, A. E., Bender, D., Dolan, R., Sanislow, C., Schaefer, E., et al. (2000). The Collaborative Longitudinal Personality Disorders Study: Reliability of axis I and II diagnoses. *Journal of Personality Disorders, 14*(4), 291–299.

THOMAS F. BABOR
REVISED BY MICHAEL B. FIRST (2009)

STUDENTS AGAINST DESTRUCTIVE DECISIONS (SADD).

In 1981, Robert Anastas, a health educator and hockey coach in Wayland, Massachusetts, stood helplessly by as two of his students died from injuries sustained in two separate alcohol-related traffic accidents. Anastas decided to act: He developed a fifteen-session high school course on driving while impaired. Rather than a curriculum focusing solely on the effects of alcohol while driving, he taught strategies for preventing driving after drinking, and he emphasized the legal consequences of getting caught while driving under the influence. In this sense, the curriculum was a significant departure from traditional driver-education approaches.

ORIGINS OF SADD AND ITS GOALS AND EFFECTS

Students who took Anastas's course reacted enthusiastically and formed an organization to reduce alcohol-related traffic deaths among their peers. They initially called the organization Students Against Driving Drunk (SADD) in order to focus attention on the act of drunk driving, not on the drivers themselves. An anecdote related by Peggy Mann (1983) captures SADD's approach and philosophy: When a student jokingly suggested that SADD involve the governor, Anastas replied, "I believe that if you dream it, it can be done," and when the governor became the honorary chairman of SADD, its motto became "If You Dream It, It Can Be Done." Within a year, chapters had been formed throughout Massachusetts and the program was gaining national attention.

Members of the early SADD chapters had a number of goals. They sought to raise awareness of impaired driving among students through the curriculum developed by Anastas. They also sought to change norms related to impaired driving. Because they realized that most of their peers did not think of drinking and driving as wrong or risky, they reasoned that changing these norms was an important component of reducing impaired driving problems. As the students put it, they wanted to change the "drinking and driving is cool" image to another image: "Drinking and driving is dumb." Finally, students in the SADD chapters sought to stimulate discussion between high school students and their parents about drinking and driving. To meet this goal, they developed a "Contract for Life," which stipulated that a student would call a parent if he or she had been drinking or if the person responsible for driving had been drinking, and the parent, in turn, agreed to provide a ride or taxi fare.

SADD was significant in three important ways. First, it was among the earliest prevention programs to emphasize student leadership. Other programs had used peer educators or peer counselors trained and supervised by adults, but SADD chapters were run by students who planned activities and took responsibility for making them happen. Second, SADD was among the first youth programs to recognize the importance of norms in impaired-driving prevention. Earlier programs had emphasized education, attitude change, or scare tactics. Third, SADD was one of the first school-based prevention programs to venture outside the classroom. Although SADD had a curriculum, it also entailed extracurricular, community, and family involvement. In this sense, SADD was the first of the so-called comprehensive school-based prevention programs.

ORGANIZATION GROWTH

SADD's early growth was rapid. By the mid-1980s, there were SADD chapters in every state in the United States and in Europe. SADD received considerable media attention and was the only alcohol-prevention program ever to be the subject of a nationally broadcast made-for-television movie, *Contract for Life: The Bob Anastas Story* (1984).

SADD was also controversial. Some vocal critics argued that SADD's emphasis on preventing drinking and driving implicitly condoned drinking by young people. They were particularly concerned about the Contract for Life. They argued that by ensuring safe transportation, parents were communicating the message that drinking itself was not a problem. Similar charges were leveled at Safe Rides and other programs that provided sober

transportation for youth. Anastas and others countered that although drinking itself *was* a problem, young people were dying from traffic crashes, not just from drinking.

This debate, which resulted in the refusal by some funding agencies to allow grant money to be used to support SADD chapters, continued throughout the 1980s. SADD was also subject to criticism because of its acceptance of funding from the alcoholic beverage industry. In 1989, SADD divorced itself from this source of funds. It also adopted a strong no-use message and amended its Contract for Life to emphasize its commitment to a drug- and alcohol-free lifestyle. The organization specifically disassociated itself from safe rides and designated driver programs. However, it continued to characterize itself as an "inclusive, not exclusive" organization, recognizing that teenagers make mistakes and should not be punished for them. Rather, it sought to "inform, educate, support and empower young people to make positive decisions in their lives."

Over the years, SADD evolved. Junior high school and college programs were added, as was an emphasis on seatbelt use. In 1997, in response to calls from its chapters, the organization amended its popular name to Students Against Destructive Decisions, incorporating in its mandate other such potentially destructive behaviors as underage drinking and drug use, teen suicide, violence, and irresponsible sexual behavior or drug use that might result in the contraction of diseases. In the early twenty-first century, SADD chapters focus primarily on education, awareness, and peer support activities on a range of issues surrounding risky behaviors. Additionally, several student safety clubs with similar approaches to those of SADD have emerged. Members of these clubs, like SADD members, encourage students to reach out to other students to reduce highway deaths.

The mission of SADD has evolved as well. It is no longer sufficient to "just say no" to drinking and driving. The twenty-first century organization focuses on other forms of positive peer pressure aimed at helping students of all ages to choose not to make destructive decisions regarding drug use, risky sexual behaviors, underage and binge drinking, school and community violence, driving while impaired in any way, dating and relationship violence, teen depression, teen pregnancy, and teen suicide.

Since the mid-1980s, SADD has been an international organization. In 1988, information on chapter creation was sent to students in the Netherlands, France, China, Japan, Iran, Jamaica, Israel, Germany, Australia, and Africa. In 1989, SADD chapters were established in the Soviet Union. In 1995, the Pruesser Group released the first systematic study of the effectiveness of SADD activities on teen decision-making. The results indicated that "students at SADD schools were more likely to hold attitudes reflecting positive reasons as to why NOT to use alcohol."

In 2000, SADD's partnership with Liberty Mutual insurance company for the purpose of creating annual surveys had its first release, which focused on communication barriers between parents and youth, the differences in how parents view critical aspects of teens' lives, and the importance of effective communication between parents and their children about making positive choices and avoiding destructive decisions.

See also Accidents and Injuries from Alcohol; Dramshop Liability Laws; Driving, Alcohol, and Drugs; Mothers Against Drunk Driving (MADD); Parent Movement, The.

BIBLIOGRAPHY

Centers for Disease Control and Prevention. (1994). Guidelines for school health programs to prevent tobacco use and addiction. *Morbidity and Mortality Weekly Report, 43*(RR-2), 1–19.

Hatcher, J. L., & Scarpa, J. (2002). *Research brief—Encouraging teens to adopt a safe, healthy lifestyle: A foundation for improving future adult behaviors.* Washington, DC: Child Trends.

Kann, K., Kinchen, S. A., Williams, B. I., Ross, J. G., Lowry, R., Grunbaum, J. A., et al. (2000). Youth risk behavior surveillance—United States, 1999. *Morbidity and Mortality Weekly Report, 49*(No. SS-5), 1–94.

Klitzner, M., Gruenewald, P. J., Bamberger, E., & Rossiter, C. (1994). A quasi-experimental evaluation of Students Against Driving Drunk. *American Journal of Drug and Alcohol Abuse, 20*(1), 57–74.

Mann, P. (1993). *Arrive alive: How to keep drunk and pot-high drivers off the highway.* New York: Woodmere Press.

Preusser Research Group. (1995). Evaluation of youth peer-to-peer impaired driving program. Washington, DC: U.S. Department of Transportation.

Sheehan, M., Schonfeld, C., Ballard, R., Schofield, F., Najman, J., & Siskind, V. (1996). A three-year outcome evaluation of a theory-based drunk-driving education program. *Journal of Drug Education, 26*(3), 295–312.

Shope, J. T., Elliot, M. R., Raghunathan, T. E., & Waller, P. F. (2001). Long-term follow-up of a high school misuse prevention program's effect on students' subsequent driving. *Alcoholism: Clinical and Experimental Research, 25*(3), 403–410.

Shults, R. A., Elder, R. W., Sleet, D. A., Nichols, J. L., Alao, M. O., Carande-Kulis, V. G., et al. (2001). Reviews of evidence regarding interventions to reduce alcohol-impaired driving. *American Journal of Preventive Medicine, 21*(4S), 66–88.

Students Against Destructive Decisions (SADD) Web site. Available from http://www.sadd.org.

U.S. Department of Health and Human Services. (2001). *Youth violence: A report of the Surgeon General.* Rockville, MD: Office of the Surgeon General.

Wagenaar, A. C., Murray, D. M., & Toomey, T. L. (2000). Communities Mobilizing for Change on Alcohol (CMCA): Effects of a randomized trial on arrests and traffic crashes. *Addiction, 95*(2), 209–217.

MICHAEL KLITZNER
REVISED BY PATRICIA OHLENROTH (2001)
PAMELA V. MICHAELS (2009)

SUBSTANCE ABUSE AND AIDS.

Acquired immunodeficiency syndrome (AIDS) is a life-threatening disease that results from severe damage to part of the body's cellular immune system, the defense system against opportunistic infections and some cancers. The disease is acquired (as opposed to genetic or hereditary) and presents a myriad of clinical manifestations (syndromes) that result from severe damage to the immune system. AIDS was first identified in 1981 among homosexual men in California and New York, and among illicit-injected-drug abusers in New York City. After 1981, the numbers and types of AIDS patients increased rapidly; it was diagnosed in millions of persons throughout the world. In the United States alone, the Centers for Disease Control (CDC) estimated in 2003 that 1.0 to 1.2 million persons in the United States were living with HIV infection.

In 2006, injecting drug use was the primary risk factor for 13 percent of known HIV/AIDS cases in the 33 U.S. states with confidential name based reporting. An additional 3 percent of cases occurred among men who have sex with men and also inject illicit drugs (MSM-IDUs). An additional 33 percent of the HIV/AIDS cases occurred among high-risk heterosexuals (who reported heterosexual relationship with persons known to be HIV infected or at high risk for HIV infection). A substantial percentage of the "high-risk heterosexual" partners are injecting drug users, though the data on the actual percentage are limited. Thus, a best estimate would be that injecting drug use is associated with one-fourth to one-third of the cases of HIV and AIDS in the United States. HIV and AIDS have also been found among non-injecting drug users—such as persons who smoke crack cocaine—but surveillance data are not available on sexual transmission of HIV facilitated by non-injecting drug use.

CAUSE

AIDS is caused by a viral infection. In the United States, the virus is called human immunodeficiency virus (HIV); it is one of a group of viruses called retroviruses (so-called because they can make DNA copies of their RNA, the reverse of what typically occurs in animal cells). In 1983, French researchers discovered the virus, which they had linked to an outbreak of enlarged lymph nodes (one early sign of HIV infection) that had been reported among French male homosexuals. The French named it the lymphadenopathy-associated virus (LAV). In 1984, U.S. researchers isolated HIV from AIDS patients and named it human T-lymphotropic virus type III (HTLV-III). American investigators found a way to grow HIV in laboratories in large amounts, which led to the development of laboratory tests that detect HIV infection.

HIV gradually destroys certain white blood cells called T-helper lymphocytes or CD4+ cells. The loss of these cells results in the body's inability to control microbial organisms that the normal immune system controls easily. These infections are called opportunistic because they take advantage of damage to part of the immune system. A few select cancers are also frequently diagnosed, such as Kaposi's sarcoma, a cancer of blood vessels, which appears as purplish spots on the skin or mucous membranes.

SIGNS AND SYMPTOMS

Early HIV Infection. The natural history of HIV disease and the time intervals between clinical events vary greatly from individual to individual. The general course, however, is one of exposure to HIV, which leads to infection. Within a few weeks or months of infection, laboratory evidence of infection can be detected as the presence of virus in the blood (viremia) or the appearance of the p24 antigen. Antibodies to HIV are found in the blood and indicate that infection has occurred. Some patients develop flu-like symptoms resembling mononucleosis or peripheral nerve abnormalities that are self-limited. This first stage of HIV infection is called the acute retroviral syndrome. Most patients have no symptoms during this period.

Latency Period. Over the ensuing years of a second, or latency, period (1–15 or more years), laboratory evidence of a decreasing number of helper T-lymphocytes can be measured. As the helper T-lymphocyte count decreases, patients are more likely to develop such signs and symptoms as enlarged lymph glands, fatigue, unexplained fever, weight loss, diarrhea, and night sweats. At about the same time or later, patients develop opportunistic infections or cancers. The diagnosis of one of the opportunistic infections or cancers indicates that the patient has developed AIDS. Pneumocystis carinii pneumonia, a fungal infection of the lung, is the most common opportunistic infection among AIDS patients. Other opportunistic infections include candidiasis of the mouth (thrush), cryptococcal meningitis, amebiasis, and cryptosporidiosis. Tuberculosis is another serious infection that has become increasingly common because of the AIDS pandemic.

Late-Stage AIDS. Late-stage AIDS is usually marked by a sharp decline in the number of lymphocytes, followed by a rise in the number of opportunistic infections and cancers. Kaposi's sarcoma is the most common cancer among AIDS patients. Kaposi's sarcoma usually arises in the skin and looks like a bruise or an area of bruises, but it grows and spreads to the internal organs. Another common type of cancer in late-stage AIDS is a form of lymphoma, or a tumor of the lymphatic system. Patients with late-stage AIDS may also develop inflammations of the muscles, arthritis-like pain in the joints, and AIDS dementia complex. AIDS dementia complex is marked by loss of reasoning ability, apathy and loss of initiative, loss of memory, and unsteadiness or weakness in walking.

DIAGNOSIS AND TREATMENT

Infection with HIV can be diagnosed with a blood test measuring antibodies to the virus. Antibodies are proteins produced by certain white blood cells in response to injection. The HIV antibody test became widely available in 1985. An enzyme-linked immunosorbent assay (ELISA) test for the presence of HIV antibody is used as the first test for detecting HIV antibody. Positive ELISA results are then tested with a western blot assay for confirmation. The use of these tests by blood banks has virtually eliminated the chances of contracting infection from transfusions.

Although a cure or vaccine for AIDS had not been discovered as of 2008, three groups of antiviral drugs are used to treat HIV infection.

Nucleoside Analogues. These drugs work by interfering with the replication process of the HIV virus. They include zidovudine (ZDV, AZT), didanosine (ddI), zalcitabine (ddC), stavudine (d4T), and lamivudine (3TC).

Nonnucleoside Reverse Transcriptase Inhibitors. These drugs work by blocking the activities of the RNA and DNA in infected cells. They include nevirapine and delavirdine. The drawback of this group of drugs is that the virus quickly develops resistance to them.

Protease Inhibitors. These are considered the most potent antiviral drugs. They inhibit the viral proteinase enzyme, which results in noninfectious particles of virus. The protease inhibitors include saquinavir, ritonavir, indinavir, and nelfinavir.

These drugs were usually given in combinations of at least two and preferably three compounds. Triple combinations, including one of the protease inhibitors, are considered the most powerful antiviral regimens. All antiviral treatment regimens must be individualized to the patient.

Because HIV frequently develops resistance to these drugs, particularly if patients do not take their medications with great consistency, there is a continuing need for developing new drugs.

HIV TRANSMISSION

HIV can be transmitted from person to person in three ways: (1) by contact with infected blood or blood components; (2) through intimate sexual contact; and (3) from an infected pregnant mother to her fetus. Drug abusers commonly become infected by sharing needles, syringes, and other injecting paraphernalia; injecting substances—such as heroin, cocaine, and amphetamines—after an HIV-infected person uses the needle and syringe causes direct inoculation of HIV. The sharing of needles and syringes can be thought of as a microtransfusion.

Sexual contact is a common route of transmission from drug abusers to their sex partners (who can transmit the virus to other sex partners, other drug abusers, or to unborn children). Various noninjected drugs, including crack cocaine and alcohol, can increase the likelihood of engaging in unprotected sexual activities. This drug use facilitated sexual transmission of HIV is a growing problem in the United States. Health care workers have also been exposed to HIV through unprotected or accidental direct contact with blood of infected patients in healthcare settings.

The World Health Organization (WHO) estimated that there were approximately 40 million persons infected with HIV in 2006, with about 4 million new infections per year. Most of these cases are in sub-Saharan Africa. Injecting drug use is not yet a major mode of HIV transmission in sub-Saharan Africa, but approximately one-third of new HIV infections outside sub-Saharan Africa are associated with injecting drug use.

PREVENTION AMONG DRUG ABUSERS

Three different types of programs have been shown to be effective in reducing HIV transmission among injecting drug users.

Community Outreach. Injecting drug users need accurate information about HIV and AIDS in order to reduce their risk behavior. While mass media can play an important role in transmitting such information, community outreach programs can be highly effective in delivering information as well as personally encouraging drug users to change behavior and providing referrals to other needed services. These outreach programs typically use former drug users.

Legal Access to Sterile Injection Equipment. As the virus is transmitted through sharing of drug injection equipment, providing good access to sterile injection equipment is critical to reducing HIV transmission among injecting drug users. Syringe exchange programs, in which drug users bring in used needles and syringes (potentially contaminated with HIV), and are then given new sterile needles and syringes in return have become the best known type of program for preventing HIV among injecting drug users. Large-scale syringe exchange programs have been effective in preventing HIV among drug injectors in many different countries. Syringe exchange programs can also provide a wide variety of other health and social services to drug users. Legal sales of needles and syringes through pharmacies is another method of reducing HIV transmission among drug injectors, and syringe exchange and pharmacy sales should be thought of as a complementary rather than an either/or choice for HIV prevention.

Methadone Maintenance Treatment (MMT). Persons who enter drug-abuse treatment usually greatly reduce their illicit drug use and therefore their risk of becoming infected with HIV through sharing needles and syringes. Methadone maintenance therapy has been shown to be an effective therapy for opiate addicts and has decreased HIV transmission among patients. Buprenophine has also been shown to be an effective treatment for narcotic addiction, though, with the exception of a few countries such as France, it has not as of 2008 been implemented on a scale large enough to affect HIV transmission. While drug abuse treatment, methadone and burprenorphine maintenance in particular, can be very effective in reducing illicit drug use, it should be considered as treatment but not cures for addiction. Certainly drug abuse treatment should be provided to everyone who needs it, but people also need to develop new treatments for addiction, particularly for cocaine and other stimulant addictions.

Comprehensive HIV Prevention Programming for Drug Users. No one type of HIV prevention programming for injecting drug users is perfect in that it will completely eliminate injection risk behavior. However, combinations of community outreach, legal access to sterile injection equipment, and drug abuse treatment have prevented HIV epidemics among drug injectors in many countries. There is no justification for not implementing such programs wherever there is a threat of HIV being transmitted among injecting drug users.

See also **Alcohol and AIDS; Complications: Route of Administration; Injecting Drug Users and HIV; Needle and Syringe Exchanges and HIV/AIDS.**

BIBLIOGRAPHY

Committee on the Prevention of HIV Infection among Injecting Drug Users in High Risk Countries. (2006). *Preventing HIV infection among injecting drug users in high risk countries: An assessment of the evidence.* Washington, DC: Institute of Medicine.

Des Jarlais, D. C., & Semaan, S. (2008). HIV prevention for injecting drug users: The first 25 years and counting. *Psychosomatic Medicine, 70,* 606–611.

McKnight, C., Des Jarlais, D. C, Perlis, T., Eigo, K., Krim, M., Ruiz, M., et al. (2007). Syringe exchange programs: United States, 2005. *Morbidity and Mortality Weekly Report, 56*(44), 1164–1167.

Open Society Institute (OSI). (2008). *Harm reduction developments 2008: Countries with injection-driven HIV epidemics. Report for OSI Public Health Program, harm reduction and drug use.* New York: Open Society Institute.

Santibanez, S. S., Garfein, R. S., Swartzendruber, A., Purcell, D. W., Paxton, L. A., & Greenberg, A. E. (2005). Update and overview of practical epidemiologic aspects of HIV/AIDS among injection drug users in the United States. *Journal of Urban Health, 83*(1), 86–100.

HARRY W. HAVERKOS
D. PETER DROTMAN
REVISED BY DON DES JARLAIS (2009)

SUBSTANCE-FREE HOUSING. *See* Alcohol- and Drug-Free Housing.

SUICIDE AND SUBSTANCE ABUSE.

Suicide is a major public health problem (Sher, 2004). With more than 30,000 annual victims, suicide is the eleventh leading cause of death in the United States. Nearly a million people around the world commit suicide every year. If every suicide affects at least six family members or friends, then every year in the world there would be about 6 million new survivors. An estimated 8 to 25 attempted suicides occur per every suicide death.

Alcohol and illicit drugs are involved in about 50 percent of all suicide attempts (Hesselbrock et al., 1988; Aharonovich et al., 2002; Conner & Duberstein, 2004; Sher, 2006; Sher et al., 2007). About 25 percent of completed suicides occur among individuals with alcoholism or drug abuse. Substance abuse among young adults is largely responsible for the increased suicide rates under age 30.

The relationship between substance abuse and suicidal behavior has been more extensively studied for alcoholism than for drug abuse. To evaluate this relationship, it is helpful to understand the statistical association between alcohol and drug abuse and suicide, to learn which substance abusers are at particular risk of attempting or committing suicide, and to appreciate how this knowledge may be used to prevent suicide.

SUBSTANCE ABUSE INCREASES SUICIDE RISK

Alcoholism and drug abuse are important risk factors for suicidal behavior (Fowler et al., 1986, Roy & Linnoila, 1986; Murphy & Wetzel, 1990, Murphy, 1992, Cornelius et al., 1996; Sher, 2006; Sher et al., 2007). It was suggested that lifetime mortality due to suicide in alcohol dependence is as high as 18 percent (Roy & Linnoila, 1986). However, Murphy and Wetzel reviewed the epidemiological literature and found that the lifetime risk of suicide among individuals with alcohol dependence treated in outpatient and inpatient settings was 2.2 percent and 3.4 percent, respectively (Murphy & Wetzel, 1990). Nonetheless, individuals with alcoholism have 60 to 120 times the suicide risk of the nonpsychiatrically ill population. Higher rates of suicide attempts among individuals with alcohol use disorders have also been reported. For example, in an urban community in the United States, 24 percent of subjects with alcoholism attempted suicide, as compared to 5 percent with other psychiatric diagnoses (Weissman et al., 1980). Forty percent of a sample of depressed subjects with alcoholism who were hospitalized had attempted suicide in the prior week, and 70 percent had attempted suicide at some point in their lives (Cornelius et al., 1996).

Suicides are not random; each occurs in a particular context. The association between specific psychiatric syndromes—such as depression or abuse of alcohol or drugs—and suicidal behavior has been studied by epidemiologists, clinicians, and neurobiologists. Since interviews with suicide completers are impossible, retrospective reviews of the circumstances predating suicides have been conducted. By using interviews of relatives and others familiar with the suicide victim, together with study of medical records, suicide notes, and coroner reports, a suicide case is subjected to a "psychologic autopsy" (Pouliot & De Leo, 2006). Factors that distinguish successful suicide cases from suicide attempters and substance abusers who have never attempted suicide are identified in the hope that differences in these factors may identify those at particular risk for attempted or completed suicide. A limitation of retrospective studies is termed *recall bias*. Informants may provide information about the suicide victim that is distorted by their attempt to explain the suicide event. Although written records and use of standardized methods to collect diagnostic information can reduce this bias, prospective studies are more reliable. However, prospective studies in the general population are not feasible because suicide is rare, occurring in only about 1 in 10,000 annually (Sher, 2004). Approximately 10 percent of suicide attempters, 15 percent of depressed people, and 3 percent of individuals with alcoholism eventually commit suicide (Murphy & Wetzel, 1990; Murphy, 1992; Sher, 2004; Sher et al., 2007). By prospective study of such high-risk groups, additional risk factors can be identified during a follow-up period.

A prospective study of Swedish military conscripts found that those who drank more than 20 drinks weekly had three times the death rate, prior to age 40, of light drinkers (Andreasson et al., 1988; Allebeck & Allgulander, 1990). Most of these premature deaths were due to suicide or accidents. Those who develop alcohol dependence or abuse are, together with drug abusers, at increased risk of death from accidents, liver disease, pancreatitis, respiratory disease, and other illnesses; however, suicide is among the most significant causes of death in both male and female substance abusers. U.S. and Swedish prospective studies, for example, showed that alcoholism increased the risk of suicide fourfold in men and twentyfold in women.

Next to depression, alcoholism and drug abuse are the psychiatric conditions most strongly associated with suicide attempts. In the U.S. Epidemiologic Catchment Area (ECA) Study, the risk of suicide attempts was increased 41-fold by depression and 18-fold by alcoholism (Moscicki et al., 1992). While cocaine users had increased rates of suicide attempts, users of marijuana, sedative-hypnotics, and amphetamines did not.

Among completed suicides, the proportion of alcoholics or drug abusers is large. Prior to 1980, alcoholism accounted for about 20 to 35 percent, and drug abuse for less than 5 percent, of suicides in a variety of countries (Sher et al., 2007). In the San Diego Suicide Study, conducted in the early 1980s, well over 50 percent of 274 consecutive suicides had alcoholism or drug abuse or dependence (Fowler et al., 1986). Much of the increase in young-adult suicide rates since the 1960s is attributable to alcoholism and drug abuse or dependence.

RISK FACTORS FOR SUICIDE ATTEMPTS

Alcoholics and drug abusers frequently threaten to kill themselves. Many, particularly women and young adults, actually attempt it. Among alcoholics studied in the ECA communities, 32.5 percent had attempted suicide during a period of active alcoholism. In a group of treated opiate addicts, 17 percent had attempted suicide (Moscicki et al., 1992). This represents at least a fivefold increased frequency of suicide attempts compared to those among non-substance abusers.

Although only about 10 percent of substance abusers who attempt suicide die in a subsequent attempt, most substance abusers who commit suicide have attempted suicide at least once before (Rosen, 1976). Thus, a review of the risks of suicide attempts may guide the identification of those substance abusers at risk of suicidal death. The risk of attempting suicide by an individual with alcohol or drug abuse is increased by co-occurring depression, bipolar disorder, antisocial personality disorder (ASP), and a history of parental alcoholism.

Even among people who do not abuse alcohol or drugs, major depression increases the risk of attempting suicide. Major depression is itself 50 percent more common among alcoholics than non-alcoholics: It was found among 5 percent of male and 19 percent of female alcoholics living in the five ECA communities (Weissman et al., 1988). Subsequently, the National Epidemiologic Survey on Alcohol and Related Conditions (NESARC) demonstrated positive and significant associations between most substance use disorders and mood and anxiety disorders (Grant et al., 2004; Compton et al., 2007; Hasin et al., 2007). It was shown that 12-month alcohol dependence was strongly and significantly associated with all 12-month substance use and psychiatric disorders, including depression controlling for sociodemographic characteristics (Hasin et al., 2007). Lifetime alcohol dependence comorbidity followed a similar pattern. Drug dependence was also associated with mood and anxiety disorders in the NESARC (Compton et al., 2007).

Depressive feelings (but not necessarily the syndrome of major depression) often motivate alcoholics and drug addicts to enter a treatment program (Sher et al., 2007). Typically 20 to 40 percent of alcoholics in such programs have had a period of major depression during their lifetime. While many people drink alcohol or use drugs such as cocaine to reduce feelings of depression, experiments show that consumption produces an initial state of euphoria, followed within a few hours by anxiety, depression, and enhanced suicide ideas. In addition to the acute effects of alcohol and drugs, which involve initial euphoria followed by dysphoria, the chronic effects of substance use appear to include a progressive worsening of mood. The latter may be the most relevant to suicide risk among substance abusers, together with the impulsivity associated with intoxication. Retrospective studies have found that depressive symptoms are more common among alcoholics who have made a suicide attempt.

Studies have found that alcoholism in a parent is associated with suicide attempts among alcoholics (Coryell et al., 1992). Depressed patients with a family history of alcoholism are at greater risk for suicidal behavior (Sher et al., 2005). In addition, ASP and drug abuse, which commonly occur in genetically predisposed males who develop alcoholism early in life, are associated with suicide attempts. Many clinicians have noted the repetitive high-risk behaviors of intravenous drug addicts, who often are quite aware that they may acquire infection or die by overdose with each injection. Overdoses occur more commonly among heroin addicts who have attempted suicide than among those who have not. Highly impulsive and aggressive alcoholics or drug abusers with ASP may be a subgroup at elevated risk of attempting suicide. Transient but intense dysphoria (feeling unwell or unhappy), though not of sufficient scope or duration to meet criteria for major depression, may nonetheless increase this group's risk of attempting suicide.

Prospective studies have found that depression, anxiety, and histories of violence and legal problems were predictive of suicide attempts in previously nonsuicidal drug addicts. Retrospective studies of alcoholics and drug addicts have found that poor social supports, occupational losses, personal losses such as divorce, and other family problems increase their risk of making a suicide attempt. Landheim and colleagues (2006) have shown that a substance use disorder with duration of more than 15 years and an early onset (less than 18 years of age) were independently associated with being a suicide attempter after controlling for other psychiatric disorders.

RISK FACTORS FOR COMPLETED SUICIDE

Individuals who attempt and those who complete suicide have somewhat different demographic, clinical, and biological characteristics. For example, women are three times more likely than men to attempt suicide, whereas men are three times more likely to commit suicide. However, there are overlapping problems: Every suicide attempt may result in completed suicide. Clinicians should take very seriously any suicide attempt.

High percentages of suicide completers with alcoholism had major depression at the end of life (Aharonovich et al., 2002; Sher, 2006). Depressed people, particularly men, typically kill themselves in young adulthood. Among alcoholics, over 90 percent of suicides occur among men (Allebeck & Allgulander, 1990; Sher, 2006). In contrast to depressives, alcoholic men typically commit suicide in their fifth and sixth decades, usually following about 20 years of alcoholism. Men with depression, but not those with alcoholism, continue to be at elevated suicide risk beyond age 60. Drug abuse shortens the interval preceding suicide: In the San Diego Suicide Study, drug addicts committed suicide after an average of only nine years of heavy use (Fowler et al., 1986). They typically did so in young adulthood, which suggests that factors other than alcoholism may shorten the suicide risk period in this group. About three of four alcoholic suicides communicate their suicidal intent prior to their deaths. Thus, middle-aged male alcoholics and young polysubstance abusers, especially those who talk of suicide, are at high risk of suicide. Bipolar disorder, schizophrenia, and ASP are also associated with suicide in substance abusers.

Ongoing substance use makes suicide more likely. Nearly all alcoholic suicides occur among active drinkers, and alcohol consumption often immediately precedes the suicide (Murphy, 1992; Sher, 2006). The abstinent alcoholic is only partly protected from suicide, however. It is likely that impulsiveness and depression contribute to suicides among abstinent alcoholics.

What determines the timing of suicide among substance abusers? Substance abusers often accumulate interpersonal problems throughout their drinking or drug-use careers, but one-third of those who commit suicide sustain a major interpersonal disruption (such as separation or divorce) within the six weeks preceding their deaths (Conner & Duberstein, 2004). They often are unemployed, living alone, and unsupported by family and friends at the time of this final and most severe disruption. In contrast, only 3 percent of nonalcoholics with depression suffer such a loss in the period before they commit suicide. Beyond psychiatric diagnoses, the strongest indicator of suicide risk in substance abusers is such an interpersonal loss. Beyond these actual losses, anticipated losses, such as impending legal, financial, or physical demise, may also increase the risk of suicide among substance abusers. Among alcoholics, those who develop serious medical problems, such as liver disease, pancreatitis, or peptic ulcers, are also at higher risk of suicide.

Availability of alcohol and guns at home may contribute to suicide risk, especially in adolescents and young adults. Overall, 28.7 percent of U.S. adolescents reported easy availability of alcohol in the home, 24.3 percent reported availability of a gun in the home, and 10.2 percent reported availability of both alcohol and a gun in the home (Swahn et al., 2002).

CLINICAL FEATURES

Substance abusers who commit suicide often see a physician or are psychiatrically hospitalized in the months prior to their deaths (Murphy, 1992; Conner & Duberstein, 2004; Sher et al., 2007). Those who talk of suicide may be ambivalent about their wish to die. They may thus be amenable to clinical interventions such as detoxification, substance-abuse rehabilitation, or psychiatric hospitalization. Conversely, those who take special precautions against discovery during a prior suicide attempt are much more likely to die in a subsequent suicide attempt.

A model of suicidal behavior among persons with alcoholism has been proposed by Conner and Duberstein (2004). Predisposing factors that are presumed to increase (moderate) risk for suicide among individuals with alcoholism are aggression/impulsivity and alcoholism severity, which represent predominantly externalizing constructs, and negative affect and hopelessness, which represent predominantly internalizing constructs. To *externalize* means to attribute inner conflicts or feelings to external circumstances or causes. To *internalize* means to take in and make an integral part of one's attitudes or beliefs. Major depressive episodes and stressful life events—particularly interpersonal difficulties—are conceptualized as precipitating factors. This model can probably also be applied to individuals with drug abuse.

PREVENTION

Prediction of those who will complete suicide remains poor in individual cases, even among high-risk groups such as substance abusers. Despite their high prevalence, alcoholism and drug abuse often go unrecognized by physicians and other health care professionals. People with psychiatric disorders, suicidal behavior, and/or substance abuse are frequently stigmatized. Even physicians and other health care professionals frequently have negative attitudes. This detrimental approach compromises dual diagnosis patient evaluations, treatment, and prognosis. Clinicians should be educated about a risk of suicidal behavior among individuals with substance abuse. Clinicians' recognition of alcohol and drug use disorders and of risk factors such as major depression that increase the risk of suicide may assist them in making preventive interventions. The substance abuser with active suicide plans or a recent suicide attempt may need hospitalization, detoxification, and/or rehabilitation designed to foster abstinence from alcohol and drugs of abuse. Firearms should be removed from the homes of substance abusers with active suicide ideation, especially adolescents and young

adults. Treatments designed to enhance social supports and foster abstinence from alcohol and drugs, together with those directed at the resolution of major depression, often reduce the risk of suicide. Careful assessment of suicide risk and appropriate treatment of comorbid psychiatric and medical disorders may reduce suicidal behavior in patients with substance abuse.

See also **Accidents and Injuries from Alcohol; Accidents and Injuries from Drugs; Complications: Mental Disorders; Epidemiology of Drug Abuse; Social Costs of Alcohol and Drug Abuse.**

BIBLIOGRAPHY

Aharonovich, E., Liu, X., Nunes, E., & Hasin, D. S. (2002). Suicide attempts in substance abusers: Effects of major depression in relation to substance use disorders. *American Journal of Psychiatry, 159*, 1600–1602.

Allebeck, P., & Allgulander, C. (1990). Suicide among young men: Psychiatric illness, deviant behaviour, and substance abuse. *Acta Psychiatrica Scandinavica, 81*, 565–570.

Andreasson, S., Allebeck, P., & Romelsjö, A. (1988). Alcohol and mortality among young men: Longitudinal study of Swedish conscripts. *British Medical Journal (Clinical Research Ed.), 296*(6628), 1021–1025.

Compton, W. M., Thomas, Y. F., Stinson, F. S., & Grant, B. F. (2007). Prevalence, correlates, disability, and comorbidity of *DSM-IV* drug abuse and dependence in the United States: Results from the national epidemiologic survey on alcohol and related conditions. *Archives of General Psychiatry, 64*(5), 566–576.

Conner, K. R., & Duberstein, P. R. (2004). Predisposing and precipitating factors for suicide among alcoholics: Empirical review and conceptual integration. *Alcoholism: Clinical and Experimental Research, 28*(5 Suppl.), 6S–17S.

Cornelius, J. R., Salloum, I. M., Day, N. L., Thase, M. E., & Mann, J. J. (1996). Patterns of suicidality and alcohol use in alcoholics with major depression. *Alcoholism and Clinical Experimental Research, 20*, 1451–1455.

Coryell, W., Winokur, G., Keller, M., Scheftner, W., & Endicott, J. (1992). Alcoholism and primary major depression: A family study approach to co-existing disorders. *Journal of Affective Disorders, 24*, 93–99.

Fowler, R. C., Rich, C. L., & Young, D. (1986). San Diego suicide study, II: Substance abuse in young cases. *Archives of General Psychiatry, 43*, 962–965.

Grant, B. F., Stinson, F. S., Dawson, D. A., Chou, S. P., Dufour, M. C., Compton, W. et al. (2004). Prevalence and co-occurrence of substance use disorders and independent mood and anxiety disorders: Results from the

National Epidemiologic Survey on Alcohol and Related Conditions. *Archives of General Psychiatry, 61*(8), 807–816.

Hasin, D. S., Stinson, F. S., Ogburn, E., & Grant, B. F. (2007). Prevalence, correlates, disability, and comorbidity of *DSM-IV* alcohol abuse and dependence in the United States: Results from the National Epidemiologic Survey on Alcohol and Related Conditions. *Archives of General Psychiatry, 64*(7), 830–842.

Hesselbrock, M., Hesselbrock, V., Syzmanski, K., & Weidenman, M. (1988). Suicide attempts and alcoholism. *Journal of the Study of Alcohol, 49,* 436–442.

Landheim, A. S., Bakken, K., & Vaglum, P. (2006). What characterizes substance abusers who commit suicide attempts? Factors related to Axis I disorders and patterns of substance use disorders. A study of treatment-seeking substance abusers in Norway. *European Addiction Research, 12,* 102–108.

Moscicki, E. K., O'Carroll, P., Rae, D. S., Locke, B. Z., Roy, A., & Regier, D. A. (1992). Suicide attempts in the epidemiologic catchment area study. *Yale Journal of Biological Medicine, 61,* 259–268.

Murphy, G. E. (1992). *Suicide in alcoholism.* New York: Oxford University Press.

Murphy, G. E., & Wetzel, R. D. (1990). The lifetime risk of suicide in alcoholism. *Archives of General Psychiatry, 47,* 383–392.

Pouliot, L., & De Leo, D. (2006). Critical issues in psychological autopsy studies. *Suicide and Life-Threatening Behavior, 36*(5), 491–510.

Rosen, D. H. (1976). The serious suicide attempt: Five year follow-up study of 886 patients. *Journal of the American Medical Association, 235,* 2105–2109.

Roy, A., & Linnoila, M. (1986). Alcoholism and suicide. *Suicide and Life-Threatening Behavior, 16*(2), 244–273.

Sher, L. (2004). Preventing suicide. *QJM: An International Journal of Medicine, 97,* 677–680.

Sher, L. (2006). Alcoholism and suicidal behavior: A clinical overview. *Acta Psychiatrica Scandinavica, 113,* 13–22.

Sher, L., Kandel, I., & Merrick, J. (Eds.). (2007). *Alcohol and suicide: Research and clinical perspectives.* Victoria, BC: Canada: International Academic Press.

Sher, L., Oquendo, M. A., Conason, A. H., Brent, D. A., Grunebaum, M. F., Zalsman, G. et al. (2005). Clinical features of depressed patients with or without a family history of alcoholism. *Acta Psychiatrica Scandinavica, 112*(4), 266–271.

Swahn, M. H., Hammig, B. J., & Ikeda, R. M. (2002). Prevalence of youth access to alcohol or a gun in the home. *Injury Prevention, 8*(3), 227–230.

Weissman, M. M., Leaf, P. J., Tischler, G. L., Blazer, D. G., Karno, M., Bruce, M. L., et al. (1988). Affective disorders in five United States communities. *Psychology Medicine, 18*(1), 141–153.

Weissman, M. M., Myers, J. K., & Harding, P. S. (1980). Prevalence and psychiatric heterogeneity of alcoholism in a United States urban community. *Journal of Studies on Alcohol, 41,* 672–681.

MICHAEL J. BOHN
REVISED BY LEO SHER (2009)

SWEDEN. *See* **Nordic Countries (Denmark, Finland, Iceland, Norway, and Sweden).**

SYNAPSE, BRAIN. The term synapse is from the Greek word *synaptein,* for "juncture" or "fasten together," by way of the Latin *synapsis.* It refers to the specialized junction found between nerve cells. It was conceived by the British pioneer neurophysiologist Sir Charles Sherrington (1857–1952) to describe the then-novel microscopic observations that the "end-feet" of one neuron physically contacted, in an intimate manner, other neurons to which it was structurally connected. A similar point of connection between peripheral nerves and their targets is usually referred to as a *junction.*

Synapses in the brain (see Figures 1 and 2) are morphologically typed by several features (1) a dilation of the presynaptic terminal (nerve ending) that contains accumulations of synaptic vesicles in various sizes, shapes, and chemical reactivities; (2) mitochondria; (3) a specialized zone of modified thickness and electron opacity in the presynaptic membrane, in which a presynaptic grid is perforated to provide maximum access of transmitter-containing vesicles to the presumptive sites of transmitter release; and (4) a specialized zone of altered thickness and opacity in the postsynaptic membrane termed the *active zone* and believed to be the site of initial response.

The synaptic vesicles have been shown to contain the neurotransmitters by a series of extensive analyses of meticuously purified vesicles. The vesicles differ in their protein content and may include the transmitter's synthetic enzymes, as well

Figure 1. Synapse. The nerve ending from one neuron forms a junction, the synapse, with another neuron (the postsynaptic neuron). The synaptic junction is actually a small space, sometimes called the synaptic cleft. Neurotransmitter molecules are synthesized by enzymes in the nerve terminal, stored in vesicles, and released into the synaptic cleft when an electrical impulse invades the nerve terminal. The electrical impulse originates in the neuronal cell body and travels down the axon. The released neurotransmitter combines with receptors on postsynaptic neurons, which are then activated. To terminate neurotransmission, transporters remove the neurotransmitter from the synaptic cleft by pumping it back into the nerve terminal that released it. (Modified from Figure 1, in M.J. Kuhar's Introduction to Neurotransmitters and Neuroreceptors in *Quantitative Imaging*, edited by J.J. Frost and H.N. Wagner. Raven Press, New York, 1990.) ILLUSTRATION BY GGS INFORMATION SERVICES. GALE, CENGAGE LEARNING

as the transporters that can concentrate the transmitter within the vesicles. For monoamine neurons, the vesicles also contain specific proteins (named for their sites of discovery in the adrenal medulla as *chromogranins* but now termed more generally *secretogranins*. These are assumed to facilitate storage and release. Superficially, synapses with a thinner postsynaptic specialization, of about the same thickness as that at the presynaptic membrane (hence termed *symmetrical*), are often inhibitory; those with a thickened postsynaptic membrane (*asymmetrical*) are often excitatory.

Monoaminergic synapses, however, are often asymmetrical, as are those for peptide-containing neurons that do not obey these simple physiological categorizations. Synapses can also be discriminated on the basis of the pairs of neuronal structures that come together at this site of functional transmission. Most typical is the *axo-dendritic* synapse in which the axon of the presynaptic neuron contacts either the smooth or spiny surface of the dendrite of the post-synaptic neuron. A second common form is the *axo-somatic* synapse in which the presynaptic axon contacts the surface of the post-synaptic neuron's cell body (or somata). Less frequently observed are axo-axonic relationships in which one axon contacts a second axon-terminal that is in its own axo-dendritic relationship; such triads of axo-axo-dendritic synapses are found most frequently in spinal cord and certain midbrain structures, in which channels of information flow are necessarily highly constrained. Most rarely, junctions between cell bodies (somato-somatic) and dendrites (dendro-dendritic) have also been described.

The nature of the proteins that provide for the thickened appearances of the active zones by electron microscopy are not completely known, but

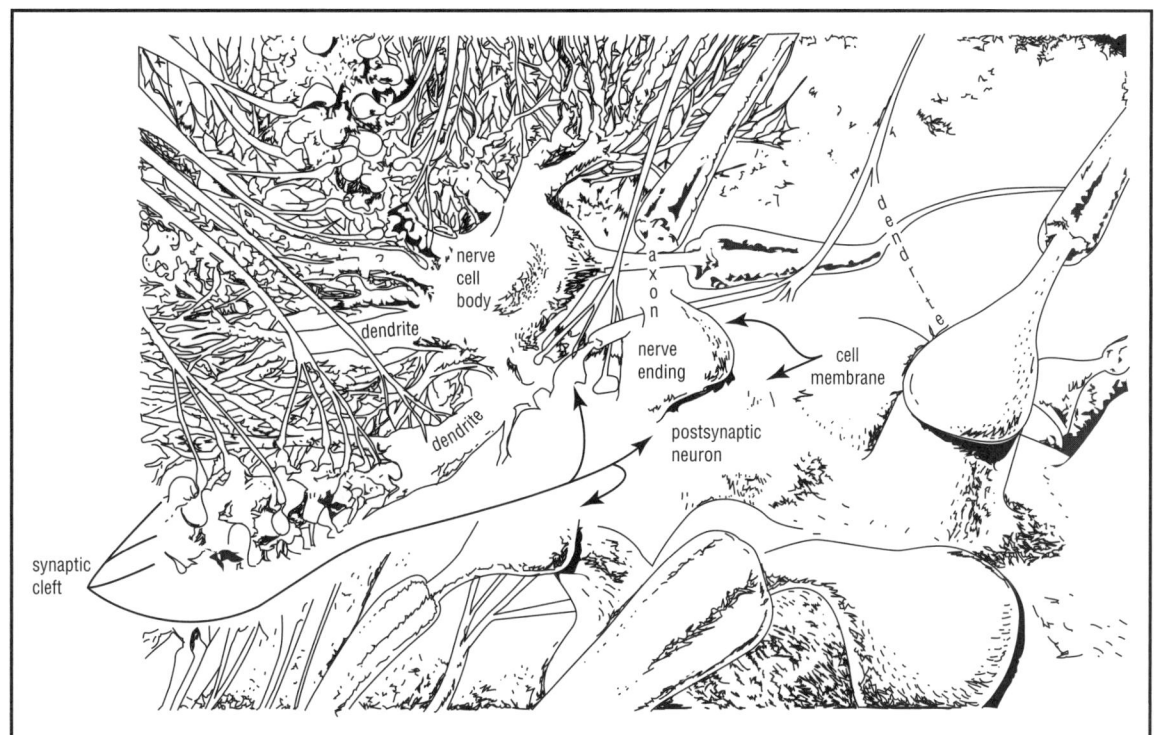

Figure 2. Neuronal complexity. The complexity of the neuronal network in the brain is demonstrated by this bundle of neurons, which form a vast and ramified structure with their cell bodies, outgrowths, and intercellular contact points. (Modified from Figure 1, in M.J. Kuhar's Introduction to Neurotransmitters and Neuroreceptors in *Quantitative Imaging*, edited by J.J. Frost and H.N. Wagner. Raven Press, New York, 1990.) ILLUSTRATION BY GGS INFORMATION SERVICES. GALE, CENGAGE LEARNING

they include the postsynaptic receptors and associated molecules that can transduce the signals from the activate receptors, as well as those molecules that serve to concentrate the receptors in such locations.

See also **Brain Structures and Drugs; Neurotransmission; Reward Pathways and Drugs.**

BIBLIOGRAPHY

Bloom, F. E. (1990). Neurohumoral transmission in the central nervous system. In A. G. Gilman et al. (Eds.), *Goodman and Gilman's the pharmacological basis of therapeutics*, 8th ed. New York: Pergamon. (2005, 11th ed. New York: McGraw-Hill Medical.)

Cooper, J. C., Bloom, F. E., & Roth, R. H. (1991). *The biochemical basis of neuropharmacology*, 6th ed. New York: Oxford University Press. (2002, 8th ed.)

Cowan, M. W. Südhof, T. C., & Stevens, C. F., Eds. (2003). *Synapses.* Baltimore, MD: The Johns Hopkins University Press.

FLOYD BLOOM

T-ACE. T-ACE is a screening test for risky drinking by pregnant women. Heavy maternal drinking is a major pregnancy risk and a significant public health problem. Fetal alcohol syndrome (FAS) was first reported as a recognizable clinical syndrome nearly thirty years ago. It is characterized by:

1. prenatal and/or postnatal growth restriction

2. central nervous system (brain) abnormalities and

3. facial dysmorphology, i.e., an abnormal appearing face characterized by underdevelopment of the midface with small eyes, a short nose and a long simple (flat) philtrum, the area below the nose and above the upper lip.

As these children grow up, they are often mildly mentally retarded, with average IQs of about 70 and disabling behavioral abnormalities. In addition, there is a continuum of abnormalities among offspring exposed before birth to alcohol, but without the full syndrome abnormalities that are much more common than full FAS. There are anatomic anomalies, called alcohol-related birth defects (ARBD) and alcohol-related neurobehavioral disorder (ARND), a set of behavioral abnormalities in offspring prenatally exposed to substantial levels of alcohol. Other adverse pregnancy outcomes related to maternal drinking during pregnancy include miscarriage and stillbirth.

A national goal to reduce the prevalence of FAS by one half by decreasing maternal drinking was set in Healthy People 2000. Unfortunately, the reported prevalence did not decrease through the 1990s but in fact increased, possibly because of improved case finding. Regardless, it is likely that heavy drinking in pregnancy did not decrease, despite warning labels required on all alcoholic beverages since 1989.

There is evidence that pregnant women are receptive to advice from their health care providers, particularly their physicians, to quit or at least cut down on both drinking alcohol and smoking cigarettes. Given that such generalized warnings as the warning label have not proven effective, a more focused approach would seem reasonable—this would focus prevention efforts on women who drink or are likely to drink enough during pregnancy to damage their offspring. Such drinking has been labeled *risk drinking*.

The precise level of drinking that might damage the embryo/fetus is unknown, but is probably variable because of differing susceptibility and differing exposures depending on exactly which adverse effect is considered and when during pregnancy the exposure occurs (critical period). Solid estimates of risk drinking have decreased over the years, as better interviewing and statistical techniques have become available. It is now reasonable to use a figure of about seven drinks per week, typically massed on one or two days, but averaging about one drink per day or 0.5 ounces of absolute alcohol per day. This is the amount of absolute alcohol in one can of beer, one glass of wine or one mixed drink of standard size. This amount of alcohol intake, while unlikely to pose any health risk to the mother, is enough to adversely affect

Question	+ Answer	Score
T	How many drinks can you hold (TOLERANCE)?	> = 6	2
A	Have people ANNOYED you by criticizing your drinking?	Yes	1
C	Have you felt you ought to CUT DOWN on your drinking?	Yes	1
E	Have you ever had a drink first thing in the morning to steady your nerves or get rid of a hangover (EYE-OPENER)?	Yes	1

The Tolerance Question is positive if the patient admits that she can hold, i.e., not get sick or lose consciousness, at least a sixpack of beer, a bottle of wine, or six standard drinks. As in the old song, (T) for two and two for (T) and, as in blackjack, each ACE is worth one. A total score of two or more is positive.

Table 1. The T-ACE Questionnaire. ILLUSTRATION BY GGS INFORMATION SERVICES. GALE, CENGAGE LEARNING

the embryo/fetus. There is not convincing evidence of clinically important effects on the offspring from an occasional drink during pregnancy.

There are, as of yet, no laboratory tests, i.e., biological markers, which will reliably identify at risk women. The only way to identify them is to obtain an appropriate history of drinking, but this is complicated by denial—the woman doesn't want to admit drinking to herself or to her doctor. Further, time is distinctly limited during prenatal visits and there are many problems to identify and address. Thus, a brief, simple questionnaire was needed. Most brief questionnaires, such as the CAGE, were developed and tested almost entirely in male populations, and do not function well for reproductive-age women.

The T-ACE questions were developed specifically as a screening test for risky drinking. They have been tested and validated over the last decade in women of multiple ethnicities, including white, African American and Native American, and across a range of socioeconomic statuses and geographic locations. The original questionnaire included the question, "How many drinks does it take to make you feel *high*?" as the (T)olerance question. An answer of greater than two standard drinks was considered positive. Several studies have now shown that substituting the *hold* question, included in Table 1, instead of the *high* question, gives better results, improving the sensitivity of the T-ACE questions.

T-ACE is a screening test, so it was designed to pick up as high a proportion of risky drinkers as possible. This version picks up about nine in ten women who drink enough in pregnancy potentially to damage their baby. If the score is less than two, i.e., the T-ACE is negative, it will correctly identify about seven in ten women who are not risky drinkers. It has a substantial false positive rate,

i.e., warning the clinician, though the patient is not, in fact, a risk drinker. It has been speculated, though, that any woman who scores positive might, in fact, be at risk to drink too much during pregnancy and should be counseled.

Screening for risky drinking is not enough. At the minimum a brief intervention to support the patient in becoming abstinent during pregnancy or at the minimum cutting way down is warranted, as is close follow-up. If alcohol abuse or dependence is present, consultation or referral may be warranted.

See also **Fetal Alcohol Syndrome; Pregnancy and Drug Dependence.**

BIBLIOGRAPHY

Chang, G. (2004). Screening and brief intervention in prenatal care settings. *Alcohol Research and Health, 28*, 2, 80–84.

Chang, G., et al. (1998). Alcohol use and pregnancy: Improving identification. *Obstetrics and Gynecology, 91*, 892–898.

National Institute on Alcohol Abuse and Alcoholism (2003). *Assessing alcohol problems: A guide for clinicians and researchers*, 2nd ed, NIH Pub. No. 03-3745. Washington, D.C.: United States Department of Health and Human Services, Public Health Service.

Russell, M., et al. (1996). Detecting risk drinking during pregnancy: A comparison of four screening questionnaires. *American Journal of Public Health, 86*, 1435–1439.

Russell, M., et al. (1994). Screening for pregnancy risk-drinking. *Alcoholism: Clinical and Experimental Research, 18*, 1156–1166.

Sokol, R. J., et al. (1989). The T-ACE questions: Practical prenatal detection of risk drinking. *American Journal of Obstetrics and Gynecology, 160*, 863–870.

ROBERT J. SOKOL

TAX LAWS AND ALCOHOL.

The first internal revenue measure adopted by the U.S. Congress, in 1790, was an excise tax on domestic whiskey; a subsequent increase in that tax from 9 to 25 cents per gallon led to an armed insurrection by the farmers of western Pennsylvania during the summer of 1794, the so-called Whiskey Rebellion.

This matter of the appropriate level for alcoholic beverage taxes has remained contentious into the early 2000s; although there is consensus that alcoholic beverages should be subject to higher taxes than other commodities, substantial disagreement remains concerning the appropriate level for such taxes. The principal impetus for raising tax rates has always been the quest for increased government revenue. Since the 1970s, however, increasing attention has been paid to the public health benefits and societal costs savings of alcohol taxes, as research has demonstrated that raising the excise tax rates, and hence the prices of alcoholic beverages, reduces traffic fatalities and other costly consequences of alcohol abuse.

HISTORY

Alcoholic beverage taxes were a major source of revenues for the federal government throughout much of U.S. history. In 1907, this source accounted for 80 percent of federal internal tax collections and was still as high as 10 percent on the eve of U.S. entry into World War II. As of 2008, the federal excise taxes and import duties continued to have a considerable effect on the prices of alcoholic beverages, but figured very lightly (less than 1%) in overall federal tax collections.

Because federal excise taxes are set in dollar terms per unit of liquid, rather than as a percentage of the price, inflation gradually erodes the real value of these taxes. For example, while Congress increased the tax per fifth of 80-proof spirits by 29 percent (to $2.16) between 1951 and 2007, the overall level of consumer prices increased by over 550 percent during this same period. The result is that the real value of the federal liquor tax has declined substantially over time. By 2006 tax revenues that accounted for 12 percent of the sales in alcohol in 1980 amounted to just 7 percent of total sales. A considerable reduction in the average price of whiskey and other spirits relative to the prices of other commodities has been the inevitable result.

Had the tax kept pace with inflation since 1965, the current $18 per-barrel tax on beer would total approximately $61.60, or $1.05 per six-pack, more than two-and-one-half times the current rate.

The states also impose special excise taxes on alcoholic beverages, as do some local governments. In addition, alcoholic beverages are generally subject to state and local sales taxes. The relative importance of these tax collections in state budgets differs widely, but as of 2006 it was less than 10 percent of government revenues everywhere. Between 2000 and 2008, however, 10 states raised excise taxes on alcohol.

TAX EFFECTS

When a legislature raises the excise tax rates on alcoholic beverages, the resulting cost to distributors is passed along to consumers in the form of higher prices. As is true for other commodities, the sales of alcoholic beverages tend to fall when prices increase. This is not to say that price is all that matters. For example, the steady decline in sales and consumption of alcohol during the 1980s cannot be explained by increased prices, since the prices of alcoholic beverages remained more or less constant (in real terms) during this period. The downward trend in consumption presumably resulted from the aging of the population and increasing public concern with healthy lifestyles, among other factors. Per capita sales and consumption of alcohol are nevertheless negatively affected by alcohol beverage prices, and if Congress had increased federal excise taxes substantially during the 1980s, sales would have declined still more rapidly than they did.

Although they differ somewhat, a number of published estimates of the price elasticity of demand for beer, wine, and liquor tend to confirm that price is one of the important variables influencing sales. One review of these estimates concluded that the price elasticity for liquor is approximately −1.0; this implies that, other things being equal, a percentage increase in the average price of liquor will result in an equal percentage reduction in the quantity of liquor sold. Beer and wine sales tend to be somewhat less responsive to price, with estimated price elasticities in the neighborhood of −0.5 (Leung & Phelps, 1993). Estimates for other developed countries are quite consistent with these conclusions (Edwards et al., 1994; Cook & Moore, 2000).

These results do not in themselves imply that a general price increase for alcoholic beverages will reduce consumption of ethyl alcohol (ethanol), the intoxicating substance in all these beverages. In the face of higher prices, consumers can switch to higher-proof brands, reduce wastage, and attempt home production of beer or wine. But in practice, research suggests that these substitutions are not large enough to negate the price effect. Ethanol consumption does tend to fall in response to a general increase in the price of alcoholic beverages.

Given the fact that higher alcohol excise taxes increase prices and reduce ethanol consumption, there remains the vital question of whether alcohol taxes are effective instruments in preventing alcohol-related harms. Of public concern are both the harms associated with the acute effects of inebriation—injuries stemming from accidents and violent crime—and the harms resulting from chronic heavy drinking, most notably the long-term deterioration in health and productivity.

There is considerable evidence that the incidence of both inebriation and chronic heavy drinking, and the associated harms, are sensitive to the prices of alcoholic beverages. For the acute effects, Cook (1981) studied 39 instances in which states increased their liquor tax between 1960 and 1975, finding strong evidence that traffic fatalities in those states fell as a result. This result was confirmed for the beer excise tax by Ruhm (1996) and Saffer and Grossman (1987), both using panel data on state traffic fatality rates. Cook and Moore (1993), also using panel data on states, found a close link between per capita ethanol consumption and violent crime rates, and direct evidence that an increase in the beer tax helped suppress rape and robbery. And Chesson and colleagues (2000) used a similar method to demonstrate that the incidence of sexually transmitted disease is inversely related to the beer tax. This literature is not without dissenters (see Dee, 1999), but the bulk of the published research results provides support for the conclusion that alcohol excises influence the incidence of inebriation and the costly consequences thereof.

There is also evidence of a link between alcohol prices and the prevalence of chronic heavy drinking. Cook and Tauchen (1982) demonstrated that changes in state liquor taxes had a statistically discernible effect on the mortality rate from cirrhosis of the liver. Since a large percentage of liver cirrhosis deaths result from many years of heavy drinking, it appears that chronic heavy drinkers are quite responsive to the price of alcohol. This conclusion is supported by evidence from clinical experiments and other sources (Vuchinich & Tucker, 1988).

Thus, there is indeed evidence that alcohol taxes are an effective instrument for preventing alcohol-related harms. The claim that alcohol taxes promote the public health is increasingly important in the public debate over raising federal and state alcohol taxes.

FAIRNESS

Although alcohol taxes reduce consumption and save some lives that would otherwise be lost to alcohol-related accidents, there remains the question of whether they are fair. Fairness is largely in the eye of the beholder (or taxpayer); nevertheless, several standards are commonly used as bases for judging the fairness of a tax. Two of the most notable standards are that a tax should fall equally on households which are in some sense equally situated and that it should not be regressive.

If equals are to be treated equally, is it fair that alcohol taxes force drinkers to pay more taxes than nondrinkers of similar incomes? Indeed, the bulk of all alcohol taxes are paid by the small minority who drink heavily: Half of all alcohol consumption is accounted for by just 6 or 7 percent of the adult population and 20 percent of drinkers consume 85 percent of all alcoholic beverages. One response is that it is fair for drinkers to pay more because drinking imposes costs on others. One estimate suggests that drinkers impose an average cost on others amounting to about 25 cents per drink (Manning et al., 1991); Miller and colleagues (1998) provide a much higher estimate. Thus, if the alcohol tax is considered a sort of *user fee*, whereby the drinker pays in proportion to the amount of alcohol consumed, then it may seem fair.

Another concern is that alcohol taxes may be regressive, meaning that on the average, wealthier households spend a smaller fraction of their income on alcohol taxes than poorer households. Although it is often taken as self-evident in political debates over raising beer taxes, the evidence on this matter is not clear (Sammartino, 1990; Cook & Moore, 1993).

Another debated issue is that of uniform taxation. A can of beer, a glass of wine, and a shot of spirits all contain approximately the same amount of ethanol, but are taxed quite differently; the federal excise tax on a shot of spirits exceeds the tax on a can of beer by a factor of 2, and on a glass of wine by a factor of 3. If special taxes on alcoholic beverages are ultimately justified by the fact that such beverages are intoxicating, then these disparities are difficult to explain. Part of the explanation may be the widespread belief that spirits are in some sense more intoxicating than beer or wine, and hence more subject to abuse, whereas beer is the *drink of moderation* and wine the *drink of connoisseurs*. But much of the evidence works against this view. Indeed, beer consumption may be more costly to society (per drink) than spirits because of the demographics of beverage choice: Young men—a group that consumes most of their ethanol in the form of beer—have by far the highest incidence of alcohol-related traffic accidents and violent crimes.

BIBLIOGRAPHY

Chaloupka, F. J., Grossman, M., & Saffer, H. (2002). The effects of price on alcohol consumption and alcohol-related problems. *Alcohol Research & Health, 26,* 22–34.

Chesson, H., Harrison, P., & Kassler, W. J. (2000). Alcohol, youth, and risky sex: The effect of beer taxes and the drinking age on gonorrhea rates in teenagers and young adults. *Journal of Law & Economics, 43,* 215–238.

Cook, P. J. (1981). The effect of liquor taxes on drinking, cirrhosis, and auto fatalities. In M. H. Moore and D. R. Gerstein (Eds.), *Alcohol and public policy: Beyond the shadow of prohibition* (pp. 255–285). Washington, DC: National Academy Press.

Cook, P. J., & Moore, M. J. (1993). Economic perspectives on alcohol-related violence. In S. E. Martin (Ed.), *Alcohol-related violence: Interdisciplinary perspectives and research directions* (NIH Publication No. 93–3496, pp. 193–212). Rockville, MD: National Institute on Alcoholism and Alcohol Abuse.

Cook, P. J., & Moore, M. J. (1993). Taxation of alcoholic beverages. In M. Hilton & G. Bloss (Eds.), *Economic research on the prevention of alcohol-related problems* (NIH Publication No. 93-3513, pp. 33–58). Rockville, MD: National Institute on Alcoholism and Alcohol Abuse.

Cook, P. J., & Moore, M. J. (2000). Alcohol. In A. J. Culyer and J. P. Newhouse (Eds.), *Handbook of health economics* (Vol. I, pp. 1–41). New York: Elsevier Science B.V.

Cook, P. J., & Tauchen, G. (1982). The effect of liquor taxes on heavy drinking. *Bell Journal of Economics, 13,* 379–390.

Dee, T. S. (1999). State alcohol policies, teen drinking and traffic fatalities. *Journal of Public Economics, 72,* 289–315.

Edwards, G., Anderson, P., Babor, T., Caswell, S., Ferrence, R., Gesibrecht, N., et al. (1994). *Alcohol policy and the public good.* New York: Oxford University Press.

Grossman, M. (1989). Health benefits of increases in alcohol and cigarette taxes. *British Journal of Addiction, 84,* 1193–1204.

Hu, T. Y. (1950). *The liquor tax in the United States 1791–1947.* New York: Columbia University Press.

Leung, S. F., & Phelps, C. (1993). The demand for alcoholic beverages. In M. Hilton and G. Bloss (Eds.), *Economic research on the prevention of alcohol-related problems* (NIH Publication No. 93–3513, pp. 1–31). Rockville, MD: National Institute on Alcoholism and Alcohol Abuse.

Manning, W. G., Keeler, E., Newhouse, J., & Sloss, E. (1991). *The costs of poor health habits.* Cambridge, MA: Harvard University Press.

Miller, T. R., Lestina, D. C., & Spicer, R. S. (1998). Highway crash costs in the United States by driver age, blood alcohol level, victim age, and restraint use. *Accident Analysis and Prevention, 30*(2), 137–150.

Pogue, T. F., & Sgontz, L. G. (1989). Taxing to control social costs: The case of alcohol. *American Economic Review, 79,* 235–243.

Rogers, J. D., & Greenfield, T. K. (1999). Who drinks most of the alcohol in the U.S.? The policy implications. *Journal of Studies on Alcohol, 60,* 78–89.

Ruhm, C. J. (1996). Alcohol policies and highway vehicle fatalities. *Journal of Health Economics, 15,* 435–454.

Saffer, H., & Grossman, M. (1987). Beer taxes, the legal drinking age, and youth motor vehicle fatalities. *Journal of Legal Studies, 16,* 51–374.

Sammartino, F. (1990). *Federal taxation of tobacco, alcoholic beverages and motor fuels.* (Congressional Budget Office Report.) Washington, DC: U.S. Government Printing Office.

Vuchinich, R. E., & Tucker, J. A. (1988). Contributions from behavioral theories of choice to an analysis of alcohol abuse. *Journal of Abnormal Psychology, 97*(2), 181–195.

PHILIP J. COOK
REVISED BY FREDERICK K. GRITTNER (2009)

TEA. Tea is the most widely consumed beverage in the world except for water, and provides over 40 percent of the world's dietary caffeine. In the United States, caffeine from tea accounts for about

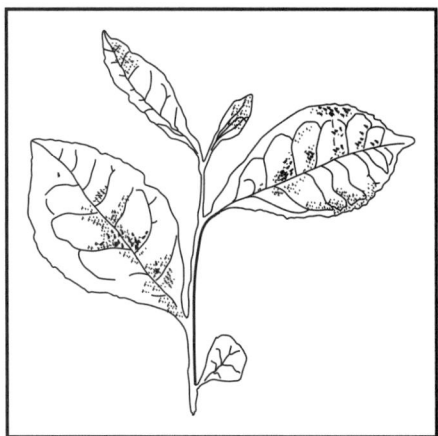

Figure 1. Tea leaf. ILLUSTRATION BY GGS INFORMATION SERVICES. GALE, CENGAGE LEARNING

17 percent of caffeine consumed; per capita caffeine consumption from tea is about 35 milligrams per day, which is a little over one-third of the daily caffeine provided by coffee beverages. Tea consumption in the United Kingdom is substantially higher, averaging 320 milligrams per capita per day and accounting for 72 percent of the United Kingdom's caffeine consumption.

Although tea contains a large number of chemical compounds, the relatively high content of polyphenols and caffeine is responsible for tea's pharmacological effects. The primary psychoactive component of tea is caffeine. Tea also contains two compounds that are structurally related to caffeine, theophylline and theobromine, however, these compounds are found in relatively insignificant amounts. On average, a 6-ounce (177-milliliter) cup of leaf or bag tea contains about 48 milligrams of caffeine, a little less than half the caffeine in the same amount of ground roasted coffee, and only slightly more than the amount found in 12 ounces of a typical cola soft drink. Six ounces of instant tea contain 36 milligrams of caffeine, on average. Individual servings of tea contain amounts of caffeine that can affect the mood and performance of adult humans.

Although the term *tea* has been used to refer to extracts from a large number of plants, only teas derived from leaves of *Camellia sinensis* plants are of special interest here, because they contain caffeine. The term *tea* has come to be used especially for extracts of *Camellia sinensis* and that restricted usage is maintained in this entry.

Consumption of *Camellia sinensis* was first documented in China (where tea is called *cha* or *chai*) in 350 CE, although there is some suggestion that the Chinese consumed tea as early as 2700 BCE. Tea was introduced to Japan around 600 CE but did not become widely used there until the 1400s. Through the China trade, tea became available in England in the 1600s, where it became the national drink. Tea was introduced into the American colonies around 1650 but in 1773 became a symbol of British rule. Americans protested the British tax on tea by raiding ships anchored in Boston harbor and dumping boxes of tea into the water. This event, referred to as the Boston Tea Party, along with other similar protests that followed, became important in shifting the predominant caffeinated beverage in North America from tea to coffee.

India, China, and Sri Lanka are the major producers and exporters tea—producing about 60 percent of the world's tea and providing about 55 percent of world tea exports. The United Kingdom, the United States, and Pakistan are the leading importers of tea.

Two types of tea, black and green tea, account for almost all the tea consumed in the world. Black tea makes up over 75 percent of the world's tea; green tea accounts for about 22 percent. The method by which tea is manufactured determines whether black or green tea is produced. Black tea is dark brown in color and is produced by promoting oxidation of a key tea constituent. Green tea is yellow-green in color and is produced by preventing such oxidation; it is therefore a less processed tea. Oolong tea, a less common type, is partially oxidized and is intermediate in appearance to that of black and green tea. Flavored teas were originally prepared by adding a range of fruits, flowers, and other plant substances to the tea prior to final packaging, although artificial flavors are often added today.

See also **Chocolate; Plants, Drugs From.**

BIBLIOGRAPHY

Barone, J. J., & Roberts, H. (1984). Human consumption of caffeine. In P. B. Dews (Ed.), *Caffeine.* New York: Springer-Verlag.

Hohenegger, B. (2007). *Liquid jade: The story of tea from east to west.* New York: St. Martin's Press.

Smith, B. D., Gupta, U., & Gupta, B. S., Eds. (2006). *Caffeine and activation theory: Effects on health and behavior.* Boca Raton, FL: CRC Press.

Spiller, G. A. (Ed.). (1984). *The methylxanthine beverages and foods: Chemistry, consumption, and health effects.* New York: Alan R. Liss.

KENNETH SILVERMAN
ROLAND R. GRIFFITHS

TEENS AND DRUG USE. *See* Adolescents and Drug Use.

TEMPERANCE MOVEMENT.

Many temperance movements and societies emerged in the United States during the nineteenth century. These movements began in the early 1800s and gained ascendancy during the mid-to-late 1800s, culminating in the prohibition movement, the prohibition-banning Eighteenth Amendment (Article 18) to the U.S. Constitution in 1919, and the start of prohibition in 1920. Joseph Gusfield, an eminent scholar of the temperance movement, has argued that the term *temperance* is not appropriate because the broad reformist ideology of the movement focused mainly on abstinence—not moderation—in the intake of alcoholic beverages (1986). Jack S. Blocker observed that the many temperance movements that emerged in the United States represented men and women from varying ethnic, religious, social, economic, and political groups who selected temperance as the solution to what they perceived as problems in their own lives and in those of others (1989). By the end of the nineteenth century, the temperance movement had evolved through several phases, characterized by differences in goals and memberships (Murdock, 1998). Proponents changed their strategies from persuasive efforts to moderate the intake of alcoholic beverages to more coercive strategies, even legislation, to bring about the control of all drinking.

EARLY PHASE: 1800–1840

In colonial America and during the early 1800s, alcoholic beverages (brewed, fermented, and distilled) were a staple of the American diet, were often homemade, and were viewed as "the good creature of God" (Gusfield, 1986). Among the colonists, the drinking of alcoholic beverages was integrated with social norms; all social groups and ages drank alcoholic beverages, and the consumption rate was very high (Gusfield, 1986). Alcohol was also traded, sold, and given to Native Americans, who had no long history of daily drinking, with almost immediate negative consequences for these peoples.

By 1840, a revolution in U.S. social attitudes had occurred, in which alcohol came to be seen as "the root of all evil" and the cause of the major problems of the early republic, such as the crime, poverty, immorality, and insanity of the Jacksonian era (Tyrrell, 1979). Temperance was advocated as the ideal solution for these problems by such people as Anthony Benezet, a popular Quaker reformer; Thomas Jefferson; and Benjamin Rush, the surgeon general of the Continental Army and a signer of the Declaration of Independence. Temperance-reform organizations, such as the American Temperance Society, emerged, committed to the eradication of these social problems.

The American Temperance Society (ATS), founded in Boston in 1826 as the American Society for the Promotion of Temperance, was the first national (as opposed to local) temperance organization. It had its roots in the processes of industrialization and the commercialization of agriculture. The people who developed the movement were committed to hastening the processes of economic and social change. These processes involved the educating of Americans to value sobriety and industry in order to create the conditions for the development of an industrial-commercial society. The movement was supported by entrepreneurs who needed a disciplined and sober workforce to help create the economic change necessary for the material improvement of the young republic.

During the Second Great Awakening, from the early 1800s until late 1830s—a period of revivalism and evangelical fervor—the evangelical clergy, as well as that of other U.S. Protestant groups, supported temperance as a means of promoting the morality needed for building a "Christian nation," through social and economic progress. According to Gusfield, these groups helped to place the issue of drinking on the public and political agenda,

Woodcut of a political cartoon showing the evils of drink, c. 1820. © BETTMANN/CORBIS.

providing their personnel as authorities on the cognitive aspects of drinking and becoming the legitimate source of public policies on drinking (1986). Also, in the early 1820s and 1830s, small-scale farmers and rural groups were active in promoting the temperance movement. They saw temperance as a way to promote social progress in a time of transition from a rural to an urban-industrial order, from small-scale farming to entrepreneurial forms of agriculture.

By 1836, more than 200,000 people belonged to the American Temperance Society (ATS), which had become an abstinence society, and ideas about problems associated with alcohol had begun to change: Inebriety or habitual drunkenness was being called a disease. The ideology of the movement placed the source of alcohol addiction in the substance itself: Alcohol was inherently addicting, a finding supported by research conducted by the medical doctor, Benjamin Rush, who in 1785 wrote *Inquiry into the Effects of Ardent Spirits upon the Human Body and Mind* (Rose, 1996). Blocker observed that the general focus of ATS was on persuading the already temperate to become abstinent rather than persuading drunkards to reform their drinking behavior (1989). According to Gusfield, abstinence became a symbol that enabled society to distinguish the industrious, steady American worker from other people, which resulted in the movement becoming democratized instead of associated only with the New England upper classes (1986). Attempts to reform and save drunkards was the focus of another temperance movement, the Washingtonians (Blumberg with Pittman, 1991).

MIDDLE PHASE: 1840–1860
Whereas well-to-do groups and Protestant evangelical clergy dominated the early phase of temperance

reform, the middle phase included the efforts of artisans and women of the lower and lower-middle classes, who promoted self-help groups among largely working-class drunkards trying to give up drinking (Tyrrell, 1979). These artisans organized into the Washingtonian societies (named for George Washington), dedicated to helping working-class drunkards who were trying to reform.

In 1840, the first Washingtonian Temperance Society was established in Baltimore, Maryland. Members took a pledge against the use of all alcoholic beverages and attempted to convert drunkards to the pledge of *teetotalism* (c. 1834, derived from total + total = abstinence). By the end of 1841, Washingtonian societies were active in Baltimore, Boston, New York, and other areas throughout the North. These groups were not socially homogeneous. Tyrrell reported that the relationships between the old organizations and the new societies culminated in various struggles for control over the Washingtonian societies, with fragmentation of these groups occurring (1979).

Washingtonian members who wanted respect from the middle-class temperance reformers, including the evangelical reformers, elected to remain with the mainstream temperance movement. The wage earners and reformed drunkards remained in their own societies, and they opposed early efforts at legal coercion; for example, the passage of the Maine Law of 1851. Gusfield interpreted support for this law as a reaction against the drinking practices of the Irish and German immigrants to the United States between 1845 and 1855 (1986). He argued that temperance reform in this period represented a "symbolic crusade" to impose existing cultural values on immigrant groups. Tyrell (1979) interpreted the Maine Law as a way for middle-class reformers to control and reform the laboring poor. From 1851 on, many local laws were passed that attempted to limit the consumption of alcohol; however, throughout the remainder of the century, these statutes were repealed, liberalized, or not enforced.

LATE PHASE: 1860–1920

The Civil War, World War I, and the rapid demographic changes that accompanied immigration during this period contributed to the support of abstinence during the last phase of the temperance movements. Urban areas were expanding, factory towns were a reality, and there was an increase in the socializing at the end of the workday as well as at the end of the workweek; consequently there was an increase in the production and consumption of alcoholic beverages. Several temperance societies that emerged during this period included the active participation of women and children, as wives and children were often neglected or abused by drunken husbands and fathers. Irish-American Catholics formed the Catholic Total Abstention Union in 1872; the Women's Christian Temperance Union (WCTU) was formed in 1874; and the Anti-Saloon League of America (ASLA) emerged in 1896. These societies were able to mobilize tremendous support for abstinence rather than mere moderation in the intake of alcoholic beverages. During these years, the ideology of the temperance movements centered upon the evil effects of all alcohol, espousing the view that alcohol had become the central problem in American life and that abstinence was the only solution for this problem (Drowne, 2005).

The WCTU was the largest women's movement of the nineteenth century and the first mainstream temperance organization to involve women and children (Blocker et al., 2003). Its creative and dynamic leaders were Annie Wittenmeyer, Frances Willard, and Carrie Nation, who also supported the feminist movement, a radical movement at the time. The WCTU began a crusade to shut down saloons and promote morality. By the late 1870s the major theme of the temperance movement was the push for legal controls on drinking. The WCTU exists into the twenty-first century and is based in Evanston, Illinois; it lists about 12,000 members in the United States, and 20,000 worldwide as of 2008 (B. Wilson, personal communication, February 14, 2008).

By the late 1800s, coercive reform became the dominant theme of the temperance movement. In 1893, the Anti-Saloon League of Ohio was organized by Howard H. Russell, a Congregational minister and temperance activist. In 1895, this group combined with a similar group in the District of Columbia, establishing a national society in 1896: ASLA. By the end of the 1800s, the ASLA, which represented a skillful political leadership resource for the prohibition movement, mobilized tremendous support for abstinence instead of just temperance. In 1896, the movement began to separate itself from a number of economic and social reforms, concentrating on the struggle of traditional rural Protestant society against developing urban systems and industrialization.

Part of the success of the ASLA was its determination to remain a single-issue (prohibition) pressure group that cut across all political party lines; the ASLA also maintained a strong relationship with the Protestant clergy. It always put its own issue first but worked peacefully with the major political parties and especially with legislators (Blocker et al., 2003). By 1912, local prohibition laws had been passed to render most of the South legally dry.

In 1917, a major event boosted the cause of national prohibition. The United States entered World War I, which prompted the ASLA to push for the suspension of the industrial distilling of alcohol (ethanol). Very shortly after the U.S. entered into the war, the selling of liquor near military bases and to servicemen in uniform was prohibited (Blocker, 1989). By 1918, the Eighteenth Amendment to the U.S. Constitution had been proposed and the ASLA had pushed prohibition through thirty-three state legislatures. Consequently, the Volstead Act—called Prohibition—was ratified on January 16, 1919. It went into effect one year later, on January 16, 1920, prohibiting the manufacture, sale, or transportation of alcoholic beverages.

TEMPERANCE MOVEMENT: IN HISTORICAL CONTEXT

Where the temperance movement was a middle-class reform movement, because it articulated the theme of self-control that was central to the middle-class ideology of the nineteenth century, some members of the working class also supported reform (Blocker, 1989). An ideology of abstinence became a rallying point for middle-class people who saw the rich as greedy, the working class as increasingly restless, and the poor as uneducated immigrants. Thus participants in the movement felt the need to restore a coherent moral order, especially after the upheaval of the Civil War and the ensuing period of industrial greed. At this time, the United States was undergoing economic expansion and deepening division along class lines. Other reform groups, such as the Progressive. Party, joined the prohibitionists in their commitment to rid cities of saloons so that the United States could move toward becoming a virtuous and moral republic. At the end of the nineteenth century, Americans seemed to be more receptive to moral than to scientific arguments for temperance reform and abstinence from alcohol.

Members of the temperance movements were concerned not only with changing the behavior of other social classes and groups but also about changing themselves (Levine, 1978). They were concerned that the pernicious effects of alcohol were also destroying the lives of people in the Protestant middle class. While some of these reform groups were not complete supporters of an abstinence ideology, they were concerned with rebuilding a national community and promoting the common welfare. Abstinence became the governing ideology of the many diverse groups that had mobilized to promote a new social order.

As more scholars turn their attention to the study of the temperance era and the various temperance movements and societies, additional knowledge and interpretations will be published. For example, Fletcher (2007), Mattingly (1998), and Rose (1996) observed that the biggest supporters of temperance have been women, a fact ignored by many scholars. Blocker and colleagues (2003) noted interests in literary criticisms and interpretations of temperance in the early twenty-first century that have the potential to create a broader and international field of study.

See also **Woman's Christian Temperance Union.**

BIBLIOGRAPHY

Blocker, J. S., Jr. (1989). *American temperance movements: Cycles of reform.* Boston: Twayne.

Blocker, J. S., Jr., Fahey, D. M., & Tyrrell, I. R. (Eds.). (2003). *Alcohol and temperance in modern history: An international encyclopedia.* Santa Barbara, CA: ABC-CLIO.

Blumberg, L. U., (with Pittman, W. L.). (1991). *Beware the first drink! The Washingtonian temperance movement and Alcoholics Anonymous.* Seattle, WA: Glenn Abbey Books.

Drowne, K. (2005). *Spirits of defiance.* Columbus: Ohio State University Press.

Fletcher, H. B. (2007). *Gender and the American temperance movement of the nineteenth century.* London: Routledge.

Gusfield, J. R. (1986). *Symbolic crusade: Status politics and the American temperance movement* (2nd ed.). Urbana: University of Illinois Press.

Levine, H. (1978). The discovery of addiction: Changing conceptions of habitual drunkenness in America. *Journal of Studies on Alcohol, 39,* 143–174.

Mattingly, C. (1998). *Well-tempered woman: Nineteenth-century temperance rhetoric.* Carbondale: Southern Illinois University Press.

Mattingly, C. (Ed.). (2001). *Water drops from women writers: A temperance reader.* Carbondale: Southern Illinois University Press.

Miller, J. (2002). *Ten nights in a bar-room.* Acton, MA: Copley.

Murdock, C. G. (1998). *Domesticating drink: Women, men and alcohol in America, 1870–1940.* Baltimore, MD: Johns Hopkins University Press.

Musto, D., ed. (2002). *Drugs in America: A documentary history.* New York: New York University Press.

Reynolds, D. S. (1997). *The serpent in the cup: Temperance in American literature.* Amherst: University of Massachusetts Press.

Rose, K. D. (1996). *American women and the repeal of prohibition.* New York: New York University Press.

Thornton, M. (1991). *The economics of prohibition.* Salt Lake City: University of Utah Press.

Tyrrell, I. R. (1979). *Sobering up: From temperance to prohibition in antebellum America, 1800–1860.* Westport, CT: Greenwood Press.

PHYLLIS A. LANGTON

TERRORISM AND DRUGS.

The links between terrorism and drugs have evolved in relation to the shifting power dynamics of various struggles that have taken place in the Cold War between the free market and Communist state-controlled economies. All sides used terror in this struggle. And narcotics played a key role in sustaining paramilitary and terrorist organizations.

The dynamics of terrorism and drugs are a phenomenon of the late twentieth century, when developing countries assumed control of the means of production to both grow and distribute illicit substances. The main destination of the products is the West, with the financial proceeds from such transactions partially used to suppress armed struggle in the areas where the drugs are grown, and also used by insurrectionist organizations to fund their own terrorist campaigns. An inherent symbiosis exists between the grower and the principal areas of consumption, Western nations. The West is involved in two contradictory ways: in stimulating the trade as consumers and in prohibiting it through national and international policy. The effects on the developing world have been spiraling rates of intravenous (IV) substance use—coupled with poor support services—creating high rates of HIV. Both public health and governance in poorer nations suffer as narcotics money based on an illicit economy corrupts civil life.

In order to understand what led to the growth of terrorism and drugs, it is necessary to examine the genealogy of narcotics distribution. Prior to World War II it was primarily the nation-state and private entrepreneurs in Great Britain, Germany, and the United States that were responsible for trade in narcotic drugs. Between the two world wars Holland and Japan took the lead in the manufacture and distribution of psychoactive drugs, particularly cocaine. Given that narcotics use was widely practiced throughout all sectors of all societies apart from prohibitionist Japan until World War I when international prohibition began to take effect, the emergence in the developing world of the local warlord whose activities were financed by trafficking in heroin and cocaine is a latter-day phenomenon.

The shaping factors of Cold War politics and the rise of independent anticolonial movements, coupled with increased prohibition and enhanced forms of communication and travel, have created new forms of distribution. Cocaine and heroin can no longer be sold openly, as they were in the 1890s when Britain dominated international trade with its "tea" clippers and steamships. The international prohibition of narcotics, which included the Chinese Communist Party's suppression of opium production from 1949 to 1955 and a similar mandate by the Shah of Iran in 1955, meant that no nation-state could openly traffic in narcotics. It has now been left to various terrorist groups in the developing world to grow, manufacture, and distribute illicit drugs.

VIETNAM

The first group to draw on heroin as a commodity to fund an armed struggle was the Hmong hill tribe of Vietnam and Laos. The Hmong were supported by the West in their armed conflicts with the majority Khinh people of Vietnam who were Communist. The Hmong grew the poppies, harvested the opium, and with French support developed their own laboratories to transform opium into heroin. In return, they were able to buy weapons to maintain their armed struggle against the Viet Cong. Western security forces also ably assisted them in their drug distribution, most notably in Operation X. This involved flying opium from Laos to a French Special Forces Camp at Cap St. Jacques in South Vietnam, where it was sold to a consortium of Vietnamese gangsters, the Kuomintang (remnants of the KMT or Chinese Nationalist Party that remained in Southeast Asia rather than retreat to Taiwan), Corsicans, and various other brokers.

This strategy began with the French colonial effort to control the Vietnamese nationalist movement, the Viet Minh. It ended with the defeat of the French at Dien Bien Phu in 1954 where, ironically, the Viet Cong were aided by Hmong tribesmen who helped guide them through the jungle. This particular Hmong clan had become embittered toward the French because the latter, instead of dealing directly with tribespeople, had instead appointed Thai overlords to act as intermediaries. This action had driven down drug prices for the Hmong as the Thai overlords, drawn from another ethnic group, took a percentage of the profits. Following France's devastating defeat in 1954, the United States assumed control of French intelligence and, as documented by a number of historians, continued to run the Southeast Asian drug connection through Cuban dictator Fulgencio Batista and American mobsters Meyer Lansky and Santo Trafficante, with socially and economically deprived U.S. urban neighborhoods as their destination marketplace.

Initially, the Hmong formed an alliance with the West to seek support for their autonomy apart from the powerful and dominant Khinh. The West viewed them as anti-Communist insurgents. In response, the Hmong built a guerrilla army backed by Western powers that operated in the mountainous jungle regions in the border country of North

Vietnam. In the early twenty-first century they continue to engage in opium production, with their subsistence economy struggling to come to terms with the opening up of Vietnam to free-market economics.

MYANMAR

In 1962 a military junta led by General Ne Win installed itself in Myanmar (formerly known as Burma), and the Shan and Karen people in Myanmar became involved in an armed struggle against it. Both of these ethnic groups were able to utilize the sale of opium poppy to purchase guns and ammunition and fund their wars of terror against (or liberation from) the Burmese state. By the 1980s the Burmese rebels produced half of the world's opium supply. As of the early twenty-first century, the Burmese government has negotiated a number of agreements with Shan warlords to cease hostilities, with the latter group shifting from opium to amphetamine production. The warlords themselves were then able to openly enjoy the benefits of their financial empires. The use of amphetamines in its various forms was extensive in 2008 in Southeast Asia, thus creating a new form of revenue.

CHINA

The KMT has supported its clandestine operations against the Chinese Communist Party through opium production. Its main focus was to create an armed rebellion in Yunnan, an area of southeast China bordering Vietnam. Initially based in Burma, the KMT operation was forced to relocate in 1961 to northern Thailand, where it took over the Thai opium trade, hauling 90 percent of Burma's export to addicted populations across the world. In return, the KMT was able to finance a terrorist operation in Yunnan province throughout the 1960s and 1970s.

AFGHANISTAN

The 1978 coup by the Communist People's Democratic Party of Afghanistan precipitated a crisis from which that country has never recovered. The initial terrorist campaign against the educated Afghani elite evolved into a wider elimination of all forms of alleged opposition, which included religious leaders, trade unionists, and anyone who posed a threat as not directly connected to the

Communist Party. The terror inflicted by the Communists created a counter-reaction to escalating atrocities, with the military eventually revolting in 1979. The former Soviet Union continued to back the Communist regime, even though it had lost popular support, and the West supported the opposing freedom fighters, the mujahideen. The rebels were able to finance their campaign against the Soviets by selling opium and heroin, whose ultimate destination was the streets of London and Berlin, in return for armaments. Although the main markets for Afghani heroin were located in the West, Soviet troops, many of whom were exposed to the drug for the first time, frequently took their drug use back to their cities, towns, and villages. This has had a devastating effect on Russian youth, for whom treatment operations hardly exist and the risk of HIV infection has seriously increased. The heroin use and addiction of young men who were drafted into the military from rural areas echo back to the American military experience in Vietnam.

Eventually in 1989, through a war of terror undertaken by both sides, the Soviets withdrew from Afghanistan, shattered by their failure to annihilate the tribal warlords and leaving behind an estimated 1.5 million Afghanis dead. Subsequent to the Soviet withdrawal, the existing government infrastructure in Afghanistan began to unravel. In the resulting power vacuum the mujahideen and various warlords fought for control. The U.S. Central Intelligence Agency (CIA) backed Gulbudding Hekmatyar, leader of the Hezbi-Ismali guerrilla group, a proto-fascist or Islamist faction, who eventually became the most influential drug warlord in the region. The result was that the Islamist Taliban emerged triumphant, able to realize its vision of an Islamic state based on the Sharia (Islamic law as derived from the Qur'an). In order to bankroll Afghanistan's shattered economy, the Taliban initially stimulated the growth of opium and then became involved in opium suppression as it tried to unsuccessfully shed its international pariah status.

Afghanistan was deemed to be a safe haven for the extremist Al Qaeda movement post 9/11, and the response was a United States-backed invasion in 2002. The invasion has yet to stem the growth in opium poppy, with Helmand province nominally controlled by the British Army becoming the opium bed of the world. The devastation in Afghanistan has created a seismic shift throughout central Asia as opium and heroin have bankrolled wars in Chechnya, Georgia, Bosnia, Croatia, and Uzbekistan while also destabilizing Pakistan. This drug trade is controlled by elements of Al Qaeda, tribal gangs, criminal warlords, and Western intelligence services.

The result has been political chaos and turmoil, with terrorism and drugs manifesting themselves in all their differing forms, and ideological or religious beliefs driving laws enacted and actions taken to control trade routes. Differing ideological gangs have fought for control and also cooperated in alliances. The financial gains derived from the opium and heroin trade have created forms of ideological drift as groups engaged in armed struggle, based on religious and political ideology, recognized the potential profits involved in narcotics supply. These far outweigh the economic gains of armed insurrection, and this becomes a key conceptual point for understanding another aspect of terrorism and drugs. The ideologies have become recruiting slogans to attract young ideologues into organizations rooted in the cause of terror. The end result, however, are narcotics gangs based on fear—whose main aim is to claim the consumer benefits of the free market, including stimulating the growth of the international sex trade—rather than a struggle against capitalism.

COLOMBIA

The rise of various political groups in Colombia is a significant conundrum for the West. Colombia became the third largest recipient of U.S. aid following the Clinton administration's commitment to a $1.3 billion military aid package to the Colombian military with the stated aim of eradicating coca plantations. Within Colombia a number of armed groups continue to vie for political power, based on various ideologies rooted in the right as well as the left. All to varying degrees are involved in the cocaine trade: its cultivation, taxing of the growers, refinement or distribution of the product.

One of the most well-armed groups of the right is a paramilitary umbrella organization called the United Self-Defence Forces of Colombia (AUC). Paramilitary forces directly participate in processing cocaine; they are also involved in its manufacture and distribution. They are able to sustain their power base through acts of terror directed against any group that challenges their hold over a defined geographical area. They coexist with the army, the police, and other state forces as they conduct terror against the Ejército de Liberación Nacional (ELN or National Liberation Army) and Fuerzas Armadas Revolucionarias de Colombia (FARC or Revolutionary Armed Forces of Colombia), two factions that wish to overthrow the Colombian state.

AUC has a special role, maintaining close links with the state but not directly funded by it. AUC is able to carry out terrorist campaigns and assassinations outside the rule of the law. Because it funds itself by drawing on a vital international commodity, the cocaine trade, AUC can exist outside of state support systems and remain unaccountable.

Plan Colombia, a United States–backed attempt to suppress drugs and terrorism, is primarily directed at groups who operate in the south of Colombia. This area is largely controlled by FARC. It is here that the war on terror—the overriding U.S. foreign policy post-9/11—conflates with the War on Drugs into the war against FARC. This group is engaged in an armed revolutionary struggle in which kidnapping, assassination, bank robberies, and extortion are viewed as strategies to raise finances and to inflict a terrorist campaign against its perceived adversaries, the state apparatus of control. Interestingly, the AUC has not been constrained by Plan Colombia and benefits from the intelligence and resources mobilized by the CIA in its wars on drugs and terror.

FARC is a group that has its origins in Cold War politics, rooted initially in Marxism, but there has been a shift to Bolivar populism as it has sought to increase peasant participation in its so-called liberation army, which also contains a significant proportion of female combatants. Bolivar populism, pioneered by Bolivian President Evo Morales, is a form of pragmatic socialism based on the Cuban model, with an emphasis on health clinics and classrooms for poor communities rather than traditional Marxist or Leninist policies based on ownership of the means of production and capture of the state. Bolivia, for example, has nationalized the oil and gas production industry, reversing the previous policy induced by the free-market economics of the International Monetary Fund (IMF). Morales has also increased the government's royalties by more than U.S. $1 billion a year. Thus far this money has been used to fund infrastructure projects that bolster popular support for the governing party as well as lift the poor out of absolute poverty. Correspondingly, he has ended credit agreements with the IMF and withdrawn from the World Bank dispute procedure, thereby lessening the chance of outside interference in Bolivia's internal affairs.

During the Cold War Marxist- and Leninist-based insurgency, groups were partially sustained by the resources of the former Soviet Union. FARC has demonstrated that even with the demise of the Soviet state, a guerrilla movement based on leftist ideology can sustain itself. In fact, FARC has consistently grown in numbers and in terms of its areas of geographical control since the official collapse of Communism.

FARC remains able to sustain its organization by taxing the cocaine growers, along with other commodities grown in the region, and also by becoming involved in cocaine distribution to middlemen who then create their own networks to distribute the drug across South America, North America, and Europe. The U.S. government's response to this trade has been the indictment of FARC leadership on charges of $25 billion worth of cocaine distribution. Until 2008 similar activities of AUC were ignored. Various official reports on drug distribution in Colombia, including one authored by Senator John Kerry in 1986, clearly indicated the complicity of the CIA in overriding the strategic aims of the Drug Enforcement Agency (DEA) to try to contain insurgency groups.

FARC was labeled as an important terrorist organization in the post-9/11 debates on U.S. security. American strategy has emphasized crop eradication as a way forward, strangling FARC's ability to raise finances. The debates surrounding the success of this form of intervention have revolved around what has had the most effect, the American aerial eradication strategy or the Colombian military approach based on manual eradication, or if the entire intervention has been counterproductive as FARC appears, to some observers, to have increased its hold. Each position is rooted within the ideology of the participants and is part of a war of words, one intended to sap the morale of the opposing side and seek funds to continue various terrorist campaigns.

The IRA in Colombia. The arrest of three provisional Irish Republican Army (IRA) members in August 2001 in Colombia highlighted the links between FARC and other groups formerly engaged in wars against the state. The senior IRA members had travelled to Colombia to allegedly provide technical knowledge about bomb making to FARC. In return, FARC was to provide funds to assist the IRA in transitioning from an insurgency group to a legitimate political group. In their past struggles the IRA had consistently patrolled its areas of the Six Counties in Northern Ireland ensuring that drugs did not penetrate the Irish Catholic Housing Estates. Punishments were meted out to those involved in the distribution of marijuana; they ranged from warnings to banishment to kneecapping. Following the ceasefire with the U.K. government, the links forged through various armed confrontations coupled with the technical knowledge gained over a twenty-year struggle allowed certain members of the former IRA to gain consultancy roles with other insurgency groups. There is some dispute over whether this was the group's official policy or if the individuals involved had operated on their own. The IRA kept its sense of purpose intact throughout twenty years of insurgency largely through strict discipline. Deviation from the leadership's aims was never tolerated, so it is inconceivable to some that senior members would have decided to participate in a nonauthorized operation.

CLOSING REMARKS

Since the beginning of the twentieth century there has been a substantial shift from state distribution of narcotics to developing nations becoming involved in their supply. The proceeds of the sale of drugs have primarily fueled conflict within supply nations, and the examples here highlight the situation in Vietnam, Myanmar, Afghanistan, and Colombia. The latent effect is that groups wishing to further their interests must be able to finance their campaigns either for or against the state. The sale of drugs allows governments and insurgents to buy weapons. These proxy wars destabilize government systems, induce campaigns of terror, and encourage the growth of the narcotics industry and narcotics use. The situation has been exacerbated by the role of Western intelligence agencies that have drawn on these various groups, asking them to fight wars based on the agencies' interests, which could not be fought conventionally. The impact of these various strategies is significant: It has ensured that drugs have become integral to the flow of international capital and are intrinsically linked to the sex trade, the arms industry, and money laundering.

See also **Crop Control Policies; Foreign Policy and Drugs, United States; International Drug Supply Systems.**

BIBLIOGRAPHY

Chomsky, N. (2001). *An American addiction.* Oakland, CA: AK Press.

Cockburn, A., & St. Clair, J. (1998). *Whiteout: The CIA, drugs, and the press.* London: Verso.

McCoy, A. (1991). *The politics of heroin.* New York: Lawrence Hill.

Parry, R. (1999). *Lost history: Contras, cocaine, the press & "Project Truth."* Arlington VA: Media Consortium.

Webb, G. (1998). *Dark alliance.* New York: Seven Stories Press.

DEAN WHITTINGTON

TETRAHYDROCANNABINOL (THC).

Tetrahydrocannabinol, or THC, is a chemical found in the hemp plant, *Cannabis sativa*, that causes the psychoactive effects of marijuana, bhang, hashish, and ganja. Hashish is derived from the resin that oozes from the flowering tips of the female plant; bhang comes from the dried leaves and flowering shoots of the female plant; and ganja comes from small leaves. THC is one of the three natural cannabinoids—chemical constituents of *Cannabis*—the other two being cannabinol (CBN) and cannabidiol (CBD).

As of the early twenty-first century, marijuana is the most commonly used nonlegal drug in the United States. Its usage peaked during the late 1970s, when about 60 percent of high school seniors reported having tried marijuana, with 11 percent reporting daily use. Usage has declined since 1979; as of 2003, 5.1 million Americans aged 12 or older described themselves as daily users.

PHARMACOLOGICAL EFFECTS

For more than 30 years, the discovery of the mechanism of THC's action had eluded the best researchers. The problem seems finally to have been resolved by the detection of specific cannabinoid-binding sites (receptors) in the brain. A further step in unraveling the mechanism of THC's action has been the cloning of the cannabinoid receptor.

The pharmacological effects of THC vary with the dose, the method of administration, the user's degree of experience with THC, the setting, and the user's vulnerability to the psychoactive effects of the drug. Most users seek to experience a "high," or "mellowing out." The high begins about 10 to 20 minutes after smoking and lasts about 2 hours. The psychological effects obtained during the high are often related to the setting in which the drug is taken.

Inhalation. THC is most commonly taken into the body by inhaling the smoke from marijuana "joints." A joint of good quality contains about 500 milligrams of marijuana, which in turn contains between 5 and 15 milligrams of THC. Blood levels of THC rise almost as rapidly after inhaling smoke as they do after intravenous administration of THC. That the drug should be so rapidly absorbed is an indication of the efficiency of the lung as a trap for the drug. THC is quickly redistributed into other tissues so that blood levels decline over the course of 3 hours to negligible amounts. The usual symptoms of marijuana intoxication are almost completely gone by that time.

Ingestion. THC is absorbed slowly and unreliably from the gut after oral administration. Blood levels of the drug peak between 1 and 2 hours after ingestion. These peak concentrations are also considerably lower than those following smoking.

THC is easily soluble in fats. It is taken up and stored in the fatty tissues of the body and in the gray matter of the brain. This pattern of storage is one reason why THC remains so long in the body.

Withdrawal. THC does not produce a severe withdrawal syndrome. Heavy users, however, frequently report insomnia, nervousness, mild stomach upset, and achy muscles—particularly if they stop their use suddenly.

DRUG TESTING AND FORENSIC ISSUES

Drug testing is an issue with respect to marijuana because of the effects of THC on coordination, sense of timing, and impairment of depth perception as well as short-term memory. It is hazardous for someone who has taken a moderate dosage of marijuana to drive or to operate heavy equipment in the workplace.

Urine testing, however, is hardly useful for determining impairment, since the metabolic products of THC are detectable for as long as 50 days in chronic users. Urine tests are also of little use in determining the patient's pattern of use.

EFFECTS OF THC

THC produces a variety of complex sensations and behavioral effects in humans. The effects on memory, coordination, and sense of time have already been noted. Some studies indicate that THC produces impairment of human cognitive functions as well. In addition, many users experience increased appetite. Psychological effects range from a pleasant sense of mellowness to negative effects that include panic reactions, anxiety, hallucinations, and schizophrenic symptoms. THC can also cause relapses in schizophrenic patients, even those who are taking antipsychotic medications. These negative effects are more common with high doses of the drug and with oral ingestion rather than smoking.

The physical effects of THC include dry mouth, abnormalities in heart rhythm, and abnormal precancerous changes in the tissues that line the airway and the lungs. People who are heavy users of marijuana often develop bronchitis and laryngitis. As of the early twenty-first century it is known that persons who smoke only marijuana have an increased risk of lung cancer, as well as those who smoke tobacco. THC lowers the sperm count in males and may produce abnormal menstrual cycles in females. Women who are pregnant or nursing are advised to avoid marijuana, as THC is secreted in human breast milk.

MEDICAL USES OF THC

THC has been used in medicine to treat the nausea that many cancer patients experience after chemotherapy. It has also been used to prevent convulsions and to lower the fluid pressure inside the eye in treating glaucoma.

In recent years, THC has been replaced in medical use by a synthetic derivative called drona-binol (Marinol). Dronabinol is used as an antinau-sea drug, an appetite stimulant in AIDS patients, and an antiglaucoma medication.

See also **Drug Metabolism; Drug Testing Methods and Clinical Interpretations of Test Results; Pharmaco-kinetics: General.**

BIBLIOGRAPHY

Beers, M. H., & Berkow, R., Eds. (1999). *The Merck manual of diagnosis and therapy*, 17th ed. Whitehouse Station, NJ: Merck Research Laboratories. (2006, 18th ed.)

Brophy, J. J. (1994). Psychiatric disorders. In L. M. Tierney et al. (Eds.), *Current medical diagnosis & treatment*, 33rd ed. Norwalk, CT: Appleton & Lange. (2007, 47th ed.)

Grotenhermen, F., & Russo, E. (2002). *Cannabis and cannabinoids: Pharmacology, toxicology, and therapeutic potential*. New York: Routledge.

Herkenham, M., et al. (1990). Cannabinoid receptor local-ization in the brain. *Proceedings of the National Acad-emy of Science, 87,* 1932–1936.

Hollister, L. E., et al. (1981). Do plasma concentrations of delta-9-tetrahydrocannabinol reflect the degree of intoxication? *Journal of Clinical Pharmacology, 21,* 1715–1755.

O'Brien, C. P. (1996). Drug addiction and drug abuse. In A. G. Gilman et al. (Eds.), *Goodman and Gilman's the pharmacological basis of therapeutics*, 9th ed. New York: McGraw-Hill Medical. (2005, 11th ed.)

SAMHSA. (2004). *The NSDUH report.* Washington, D.C.: Department of Health and Human Services. Available from http://www.oas.samhsa.gov/.

Wilson, B. A., Shannon, M. T., & Stang, C. L., Eds. (1995). *Nurses drug guide*, 3rd ed. Norwalk, CT: Appleton & Lange. (B. A. Wilson, et al. [2008]. *Pren-tice Hall nurse's drug guide 2008.* Upper Saddle River, NJ: Prentice Hall.)

LEO E. HOLLISTER
REVISED BY REBECCA J. FREY (2001)

THEOBROMINE. This alkaloid belongs to the class of drugs called methylxanthines; it is similar to theophylline and to caffeine. Theobro-mine (3,7-dimethylxanthine), however, is somewhat weaker than these two compounds and currently has almost no practical use in medicine.

Theobromine is found in the seeds of the plant *Theobroma cacao*, which is the well-known source of chocolate and cocoa. The cacao seeds have caf-feine too (as does tea, which contains small amounts of theobromine and theophylline). Caf-feine has powerful stimulant effects on the brain, whereas theobromine has very little (although pop-ular articles alleged for years that theobromine makes one feel "happy"). High doses of theobro-mine can, however, affect several physiological functions in the body, such as increasing the for-mation of urine in the kidney.

See also **Alkaloids; Caffeine; Chocolate.**

BIBLIOGRAPHY

Serafin, W. E. (1996). Drugs used in the treatment of asthma. In J. G. Hardman et al. (Eds.), *The pharmaco-logical basis of therapeutics*, 9th ed. New York: McGraw-Hill Medical (2005, 11th ed.).

Taubert, D., Roesen, R., &amp: Schömig, E. (2007). Effect of cocoa and tea on blood pressure. *Archives of Inter-nal Medicine, 167, 7,* 626–634.

MICHAEL J. KUHAR

TOBACCO

This entry includes the following essays:
AN INTERNATIONAL OVERVIEW
A HISTORY OF TOBACCO
TOBACCO INDUSTRY
DEPENDENCE
MEDICAL COMPLICATIONS
SMOKELESS
SMOKING CESSATION AND WEIGHT GAIN

A HISTORY OF TOBACCO

The term *tobacco* generally refers to the leaves and other parts of certain South American plants that were domesticated and used by Native Americans for the alkaloid nicotine. Tobacco plants are a spe-cies of the genus Nicotiana, belonging to the So-lanaceae (nightshade) family, which also includes potatoes, tomatoes, eggplants, belladonna, and petunias. Including plants used for tobacco, there are 64 Nicotiana species. The two widely cultivated for use as tobacco are Nicotiana tabacum and

Nicotiana rustica, the latter of which contains the higher levels of nicotine.

Nicotiana tabacum is, however, the major source of commercial tobacco, although it has been hybridized with other Nicotiana species and its chemical composition altered in the process. Nicotiana tabacum is a broad-leaf plant that grows from three to ten feet (1–3m) tall and produces ten to twenty leaves radiating from a central stalk. Nicotiana rustica, also known as Indian tobacco, was first cultivated by Native Americans and was probably the tobacco offered to Columbus. The word *tobacco* came into English about 1565 from the Spanish word *tabaco*, which probably derives from the Taino word for the roll of leaves containing the N. rustica that the indigenous people of the Antilles smoked.

HISTORY OF TOBACCO USE IN EUROPE

Tobacco was introduced to Europeans by Native Americans at the time Columbus explored the New World (1492–1506). The first written records of tobacco use date from this time, but there is archaeological evidence for tobacco's wide use in the Americas as early as 600 to 900 CE. Native Americans considered tobacco to be sacred, and the plant was used in social, fertility, and spiritual rituals. For example, tobacco was used for seasonal ceremonies, for sealing friendships, preparing for war, predicting good weather or good fishing, planting, courting, consulting spirits, and preparing magical cures. The desired effect of tobacco was a trance state, achieved by using the leaves in various ways, including smoking, chewing, snuffing, drinking (tobacco juice or tea), licking, and injecting in enemas.

Tobacco Use Spread from the Americas to Europe. Acute nicotine poisoning was a central aspect of the practice of shamanism in many parts of South America. South American shamans would smoke or ingest tobacco to the point of producing a nicotine-mediated trance or coma. The dose of nicotine could be titrated to produce a coma state resembling death, but from which the shaman would recover. Recovery from apparent death was believed to enhance the perception of the shaman's magical powers.

Tobacco use spread widely through all the Americas, and most tribes had ceremonial traditions related to tobacco. Although tobacco ceremonies were common among native tribes in the Americas from Canada to Argentina, the traditions and stories about the origin of tobacco vary greatly. In 1492 Columbus encountered natives in Hispaniola smoking tobacco in the form of large cigars. Enticed by the sacred and special regard in which they held tobacco, Columbus's crew experimented with tobacco smoking and soon became enthusiastic users. In the early 1500s tobacco cultivation began in Portugal. By the late 1500s, France had introduced tobacco cultivation to Holland and later to Italy. By 1570 tobacco had been introduced to Germany, Switzerland, Austria, and Hungary. In central Europe tobacco was primarily used for medicinal purposes. Tobacco was said to be useful in the prevention of plague and as a cure for headache, asthma, gout, ulcers, scabies, labor pains, and even cancer.

Objections by James I to Tobacco. In 1570 the tobacco plant was named Nicotiana after Jean Nicot, the French ambassador to Portugal who introduced tobacco to France. In the late 1500s, Sir Walter Raleigh popularized the smoking of tobacco for pleasure in the court of Queen Elizabeth I (reigned 1558–1603); from there it spread to other parts of England.

James I of England (reigned 1603–1625), who succeeded Elizabeth, was strongly opposed to tobacco use and in 1604 wrote the first major anti-tobacco treatise, *A Counterblaste to Tobacco.* King James described tobacco as "a custome loathsome to the eye, hateful to the nose, harmful to the brain, dangerous to the lungs, and in the black stinking fume thereof nearest resembling the horrible stygian smoke of the pit that is bottomless." Despite James's opposition, however, tobacco use flourished. Eventually, even James lessened his opposition to tobacco because of the lucrative income from its taxation. Governments often became addicted to the tax revenues from tobacco much like people became addicted to the chemicals being taxed. These revenues were often used to fund wartime efforts and support the economy during desperate times (Courtwright, 2001, p. 156).

Throughout Europe pipe use became the popular method of consuming tobacco, and the first vending machine for pipe tobacco was introduced in England in 1610. During the Thirty Years War (1618–1648), which began as a struggle for religious supremacy that grew into a large-scale non-religious struggle for political dominance in Europe, tobacco use expanded primarily through the ranks of warring armies. With Germany being the primary battle area for the war, historians estimate that nine out of every ten peasant homes had a tobacco user (Corti, 1932, p. 108). Also during this time, medical practitioners began treating many common ailments with tobacco, leading to increased use of the pipe.

Tobacco as Big Business, and Its Critics. In the early 1600s, Spain, Portugal, and England increased their financial investment in tobacco through cultivation in their North American territories. In 1614, King Phillip III of Spain declared Seville the tobacco center of the world and had all Spanish crops in the Americas funneled through Seville. Simultaneously, the English expanded cultivation in their colony of Virginia. In 1619, the first slaves arrived in Virginia to cultivate English tobacco crops. Rapidly expanding tobacco production by the English was credited for the slave trade industry in the seventeenth and eighteenth centuries. Tobacco growers in the Americas realized that growing tobacco required large numbers of permanent laborers and found inexpensive labor from the Africans being shipped from West Africa. Although many were originally brought to the Americas as indentured servants, the practice transformed into slavery as profit-minded plantation owners institutionalized the practice of owning permanent laborers and providing only for their basic needs plantation owners.

Throughout the 1600s increasing numbers of antismoking regulations spread throughout Europe and east to Russia. The Russian Czar Michael Feodorivich (1596–1645) declared tobacco use a deadly sin and established harsh punishments for offenders. Murad the Cruel of Turkey (1623–1640) ordered that tobacco users be beheaded, quartered, and/or hanged. As the anti-tobacco pressures increased in Europe and Russia, tobacco trade moved into Asia. By the mid-1600s, smoking was a pastime in China, Japan, Korea, and India. Shortly, antismoking pressures increased, leading Persia and India to enact death penalties for tobacco use. In 1620 Japan banned smoking for the first time. Nevertheless, smoking persisted. Government prohibitions became costly to national economies as the trade of tobacco moved to black markets.

India's tobacco bans in the late 1800s alone created a significant negative impact on government revenue as tobacco revenue dropped from 14 percent in 1880 to 7 percent in 1905 (Courtwright, 2001, p. 183).

Due to the enormous profit in tobacco trade, smuggling and black markets for tobacco increased greatly during the 1700s. Ireland and Scotland became gateways for tobacco smuggling. Tobacco created an economic boom leading to population growth and prosperity in Glasgow. During the early 1700s, England's state of war with France and Spain contributed to Scotland and Ireland's prosperity in tobacco as their ports provided safer transport than England's.

Despite countervailing pressures, tobacco was also recognized as having medicinal properties. During an outbreak of the bubonic plague (Black Death) in England in the mid-1600s, tobacco was recognized as a preventive measure. Young men during this period were encouraged to smoke a daily pipe at Eton College and were routinely punished for not doing so.

Royal Support of Tobacco. During the 1700s, Europe saw a resurgence of tobacco use among European elites. Smoking had become primarily a pastime of the lower and middles classes following the Thirty Years War and the social elite turned to using tobacco in the form of snuff, a finely ground tobacco powder inhaled through the nose. Opposed to smoking, Louis XIV of France promulgated the use of snuff as a discreet habit that did not offend others with smoke. Snuff-taking throughout the 1700s increased dramatically. In contrast to most of Europe, Frederick I and Frederick William I of Prussia were avid pipe smokers who began the first tobacco club with the sole purpose of promoting smoking.

PRODUCTION OF CIGARETTES IN NORTH AMERICA

In France and England, snuff-taking continued to grow in popularity among the aristocracy. Even Napoleon I was rumored to consume up to seven pounds of snuff a month. Expensive to produce and package, snuff was used mostly by the upper classes. Snuff-taking was popular until the mid-1800s when smoking was reintroduced with the emergence of cigars from the Spanish colonies. Various ancestors to the modern cigarette first appeared in the mid-seventeenth century. For example, the famed Casanova (1725–1798) in Italy helped popularize the hand-rolled cigarette. Not until 1843, however, did Manufacture Francaise des Tabacs produce the first commercial cigarette. Napoleon III (1808–1873) helped popularize the cigarette with his own 50-per-day habit. With the introduction of mass production of commercial cigarettes, large manufacturing plants began to appear in Europe and North America. In 1847 Phillip Morris opened his first production plant in England, producing hand-rolled Turkish cigarettes.

Tobacco production was a mainstay of American capitalism. In contrast to Europe, the U.S. public preferred chewing tobacco to smoking in the early 1800s. By 1860, the U.S. business census listed 348 tobacco factories producing chew tobacco in North Carolina and Virginia alone. However, cigar smoking also grew in popularity in the United States after soldiers in the Mexican War (1846–1848) returned with a desire for the darker, richer tobacco found in Latin cigars. Most tobacco was smoked as cigars or in pipes or used as snuff. Cigarettes were hand rolled. A skillful worker could roll four cigarettes per minute. Cigarette smokers were primarily boys or women, and smoking was a behavior confined to the lower socioeconomic class.

The gold rush of 1849 in California spurred an American interest in finer tobaccos and liquors. San Francisco became known as the capital for the *best bad things* in the United States. The Civil War contributed to the U.S. growth in tobacco consumption in two ways. First, the ration packs for soldiers in both the Confederate and Union armies contained tobacco products. Second, the U.S. government imposed the first excise tax on tobacco to help fund the Civil War for the Unionists.

Introduction of the match in 1852 and mass production of commercial cigarettes caused cigarette consumption to rise in the latter half of the 1800s. Increased smoking led to resurgence in antismoking regulations. In 1868, the British Parliament banned smoking on all commercial trains. In 1871, the U.S. House of Representatives voted to ban smoking in its own chambers. The U.S. Senate was able to enact the ban in its chamber in 1914. Nonetheless, smoking prevailed.

Cigarette Rolling Machine. The invention of the cigarette rolling machine by James Bonsack in 1880 made tobacco use inexpensive and convenient. Bonsack went into business with W. B. Duke and Sons in Durham, North Carolina. Together they improved the machine; by April 30, 1884, the device could roll 120,000 cigarettes per day. Duke used his competitive edge in manufacturing with an exclusive agreement with Bonsack to drive the price down, making cigarettes more affordable for the general public. Duke's American Tobacco Company dominated tobacco through the late 1800s but eventually collapsed in an anti-trust action in 1911.

Popular Culture and the Cigarette. By the late 1800s, tobacco had entered the world of popular entertainment and had begun to appear in popular fiction. Mérimée's 1865 novel about a cigarette girl in Seville became the basis for the opera *Carmen*. In 1878, trading cards and coupons began to appear in packs of cigarettes. Sports figures became the first trading cards to link tobacco and celebrity. By the beginning of the 1900s cigarette consumption in the United States had increased more than fourfold. At the same time, chewing tobacco had reached its peak consumption.

Ironically, as pressures increased in the U.S. Congress to ban or control tobacco, the government listed tobacco in the *U.S. Pharmacopoeia*. This government endorsement of tobacco as a medicinal agent led to partnerships between the tobacco companies and the medical community. In 1899, the first *Merck Manual*, a widely used reference book for physicians, listed tobacco as a treatment for bronchial distress and asthma.

Mass media opened doors to tobacco never experienced before the first half of the twentieth century. The glamorization of cigarette smoking increased through the use of entertainment celebrities as spokespersons and the inclusion of smoking in the new motion picture industry. Both world wars provided a venue for increasing tobacco use by soldiers, who received cigarettes as rations. Tobacco advertising also included doctors among the role models depicted as smoking cigarettes. Despite the fact that tobacco had been removed from the *U.S. Pharmacopeia* by 1905, smoking was considered sophisticated, glamorous, individualistic, and even healthful. Across the world, the average person was spending 3 to 5 percent of his or her total income on tobacco by 1951, according to John B. Hutson, president of Tobacco Associates in a paper published in that same year.

HISTORY OF OPPOSITION TO TOBACCO USE

Strong opposition to tobacco consumption emerged by the turn of the twentieth century with 43 of the 45 states addressing tobacco as a menace. Business owners joined ranks in 1908 and began refusing employment for people who smoked. However, bans on sales of tobacco to minors were the only successful national regulation in the United States, Canada, and England. Despite antismoking regulations, tobacco consumption in the first half of the 1900s increased, peaking in 1955 in the United States with 50 percent of men smoking and in 1966 for women, with 32 percent of women smoking. By the 1960s nearly half of Americans were addicted to nicotine.

Health Hazards and Legal Action. While there had been occasional reports on the health hazards of cigarette smoking from the time of King James, the first large-scale studies documenting the link between cigarette smoking and cancer appeared in 1950 (Doll & Hill, 1950; Wynder & Graham, 1950). Subsequently, hundreds of studies have shown that cigarette smoking accounts for 30 percent of cancers—including some cancers of the lung, mouth, throat, esophagus, bladder, and kidney, as well as some leukemia; and that it is the cause of some heart and vascular disease, stroke, emphysema, chronic obstructive lung disease, and other health problems. The U.S. Office of the Surgeon General regularly publishes findings regarding the health consequences of tobacco use with the most comprehensive report released in 2004. The first comprehensive review of the scientific research regarding the health consequences for nonsmokers regularly exposed to smoke in their work, home, and social environments was published by the U.S. Office of the Surgeon General in 2006. This report has been paramount in supporting tobacco bans worldwide.

Unprecedented scientific and legal efforts to reduce the use of tobacco emerged in the second half of the twentieth century. With mounting support that tobacco causes different types of cancer, multiple lawsuits were filed in the 1950s in the United States against tobacco companies. The increase in scientific literature led to the 1962 report by the Royal College of Physicians in Britain and the 1964 Surgeon General's Report in the United States linking tobacco with lung cancer. The largest public health campaign related to any one issue began with these reports.

The 1960s in the United States started the era of comprehensive tobacco control. Regulations were passed that limited advertising by tobacco companies. Tobacco advertising on television was banned in the United Kingdom. Warning labels about the dangers of tobacco had to be placed on all tobacco products in the United States. The U.S. Surgeon General released three more reports on the dangers of smoking. By the 1970s legislation was introduced in the United States and the United Kingdom that banned smoking in public places, including airlines. Individual states within the United States began to draft legislation to control where people would be allowed to smoke.

During this same time, in stark contrast to many of the industrialized nations moving toward smoking bans, Japan stood out for its political support of smoking. Emperor Hirohito started a tradition of passing out cigarettes to all of his employees on his birthday. He also provided free cigarettes to the elderly on a holiday honoring them. Japan's consumption of tobacco peaked in 1966 with 84 percent of men smoking, according to the World Health Organization in 1998.

Federal Restrictions. In the 1990s the United States and other industrialized nations moved to reduce both the affordability and convenience of smoking. Federal and state governments began placing large taxes on tobacco products that significantly increased the cost of tobacco. With smoke-free laws being regulated, making smoking less convenient, more regular smokers quit. By the end of the 1990s, according to the Centers for Disease Control, smoking rates in the United States had dropped to about 25 percent in the adult population.

In 1997 the United States Attorney General's Office and the tobacco companies came to the largest agreement ever settled by the tobacco industry. The master settlement agreement severely restricted advertising, required bold warnings on tobacco, and limited damages against tobacco companies in lawsuits. The tobacco companies admitted they knew tobacco was addictive and company executives lied about the dangers of using tobacco.

Tobacco control efforts had mixed impact in Asia. In 2000, Japan demonstrated the effect of pressures to control tobacco use as Emperor Akihito repealed the tradition of handing out cigarettes to staff on his birthday. Smoking rates dropped to 47.7 percent that year. With all the tobacco control efforts across the globe during this time, China National Tobacco Company accounted for 31 percent of the tobacco market, representing 385 million smokers in China in 2000, making it the dominant tobacco trader in the world.

In February 2005 the Framework Convention on Tobacco Control (FCTC) took effect in the 40 countries that ratified it. The convention sought to protect the world's citizens from the dangers of secondhand smoke. By 2008 over 65 countries had established smoke-free laws that limit or ban smoking in public places. In the United States, according to the 2007 *Morbidity and Mortality Weekly Report*, rates dropped from 25 percent in 1999 to 21 percent in 2004. In the United States smoking rates among teenagers dropped from 28 percent in 1991 to 23 percent in 2005. Although the overall smoking rate dropped through the early years of the twenty-first century, the U.S. Centers for Disease Control reported a disproportionate number of smokers among African Americans, Asian Americans, and the gay/lesbian populations.

While smoking rates continued to drop in industrial nations, WHO noted that smoking rates in developing countries were on the increase in the early years of the twenty-first century. With the increased restrictions for marketing in industrial nations, the largest tobacco companies looked elsewhere for profits, developing multinational offices to increase marketing efforts in developing markets.

See also **Advertising and Tobacco Use; Nicotine; Nicotine Delivery Systems for Smoking Cessation.**

BIBLIOGRAPHY

Corti, C. (1932). *A history of smoking*. Translated by Paul England. New York: Harcourt, Brace and Company.

Courtwright, D. T. (2001). *Forces of habit: Drugs and the making of the modern world*. Cambridge, MA: Harvard University Press.

Doll, R., & Hill, A. B. (1950). Smoking and carcinoma of the lung: Preliminary report. *British Medical Journal, 2*, 739–748.

Gilman, S., & Zun, X. (2004). *Smoke: A global history of smoking*. London: Reaktion Books.

George Washington's Fredericksburg Foundation Fellows. (2000–2001). *Tobacco and slavery in the Virginia Colony. History in your own backyard. Primers to the past: Teaching our history*. Central Rappahannock Regional Library. Available from http://www.historypoint.org/.

John B. Hutson Papers (#220), Special Collections Department, J. Y. Joyner Library, East Carolina University, Greenville, North Carolina.

Leavey, James. *A history of tobacco*. Available from http://www.forces.org/.

Royal College of Physicians. (1962) *Smoking and Health. Summary and Report of the Royal College of Physicians of London on smoking in relation to cancer of the lung and other diseases*. New York: Pitman Publishing.

Shafey, O., Dolwick, S., & Guindon, G. E. (Eds). (2003). *Tobacco control: Country profiles*. Atlanta, GA: American Cancer Society. Available from http://www.cancer.org/.

U.S. Centers for Disease Control. (2007). Cigarette smoking among adults: United States, 2006. *Morbidity and Mortality Weekly Report, 56*(44), 1157–1161.

U.S. Centers for Disease Control. Cigarette use among high school students: United States, 1991–2005. *Morbidity and Mortality Weekly Report, 200*(55), 724–726.

U.S. Department of Health, Education and Welfare. (1964). Smoking and Health: *Report of the Advisory Committee to the Surgeon General of the Public Health Service*. Atlanta, GA: Public Health Service, Centers for Disease Control. Publication No. 1103.

U.S. Department of Health, Education and Welfare. (1967). Smoking and Health: *The health consequences of smoking, a Public Health Service review*. Atlanta, GA: Public Health Service, Centers for Disease Control. Publication No. 1696.

U.S. Department of Health, Education and Welfare. (1968). Smoking and Health: *The health consequences of smoking: 1968 supplement to the 1967 Public Health Service review*. Atlanta, GA: Public Health Service, Centers for Disease Control. Supplement to Publication No. 1696.

U.S. Department of Health, Education and Welfare. (1969). Smoking and Health: *The Health Consequences of Smoking: 1969 supplement to the 1967 Public Health Service review*. Atlanta, GA: Public Health Service, Centers for Disease Control. Publication No. 1696-2.

U.S. Department of Health and Human Services. (2004). *The health consequences of smoking: A report of the Surgeon General*. Atlanta, GA: U.S. Department of Health and Human Services, Centers for Disease Control and Prevention, National Center for Chronic Disease

Prevention and Health Promotion, Office on Smoking and Health.

U.S. Department of Health and Human Services. (2006) *The health consequences of involuntary exposure to tobacco smoke: A report of the Surgeon General.* Atlanta, GA: U.S. Department of Health and Human Services, Centers for Disease Control and Prevention, Coordinating Center for Health Promotion, National Center for Chronic Disease Prevention and Health Promotion, Office on Smoking and Health.

World Health Organization. Tobacco use introduction for Japan. World Health Organization Infobase. Available from http://www.who.int/.

World Health Organization. (2008). Report on the global tobacco epidemic, 2008: The MPOWER package (p. 16). Geneva: Author.

Wynder, E. L., & Graham, E. A. (1950). Tobacco smoking as a possible etiologic factor in bronchogenic carcinoma. *Journal of the American Medical Association, 143,* 329–336.

NEIL L. BENOWITZ
ALICE B. FREDERICKS
REVISED BY RONALD ROSS WATSON (2009)
STEPHEN S. MICHAEL (2009)

AN INTERNATIONAL OVERVIEW

The tobacco plant (*Nicotiana tabacum*) is native to the western hemisphere where it has grown from 6000 BC to 3000 BC and was used by indigenous peoples for religious and medicinal purposes. Since the seventeenth century, the cultivation and use of tobacco has spread worldwide. By the early twenty-first century, tobacco had become an industry worth $400 billion in annual revenues. Around one in three adults uses tobacco.

PHARMACOLOGY OF TOBACCO AND ITS EFFECTS

Tobacco, in its natural form, contains over three thousand compounds. Its cultivation, processing, and manufacture into various products; combination with other compounds; and routes of delivery; in turn, result in differences in absorption into the body. Tobacco smoke, for instance, contains over five thousand known chemical compounds, including highly volatile gaseous and vapor components and larger smoke particles (tar). There are at least fifty carcinogens released when a cigarette is smoked, including benzene, formaldehyde, and hydrogen cyanide. Some compounds increase the addictive properties of smoking, alter behavioral patterns, or produce additional effects in the brain and central nervous system (CNS).

The key substance found in tobacco is nicotine, a liquid alkaloid first isolated in 1828 by German chemists Wilhelm Heinrich Posselt and Ludwig Reimann. Nicotine makes up about 0.6 to three percent of dry weight of tobacco. It readily diffuses through the skin, lungs, and mucous membranes (such as the lining of the nose or gums), with the amount absorbed dependent on the type of tobacco leaf, method of use, and specific product. For example, cigarettes contain eight to twenty milligrams of nicotine, of which around one milligram is absorbed when smoked. Smokeless tobacco products (snuff and chewing tobacco) deliver three to four times the amount of nicotine delivered by a cigarette, which is absorbed more slowly but remains in the bloodstream longer.

The most common and expedient way to get nicotine into the bloodstream is through inhalation. Alveoli (tiny air sacs in the lungs where gas exchange occurs) provide an enormous surface area for access by nicotine. Once in the bloodstream, nicotine travels to the brain, taking an average of seven seconds. The nicotine then acts upon two nicotinic acetylcholine receptors in the brain—a ganglion type nicotinic receptor and a CNS type nicotinic receptor—increasing their activity. By binding to ganglion type nicotinic receptors, the adrenal medulla increases the flow of adrenaline (epinephrine), a stimulating hormone. This, in turn, causes an increase in heart rate, blood pressure, and respiration, as well as higher blood glucose levels. By binding to CNS type nicotinic receptors, dopamine levels in the reward circuits of the brain are increased, generating feelings of pleasure similar to that caused by cocaine and other stimulants. Other chemical messengers released by nicotine are acetylcholine, norepinephrine, vasopressin, arginine, and endorphins (small proteins that are often called the body's natural painkiller).

For the user, the amount of specific chemical messengers released, and the resultant feelings they induce, depend on the level of nicotine in the bloodstream. If a smoker takes short quick puffs on a cigarette, this will produce a low level of blood nicotine. Low doses enhance the actions of norepinephrine and dopamine in the brain, causing a stimulating effect that increases alertness and concentration. In contrast, deep puffs produce a high level of blood nicotine that enhances the effect of serotonin and opiate activity. This leads to an increase of acetylcholine and beta-endorphin, and a depression of the passage of nerve impulses. The result is a mild sedative effect, decreasing anxiety and producing a calming, even painkilling effect. Nicotine is thus unique in comparison to most drugs because its profile can change from stimulant to sedative/painkiller depending on dosage and use.

Nicotine has a half-life of one to two hours. The user must therefore self-dose with nicotine again to sustain its pharmacological effects. This repeated use is prompted by two further factors. First, tolerance develops over time so that users must absorb more nicotine to achieve the same effect, which explains how users can rapidly move to using increasing amounts of tobacco. Second, tobacco use leads to strong dependence or addiction. The pharmacological and behavioral characteristics that determine tobacco addiction are similar to those that determine addiction to such drugs as heroin and cocaine. While using nicotine-containing products, the body adapts the way it works to compensate for the effects of the nicotine. For example, neurons in the brain might increase or decrease the number of receptors or the amount of different neurotransmitters affected by the presence of nicotine. When there is no longer nicotine in the body, these physiological adaptations remain. The net result is that the body cannot function the same way in the absence of the drug as it did before, at least in the short term. Withdrawal symptoms include irritability, anxiety, depression and, above all, craving for nicotine. It is for this reason that, of the millions of people who try to stop smoking annually, only 10 percent succeed. In about a month, these feelings subside as physiological and psychological re-adaptation occurs.

SPREAD OF TOBACCO CULTIVATION

Tobacco was first cultivated by the peoples of the pre-Columbian Americas, with large-scale cultivation beginning in the sixteenth century. In 1527 the first tobacco plantation was established in Haiti by the Spanish. In 1612 John Rolfe raised the first commercial crop of wild tobacco (*Nicotiana rustica*) in the English colony of Jamestown, Virginia, founded by Sir Walter Raleigh, for export to England. Growers soon switched to common tobacco

(*Nicotiana tabacum*), a milder variety with rapidly growing demand in Europe. Within seven years, tobacco became the most valuable cash crop of the day, without which the American colonies would have failed. As tobacco farming expanded throughout the colonies, growers brought British prisoners, debtors, and eventually African slaves to work on the plantations.

In 1492 the South American Arawak tribe gave Christopher Columbus dried tobacco leaves, which he took back to Europe along with seeds. It was not until the mid-sixteenth century, however, that tobacco became popularized in Europe by sailors, explorers, and diplomats, such as Sir Frances Drake, Jean Nicot (after whom nicotine is named), and Francisco Hernández de Toledo. By the 1600s, tobacco cultivation in Europe began to be established. Sir Walter Raleigh is attributed with establishing one of the first tobacco farms in England.

Tobacco was first introduced to the Middle East by the Turks who took it to Egypt in the early 1500s. It was introduced to China in the late 1500s via Japan and the Philippines, and in 1560 Portuguese and Spanish ships brought tobacco to East Africa where it then spread to Central and West Africa. Tobacco exports from South America to South Asia via Europe, through the British East India Trading Company and Dutch East Indies Company, commenced in the eighteenth century. This early trade arrived in eastern Mediterranean ports and was taken overland along the great Silk Road to Persia, Mughal, and China. The Portuguese colony of Goa was also supplied by sea. Under the Raj (1700–1800), widespread use of tobacco was established in South Asia, fuelled by an export drive by British merchants connected to the Virginian tobacco farmers. Initially smoked in pipes and hookahs, tobacco gradually became indigenized, mixed with local spices and additives to produce such products as *gutka*. During the U.S. Revolutionary War in 1776, problems with supply led to large-scale tobacco farming in Africa and Asia by the 1800s. The glut in world production that resulted led to a decline in prices, making the hitherto luxury product more affordable, and thus fueling even greater demand.

In the early twenty-first century, tobacco was the world's most widely cultivated non-food crop, cultivated in about 120 countries of diverse climates. It is favored by farmers because of its performance under widely varying climatic and soil conditions. The largest producers of tobacco leaf as of 2008 were China, the United States, India, Brazil, Turkey, Malawi, and Zimbabwe.

TECHNOLOGICAL DEVELOPMENTS IN THE PRODUCTION OF TOBACCO PRODUCTS

As tobacco has become a valuable commercial crop, techniques for growing and curing the leaf developed in sophistication. Different varieties of leaf are grown, varying in the growing conditions needed, taste (due to level of dextrose), and burning properties. Among the most popular are Virginia, Burley, and various Oriental tobaccos, with most products blending different leaf varieties. Once harvested, tobacco leaf is subject to various methods of processing. The most important is curing, which enhances the flavor of tobacco and increases its preservation by reducing the moisture level of the leaf. Initially leaf was naturally cured in the sun or by air, but artificial methods using fires or flues were used for larger-scale production. In 1839 it was discovered that flue-curing turns leaf grown on infertile sandy soil a bright yellow and orange color, thus establishing the lucrative *brightleaf* industry. Over time, various fuels to cure tobacco came to be used, including coal, oil, gas, and wood. There has been an ongoing search for more cost-effective and energy-efficient uses of oil and gas, alongside improvements in barn and furnace design, to reduce fuel requirements. In the early 2000s, many countries bulk-cure their tobacco in barns constructed out of metal that guarantee better pane insulation, more precise atmospheric control, reduced labor requirements, and more efficient energy use.

There are many ways that tobacco can be consumed. Smokeless tobacco products can be sniffed through the nose (powdered snuff), chewed, or dipped (placed between the cheek and gum). In Europe, snuff remained the most popular way of consuming tobacco until the nineteenth century. Chewing tobacco was also popular; in the United States, it was associated with cowboys from the nineteenth century, and in many parts of Asia, as part of everyday social life for men and women.

Smoking tobacco has been the main method of consumption since the late nineteenth century.

Pipes were first used by North American Indians for medicinal and ceremonial purposes, and clay pipes became fashionable in Europe from the sixteenth century among both men and women. In East Asia, pipes were made of bamboo and sometimes ivory, whereas throughout the Ottoman Empire, men smoked waterpipes (also known as narghile, hookah, and shisha). The discovery of *meerschaum* (a soft white mineral) in the eighteenth century led to the production of fine quality carved pipes. For common use, wooden pipes progressively replaced fragile clay pipes, with briar burl becoming the material of choice.

The first cigars (from the Mayan word for smoking) originated in Cuba, which still produces the most sought-after cigars. Imported to Europe and the United States in the eighteenth century, cigars became popular among the wealthier classes. By the nineteenth century, smoking rooms began to be introduced on trains, and in private clubs and hotels, and the smoking jacket became fashionable. During the twentieth century, cigarillos (mini cigars) became a fast growing segment of the tobacco market, especially among cigarette smokers seeking to reduce the amount smoked, and by cigar smokers wanting to reduce costs.

The most common way of consuming tobacco since the late nineteenth century has been the cigarette. While early forms of cigarettes are believed to date from Central America in the ninth century, the rolling or stuffing of paper-wrapped cylinders with cured and finely cut tobacco leaves is attributed to Ottoman Turks around the 1830s. In 1843 the French tobacco monopoly began to manufacture cigarettes. In 1847 Philip Morris opened a shop in London selling hand-rolled Turkish cigarettes, switching to making his own in 1854. Because the process of hand rolling was slow (four cigarettes per minute) and labor intensive, cigarettes remained relatively expensive. The invention of the cigarette rolling machine in 1880 by James Bonsack, which could produce 12,000 cigarettes an hour, opened the way for mass production and consumption. James Buchanan Duke, later the first chairman of British American Tobacco (BAT), licensed the machine and by the late 1880s, the Duke Company was producing four million cigarettes per day. Alongside increased production, manufacturers developed new blends of tobacco leaf and other ingredients, which gave specific brands a distinct flavor. One key ingredient was reconstituted tobacco which, given additives to make nicotine more volatile when burned, also made cigarettes more addictive.

In 2007, cigarette companies worldwide produced around 5.5 trillion cigarettes, representing around 96 percent of the world tobacco market. The top five consuming countries are China (1,643 billion), United States (451 billion), Japan (328 billion), Russia (258 billion) and Indonesia (215 billion). While the global cigarette market continues to grow, awareness of the harmful health effects of smoking has led to efforts to develop products of varying effect that seek to reduce harm, including the introduction of filters, lowering tar levels, nicotine replacement therapy (NRT), and smokeless products.

OPPOSITION TO TOBACCO USE AND ITS CHANGING RATIONALE

Efforts to control tobacco use largely date from the seventeenth century and initially focused on immorality and economic protectionism. Catholic and other spiritual leaders denounced the increasingly popular practice, some banning it from religious venues. King James I published *A Counterblaste to Tobacco* in 1604, introduced a 4,000 percent tobacco import tax to stem debauchery, and made imports a royal monopoly in 1614. In 1612 the Chinese emperor Kangxi passed an edict forbidding the planting and use of tobacco. Prohibition was introduced in Japan around 1620, and in Russia under the Romanoffs between 1613 and 1689. In 1683 Massachusetts and Pennsylvania forbid the smoking of tobacco outdoors for fear of fire. Various penalties were introduced, ranging from excommunication to execution.

The rapid growth in tobacco's popularity, and the lucrative profits generated, led to the repeal of most restrictions until the early twentieth century. In many countries, governments sought to exert monopoly control over production and trade, while the medical professions even claimed tobacco offered health benefits. *The Lancet*, for instance, stated that smoking cigarettes in moderation could help sufferers of tuberculosis. There remained limited opposition to tobacco use until the late 1800s when antismoking organizations began to form in

Europe and the United States to encourage moderate use among adults. These organizations failed to attract mass support until the early 1900s when attention switched to smoking among children as a detriment to their physical fitness and morality. Legislation prohibiting the sale of tobacco products to children was first adopted at this time.

Health-based concerns about tobacco began to influence broader regulation from the 1930s onward. Statisticians for insurance companies began to link smoking to cancer and reduced life expectancy. German scientists, as part of the Third Reich's so-called Gesundheitspflicht (duty to be healthy) campaign, were among the first to link tobacco to lung cancer. By the end of the Second World War, alarming increases in morbidity and mortality from lung cancer brought more scientific and medical evidence to the fore. The work of Argentinian Angel Honorio Roffo showed that cancer all along the "smoking highway" (lips, tongue, throat, cheek, bronchial passages) was caused by exposure to tars released in the course of smoking (Proctor, 2006, p. 494). In Britain, Richard Doll and Austin Bradford Hill published their seminal paper in 1950 linking smoking to carcinoma of the lung. Ernst Wynder and E. A. Graham reported similar findings in the United States the same year. Over the next ten years, rapidly accumulating evidence of harmful health effects led to the publication of *Smoking and Health* by the Royal College of Physicians in 1962, and the *Report of the U.S. Surgeon General* in 1964.

By the 1980s, accumulated medical and scientific evidence showed smoking to be a known or probable cause of around twenty-five diseases, including various cancers, heart disease, and emphysema. Policy measures aimed at reducing demand by tobacco users, such as higher taxation, health warnings, and education, were widely introduced in established markets such as the United States and Europe. The health risks to nonsmokers (notably children, spouses, and coworkers) from secondhand smoke prompted measures to ban smoking in public places from the early 1990s. Other measures to regulate tobacco use included restrictions on marketing, advertising, and promotion; product design; and ingredients disclosure.

Throughout the second half of the twentieth century, public health advocates decried the pace and strength of regulation, weakened by the economic importance and political influence of the tobacco industry. The release of internal documents of the tobacco industry in the late 1990s revealed a well-organized and resourced campaign by the industry to undermine tobacco control efforts. The strategy included the funding of scientists to generate contrary evidence, lobbying of policy makers, and mobilizing of diverse allies to argue for the protection of civil liberties. The exposure of these tactics, along with data by the World Health Organization (WHO) attributing five million deaths annually to tobacco worldwide, led to growing support for stronger supply-side measures to control tobacco use. The adoption of the WHO Framework Convention on Tobacco Control (FCTC) in 2005 signalled recognition of the need for collective efforts across countries to strengthen both supply and demand side measures.

NEW SCIENTIFIC DEVELOPMENTS AND THE CONCEPT OF ADDICTION

In 1527 Archbishop Bartolomé de Las Casas Cuzco of Spain is believed to be the first to write about tobacco's adverse effect on the brain, notably the inability of American Indians to stop smoking. However, nicotine addiction or dependence is a relatively recent concept whose definition has evolved over time. Prior to the 1920s, addiction was seen largely as a type of excessiveness, attributable by some to moral vice. From the late 1920s, research sought to find psychological correlates with the withdrawal of narcotic drugs, such as morphine, after prolonged use. This approach remained popular into the early 2000s, with addiction conceptualized as an uncontrollable disease and applied to the use of other substances, notably alcohol. A popular view of addiction in the 1960s, based on an assumption of physiological dependence by the user, refers to a state in which an individual needs to continue to take a drug in order to stave off unpleasant or dangerous withdrawal effects. The main shortcoming of this approach is that this motive plays a relatively modest role in the apparently unreasonable continued use of a drug. While many addicts experience withdrawal discomfort, this is only one aspect of a wider problem. Indeed, individuals attempting to stop using drugs, including nicotine, continue to relapse at a high rate long after withdrawal symptoms have resolved and controlling such symptoms may be insufficient to prevent relapse. Another outmoded definition of addiction is inclusion of the concept of *intoxication*. This view holds that addictive drugs

lead to changes in users' psychological state, leaving some degree of impairment.

Since the late 1980s, generic criteria for defining substance dependence, such as those developed by the American Psychiatric Association and the WHO, focused on difficulties in controlling the use of the drug, of giving priority to drug use over other important obligations, to continued use of the drug in the knowledge of harmful consequences, and tolerance to the effects of the drug. While the criteria apply generically to substance abuse, they are seen as a suitable framework for determining the addictive or dependent nature of nicotine and smoking. On the basis of these criteria, the UK Royal College of Physicians concludes that "nicotine delivered through tobacco smoke should be regarded as an addictive drug, and tobacco use as the means of nicotine self-administration" (2000, p. 85). Nicotine replacement therapies have come to be accepted as part of the support needed by tobacco users seeking to stop.

See also **Advertising and Tobacco Use; Britain: Tobacco Use and Policy.**

BIBLIOGRAPHY

Ferrence, R., Slade, J., Room, R. & Pope, M. (Eds.) (2000). *Nicotine and public health.* Washington, DC: American Public Health Association.

Gilman, S. L., & Zhou X. (Eds.). (2004). *Smoke: A global history of smoking.* London: Reaktion Books.

Goodman, J., Norton, M., & Parascandola M., (2005). *Tobacco in history and culture: An encyclopedia.* Farmington Hills, MI: Charles Scribner's Sons.

Kluger, R. (1996). *Ashes to ashes.* New York: Vintage Books.

Peele, S. (1990). Addiction as a cultural concept. *Annals of the New York Academy of Sciences, 602,* 206–220.

Proctor, R. N. (2006). Angel H. Roffo: The forgotten father of experimental tobacco carcinogenesis. *Bulletin of the World Health Organization, 84*(6), 494–496.

Royal College of Physicians. (2000). *Nicotine addiction in Britain.* London: Tobacco Advisory Group.

World Health Organization. (1964). Nomenclature and classification of drug- and alcohol-related problems: A WHO memorandum. *Bulletin of the World Health Organization, 90,* 225–242.

KELLEY LEE

TOBACCO INDUSTRY

The tobacco industry is made up of the complex of primary suppliers, manufacturers, distributors (both wholesale and retail), advertising agencies, and media outlets that produce, promote, and sell tobacco products. It also includes the law, public relations, and lobbying firms that work to protect these products from stringent public-health regulation and control.

The industry evolved in the late nineteenth and early twentieth century from many relatively small enterprises that produced tobacco products for puffing, snuffing, and chewing. The products of these small firms delivered nicotine to the nasal and oral mucosa. With the evolution and refinement of the cigarette, the industry developed first into a monopoly and then into an oligopoly in which a handful of major producers made a more sophisticated nicotine delivery system: a device that delivers nicotine by inhalation to the lungs and thence rapidly to the brain. Although its popularity is declining in the United States, cigarette use is increasing worldwide at over 2 percent per year, especially in much of Asia, Eastern Europe, and the former Soviet Union. An integrated system of suppliers, manufacturers, marketers, and sales outlets is constantly evolving to supply this vast and growing market. In the past, sophisticated legal and lobbying enterprises managed to protect this industry from the sort of regulation advocated by a number of public health groups—regulations that governments routinely impose on far less toxic products—but an admonition from an internal source as to the effects of tobacco led to a dramatic increase of public and regulatory pressure on the tobacco industry.

PRIVATE ENTERPRISE VERSUS STATE MONOPOLY

Tobacco (nicotiana) is a plant of the nightshade family (genus *Nicotiana*) and is native to the Americas; it was a major commodity of commerce in colonial times. Cigar tobaccos were key exports from the Spanish and Portuguese colonies of the Caribbean and South America, while tobaccos for snuff, pipe, and chew were the economic mainstays of the English colonies in Virginia, Maryland, and the Carolinas. Whereas most of Europe (and the rest of the world) established state-run monopolies for tobacco distribution, private enterprise was the vehicle of tobacco commerce in Great Britain (and eventually in the United States). The state monopolies provided both a popular product for the populace and revenue

for the national treasury—but private enterprise, which always paid excise tax in Great Britain, was more resourceful in expanding the market. This phenomenon was exploited in the twentieth century and was especially apparent in the 1990s, with the remaining state monopolies becoming privatized and adopting the marketing techniques of the by-now enormous transnational tobacco companies, often actually merging with them.

FROM COTTAGE INDUSTRY TO MONOPOLY TO OLIGOPOLY

Relatively expensive, hand-rolled cigarettes became popular novelties in the United States and Europe in the mid-nineteenth century. The novelty came to dominate the industry over a period of forty years, from the mid-1880s to the mid-1920s, when, for the first time, more tobacco in the United States was used for cigarettes than for chewing tobacco.

A number of changes in the nineteenth century laid the groundwork for the cigarette's commercial success. The development of flue-cured tobacco and air-dried burley tobacco—easily processed into tobaccos for smoking (where the smoke might be inhaled) were major factors (Slade, 1993). Cigarette-making machines—first used commercially in 1883 by the American Tobacco Company—the development of safe matches, and an extensive railroad network to transport centrally manufactured cigarettes throughout the United States were among the other key factors responsible for this product's success.

Duke of Durham, North Carolina. These elements were successfully harnessed by Benjamin Newton (Buck) Duke, head of the American Tobacco Company. A working cigarette-making machine had been invented in 1881 by James Bonsack in response to a contest held by the cigarette maker Alan & Ginter of Richmond, Virginia (Smith, 1990). But the contest sponsors decided against using the invention since they did not know how to sell as many cigarettes as the machine was capable of making. Duke, however, realized that the low prices made possible by mass production, together with advertising to stimulate demand, would create a large enough market to absorb the vastly expanded production. He obtained favorable terms for using the machine in exchange for technical assistance in perfecting it. The machine Duke put on line in 1883 produced 120,000 cigarettes per day, the equivalent of 60 expert hand rollers. Duke's competitors had to pay more for Bonsack machines than he had, and Duke engaged in price wars to further weaken other manufacturers. Gradually, he bought out his competitors and monopolized the U.S. cigarette industry. By 1890, Duke controlled the cigarette market, and by 1910, just before his monopoly was broken, he controlled more than 80 percent of all tobacco products manufactured in the United States, except for cigars (Robert, 1952).

Seeking further growth, Duke began to expand his cigarette business overseas (Robert, 1952). By 1900, a third of the U.S. domestic production was being sent to Asia, and company factories were operating in Canada, Australia, Germany, and Japan. In 1901, Duke purchased a cigarette factory in Liverpool, England. Alarmed British manufacturers, seeking to avoid the fate of their U.S. compatriots, banded together as the Imperial Tobacco Company. The resulting trade war between American and Imperial ended in a truce. American was given exclusive trading rights in the United States and Cuba, and Great Britain became Imperial's exclusive territory. A new company, jointly controlled by both giants, was to sell cigarettes to the rest of the world. This modest sinecure was the birthright the parent companies gave the British-American Tobacco Company (BAT).

Antitrust Litigation. In 1907, the U.S. government filed an antitrust case against the American Tobacco Company. The result of this litigation was the dissolution of the trust four years later into a number of successor companies, some of which retain major roles in the U.S. cigarette market. These companies were the American Tobacco Company, the R. J. Reynolds Tobacco Company, Liggett & Myers, and P. Lorillard.

Once it had emerged from the confines of the trust, R. J. Reynolds, which had never before made cigarettes, developed and introduced Camel, a novel brand, in 1913 (Tilley, 1985). Camel was the first brand to combine air-dried burley, which had previously been important in chewing-tobacco products, with the then-conventional cigarette tobaccos—the flue-cured and Turkish (Oriental) varieties (Slade, 1993). Camel featured a coherent, national advertising campaign from N. W. Ayer that relied entirely on mass-media outlets in magazines and

on billboards instead of on package-based promotions such as cigarette cards, coupons, and premiums. The legacy of this startling departure from the conventional cigarette-marketing techniques of the time is captured by the sly legend that still graces each pack of twenty unfiltered Camels sold in the United States: "Don't look for premiums or coupons, as the cost of the tobaccos blended in CAMEL Cigarettes prohibits the use of them."

The other factor that distinguished Camel from its competitors was its price. While the leading brands of the time, such as Fatima, sold for fifteen cents per pack of twenty, a pack of Camel sold for a dime. In short order, Camel overwhelmed the competition and ushered in a dramatic expansion of the domestic cigarette market. American Tobacco copied the Camel formula with Lucky Strike, and Liggett & Myers followed with its copycat product Chesterfield. Cigarette cards, premiums, and coupons were abandoned in favor of the mass media, and prices fell. Cigarette use, then only rising slowly, began an unprecedented increase. This growth continued virtually unabated for forty years or so, until it finally slowed and eventually reversed by alarms that lung cancer and other major diseases could be caused by cigarettes (Fiore et al., 1993).

Only two firms that had no roots in the tobacco trust have played major roles in the U.S. cigarette market (Sobel, 1978). After Buck Duke's death in 1929, BAT purchased the Brown & Williamson Tobacco Company in Louisville, Kentucky. BAT gradually built this company into a major cigarette producer. For decades, its Kool brand dominated the menthol category, and during the 1930s and 1940s, its Wings brand gained market share by undercutting the prices of the majors. Brown & Williamson continues to offer a full range of cigarettes for the U.S. market in the early 2000s. It also produces cigarettes for export to many of BAT's international markets.

The other upstart company was Philip Morris, which began its U.S. operations as a specialty cigarette maker in New York in the first quarter of the twentieth century. In addition to its standard brand called Philip Morris, it produced Marlboro—a cigarette for "ladies." The company expanded in the 1930s with a low-priced brand (Paul Jones) and a clever pricing scheme for Philip Morris English Blend (Robert, 1952; Sobel, 1978). It suggested a retail price for the latter slightly above that for the major brands, but it gave retailers a larger margin, thus encouraging prominent display of the brand in stores. In the mid-1950s, Philip Morris gave Marlboro a filter and had the Leo Burnett advertising agency remake its image entirely to one of rugged masculine outdoor daring on horseback. (The entire sweep of Marlboro advertising is included in the special advertising collection of the American Museum of National History in Washington, D.C.) By the mid-1970s, Marlboro was the leading U.S. cigarette and by the 1990s, thanks to the strength of Marlboro's appeal to teens and young adults, Philip Morris overtook R. J. Reynolds to become the nation's largest tobacco-product manufacturer.

Smokeless Tobacco. Moist snuff and chewing tobacco enjoyed a 1980s and 1990s resurgence in popularity—this is based on the successful efforts of U.S. Tobacco (UST). It sells oral tobacco (e.g., Skoal Bandits, Skoal, Copenhagen) to adolescents and preadolescents (Denny, 1993). Oral tobacco is the only category of tobacco product whose consumption increased in the 1990s and early 2000s in the United States. This increase is attributable to UST's innovative marketing of moist snuff to adolescent boys and to imitation products from other manufacturers. Although UST envisions a global market for snuff, the World Health Organization has declared that countries in which oral tobacco is not a traditional product should ban it. A number of countries—including Australia, New Zealand, Hong Kong, and the European Community—have taken this step, often defying intense pressure from the U.S. government when doing so.

INNOVATION

The tobacco industry adapts to changing circumstances in many ways. Product innovation is a key strategy. Since the early 1950s, the major changes in cigarette design have come in response to public-health concerns that cigarettes constitute a leading cause of illness and death (McGinnis, 1993; Slade, 1993). Most of these innovations have been variations on filters and so-called low-tar designs. Ballyhooed with multibillion-dollar advertising budgets, these innovations propped up cigarette consumption over the years despite the complete absence of demonstrated benefit at the time they were introduced. Years of study (and as many years

of unregulated sale) have only produced evidence for decidedly marginal benefits, yet the innovations have become firmly established. These supposed advances have been criticized by some as being nothing more than public relations gimmicks in the face of and in mocking response to profound public-health problems.

The cigarette companies continue in the early twenty-first century to invent novel ways to deliver nicotine to the brain. Electronic devices, smokes with charcoal fuel elements, and tiny aerosol cans are but some of the gimmicks the companies have patented to facilitate the inhalation of nicotine. Despite these efforts, the industry remains dependent on smoking, with variations of the tobacco-filled cigarette the mainstay of its business for the foreseeable future.

INTERNATIONAL EXPANSION

Cigarette smoking has been declining in the United States, Canada, and Western Europe. Since the 1960s, however, the biggest cigarette manufacturers (BAT, Philip Morris, RJR/Nabisco, and, later, Japan Tobacco Incorporated) have steadily increased their business in international markets (Taylor, 1984). This expansion has been accompanied by the weakening and dissolution of both national private and state-owned tobacco companies. The process got under way in Latin America in the 1960s, spread to eastern Asia in the late 1980s, and developed into a frenzy of deal making in Eastern Europe and the republics of the former Soviet Union in the early 1990s (Shepherd, 1985; Sesser, 1993).

Shepherd has described the process whereby a transnational corporation moves toward dominating a formerly self-contained market through product innovation, smuggling, aggressive advertising, and pricing policies. The result is a larger market for tobacco products than existed previously and a corporate management that is better able to oppose public-health efforts at regulation and control. Although cigarette consumption is down in the United States, Canada, and Western Europe, it is rapidly growing in most of the world—especially the so-called third world. The transnational companies have positioned themselves to both fuel and profit from this trend. In an effort to reduce the public health impact from global expansion, the

World Health Organization created the Framework Convention on Tobacco Control in 2007, giving support from wealthier nations to those in mid-low income nations to fight against tobacco company marketing efforts.

DIVERSIFICATION

The giant cigarette makers have invested their tobacco profits in other enterprises for more than twenty years, ranging from soft drinks and cookies to office products, insurance, and real estate. This process has resulted in the ownership by tobacco companies of some widely known consumer-product companies, including Kraft and Nabisco. Although the parent tobacco companies pretend that this phenomenon makes them somehow less involved in tobacco (none now has the word "tobacco" in its corporate name), a thoughtful examination of these businesses reveals the following:

- Tobacco products remain by far the most profitable sector of each of these conglomerates; and tobacco products are always responsible for most of the company profits.

- Not one of these companies has backed away from any available opportunity to sell tobacco products. Indeed, the strongest companies continue to invest in domestic and overseas ventures that have as their goal the expansion of tobacco consumption.

- These companies make ready use of nontobacco subsidiaries to support their tobacco businesses. For example, RJR/Nabisco fired the ad agency that did their Oreo Cookie advertising after that agency also produced ads promoting an airline offering smoke-free flights. Philip Morris has used one of its Kraft-General Foods warehouses for its coupon-redemption program for the Marlboro Adventure Team.

Tobacco companies do not diversify to get out of the tobacco business. They diversify because tobacco has given them profits, the acquisitions seem to be sound investments, and the resulting product mix complements the core business in some manner.

PRICE WARS

Price competition has long been part of the tobacco industry strategy. It was the major tool for the achievement of monopoly power in the 1880s and was a key element in the early twentieth-century dominance of the market by Camel. In the 1930s, price competition, made possible by overly aggressive price increases by the majors, contributed to the emergence and growth of Brown & Williamson and Philip Morris (Sobel, 1978). From the end of World War II (1945) until 1980, however, price competition was virtually absent from the U.S. cigarette market.

In 1980, tiny Liggett & Myers, a firm that had become too small to enjoy oligopolistic profits, broke ranks with its fellows by introducing generic cigarettes. The strategy was made possible by the pattern of price increases in the industry—increases that had exceeded the rate of inflation for years. Brown & Williamson soon followed suit with its own generic brands, and within a few years every cigarette manufacturer had a multitiered pricing structure, with the heavily advertised, standard brands at the top. Prices for the major brands continued to rise steeply, far faster than inflation, through early 1993. Customers who might have stopped smoking because of high prices were kept in the market by the increasingly available lower priced offerings. By early 1993, however, investment analysts had become concerned because lower priced brands accounted for more than 25 percent of all cigarette purchases—with attendant threats to profits—and Philip Morris had become alarmed by the market share losses sustained by its cash cow, Marlboro, to less than 25 percent of all cigarettes sold.

Philip Morris had a number of key strengths that gave it a flexibility not possessed by its competitors, including market leadership, an absence of corporate debt, and a strong youth market for Marlboro. Its principal competitor, RJR/Nabisco, had an enormous corporate debt—and although Camel had been making inroads into Marlboro's youth market, it was still far from the dominant cigarette. These factors led Philip Morris to cut prices substantially (while mounting the most elaborate promotional campaign ever seen in the industry). The competition was forced to follow suit with lower prices. Marlboro's brand share surged; the threat to profitability from lower priced brands subsided; and the competition was left somewhat weakened.

LOBBYING AND PUBLIC RELATIONS

In 1915, the U.S. tobacco industry formed the Tobacco Merchants Association (TMA) to lobby against the anticigarette laws that had become a problem for the industry in a number of states (Robert, 1952). These laws came about as a result of the efforts of antitobacco advocates, including Henry Ford and Thomas Edison. The TMA accomplished its objectives: By 1930, the state prohibitions on cigarettes had been diminished to easily ignored prohibitions that only barred the sale of cigarettes to minors.

In the 1950s, the industry faced a more substantial challenge—proof that cigarettes caused lung cancer. In addition to putting cosmetic filters on the product and making outrageous claims for their benefit (P. Lorillard trumpeted its asbestos-filtered Kent as "the greatest health protection in cigarette history"), the industry developed a sophisticated public relations and lobbying capability (Wagner, 1971). The public relations firm of Hill & Knowlton organized the Tobacco Institute to meet the industry's public relations and lobbying needs. The cigarette makers also formed the Tobacco Industry Research Committee (later reorganized and renamed the Council for Tobacco Research) to create the pretense that the industry was conscientiously involved in biomedical research to get to the bottom of the smoking and health question (Freedman & Cohen, 1993).

Although speculation existed as to how diligently the tobacco industry would pursue smoking research, they did in fact do so, but their conclusions, giving more light to the fact that tobacco is addictive and harmful, were not released. Routinely called the *tobacco cover-up* it resurfaced in later years with much of its strength coming from Bennett S. LeBow's agreeing, in 1997, to put warnings on cigarette packs stating that smoking is addictive. Leaked internal documents also served as evidence of the dangers. In 1998, however, other tobacco companies still contested that tobacco was not an addictive drug. Discovery, through LeBow, of the industry's nondisclosure and the understanding that the industry had evidence of the threat of smoking, however, caused severe public attacks on the tobacco industry to be more common. Public campaigns have also been more potent with reducing youth smoking. Between 1998 and 2000 smoking had declined 54 percent in middle schools and 25.2 percent in high schools. Then, too, tobacco advertising legislation has weakened the strength of tobacco propaganda

Company	Home office	Major brands
Cigarettes		
Phillip Morris (Altria)	Richmond, VA	Marlboro
		Basic
		Benson & Hedges
		Merit
		Virginia Slims
RJ Reynolds (Nabisco)	Winston-Salem, NC	Camel
		Kool
		Pall Mall
		Winston
		Salem
		Doral
		Natural American Spirit
Lorrillard (Loew's Corp)	Greensboro, NC	Kent
		Newport
Moist snuff		
UST	Stamford, CT	Copenhagen
		Skoal Bandits
		Skoal Classic

Table 1. Leading U.S. tobacco companies. Major tobacco-product manufacturers in the United States, the location of their corporate headquarters, and the major tobacco brands they market. ILLUSTRATION BY GGS INFORMATION SERVICES. GALE, CENGAGE LEARNING

among youth populations by banning all advertising that is determined to be too appealing to a minor.

As of 2008 more legislation was being proposed and being worked on to make nicotine a drug regulated by the FDA. Previously, the FDA has tried to apply regulations to tobacco and cigarettes as a nicotine delivery agent, but the courts had determined that Congress had not yet given the regulatory administration such authority, so new legislation must be passed for successful and lawful regulation. If such a bill is passed tighter control will be possible so that tobacco can be prohibited at public events where minors may be part of the targeted demographic, in response to public outcry. Furthermore, tobacco companies are prohibited from sponsoring public events and athletic competitions. In some states, legislation has also already been passed, and tried, winning large cash settlements to recover lost health costs suspected to be tobacco-use related. Included in some of these settlements have also been requirements for the tobacco companies to pay for more advertisements intended to reduce youth smoking. Despite the research, such as it was, the mounting costs to the tobacco companies because of law suits and penalties, and in the face of growing evidence of harm from a variety of other quarters, the smoking epidemic continues into the early twenty-first century.

The Tobacco Institute, in alliance with the various branches of the industry, stood as a bulwark against public-health activities for a generation. After the Master Settlement Agreement in 1998, the Tobacco Institute was reduced to a Web site of searchable documents directly related to tobacco industry lawsuits. The Council for Tobacco Research has funded studies of marginal importance for public relations gain while operating a Special Projects branch for the benefit of tobacco-product liability defense. In these and other ways, the tobacco industry has attempted to insulate itself from significant regulation and from acceptance of any responsibility for the harm its products cause. Similar organizations exist to protect the interests of oral-tobacco manufacturers.

OWNERSHIP

The major tobacco-product manufacturers are publicly owned and traded corporations. As such, they are owned by their investors. Major institutions, including banks, insurance companies, and pension funds, hold the majority of shares in the tobacco industry.

The tobacco industry is a powerful oligopoly of product manufacturers in alliance with a network of suppliers and associated service organizations. Although its products form the leading cause of preventable death, it continues despite public sentiment and attempts to protect itself against appropriate regulation by extensive legal, public relations, and lobbying efforts. The industry is understandably driven by an interest in making money. It has never acted out of a primary concern for the health of its customers or the health of those around them. For a variety of reasons, including clever intervention by the industry, government has utterly failed to provide the sort of regulatory control expected when it comes to something as addicting and toxic as nicotine-containing tobacco products until a critical documentation leak occurred from within the companies of the tobacco industry.

See also **Advertising and Tobacco Use; Nicotine.**

BIBLIOGRAPHY

Brooks, J. E. (1949). The mighty leaf. New York: Little, Brown.

Cannon, A. (1997). Liggett owner settles lawsuits by agreeing to warn smokers that tobacco is addictive. *Knight-Ridder/Tribune News Service.* Available from www.highbeam.com/doc/1G1-19227292.html.

Conference of State Legislatures. (1996, March 1). States try to recoup health costs of smoking. Available from http://www.thefreelibrary.com/.

Denny, J. (1993). The king of snuff. *Common Cause Magazine, 19*(2), 20–27.

Federal Trade Commision. (2007). *Federal Trade Commission Cigarette Report for 2004 and 2005.* Available from http://www.ftc.gov/.

Fiore, M. C., Newcombe, P., & Mcbride, P. (1993). Natural history and epidemiology of tobacco use and addiction. In C. T. Orleans & J. Slade (Eds.), Nicotine addiction: Principles and management (pp. 89–104). New York: Oxford University Press.

Freedman, A. M., & Cohen, L. P. (1993, February 11). How cigarette makers keep health question "open" year after year. *Wall Street Journal,* p. A1.

Ganske, G. (2000, April 5). The Nation's Number One Health Problem. Congressional Record (pp. H1847–H1849). Available from http://www.access.gpo.gov, DOCID:CR05AP00-89.

Mcginnis, J. M., & Foege, W. H. (1993). Actual causes of death in the United States. *Journal of the American Medical Association, 270*(18), 2207–2212.

Mishra, R. (1998, February 24). Tobacco CEOs refuse to be pinned down on whether tobacco is addictive. *Knight-Ridder/Tribune News Service.* Available from www.highbeam.com/doc/1G1-20324375.html.

Robert, J. C. (1952). *The story of tobacco in America.* New York: Alfred A. Knopf.

Sesser, S. (1993). Opium war redux. *New Yorker, 69*(29), 78–89.

Shepherd, P. L. (1985). Transnational corporations and the international cigarette industry. In R. S. Newfarmer (Ed.), *Profits, progress and poverty* (pp. 63–112). Notre Dame, IN: University of Notre Dame Press.

Slade, J. (1993). Nicotine delivery devices. In C. T. Orleans & J. Slade (Eds.), *Nicotine addiction: Principles and management* (pp. 3–21). New York: Oxford University Press.

Smith, J. W. (1990). *Smoke signals.* Richmond, VA: The Valentine Museum.

Sobel, R. (1978). *They satisfy.* Garden City, NY: Anchor Press/Doubleday.

Taylor, P. (1984). *The smoke ring: Tobacco, money, and multi-national politics.* New York: Pantheon.

Tilley, N. M. (1985). *The R. J. Reynolds Tobacco Company.* Chapel Hill: University of North Carolina Press.

Tobacco: The anti-smoking bandwagon rolls on. (2007, July 7). *Economist, 384*(8536), 60.

'Truth' puts dent in Florida teen smoking. (2000, March 6). Adweek. Available from http://www.adweek.com/

Wagner, S. (1971). *Cigarette country*. New York: Praeger.

Waxman, H. (2000, March 21) Congressional Record (PP. H1127). Available from http://www.access.gpo.gov, DOCID:CR21MR00-56.

JOHN SLADE
REVISED BY ANDREW J. HOMBURG (2001)
STEPHEN S. MICHAEL (2009)
RONALD R. WATSON (2009)

DEPENDENCE

As of 2006, there were about 45 million cigarette smokers in the United States, representing 21 percent of the adult population. Another 2 percent were cigar smokers, and 2 percent used smokeless tobacco (chewing tobacco or snuff) (*Morbidity and Mortality Weekly Report*, 2007). More than half of tobacco users are dependent on (addicted to) nicotine, an alkaloid that is the main psychoactive ingredient in tobacco. Most of them will have to try to quit several times before they are successful. Both the direct effects of nicotine on the body and behavioral associations with those effects learned over the years of tobacco use keep people smoking even when they want to quit.

The role of nicotine in tobacco use is complex. Nicotine acts on the body directly to produce effects such as pleasure, arousal, enhanced vigilance, relief of anxiety, reduced hunger, and body-weight reduction. Nicotine (whether in tobacco or nicotine-containing medications) can reverse the withdrawal symptoms that occur in a nicotine-dependent person trying to quit, when nicotine levels in the body fall. These symptoms include anxiety, irritability, difficulty concentrating, restlessness, hunger, depression, sleep disturbance, and craving for tobacco. Nicotine also acts indirectly, through a learning process that occurs when the direct effects of nicotine occur repeatedly in the presence of certain features of the environment. As a result of this learning process, called conditioning, formerly insignificant environmental factors become cues for the direct actions of nicotine. These factors can become pleasurable in themselves or they can serve as a triggering mechanism for lighting up a cigarette. For example, the taste, smell, and feel of tobacco often evoke a neutral response and sometimes repugnance in a nonsmoker. After years of experiencing the direct effects of nicotine in the presence of tobacco, however, a smoker finds the sensory aspects of tobacco pleasurable.

The indirect or conditioned effects of nicotine can be responsible for much more complicated learning than the learning associated with nicotine's direct effects. Conditioning is also the process whereby the situations in which people often smoke, such as after a meal, with a cup of coffee, with an alcoholic beverage, while doing a task at work, while talking on the telephone, or with friends who also smoke, become in themselves powerful cues for the urge to smoke. When people stop using tobacco, therefore, the direct effects of nicotine are not the only pleasures they must give up. They must also learn to forgo the indirect effects of nicotine: those experiences that, through learning, have become either pleasurable in themselves or a cue to smoke.

QUITTING

Many nicotine dependent smokers want to quit smoking; however, once dependence on nicotine or tobacco is established, cessation becomes difficult. The reasons for wanting to quit vary. The most common include (1) a concern for one's health, (2) a concern for the health of family members and others due to the harmful effects of secondhand smoke, (3) social pressure exemplified in laws by state or municipal governments prohibiting smoking in certain indoor locations (such as restaurants and bars) and outdoor environments (such as in areas within the vicinity of hospitals or schools); and (4) economic factors (cigarettes have become increasingly expensive).

Successful quitting of tobacco use usually occurs through a series of mental stages or steps (Prochaska & DiClemente, 1983): (1) *Precontemplation*: the smoker has no intention to stop smoking during this stage; (2) *Contemplation*: the person is thinking of quitting but not within the next six months; (3) *Action*: the smoker has a stop date and a plan that is or will be implemented within one month; (4) *Maintenance*: the person has discontinued the regular, daily use of tobacco for a minimum of one month. Most regular tobacco users go through these stages of change several times before they are successful. Although developed in relation to smoking cessation, these stages of change have been applied to the process of stopping other addictive behaviors.

RELAPSE

Relapse is a cardinal feature of substance dependencies, including nicotine dependence. To paraphrase Mark Twain: Quitting smoking is easy, I've done it a thousand times. Most quit attempts that are successful in the short-term are followed by a return to smoking or other tobacco use within a few weeks, sometimes days, of stopping. For example, 66 percent of smokers who try to quit on their own or with minimal outside help relapse within two days, 90 percent relapse within three months, and 95 to 97 percent relapse within one year of quitting. The key to successful smoking cessation is an understanding of the particular triggers that provoke relapse and the strategies that are effective in preventing relapse. Withdrawal symptoms, which can begin within hours of the last use of tobacco, are important triggers for cravings to smoke again. Emotional reactions to stress, such as depression and anxiety, and environmental cues that have acquired an association with smoking can also serve as powerful triggers of urges to smoke.

MANAGING URGES TO SMOKE

To avoid succumbing to urges to smoke, former tobacco users must develop ways of coping with and managing triggers for smoking. Shortly after quitting, when the strength of withdrawal symptoms and environmental cues is greatest, behavioral techniques such as the following are helpful: (1) removing ashtrays from one's home and office, (2) leaving the table as soon as possible after meals and engaging in other activities such as talking, walking, or doing the dishes; (3) avoiding (at least temporarily) situations that used to occur with smoking, such as drinking alcohol, coffee, or other beverages linked with smoking; (4) avoiding situations in which other smokers are likely to be around, and (5) actively seeking social support for smoking cessation. The encouragement of a spouse, family members, or friends who are nonsmokers or who are in the process of quitting, can make it easier to avoiding lighting up again. Smokers who enjoy having something in their mouths or handling cigarettes can substitute

something for these smoking-related tactile behaviors. They can chew gum, toothpicks, or sunflower seeds; munch low-calorie snacks; and snap, roll, or twist rubber bands on their wrist. What people think about while quitting is also an important factor for preventing relapse. Instead of thinking about the expected pleasures of a cigarette, the would-be quitter can substitute thoughts about the health hazards of smoking, the health benefits of not smoking, or the pleasures of an anticipated reward for not smoking.

These urges to smoke, or cravings, can re-occur long after the nicotine withdrawal period has ended, usually provoked by conditioned cues to smoking, frequently the onset of strong emotional events formerly managed by smoking. Applying the strategies learned during the weeks shortly after quitting can help the former smoker to overcome temptations to smoke that challenge one's ability to maintain abstinence in the long term.

INDEPENDENT QUITTING

Most efforts to quit occur without professional help. Persistence in avoiding a return to smoking is essential; most smokers try to quit several times before they are successful. Many aids are available to tobacco users who quit on their own. Smoking-cessation program guides and motivational and educational audiotapes and videotapes are obtainable from physicians, hospitals, or organizations such as the American Lung Association, the American Cancer Society, or the American Heart Association, or they may be found in bookstores and libraries.

ASSISTED QUITTING

Smoking-Cessation Programs. Resources for smokers who seek help for quitting are available in most communities in the United States. Smoking cessation clinics can be found in most hospitals and community health centers. Information regarding the location and availability of smoking cessation programs can be obtained from a nationally based telephone resource at 1-800-QUIT-NOW (1-800-784-8669).

Physician- and Clinic-Assisted Quitting. Physicians' offices and hospital clinics that offer smoking cessation assistance are particularly useful for people who have medical problems, for people who have tried before and failed to quit, or for people who may benefit from smoking cessation medications. Smokers can turn to these health-care facilities for advice on how to quit, for self-help material, for support and information about other cessation resources that could be more suited to their needs, and if necessary, prescriptions for medications to ease the difficulties of withdrawal and increase their chance of successfully quitting.

Pharmacotherapies for Tobacco Dependence.

Smokers who have tried to stop smoking on their own but failed are candidates for treatments with smoking cessation medications. First-line medications approved as cessation aids by the U.S. Food and Drug Administration (FDA) include the various nicotine replacement systems, such as nicotine chewing gum, nicotine patch, nicotine nasal spray, nicotine inhaler, and nicotine lozenge; and two non-nicotine medications, bupropion (Zyban) and varenicline (Chantix). Second-line medications, which are not FDA-approved for this indication, include nortriptyline and clonidine, and combination pharmacotherapy (United States Department of Health Human Services, 2008).

FIRST-LINE MEDICATIONS

The nicotine replacement therapies (NRT) when used as directed all approximately double the likelihood that a person will successfully quit smoking. NRT can reduce the severity of nicotine withdrawal. Research has suggested that prolonged use of these medications can extend the period of abstinence. Some tobacco users are concerned about the hazards of nicotine, but the hazards of NRT are much less than those associated with smoking. First, the amount of nicotine ingested through the replacement therapies is less than that taken in from cigarettes. Second, nicotine-replacement medications do not expose smokers to the other hazards of cigarette smoke, which include carbon monoxide, tar, cyanide, and a number of other toxic substances. On balance, using the nicotine replacement systems is much safer than smoking cigarettes. The nicotine-replacement medications are particularly useful with more seriously addicted smokers, but they are not a simple cure; rather, they should be used as part of a program of learning to live a tobacco-free lifestyle.

Nicotine Chewing Gum.

The chewing gum is available without a prescription and comes in strengths of 2 and 4 milligrams (mg), although the dose actually delivered to the chewer is 1 mg and 2 mg, respectively. The 4-mg formulation has greater utility for heavier smokers (those smoking more than twenty cigarettes daily). Nicotine is absorbed from the gum gradually over twenty to thirty minutes, in the course of which blood nicotine levels are similar to those seen after smoking a cigarette. The gum should be chewed intermittently, to allow time for the nicotine in the saliva to be absorbed. Nicotine gum should be chewed regularly throughout the day, and when urges to smoke are felt. For maximum benefit, nicotine gum should not be chewed within ten minutes of drinking any beverage because certain beverages such as coffee, fruit juice, or cola drinks reduce the absorption of nicotine. Most people need to chew eight to ten pieces per day to obtain optimal benefits, usually for three to six months, but fewer pieces can be used during the later period of nicotine gum use. Side effects from chewing nicotine gum may include fatigue and soreness of the jaw, loosening of dental fillings, and occasionally nausea, indigestion, gas, or hiccups, particularly if one has chewed the gum so rapidly as to swallow nicotine-rich saliva.

Nicotine Patches.

This formulation of nicotine treatment is also available as an over-the-counter medication. Patches deliver nicotine in its un-ionized (uncharged) chemical form, thereby allowing the drug to pass through the skin readily. Various patches deliver different doses and are applied to the skin once a day for periods that range from sixteen to twenty-four hours within the day. The higher dose patches (usually 21 mg) are used during the initial four weeks of quitting, and lower-dose patches (14 mg and 7 mg) are available for subsequent tapering. A single-dose nicotine patch (15 mg) used for sixteen hours during the day, which is recommended for eight weeks' use, is also available. Smokers who want to quit are instructed to first stop smoking and then to apply the patch daily, usually upon waking up. Side effects from nicotine patches may include itching or burning over the patch site, which usually subsides within an hour, and local redness and mild swelling. Some people experience a sense of stimulation, and occasionally, insomnia and vivid dreams. These effects tend to occur during the first few days of patch use but diminish with longer patch use. There was initial concern regarding the cardiovascular safety of smoking while using the patch, though this has not been borne out. Nicotine patch users who are unable to resist one or two cigarettes are much better off keeping the patch on, to prevent a full-blown return to smoking, rather than removing the patch.

Nicotine Lozenge. The nicotine lozenge, like the nicotine gum, is an oral form of nicotine replacement and is also available as an over-the-counter medication. The nicotine lozenge comes in the form of hard candy, and should be dissolved in the mouth rather than chewed or swallowed. Patients are advised to use one lozenge every one to two hours, or a minimum of nine lozenges per day for the first six weeks, then to reduce to one lozenge every two to four hours during the seventh to the ninth week, and one lozenge every four to eight hours for weeks ten to twelve. Use beyond twelve weeks is not recommended. Patients should not drink or eat immediately before using the lozenge or while it is in the mouth. The most common side effects from nicotine lozenge are nausea, hiccups, heartburn, coughing, and headache. More nicotine is delivered through the lozenge than the gum because the lozenge dissolves completely whereas a residual amount of nicotine is retained in the gum. A comparison of safety profiles showed similar tolerability of the nicotine lozenge and the nicotine chewing gum.

Nicotine Inhaler. The nicotine inhaler consists of a plastic tubelike mouthpiece into which is placed a cartridge containing a nicotine-impregnated plug. Nicotine vapor is produced when warm inhaled air passes through the plug and nicotine is delivered through the buccal mucosa. The inhaler produces a rate of nicotine delivery similar to the nicotine gum. Eating and drinking acidic beverages such as coffee and juice should be avoided fifteen minutes before or after use of the inhaler. Dose is related to temperature; low temperatures will inhibit the release of nicotine. Use of the inhaler for up to six months with gradual reduction in frequency during the last two months is recommended. Clinical trials of the nicotine inhaler have shown that it doubles quit rates obtained with placebo, similar to the effects observed with the other nicotine replacement systems. Side effects from the inhaler include mild irritation of the mouth and throat, coughing, and runny nose. The frequency and severity of these symptoms decline with continued use of the inhaler.

Nicotine Nasal Spray. The nicotine nasal spray was designed as a more rapid means of delivering nicotine to the smoker than the gum or the patch. The nasal spray consists of a small bottle containing a 10-mg/ml nicotine solution. A 50-milliliter spray containing 0.5 mg nicotine can be conveniently delivered using an accompanying manual pump. Each dose consists of two squirts, one to each nostril. This mechanism can deliver nicotine to the brain within ten minutes, providing the most rapid nicotine delivery among the currently available nicotine replacement delivery systems. Patients are advised to use one or two doses per hour and may increase as needed. The minimum treatment is eight doses per day, with a maximum limit of forty doses per day or five doses per hour. The recommended duration of therapy is three to six months. The nicotine nasal spray has some potential to produce dependence manifested either in increased frequency of use or in longer duration of use than recommended, associated with its greater rapidity in producing nicotine effects compared to the other forms of NRT. The side effects associated with the nasal spray are irritation of the nose and throat, sneezing, coughing, and teary eyes. These symptoms often occur during the first week of use but typically decline with continued use.

Bupropion. Bupropion sustained release (SR) is a non-nicotine medication that is available by prescription only. Bupropion was originally marketed as an antidepressant (Wellbutrin). On the strength of evidence from several placebo-controlled trials, the FDA approved the marketing of bupropion (SR), under the trade name Zyban, as a treatment aid for smoking cessation. The mechanism by which bupropion assists smokers is not clear but it is thought to be related to both noradrenergic and dopaminergic activity in the brain. Patients are advised to begin using bupropion at a dosage of 150 mg per day for three days, then to increase to 150 mg twice a day for one to two weeks prior to a selected quit date, with continued treatment for seven to twelve weeks following the quit date. Bupropion has been shown to reduce withdrawal symptoms and to reduce the weight gain usually associated with stopping smoking. The most common side effects reported by bupropion users have been insomnia and dry mouth. Bupropion is contraindicated in persons with a history of seizures, or of eating disorders, and those who have used a monoamine oxidase inhibitor in the past fourteen days. Recent research has suggested that extending bupropion use beyond eight to twelve weeks can increase the period of abstinence, although the risk of smoking again appears to return once the medication is no longer used (Covey et al., 2007).

Varenicline. Varenicline was approved by the FDA under the trade name Chantix as a treatment for nicotine dependence. The development of varenicline for smoking cessation was based on knowledge regarding the pharmacology of nicotine addiction, specifically the role of acetylcholine-receptor subtypes in the mediation of nicotine addiction. Through high affinity and high selectivity at the alpha4beta2 nicotinic acetylcholine receptor site, varenicline exerts agonist effects—reducing withdrawal symptoms, and antagonizing the effects of ingested nicotine—limiting the reward and pleasure associated with smoking. Industry-sponsored trials of varenicline, conducted among healthy smokers aged eighteen years or more who smoked at least ten cigarettes daily, showed that compared to placebo treatment, varenicline more than doubled the abstinence rate at the end of twelve weeks of treatment and at fifty-two weeks after the initial quit date (Lam & Patel, 2007). In addition, head-to-head trials showed higher abstinence rates at the end of twelve-week treatments and one year after quitting with varenicline compared to bupropion. A maintenance treatment trial showed that extending the treatment period by another twelve weeks modestly increased the abstinence rate, although the protective effect of varenicline seemed to abate upon discontinuing its use. The recommended dosing regimen is 0.5 mg once daily for the first three days, then 0.5 mg twice daily for days four to seven, and 1 mg twice daily to complete twelve weeks of treatment. Mild-to-moderate nausea was the most commonly reported side effect (about 30 percent of trial participants); other adverse events reported by more than 10 percent of study participants were headache, insomnia, and abnormal dreams.

Unlike bupropion, which had been available for several years as an antidepressant medication, the post-marketing information about the side effects of varenicline has been limited. Concerns have been raised regarding possible adverse reactions among smokers with comorbid psychiatric conditions, for example, schizophrenia and bipolar disorder, who were excluded in the pivotal clinical trials; further research to determine varenicline's safety and efficacy among such populations is needed.

SECOND-LINE MEDICATIONS

Clonidine (Catapres) is an alpha2-noradrenergic agonist that was initially used for the treatment of hypertension, and subsequently found to diminish symptoms of both opiate and alcohol withdrawal. The efficacy of clonidine as a short-term smoking cessation aid was demonstrated in several studies in which clonidine was delivered either orally or in patch form. This drug has not received FDA approval as a smoking cessation aid, however, and should be considered to be a second-line treatment to be used when first-line pharmacotherapies have not been successful. Clonidine use is associated with reductions in pulse rate and blood pressure, and abrupt discontinuation could result in a rapid rise in blood pressure and catecholamine levels. Side effects reported with clonidine use include dry mouth, drowsiness, dizziness, and sedation. Appropriate dosage levels have not been established as of 2008.

Nortriptyline is used primarily as an antidepressant (Pamelor). Results from several trials of nortriptyline as a smoking cessation aid have found that it can double the abstinence rate at the end of treatment, similar to the effect of bupropion. Nortriptyline has not been approved by the FDA for the treatment of tobacco dependence, mainly because of a more complicated side effect profile than the first-line medications (including cardiovascular changes), and the small number of trials that have evaluated nortriptyline for smoking cessation. In the smoking cessation trials, nortriptyline use was initiated at a dosage of 25 mg/day, and increased gradually to 75 to 100 mg per day over twelve weeks. Sedation, dry mouth, blurred vision, urinary retention, lightheadedness, and shaky hands are the most commonly reported side effects of nortriptyline use.

Other Treatments. A number of other treatments have been used to aid in smoking cessation: hypnosis, acupuncture, lobeline and silver acetate medications. The effectiveness of these treatments has not been established by medical research, although some individuals may benefit from them. None of these treatments, however, can cure smokers of their tobacco addiction without the commitment and effort that are usually required to quit.

Combination Pharmacotherapies. Evidence from multiple published studies support the effectiveness of several types of combination treatments; these include nicotine patch + bupropion, nicotine patch + nicotine inhaler, long-term nicotine patch use (eighteen to twenty-four weeks) + ad libitum nicotine gum or nasal spray, nicotine patch + nortripyline, and nicotine patch + antidepressants (paroxetine and venlafaxine). All of these combination treatments significantly increased abstinence at the end of treatment and at twelve months follow-up. Individual patient characteristics, for example, depressed mood at the time of making the cessation attempt, and patient preference are useful indicators for selecting the appropriate type of combination treatment.

SMOKERS WITH PSYCHIATRIC CONDITIONS

There has been increasing recognition that tobacco use and nicotine dependence are more prevalent among individuals with psychiatric illness and substance use (alcohol or drugs) disorders. Persons with mental disorders comprise 20 percent of the population yet consume 44 percent of cigarettes and tobacco in the United States. The prevalence of nicotine dependence in the general population is about 13 percent but significantly higher among persons with mental illness or alcohol and substance use (other than nicotine) disorders (Grant et al., 2004). Several explanations for the high comorbidity of psychiatric illnesses and nicotine dependence have been considered: (1) because nicotine can affect brain structure, tobacco use, which typically starts during adolescence, can cause susceptibility to mental illness and drug dependence; (2) because nicotine exerts positive effects on

mood as well as reduces psychiatric symptoms, nicotine could be used for self-medication; and, (3) common factors, such as genetics or shared environment, account for the susceptibility to nicotine dependence and mental illnesses. Empirical support for these mechanisms has been reported, making it possible that any single one of them or combinations thereof are applicable in individual cases where tobacco dependence and psychiatric conditions co-occur.

Although it is clear that there is a higher prevalence of tobacco use among mentally ill and drug dependent populations, the likelihood as well as the consequences of smoking cessation when psychiatric illness is present remain controversial. Epidemiological evidence has tended to show lower smoking cessation rates among persons with affective and anxiety disorders as well as persons with current alcohol and drug disorders, but contrary evidence has also been reported. Findings from clinical trials of smokers have also been mixed. It is possible that variation in severity or treatment of the comorbid disorder affects the likelihood of successful cessation. For example, a meta-analysis showed that among individuals who receive active treatments, for example, clonidine, bupropion, nortriptyline, or nicotine replacement therapy, or cognitive therapy for mood management, smokers stopped smoking at similar rates irrespective of whether they had a past history of major depression. However, among individuals who did not receive an active treatment (for example, those treated with placebo), a lower smoking cessation rate was observed among those with past major depression, particularly, the more severe, recurrent type of major depressive disorder (Covey, Bomback, & Yan, 2006).

Another clinically important but unresolved issue is the effect of smoking cessation on recurrence of mental illness or substance use relapse. Although more work remains to be done and exceptions have occurred, studies of persons with past major depression and schizophrenia have suggested that smoking cessation can occur without risk of exacerbating symptoms of the comorbid psychiatric condition (Hall, 2007). Studies of smokers with substance dependencies have also produced mixed results. A meta-analysis of nineteen trials of smokers who were either in treatment or recovering from substance dependence found that smoking cessation treatment enhanced rather than impeded long-term sobriety (Prochaska, Delucchi, & Hall, 2004). Further studies of this important question are needed; however, a well-controlled trial of 499 persons receiving treatment for alcohol dependence showed that concurrent smoking cessation treatment resulted in higher rates of alcohol relapse compared to delayed smoking cessation treatment (Joseph et al., 2004).

Many persons who are dependent on tobacco want to quit but multiple barriers to tobacco cessation treatment remain. These include lack of knowledge about the availability of efficacious treatments, and lack of confidence on the part of smokers and health practitioners that tobacco cessation efforts will be successful. Removing these barriers are challenges to the public health and medical community. A significant barrier as well is the perception that cessation treatments are too expensive. In fact, tobacco cessation is one of the most cost-effective health interventions (Croghan et al., 1997) and, through its effect on reducing the morbidity and mortality of tobacco-related diseases, has the most far-ranging effects of any medical service in improving longevity and the overall quality of life (National Cancer Institute, 1997).

See also **Addiction: Concepts and Definitions; Nicotine; Nicotine Delivery Systems for Smoking Cessation; Treatment, Stages/Phases of: Relapse Prevention; Withdrawal: Nicotine (Tobacco).**

BIBLIOGRAPHY

Covey, L. S., Bomback, A., & Yan, G. W. (2006). History of depression and smoking cessation: A rejoinder. *Nicotine and Tobacco Research, 8*(2), 315–319.

Covey, L. S., Glassman, A. H., Jiang, H., Fried, J., Masmela, J., Loduca, C., et al. (2007). A randomized trial of bupropion and/or nicotine gum as maintenance treatment for preventing smoking relapse. *Addiction, 102*(8), 1292–1302.

Croghan, I. T., Offord, K. P., Evans, R. W., Schmidt, S., Gomez-Dahl, L. C., Schroeder, D. R., et al. (1997). Cost-effectiveness of treating nicotine dependence: The Mayo Clinic experience. *Mayo Clinic Proceedings, 72*(10), 917–24.

Grant, B. F., Hasin, D. S., Chou, S. P., Stinson, F. S., & Dawson, D. A. (2004). Nicotine dependence and psychiatric disorders in the United States: Results from the national epidemiologic survey on alcohol and related conditions. *Archives of General Psychiatry, 61*(11), 1107–1115.

Hall, S. M. (2007). Nicotine interventions with comorbid populations. *American Journal of Preventive Medicine, 33*(6), Suppl 1, S406-S413.

Joseph, A. M., Willenbring, M. L., Nugent, S. M., & Nelson, D. B. (2004). A randomized trial of concurrent versus delayed smoking intervention for patients in alcohol dependence treatment. *Journal of Studies on Alcohol, 65*(6), 681–691.

Lam, S., & Patel, P. N. (2007). Varenicline: a selective alpha4beta2 nicotinic acetylcholine receptor partial agonist approved for smoking cessation. *Cardiology Review, 15*(3), 154–161.

Morbidity and Mortality Weekly Report. (2007, November 9). *56*(54), 1157–1161.

National Cancer Institute. (1997). Changes in cigarette-related disease risks and their implication for prevention and control. NIH Publication No. 97-4213.

Prochaska, J. J., Delucchi, K., & Hall, S. M. (2004). A meta-analysis of smoking cessation interventions with individuals in substance abuse treatment or recovery. *Journal of Consulting and Clinical Psychology, 72,* 1144–1156.

Prochaska, J., & DiClemente, C. C. (1983). Stages and processes of self-change of smoking: Toward an integrative model of change. *Journal of Consulting and Clinical Psychology, 51,* 390–395.

United States Department of Health Human Services. (2008). Evidence. In *Treating tobacco use and dependence. Clinical practice guidelines.*

NEAL L. BENOWITZ
ALICE B. FREDERICKS
REVISED BY ANDREW J. HOMBURG (2001)
LIRIO S. COVEY (2009)

MEDICAL COMPLICATIONS

The notion that smoking tobacco is injurious to the body is not recent. King James I of England, in his classic *Counterblaste to Tobacco*, written in 1604, outlined a number of beliefs about tobacco's ill effects on health and urged his subjects to avoid it. He called smoking a "filthie noveltie...A custome lothsome to the eye, hatefull to the nose, harmefull to the braine, dangerous to the Lungs." Opinions on the possible benefits and health damage caused by use of tobacco varied over the next three hundred years. Some nineteenth-century arguments that tobacco use injured health were linked to moral arguments against its use rather than to medical evidence (Corti, 1932).

In 1926, Sir Humphrey Rolleston of Cambridge University, who headed a committee on the use of opioids, addressed the Harrogate Medical Society on the subject of medical aspects of tobacco and the possible toxic effects of nicotine (Rolleston, 1926). He drew few conclusions. Only a few health problems were clearly linked to tobacco: irritation of the throat and upper air passages by furfural, pyridine derivatives, ammonia, and carbon monoxide, which he ascribed to combustion of vegetable material and "not, like nicotine, in any way special to tobacco." Among the heart disorders Rolleston mentioned were extrasystoles (irregular heartbeats) and angina (pain caused by insufficient blood reaching the heart muscle). He noted that nicotine constricted the coronary arteries but suggested that people who suffered from extrasystoles might consider giving up coffee and tea before tobacco. He observed that cigarette smoking could cause arterial spasms and it was linked to obliterative diseases of the large arteries among young Jews living in London's East End. Rolleston believed that cancers of the lip and oral cavity observed in smokers were probably caused by syphilis and therefore not firmly linked to smoking. He devoted only a few lines to smoking's adverse effects on the respiratory tract, observing that smoking was responsible for "causing cough, hoarseness, bronchial catarrh, and so emphysema of the lungs." In general, Rolleston observed that considering "the large number of heavy smokers, the comparative rarity of undoubted lesions due to smoking is remarkable." He concluded that "to regard tobacco as a drug of addiction may be all very well in a humorous sense, but it is hardly accurate."

By the late nineteenth century, tobacco use was widespread, but people used very small amounts, mostly in the form of pipes, hand-rolled cigars, chew, and snuff; smoking was rare. The low level (by twenty-first century standards) of cigarette consumption changed dramatically at the beginning of the twentieth century with the invention of the cigarette rolling machine and the safety match. In addition to these technological innovations, the aggressive marketing campaign beginning in the late 1880s led to a dramatic increase in cigarette consumption. Before 1925, marketing was targeted exclusively at men; afterward, marketing was also targeted at women.

The turning point in the public's perception of the adverse consequences of tobacco smoking came with the publication of the Report of the Royal

College of Physicians in England in 1962 and the Report of the Surgeon General in the United States in 1964. These two reports documented the experimental, epidemiological, and pathological evidence linking tobacco smoking to a variety of diseases, the most notable of which were chronic obstructive pulmonary disease (COPD), lung cancer, and illness and death from heart disease. Many more reports on the health consequences of smoking followed these two pivotal publications. Since 1969, the Office of Smoking and Health of the U.S. Public Health Service has coordinated the annual publication of a Surgeon General's Report on the health consequences of smoking, with several of the reports focusing on specific topics. In approaching such major reviews of specific health consequences of smoking, the Office of Smoking and Health assigns recognized experts to review and summarize all the existing scientific literature on the topic and then draw some conclusions from it. Some of the special topics that have been considered are the changing cigarette (the implications for health of low tar/nicotine cigarettes and filters) (1981), chronic obstructive lung disease (1984), cancer and chronic lung disease in the workplace (1985), nicotine addiction (1988), tobacco use among young people (1994), women and smoking (2001), and the health consequences of involuntary exposure to tobacco smoke (2006).

The 1979 and 1989 reports were overall reviews of the field, marking the fifteenth and twenty-fifth anniversaries of the landmark 1964 report produced when Dr. Luther Terry was Surgeon General. The 1979 report described tobacco smoking as "the largest preventable cause of death in America." In a 2004 report, tobacco smoking was expected to cause 170,000 cancer deaths; up to 200,000 deaths from cardiovascular disease; and more than 101,000 deaths from chronic pulmonary disease in 2008 (U.S. Department of Health and Human Services, 2004). As of 2008, cigarette smoking remained the most important cause of preventable disease and premature death in developed countries. It is estimated that, depending on the age at which a person starts to smoke, seven to thirteen years of life are lost to smoking-related diseases. Nonetheless, nearly forty-five million Americans continue to smoke and the economic costs of smoking are estimated at $167 billion annually (Centers for Disease Control and Prevention, 2007).

Other agencies, national (U.S. Environmental Protection Agency [EPA] and California Environmental Protection Agency [CalEPA]) and international (International Agency on Cancer Research [IARC]), have published comprehensive reports on tobacco and health. In particular, the CalEPA analyses tend to lead conclusions by the Surgeon General. For example, the CalEPA identified second-hand smoke (SHS) as a cause of heart disease in 1997; the Surgeon General did not do so until 2006. In 2005, the CalEPA concluded that SHS caused breast cancer in younger, primarily premenopausal women; in 2006 the Surgeon General concluded that the evidence is suggestive (one step below causal) (California Environmental Protection Agency, 2005, p. ES-4).

THE PHARMACOLOGICAL ACTIONS OF NICOTINE

Nicotine, the addictive component in tobacco, is responsible for the effects of tobacco use on the neural, cardiovascular, endocrine, and skeletal muscle systems. The most important effects are on the brain. It has stimulant (increased attentiveness, heart rate, and blood pressure) and mild depressant effects. Its effects are determined by the dose and rate of administration, hosts' tolerance, and rate of elimination. The addictive nature of nicotine is demonstrated by the return to smoking by those who have had serious smoking-related illnesses. Further, among those who quit, fewer than 10 percent are abstinent one year later (Benowitz, 2008). Pure nicotine is a poison that can kill within minutes by causing respiratory failure. Nicotine poisoning most commonly results from accidental ingestion of insecticides containing nicotine. A fatal dose of nicotine for an adult is forty to sixty milligrams.

Nicotine is quickly absorbed through the skin, mucous membranes, and lungs. Absorption through the lungs produces measurable effects on the central nervous system in as little as seven seconds. This rapid rate of absorption means that each puff on a cigarette produces some reinforcement of the smoking habit.

As early as 1963, scientists within Brown & Williamson and BAT Industries (formerly British American Tobacco) recognized that nicotine was addictive (Slade et al., 1995). In response to the public concerns about the health dangers of smoking, the tobacco industry has developed and marketed low tar and low nicotine cigarettes. Given nicotine's addictive nature, people smoke to maintain a target level of nicotine in their blood, and respond to low nicotine cigarettes by increasing their amount smoked or the number of puffs per cigarette, or by puffing more deeply or inhaling longer. Therefore, any possible benefits from switching to lower tar or nicotine cigarettes may be offset by this tendency of smokers to adjust their smoking behavior to maintain blood nicotine levels.

TOBACCO-RELATED DISEASES

Cancer. Tobacco smoking has been shown to be the major cause of lung cancer in both men and women. The increased risk for lung cancer depends on the number of cigarettes smoked per day, the degree of inhalation, and the age at which the adult began smoking. The risk of death from lung cancer is about twenty times greater for men who smoke two packs a day than for those who have never smoked. It is about ten times higher for those who smoke one-half to one pack a day. Mentholated and low tar cigarettes have also been shown to increase the risk of lung cancer. Tobacco smoking is synergistic (produces a multiplier effect) with the effects of other carcinogenic risks, such as exposure to radon or asbestos. Smoking is also synergistic with alcohol in causing cancers of the oral cavity, larynx, pharynx, and esophagus. In addition, smoking has been found to increase the risk of breast cancer, particularly in young premenopausal women and those who start smoking in their teen years when the breast is still developing.

Cardiovascular Disease. Smoking is the major cause of coronary heart disease (CHD); risk of death from CHD is 70 percent higher for men who smoke, with a similar effect for women. The risk of CHD from smoking is mediated through increases in blood pressure, oxygen demand, heart rate, and oxidative stress. In addition, it decreases the blood's oxygen carrying capacity and the ability of muscle to convert oxygen into energy. Smoking increases the risk for stroke. For example, women who smoke twenty-five cigarettes or more per day have a risk for stroke almost four times higher than nonsmokers. Smoking also increases the risk of atherosclerosis (formation of plaques) in the peripheral arteries and the aorta. In addition, it leads to arterial endothelial dysfunction. The endothelium, which is the arterial layer that comes into direct contact with blood, is vital for arterial dilation and contraction, and prevents cholesterol from sticking to the arterial wall.

Lung Disease. Chronic obstructive pulmonary disease (COPD) includes three related disorders: chronic mucous hypersecretion that causes cough and phlegm production; airway thickening and obstruction of expiratory airflow; and emphysema—abnormal dilation of alveoli (air sacs responsible for gas exchange) and destruction of their walls. Cigarette smoking is the major cause of COPD. Compared to nonsmokers, male smokers are three times more likely and female smokers are twice as likely to have a persistent cough.

Other Medical Disorders. Other medical disorders include peptic ulcers, upper respiratory infections, osteoporosis, erectile dysfunction, dental and eye diseases, and cancers of the pancreas, bladder, and esophagus.

Conclusions Regarding Causality. Over time, the strength of the evidence linking tobacco with disease has mounted, new conclusions have been added, and older conclusions strengthened. To summarize conclusions regarding causality, both the Surgeon General and the CalEPA have followed the classification used by the Institute of Medicine and IARC. In this classification, a four-level hierarchy is established based on the available evidence (U.S. Department of Health and Human Services, 2004, pp. 17–29).

Category A. Evidence is sufficient to infer a causal relationship: Cancers of the lung, larynx, pharynx (oral cavity), esophagus, pancreas, bladder and kidney, cervix, stomach, and acute myeloid leukemia. Coronary heart disease (including heart attacks), stroke, and aortic aneurysms are also under this category. In addition, acute respiratory illnesses (including pneumonia) and chronic obstructive pulmonary disease are included. Breast cancer, as evidenced by research published after the year 2000, has also been found to be increased by smoking (Johnson, 2005).

Category B. Evidence is suggestive of a causal relationship: Cancers of the colon and liver, and erectile dysfunction.

Category C. Evidence is inadequate to infer the presence or absence of a causal relationship: Ovarian cancer, asthma onset in adulthood, and congenital malformations in general.

Category D. Evidence is suggestive of no causal relationship: Prostate cancer.

The effects of tobacco use are not limited to specific diseases that lead to death. Tobacco use can stimulate enzymes in the liver, which can result in alterations in the way various medications are metabolized. This alteration in metabolism can mean that the levels of medications in the body will not be high enough to be optimally therapeutic.

The risk for most diseases can be decreased by smoking cessation, but not all risks decline at the same rate. Cardiovascular disease risk falls halfway back to that of a never-smoker in just one year, and is almost (but not entirely) gone within three to five years. The risk of cancer declines more slowly, with some elevated risk still evident ten years after cessation. Within five years of quitting, overall risk of premature death drops by 50 percent (Shopland & Burns, 1993).

Pipe and cigar smokers are also at an increased risk of premature death, with approximately the same relative risk as cigarette smokers of getting laryngeal and esophageal cancers. The mortality risk for users of smokeless tobacco (oral snuff and chewing tobacco) comes primarily from cancers of the oral cavity and throat (U.S. Department of Health and Human Services, 2004).

Psychiatric Disorders. Dependence on tobacco is associated with dysthymic disorder and other forms of depression. As of 2008, it is not known, however, whether depression prompts people to begin smoking or whether it develops in the course of dependence on tobacco. Mood disorders increase significantly during withdrawal from nicotine, and are common reasons for relapse.

WOMEN AND SMOKING

Women who smoke tobacco have the same risks for adverse effects as men. In 2007, deaths due to lung cancer among women exceeded deaths from breast cancer, becoming the leading cause of cancer death for women. Some women are at special risk. Women who smoke and use oral contraceptives have an increased risk of cardiovascular disease, as well as cerebrovascular disease, including subarachnoid hemorrhage (bleeding between the brain and its protective covering inside the skull). In addition, women who start smoking early in their teen years also have an increased risk of breast cancer compared to nonsmoking women (California Environmental Protection Agency, 2005, p. ES-4).

Women who smoke have higher infertility rates than those who do not and are also more likely to have menstrual irregularities. They also have higher rates of ectopic pregnancy (abnormal implantation of the fertilized ovum outside of the uterus). Nicotine crosses the placenta, and because it constricts blood vessels, a decreased amount of oxygen is delivered to the fetus. In addition, smoking elevates the amount of carbon monoxide in the mother's blood so that it carries less oxygen to the fetus. Women who smoke during pregnancy have higher rates of premature detachment of the placenta (*abruptio placentae*), premature rupture of membranes, and preterm delivery. The greater the amount of tobacco smoked during the pregnancy, the higher the frequency of spontaneous abortion and fetal death and the greater the likelihood of delivering an infant that is smaller than normal. In the United States, smoking has been associated with a 20 percent increase in preterm births among women who smoked a pack a day or more compared with those who did not smoke. Women who stop smoking early in pregnancy increase their likelihood of having normal deliveries and normal birth weight babies (U.S. Department of Health and Human Services, 2001).

SECONDHAND SMOKE

Secondhand smoke, also known as environmental tobacco smoke, is the smoke breathed by nonsmokers and is a mixture of mainstream (inhaled by the smoker) and sidestream (emitted from the tip of the cigarette) smoke. SHS accounts for approximately fifty thousand deaths annually, including three thousand deaths from lung cancer and forty-six thousand deaths from heart disease (U.S. Department of Health and Human Services, 2006). It has been established as a cause of heart disease, lung and sinus cancer, respiratory problems in children

(bronchitis and pneumonia, middle ear infections) and adults (asthma induction), and low birth weight and sudden infant death syndrome in newborns. Passive smoke exposure during pregnancy (e.g., living with a smoker) can adversely affect the birth weight of the baby. In addition, SHS is a cause of breast cancer in young, primarily premenopausal, women (California Environmental Protection Agency, 2005, p. ES-4). The cardiovascular system is particularly sensitive to the harmful effects of SHS (just thirty minutes of exposure is enough to harm the exposed individual's arteries) (Barnoya & Glantz, 2005).

Exposure to SHS during pregnancy is associated with a decrease in birth weight of twenty to one hundred grams. Infants born to mothers who smoke are far more likely to die before their first birthday, primarily as a result of respiratory complications and sudden infant death syndrome. Children of mothers who smoke seem in general more likely to suffer from colds, asthma, bronchitis, pneumonia, and other respiratory problems (California Environmental Protection Agency, 2005).

Tobacco control programs (tax increases, banning smoking in the workplace and advertising, smoking cessation programs, and other strategies) have led to a reduction in the prevalence of smoking in the United States. Banning smoking in the workplace has proven to be one of the most effective tobacco control strategies, as it decreases smoking prevalence, the number of cigarettes smoked by continuing smokers, and exposure to SHS (Fichtenberg, 2002). In addition, heart disease and lung cancer mortality decrease after the implementation of smoke-free environments (Fichtenberg, 2002; Barnoya & Glantz, 2004). To halt the spread of smoke-free legislation in the United States and worldwide, the tobacco industry has implemented several strategies, including hiring scientists to redirect public attention from SHS toward other sources of air pollution, lobbying politicians, and creating useless smoking and nonsmoking sections in public places.

In general, white males in higher socioeconomic groups have lowered their smoking rate more than women and members of ethnic and racial minorities and lower socioeconomic groups. Adult smoking prevalence in the United States remained unchanged during the early 1990s but decreased from 1997 (24.7%) to 2004 (20.8%). Smoking prevalence by ethnic group is highest among American Indians/Alaska Natives (32%), followed by African Americans (23%), Whites (22%), Hispanics (15%), and Asians (10%) (Centers for Disease Control and Prevention, 2007). An estimated 20 percent of high school students (ninth to twelfth grades) were current smokers in 2005 (Centers for Disease Control and Prevention, 2006).

In contrast to the general decline in the prevalence of smoking in developed nations, the prevalence of smoking is increasing in developing and newly industrialized countries. By the year 2030, cigarettes will kill ten million people per year; 70 percent of this total will be in low- and middle-income countries (Jha & Chaloupka, 1999). In most of these countries, the tobacco industry has been successful in preventing the implementation of sound tobacco control measures.

See also **Advertising and Tobacco Use; Complications; Nicotine; Treatment, Behavioral Approaches to; Treatment, Pharmacological Approaches to; Treatment, Specialty Approaches to.**

BIBLIOGRAPHY

Barnoya, J., & Glantz, S. A. (2004). Association of the California tobacco control program with declines in lung cancer incidence. *Cancer Causes Control, 15,* 689–695.

Barnoya, J., & Glantz, S. A. (2005). Cardiovascular effects of secondhand smoke: nearly as large as smoking. *Circulation, 111,* 2684–2698.

Benowitz, N. L. (2008). Neurobiology of nicotine addiction: Implications for smoking cessation treatment. *The American Journal of Medicine Update on Smoking Cessation Interventions for the Primary Care Physician, 121,* S3–S10.

California Environmental Protection Agency. (2005). *Proposed identification of environmental tobacco smoke as a toxic air contaminant.* State of California: Office of Environmental Health Hazard Assessment.

Centers for Disease Control and Prevention. (2007). *Cigarette smoking among adults: United States, 2006, 53,* 1157–1161. Atlanta, GA: Author.

Centers for Disease Control and Prevention. (2006). *Cigarette use among high school students: United States 1991–2005, 55,* 724–726. Atlanta, GA: Author.

Corti, E. (1932). *A history of smoking* (P. England, Trans.). New York: Harcourt, Brace.

Fichtenberg, C. M., & Glantz, S. A. (2002). Association of the California Tobacco Control Program with declines in cigarette consumption and mortality from heart disease. *New England Journal of Medicine, 343,* 1772–1777.

Fichtenberg, C. M., & Glantz, S. A. (2002). Effect of smoke-free workplaces on smoking behaviour: Systematic review. *British Medical Journal, 325,* 188–191.

Jha, P., & Chaloupka, F. J. (1999). *Curbing the epidemic. Governments and the economics of tobacco control.* Washington, DC: The World Bank.

Johnson, K. C. (2005). Accumulating evidence on passive and active smoking and breast cancer risk. *International Journal of Cancer, 117,* 619–628.

Rolleston, H. (1926, May 22). Medical aspects of tobacco. *Lancet, 1,* 961–965.

Shopland, D. R., & Burns, D. M. (1993). Medical and public health implications of tobacco addiction. In C. T. Orleans & J. Slade (Eds.), *Nicotine addiction: Principles and management.* New York: Oxford University Press.

Slade, J., Bero, L. A., Hanauer, P., Barnes, D. E., & Glantz, S. A. (1995). Nicotine and addiction. The Brown and Williamson documents. *Journal of the American Medical Association, 274,* 225–233.

U.S. Department of Health and Human Services. (2001). *Women and smoking: a report of the Surgeon General.* Washington, DC: Office of the Surgeon General.

U.S. Department of Health and Human Services. (2004). *The health consequences of smoking. A report of the Surgeon General.* Washington, DC: Centers for Disease Control and Prevention; National Center for Chronic Disease Prevention and Health Promotion; Office on Smoking and Health.

U.S. Department of Health and Human Services. (2006). *The health consequences of involuntary exposure to tobacco smoke: A report of the Surgeon General.* Atlanta, GA: U.S. Department of Health and Human Services, Centers for Disease Control and Prevention, Coordinating Center for Health Promotion, National Center for Chronic Disease Prevention and Health Promotion, Office on Smoking and Health.

JEROME H. JAFFE
DONALD R. SHOPLAND
REVISED BY REBECCA J. FREY (2001)
JOAQUIN BARNOYA (2009)

SMOKELESS

Tobacco has been used in various nonsmoked forms throughout its long history. Indeed, before the introduction of the mass-produced cigarette in the early twentieth century, smokeless tobacco, including chewing tobacco and snuff, was the predominant form of tobacco use, and in some regions of the world, such as India, it remains so in the early twenty-first century.

The earliest uses of tobacco, dating back thousands of years, were probably through chewing the leaves of the plant or inhaling powdered tobacco through the nose (snuffing). Tobacco was held to have many uses among Native Americans, including as a medicine, wound healer, appetite suppressant, psychoactive agent, and as an aid to religious rituals.

Early Spanish explorers recorded their observations of the practice of chewing and snuffing tobacco among the natives as well as smoking. When tobacco was brought back to Europe it was used both in smoked form (cigars and pipes) and in smokeless forms. However, during the eighteenth and early nineteenth centuries, tobacco use in European society was most commonly in the form of snuff. The practice of snuffing became fashionable among the French aristocracy at the time. The offering and taking of snuff in social settings became highly stylized, and elaborate snuff boxes served to display one's refinement, rank and wealth. Snuff use subsequently gained broader popularity in other European countries, including England, and outside the elite circles.

In late nineteenth century America, chewing tobacco was widespread and at its peak of popularity. Spittoons became a fixture in many public places, such as public buildings and trains. In the early twentieth century, however, use of chewing tobacco declined as machine-rolled cigarettes, which were seen as more convenient and hygienic, gained popularity. Around 1900, 52 percent of all tobacco used in the United States was smokeless, but by 1952 that number had dropped to 6 percent (Lewis et al., 1999).

USE OF SMOKELESS TOBACCO PRODUCTS

The term *smokeless tobacco* refers to an extremely diverse range of products, including mass-produced manufactured products as well as traditional and handmade products. While smokeless tobacco products by definition contain tobacco as the principal ingredient, the tobacco may also be mixed with other ingredients. For example, the primary ingredients in *gutka*, which is widely used in the Indian subcontinent, include betel leaf, areca nut, and a variety of

spices and flavors in addition to tobacco. Even within the United States, a wide range of different types of smokeless tobacco products with different characteristics are used, including chewing tobacco, dry and moist snuff, traditional oral tobacco products, such as *iqmik*, and novel products, such as tobacco lozenges. The popularity of different product types has evolved over time. For example, use of moist snuff or dip increased substantially toward the end of the twentieth century, making up over half of the smokeless tobacco market, whereas sales of chewing tobacco and dry snuff fell (Maxwell, 2004).

Overall sales in pounds of smokeless tobacco products in the United States have remained relatively unchanged, or saw only a slight decline, between 1988 and 2008. However, revenues and advertising and promotional expenditures increased steadily over the same period. In 2005, the five largest tobacco manufacturers spent $250.76 million on smokeless tobacco advertising and promotion; over 40 percent of that was spent on price discounts paid to retailers and wholesalers to reduce the price to consumers for smokeless tobacco products (Federal Trade Commission, 2007, pp. 3, 5).

According to the 2006 National Survey on Drug Use and Health, there are approximately 8.2 million people aged 12 or older in the United States who use smokeless tobacco. The prevalence of smokeless tobacco use in the U.S. population overall is substantially lower (3.3%) than that for cigarette smoking (25%). However, there are substantial disparities in smokeless tobacco use among subgroups of the population. While 6.6 percent of American males report current smokeless use, only 0.3 percent of American females report the same. Smokeless tobacco use is also substantially higher among whites (4.2%) and American Indian/Alaska Natives (6.5%) than among African Americans (1.7%), Asians (1.2%), and Hispanics (0.9%). Smokeless tobacco use is greater in rural areas; the proportion of smokeless tobacco use ranges from 10 percent in rural counties to only 2 percent in large metropolitan counties (Substance Abuse and Mental Health Services Administration, 2007). High prevalence of smokeless tobacco use has also been found among U.S. military personnel (24% reported use; Chisick et al., 1998) and among some athletes, particularly major league baseball players (36% reported use; Severson et al., 2005).

Use of smokeless tobacco among youth warrants particular attention both because its prevalence is higher and because it may serve as a pathway to nicotine addiction and use of other tobacco products. A national survey found that 12.6 percent of twelfth grade boys reported having used smokeless tobacco in the past 30 days, and prevalence was even higher among white boys in southern states (Nelson et al., 2006, p. 900). Moreover, some smokeless tobacco products may be more accessible to new users and more likely to appeal to adolescents. During the 1970s, smokeless tobacco use increased substantially among teens and young adults when new products were introduced that were more accessible to new users, with lower nicotine content and attractive flavorings (Connolly, 1995). And evidence suggests that users who begin with starter products, that are low in nicotine, are more likely to graduate subsequently to products with higher nicotine content (Tomar et al., 1995).

A number of studies suggest that adolescents who use smokeless tobacco may be more likely to progress to cigarette smoking, although the evidence is not consistent (Tomar, 2003; O'Connor et al., 2005; Haddock et al., 2001). Smokeless tobacco also poses a global public health challenge. In many regions of the world, such as in India, smokeless tobacco use is the predominant form of tobacco use. In the Indian National Family Health Survey, 20 percent (28.1% of men and 12.0% of women) of respondents reported chewing tobacco and/or *pan masala*, though these figures varied widely by region (Rani et al., 2003, p. 3). Also, data from the Global Youth Tobacco Survey show that students aged 13 to 15 surveyed in 132 countries were more likely to report using non-cigarette tobacco products (11.2%) than to report smoking cigarettes (8.9%; MMWR, 2006).

HEALTH EFFECTS

One International Agency for Research on Cancer (IARC) monograph on smokeless tobacco reported that there is sufficient evidence, based on epidemiologic and laboratory studies, to conclude that smokeless tobacco causes oral cancer and pancreatic cancer in humans (Cogliano et al., 2004). At least 28 different carcinogens have been identified in smokeless tobacco products (National Cancer Institute, 1992, p. 115). Additionally, measurements of carcinogen by-products in humans show that smokeless tobacco

users are exposed to levels of tobacco-specific nitrosamines, among the most important tobacco carcinogens, that are as high or higher than cigarette smokers (Kresty et al., 1996). There is also limited but inconsistent evidence suggesting that smokeless tobacco use may be associated with cardiovascular disease (Gupta et al., 2004). And smokeless tobacco use is associated with other health outcomes, including oral mucosal lesions, leukoplakia, and periodontal disease.

However, assessing the health risks of smokeless tobacco products is complicated given the diversity of traditional and manufactured products in use and their different characteristics. One study of eleven smokeless tobacco product brands available in the United Kingdom found that levels of tobacco-specific nitrosamines varied 130-fold across the products and nicotine content ranged from 0.1 mg/g to 63.2 mg/g (McNeill et al., 2006). Additionally, moist snuff sold in Sweden has relatively low levels of nitrosamines compared with some other smokeless tobacco products, such as American chewing tobacco (Hoffman et al., 1995) or *toombak*, a moist snuff product found in Sudan (Idris et al., 1991). Moreover, the health risks experienced by any tobacco user vary depending not only on the type of product used but on how it is used, when the person started and/or quit, and concurrent use of other harmful substances.

ADDICTION AND TREATMENT

Smokeless tobacco products contain nicotine as a major constituent and users of smokeless tobacco products demonstrate signs of dependence similar to those in cigarette smokers, including tolerance with repeated use and symptoms of withdrawal upon cessation of use. Moreover, individuals who are dual users (those who use both cigarettes and smokeless tobacco) tend to have higher nicotine exposure levels and find cessation even more difficult to achieve than those who use only one type of product (Wetter et al., 2002).

However, the most promising strategies for helping smokeless tobacco users to quit are different than those for cigarette smoking. While drug interventions, including nicotine replacement therapy (such as nicotine patch or gum) and bupropion, have been shown to be effective in helping cigarette smokers to quit, studies in smokeless tobacco users have not found a similar benefit (Ebbert et al., 2004). These treatments may help reduce unwanted side effects associated with nicotine withdrawal, such as feelings of craving or weight gain, but they have not been shown to have any impact on successful quitting over the long term (Dale et al., 2007). Yet there is strong evidence that behavioral counseling interventions are effective for helping smokeless tobacco users to quit. In particular, counseling patients in dental offices, where the effects of smokeless tobacco use on the mouth can be detected and explained, has been shown to increase success in quitting. Interestingly, similar interventions have not been found to be effective for cigarette smokers (Carr & Ebbert, 2006). Telephone counseling may also be useful in assisting smokeless tobacco users to quit, although larger studies are needed to support more specific recommendations. In general, the evidence regarding cessation in smokeless tobacco users is very limited compared to that for cigarette smoking.

HARM REDUCTION

While smokeless tobacco use causes cancer and other diseases, it is associated with a lower overall risk profile compared with cigarette smoking. Indeed, according to some estimates, the magnitude of this difference is vast (i.e., "consumption of non-combustible tobacco is of the order of 10-1,000 times less hazardous than smoking" according to Royal College of Physicians, 2002, p. 5). This difference has led some scientists to suggest that smokeless tobacco has promise as a *harm reduction* intervention for cigarette smokers. That is, smokers who have trouble quitting might reduce their risk by switching to a smokeless tobacco product in place of cigarettes. However, there is not sufficient evidence as of 2008 to demonstrate that this strategy is effective in practice. In other words, even if the product is less toxic, it is not clear whether smokers will successfully switch without relapsing or continuing to smoke. Critics of this approach have also suggested that promoting the use of smokeless tobacco as less harmful might lead to an increase in initiation of smokeless tobacco use by adolescents and other new users or have a negative impact on tobacco use cessation efforts (Hatsukami et al., 2004).

The Swedish Experience is often referred to as a sort of natural experiment in the use of smokeless tobacco for harm reduction (Foulds et al., 2003).

Sweden has the lowest male smoking prevalence of any country in Europe (14% of adult men are daily smokers) and the lowest levels of tobacco related mortality (about half that of the EU overall). However, a significant portion of men (22%) report using oral smokeless tobacco, typically in the form of *snus*, a moist oral tobacco product. Some scientists have suggested that the low smoking prevalence (and lower mortality) is due to the use of snus in place of cigarettes. However, this trend may also be a result of broader social and policy influences. For example, in the early 1960s Sweden was one of the first countries to fund an organized tobacco control effort, including the development of cessation clinics and antismoking education programs (Mitchell & Wellings, 1998). Changes in popular culture also likely had an impact on behavior and national smoking trends, as popular portrayals of smoking shifted from accepting to negative (Torell, 2002).

EVOLVING MARKETPLACE AND POLICIES

In the late 1990s and early twenty-first century, a range of new smokeless tobacco products were introduced and marketed that may be more likely to appeal to new users, including youth. Some new smokeless products use attractive flavorings, such as mint or fruit flavors, and new delivery methods, such as lozenges or small pouches that eliminate the need to spit. Major cigarette manufacturers Philip Morris and R. J. Reynolds have also introduced new smokeless tobacco products using the familiar brand names Marlboro and Camel. Moreover, some smokeless tobacco manufacturers have introduced new marketing strategies, such as marketing smokeless tobacco products to smokers for situations in which they cannot smoke, given the increase in smoking restrictions in workplaces and public spaces (O'Hegarty et al., 2007). It remains to be seen as of 2008 whether these new strategies will lead to increased use of smokeless tobacco.

Policies and regulations around smokeless tobacco products vary widely across countries. Additionally, the policies and regulations applying to smokeless tobacco products are in many cases different than those for cigarettes. For example, in the United States smokeless tobacco product packages carry a different set of mandated health warnings than cigarette packages. Additionally, smokeless tobacco products are taxed differently than cigarettes; in general they are taxed at a lower level and states use different formulas for calculating the taxes. Since 2001, the European Union has prohibited marketing of snuff products (but not cigarettes or chewing tobacco) in all affected countries except Sweden and Norway. However, the World Health Organization Framework Convention on Tobacco Control, the first global public health treaty, broadly applies to all tobacco products, including traditional and manufactured forms of smokeless tobacco.

See also **Advertising and Tobacco Use; Withdrawal: Nicotine (Tobacco).**

BIBLIOGRAPHY

Carr, A. B., & Ebbert, J. O. (2006). Interventions for tobacco cessation in the dental setting. *Cochrane Database of Systematic Reviews*, Issue 1. Art. No.: CD005084. DOI: 10.1002/14651858.CD005084.pub2.

Chisick, M. C., Poindexter, F. R., & York, A. K. (1998). Comparing tobacco use among incoming recruits and military personnel on active duty in the United States. *Tobacco Control, 7,* 236–240.

Cogliano, V., Straif, K., Baan, R., Grosse, Y., Secretan, B., & El Ghissassi, F. (2004). Smokeless tobacco and tobacco-related nitrosamines. *Lancet Oncology Journal, 5,* 708.

Connolly, G. (1995). The marketing of nicotine addiction by one oral snuff manufacturer. *Tobacco Control, 4,* 73–79.

Dale, L. C., Ebbert, J. O., Glover, E. D., Croghan, I. T., Schroeder, D. R., Severson, H. H., et al. (2007). Bupropion SR for the treatment of smokeless tobacco use. *Drug and Alcohol Dependence, 90,* 56–63.

Ebbert, J. O., Rowland, L. C., Montori, V., Vickers, K. S., Erwin, P. C., Dale, L. C., et al. (2004). Interventions for smokeless tobacco use cessation. *Cochrane Database of Systematic Reviews*, Issue 3. Art. No.: CD004306. DOI: 10.1002/14651858.CD004306. pub2.

Federal Trade Commission. (2007). *Smokeless tobacco report for the years 2002–2005.* Washington, DC: Author. Available from http://www.ftc.gov/reports/tobacco/02-05smokeless0623105.pdf

Foulds, J., Ramstrom, L., Burke, M., & Fagerström, K. (2003). Effect of smokeless tobacco (snus) on smoking and public health in Sweden. *Tobacco Control, 12*(4), 349–359.

Gupta, R., Gurm, H., & Bartholomew, J. R. (2004). Smokeless tobacco and cardiovascular risk. *Archives of Internal Medicine, 164,* 1845–1849.

Haddock, C., Weg, M., DeBon, M., Klesges, R., Talcott, G., Lando, H., et al., (2001). Evidence that smokeless

tobacco use is a gateway for smoking initiation in young adult males. *Preventive Medicine, 32,* 262–267.

Hatsukami, D. K., Lemmonds, C., & Tomar, S. L. (2004). Smokeless tobacco use: Harm reduction or induction approach? *Preventive Medicine, 38*(3), 309–317.

Hoffmann, D., Djordjevic, M. V., Fan, J., Zang, E., Glynn, T., & Connolly, G. N. (1995). Five leading U.S. commercial brands of moist snuff in 1994: Assessment of carcinogenic N-nitrosamines. *Journal of the National Cancer Institute, 87,* 1862–1869.

Idris, A. M., Nair, J., Oshima, H., Friesen, M., Brouet, I., Faustman, E. M., et al., (1991). Unusually high levels of carcinogenic nitrosamines in Sudan snuff (Toombak). *Carcinogenesis, 12,* 1115–1118.

Kresty, L. A., Carmella, S. G., Borukhova, A., Akerkar, S. A., Gopalakrishnan, R., Harris, R. E., et al. (1996). Metabolites of a tobacco-specific nitrosamine, 4-(methylnitrosamino)-1-(3-pyridyl)-1-butanone (NNK), in the urine of smokeless tobacco users: Relationship between urinary biomarkers and oral leukoplakia. *Cancer Epidemiology Biomarkers and Prevention, 5*(7), 521–525.

Lewis, P. C., Harrell, J. S., Deng, S., & Bradley, C. (1999). Smokeless tobacco use in adolescents: The cardiovascular health in children (CHIC II) study. *Journal of School Health, 69,* 320–335.

Maxwell, J. C., Jr. (2004). *The Maxwell report: The smokeless tobacco industry in 2003.* Richmond, VA: John C. Maxwell Jr.

McNeill, A., Bedi, R., Islam, S., Alkhatib, M. N., & West, R. (2006). Levels of toxins in oral tobacco products in the UK. *Tobacco Control, 15*(1), 64–67.

Mitchell, K., & Wellings, K. (1998). *Improving health status in Europe: A case study approach to the identification of best practice. Best practice in smoking: The Swedish Case Study.* London School of Hygiene and Tropical Medicine.

Morbidity and Mortality Weekly Report. (2006). Use of cigarettes and other tobacco products among students aged 13–15 years worldwide, 1999–2005. *Morbidity and Mortality Weekly Report, 55,* 553–556.

National Cancer Institute. (1992). Monograph 2: Smokeless tobacco or health: An international perspective. Bethesda, MD: U.S. Department of Health and Human Services, National Cancer Institute. Available from http://www.cancercontrol.cancer.gov/.

Nelson, D. E., Mowery, P., Tomar, S., Marcus, S., Giovino, G., & Zhao, L. (2006). Trends in smokeless tobacco use among adults and adolescents in the United States. *American Journal of Public Health, 96,* 897–905.

O'Connor, R. J., Kozlowski, L. T., Quinio Edwards, B., & Flaherty, B. P. (2005). Most smokeless tobacco use does not cause cigarette smoking: Results from the

2000 National Household Survey on Drug Abuse. *Addictive Behaviors, 30,* 325–336.

O'Hegarty, M., Richter, P., & Pederson, L. L. (2007). What do adult smokers think about ads and promotional materials for PREPs? *American Journal of Health Behaviors, 31,* 526–534.

Rani, M., Bonu, S., Jha, P., Nguyen, S. N., & Jamjoum, L. (2003). Tobacco use in India: Prevalence and predictors of smoking and chewing in a national cross sectional household survey. *Tobacco Control, 12*(4), e4.

Royal College of Physicians, Tobacco Advisory Group. (2002). *Protecting smokers, saving lives: The case for a tobacco and nicotine regulatory authority.* London: Royal College of Physicians.

Severson, H. H., Klein, K., Lichtenstein, E., Kaufman, N., & Orleans, C. T. (2005). Smokeless tobacco use among professional baseball players: Survey results, 1998 to 2003. *Tobacco Control, 14,* 31–36.

Substance Abuse and Mental Health Services Administration. (2007). Results from the 2006 National Survey on Drug Use and Health: Detailed tables. Available from http://www.oas.samhsa.gov/NSDUH/.

Tomar, S. (2003). Is use of smokeless tobacco a risk factor for cigarette smoking? The U.S. experience. *Nicotine & Tobacco Research, 5(4),* 561–569.

Tomar, S. L., Giovino, G. A., & Eriksen, M. P. (1995). Smokeless tobacco brand preference and brand switching among U.S. adolescents and young adults. *Tobacco Control, 4,* 67–72.

Torell, U. (2002). *Den rökande människan: bilden av tobaksbruk i Sverige mellan 1950- och 1990-tal.* Stockholm: Carlsson bokförlag.

Wetter, D. W., McClure, J. B., de Moor, C., Cofta-Gunn, L., Cummings, S., Cinciripini, P. M., et al. (2002). Concomitant use of cigarettes and smokeless tobacco: Prevalence, correlates, and predictors of tobacco cessation. *Prevention Medicine, 34*(6), 638–648.

MARK PARASCANDOLA

SMOKING CESSATION AND WEIGHT GAIN

Successful smoking cessation is associated with modest weight gain. The amount of weight gain tends to average 10 to 13 pounds in the first year after quitting, with most of this occurring within the first six months of abstinence. Individual characteristics influencing the amount of weight gain include gender and initial body weight, length and frequency of smoking behaviors, and other lifestyle factors such as type of diet and physical activity. The exact mechanism through which cigarette smoking affects energy expenditure and body weight is not fully understood and is likely a combination of several factors:

- There is a slight metabolic advantage to cigarette smoking, meaning that smoking increases heart rate and the overall level of energy that the body uses to function. Following cessation, basal metabolic level slows, which promotes weight gain.
- Smoking suppresses appetite and food intake. Animal research has shown that mice administered nicotine initially eat less than control mice but that meal size eventually increases. Similarly, some dieters attempt to use the appetite-suppressing effects of smoking to resist urges to eat and to help them eat less. However, over the long term smokers do not tend to eat less than nonsmokers.
- Following smoking cessation, food smells and tastes better and is, therefore, more desirable. In general, smoking serves as an appetite suppressant and during withdrawal from nicotine, appetite increases. Laboratory experiments have shown that during smoking withdrawal, people are likely to manage cigarette cravings with food and to report more enjoyment in the experience of eating. Among current smokers, short-term abstinence from smoking is associated with heightened cravings for cigarettes and food, as well as increased calorie and fat intake.

Through a combination of these factors, smoking suppresses body weight, and following cessation weight reverts to a higher natural set point. On the population level, smokers tend to weigh less than former-smokers, who in turn weigh less than never-smokers. It should be noted that although there are certain health benefits to lower weight, these benefits are greatly offset by the negative health impact of smoking.

SMOKING FOR WEIGHT CONTROL

For some smokers, concerns about weight may motivate the decision to begin smoking. Initiation of smoking by adolescent girls has been linked to weight concerns, and among young adults smoking is more common among those who are trying to lose weight. The cigarette industry appears to capitalize on the weight concerns of its target market by producing advertisements that equate smoking with being slim. There is some evidence to suggest that smokers who are especially concerned about their weight have magnified beliefs in the ability of smoking to suppress weight; that is, they believe smoking to be much more effective at controlling weight than it actually is. Consequently, smokers who are especially weight concerned are less likely to report a desire to quit.

Weight concerns are also associated with unsuccessful attempts to quit smoking. One of the commonly reported reasons for smoking relapse is weight gain. Although concerns about weight gain are more common for female smokers than male, a significant portion of male smokers also report fear of cessation-associated weight gain.

TREATMENTS GEARED TOWARD WEIGHT CONCERNS

Smoking cessation treatments that include a component to address weight gain may be more successful for some individuals, especially those with heightened concerns about weight gain. Several treatment options have shown some promise, whereas others have been less successful.

Behavioral treatments for weight control may be effective for weight-concerned smokers. Examples of behavioral weight control treatments include moderate calorie-reducing diets and programs to promote physical activity. These treatments are most successful when administered as a supplement to standard smoking-cessation treatment and when promoting behavioral changes intended to result in very modest weight change. The DHHS 2000 *Clinical Practice Guideline* for treating tobacco use and dependence recommends that patients not attempt weight control until after they are confident that they will not resume smoking. Patients should be advised that strict dieting during a quit attempt could hinder successful cessation.

Cognitive Behavioral Therapy. Cognitive behavioral therapy (CBT) and other treatments to address body image and weight concerns aim to establish healthier body image, thus reducing the psychological distress associated with slight weight gain. CBT for cessation-related weight gain draws from treatments for eating disorders and body image

disturbances and helps patients learn to modify maladaptive thoughts that lead to unhealthy weight control. Examples of these maladaptive thoughts include overvalued ideas of the importance of thinness, and all-or-nothing thinking (e.g., that one can be only thin or overweight, or there are good and bad foods). CBT may be particularly effective as a supplement to standard treatment for women who are weight-preoccupied.

Pharmacological Treatments. Certain medications may be especially helpful for weight-concerned smokers by helping to reduce weight gain. Bupropion is an antidepressant (selective reuptake inhibitor of dopamine and noradrenalin) that is an efficacious treatment for smoking cessation. Theorized mechanisms of its effectiveness in assisting smoking cessation include its antidepressant effects and its effectiveness in reducing nicotine cravings. Bupropion also reduces appetite for food, and may effectively curb weight gain following cessation, thereby increasing the likelihood of prolonged abstinence. Research has shown that smokers experience heightened food reward following smoking cessation and that bupropion effectively attenuates this increase. Research reviews indicate that bupropion is an effective and well-tolerated first-line treatment for smoking cessation. Naltrexone hydrochloride is an opiate antagonist and may be particularly effective for reducing post-cessation weight gain due to its regulation of appetitive behaviors. When administered in conjunction with the nicotine patch, low-dose naltrexone results in less post-cessation weight gain.

Smoking cessation is associated with modest weight gain. The exact mechanism of weight gain is not fully understood but is likely a combination of physiological and behavioral factors. There is some evidence that weight-preoccupied smokers have a more difficult time quitting due to their unwillingness to tolerate minimal weight gain. Although concerns about weight gain are more common for female smokers than male smokers, a significant portion of male smokers also report fear of cessation-associated weight gain. Treatments that address weight gain may be more successful for some individuals, especially those with heightened concerns about weight gain, and may increase interest in making a quit attempt.

See also **Advertising and Tobacco; Nicotine Delivery Systems for Smoking Cessation; Treatment, Behavioral Approaches to: Cognitive-Behavioral Therapy.**

BIBLIOGRAPHY

Cavallo, D. A., Duhig, A. M., McKee, S., & Krishnan-Sarin, S. (2006). Gender and weight concerns in adolescent smokers. *Addictive Behaviors, 31*(11), 2140–2146.

Clark, M. M., Hurt, R. D., Croghan, I. T., Patten, C. A., Novotny, P., Sloan, J. A., et al. (2006). The prevalence of weight concerns in a smoking abstinence clinical trial. *Addictive Behaviors, 31*(7), 1144–1152.

Copeland, A. L., Martin, P. D., Geiselman, P. J., Rash, C. J., & Kendzor, D. E. (2006). Smoking cessation for weight-concerned women: Group vs. individually tailored, dietary, and weight-control follow-up sessions. *Addictive Behaviors, 31*(1), 115–127.

Filozof, C., Fernandez Pinilla, M. C., & Fernandez-Cruz, A. (2004). Smoking cessation and weight gain. *Obesity Reviews, 5*(2), 95–103.

Fiore, M., Bailey, W. C., Cohen, S. J., Dorfman, S. F., Goldstein, M. G., Gritz, E. R., et al. (2000). *Treating tobacco use and dependence: Clinical practice guideline.* Rockville, MD: U.S. Department of Health and Human Services, Public Health Service.

John, U., Meyer, C., Hanke, M., Volzke, H., & Schumann, A. (2006). Smoking status, obesity, and hypertension in a general population sample: A cross-sectional study. *Quarterly Journal of Medicine, 99*(6), 407–415.

Perkins, K. A. (1993). Weight gain following smoking cessation. *Journal of Consulting and Clinical Psychology, 61*(5), 768–777.

Perkins, K. A., Marcus, M. D., Levine, M. D., D'Amico, D., Miller, A., Broge, M., et al. (2001). Cognitive-behavioral therapy to reduce weight concerns improves smoking cessation outcome in weight-concerned women. *Journal of Consulting and Clinical Psychology, 69*(4), 604–613.

MARNEY A. WHITE
STEPHANIE S. O'MALLEY

TOBACCO, ADVERTISING AND. *See* Advertising and Tobacco Use.

TOLERANCE AND PHYSICAL DEPENDENCE.

In physical dependence, the brain and body chemistry undergo changes to adapt to the consistent presence of the drug, and this adaptation causes withdrawal symptoms if the concentration of the drug present is sharply reduced or removed altogether. Withdrawal symptoms are determined by the type of drug upon which the individual has developed physical dependence, but they are consistent for specific substances. That is, withdrawal from opioids is different than withdrawal from antidepressants or amphetamines, but withdrawal from a particular type of drug is consistent across individuals. So, the signs and symptoms of withdrawal from a specific substance will be largely consistent across persons who are physically dependent on it but may vary somewhat in terms of severity, speed of onset, and duration of effects.

As a rule, withdrawal symptoms are opposite of the drug's effects on the central nervous system: If physical dependence produces drowsiness, calm, and constipation, withdrawal will likely include agitation, insomnia, anxiety, and diarrhea (among a constellation of other symptoms). Those physiological functions or chemical processes that are altered or suppressed by the drug will usually be hyper-stimulated during withdrawal. Because tolerance leads an individual to use progressively more of a substance to achieve the same effect, withdrawal symptoms will typically correlate with both the amount and length of use.

Physical dependence is distinct from addiction in that the person who is physically dependent often uses to reduce pain or maintain homeostasis—not necessarily to achieve intoxication or a high. Persons who use pain medication may become physically dependent on the drug in order to manage symptoms but might not overuse or wish to continue substance use if the source of the pain no longer exists. Persons who are physically dependent on a drug may not experience adverse impacts on their social, familial, or occupational functioning as a result of the substance use and may not exhibit the drug-seeking behavior (willingness to take risks, compromised functioning, or making unwise decisions) that is typically present in persons with substance addiction.

TOLERANCE

Tolerance is the process that occurs when a drug is repeatedly administered over time; the body becomes accustomed to its presence and experiences progressively less effect from the drug. As a result, the person needs to use progressively more of the substance over time to achieve the desired effect, whether that effect is a *buzz*, a *high*, or simply a sense of relief from troubling symptoms (such as pain, anxiety, or depression). Tolerance and physical dependence are common consequences of drug self-administration. To understand and modify alcohol and drug abuse and the problems they cause, people need to recognize how tolerance and physical dependence determine drug self-administration. Some alcoholics, for example, can appear unaffected at blood alcohol concentrations that would prostrate most social drinkers. For these alcoholics, tolerance makes possible escalation in drug use and in medical and psychological problems caused by heavy drug use. In addition to being highly tolerant, alcoholics will probably be physically dependent on alcohol, though tolerance and dependence have been shown to be distinct in their neurobiology.

Tolerance has to do with habituation: Over time, the same amount of a substance produces less effect. To obtain the desired substance-use effect, it is therefore necessary to increase the amount of substance used. There are several different types of tolerance. Acute tolerance occurs with a single exposure to the substance. For example, alcohol-induced impairment can be greater when measured soon after drinking begins than when measured later in the drinking session, even at the same blood alcohol concentration. Functional tolerance occurs with substance ingestion over time and reflects the development of different mechanisms by the brain and body to compensate for prolonged exposure to the substance. For example, chronic drinkers of alcohol can appear completely sober after drinking an amount that would inebriate or even kill other individuals, despite having a blood alcohol level that greatly exceeds the legal limit for intoxication. Functional tolerance increases the possibility for physiological damage because the substance user may ingest amounts that cause considerable damage without being aware of any bodily changes.

Environment dependent tolerance develops over time when the individual always uses the substance in the same place, under the same or similar conditions, and with the same cues. Tolerance is increased, or occurs more rapidly, when all of the conditions around the substance use remain relatively constant. In contrast, environment independent tolerance occurs when an individual habitually

consumes large amounts of a substance (typically alcohol) and becomes functionally tolerant, regardless of where the consumption occurs or under what circumstances. The latter form of tolerance develops more gradually than the former.

Some aspects of tolerance may be influenced by genetics. One study compared sons of alcoholic fathers with sons of non-alcoholic fathers on a variety of measures. The results indicated that sons of alcoholic fathers were generally less functionally impaired by ingesting alcohol than were sons of non-alcoholic fathers. It is thought that sons of alcoholic fathers are more apt to demonstrate acute tolerance while drinking than the sons of non-alcoholic fathers. The predisposition to be less impaired by alcohol consumption and to develop acute tolerance may be associated with a genetic propensity to drink more and to develop alcoholism.

PHYSICAL DEPENDENCE

Physical dependence is defined as a physiologic state of adaptation to a substance. The absence of this substance produces symptoms and signs of withdrawal. The withdrawal syndrome is often characterized by over activity of physiological functions that were suppressed by the drug and/or depression of functions that were stimulated by the drug. Physical dependence requires a period of exposure to the substance adequate to produce adaptation to its effects. The duration and extent of exposure required varies among different substances. In an individual who is physically dependent on a substance, sudden cessation or a dramatic reduction in substance use causes withdrawal symptoms. These are typically uncomfortable but may be life threatening at times. Depending on their severity, the withdrawal symptoms may motivate the individual to use drugs or alcohol to alleviate discomfort.

The withdrawal symptoms experienced by persons who are physically dependent on alcohol include the following: feelings of craving for alcohol, nausea, sweatiness, shakiness, and anxiety, along with elevated blood pressure, pulse, and temperature. Symptoms of alcohol withdrawal become evident within 6 to 24 hours of the last drink. At its extreme, withdrawal from alcohol is accompanied by delirium, referred to as *delirium tremens*, which can be life threatening.

Common symptoms of withdrawal from opioids include yawning, sweating, watery eyes, stuffy and runny nose, abdominal cramps, nausea and vomiting, diarrhea, extreme feelings of weakness, dilated pupils, goose bumps and chills, muscle twitching, muscle aches and muscle pains, anxiety, insomnia, rapid pulse, rapid and shallow breathing, and increased blood pressure. The length of time until withdrawal begins varies by type of opioid and how long it took to metabolize out of the body. For example, users of morphine (or any of its derivatives) or oxycodone generally begin to experience withdrawal symptoms within 6 to 12 hours after the last use, whereas persons who abruptly cease using methadone may not experience withdrawal symptoms until 72 to 96 hours after the last use. The more severe the physical dependence, the longer lasting and more uncomfortable the withdrawal symptoms.

Persons who are physically dependent on benzodiazepines experience very similar withdrawal symptoms to those with alcohol dependence, but they are significantly longer lasting. Symptoms commonly associated with benzodiazepine withdrawal are anxiety and depressed mood. The major medical risk to individuals withdrawing from benzodiazepines is increased likelihood of having a seizure. People who use short-acting benzodiazepines experience withdrawal more rapidly than those who use long-acting varieties.

Between 1998 and 2008, researchers determined that withdrawal syndrome occurs with abrupt cessation of antidepressants, though these drugs are rarely abused. The withdrawal symptoms experienced by individuals physically dependent on antidepressants typically include acute anxiety and panic, followed by feelings of depression and (sometimes) suicidal ideation.

The general principle guiding the treatment of withdrawal is to use a long-acting substance from the same class (e.g., an opiate such as buprenorphine for heroin withdrawal) or a medication with similar pharmacological effects (e.g., a benzodiazepine for alcohol withdrawal) to suppress withdrawal symptoms. The medication dose is then gradually reduced, giving the body and brain adequate time to adjust to the drug's elimination.

See also **Addiction: Concepts and Definitions; Research, Animal Model: An Overview; Risk Factors for Substance Use, Abuse, and Dependence: An Overview.**

BIBLIOGRAPHY

Adams, L. L., Gatchel, R. J., Robinson, R. C., Polatin, P., Garraj, N., Deschner, M., et al. (2004). Development of a self-report screening instrument for assessing potential opioid medication misuse in chronic pain patients. *Journal of Pain Symptom Management, 27*(5), 440–459.

American Psychiatric Association. (2000). *Diagnostic and statistical manual of mental disorders* (4th ed., text rev.). Arlington, VA: Author.

Cann, W., & De Belleroche, J. (Eds.). (2002). *Drink, drugs, and dependence: From science to clinical practice.* New York: Routledge.

Center for Substance Abuse Treatment. (2006, Summer). *Pain management without psychological dependence: A guide for healthcare providers* (Substance Abuse in Brief Fact Sheet, Vol. 4, Issue 1). Rockville, MD: SAMHSA National Clearinghouse for Alcohol and Drug Information.

Friedman, R., Li, V., & Mehrotra, D. (2003). Treating pain patients at risk: Evaluation of a screening tool in opioid-treated pain patients with and without addiction. *Pain Medicine, 4*(2), 182–185.

Graham, A. W., Schultz, T. K., Mayo-Smith, M. F., Ries, R. K., & Wilford, B. B. (2003). *Principles of addiction medicine* (3rd ed.). Chevy Chase, MD: American Society of Addiction Medicine.

Heit, H. A. (2003). Addiction, physical dependence, and tolerance: Precise definitions to help clinicians evaluate and treat chronic pain patients. *Journal of Pain & Palliative Care Pharmacotherapy, 17*(1), 15–29.

Jones, E. M., Knutson, D., & Haines, D. (2003). Common problems in patients recovering from chemical dependency. *American Family Physician, 68*(10), 1971–1978.

O'Brien, C. P. (1996). Recent developments in the pharmacotherapy of substance abuse [Special Section: The contribution of psychotherapy and pharmacotherapy to national mental health care]. *Journal of Consulting and Clinical Psychology, 64,* 677.

Savage, S. R. (2002). Assessment for addiction in pain-treatment settings. *Clinical Journal of Pain, 18*(Suppl. 4), S28–S38.

Substance Abuse and Mental Health Services Administration, Office of Applied Studies. (2006). *Treatment episode data set (TEDS). Highlights 2004. National admissions to substance abuse treatment services.* (DASIS Series: S-31, DHHS Publication No. SMA 06–4140). Rockville, MD: Author.

Substance Abuse and Mental Health Services Administration, Office of Applied Studies. (2007). *Drug abuse warning network: 2005 National estimates of drug-*

related emergency department visits. (DAWN Series D-29, DHHS Publication No. SMA 07–4256). Rockville, MD: Author.

Substance Abuse and Mental Health Services Administration, Office of Applied Studies. (2007). *National Survey of Substance Abuse Treatment Services (N-SSATS): 2006 Data on substance abuse treatment facilities.* (DASIS Series: S-39, DHHS Publication No. SMA 07–4296). Rockville, MD: Author.

Substance Abuse and Mental Health Services Administration, Office of Applied Studies. (2007). *Results from the 2006 National Survey on Drug Use and Health: National findings* (NSDUH Series H-32, DHHS Publication No. SMA 07–4293). Rockville, MD: Author.

HOWARD D. CAPPELL
REVISED BY MARY CARRLIN (2001)
PAMELA V. MICHAELS (2009)

TOUGHLOVE. The generic term *toughlove* (or tough love) describes a style of caring applied in diverse interpersonal contexts whereby one person or group reasserts power over another for whom he or she is responsible. Claire Kowalski was the first person to use the term in published material in 1976, to differentiate a respectful means of caring for elderly people that preserves self-mastery from a smothering style that promotes dependence. Since that first use, others have found the term useful. The Association of the Relatives and Friends of the Mentally Ill endorses the concept (Roberts, 1985). In its most common use today, the term describes the means by which parents of abusive, delinquent, or drug-abusing children can regain parental control. Toughlove is also the name of a self-help program for these parents and their children.

Toughlove, the self-help program, was developed by Phyllis and David York in 1980. They found that rescuing their daughter, who engaged in highly destructive behavior, did more harm than good. Instead, they permitted natural and logical consequences to correct their daughter's behavior while they sought emotional support from their friends. They wrote and published *Toughlove* (1980) and founded an organization called the Toughlove Support Network (which is described in their later book, 1984). The network's mission is to promote what they view as a mode of intervention for individuals, families, and communities.

According to the Toughlove philosophy, parents are the ones with the dominant power in a family. Children misbehave when parents fail to assert themselves or to take responsibility for their role as parents; but when parents' expectations are stated clearly, a child will no longer control the family. Parents are urged to describe the behavior they expect from their children. Speculation about the causes of child misbehavior is discouraged. Parents do not need to understand why their child misbehaves. Instead, they must act in coalition with other parents to assert control of themselves and their home environment.

Toughlove parents are taught not to feel guilty about their child's misbehavior because children are responsible for their own actions. A Toughlove parent of a destructive child might say: "We have had enough. We are not rescuing you from the trouble you have caused. We love you enough to say no." Proponents of Toughlove believe that drug and alcohol abuse is the most important causative factor in the disruptive behavior among teens. Once parents suspect drug and alcohol abuse, it is important that they investigate by questioning their child's friends, school officials, other family members, and anyone else their child meets frequently. When parents find drug and alcohol abuse, they must require abstinence. Strict discipline and limit setting are seen as the only means of enabling children to behave and to have a chance of regaining control of their lives.

Parents must confront their child about the drug and alcohol abuse and stipulate the behavior they expect. Toughlove recommends that they require the child to stop using drugs and seek treatment if needed. If a child refuses to comply, he or she is to be ejected from the home. Many uncooperative children are sent to live with another Toughlove family until they are serious about meeting their own parents' stipulations. Children who refuse to live with another Toughlove family are out on their own until they agree to their parents' rules.

To gain help in maintaining firmness and setting appropriate rules, parents attend a support group consisting of other parents who endorse the Toughlove principles. Toughlove support groups are organized by the parents without any professional leadership. Besides providing support for parents, Toughlove groups evaluate the effectiveness of treatment programs and the effectiveness of professionals who treat children for alcohol and drug abuse.

Hollihan and Riley (1987) used qualitative research methods to study a Toughlove parent group. They found that several themes characterized group sessions and defined the Toughlove program experience for parents. First, the lay-led group emphasized that old-fashioned values are superior to those inherent in more permissive methods of raising children. Second, members regarded child-development professionals as advocates for modern child-raising methods that blame parents for child misbehavior. Third, they described the Toughlove group as their island of support within a pro-child social environment made up of the police, educators, social workers, and the courts. Last, the group provided successful models of rule setting by parents and enforcement of strict discipline—including as a final resort forcing a child to leave home. The group presented a persuasive and comforting rationale for the use of strict discipline that addressed the needs of parents who were experiencing great stress and feelings of failure (Hollihan & Riley, 1987).

Toughlove has been criticized as being simplistic and heavy-handed. According to Hollihan and Riley (1987), parents in the group they observed who did not believe their child was abusing drugs or alcohol were nevertheless instructed in ways to document such abuse. Other possible causes of their child's misbehavior were ignored, because the Toughlove solution is supposed to apply in all situations. The tactic of throwing an unruly child out of the house is especially controversial. Although most children go to live with other Toughlove families, some are forced to leave with nowhere to go and can become homeless, a predator or a victim, or a threat to themselves and others. For example, John Hinckley, who attempted to kill President Ronald W. Reagan in 1982, had been cast out of his home by parents who endorsed Toughlove and who later warned other parents to be cautious in disciplining their children.

Neither the Toughlove program nor the style of caring identified with it has been evaluated. On the one hand, there is anecdotal evidence from parents to vouch for it. On the other, as illustrated by the Hinckley family, Toughlove solutions can make matters worse. At present, we do not know whether the positive or the negative is the more common outcome, or whether positive outcomes result from factors having nothing to do with Toughlove.

See also **Adolescents and Drug Use; Parent Movement, The; Prevention, Education and.**

BIBLIOGRAPHY

Hollihan, T., & Riley, P. (1987). The rhetorical power of a compelling story: A critique of a "Toughlove" parental support group. *Communication Quarterly, 35*, 13–25.

Klug, W. (1990). *A preliminary investigation of Toughlove: Assertiveness and support in a parents' self-help group.* Paper presented at the Annual Convention of the American Psychological Association, Boston.

Kowalski, C. (1976). Smother love vs. tough love. *Social Work, 21*, 319–321.

Lawton, M. (1982). Group psychotherapy with alcoholics: Special techniques. *Journal of Studies on Alcohol, 43*, 1276–1278.

Milhorn, H. T. (2007). *Drug and alcohol abuse: The authoritative guide for parents, teachers, and counselors.* Cambridge, MA: Da Capo.

Nemy, E. (1982). For problem teenagers: Love, toughness. *New York Times*, April 26, p. B12.

Roberts, A. (1985). A.R.A.F.M.I.: Association of the Relatives and Friends of the Mentally Ill. *Mental Health in Australia, 1*, 37–39.

Szalavitz, M. (2006). The trouble with tough love. *Washington Post*, January 29, p. B01.

Westreich, L. (2007). *Helping the addict you love: The new effective program for getting the addict into treatment.* New York: Fireside.

Wohl, L. (1982). The parent training game—from Toughlove to perfect manners. *Ms.*, May, pp. 40–44.

York, P., & York, D. (1980). *Toughlove.* Sellersville, PA: Community Service Foundation.

York, P., York, D., & Wachtel, T. (1984). *Toughlove solutions.* Garden City, NY: Doubleday.

GREGORY W. BROCK
ELLEN BURKE

TREATMENT

This entry includes the following essays:
AN OVERVIEW
AN OVERVIEW OF ALCOHOL ABUSE/DEPENDENCE
AN OVERVIEW OF DRUG ABUSE/DEPENDENCE
A HISTORY OF TREATMENT IN THE UNITED STATES

AN OVERVIEW

The sections below cover a wide range of topics relative to the treatment of drug and alcohol problems. They are organized within 4 major subheadings. The first section, Behavioral Approaches, covers the range of *talk* therapies or psychotherapies as well as some of the common formats (long-term versus brief, group therapies). The next section includes articles on the major pharmacological strategies (medications) for treatment including newer approaches such as vaccines and long-acting (injectable) preparations. The third section covers specialty approaches (acupuncture, therapeutic communities) and populations (adolescents, older adults). The fourth section addresses treatment more broadly, reflecting the different stages of interventions and increasing the acceptance that addiction is a chronic, relapsing disorder similar to other chronic disorders such as diabetes and hypertension. This organization reflects the increasing recognition of commonalities across substance of abuse in terms of risk factors, co-occurring psychiatric disorders, and treatment approaches. Thus, treatments of specific drug and alcohol use disorders are covered within the major subheadings and to a lesser extent within the entries for each type of substance. In addition, brief overview sections that summarize the current state of knowledge on the treatment of alcohol and drug use disorders are included.

See also **Accidents and Injuries from Alcohol; Coerced Treatment for Substance Offenders; Criminal Justice System, Treatment in the; Substance Abuse and AIDS; Treatment: A History of Treatment in the United States.**

KATHLEEN M. CARROLL

AN OVERVIEW OF ALCOHOL ABUSE/ DEPENDENCE

Early-twenty-first century treatment options for alcohol use disorders include psychotherapeutic interventions and medications. In addition, those individuals suffering from an alcohol use disorder can avail themselves of a unique network of self-help movements to support their efforts at recovery.

Besides the two broad types of interventions for alcoholism (psychotherapy and medications), treatment may be also conceptualized in terms of the phases or goals of the intervention. For example, this may include interventions whose primary goals are prevention and harm reduction, such as brief interventions for certain populations at risk, like college students, heavy drinkers, and adolescents or adults with additional psychiatric conditions. Interventions may also be aimed at acute stabilization, which might involve medically supervised inpatient care to stabilize and treat the alcohol withdrawal syndrome and any associated psychiatric or medical condition. Interventions aimed at maintenance and recovery may involve ambulatory care, and have short-term goals of reducing drinking behavior, achieving abstinence, and preventing relapse, and the long-term goals of recovery and health restoration. Typically, treatment is a combination of psychotherapeutic interventions, medication, and encouragement to become involved in self-help groups when feasible.

The self-help movement has a unique supportive role and tradition in the treatment of alcoholism. It emerged during the first half of the twentieth century as an independent self-help movement within the community of affected individuals (William, 1949; Khantzian & Mack, 1994). From that self-help tradition, empirically based psychotherapeutic interventions, such as twelve-step facilitation therapy and individual and group drug counseling, have evolved. These traditions have also enriched the treatment interventions by emphasizing broader elements related to recovery, such as promoting wellness behavior, spirituality, and personal growth. Self-help groups have, in addition, become more cognizant of the need to treat alcohol dependence with medication for a variety of reasons.

MEDICATIONS USED TO TREAT ALCOHOLISM

There are primary indications for which medications are commonly used in treating alcoholism. For the most part, they are used to treat alcohol withdrawal, to reduce or stop drinking behavior, and to treat associated psychiatric and medical conditions.

Medications for Alcohol Withdrawal. Alcohol withdrawal syndrome usually develops in people with a long history of sustained heavy drinking. This syndrome starts a few hours after such an individual stops drinking or attempts to reduce significantly his or her intake of alcohol. The syndrome may range in severity from mild anxiety, insomnia, tremors, and mild changes in vital signs, to severe complications such as the development of alcohol withdrawal seizures and delirium tremens, with the latter still associated with a high degree of mortality if untreated. It is well known that the greater the number of previous withdrawals, the more severe the current withdrawal will be. The primary goals of the treatment of alcohol withdrawal syndrome are to prevent the severe complications mentioned earlier, to make the patient as comfortable as possible, and to help the patient address his or her alcohol problem and opt for follow-up treatment, as the phase of withdrawal may represent a window of opportunity, prompting the patient to commit to rehabilitation.

Benzodiazepine medications have been the standard treatment for alcohol withdrawal syndrome. Long- and intermediate-acting benzodiazepines are the most commonly used. Long-acting compounds allow less frequent dosing and produce a self-tapering effect, whereas intermediate-acting compounds with no active metabolites are the preferred medications in patients with compromised liver. In many settings, a withdrawal assessment scale is used in combination with medication to provide more comprehensive monitoring of the withdrawal syndrome and to guide medication dosing. Anticonvulsant medications, such as carbamazepine, sodium valproate, and gabapentin, are being used increasingly for the treatment of alcohol withdrawal. Preliminary research suggests that these medications may also be helpful in decreasing alcohol use subsequent to withdrawal, especially in people who have experienced previous episodes of alcohol withdrawal (Malcolm et al., 2002).

Medications for Reducing or Stopping Drinking Behavior. The U.S. Food and Drug Administration (FDA) has thus far approved three medications to treat alcoholism: disulfiram, naltrexone (both oral and intramuscular forms), and acamprosate. A number of other medications have also been tested, and some of them, such as topiramate, have shown efficacy in well-designed studies. Following is a brief description of the medications used to reduce or stop drinking behavior:

- Disulfiram is known as an aversive, or alcohol-sensitizing, agent. Aversive agents are compounds that produce a toxic reaction if alcohol is consumed. Disulfiram blocks the breakdown

of ethanol by irreversibly inhibiting the enzyme aldehyde dehydrogenase (ALDH), which is responsible for the metabolism of acetaldehyde, a toxic by-product of alcohol. The resultant accumulation of acetaldehyde in the blood produces what is termed as the disulfiram-ethanol reaction (DER). The DER develops within a few minutes and may last 30 minutes or more. It ranges in severity from mildly increased heart rate and blood pressure, chills, nausea, vomiting, hypertension, and shortness of breath to moderate, and in some cases extreme, severity with convulsions, congestive heart failure, and cardiovascular collapse. The severity of the syndrome also depends on the dose of disulfiram and the amount of alcohol ingested. Disulfiram is useful in the treatment of alcoholism in a select group of patients, especially those with supervised medication ingestion. Disulfiram, like most medications, produces side effects; including worsening of psychotic symptoms. Calcium carbimide is another aversive agent. However, it is not available in the United States.

- Naltrexone is a pure, reversible opioid antagonist, approved by the FDA, initially for opiate dependence, and subsequently for alcohol dependence; it is available in oral and long-acting (1-month) intramuscular injection forms. This medication decreases drinking by reducing the positive reinforcing effect of alcohol. Studies have shown that naltrexone decreases drinking, improves abstinence rates, reduces craving, and therefore reduces the risk for relapse. Patients who continue to drink alcohol while on naltrexone report experiencing less of a "high." Naltrexone appears to reduce the desire to drink in alcohol-dependent patients as well as social drinkers. Multiple studies, but not all, have demonstrated the efficacy of naltrexone in its oral form when taken on a daily basis. Studies have also shown the effectiveness of targeted naltrexone use among problem drinkers to reduce their heavy drinking (Kranzler et al., 2003). In such a targeted scenario, the drinking patient takes naltrexone only in anticipation of exposure to a high-risk situation for heavy drinking. An intramuscular monthly injection of naltrexone (at a dosage of 380 milligrams) was also found effective in reducing alcohol use (Garbutt et al., 2005). In addition, naltrexone appears to be effective in combination with different psychotherapies, including cognitive-behavioral therapy (CBT), supportive treatment, and medication management therapy (Anton et al., 2005, 2006). Nalmefene is another opioid antagonist, one which has been much less studied than naltrexone, and evidence of its efficacy in treating alcoholism is mixed, with some studies showing it to be efficacious and one other showing it to be no better than placebo.

- Acamprosate or calcium acetyl homotaurinate is the third FDA-approved medication for treating alcoholism. This medication decreases alcohol use by reducing the negative reinforcing effect of alcohol. Acamprosate is thought to normalize the glutamatergic excitation that occurs during alcohol withdrawal and early abstinence, leading to a reduction in craving, distress, and the need to consume alcohol. Several European trials have shown that acamprosate approximately doubles the abstinence rate over a 12-month period compared to a placebo, although studies in the United States have not shown it to be superior to placebo. Acamprosate is not metabolized in the body; it is excreted primarily by the kidney. It also has a good safety profile, with the main side effects being headache and diarrhea.

- Topiramate is an anticonvulsant medication approved by the FDA for the treatment of certain forms of seizure disorders and for the prevention of migraine headache, but not for alcoholism. It has been hypothesized that topiramate decreases the craving for alcohol and its rewarding effect by facilitating gamma-amino butyric (GABA) neurotransmission and dampening glutamate-related excitatory effects. Two rigorously conducted, double-blind, placebo-controlled studies; one single-site and one multisite; demonstrated the efficacy of topiramate in treating alcohol dependence (Johnson et al., 2003, 2007). A salient feature of these studies is that patients were still drinking a large amount of alcohol when the study drug was started. Thus, topiramate has proven efficacious in treating patients who continue drinking, and a period of abstinence is not required before starting the medication. Preliminary evidence also points to the usefulness of other anticonvulsants, such as sodium valproate, carabamazepine, and gabapentin, in decreasing alcohol use.

- A number of medications that affect the serotonergic system have shown efficacy in a subgroup of patients. For example, a low-risk low-alcohol severity subgroup was found to respond better to the antidepressant sertraline than placebo (Pettinati et al., 2000), whereas those with early-onset alcoholism (below the age of 25 years) responded better to ondansetron than placebo (Johnson et al., 2000).

Medications for Comorbid Psychiatric Disorders. Additional psychiatric difficulties such as major depression, bipolar disorder, anxiety disorders, or psychotic disorders requiring medication are often encountered among patients suffering from alcoholism. Several antidepressants have been tested on patients with major depression and alcoholism with mixed results, particularly in terms of the effects on drinking. A reduction in drinking was most evident in those groups that had experienced the greatest improvement in depressive symptoms.

Few studies have been conducted among subjects with both bipolar disorder and alcoholism. Sodium valproate was found effective in decreasing heavy drinking in this population (Salloum et al., 2005), but a recent controlled trial reported that quetiapine was no better than a placebo in improving the alcohol outcome (Brown et al., 2008). Paroxetine, a serotonin reuptake inhibitor, appears to be helpful in treating the symptoms of anxiety but not in decreasing alcohol use among patients with alcoholism and anxiety disorders. Open-label, follow-up studies have reported an improved alcohol outcome for patients with schizophrenia and alcoholism who were taking clozapine.

PSYCHOTHERAPY FOR ALCOHOL DEPENDENCE

There are many modalities of psychotherapy, and diverse techniques and theoretical approaches available to intervene in alcoholism. These include individual, group, and family therapy formats as well as self-help groups, all of which could take place with different intensity and frequency, in diverse treatment settings such as inpatient, residential, and ambulatory programs. Many therapeutic approaches have also been developed, including dynamically oriented psychotherapy, cognitive behavioral therapy (CBT), relapse-prevention therapy, motivational enhancement therapy, contingency management therapy, network therapy, and disease management/ medication adherence therapy. Furthermore, a number of these therapies have been empirically tested in large multicenter, randomized trials. Overall, although there is good evidence that the use of such psychosocial interventions is superior to no or minimal treatment, there is only limited evidence that one type of intervention is superior to the others.

A combination of psychotherapy and pharmacotherapy has also been studied in randomized controlled trials. Different manual-guided therapies for alcoholism, such as CBT, motivational enhancement therapy, and twelve-step facilitation therapy, among others, have been found effective in reducing alcohol use. Some therapies may be more apt to yield a better outcome than others. For example, exposure to the twelve-step facilitation therapy in Project MATCH (Project MATCH Research Group, 1998), a large multicenter study of psychotherapies for alcohol dependence, produced a higher abstinence rate at follow-up (Miller, 2005). The combination of psychotherapy and medication may be associated with improved outcome (O'Malley et al., 1992; Anton et al., 2005). For example, in the COMBINE study (Anton et al., 2006), as of 2008 the largest pharmacotherapy trial conducted to study alcoholism in combination with psychotherapy, showed that a combination of disease management therapy with naltrexone was among the most effective treatment of nine different kinds of treatment assignments.

Furthermore, brief interventions for alcoholism have been extensively studied and found effective in decreasing alcohol use among samples of drinkers with alcohol-related problems, including individuals who were not seeking treatment (Moyer et al., 2002; Vasilaki et al., 2006). Brief interventions appear to be effective when they are delivered using available technologies like telephone counseling or Web-based counseling (Blow et al., 2006; Mello et al., 2008). The key advantage to using such an alternative technology is the ability to reach a wider audience of affected individuals at a lower cost.

See also **Accidents and Injuries from Alcohol; Treatment: A History of Treatment in the United States.**

BIBLIOGRAPHY

Anton, R. F., Moak, D. H., et al. (2005). Naltrexone combined with either cognitive behavioral or motivational enhancement therapy for alcohol dependence. *Journal of Clinical Psychopharmacology, 25*(4), 349–357.

Anton, R. F., O'Malley, S. S., et al. (2006). Combined pharmacotherapies and behavioral interventions for alcohol dependence. The COMBINE study: A randomized controlled trial. *Journal of the American Medical Association, 295*(17), 2003–2017 [see comment].

Blow, F. C., Barry, K. L., et al. (2006). The efficacy of two brief intervention strategies among injured, at-risk drinkers in the emergency department: Impact of tailored messaging and brief advice. *Journal of Studies on Alcohol, 67*(4), 568–578.

Brown, E. S., Garza, M., et al. (2008). A randomized, double-blind, placebo-controlled add-on trial of Quetiapine in outpatients with bipolar disorder and alcohol use disorders. *Journal of Clinical Psychiatry.* Available from http://www.psychiatrist.com.

Garbutt, J. C., Kranzler, H. R., et al. (2005). Efficacy and tolerability of long-acting injectable naltrexone for alcohol dependence: A randomized controlled trial. *Journal of the American Medical Association, 293*(13), 1617–1625 [erratum appears in *293*(16), 1978].

Johnson, B. A., Ait-Daoud, N., et al. (2003). Oral topiramate for treatment of alcohol dependence: A randomised controlled trial. *The Lancet, 361*(9370), 1677–1685.

Johnson, B. A., Roache, J. D. P., et al. (2000). Ondansetron for reduction of drinking among biologically predisposed alcoholic patients: A randomized controlled trial. *Journal of the American Medical Association, 284*(8), 963–971.

Johnson, B. A., Rosenthal, N., et al. (2007). Topiramate for treating alcohol dependence: A randomized controlled trial. *Journal of the American Medical Association, 298*(14), 1641–1651.

Khantzian, E. J., & Mack, E. (March–April 1994). How AA works and why it's important for clinicians to understand. *Journal of Substance Abuse Treatment, 11*(2), 77–92.

Kranzler, H. R., Armeli, S., et al. (2003). Targeted naltrexone for early problem drinkers. *Journal of Clinical Psychopharmacology, 23*(3), 294–304.

Malcolm, R., Myrick, H., et al. (2002). The effects of carbamazepine and lorazepam on single versus multiple previous alcohol withdrawals in an outpatient randomized trial. *Journal of General Internal Medicine, 17*(5), 349–355.

Mello, M. J., Longabaugh, R., et al. (2008). DIAL: A telephone brief intervention for high-risk alcohol use with injured emergency department patients. *Annals of Emergency Medicine, 51*(6), 755–764.

Miller, W. R. (2005). Are alcoholism treatments effective? The Project MATCH data: Response. *BMC Public Health, 5*, 76.

Moyer, A., Finney, J. W., et al. (2002). Brief interventions for alcohol problems: A meta-analytic review of controlled investigations in treatment-seeking and non-treatment-seeking populations. *Addiction, 97*(3), 279–292.

O'Malley, S. S., Jaffe, A. J., et al. (1992). Naltrexone and coping skills therapy for alcohol dependence. A controlled study. *Archives of General Psychiatry, 49*(11), 881–887.

Pettinati, H. M., Volpicelli, J. R., et al. (2000). Sertraline treatment for alcohol dependence: Interactive effects of medication and alcoholic subtype. *Alcoholism: Clinical & Experimental Research, 24*(7), 1041–1049.

Project MATCH Research Group. (1998). Matching alcoholism treatments to client heterogeneity: Project MATCH three-year drinking outcomes. *Alcoholism: Clinical & Experimental Research, 22*(6), 1300–1311.

Salloum, I. M., Cornelius, J. R., et al. (2005). Efficacy of valproate maintenance in patients with bipolar disorder and alcoholism: A double-blind placebo-controlled study. *Archives of General Psychiatry, 62*(1), 37–45.

Vasilaki, E. I., Hosier, S. G., et al. (2006). The efficacy of motivational interviewing as a brief intervention for excessive drinking: A meta-analytic review. *Alcohol & Alcoholism, 41*(3), 328–335.

William, W. (1949). The society of Alcoholics Anonymous. *American Journal of Psychiatry, 105*(5), 370–375.

IHSAN SALLOUM

AN OVERVIEW OF DRUG ABUSE/DEPENDENCE

Drug addiction is a medical and public health problem that affects everyone, either directly or indirectly. It has been estimated that drug abuse and addiction cost the United States more than $110 billion per year. If one adds the cost of nicotine to this figure, the number dramatically soars. Added to the economic costs are the personal, family, and medical problems associated with smoking and the use and abuse of other drugs. Improved prevention and treatment are the best ways to reduce all of these problems. Fortunately, advances in science have revolutionized the fundamental understanding of the nature of drug abuse and addiction and what to do about it.

Extensive data show that addiction is eminently treatable if the treatment is well delivered and tailored to the needs of a particular patient. An array of both behavioral and pharmacological treatments can effectively reduce drug use, help manage drug cravings, prevent relapses, and restore people as productive members of society.

Three decades of scientific research and clinical practice have yielded a variety of effective approaches to drug addiction treatment. Extensive data document that drug addiction treatment is as effective as treatments for most other chronic medical conditions. In spite of scientific evidence that establishes the effectiveness of drug abuse treatment, many people believe that treatment is generally ineffective. In part, this is because of unrealistic expectations. Many people equate addiction with simply using drugs, and they therefore expect that addiction will be cured quickly and permanently, so they view treatment as a failure if it is not. In reality, because addiction is a chronic disease, the ultimate goal of long-term abstinence often requires sustained and repeated treatment episodes.

Drug-abuse treatment programs using medications and/or behavioral techniques can and do work. The most successful treatment programs are a complex mix of medical, psychosocial, and rehabilitation services, including the use of self-help groups like Narcotics Anonymous and Cocaine Anonymous that attempt to deal with the unique needs of each individual. However, effectiveness of treatment can differ because of complex variables such as the type(s) of drug(s) to which a person is addicted, the dysfunctional lifestyles of many addicts, and time and treatment resources available to both addicts and treatment personnel. Many Americans affected by drug addiction have been restored to healthy and productive lifestyles through appropriate treatment.

NEW AND IMPROVED TREATMENTS

The National Institute on Drug Abuse (NIDA) has already made considerable progress in developing a variety of effective behavioral and pharmacological addiction treatments and making them widely available to the public. For example, NIDA has taken the lead in developing readily available nicotine addiction therapies. They have also brought to the world the most effective medications to date for heroin addiction, including methadone and buprenorphine and have standardized behavioral interventions that have been effective in treating both adults and adolescents.

NIDA supports research to develop additional new and improved pharmacological and behavioral treatments. To this end, NIDA sponsors both a medications development program and a behavioral therapies development program. The NIDA medications development program brings the critical mass of knowledge of medicinal chemistry, molecular biology, brain function, and behavior to bear on the urgent public health problem of drug addiction to provide new medications as an effective adjunct to conventional psychosocial treatment by helping to stabilize addicts and allow them to succeed in their overall treatment program. Specifically, new medications are being researched to:

- block the effects of abused drugs;
- reduce the craving for abused drugs;
- moderate or eliminate withdrawal symptoms;
- block or reverse the toxic effects of abused drugs;
- or prevent relapse in persons who have been able to initiate abstinence (e.g., through medical or other means).

Because psychosocial interventions are the most common and sometimes the only treatments administered to individuals with drug addiction, NIDA also has a robust behavioral therapies development program to complement its medications portfolio. Researchers are working to develop new behavioral treatments for drug abuse and addiction and enhance the efficacy of existing ones. Psychotherapies, behavior therapies, cognitive therapies, family therapies, and counseling strategies are among the approaches currently being studied under this program. Once these treatments are proven to be safe and effective in small trials, they are tested in larger and more diverse populations through the NIDA National Drug Abuse Treatment Clinical Trials Network. This network enables the rapid, concurrent testing of a wide range of promising science-based medications and behavioral therapies across a spectrum of real-life patient populations, treatment settings, and community environments.

CONCLUSION

Addiction is a treatable disease. However, there is no one-size-fits-all treatment program. Treatment, which is delivered in outpatient, inpatient, and residential settings, has been shown to be effective in reducing drug use, but the settings and modalities of treatment must be tailored to the individual's needs. Drug addiction treatment can include behavioral therapy (such as counseling, cognitive therapy, or psychotherapy), medications, or a combination of both. Behavioral therapies, such as cognitive behavioral coping skills treatment, offer addicts ways to cope with their drug cravings, teach them to avoid drugs and relapse, and help them deal with relapse if it occurs. Medications and self-help group participation can augment these beneficial effects. The best programs provide a combination of therapies and other services, such as referral to other medical, psychological, and social services, to meet the needs of the individual patient.

See also **Alcohol: Chemistry and Pharmacology; Clinical Trials Network; Drug Interaction and the Brain; Economic Costs of Alcohol and Drug Abuse; Funding and Service Delivery of Treatment; Heroin; Methadone Maintenance Programs; Myths About Addiction and Its Treatment; Narcotics Anonymous (NA); Research: Aims, Description, and Goals; Research: Developing Medications to Treat Substance Abuse and Dependence; Tobacco: Dependence; Treatment, Behavioral Approaches to: Cognitive Therapy; Treatment, Behavioral Approaches to: Cognitive-Behavioral Therapy; Treatment, Behavioral Approaches to: Couples and Family Therapy; Treatment, Behavioral Approaches to: Self-Help and Anonymous Groups; Treatment, Pharmacological Approaches to: Buprenorphine; Treatment, Pharmacological Approaches to: Methadone; Treatment, Specialty Approaches to: Adolescents; Treatment: Outpatient Versus Inpatient Setting; Treatment: An Overview; Treatment, Pharmacological Approaches to: An Overview; U.S. Government Agencies: National Institute on Drug Abuse (NIDA); U.S. Government: Agencies Supporting Substance Abuse Research.**

BIBLIOGRAPHY

American Psychiatic Association. (2006). Work Group on Substance Use Disorders. Treatment of patients with substance use disorders. (2nd ed.). *American Journal of Psychiatry, 163*(8 Suppl), 5–82.

Hatsukami, D. K., Stead, L. F., & Gupta, P. C. (2008). Tobacco addiction. *Lancet, 371*(9629), 2027–2038.

Humphreys, K. (2003). *Circles of Recovery: Self-help organizations for addictions.* Cambridge, UK: Cambridge University Press.

National Institute on Drug Abuse. (2000). *Principles of drug addiction treatment: A research based guide.* Bethesda, MD. Available from http://www.drugabuse.gov/.

National Institute on Drug Abuse. (2008, July 16). *Clinical trials network*. Available from http://www.drugabuse.gov/.

ALAN I. LESHNER
HENRY R. KRANZLER

A HISTORY OF TREATMENT IN THE UNITED STATES

The history of the treatment of alcohol and other drug problems is often assumed to be a straightforward story of progress—moralism, neglect, and brutality were displaced by scientific knowledge, medical activism, and professional civility. A view that the addict freely chose continued drinking and drug use was succeeded by an understanding of how a disease or disorder could overrule the capacity to choose.

This assumption is historically incorrect. First, it neglects the coexistence and mutual influence of views emphasizing free will or social or biological determinism. Although one view may have enjoyed greater influence at a given time, its competitors have never been vanquished. No generation has any more solved the puzzle of addiction than it has resolved the related enigmas of the relationship between mind and body, choice and compulsion. Second, it is equally incorrect to associate condemnation and neglect with the free-will position, or kindness and activism with the determinist perspective. The historical truth is more complicated.

As various studies have demonstrated, there is a tenacious American folk wisdom about addiction. Simply put, it goes as follows: While addicts experience a compulsion to take a drug, this develops as the result of repeated bad choices that are socially influenced; further, addicts can rid themselves of compulsion only by developing self-discipline, perhaps with some skilled influence in the form of treatment. Thus, in contemporary culture, and despite the modern message that "addiction is a disease like hypertension or diabetes," addicts are understood to be sick *and* immoral, blameless *and* culpable, free *and* determined. In the popular mind, and among treatment professionals, addicts are ambiguous characters.

The history of treatment in the United States reflects this cultural dilemma. Cultures limit the range of possible responses to a problem, and because they tend to change slowly in fundamental ways, to the extent that an important problem recurs or remains unsolved, the range of possible responses will be explored repeatedly as new generations search for fresh insights and effective methods of intervention. At various times, treatment has embraced exhortation and coercion, sermons and miracle drugs, democratic mutual aid, and autocratic professional prerogative—often simultaneously. This entry will emphasize enduring cultural tensions and the therapeutic pluralism that continues to reflect them.

This approach to bounding a very large subject has at least one serious drawback that needs explanation at the outset. Sociologists and political scientists, in particular, often distinguish between "culture" as a value-laden, meaning-making process and "structure" as a pattern of relationships that generates its own imperatives. For example, any successful political system reflects to some extent the values of those it represents, but governance is achieved through structured relationships and processes that translate diffuse values and ideas into relatively specific social practices. The various processes and constituencies involved in sorting through values, reasoning about priorities, considering technical problems and group interests, and fitting proposals to the demands of political survival are fundamental to a thorough understanding of the history of treatment. And yet considering these processes is a huge analytic task due to the complexity of the modern American state (with its bewildering field of interorganizational relationships involving several layers of government and substantial fragmentation within each layer) and the existence in the United States of the world's most elaborate field of nongovernmental organizations (NGOs) that both influence the policy processes and provide the services. Thus, although structural factors will be discussed here, this entry is of necessity not a history of policy, public administration, or competitive strife among NGOs. Humbly stated, it is an introduction to some of the overarching sources of ideas about treatment and the institutional forms it has taken.

By way of further introduction, choices about periodization and terminology also need to be clarified. Modernity has different meanings with respect to the treatment of habitual drunkenness and drug addiction. In the case of habitual drunkenness, the modern era is traceable to the birth of Alcoholics Anonymous (AA) in 1935. In the case of drug addiction, the modern era begins with the introduction of methadone maintenance (for heroin dependence) in 1965.

The terms *alcoholism* and *alcoholic* date from the mid-nineteenth century, but they did not come into common professional use until the early twentieth century and were not embedded in the American vernacular until after the rapid growth of AA during the 1940s. The more common professional terms in the premodern era were *inebriety* and *inebriate*, but as these often were used to refer to a heterogeneous group now called *substance abusers*, the durable term *drunkard* is most appropriate when writing about this era. Similarly, the term *drug addict* was not in common use until the early 1900s. Before this time habitual users of drugs were known by terms that reflected their preferences: They were *morphinists*, *cocainists*, and so forth (even though the use of multiple substances was common). Sometimes, they were known more generally as *dope fiends*, but to speak generally and to avoid pejorative (if historically accurate) terminology, the term *drug addict* is most useful. The terms *addict* and *addiction* are acceptable when speaking of both habitual drunkards and drug addicts.

PREMODERN TREATMENT OF HABITUAL DRUNKARDS

Colonials and Americans of the early republic drank astonishing quantities of alcohol. Quite unapologetically, men, women, and children drank morning, noon, and night. Their food was fatty and salty, the water was unhealthy around settlements, and the land was full of fruits and grains that could be converted into fermented and distilled beverages for drinking and transport without spoilage to sometimes distant trading centers. For these and other reasons, we were, in the famous phrase of historian William Rorabaugh, "an alcoholic republic."

As transplanted from England around 1810, the early American temperance movement was indifferent to reclaiming drunkards. Led by clerics such as Lyman Beecher, the movement aimed principally to shore up the respectability of the wobbly postcolonial elite by redefining the proprieties concerning alcohol consumption and the requirements of self-possession and cultural stewardship. Over two

generations, such efforts were remarkably successful. By the first state prohibition law in Maine in 1851, drinking distilled spirits, especially, had become disreputable among aspiring young people—not unlike cigarette smoking in the early twenty-first century—and the per capita consumption of alcohol had declined significantly. Throughout the nineteenth century—indeed, until the so-called wet generation that followed national Prohibition (1920–1933)—abstention from alcohol remained a hallmark of respectability among the Protestant middling classes. Even as of 2008, about one-third of American adults do not drink, and this abstinent minority is concentrated among the Protestant faithful.

Tradition of Mutual Aid. The organized, specialized effort to help habitual drunkards began with the Washington Total Abstinence Movement in 1842. The Washingtonian Movement stands at the head of a tradition of mutual aid that developed throughout the remainder of the century in close connection to American Protestantism, particularly its evangelical expressions. The Salvation Army, which traces its American incarnation to the mid-1870s, also falls in this line, as does AA and the many "Anonymous" fellowships it inspired.

Washingtonian societies were dedicated to sobering up hard drinkers, usually (but not always) men. The societies intended to foster a solidarity based on shared experience with suffering that transcended profound social divisions. (Unlike the kindred Sons of Temperance, they were neutral on the divisive question of prohibition laws.) Although some famous teetotalers such as Abraham Lincoln were members, the societies included the disreputable, the unlettered, and sometimes nonwhites and women as equals. Their motives were couched in terms of Christian charity, economic self-improvement, and democratic principles. They had, one might say, one eye on the Almighty and the other on His worldly goods.

The hallmark of mutual aid is the banding together of people in similar circumstances to help one another. (The popular term *self-help* is thus misleading.) The Washingtonians and their successors did not invent the methods by which they fostered solidarity and mutual support. However, in adapting the voluntary association to the reform of drunkards, the Washingtonians introduced new elements.

Owing its provenance to the revival meeting, the most striking and controversial (some found it distasteful) Washingtonian innovation was the confession of drunkards before their peers, and sometimes before a general audience. Its contemporary form is familiar: "I am Jim B., and I am an alcoholic," but the practice dates from Washingtonian *experience lectures*, forums for telling so-called drunkard's tales, stories of degradation, struggle, and redemption through sobriety that nowadays form a common literary trope. These introduced the drunkard's tortured inner life to the polite public. "You all know me and what I used to be," Salvation Army lecturers often began.

Some Washingtonian societies also established temporary homes, or refuges, for drunkards. These were places where drunkards could live for a short time while they sobered up and were introduced to the Washingtonian fellowship, whose members found them jobs and other necessities. A century later AA would reinvent this institution (the *recovery home*) as part of its twelve-step work—the commitment to help other drunks.

Although not continuous with these early refuges, beginning in Boston (1857), San Francisco (1859), and Chicago (1863), a number of formal inebriate homes were established to treat drunkards in the Washingtonian tradition of therapeutic temperance. Typically, these were small institutions (fewer than 50 beds), operated as private charities, sometimes under religious or temperance auspices. They relied on the voluntary cooperation of their residents and used temperance fellowship as a form of what is now called aftercare. They were located in urban environments and did not isolate their residents from community life. Although often superintended by physicians, residence rarely exceeded three weeks and medical treatment was considered important only in managing withdrawal symptoms or delirium tremens (DTs). The terms *disease* and *vice*, *cure* and *reformation* were used interchangeably, and sober outcomes were attributed to the influences of family, friends, and the fellowship, not to medical intervention. Inebriate homes practiced a profoundly social (and sometimes spiritual) form of treatment based on the belief that the human capacity for transformation was never extinguished, no matter how "despotic" the appetite for alcohol.

For those in the Washingtonian line, the source of such optimism was their belief in the presence of an immortal God in the human mind. The mind, they believed, was distinct from the brain and other corruptible flesh and formed in God's image. By the mid-1800s the image of God was far more benign and rational than the often wrathful, finally inscrutable deity of even the early 1700s. This gradual change in the conception of God owed much to the spread of the market as arbiter of economic affairs and social relations. The rigorous logic of the market reordered economics from the academy to the workshop. In its train, a disciplined, optimistic rationalism—and the ideas of moral progress and human perfectibility—suffused popular culture and theology.

At the same time, another form of rationalism, that of natural science, was pervading popular discourse and causing tumult in seminary and pulpit. Science did not overthrow religion so much as assume a place alongside it. For believers, scientific order was a wonder of the divine plan. The natural *laws of health*, as various rules of disciplined self-denial were known, were signals of divine intent, of God's ideas about right living. The drunkard was therefore both sinful and sick, having contracted the disease as the result of moral transgression. (A common analogy of the time was to syphilis; today some religious leaders speak similarly of AIDS.) Thus, although Washingtonians and their successors spoke of addiction as a disease—by which they meant an organically based compulsion—they also employed religious images, for they believed in the power of the divinely inspired human mind to choose the rational good (total abstinence from alcohol) and to thus achieve health. In the Washingtonian tradition, the languages of morality and disease became assimilated, and remain so in the many contemporary Anonymous fellowships' claim that addiction is in part a "spiritual disease."

Although the Washingtonian Movement as such was defunct by 1850, Washingtonianism was extremely influential until about 1865. The tradition did not disappear, but in the decades following the Civil War (1861–1865), profound changes in American culture and society, and related changes in the temperance movement, blunted Washingtonian influence and gave new prominence to a competing philosophy of treatment and its attendant practices and institutional embodiment. The philosophy was that of biological determinism or *somaticism*, and its institutional expression was the *inebriate asylum*.

Asylum Tradition. In 1810 Benjamin Rush, a Philadelphia physician, signer of the Declaration of Independence, and first formulator of a disease theory of addiction (although not the inventor of the idea), proposed "sober houses" for drunkards. However, Samuel Woodward, a Massachusetts insane asylum superintendent and temperance orator, was the father of institutional treatment based on a somatic explanation of habitual drunkenness. In a tract written in 1835, Woodward contributed two critical ideas to what would become the inebriate asylum movement of the nineteenth and early twentieth centuries. The first was that drunkards could not be treated successfully on a voluntary basis. The second, which flowed from the first, was that they needed legal restraint in a "well-conducted institution"—by which Woodward meant something like the insane asylum that he superintended.

The course staked out by Rush and Woodward had no institutional realization until an inebriate asylum subsidized by the State of New York opened in Binghamton in 1864. Another was opened in Kings County, New York, in 1869. In subsequent decades, pursuant to arduous promotion by the American Association for the Cure of Inebriates (AACI, founded in 1870), public inebriate asylums opened in Massachusetts (1893), Iowa (1904), and Minnesota (1908). Other jurisdictions chartered inebriate asylums but never built them (Texas and Washington, D.C.). Indeed, Binghamton was converted to an insane asylum in 1879. By the advent of Prohibition in 1920, all public inebriate asylums had been closed or converted to other use. Prevention, it seemed, would be the cure.

The inebriate asylum movement spawned dozens of private sanatoriums that treated well-to-do drunkards and, by the 1890s, drug addicts. (The most famous of these—the Betty Ford Clinic of its day—was the Townes Hospital in New York City.) However, judged by its manifestation in brick and mortar, the movement for public treatment was a failure.

For two related reasons, the AACI was notably unsuccessful in converting legislatures to its cause.

First, its physician members never could produce a strictly medical "cure" for addiction. Although its theorist-practitioners developed rigorously somatic explanations of addiction that dispensed with will power, spirituality, and the therapeutic necessity of fellowship, they relied on recuperation by bed rest, a healthy diet, and therapeutic baths (hydrotherapy), followed by the discipline of useful labor. This regime was highly structured (military analogies were popular), medically supervised, and set in a context of prolonged legal restraint (involuntary commitment). However, there was nothing particularly innovative or medical about this approach. Its methods already were the staples of lunatic asylums (called mental hospitals in most states after about 1900), almshouses, and county jails, institutions that managed huge numbers of habitual drunkards and, after the 1880s, drug addicts. Second, the inebriate asylum was an ambitious undertaking: Like the insane asylum, it was to accommodate several hundred patients on a sequestered rural estate. Few legislatures could be persuaded that such costly new institutions were worth the price. In a word, the inebriate asylum was viewed as redundant.

The ideology of the inebriate asylum movement—its adherents' view of the world—was shaped by two profound, contemporaneous developments in American culture and society: (1) the rising esteem and secularism of science and (2) the growing disorder and complexity of American society after the Civil War. The movement reflected the grand aspirations of Gilded Age science, whose practical applications were transforming American life: railroads and streetcars, the telephone, gas and electrical lighting—all attested to the power of science and human ingenuity. It was a time when "scientific" understanding became the basis for professional status for all manner of occupational groups, from proto-social workers to plumbers. The metaphor of disease and the optimistic message implicit in its use—that all defects could be cured—became popular among forward thinkers. In the most widely read book of its time, the utopian novel, *Looking Backward* (1888), Edward Bellamy characterized all sorts of misconduct as disease, and his near-perfect world of the year 2000 cured its rare wayward citizens in public hospitals.

If Washingtonians assimilated the languages of morality and disease, the rising generation of inebriate asylum enthusiasts radically separated them and often reduced human volition to a by-product of neurology. (In the work of George Miller Beard, human nature had more in common with an electrical circuit than the image of God.) In the United States and Europe, they initiated research on the biology (and later, the genetics) of addiction. Primitive by early-twenty-first-century standards, it nonetheless established a robust tradition of inquiry that remains lively and influential.

The inebriate asylum movement appealed to American aspirations to create a better world through science, but it also addressed growing fears of social disorder. The extent of such disorder should not be exaggerated, however; preindustrial America was more disorderly than nostalgic chroniclers have made it seem, and urbanization and industrialization were less chaotic than critics sometimes contend. On the whole, though, life after the Civil War was more complex, more anonymous, and less certain.

Immigration from abroad was an important fuel for such change and promoted nativist fear. In the 1830s free Americans were overwhelmingly Anglo-Saxon in origin and Protestant in belief. By the 1880s this was changing dramatically. Burgeoning northern and western cities were becoming testing grounds for the promise and limits of diversity—indeed, for explanations of diversity. Amid glaring inequality of wealth and opportunity, cultural conflicts often were played out around practices of consciousness alteration. Protestant, native-born Americans (including African Americans) were remarkably abstemious (a notable success of the Protestant-driven temperance movement); the mostly Roman Catholic Italians and French were daily wine drinkers; Poles, Germans, and some Scandinavians drank large quantities of beer (some on Sunday—in public beer gardens, no less!).

Of Irish Catholics, who had a large temperance movement of their own but also a penchant for drunkenness (what is known as a *bi-modal distribution* of drinking habits), a California temperance editor wrote in 1883: "They are by far the worst and meanest material in which to store whisky." Native Americans had been introduced to alcohol by traders and government agents from colonial times, and the corruption of indigenous ways by whisky became a factor in the appropriation of western tribal lands and the ensuing Indian Wars. The "idolatrous" (non-Judeo-Christian) Chinese introduced opium smoking to America, a practice that crossed the color line during the 1870s and became popular among young white men and women during the 1880s. Then from 1900 to 1920 Mexicans became associated with marijuana use in the West and Southwest. In the South, African American men frequently were accused of the riotous use of cocaine, with subsequent designs on white women.

The increasing diversity of the U.S. population became a source of conflict and disorder; the continuing tempest of industrial capitalism was another. The United States experienced two prolonged economic depressions (then called *panics*) between the Civil War and the turn of the century—from 1873 to 1878 and from 1893 to 1898. In between, a short but sharp slump during the mid-1880s took its toll on stability. During these years the noun *tramp* entered the American language; the country experienced its first pronounced labor violence and political bombings (dynamite being an 1860s product of scientific ingenuity); in the spring of 1894 so-called armies of the unemployed converged on Washington, D.C., from all over the country.

This era of mounting diversity and instability was marked by a failing faith in exhortation as a method to achieve social regulation and by a concomitant exaltation of coercive means. Although never abandoning altogether its sympathy for drunkards, the temperance movement made securing prohibitionist measures its primary objective. Although never withdrawing their support from surviving Washingtonian institutions, temperance adherents simultaneously supported the more stringent regime promoted by inebriate asylum enthusiasts, some of whom believed that an orderly, peaceful society required the lifetime detention of incurable addicts. Indeed, the temperance movement helped to popularize theories that purported to demonstrate a biological basis for the failure of certain racial and ethnic groups to live up to the abstemious standard of so-called native stock—or to benefit from treatment. In the name of prevention, such views justified not only prohibition laws but also statutes that in a few states permitted the forced sterilization of addicts.

In sum, the legacy of the inebriate asylum movement was the biologically based approach to understanding addiction, the corollary claim that addiction is the special province of medicine and physicians, the notion that successful treatment requires legal coercion, and the assertion that treatment is both a responsibility of government and a commodity to be sold on the market. These ideas endure as part of the complex intellectual, professional, and political fabric of treatment.

Tradition of Mental Hygiene. The mental hygiene movement, customarily dated from the 1908 publication of Clifford Beers's *A Mind That Found Itself*, represented a departure from the somatic tradition of thought about mental disorder and addiction. At the same time, it did not appeal to spiritual explanations nor did it dwell on will power. Rather, mental hygienists employed a socio-biological determinism: Although addiction could be the result of hereditary biological defect and might be incurable, its origins were mainly familial and social, and if the condition was addressed early on, it could be arrested. Mental hygienists stressed the important roles of family, friends, and occupation in creating a salubrious environment for an addict's continuing sobriety. Mental hygiene did not speak the language of mutual aid, but it was similarly environmental in outlook. This was the beginning of what later would be called community mental health, and its point of view virtually defines what we understand to be "modern" about treatment and the biopsychosocial perspective.

The environmentalism of mental hygiene challenged the rationale of the asylum model of treatment. Mental hygienists criticized the asylum's lack of connection with community life and its reliance on involuntary treatment, claiming that only voluntary access to free or inexpensive care would attract patients in the early stages of drinking or drug-taking. The history of the Massachusetts Hospital for Dipsomaniacs and Inebriates (1893–1920) illustrates well the influence of mental hygiene philosophy and practice. Between 1893 and 1907 the hospital was run on the asylum model. After a complete reorganization in 1908, it followed a mental hygiene course: Most of its admissions were legally voluntary; the hospital established a statewide network of outpatient clinics; it worked closely with local charities, probation offices, employers, and the families of patients. Known finally as Norfolk State Hospital, it was a preview of what treatment would become beginning in the 1940s.

Even so, Norfolk created on its campus a "farm" for the long-term detention of so-called incurables. The mental hygiene movement modified the emphasis of the asylum tradition but did not entirely abandon its practices. Indeed, under the banner of mental hygiene, between 1910 and 1925, many local governments across the United States established farms to segregate repeated public drunkenness offenders and drug addicts. Some of these persisted until the 1960s, and some have been reopened in recent years to accommodate homeless people with alcohol and drug problems. As discussed below, the asylum tradition remained particularly important in the treatment of drug addicts.

PREMODERN TREATMENT OF DRUG ADDICTS

Although the San Francisco Home for the Care of the Inebriate (1859–1898) treated a few opium addicts as early as 1862, Washingtonian institutions mainly treated drunkards. The few reborn drug addicts among the legions of the Salvation Army and other urban missions were vastly outnumbered by reformed drunkards. Until the formation of Narcotics Anonymous (NA) in 1953, there was no large or well-defined group of addicts involved in the practices of mutual aid, and there were several reasons for this.

Drug addiction was not a matter of widespread concern until after the Washingtonian philosophy was eclipsed by the asylum model of treatment. Furthermore, drug addicts were quickly perceived to be more exotic and ominous than habitual drunkards. Although there were many people addicted to morphine as a result of ill-advised medical treatment or attempts at self-treatment during the late 1800s, this more or less respectable population declined after the turn of the century as physicians and pharmacists reformed their dispensing practices and new laws required disclosure of the content of proprietary (or patent) medicines and nostrums. At the same time, a growing number of urban young people began to experiment with drugs, especially smoking opium, morphine, and cocaine. By 1910 drug addiction was popularly associated with petty thieves, dissipated actors, gamblers, prostitutes, and other nightlife aficionados, and with racial minorities and dissolute youth. Unlike habitual drunkards, drug addicts never were caricatured as boisterous and occasionally obstreperous nuisances or buffoons. Especially after 1900 they usually were portrayed as dangerous predators and corrupters of society, alternating between drug-induced torpor (in the case of opiates) or hyperactivity and hallucination (in the case of cocaine) and a craving that propelled them on relentless and unscrupulous searches for drugs and the means to buy them.

The "criminal" taint of drug addiction made mutual aid risky for participants, and the widespread view that most addicts were incurable and would do anything to alleviate withdrawal symptoms provided a powerful rationale for their prolonged confinement under strict conditions. Even the mental hygienists at Norfolk State Hospital had no expectation that addicts would remain sober and favored incarcerating them in the Massachusetts State Farm at Bridgewater, a correctional facility. Indeed, state hospitals were generally more opposed to admitting drug addicts than habitual drunkards, preferring to have them incarcerated in jails. Even more than drunkards, addicts disturbed the routine and good order of state hospitals, in no small part because they were, as a group, considerably younger and less conventional than other hospital patients. They pursued sexual liaisons in violation of institutional rules against fraternization; they smuggled drugs into the hospitals; and once through withdrawal, they escaped in droves.

Nor were jails and prisons anxious to take in addicts, mainly because of the problem of smuggling. By the 1870s opium was a customary (although illicit) medium of exchange at San Quentin Prison in California, and it was routinely available in the big county jails of the United States at the turn of the century.

As state laws against the sale or possession of opiates and cocaine proliferated in the 1890s, and as they began to be more strictly worded and enforced after 1910, county jails and state prisons faced a major problem of internal order. This intensified with the implementation of the federal Harrison Narcotics Tax Act (passed in 1914 to take effect in March 1915), particularly after a U.S. Supreme Court decision in 1919 made it illegal for physicians to prescribe opiates for the purpose of maintaining an addict's habit. The vast majority of drug offenders, even those arrested by federal agents, were prosecuted under state drug and vagrancy laws and sent to state and county lockups. The resulting crisis led jailers to support two related treatment strategies.

The first of these was the creation of special institutions for drug addicts. Thus, the aforementioned county farms were created, or laws were passed to allow addicts to be committed to existing state or county hospitals with wards designated for this purpose. Mendocino State Hospital in California, Worcester State Hospital in Massachusetts, Norwich State Hospital in Connecticut, and Philadelphia General Hospital, to name a few, treated significant numbers of addicts in the 1910s and 1920s. Later, California (1928) and Washington (1935) opened state-sponsored variations on the jail farm, although under the auspices of their state hospital systems.

Jailers were also important to local political coalitions in support of a short-lived and controversial treatment strategy of the early 1920s—drug dispensaries for registered addicts. At least 44 such clinics were established nationwide, most in late 1919 or early 1920, following the Supreme Court's antimaintenance ruling.

In principle, these were not to be maintenance clinics. Addicts initially were to receive their customary dosages of morphine (occasionally heroin and, very rarely, smoking opium) and were then to be "reduced" over a short time to whatever dosage prevented withdrawal. At this point, abstinence was to be achieved.

In practice, few of the clinics worked this way. Many clinic operators believed that their primary aim was to mitigate drug peddling by supplying addicts through medical channels. This implied a maintenance strategy at odds with the Supreme Court's interpretation of the Harrison Act and with some earlier state laws forbidding maintenance (in California and Massachusetts, e.g.). Furthermore, most clinic operators agreed with the American Medical Association that dispensaries could only work effectively within the law if prolonged institutional treatment was available once the addict's dosage had been reduced to the brink of withdrawal. In the absence of such institutional capacity, reduction was useless, and so clinic doctors rarely bothered. The Prohibition Unit of the U.S. Department of the Treasury (which enforced the Harrison Act), state boards of pharmacy (which typically enforced state drug laws), and local medical societies and law enforcement agencies regarded the clinics as stopgaps, valuable only until adequate public hospitals could be opened.

In the midst of the inflation following World War I, localities looked to the states to finance such institutions and states looked to the federal government, particularly the U.S. Public Health Service, which had operated hospitals for merchant mariners since 1792. But the first proposed legislation to create a federal treatment program along mental hygiene lines failed to pass and the states were thrown on their own resources. The Prohibition Unit, convinced that the clinics were doing more harm than good, moved to close them, threatening dispensing physicians with prosecution. The clinics closed rapidly. The last one, at Shreveport, Louisiana, closed in 1923. Addicts were consigned to their customary ports of call in jails, prisons, or for the fortunate few, private sanatoriums.

The growing number of addict prisoners in the federal system also led to their segregation, first at Leavenworth, Kansas (mainly), and then at two narcotic hospitals opened at Lexington, Kentucky (1935), and Fort Worth, Texas (1938). (Women were sent to a federal prison in Aldersen, West Virginia, where singer Billie Holiday served time.) Operated by the U.S. Public Health Service, these hospitals were in fact more like jails, although they were authorized to admit voluntary patients of supposed good character whose applications were approved by the U.S. Surgeon General. Initially, these patients were kept involuntarily once they had been admitted, but a federal district court ruling in 1936 affirmed that voluntary patients could leave after giving notice. Before they were closed in the 1970s, the two facilities admitted more than 60,000 individuals, accounting for over 100,000 admissions.

The controversy over maintenance did not disappear, however, particularly on the West Coast, where efforts to loosen its prohibition in the states of California and Washington continued until the United States entered World War II in 1941.

Furthermore, both federal and state governments permitted the maintenance of a small number of addicts, usually of middle age or older, suffering from severe pain related to a terminal illness or an incurable condition. However, the period from 1923 through 1965 was generally characterized by the strict enforcement of increasingly severe laws against drug possession and sales, by relentless opposition to maintenance, and by treatment that was essentially in the asylum tradition, supplemented by the mental hygiene innovation of supervised probation. In 1961 California passed legislation permitting the compulsory treatment of drug addicts (including marijuana users) and established the California Civil Addict Program within its Department of Corrections. From 1962 to 1964 more than 1,000 people were committed to a 7-year period of supervision, which typically involved an initial year of residential treatment in a facility surrounded by barbed wire to discourage premature departure. In 1964 New York passed similar legislation but assigned its implementation to a special commission rather than the Department of Corrections. As in California, New York's residential treatment facilities were "secure." As late as 1966, the federal Narcotic Addict Rehabilitation Act (NARA), in most respects a piece of modern legislation, nonetheless provided for the compulsory treatment of addicts and made the hospitals at Lexington and Fort Worth into the institutional bases of the NARA program.

THE MODERN ERA

The modern history of alcohol and drug treatment has been shaped by the therapeutic pluralism descended from the mutual-aid, asylum, and mental hygiene traditions; the coexistence of public and private sectors of treatment; and an increasingly complex field of interorganizational relationships involving several layers of government and myriad NGOs. As well, drugs with modest effects on consciousness (such as nicotine), and even pleasurable behaviors that have the potential to become obsessive (such as sex and gambling), are often brought together with drinking and drugging under the rubric of behavioral health problems.

Consolidating terms like *behavioral health* reflect important changes in the organization of treatment practices as well as the reorganization of the bureaucratic entities that fund and study intervention and train practitioners. In the early twenty-first century substance abusers of all sorts are treated together in most programs (opiate maintenance is the obvious exception), but this is a development of the last 30 years. When in the mid-1970s a hospital in Pennsylvania advocated the joint treatment of alcoholics and drug addicts, the idea was controversial.

Although the accumulating insights of brain science and research on intervention provide reasons to treat substance abusers together (as well as some reasons to develop separate clinical regimes), the change on the ground probably originated in generational experience. Drugs other than alcohol are no longer exotic and their users and abusers have a more domesticated image. Even if they have not themselves been users, most Americans who have come of age after about 1970 know people who have been and some whose lives have been derailed by such use. Dabbling in various substances is now a commonplace experience of development, and choice of drugs is no longer such a reliable predictor of divisions among America's social worlds. The former antagonism in treatment programs between the "respectable" drunks and the "degenerate" drug addicts is no longer of much importance. The training of addiction specialists within the major human service professions and their separate licensing as addiction counselors in many states since the 1980s have institutionalized this change of perspective.

But access to treatment—like access to health care more generally in the United States—remains keenly divided by the existence and nature of job-related benefits. In 1990 the Institute of Medicine described U.S. treatment arrangements as a two-tiered system, composed of public and private sectors in which the private sector garnered a disproportionate share of expenditures. This characterization is as true in 2008 as it was then. To understand recent developments in treatment, it is important to understand some things about the history of this system.

A Two-Tiered System. By Repeal in 1933 nothing remained of the U.S. public treatment system save the specialty wards of a few state and county hospitals. Treatment was a commodity to be purchased by those who could afford it, and although few specialized private treatment institutions survived Prohibition, a number of private sanatoriums

around the country treated alcoholics and addicts along with psychiatric patients. (The superintendents of these institutions did not like addicts as patients any more than physicians in public hospitals, but these patients or their families paid quite handsomely.) Before the 1960s, only the creation of the federal hospitals at Lexington and Fort Worth had much impact on public treatment capacity.

In addition, insurance companies worked assiduously to reduce their risk on life and disability policies by excluding known alcoholics or drug addicts. Abstainers were offered lower rates than drinkers, as nonsmokers are today. As health insurance developed within the industry, addiction treatment was systematically excluded from benefits due to skepticism about its efficacy and concerns about its cost.

Beginning in 1964 (with Kemper Insurance Companies), and expanding over the next decade to include a few insurance industry leaders such as The Travelers, health insurance policies began to provide coverage for the treatment of alcohol and drug dependence. Sometimes this was the result of industry investment in early detection intended to reduce long-term costs; sometimes it resulted from labor negotiations; sometimes it was the result of state insurance commission mandates for its inclusion. Whatever the impetus, in response to the availability of support, private hospitals (both nonprofit and for-profit) expanded their treatment capacities dramatically. There had been no such growth in the private treatment sector since the boom of the inebriate asylum era.

Commonly, treatment programs within the private sector were based on the Minnesota model, emphasizing twelve-step principles and employing recovering people. Such programs typically consisted of a brief period of inpatient detoxification followed by several weeks of inpatient rehabilitation. Twenty-eight days was such a common duration of inpatient care that the programs often were referred to as 28-day programs. The posthospital phase of treatment usually consisted of participation in AA, NA, or Cocaine Anonymous (CA).

Such programs—often called chemical dependency programs because they admitted people with drug *and* alcohol problems—catered almost exclusively to those with health insurance. (In many instances, they represented important profit centers for medical institutions needing to subsidize financial losses from other services, such as emergency rooms.) Those without insurance either had no access to treatment or made use of the network of publicly supported programs—a network that became increasingly thin during the 1980s and increasingly under pressure to find sources of funds other than public grants and contracts and payments from medical programs for the indigent (such as Medicaid, established in 1965). During the 1980s sliding fee scales became more commonly used in public programs, and in some places scarce public treatment slots were absorbed by fee-paying drinking drivers mandated to treatment by stricter penalties for drunk driving and more systematic enforcement of such laws.

The growth of the private sector was spurred as well by employee assistance programs (EAPs), efforts to intervene in alcohol and/or drug problems at places of employment. This strategy goes back at least to the Washingtonian movement, but formal EAPs date from the 1940s, when wartime employers, faced with labor shortages, struggled to keep impaired workers on the job. Insurance companies such as Kemper and The Travelers were pioneers in EAP development during the 1950s and 1960s, and with insurance coverage available for treatment, the number of EAPs swelled during the 1970s and 1980s. Generally, EAPs referred people with more serious alcohol and drug problems to formal—usually private—treatment programs, which were paid primarily by fees derived from third parties such as insurance companies, who in turn derived their funds from policies paid for or subsidized by employers.

By the 1990s the ambitions of many private treatment programs fueled a constant search for clients and fierce competition among for-profit providers especially. Very quickly, the sharply rising cost to employers of providing alcohol and drug treatment became a major factor in the development of managed care, which was aimed initially at controlling the cost of mental health and alcohol and drug treatment. The major mechanism by which the managed-care industry addressed the cost of treatment was to challenge the practice of using several weeks of inpatient care as the initial phase of treatment for alcohol and drug dependence.

In practice, treatment providers were told that inpatient treatment beyond a few days could not be justified by research and would not be paid for under the insurance policy.

The success of managed care in reducing costs by constraining the use of inpatient treatment resulted in a dramatic growth of managed-care organizations and an equally significant contraction and restructuring of the private alcohol and drug treatment system. By the early 1990s a number of states had obtained federal permission to use managed-care approaches to contain the costs of treatment for individuals covered by federal programs such as Medicaid. (Each state determines whether and to what extent alcohol and drug treatment is covered by its Medicaid program.) The result of this industry shake out and the adoption of cost-containment measures in the public sector radically altered available alcohol and drug treatment, as discussed below.

MODERN ALCOHOLISM TREATMENT

It is hard to exaggerate the influence of AA on the nature of modern treatment. Whatever its therapeutic success—a point of warm debate among scholars—AA has profoundly affected the treatment of people now regularly known as alcoholics. Indeed, AA and its Anonymous cousins have changed how recent generations think about the compulsive consumption of almost anything, from intoxicating substances to food or exhilarating experiences.

AA's impact has been both ideological and institutional; that is, its promotion of "disease theory" within the mutual-aid tradition has changed the perception of excessive or problem-causing consumption and treatment methods, and the penetration of policymaking bodies and treatment institutions by recovering people has shaped the funding and practices of treatment. The somaticist entrepreneurs of the inebriate asylum movement cast out sufferers as potential sources of therapeutic wisdom; AA brought them back.

AA's impact was facilitated by the growing influence of the mental hygiene movement during the 1920s and 1930s, for AA provided the critical therapeutic bridge between the segregating institution and the community at large. This was recognized quickly by men such as Clinton Duffy, the "reform" warden of San Quentin, who encouraged the establishment of AA groups in his prison in 1942. Much early twelve-step work was done in U.S. county jails. Harvard psychiatrist Robert Fleming opined in 1944 that the prolonged institutionalization of alcoholics was no longer necessary; a week's medical care in a general hospital followed by community-based psychotherapy and AA participation was his new prescription. The growth of AA permitted the first substantial stirrings of community care since the Washingtonian Movement.

During the early 1960s some state hospitals, particularly in Minnesota, incorporated recovering alcoholics and the principles of AA into their treatment programs. What became known as the Minnesota model of short-term inpatient care and subsequent AA fellowship and recovery-home living spread slowly but discernibly among private treatment providers such as the Hazelden Foundation, also in Minnesota, and the Mary Lind Foundation in Los Angeles. Across the country, local councils on alcoholism, dominated by people recovering from alcoholism and encouraged by the National Council on Alcoholism (now, fittingly, the National Council on Alcoholism and Drug Dependence) and the National Institute of Mental Health (NIMH, created in 1946, was an ardent promoter of community psychiatry), began to press states and localities for outpatient clinics, diversion of alcoholics from jail, and other methods consistent with the traditions of mutual aid and mental hygiene. (Even so, a survey in 1967 found only 130 outpatient clinics and only 100 halfway houses and recovery homes dedicated to serving alcoholics, and alcoholics continued to be barred from most hospital emergency rooms.)

The intellectual warrant for such advocacy and organizing was E. M. Jellinek's *The Disease Concept of Alcoholism* (1960). Jellinek was more provisional in his use of the term than most of his readers appreciated, but he understood the important strategic value of such a claim. In the first instance, the language of disease challenged the legal and correctional system's jurisdiction over alcoholics; in addition, it provided a rationale for the increased availability of services within established medical facilities and under the aegis of public health. Several important court decisions in the 1960s endorsed the view that alcoholism was a disease.

In 1967 a presidential commission on law enforcement concluded that it was both ineffective and inhumane to handle public drunkenness offenders within the criminal justice system and recommended creating a network of detoxification centers instead. In 1970 Congress passed the Comprehensive Alcohol Abuse and Alcoholism Prevention, Treatment and Rehabilitation Act (the Hughes Act). This legislation made federal funds available for the first time specifically for alcoholism treatment programs.

The Hughes Act effectively redefined alcoholism as a primary disorder, not a symptom of mental illness. Based on this distinction, it created a federal agency—the National Institute on Alcohol Abuse and Alcoholism (NIAAA)—that would not be dominated by the mental health establishment competing for the same resources. NIAAA aggressively sought state adoption of the model Uniform Alcoholism and Intoxication Treatment Act. Section 1 of the Uniform Act stated that "intoxicated persons may not be subject to criminal prosecution because of their consumption of alcoholic beverages but rather should be afforded a continuum of treatment." By 1980, 30 states had adopted some version of the Uniform Act, thereby decriminalizing public drunkenness.

The thrust of federal and state grant making was to create an effective system of community-based alcoholism treatment services. This occurred in tandem with the deinstitutionalization process that was rapidly depopulating state mental hospitals. Although state hospital depopulation is customarily thought to affect only persons with mental illness, it had an important impact on alcoholics. In 1960, a decade before deinstitutionalization began in earnest, 36 states had provisions specifically for the involuntary hospitalization of so-called alcoholics, habitual drunkards, or inebriates. In addition, many states had voluntary admission statutes. By the mid-1970s, however, these laws were history. Prepared or not, local communities had to provide.

They did so within a unified substance abuse, chemical dependency, or behavioral health framework and the tiered system described above. With managed care, treatment became based almost entirely on outpatient measures supplemented by participation in an Anonymous group; long-stay residential treatment became an experience for the rich, who could pay out of pocket. Moreover, because outpatient treatment typically was voluntary, initial and continuing participation rates declined. Whatever its therapeutic implications, lagging participation triggered more financial distress for treatment agencies, which looked to captive clients—that is, those mandated to treatment by criminal justice and child welfare authorities, mainly, and sometimes by employers using treatment as the carrot on the stick of workplace drug testing. Coerced treatment, once a matter of bitter controversy in AA, is now widely accepted in Anonymous circles as a means to "bring the bottom up"—that is, as a way to quicken the addict's disgust with his or her life.

MODERN DRUG TREATMENT

By the late 1950s the antimaintenance consensus of an earlier era of drug control and treatment was breaking down. A joint report of the American Bar Association and the American Medical Association in 1958 cautiously favored outpatient treatment and limited opiate maintenance as alternatives to "threats of jail or prison sentences." In 1962, appealing to disease theory, the U.S. Supreme Court struck down a California statute that made drug addiction per se a crime. Medical treatment, not the "cruel and unusual punishment" of incarceration, was the Court's desideratum. In 1963 the President's Advisory Commission on Narcotic Drug Abuse made substantially similar recommendations.

Although now supplemented by other maintenance drugs (including heroin in a few countries), the experimental success of methadone finally altered the discussion of opiate maintenance that had been quashed with the closing of the clinics from 1919 through 1923 and the prosecution of dissenting physicians in the years that followed. Methadone, a synthesized drug with opiate properties, was invented by German pharmacologists during World War II and had been used at Lexington to block addicts' withdrawal symptoms. In 1963 and 1964, with the support of the prestigious Rockefeller University, medical researchers Vincent Dole and Marie Nyswander began to study its wider use in the treatment of heroin addiction. Their research, first published in 1965, proceeded despite opposition by the federal Bureau of Narcotics. They observed remarkable changes in their patients that soon were replicated by other scholars. Methadone maintenance attracted considerable notoriety and generated new enthusiasm for maintenance as a strategy of treatment.

Nevertheless, methadone maintenance has never been without controversy. The fundamental criticism of maintenance—by whatever drug—has always been that it presumes "incurability," encourages users to continue to remain dependent on a drug, and thereby undermines abstinence-based approaches. During the 1960s, and especially during the 1970s, when methadone maintenance programs expanded rapidly, this criticism derived mainly from two sources: (1) abstinence-based programs run by recovering addicts more or less in the mutual-aid tradition and (2) African American and Hispanic poverty activists who saw in maintenance a palliative strategy to treat a symptom of economic deprivation without addressing its causes.

Opposition from those working in the mutual-aid tradition came chiefly from veterans of therapeutic communities inspired by Synanon (established in Southern California in 1958) and Daytop Village (opened in New York City in 1964). The term *therapeutic community* (TC) covers a wide range of practices that have changed considerably over the last 50 years as most TCs have become far more influenced by professional insights and standards, in part as the result of funding requirements. The common denominators among TCs, however, are the ideas that recovery from addiction involves a wholesale reconstitution of behavior, thinking, and feeling; that the processes of a community of residents are the treatment itself; and that abstinence from substances is the only desirable outcome. Unlike mutual aid in the Washingtonian tradition, TCs tend to carefully control their residents' participation in local communities. They are sometimes isolated worlds. Indeed, in one infamous case, Synanon became a separatist cult that sought legal standing as a religion. In this sense, then, the TC has some asylumlike characteristics, and "graduation" often marks a transitional process facilitated by an Anonymous fellowship.

Most therapeutic communities work in the assimilated languages of morality and disease, but from their beginning a few have also relied on an analysis of addiction that locates its social sources in adaptations to poverty. This was an important theme of much scholarship on drug addiction during and after the late 1950s. In this analysis, still vital in the early twenty-first century, no form of treatment is effective without job and community development to support aftercare and prevent relapse. Descending from the mental hygiene tradition, this view provides a rationale for great skepticism about any narrow medical approach proclaimed as a solution rather than a first step.

There was (and remains) no inherent contradiction between maintenance and antipoverty strategies. In the 1960s many antipoverty workers embraced methadone as a viable and useful treatment. But many did not, and the result was an uneasy pluralism in drug-treatment approaches. In 1966, when New York City launched a major expansion of treatment for drug addiction, it chose to make drug-free therapeutic communities the centerpiece of its effort.

Despite the variety of approaches, accessibility to voluntary treatment remained limited to the federal narcotic farms and some state and local hospitals throughout the 1960s. The Narcotic Addict Rehabilitation Act of 1966 authorized NIMH to make grants to establish community-based treatment programs. The first of these grants was awarded in 1968; ecumenically, they provided federal support for therapeutic communities and methadone maintenance. This expansion of treatment capacity was also notable for its attention to problems associated with a variety of drugs. It came at a time of sharp increase in marijuana use among middle-class youth, an epidemic of amphetamine use, growing experimentation with LSD, and media preoccupation with the counterculture or "youth revolt." Thus, the political urge to provide treatment was fueled by two enduring concerns of Americans: unconventional and disorderly behavior by young people and minority group members; and the connection between drug use and crime.

For a short time in the early 1970s federally supported treatment expanded rapidly. Anything that might work was tried. In early 1971 there were 36 federally funded treatment programs in the United States. By January 1972 there were 235, and by January 1973 almost 400. This heyday did not last long, however. Buffeted by a terrible economy (the infamous period of stagflation and the near bankruptcy of several big cities, including New York), subsequent federal regimes allowed the real value of federal treatment spending to be eroded by

inflation. Measured in 1976 dollars, the level of federal support for treatment was cut almost in half between 1976 and 1982. At the same time, as the result of the impact of inflation on the cost of state and local government, these jurisdictions also curtailed their support, thus aggravating the impact of federal reductions.

Since 1980 federal money for treatment has flowed to the states in the form of a *block grant*, a fixed sum that the states may spend as they see fit but within a set of federal priorities. Despite some increases in the amount of these grants, particularly during the second Clinton administration, access to public treatment remains constrained and dependent largely on the willingness of states and localities to supplement federal funds. Put another way, access to public treatment in the United States has a lot to do with where one lives. (A few states do not permit methadone maintenance.) Absent public treatment, access depends largely on one's health insurance. The federal Substance Abuse and Mental Health Services Administration found that from 2004 to 2006, among persons who needed but did not receive treatment for illicit drug or alcohol use, and made an effort to get it, 36.3 percent had no health insurance and could not afford the cost.

The future of treatment is inseparable from the broader debates on the financing of health care and the management of nonviolent drug offenders. California's Proposition 36 (the Substance Abuse and Crime Prevention Act of 2000) diverts nonviolent drug offenders to mandatory treatment and has saved the state hundreds of millions of dollars compared to previous business as usual in the prison system. Even so, the California approach has gaps and capacity problems and has faced some political opposition.

It remains to be seen what the balance of public and private treatment will be in the years ahead, what innovations or reinventions will be born of financial necessity, practical applications of neuroscience, or as the result of homeless addicts and a groaning correctional system. History allows one to predict the likely questions, but it is not a very reliable guide to specific answers.

BIBLIOGRAPHY

Baumohl, J. (1986). On asylums, homes, and moral treatment: The case of the San Francisco Home for the

Care of the Inebriate, 1859–1870. *Contemporary Drug Problems, 13*, 395–445.

Baumohl, J. (1993). Inebriate institutions in North America, 1840–1920. In C. Warsh (Ed.), *Drink in Canada: Historical essays*. Montreal: McGill-Queens University Press.

Baumohl, J. (2004). Maintaining orthodoxy: The Depression-era struggle over morphine maintenance in California. In S.W. Tracy & C. J. Acker (Eds.), *Altering American consciousness: The history of alcohol and drug use in the United States, 1800–2000*. Amherst: University of Massachusetts Press.

Baumohl, J., & Tracy, S. W. (1994). Building systems to manage inebriates: The divergent paths of California and Massachusetts, 1891–1920. *Contemporary Drug Problems, 21*, 557–597.

Courtwright, D. T. (1982). *Dark paradise: Opiate addiction in America before 1940*. Cambridge, MA: Harvard University Press.

Courtwright, D., Joseph, H., & Des Jarlais, C. (1989). *Addicts who survived: An oral history of narcotic use in America, 1923–1965*. Knoxville: University of Tennessee Press.

Gerstein, D. R., & Harwood, H. J. (Eds.). (1990). *Treating drug problems*. Committee for the Substance Abuse Coverage Study, Division of Health Care Services, Institute of Medicine. Washington, DC: National Academy Press.

Institute of Medicine. (1990). *Broadening the base of treatment for alcohol problems*. Report of a Study by a Committee of the Institute of Medicine, Division of Mental Health and Behavioral Medicine. Washington, DC: National Academy Press.

Musto, D. F. (1999). *The American disease: Origins of narcotic control*. New York: Oxford University Press.

Rorabaugh, W. J. (1979). *The alcoholic republic*. New York: Oxford University Press.

Substance Abuse and Mental Health Services Administration (SAMSA). (2007). *Results from the 2006 National Survey on Drug Use and Health: National Findings*. Office of Applied Studies, NSDUH Series H-32, DHHS Publication No. SMA 07-4293. Rockville, MD: Author.

Tracy, S. W. (2005). *Alcoholism in America: From Reconstruction to Prohibition*. Baltimore: Johns Hopkins University Press.

UCLA Integrated Substance Abuse Programs. (2007). *Evaluation of the Substance Abuse and Crime Prevention Act: Final report*. Available from http://www.uclaisap.org/.

White, W. L. (1998). *Slaying the dragon: The history of addiction treatment and recovery in America*. Bloomington, IL: Chestnut Health Systems/Lighthouse Institute.

JIM BAUMOHL

TREATMENT, BEHAVIORAL APPROACHES TO

This entry includes the following essays:

AN OVERVIEW

Behavioral treatments encompass a wide range of nonpharmacologic approaches to the treatment of substance-related problems. These approaches are also often referred to as "psychotherapy," "psychosocial approaches," "counseling," and "talk therapies." Behavioral therapies may be combined with other approaches (e.g., medications, case management), which are delivered in a range of settings (e.g., inpatient, outpatient, residential, and prisons) and at various stages of treatment (e.g., assessment, engagement, stabilization, aftercare). In addition, they can be delivered by a range of different clinicians, such as psychiatrists, psychologists, social workers, counselors, or ministers. Generally, however, behavioral treatment refers to an intervention wherein the individual meets with a clinician and, together, they determine the aims and goals of the intervention and the steps to be taken to reach those goals. They will both then monitor the individual's progress in meeting the established goals.

In general, although they vary greatly in their theoretical foundation, approach, and duration, well-defined, competently administered behavioral therapies tend to be associated with positive treatment outcomes. (Behavioral therapies that have been proven to work in clinical trials are often referred to as "empirically evaluated" or "evidence-based" approaches.) Further, retention in treatment is a key factor associated with improved outcomes. The sections that follow provide a survey, with a brief description and evidence for effectiveness, of some of the most commonly used and studied behavioral approaches in the treatment of substance use and related disorders.

BIBLIOGRAPHY

Dutra, L., Stathopoulou, G., Basden, S. L., Leyro, T. M., Powers, M. B., & Otto, M. W. (2008). A meta-analytic review of psychosocial interventions for substance use disorders. *American Journal of Psychiatry, 165*(2), 179–187.

Simpson, D. D., Joe, G. W., & Brown, B. S. (1997). Treatment retention and follow-up outcomes in the Drug Abuse Treatment Outcome Study (DATOS). *Psychology of Addictive Behaviors, 11*(4), 294–307.

KATHLEEN M. CARROLL

COGNITIVE THERAPY

Cognitive treatment is based on the assumption that the way one thinks is a primary determinant of feelings and behavior. Developed from Beck's research (Beck et al., 1979, 1993), cognitive treatment is approached as a collaborative effort between the client and therapist to examine the client's errors and distortions in thinking that contribute to problematic behavior. This examination is fostered through a combination of verbal techniques and behavioral experiments to test the underlying assumptions the client holds about the problematic behavior.

Cognitive treatment in the substance abuse field was a direct extension of Beck's work. Beck's catalog of distorted thoughts examined in depression were found to be applicable to cognitive distortions and errors that accompany addictive disorders. Various cognitive treatments for substance abuse focus on these distortions and vary primarily in the techniques used to change these thought processes.

In relapse prevention (Marlatt & Gordon, 1985), cognitive distortions are viewed as instrumental in the process that leads to relapse. By helping the client thoroughly examine the thoughts that accompany substance use, therapy can reduce the likelihood of a lapse (single use), as well as help prevent a lapse from becoming a relapse (return to uncontrolled use). This is accomplished by examining the following cognitive errors:

1. Overgeneralizing—this is one of the most frequently occurring cognitive errors that helps a single lapse become a full-blown relapse. By viewing the single use as a sign of total relapse, the client overgeneralizes the single use of a substance as a symptom of total failure, thereby allowing for increasing use over time and in a variety of situations. This is sometimes referred to as the abstinence violation effect (AVE).

2. Selective abstraction—by excessively focusing on the immediate lapse, with an accompanying neglect of all past accomplishments and learning, the client interprets a single slip as equivalent to total failure. The individual measures progress almost exclusively in terms of errors and weaknesses.

3. Excessive responsibility—by attributing the cause of a lapse to personal, internal weaknesses or lack of willpower, the client assumes total responsibility for the slip, which in turn makes reassuming control more difficult than when environmental factors are considered partially responsible for the slip.

4. Assuming temporal causality—here, the client views a slip as the first of many to come, thereby dooming all future attempts at self-control.

5. Self-reference—when the client thinks that a lapse becomes the focus of everyone else's attention, believing that others will attribute blame for the event to the client, this adds to feelings of guilt and shame that may already be present within the person.

6. Catastrophizing—the client believes the worst possible outcome will occur from a single use of the substance instead of thinking about how to cope successfully with the initial lapse.

7. Dichotomous thinking—by viewing events in "black and white," clients view their addictive behavior exclusively in terms of abstinence or relapse and leave no logical room for "gray" areas, where they can get back on track once a slip has occurred.

8. Absolute willpower breakdown—here, the client assumes that once willpower has failed, loss of control is inevitable, never to be regained.

9. Body over mind—the cognitive error here is assuming that once a single lapse has occurred, the physiological process of addiction has exclusive control over subsequent behavior, making continued use inevitable.

These errors in thinking are targeted for change in relapse prevention by helping the client learn how to reattribute the cause of a lapse from internal, stable, personal causes to mistakes or errors in the learning process. To facilitate the client's sense of personal control, lapses are viewed as opportunities for corrective learning, instead of indications of total failure. Congruent with the research in the area (Shiffman, 1991), the therapist presents a lapse as a frequently occurring event in the journey toward recovery. The therapist therefore encourages the client to examine the thoughts and expectancies that surround the lapse closely, with the aim of learning alternative coping skills for similar situations that may arise in the future. By reframing a lapse as a learning opportunity, the client is encouraged to view the event as a chance to hone the skills required for abstinence, thereby countering the cognitive errors of selective abstraction.

To intervene with the errors of overgeneralization and temporal causality, the client is taught to view a lapse as a specific, unique event in time and space, instead of as a symptom with greater significance attached to it (e.g., the beginning of the inevitable end). The errors of self-reference and willpower breakdown can be countered by teaching the client to reattribute a lapse to external, specific, and controllable factors. By examining the difficulty of the high-risk situation, the appropriateness of the coping response employed, and any motivational deficits (fatigue or excessive stress), the client can maintain a sense of control over the event and the process of recovery.

Each of these techniques is aimed at conveying the idea that abstinence is the result of a learning process, requiring an acquisition of skills similar to many other skills one learns. This general metaphor can help the client reverse catastrophizing, by reframing a relapse as a "prolapse," as a fall forward rather than backward. This view, combined with viewing a lapse as a unique event in time, helps the client maintain a sense of personal control, since abstinence or control is framed as just a moment away if use is discontinued.

Several skills are taught to the client in relapse prevention to facilitate these cognitive changes and prevent future lapses. Identifying specific sources of stress that contribute to urges, cravings, or lapses helps isolate the event in time as well as identify other distortions that may be present. For example, clients may identify discussing money with one's spouse as the high-risk situation that preceded a lapse. While discussing the lapse with a therapist, clients can learn to anticipate that discussing money in the marriage may trigger an urge or craving to drink. Teaching clients to use visual imagery, such as viewing the urge as a wave that they can surf, can help manage the feeling that urges will continue to build until they must inevitably be given in to. Self-talk is encouraged if a client believes this will help gain a sense of personal control (such as reciting a phrase to oneself about the goal of abstinence or remembering who can be telephoned when an urge is experienced). In addition, clients are taught to be alert for "apparently irrelevant decisions," which can inadvertently lead to relapse. For example, an abstinent gambler may decide to take a scenic drive through Reno, only to find a situation that would be extremely difficult for many to ignore, thus in this case causing a relapse.

Other theorists have developed treatments based exclusively on changing irrational thinking. Ellis and colleagues (1988) founded a self-help group network called Rational Recovery (RR), based on the principles of rational emotive therapy. Developed as an alternative to the Alcoholics Anonymous network, RR focuses on "addictive thinking" and views abstinence as possible—purely as a result of changing these thought processes. This differs from the relapse prevention model described above, which in its entirety combines cognitive and behavioral techniques. Ellis's RR movement teaches addicts how to identify their own faulty thinking through a self-help manual (Trimpey, 1989) and the attendance at support groups.

See also **Models of Alcoholism and Drug Abuse; Risk Factors for Substance Use, Abuse, and Dependence: An Overview.**

BIBLIOGRAPHY

Beck, A. T., et al. (1993). *Cognitive therapy of substance abuse*. New York: Guilford Press.

Carroll, K. M. (1998). *A cognitive behavioral approach: Treating cocaine addiction. Therapy Manuals for Drug Addiction*. U.S. Department of Health and Human Services: National Institute on Drug Abuse.

Ellis, A., McInerney, J. F., DiGiuseppe, R., & Yeager, R. J. (1988). *Rational-emotive therapy with alcoholics and substance abusers*. New York: Pergamon Press.

Freeman, A., et al. (2004). *Clinical applications of cognitive therapy.* New York: Springer.

Kouimtsidis, C., et al. (2007). *Cognitive behavioral therapy in the treatment of addition: A treatment planner for clinicians.* Indianapolis, IN: Wiley.

Leahy, R. L. (2003). *Cognitive therapy techniques: A practitioner's guide.* New York: Guilford Press.

Liese, B. S., & Beck, A. T. (2002). Back to basics: Fundamental cognitive therapy skills for keeping drug-dependent individuals in treatment. In D. W. Brook & H. I. Spitz (Eds.), *The group therapy of substance abuse.* New York: Informa Healthcare.

Marlatt, G.A., & Gordon, J.R., eds. (1985). *Relapse prevention: maintenance strategies in the treatment of addictive behaviors.* New Guilford Press: 1985.

Shiffman, S. (1991). Relapse process and relapse prevention in addictive behaviors. *Behavior Therapists,* pp. 9–11.

Trimpey, J. (1989). *Rational recovery from alcoholism: The small book.* Lotus, CA: Lotus Press.

MOLLY CARNEY
REVISED BY REBECCA HORN (2001)

COGNITIVE-BEHAVIORAL THERAPY

Cognitive-behavioral treatments (CBT) include a group of approaches, grounded in social learning theories of substance abuse (that is, based on classical and operant conditioning, as well as cognitive theory), which emphasize changes in thoughts and behaviors as a means of behavior change. Cognitive-behavioral treatments have been among the most well-defined and rigorously studied psychosocial treatments for substance abuse and dependence. Meta-analysis (Irvin et al., 1999) and reviews of the effectiveness of treatments for substance abuse (APA Workgroup on Substance Use Disorders, 1996; DeRubeis & Crits-Christoph, 1998) have reported that cognitive-behavioral approaches have among the highest level of empirical support for the treatment of substance use disorders and related problems.

OVERVIEW AND STRUCTURE OF CBT

CBT are typically highly structured compared to other approaches used to treat substance use disorders. These treatment approaches are typically comparatively brief (12–24 weeks) and organized closely around well-specified treatment goals. There is typically an articulated agenda for each session and discussion remains focused on issues directly related to substance use. Progress toward treatment goals is monitored closely and frequently, and the therapist takes an active stance throughout treatment.

Cognitive-behavioral approaches typically include a range of skills to foster or maintain abstinence and to prevent relapse, including strategies for issues such as the following:

1. Understanding the individual's patterns of substance use (e.g., factors that precede substance use or change after or during an episode of substance use), sometimes referred to as *functional analysis.*

2. Reducing availability and exposure to the substance and related cues (e.g., people, places, and states that are associated with substance use by its being paired with them during previous episodes of substance use).

3. Fostering the individual's resolution to stop substance use by exploring positive and negative consequences of continued use.

4. Self-monitoring (keeping a diary of activities, craving, and substance use) to identify high-risk situations and to conduct functional analyses of substance use.

5. Recognizing conditioned craving (urges and thoughts about drug use that may be paired with particular cues) and developing strategies to cope with craving.

6. Identifying decisions and thinking styles that can make substance use more likely and learning new strategies to modify those thoughts.

7. Preparing for emergencies and coping with relapse to substance use.

8. Learning substance refusal skills (how to avoid offers of drug and respond assertively).

9. Learning and practicing new behavioral strategies so that the individual can cope more effectively with a range of situations without resorting to substance use or other unhealthy behaviors.

Techniques for teaching these coping responses include direct verbal instruction, modeling appropriate skills through role play, and practice of skills and strategies within the therapy session (Marlatt & Gordon, 1985). Material discussed during sessions is typically supplemented with extra-session tasks (i.e., homework) intended to foster practice and mastery of coping skills.

Broad-spectrum cognitive-behavioral approaches such as that described by Monti and colleagues (1989) also include interventions directed to other problems in the individual's life that are seen as functionally related to substance use. These may include general problem-solving skills, assertiveness training, strategies for coping with negative affect, awareness of anger and anger management, coping with criticism, increasing pleasant activities, enhancing social support networks, and job seeking skills.

Various manuals (Monti et al., 1989; Kadden et al., 1992; Carroll, 1998) describe key cognitive-behavioral treatment strategies and techniques, as well as guidelines for their implementation with a variety of types of substance users. The classic resource in this area remains the landmark book by Marlatt and Gordon, *Relapse Prevention: Maintenance Strategies in the Treatment of Addictive Behaviors,* which appeared in a second edition in 2005.

The goals of CBT tend to be somewhat broader than those of *strict* behavioral approaches, and the choice of treatment goals dictates the specific interventions implemented with a particular individual. For example, in broad spectrum cognitive-behavioral treatments (e.g., Azrin et al., 1976; Monti et al., 1989), the patient and therapist may select a wide range of target behaviors in addition to a treatment goal of abstinence, including improved social skills or social functioning, reduced psychiatric symptoms, reduced social isolation, and entry into the workforce. Cognitive-behavioral therapy also differs from cognitive therapy through its greater emphasis on building specific behavioral skills (e.g., coping with craving, avoiding high risk situations, understanding behavioral patterns) and somewhat less emphasis on targeting and challenging maladaptive cognitions in the earlier stages of treatment.

STRENGTHS AND WEAKNESSES

Strengths of cognitive-behavioral approaches have been summarized by Rotgers (1996) and include the following:

1. Flexibility in meeting individual needs.
2. Acceptability to a wide range of substance abusing individuals seen in clinical settings.
3. Grounding in established principles of behavior theory and behavior change.
4. Emphasis on linking science to treatment.
5. Well-specified treatment goals and clear guidelines for assessing treatment progress.
6. Emphasis on building self-efficacy.
7. A comparatively strong level of empirical support.

Cognitive-behavioral treatments are highly flexible and can be used in a number of treatment modalities and settings, can be applied across different types of substance use with minor modifications, and are compatible with a wide range of other treatment approaches, including family therapy and pharmacotherapy.

Disadvantages of this group of approaches include the following:

1. Research on these approaches has tended not to emphasize the importance of isolating and evaluating the specific *active ingredients* associated with behavior change.
2. These approaches have tended not to be used much outside academic treatment settings (Rotgers, 1996).
3. Patient motivation and specific procedures for addressing the patient's readiness for change have not been emphasized.

Cognitive-behavioral treatments emerged as a leading approach to the treatment of substance use disorders. Solidly grounded in well-established principles of behavior change, with strong empirical support, and applicable to a wide range of individuals with substance use disorders, these well-defined approaches should be a part of any clinician's treatment repertoire.

See also **Addictive Personality and Psychological Tests; Psychoanalysis.**

BIBLIOGRAPHY

American Psychiatric Association, Work Group on Substance Use Disorders. (1995). Practice guideline for the treatment of patients with substance use disorders: Alcohol, cocaine, opioids. *American Journal of Psychiatry, 152* (Suppl.), 2–59.

Azrin, N. H. (1976). Improvements in the community reinforcement approach to alcoholism. *Behavior Research and Therapy, 14,* 339–348.

Carroll, K. M. (1998). *A cognitive-behavioral approach: Treating cocaine addiction* (NIH Publication No. 98–4308). Rockville, MD: National Institute on Drug Abuse.

Carroll, K. M. (1999). Behavioral and cognitive behavioral treatments. In B. S. McCrady & E. E. Epstein (Eds.), *Addictions: A comprehensive guidebook* (pp. 250–267). New York: Oxford University Press.

Chaney, E. F., O'Leary, M. R., & Marlatt, G. A. (1978). Skill training with problem drinkers. *Journal of Consulting and Clinical Psychology, 46,* 1092–1104.

Derubeis, R. J., & Crits-Christoph, P. (1998). Empirically supported individual and group psychological treatments for adult mental disorders. *Journal of Consulting and Clinical Psychology, 66,* 37–52.

Irvin, J. E., Bowers, C. A., Dunn, M. E., & Wong, M. C. (1999). Efficacy of relapse prevention: A meta-analytic review. *Journal of Consulting and Clinical Psychology, 67,* 563–570.

Marlatt, G. A., & Donovan, D. M. (Eds.). (2005). *Relapse prevention: Maintenance strategies in the treatment of addictive behaviors* (2nd ed.). New York: Guilford.

Marlatt, G. A., & Gordon, J. R., (Eds.). (1985). *Relapse prevention: Maintenance strategies in the treatment of addictive behaviors.* New York: Guilford.

Monti, P. M., Abrams, D. B., Kadden, R. M., & Cooney, N. L. (1989). *Treating alcohol dependence: A coping skills training guide in the treatment of alcoholism.* New York: Guilford.

Rotgers, F. (1996). Behavioral theory of substance abuse treatment: Bringing science to bear on practice. In F. Rotgers, D. Keller, & J. Morgenstern (Eds.), *Treating substance abusers: Theory and technique* (pp. 174–201). New York: Guilford.

KATHLEEN M. CARROLL

CONTINGENCY MANAGEMENT

Between 1998 and 2008, research progress on contingency management (CM) accelerated substantially, resulting in a sizable literature demonstrating the effectiveness of CM in the treatment of substance use disorders (Higgins, Silverman, & Heil, 2008). CM is effective for increasing abstinence from a variety of drugs of abuse both during and after treatment, increasing compliance with other substance abuse treatment goals, and improving substance abuse treatment outcomes with special populations. After a brief introduction to the theoretical rationale for CM, research in each of these three areas is summarized below.

CM interventions are based on principles of operant conditioning, which is an area of psychology that studies how environmental contingencies of reinforcement and punishment alter the probability of future behavior. There is extensive basic scientific research showing that operant conditioning is involved in important ways in the development of substance use disorders. That is, the drugs that people abuse stimulate the brain's basic reward centers, thereby increasing the likelihood that people will want to take them again, in terms of operant conditioning, an example of positive reinforcement contingency. That is, the consequence of taking the drug is stimulation of the brain reward centers, which increases the likelihood that the person will again take the drug, which produces still further brain reward, and so on. What CM attempts to do is to use similar positive reinforcement contingencies, along with other principles of operant conditioning, to promote therapeutic changes in behavior such as abstaining from drug use, attending therapy sessions, and taking prescribed medications.

The most common use of CM with drug-dependent individuals is to reinforce abstinence from drug use (Lussier et al., 2006; Higgins et al., 2008). Although compelling evidence regarding the efficacy of CM has been available since the 1970s, interest in this treatment approach was bolstered substantially by successes achieved with CM in the treatment of cocaine dependence. In a seminal study on that topic, thirty-eight cocaine-dependent adults were randomly assigned to twenty-four weeks of behavior therapy, including CM, or to drug abuse counseling (Higgins et al., 1993). The CM program used in that study is the model on which many contemporary CM interventions are based. The CM intervention was twelve weeks in duration and explicitly integrated with routine urine toxicology testing. Urine specimens were analyzed at the clinic to minimize delay between obtaining the specimen and delivering appropriate consequences. Cocaine-negative test results earned points that were recorded on vouchers and provided to patients. Points were worth $0.25 each, with the first negative test results earning 10 points or $2.50 in purchasing power. To promote sustained abstinence in the outpatient setting where opportunities to resume drug use are ubiquitous, the number of points earned increased by five with each consecutive cocaine-negative test result, and each three consecutive negative test results earned a $10 bonus voucher. Moreover, a cocaine-positive test result or failure to provide a scheduled specimen reset the value of the vouchers back to the initial low level from which it could escalate again according to the same schedule. Vouchers were often used to purchase retail items such as gym memberships, fishing licenses, or gift certificates to local restaurants. If a patient earned all of the points available across twelve weeks, the individual could earn a total of $997.50 in purchasing power, although average earnings were approximately half of the total possible, which was later determined to be typical in these interventions.

More than 50 percent of patients in the CM condition remained in treatment for the recommended twenty-four weeks and achieved several months of continuous cocaine abstinence whereas only 11 percent of patients in the comparison condition did so. These positive results with CM were particularly encouraging because so few other treatment approaches had been shown to be efficacious with cocaine dependence.

Subsequent studies of CM treatment of cocaine dependence replicated those findings. Studies also have shown that benefits of treatment can persist for almost two years after termination of the CM intervention and that the amount of abstinence achieved during the treatment period is the best predictor of whether the treatment benefits are sustained post-treatment (Higgins et al., 2000; Higgins et al., 2007).

Research has demonstrated effectiveness of CM for increasing abstinence from other drugs of abuse. Also important to note is that reinforcers other than vouchers have been used successfully in CM, such as abstinence-contingent housing employment, take-home medication privileges, and draws from a prize bowl, with the possibility of winning prizes of varying amounts with each draw.

Typically, but not always, CM is used as part of a more comprehensive treatment plan. CM can be used to improve compliance with other treatment goals such as with recommended medication regimens (Rounsaville et al., 2008). Adherence to medications to reduce drug use, such as naltrexone and disulfiram for opioid and alcohol use, can be improved with CM (Carroll et al., 2001). Studies also have demonstrated efficacy of CM in improving medication compliance among tuberculosis-exposed and HIV-infected drug abusers (Elk, 1999). Besides medication compliance, CM can also improve attendance at therapy sessions (Jones et al., 2001) and compliance with participation in therapy-related activities between therapy sessions (Bickel et al., 1997; Iguchi et al., 1997). In these latter applications, patients earn vouchers by completing some minimum number of therapy-related activities weekly. The activities might include attending a job interview if the goal was gaining employment or attending a self-help meeting if the goal was to increase contact with a social network to support sobriety. Vouchers are provided when patients submit documentation verifying that they had completed a designated therapeutic activity. Completion of therapeutic activities is associated with greater drug abstinence.

CM also is capable of improving outcomes with important special populations of drug abusers. For example, effective treatments are sorely needed for drug-dependent pregnant women. A voucher-based CM intervention has been demonstrated to significantly increase abstinence from cocaine and heroin use while simultaneously increasing vocational skills among pregnant women who were both drug dependent and chronically unemployed (Silverman et al., 2002). Vouchers delivered contingent on abstinence from cigarette smoking increased cessation rates during pregnancy and postpartum (Donatelle et al., 2000; Higgins et al., 2004) and increased fetal growth (Heil et al., in press). Other special populations for whom CM interventions show promise are adolescents (Kamon et al., 2005; Krishnan-Sarin et al., 2006), the homeless (Milby et al., 2000), and people with serious mental illness (Roll et al., 2004).

Sufficient research has been conducted to glean some rules about effective implementation of CM. Below are ten features of effective CM interventions:

1. The details of the intervention must be explained carefully to patients prior to beginning treatment, with written contracts being very helpful.

2. The response being targeted by the CM intervention (e.g., drug abstinence) should be defined in objective terms (e.g., drug-negative urine toxicology results).

3. The objective methods to be used for verifying that the target response occurred (e.g., urine toxicology testing) should be identified in advance.

4. The schedule for monitoring progress (e.g., Monday, Wednesday, & Friday) should be outlined clearly.

5. The schedule for monitoring progress should include frequent opportunities for patients to experience the programmed consequences.

6. The duration of the intervention should be clearly stipulated in advance.

7. Focusing on a single target (e.g., abstinence from a single substance) on average produces larger treatment effects than those that target multiple targets (e.g., abstinence from multiple substances).

8. The consequences that will follow success and failure have to be clear.

9. There should be minimal delay in delivering designated consequences. Delivering the consequence on the same day that the target response is verified produces larger treatment effects than delivering the consequence at a later time.

10. Larger value incentives on average produce larger treatment effects.

CM is effective in increasing drug abstinence and in improving compliance with treatment regimens for various types of drug dependence and populations. Positive outcomes have been achieved even with some of the most challenging and recalcitrant subgroups of drug abusers. Though there is a loss of treatment gains when the intervention is terminated, beneficial carryover effects have been demonstrated for a year or more post-treatment and the rates of relapse appear to be comparable to other interventions. Nevertheless, prevention of relapse is an important problem needing improved methods to manage it. Systematic use of multimodal interventions designed to address the many changes likely to be necessary for longer-term success is one reasonable approach, as is the development of longer-term CM interventions that can be kept in place until the patient gains the requisite skills to sustain abstinence without CM support.

BIBLIOGRAPHY

Bickel, W. K., Amass, L., Higgins, S. T., Badger, G. J., & Esch, R. A. (1997). Effects of adding behavioral treatment to opioid detoxification with buprenorphine. *Journal of Consulting and Clinical Psychology, 65,* 803–810.

Carroll, K. M., Ball, S. A., Nich, C., O'Connor, P. G., Eagan, D., Frankforter, T. L. et al. (2001). Targeting behavioral therapies to enhance naltrexone treatment of opioid dependence: Efficacy of contingency management and significant other involvement. *Archives of General Psychiatry, 58,* 755–761.

Donatelle, R., Prows, S. L., Champeau, D., & Hudson, L. D. (2000). Randomized controlled trial using social support and financial incentives for high-risk pregnant smokers: The Significant-Other Supporter (SOS) Program. *Tobacco Control, 9* (Suppl. III), iii67–iii69.

Elk, R. (1999). Pregnant women and tuberculosis-exposed drug abusers: Reducing drug use and increasing treatment compliance. In S. T. Higgins & K. Silverman (Eds.), *Motivating behavior change among illicit-drug abusers: Research on contingency management interventions* (pp. 123–144). Washington, DC: American Psychological Association.

Heil, S. H., Higgins, S. T., Bernstein, I. M., Solomon, L., Rogers, R. E., Thomas, C. S., et al. (in press). Effects of voucher-based incentives on abstinence from cigarette smoking and fetal growth among pregnant women. *Addiction.*

Higgins, S. T., Budney, A. J., Bickel, W. K., Hughes, J. R., Foerg, F., & Badger, G. (1993). Achieving cocaine abstinence with a behavioral approach. *American Journal of Psychiatry, 150,* 763–769.

Higgins, S. T., Heil, S. H., Dontona, R. L., Donham, R., Matthews, M., & Badger, G. J. (2007). Effects of varying the monetary value of voucher-based incentives on abstinence achieved during and following treatment among cocaine-dependent outpatients. *Addiction, 102,* 271–281.

Higgins, S. T., Heil, S. H., Solomon, L. J., Bernstein, I. M., Lussier, J. P., Able, R. L., et al. (2004). A pilot study on voucher-based incentives to promote abstinence from cigarette smoking during pregnancy and postpartum. *Nicotine & Tobacco Research, 6,* 1015–1020.

Higgins, S. T., & Silverman, K. (2008). Contingency management. In M. Galanter & H. D. Kleber (Eds.), *Textbook of substance abuse treatment* (4th ed.). Washington, DC: American Psychiatric Press.

Higgins, S. T., Silverman, K., & Heil, S. H. (2008). *Contingency management in substance abuse treatment.* New York: Guilford Press.

Higgins, S. T., Wong, C. J., Badger, G. J., Haug Ogden, D., & Dantona, R. L. (2000). Contingent reinforcement increases cocaine abstinence during outpatient treatment and one year of follow-up. *Journal of Consulting and Clinical Psychology, 68,* 64–72.

Iguchi, M. Y., Belding, M. A., Morral, A. R., Lamb, R. J., & Husband, S. D. (1997). Reinforcing operants other than abstinence in drug abuse treatment: An effective alternative for reducing drug use. *Journal of Consulting and Clinical Psychology, 65,* 421–428.

Jones, H. E., Haug, N., Silverman, K., Stitzer, M., & Svikis, D. (2001). The effectiveness of incentives in enhancing treatment attendance and drug abstinence in methadone-maintained pregnant woman. *Drug and Alcohol Dependence, 61,* 297–306.

Kamon, J., Budney, A., & Stanger, C. (2005). A contingency management intervention for adolescent marijuana users. *Journal of the American Academy of Child and Adolescent Psychiatry, 44,* 512–521.

Krishanan-Sarin, S., Duhig, A., Mckee, S., McMahon, T. J., Liss, T., McFetridge, A., et al. (2006). Contingency management for smoking cessation in adolescent smokers. *Experimental and Clinical Psychopharmacology, 14,* 306–310.

Lussier, J. P., Heil, S. H., Mongeon, J. A., Badger, G. J., & Higgins, S. T. (2006). A meta-analysis of voucher-based reinforcement therapy for substance use disorders. *Addiction, 101,* 192–203.

Milby, J. B., Schumacher, J. E., McNamara, C., Wallace, D., Usdan, S., & Michael, M. (2000). Initiating abstinence in cocaine abusing dually diagnosed homeless persons. *Drug and Alcohol Dependence, 60*(1): 55-67.

Roll, J. M., Petry, N. M., Stitzer, M. L., Brecht, M. L., Peirce, J. M., McCann, M. J., et al. (2004). Contingency Management for the Treatment of Methamphetamine Use Disorders. *American Journal of Psychiatry 163,* 1993–1999.

Rounsaville, B. J., Rosen, M., & Carroll, K. M. (2008). Medication compliance. In S. T. Higgins, K. Silverman, & S. H. Heil (Eds.), *Contingency management in substance abuse treatment* (pp. 140–158). New York: Guilford Press.

Silverman K., Robles E., Mudric T., Bigelow G. E., & Stitzer, M. L. (2004). A randomized trial of long-term reinforcement of cocaine abstinence in methadone-maintained patients who inject drugs. *Journal of Consulting and Clinical Psychology, 72,* 839–854.

Silverman, K., Svikis, D., Wong, C. J., Hampton, J., Stitzer, M. L., & Bigelow, G. E. (2002). A reinforcement-based therapeutic workplace for the treatment of drug abuse: Three-year abstinence outcomes. *Experimental and Clinical Psychopharmacology, 10,* 220–240.

STEPHEN T. HIGGINS
SARAH H. HEIL
RANDALL E. ROGERS

COUPLES AND FAMILY THERAPY

Since the late 1970s, there has been growing recognition that relationship factors between couples and among families play a crucial role in maintaining substance abuse. Substance misuse and relationship problems have a reciprocal relationship where each exacerbates problems in the other, producing a vicious cycle that is difficult to escape.

Among couples, ineffective problem-solving, poor communication, conflict, financial strain, and nagging are common antecedents to substance use and abuse. Caretaking by the non-substance-abusing spouse following drinking or drug use can inadvertently reinforce substance use. Additionally, spouses' resentments, while understandable, can lead to ignoring rather than reinforcing abstinence.

BEHAVIORAL COUPLES THERAPY TREATMENT

Behavioral couples therapy (BCT) was founded upon two fundamental assumptions. First, family members can reward abstinence. Second, relationship distress and conflict are powerful antecedents to substance use, and reduction of these antecedents improves treatment outcomes. The following is an overview of some of the defining approaches used in behavioral couples therapy (see O'Farrell and Fals-Stewart [2006] for more details).

Supporting Abstinence with Recovery Contract. In early treatment phases, the therapist and the couple collaboratively develop a Recovery Contract, consisting of a daily Trust Discussion in which the substance-abusing partner expresses the intention to refrain from alcohol or drugs, and the non-substance-abusing partner verbally supports the patient's efforts. For patients medically cleared and willing, daily use of medications supporting sobriety (i.e., disulfiram, naltrexone) is witnessed and verbally supported by the spouse. Completion of Recovery Contract components, including the Trust Discussion, medication adherence, and additional components (e.g., Alcoholics Anonymous, Al-Anon attendance) are recorded daily on a calendar provided by the therapist. Both partners agree to limit discussions of past substance use to the therapy session where communication can be monitored and mediated as necessary to reduce substance-related conflicts, which may trigger relapse.

Improving Couple Relationship Functioning.
Through standard couple-based behavioral assignments, BCT aims to increase positive feelings, shared activities, and constructive communication. Exercises include noticing and acknowledging pleasing behaviors performed by one's partner daily, planning ahead to surprise the partner through activities that demonstrate caring, and engaging in rewarding shared activities. Additionally, communication skills training (e.g., paraphrasing, empathizing, validating) can help the couple better address stressors as they arise, reducing the risk of relapse.

Relapse Prevention and Maintenance.
The final stages of BCT involve relapse prevention including ongoing sobriety-related activities (e.g., daily Trust Discussion, self-help support meetings) and contingency plans for relapses (e.g., contacting the therapist and a sponsor).

EMPIRICAL BASIS FOR BCT
Multiple studies indicate that participation in BCT (O'Farrell & Fals-Stewart, 2006) is associated with positive outcomes for alcoholic and drug-abusing patients. BCT produced better outcomes than more typical individual-based treatment for married or cohabiting alcoholic and drug-abusing patients in a meta-analysis of 12 controlled studies (Powers et al., 2008), some of which are summarized below, and details are provided in O'Farrell and Fals-Stewart (2003, 2006).

Primary Clinical Outcomes.
Fourteen studies comparing substance use and relationship outcomes for primarily male, substance-abusing patients show a fairly consistent pattern of greater rates of abstinence and fewer substance-related problems, happier relationships, and lower risk of divorce and separation among those who receive BCT than patients who receive individual-based treatment.

Benefit-to-Cost Ratio.
Three BCT studies (two in alcoholism and one in drug abuse) examined social costs due to substance abuse and found savings that averaged $5,000–$6,500 per case, with every dollar spent delivering BCT saving five dollars in social costs. BCT was more cost effective than individual treatment for drug abuse or interactional couples therapy for alcoholism.

Domestic Violence Outcomes.
Two studies with male alcoholics found male-to-female violence was significantly reduced after BCT and nearly eliminated with abstinence. Two studies showed that BCT reduced partner violence and couple conflicts better than individual treatment.

Impact of BCT on Children.
Two studies (one in alcoholism, one in drug abuse) demonstrated greater improvements in functioning among children when parents received BCT for substance abuse than among children when parents received individual-based treatment or couple psychoeducation. Significant reductions in the number of impaired children were found only for those receiving BCT.

Integrating Recovery-related Medication.
Among male opioid patients taking naltrexone, BCT patients had better naltrexone compliance, greater abstinence, and fewer substance-related problems than those in individual treatment. BCT also resulted in improved compliance with HIV medications and with disulfiram and naltrexone for alcoholic patients.

BCT with Other Family Members.
While most BCT studies involve traditional couples, some recent studies, including those described above, successfully expanded the use of BCT to include family members beyond spouses. For example, in the studies of BCT with HIV medications among drug abusers and naltrexone use for opioid patients, family members included heterosexual partners, homosexual partners, parents, siblings, and roommates. The outcomes for nonspousal dyads resulted in as much success as those for spousal dyads. Specifically, Fals-Stewart and O'Farrell (2003) found no significant differences across outcome measures between the spousal and nonspousal dyads for opioid patients.

CONTRAINDICATIONS FOR BCT

Contraindications to consider in the use of BCT include current psychosis for either member of the couple, acute risk of severe family violence, or an active court order requiring the couple to have no contact. Cases with less severe forms of family violence can be treated successfully in BCT with conflict containment as an explicit goal from the outset and with specific steps taken to avoid violence (for more details see O'Farrell & Murphy, 2002). Finally, if both members of the couple have a current substance use problem, BCT may not be effective; possible exceptions to this are when one member has at least 90 days of abstinence or both members decide to change their substance use within the first few treatment sessions.

Future Directions for BCT. Research is needed to replicate and extend recent advances, particularly for women and broader family constellations. There is a great need for research on BCT for dual-using couples, as this difficult clinical challenge has yet to be addressed empirically. Finally, there is a need for technology transfer so that additional families can benefit from existing knowledge about the effectiveness of BCT for alcoholism and drug abuse.

See also **Al-Anon; Alcoholics Anonymous (AA); Families and Drug Use; Intimate Partner Violence and Alcohol/Substance Use; Naltrexone; Opiates/ Opioids; Treatment, Pharmacological Approaches to: Disulfiram; Treatment, Pharmacological Approaches to: Naltrexone.**

BIBLIOGRAPHY

Fals-Stewart, W., & O'Farrell, T. J. (2003). Behavioral family counseling and naltrexone for male opioid dependent patients. *Journal of Consulting and Clinical Psychology, 71,* 432–442.

O'Farrell, T. J., & Fals-Stewart, W. (2003). Marital and family therapy. In R. Hester & W. R. Miller (Eds.), *Handbook of alcoholism treatment approaches* (3rd ed., pp. 188–212). Boston: Allyn and Bacon.

O'Farrell, T. J., & Fals-Stewart, W. (2006). *Behavioral Couples Therapy for alcoholism and drug abuse.* New York: Guilford Press.

O'Farrell, T. J., & Murphy, C. M. (2002). Behavioral Couples Therapy for alcoholism and drug abuse: Encountering the problem of domestic violence. In C. Wekerle & A. M. Wall (Eds.), *The violence and addiction equation: Theoretical and clinical issues in substance abuse and relationship violence* (pp. 293–303). New York: Brunner-Routledge.

Powers, M. B., Vedel, E., & Emmelkamp, P. M. G. (2008). Behavioral Couples Therapy (BCT) for alcohol and drug use disorders: A meta–analysis. *Clinical Psychology Review, 28*(6), 952–962.

TIMOTHY J. O'FARRELL
LAURA A. MEIS
WILLIAM FALS-STEWART

GROUP THERAPY

Group therapy is the most common treatment modality for substance use disorders (SUDs). Broadly defined, group therapy for SUDs consists of two or more unrelated patients and a therapist who meet together regularly, with the primary goal of reducing or eliminating substance use or addressing behaviors related to substance use.

A 1988 study indicated that 94 percent of SUD treatment facilities in the United States offered group therapy of some type (Price et al., 1991). It is unlikely that this figure has decreased since that time, given the increased emphasis on reducing costs in such facilities. Group therapy is a popular choice for patients with SUDs because of its perceived cost-effectiveness, and because of the powerful influence of self-help (also called mutual-help) groups such as Alcoholics Anonymous (AA), Narcotics Anonymous (NA), and SMART Recovery. A key idea behind these groups is that the influence of group members with similar experiences can help to reduce the denial frequently associated with substance use. Other central ideas behind self-help groups are the beliefs that members can benefit from: (1) developing supportive interpersonal relationships with others, (2) recognizing and expressing needs and emotions, and (3) identifying and changing maladaptive patterns of behavior. It is likely that nearly all forms of group therapy share these benefits to varying degrees.

TYPES OF GROUP THERAPY

There are five basic models of group therapy:

1. the group education model, in which the group leader serves as a teacher and instructs patients about the effects of drug and alcohol use on the brain and body as well as the natural course of addiction and recovery.

2. recovery skills training (also educationally based), which has the aim of teaching specific behavioral and cognitive-behavioral skills. These include recognizing, avoiding, and coping with triggers to substance use; drug-refusal skills; problem solving; and cognitive restructuring.

3. the group process model, in which the therapeutic effect is related to the nature of the interaction (either supportive or confrontational), both among group members themselves and between group members and the group leader. These groups emphasize the parallels between such interactions and relationships outside of the group therapy setting.

4. the check-in group, which essentially consists of brief individual treatment, including goal-setting and a review of progress toward goals, conducted in a group format.

5. group treatment that addresses other issues that are relevant to substance use, including anger management, communication, assertiveness, relaxation, or parenting skills.

EFFECTIVENESS

A review of 30 studies examining the effectiveness of group therapy for SUDs revealed three primary findings. First, the results of several studies suggest that group therapy is generally more effective than no treatment, and that group therapy can increase the effectiveness of existing treatments. This finding may be reassuring to those who may fundamentally question whether group therapy is helpful at all.

Second, no specific type of group therapy has been found to be generally most effective at improving SUD outcomes. However, several promising interventions have shown at least some evidence of being more effective than others, usually in treating specific populations. For example, there is evidence that integrated group therapy is superior to group drug counseling in reducing substance use in patients diagnosed with both bipolar disorder and SUD (Weiss et al., 2007). Preliminary data also indicate promise for women's recovery groups when compared to mixed-gender group drug counseling in treating women with a SUD (Greenfield et al., 2007). Solution-focused group therapy has demonstrated superior results to problem-focused group therapy in reducing substance use in people

identified as having a substance abuse problem that requires less than nine hours per week of treatment (Smock et al., 2008). Similarly, a family systems intervention for adolescents yielded superior substance use outcomes when compared to either group drug education or a process-oriented group therapy (Joanning et al., 1992).

There have also been promising results for a substance abuse-domestic violence group treatment compared to a twelve-step facilitation group for men exhibiting domestic violence and SUD (Easton et al., 2008). Multidimensional family therapy has demonstrated superior outcomes to peer group therapy in measures of substance use and behavioral problems with low-income, ethnically diverse young adolescents (Liddle et al., 2007). Finally, a behavioral skills intervention was superior in effectiveness to transactional analyses in treating adult males with an alcohol use disorder (Olson et al., 1981).

The third finding is that there is no evidence that group therapy is superior to individual therapy, or that individual therapy is superior to group therapy, when the content, intensity, and length of treatment are equivalent. This is an important finding for the proponents of group therapy, given its presumed cost-effectiveness and its widespread inclusion in SUD treatment throughout the country. Conversely, it also supports the idea that group therapy is not intrinsically superior to individual approaches.

However, a failure to find differences between treatments does not necessarily mean that the treatments compared are equally effective. These outcomes may have arisen from several factors, all of which can influence statistical power, or the ability to detect a difference when it exists. The size of the measured treatment effect is one determinant of statistical power, which is in turn influenced by the treatment intensity and duration. Statistical power is also influenced by the number of participants in a study, as well as by variations in how treatment is delivered.

Perhaps the most important finding in examining the treatment literature on group therapy is that so few studies of this treatment modality have been conducted. Given how frequently group therapy is used to treat SUDs, this is particularly noteworthy. Between 1978 and 2008, there were only 30 published papers from prospective treatment studies comparing group therapy to other treatments. Unfortunately, with the few exceptions noted earlier, it is difficult to establish firm conclusions about what frequency, duration, or type of group treatment is most effective with particular populations. Despite the widespread clinical acceptance of group therapy for SUDs, relatively little is really known about its effectiveness. The outcome studies on this topic are limited in number, and the findings are generally mixed.

See also **Families and Drug Use; Risk Factors for Substance Use, Abuse, and Dependence: An Overview; Sobriety; Toughlove.**

BIBLIOGRAPHY

Easton, C. J., Mandel, D. L., Hunkele, K. A., Nich, C., Rounsaville, B. J., & Carroll, K. M. (2008). A cognitive behavioral therapy for alcohol-dependent domestic violence offenders: An integrated substance abuse-domestic violence treatment approach (SADV). *American Journal on Addictions, 16*(1), 24–31.

Greenfield, S. F., Trucco, E. M., McHugh, R. K., Lincoln, M., & Gallop, R. J. (2007). The women's recovery group study: A stage I trial of women-focused group therapy for substance use disorders versus mixed-gender group drug counseling. *Drug and Alcohol Dependence, 90*(1), 39–47.

Joanning, H., Thomas, F., Quinn, W., & Mullen, R. (1992). Treating adolescent drug abuse: A comparison of family systems therapy, group therapy, and family education. *Journal of Marital and Family Therapy, 18*(4), 345–356.

Liddle, H. A., Rowe, C. L., Dakof, G. A., Ungaro, R. A., & Henderson, C. E. (2007). Early intervention for adolescent substance abuse: Pretreatment to post-treatment outcomes of a randomized clinical trial comparing multidimensional family therapy and peer group treatment. *Journal of Psychoactive Drugs, 36*(1), 49–63.

Olson, P. R., Devine, V. T., Ganley, R., & Dorsey, G. C., Jr. (1981). Long-term effects of behavioral versus insight-oriented therapy with inpatient alcoholics. *Journal of Consulting and Clinical Psychology, 49*(6), 866–877.

Price, R. H., Burke, A. C., D'Aunno, T. A., Klingel, D. M., McCaughrin, W. C., & Rafferty, J. A. (1991). Outpatient drug abuse treatment services, 1988: Results of a national survey. In R. W. Pickens, C. G. Leukefeld & C. R. Schuster (Eds.), *Improving drug abuse treatment* (NIDA research monograph 106). Washington, DC: National Institute on Drug Abuse.

Smock, S. A., Trepper, T. S., Wetchler, J. L., McCollum, E. E., Ray, R., & Pierce, K. (2008). Solution-focused group therapy for level 1 substance abusers. *Journal of Marital and Family Therapy, 34*(1), 107–120.

Weiss, R. D., Griffin, M. L., Kolodziej, M. E., Greenfield, S. F., Najavits, L. M., Daley, D. C., et al. (2007). A randomized trial of integrated group therapy versus group drug counseling for patients with bipolar disorder and substance dependence. *American Journal of Psychiatry, 164*, 100–107.

WILLIAM B. JAFFEE
ROGER D. WEISS

LONG-TERM VERSUS BRIEF

For many people, alcohol and drug abuse has the characteristics of chronic disorders, such that people experience recurring cycles of cessation and relapse (Hser, Anglin, Grella, Longshore, & Prendergast, 1997). Therefore, researchers and practitioners have increasingly accepted the idea that substance dependence is a chronic disorder (Donovan, 1998; McLellan, 2002). Like substance use disorders (SUDs), many medical and psychiatric disorders have a chronic course. With such disorders, longer-term treatments are usually found to be much more effective than short interventions. For example, most patients with disorders such as hypertension, elevated cholesterol, diabetes, or schizophrenia have the best clinical course if they maintain lifestyle modifications and remain on their medications for extended periods of time. One would therefore think that individuals with SUDs who seek treatment would have better outcomes if they received longer, as opposed to shorter, episodes of care. However, research findings in the addictions have indicated that the relationship between length of treatment and outcome is not particularly straightforward.

There is considerable evidence that patients who stay in treatment longer have better outcomes (Simpson, 2004). That is, when patients with similar demographic characteristics and pretreatment substance use severity all enter the same treatment program, those who stay in treatment longer will, on average, have better treatment outcomes that those who leave early. However, it is not clear how much the better outcomes should be attributed to longer stays in treatment or to individual characteristics such as motivation and initial success in treatment. The most direct way to untangle treatment from motivation effects and other patient characteristics is to conduct studies in which patients are randomly assigned to the same or similar treatments of different lengths, and their outcomes examined over time. Studies of this sort have produced very little evidence to indicate that treatments with longer durations produce better substance-abuse outcomes than those with shorter durations (Miller & Hester, 1986; McCusker et al., 1995; Kamara & Van Der Hyde, 1997; Long, Williams, & Hollin, 1998; Trent, 1998; Stephens, Roffman, & Curtin, 2000). One potential factor contributing to this result is that treatments in these studies are relatively short, such that the long conditions seldom exceed 90 days. Hence, these studies have not directly examined if extended interventions generate better outcomes than standard-length (i.e., 90-day) treatments (McKay, 2005).

In addition, it should also be stressed that many substance-abuse treatment programs feature a continuum of care, in which patients spend a certain amount of time in an initial higher-intensity treatment and then "step down" to a lower-intensity level of care, such as aftercare. Would participation in and completion of aftercare following initial treatment have greater prognostic significance than the duration of a single level of care? Earlier research suggested that such was not the case (McKay, 2001). In the majority of the relatively few studies that examined this issue, patients who were randomly assigned to active aftercare treatments did not have better substance use outcomes than those who were randomized to either no aftercare or minimal aftercare conditions. In a more recent study that examined new continuing care approaches, McKay (2006) summarized the key findings:

> 1) Continuing care interventions of a year or longer are more likely to show significant positive effects; 2) continuing care treatments that are less burdensome to patients appear to promote higher rates of sustained engagement; 3) more structured and intensive continuing care may be more effective for patients with severe substance dependence and associated problems and for those who fail to achieve reasonable progress while in the initial phase of treatment; and 4) use of medications as part of continuing care is increasing. (p. 355)

In a recent review of extended interventions (i.e., therapeutic protocols that have a planned duration of longer than 6 months) for alcohol and drug use disorders, McKay (2005) examined interventions in two categories: (1) Interventions contained either behavioral or pharmacological treatments, which were provided over periods of greater than 6 months. These interventions consisted of face-to-face contact with counselors or therapists and were provided primarily in clinics and other treatment facilities. This category included some studies reviewed by McKay in 2001. (2) Lower-intensity interventions involved the regular monitoring of patients' symptoms and status throughout extended periods of time. Monitoring was conducted through face-to-face contacts with research or treatment personnel or through telephone contacts using an interactive voice response system. In some of these monitoring protocols, patients were linked to services or were provided with brief counseling when their conditions warranted additional support.

The results of this comprehensive review indicated that maintaining therapeutic contact with individuals with SUDs for extended periods of time seemed to promote better long-term outcomes than "treatment as usual." Although most of the extended behavioral and pharmacological interventions reviewed in this article yielded positive effects, two studies did not (Prendergast, Hall, Wexler, Melnick, & Cao, 2004; Krystal, Cramer, Krol, & Kirk, 2001) and several other studies with various methodological limitations produced mixed results (Braukmann et al., 1985; Dahlgren & Willander, 1989; Ojehagen et al., 1992; Tomson, Romelsjo, & Aberg, 1998; McCrady, Epstein, & Kahler, 2004). In addition, McKay pointed out an important issue regarding study design: "In many studies the extended interventions were compared to relatively low intensity or placebo control conditions rather than to shorter versions of the same intervention, which raises questions about how 'extended' an extended intervention needs to be for effective addiction management" (2005, p. 1603). Therefore, before any firm conclusions can be drawn about the utility of extended treatment in the addictions, future research that directly compares extended behavioral and pharmacological interventions to treatment as usual or shorter versions of the same interventions is needed (McKay, 2005).

Overall, consensus exists among clinicians and clinical researchers that sustained recoveries from

SUDs generally require ongoing efforts by those who have these disorders. Some of the behaviors associated with good long-term outcomes include regular attendance of self-help groups such as Alcoholics Anonymous, treatment for family or marital problems, employment, involvement with a religious group, and a commitment to new interests or hobbies. These findings are consistent with the notion that formal treatment, whether of short or long duration, is useful to begin a process of change that must be sustained over long periods of time to be successful and that ultimately involves many areas of functioning.

See also **Diagnosis of Substance Use Disorders: Diagnostic Criteria; Research: Motivation.**

BIBLIOGRAPHY

Braukmann, C. J., Bedlington, M. M., Belden, B. D., Braukmann, P. D., Husted, J. J., Ramp, K. K., et al. (1985). Effects of community-based group-home treatment programs on male juvenile offenders' use and abuse of drugs and alcohol. *American Journal of Drug and Alcohol Abuse, 11*, 249–278.

Dahlgren, L., & Willander, A. (1989). Are special treatment facilities for female alcoholics needed? A controlled 2-year follow-up study from a specialized female unit (EWA) versus a mixed male/female treatment facility. *Alcoholism: Clinical and Experimental Research, 13,* 499–504.

Donovan, D. M. (1998). Continuing care: Promoting the maintenance of change. In W. R. Miller & N. Heather (Eds.), *Treating addictive behaviors* (2nd ed., pp. 317–336). New York: Plenum.

Hser, Y. I., Anglin, M. D., Grella, C., Longshore, D., & Prendergast, M. L. (1997). Drug treatment careers: A conceptual framework and existing research findings. *Journal of Substance Abuse Treatment, 14*(6), 543–558.

Kamara, S. G., & Van Der Hyde, V. A. (1997). Outcomes of regular versus extended alcohol/drug out-patient treatment. *Medicine and Law, 16,* 607–620.

Krystal, J. H., Cramer, J. A., Krol, W. F., & Kirk, G. F. (2001). Naltrexone in the treatment of alcohol dependence. *New England Journal of Medicine, 345,* 1734–1739.

Long, C. G., Williams, M., & Hollin, C. R. (1998). Treating alcohol problems: A study of program effectiveness and cost effectiveness according to length and delivery of treatment. *Addiction, 93,* 561–571.

McCrady, B. S., Epstein, E. E., & Kahler, C. W. (2004). Alcoholics Anonymous and relapse prevention maintenance strategies after conjoint behavioral alcohol treatment for men: 18-month outcomes. *Journal of Consulting and Clinical Psychology, 72,* 870–878.

McCusker, J., Vickers-Lahti, M., Stoddard, A., Hindin, R., Bigelow, C., Zorn, M., et al. (1995). The effectiveness of alternative planned durations of residential drug abuse treatment. *American Journal of Public Health, 85,* 1426–1429.

McKay, J. R. (2001) The role of continuing care in out-patient alcohol treatment programs. In M. Galanter (Ed.), *Recent developments in alcoholism, Vol. 15. Services research in the era of managed care,* (pp. 357–372). New York: Kluwer Academic/Plenum.

McKay, J. R. (2005). Is there a case for extended interventions for alcohol and drug use disorders? *Addiction, 100,* 1594–1610.

McKay, J. R. (2006). Continuing care in the treatment of addictive disorders. *Current Psychiatric Reports, 8*(5), 355–362.

McLellan, A.T. (2002). Editorial: Have we evaluated addiction treatment correctly? Implications from a chronic care perspective. *Addiction, 97,* 249–252.

Miller, W. R., & Hester, R. K. (1986). In-patient alcoholism treatment: Who benefits? *American Psychologist, 41,* 794–805.

Moos, R. H., Finney, J. W., & Cronkite, R. C. (1990). *Alcoholism treatment: Context, process, and outcome.* New York: Oxford University Press.

Ojehagen, A., Berglund, M., Appel, C. P., Andersson, K., Nilsson, B., Skjaerris, A., et al. (1992). A randomized study of long-term out-patient treatment in alcoholics: Psychiatric treatment versus multimodal behavioral therapy, during 1 versus 2 years of treatment. *Alcohol and Alcoholism, 27,* 649–658.

Prendergast, M. L., Hall, E. A., Wexler, H. K., Melnick, G., & Cao, Y. (2004). Amity prison-based therapeutic community: 5-year outcomes. *Prison Journal, 84,* 36–60.

Simpson, D. D. (2004). A conceptual framework for drug treatment process and outcomes. *Journal of Substance Abuse Treatment, 27,* 99–121.

Simpson, D. D., Joe, G. W., & Brown, B. S. (1997). Treatment retention and follow-up outcomes in the Drug Abuse Treatment Outcome Study (DATOS). *Psychology of Addictive Behaviors, 11*(4), 294–307.

Stephens, R. S., Roffman, R. A., & Curtin, L. (2000). Comparison of extended versus brief treatments for marijuana use. *Journal of Consulting and Clinical Psychology, 68,* 898–908.

Tomson, Y., Romelsjo, A., & Aberg, H. (1998). Excessive drinking—brief intervention by a primary health care nurse: A randomized controlled trial. *Scandinavian Journal of Primary Health Care, 16,* 188–192.

Trent, L. K. (1998). Evaluation of a four- versus six-week length of stay in the Navy's alcohol treatment program. *Journal of Studies on Alcohol, 59,* 270–279.

James R. McKay
Revised by Sharon Hsin Hsu (2009)
G. Alan Marlatt (2009)

MINNESOTA MODEL

Origins of the Minnesota Model of alcohol and drug abuse treatment are found in three independent Minnesota treatment programs: Pioneer House in 1948, Hazelden in 1949, and Wilmar State Hospital in 1950. The Hazelden Clinics remain in existence as of 2008 and are located in Minnesota, New York, Illinois, Oregon, and Florida. The original treatment programs recognized Alcoholics Anonymous (AA) as having success in bringing about recovery from alcoholism. Unique to this early stage of the Minnesota Model was the blending of professional behavioral science understandings with AA's principles. Important in the development of the Minnesota Model is the way treatment procedures emerged, from trial and error, from acknowledgment of the mutual help approach of AA, and from the use of elementary clinical assumptions rather than a well-developed theoretical position. In many ways, the Minnesota Model developed from a grassroots, pragmatic movement.

ASSUMPTIONS OF MINNESOTA MODEL

Because of its noncentralized development, the Minnesota Model is not a standardized set of procedures but an approach organized around a shared set of assumptions. They were articulated by Dan Anderson, the former president of Hazelden Foundation and one of the early professionals working with the Minnesota Model at Wilmar State Hospital. The assumptions indicate that alcoholism is (1) a cluster of symptoms; (2) an illness characterized by an inability to determine time, frequency, or quantity of consumption; (3) non-volitional (alcoholics should not be blamed for their inability to drink alcohol moderately); (4) a physical, psychological, social, and spiritual illness; and (5) a chronic primary illness, meaning that once manifest, a return to non-problem drinking is not possible. Although these assumptions are phrased as pertaining to alcoholism, early experience with the Minnesota Model demonstrated that drug addiction can also be understood and treated within these assumptions. *Chemical dependency* is the term generally used by clients and treatment providers when referring to substance use disorders in this model. The Minnesota Model provides treatment for chemical dependency for both alcohol and other drugs.

A twenty-four- to twenty-eight-day inpatient treatment stay, or approximately eighty-five hours in outpatient rehabilitation, characterizes Minnesota Model treatment. Inpatient treatment may occur in hospital settings or free-standing facilities and may be run by for-profit or nonprofit organizations. Different treatment settings have different mixes of staff positions, but the multidisciplinary team of medical and psychological professionals plus clergy and counselors are frequently found, either in a close interacting network or a more diffuse working arrangement.

Primary counselors have either received specific training in the Minnesota Model approach to treatment or have learned their counseling skills in an apprentice-like placement. Most counselors are not mental-health-degreed professionals or holders of medically related degrees, but they are commonly working on their own twelve-step programs because of life experience with chemical dependency or other addictions. As in AA, this shared personal experience of both clients and counselors is important for the client/counselor relationship and the modeling the counselor provides for the client.

Minnesota Model treatment programs vary in the centrality of counseling staff and the programmed autonomy of the treatment experience. Some treatment programs have the counselor facilitating the majority of the groups and actively directing the treatment experience. Other programs have the group members carrying out the treatment experience while the counseling staff maintains a low profile as they seek to empower clients to acquire the insights and resources necessary for their recovery. Treatment also varies in the amount of confrontation employed, the presence of a family program requirement (which is central with adolescents), the extent of assigned reading, the detail of client record documentation, and other attributes.

Minnesota Model treatment is without exception characterized by the use of AA principles and understandings (steps and traditions) at the core of the treatment experience. Clients are provided with the *AA Big Book* (Alcoholics Anonymous) and *The Twelve Steps and Twelve Traditions*. Both of these books are required reading. Spirituality is emphasized as important to recovery, which is consistent with the AA understanding. AA group meetings occur in the schedule of rehabilitation activities, and clients may visit a community AA meeting as part of their treatment experience. Clients work on AA steps during their treatment experience; some programs focus on the first five steps whereas others emphasize all twelve steps.

Treatment is not just an intensive exposure to AA. It motivates treatment participants to develop mutual trust and to share and be open about how the use of substances has come to control their lives. Clients are told that they have a chronic disorder. Their behavior has been directed by the disorder, but they have been unable to see the consequences of their behavior because the disorder can give rise to denial.

Treatment plans are individualized based on assessments by the multidisciplinary staff. Generally, the first goal of treatment is to break the client's denial, and the second goal is for the client to accept the disease concept. Because treatment has clients ranging from new admissions to those ready to complete their program, senior peers are influential in helping clients who are in the early stages of treatment to understand denial and the disease concept.

The message in the final treatment stage is acceptance and awareness that individuals are able to change if they take appropriate action to deal with a chronic condition. The rehabilitation staff develops an aftercare plan with clients that will continue to support some of the changes that have taken place during treatment and to encourage changes that will promote ongoing recovery. Characteristically, clients comment on their increased awareness of the simple pleasures of life. They are told that they must continue to work the AA steps, attend AA meetings, and address other problems of living if they are going to experience recovery. It is emphasized that primary treatment is just one part of an ongoing continuum of care. Recovery is hard work made even more difficult by possible bouts of craving to drink or use drugs, by periods of depression, problems of regaining trust from their family,

and establishing new friends and activities not tied to alcohol and drug use.

There have been few published reports of the effectiveness of Minnesota Model treatment programs. These include outcome studies prepared by Hazelden for treatment programs in the Hazelden Evaluation Consortium and peer-reviewed publications. This body of work generally indicates that for clients treated with the Minnesota Model, about 50 percent of those treated, including non-completers, are abstinent for one year following discharge from treatment. This percentage is higher for treatment completers and for clients having fewer complications and more stability in their lives. About one-third of the clients return to heavy use patterns within the year, and the remainder has slips or a period of resumed drinking/use but also sustained periods of abstinence. Abstinent clients have fewer legal, health, interpersonal, and job-related problems, and about 75 percent attend AA and/or continuing care.

The Minnesota Model is a label applied to a broad range of programming that is primarily based in the principles of AA. While its suitability for all addicts merits further study, this approach represents a highly visible treatment modality serving a large number of clients, including adolescents, throughout the United States. It has a counterpart known as the Icelandic Model, and both of these treatment models have significantly influenced treatment in Sweden and other parts of Scandinavia. International interest in adopting the Minnesota Model appears to be growing, with scattered treatment programs appearing in many countries. Little research has been done as of 2008 on the transportability of this treatment model to other cultures.

See also **Treatment: An Overview of Alcohol Abuse/ Dependence; Treatment: A History of Treatment in the United States.**

BIBLIOGRAPHY

Anderson, D. J. (1981). *Perspectives on treatment: The Minnesota experience.* Center City, MN: Hazelden Educational Services.

Cook, C. C. H. (1988). The Minnesota Model in the management of drug and alcohol dependency: Miracle, method or myth? Part I. The philosophy and programme. *British Journal of Addiction, 83,* 625–634.

Cook, C. C. H. (1988). The Minnesota Model in the management of drug and alcohol dependency: Miracle, method or myth? Part II. Evidence and conclusions. *British Journal of Addiction, 83*, 735–748.

Laundergan, J. C. (1982). *Easy does it: Alcoholism treatment outcomes, Hazelden, and the Minnesota Model.* Center City, MN: Hazelden Educational Services.

Stinchfield, R., & Owen, P. (1998). Hazelden's model of treatment and its outcome. *Addictive Behaviors, 23,* 669–683.

Walters, G. (2002). Twelve reasons why we need to find alternatives to Alcoholics Anonymous. *Addictive Disorders & Their Treatment, 1,* 53–59.

J. CLARK LAUNDERGAN
REVISED BY KEN C. WINTERS (2009)

MOTIVATIONAL AND BRIEF

Brief interventions can be used as preventive interventions for individuals at risk of developing an alcohol or drug use disorder or as treatment for those meeting the diagnostic criteria of the American Psychiatric Association (APA) for a substance use disorder (SUD). These interventions, which can be delivered one-on-one or in a group setting, can often increase an individual's readiness to change his or her substance use behavior and motivate that individual to enter longer-term treatment. Although facilitators can deliver brief interventions using a variety of styles, the discussion here will focus on brief interventions that utilize a motivational interviewing style.

Motivational interviewing, devised by Drs. William Miller and Stephen Rollnick, is a nonjudgmental and nonconfrontational counseling style. It emphasizes client-centeredness and uses a direct but collaborative approach to help clients explore and resolve their ambivalence about changing their substance use. Facilitators elicit behavior change from the client's own resources instead of imposing their views on the client. In contrast to an expert or authoritarian role that confronts, educates, and convinces clients to change, facilitators using motivational interviewing assume a partnership role with clients and respect a client's autonomy and freedom to change.

Motivational interviewing techniques overlap with other forms of therapy and have been captured in the acronym OARS. Facilitators ask or make *open-ended* questions and statements (e.g.,

"Tell me more about your drinking"), praise and sincerely *affirm* the client (e.g., "I appreciate you taking the time to come in today"), *reflect* back to the client what he or she has expressed (e.g., "From what I hear you saying, you have been worried about your health for quite a while"), and *summarize* periodically and at the end of the session (e.g., "You like drinking because you feel it helps you relax, improves your mood, and makes it easier to talk with people in social situations"). The facilitator selectively uses OARS to elicit client "change talk" or language related to the client's desire, ability, reason, and need to change.

Brief interventions that utilize motivational interviewing typically range between one and four sessions and vary in the amount of structure. As an unstructured preventive intervention, the facilitator and client discuss a client's substance use in an open-ended manner (i.e., without a manual to follow). As a structured treatment, the facilitator uses a manual or guide and discusses specific components of the intervention (e.g., normative feedback and drinking expectancies). Motivational enhancement therapy, developed by Miller and colleagues, is an example of a four-session manualized brief intervention for Project MATCH (Matching Alcoholism Treatments to Client Heterogeneity). The key components of motivational enhancement therapy are described in the acronym FRAMES: Facilitators provide *feedback* to an individual about the costs and consequences of alcohol and drug use (e.g., "Compared to other women your age, you drink at the 75th percentile"), encourage *responsibility* for the change to come from the client rather than the facilitator (e.g., "This information is just for you, it's up to you what you'd like to do with it"), give *advice* to change as part of talking about change and setting goals (e.g., "You've discussed several methods of drinking less to improve your health. If it's okay with you, I'd also recommend that you make an appointment with your physician to have your liver evaluated"), offer clients a *menu* of alternative self-help or treatment options, use an *empathetic* style, and enhance the client's *self-efficacy* (e.g., client's belief that he or she has the ability to change). Brief interventions vary in the amount of structure when used as a preventive intervention or treatment.

EFFECTIVENESS OF BRIEF INTERVENTIONS AND MOTIVATIONAL INTERVIEWING

Research suggests that brief interventions are effective in reducing substance use and related consequences and facilitating treatment entry and aftercare. Brief interventions are most effective for individuals with at-risk drinking and drug-related problems that have not yet developed into alcohol or drug dependence. In these studies, heavy use and substance-related consequences tend to improve. However, studies such as Project MATCH have shown that brief interventions can be helpful for individuals with alcohol dependence. In Project MATCH, individuals who received motivational enhancement therapy showed treatment outcomes (e.g., abstinence from alcohol one and three years after treatment) similar to those of individuals who received twelve-session cognitive-behavioral therapy (CBT) or twelve-step facilitation therapy. Although brief interventions are often associated with positive lifestyle improvements and a decrease in negative consequences from substance use, these effects tend to diminish over time. Brief interventions have also been shown to enhance treatment entry, program attendance, treatment adherence, and aftercare compliance for substance use. Thus, they can help to engage clients at multiple levels of treatment.

The flexibility of brief interventions allows them to be delivered by facilitators of diverse backgrounds and in diverse settings. For example, research suggests that brief interventions can effectively be delivered by facilitators who do not specialize in addiction treatment. With the proper training and supervision, brief interventions that utilize a motivational interviewing style can be equally effective when delivered by therapists, physicians, social workers, nurses, or peers. Brief interventions are also efficacious in a variety of settings, including medical settings (e.g., during routine visits as part of primary care, prenatal care, or other hospital stays), emergency departments (e.g., when individuals are being treated for alcohol- or drug-related consequences in emergency rooms and trauma centers), and other nonmedical settings (e.g., the criminal justice system, police stations, college settings, or employee assistance programs). These interventions may also be used with both adults and adolescents. Adolescents receiving a brief intervention tend to have decreased substance use, fewer negative consequences, and increased treatment adherence. In summary, research supports the use of brief interventions across a variety of settings that can be delivered by diverse facilitators and utilized by adults and adolescents alike.

Additional research is needed in the area of brief motivational interviewing interventions that examine outcomes with different populations (e.g., different racial or ethnic groups, different age groups, and other addictive behaviors), investigate methods of sustaining longer-term outcomes, and compare the effectiveness of different components of brief interventions (e.g., frames and in-person versus phone delivery). Brief interventions and motivational interviewing are an innovative and cost-effective approach to addressing alcohol and drug problems.

BIBLIOGRAPHY

Dunn, C., Deroo, L., & Rivara, F. P. (2001). The use of brief interventions adapted from motivational interviewing across behavioral domains: A systematic review. *Addiction, 96,* 1725–1742.

Miller, W. R., & Rollnick, S. (2002). *Motivational interviewing: Preparing people for change* (2nd ed.). New York: Guilford Press.

Miller, W. R., Zweben, A., DiClemente, C. C., & Rychtarik, R. G. (1994). *Motivational enhancement therapy manual: A clinical research guide for therapists treating individuals with alcohol abuse and dependence, Volume 2.* In M. E. Mattson (Ed.), Project MATCH Monograph Series. Publication No. 94-3723. Rockville, MD: National Institutes of Health.

Moyer, A., Finney, J. W., Swearingen, C. E., & Vergun, P. (2002). Brief interventions for alcohol problems: A meta-analytic review of controlled investigations in treatment-seeking and non-treatment-seeking populations. *Addiction, 97,* 279–292.

Project MATCH Research Group. (1998). Matching alcoholism treatments to client heterogeneity: Project MATCH three year drinking outcomes. *Alcoholism: Clinical and Experimental Research, 22*(6), 1300–1311.

STEFANIE A. STERN
KAREN CHAN OSILLA

SELF-HELP AND ANONYMOUS GROUPS

The recovery process does not end when an individual completes a drug rehabilitation program. Due to the relapsing nature of substance abuse, individuals receiving treatment for the disorder are generally urged to participate in some form of continuing care after their initial phase of treatment has ended

(McKay et al., 2004). Self-help (also known as mutual aid) support groups play a vital role: The great strain on health care resources has led the treatment system to become increasingly reliant on these groups as complements or alternatives to professional treatment (Atkins & Hawdon, 2007).

TWELVE-STEP MODEL

Support groups using the twelve-step model are the most widely known and play a major role in the treatment protocols of many treatment facilities. The original twelve-step program, Alcoholics Anonymous (AA), is the most widely used treatment in the United States for those with alcohol problems. Similar groups include Narcotics Anonymous, Cocaine Anonymous, Emotions Anonymous, Gamblers Anonymous, and others. The twelve steps were devised in the late 1930s by William Griffith Wilson (1895–1971), known as Bill W., a major cofounder of AA, in conjunction with a small group of his early followers. The Twelve Steps of Alcoholics Anonymous (Alcoholics Anonymous, 2001) are as follows:

1. We admitted we were powerless over alcohol— that our lives had become unmanageable.
2. Came to believe that a Power greater than ourselves could restore us to sanity.
3. Made a decision to turn our will and our lives over to the care of God as we understood Him.
4. Made a searching and fearless moral inventory of ourselves.
5. Admitted to God, to ourselves, and to another human being the exact nature of our wrongs.
6. Were entirely ready to have God remove all these defects of character.
7. Humbly asked Him to remove our shortcomings.
8. Made a list of all persons we had harmed, and became willing to make amends to them all.
9. Made direct amends to such people wherever possible, except when to do so would injure them or others.
10. Continued to take personal inventory, and when we were wrong, promptly admitted it.
11. Sought through prayer and meditation to improve our conscious contact with God as we understood Him, praying only for knowledge of His will for us and the power to carry that out.
12. Having had a spiritual awakening as the result of these steps, we tried to carry this message to others, and to practice these principles in all our affairs.

Twelve-step programs offer an informal treatment adjunct to professional care, using a support community of peer volunteers. There are no dues or fees for AA membership, and the only requirement for membership is a desire to stop drinking. The AA organization focuses exclusively on helping individuals recover from alcoholism, and as a matter of policy has no opinions on outside issues of any kind. It is fully self-supporting and declines outside contributions, with the intention of minimizing distraction, controversy, and disunity (Kelly, 2003).

Related groups include Al-Anon, a group dedicated to helping the friends and relatives of alcoholics, and Ala-teen, which is aimed at teenagers who have a family member or friend who is alcoholic.

Although AA does not affiliate with outside facilities, in the 1950s its philosophy was borrowed by and incorporated into professional drug treatment programs in the United States. This influential approach, dubbed the *Minnesota Model*, uses a treatment package encompassing abstinence, behavior change, and attending AA meetings. A 1998 study found that 90 percent of private substance use disorder treatment centers in the United States based their treatment on the twelve-step model (Kelly, 2003).

CONTROVERSY OVER AA

Despite its popularity, AA remains one of the more controversial and least understood and assessed approaches to alcoholism treatment (Morgenstern et al., 1997). Some have argued that it is difficult to assess the independent effects of self-help groups, due to their integration with professional treatment. Research shows a high sobriety rate for alcoholics strongly devoted to the AA program, but adherence is a problem: Those who attend frequently and actively participate seem to benefit but the dropout rate is high.

Spiritual Component. The twelve-step approach has a strong spiritual component, as treatment recovery steps include admitting powerlessness over the addiction and surrendering to a "higher power." This powerlessness is seen as a lifetime condition, and the twelve steps are seen as providing a mechanism for ensuring a lifetime cessation of the compulsive behavior. Some argue that non-religious individuals might be turned off by the perceived spiritual or religious emphasis. Others suggest that a moderation approach works better than abstinence-only with some individuals. These different opinions have led to increased interest in answering the question: For whom are twelve-step meetings particularly helpful or not helpful?

In the early twenty-first century, some members of AA have made an effort to separate AA from its original quasi-religious roots. For example, Griffin (2004) writes that a Higher Power can be interpreted as God, or as a non-monotheistic object, including the AA group itself. This movement may help improve AA attendance among atheists and agnostics, as these individuals were less likely to initiate and sustain AA attendance compared to those who identify themselves as religious. Interestingly, belief in God prior to AA attendance did not provide any advantage in obtaining AA-related benefits (Tonigan, 2007).

ALTERNATIVE VERSIONS OF TWELVE-STEP PROGRAMS

Studies have revealed that substance use disorders frequently co-occur with psychiatric illnesses such as depression, anxiety, or personality disorders. To address the needs of this population, self-help groups specifically designed for dual diagnosis patients have emerged, such as Double Trouble in Recovery and Dual Recovery Anonymous. These groups follow a modified twelve-step approach, incorporating specific components for addressing the mental health needs of the participants. For example, participating in Double Trouble in Recovery meetings has been associated with better medication compliance, which may be particularly helpful for individuals with serious mental illnesses, such as schizophrenia and bipolar disorder that also have a high rate of co-occurring substance abuse.

While twelve-step groups dominate treatment centers, there are also a number of important mutual-aid support groups using alternative approaches to recovery. In contrast to the acceptance of a "Higher Power," Secular Organizations for Sobriety (SOS) groups emphasize a secular approach, using cognitive tools to support recovery. Founded in 1985, SOS emphasizes personal responsibility and self-reliance in its abstinence-

based program. Participants commit to a lifelong Sobriety Priority, agreeing to abstain from all drugs or alcohol. SOS does have a suggested meeting format, but each meeting is autonomous, and formats vary considerably, reflecting the desires of the individual group. For example, the largest chapter of SOS (centered in northern California) changed its name to LifeRing Secular Recovery in 1999 but remains integrated within SOS as a whole.

Women for Sobriety. Another alternative to the twelve steps is Women for Sobriety (WFS). Founded in 1976, WFS rests on the belief that women have different needs than men in recovery. WFS groups are run by a certified moderator in a conversation format and generally take place at least once per week. The New Life Program provides structure to the meetings, including a statement of purpose, weekly topic guide, and other literature. WFS seeks to develop in female alcoholics a strong feeling of self-worth while acknowledging that they have symptoms of a serious disease.

Rational Recovery and SMART Recovery. In 1988, licensed social worker Jack Trimpey founded Rational Recovery (RR), an organization sharply critical of Alcoholics Anonymous. He based his program on cognitive-behavioral techniques influenced by the rational-emotive therapy of Albert Ellis. RR uses the Addictive Voice Recognition Technique, which helps the addicted person recover on his or her own by recognizing and controlling compulsive thoughts and desires. An RR participant defeats addiction by rational self-control rather than spiritual change. RR self-help groups meet once a week and participants discuss how to control irrational beliefs.

In the mid-1990s, Trimpey publicly denounced all self-help groups and treatment centers (including RR groups), and RR became an individual treatment program. The former RR self-help groups broke off and changed its name to SMART Recovery. SMART intends to provide an alternative to AA but is not as explicitly anti-AA as RR. Like RR, SMART views addiction as a learned behavior that can be changed using cognitive-behavioral principles. SMART recommends abstinence for its participants, but acknowledges that all of its members do not share this goal. SMART explicitly acknowledges science as the ultimate authority, adapting its program to match research findings in relapse prevention, motivational enhancement, stress management, mood management, and other areas.

Moderation Management. In contrast to the abstinence-only programs, Moderation Management (MM) supports moderate use as a goal for its members. MM explicitly targets beginning stage problem drinkers, rather than seriously alcohol-dependent individuals. MM views non-dependent problem drinking as a bad habit, one controllable by following a nine-step cognitive-behavioral change program. Participants are encouraged to complete a 30-day abstinence period and then evaluate the positive and negative aspects of alcohol in their lives.

Overall, research indicates that being actively involved in a support group significantly improves one's chances of remaining clean and sober, but which mutual-aid support group one attends is not as important. Provided one participates in a mutual-aid support group, his or her religiosity does not directly influence the chances of remaining sober. Involvement in a group directly increases the amount of time one stays clean and sober (Atkins, 2007).

See also **Alcoholism: Abstinence versus Controlled Drinking; Models of Alcoholism and Drug Abuse; Women and Substance Abuse.**

BIBLIOGRAPHY

Alcoholics Anonymous. Available from http://www.alcoholics-anonymous.org.

Alcoholics Anonymous. (2001). Chapter 5: How it works. In *The big book* (pp. 58–71). New York: Alcoholics Anonymous World Services.

Atkins, R., & Hawdon, J. (2007). Religiosity and participation in mutual-aid support groups for addiction. *Journal of Substance Abuse Treatment, 33,* 321–331.

Gossop, M., Stewart, D., & Marsden, J. (2008). Attendance at Narcotics Anonymous and Alcoholics Anonymous meetings, frequency of attendance and substance use outcomes after residential treatment for drug dependence: A 5-year follow-up study. *Addiction, 103,* 119–125.

Griffin, K. (2004). *One breath at a time: Buddhism and the twelve steps.* New York: Rodale Press.

Kelly, J. (2003). Self-help for substance-use disorders: History, effectiveness, knowledge gaps, and research opportunities. *Clinical Psychology Review, 23,* 639–663.

McKay, J., Foltz, C., Leahy, P., Stephens, R., Orwin, R., & Crowley, E. (2004). Step down continuing care in the treatment of substance abuse: Correlates of participation and outcome effects. *Evaluation and Program Planning, 27*(3), 321–331.

Morgenstern, J., Labouvie, E., McCrady, B., Kahler, C., & Frey, R. (1997). Affiliation with Alcoholics Anonymous after treatment: A study of its therapeutic effects and mechanisms of action. *Journal of Consulting and Clinical Psychology, 65*(5), 768–777.

Tonigan, J. S. (2007). Spirituality and Alcoholics Anonymous. *Southern Medical Journal, 100*(4), 437–440.

G. Alan Marlatt
Joel Grow

TRADITIONAL DYNAMIC PSYCHOTHERAPY

Dynamic psychotherapy is the term for the various psychological treatments, primarily talking treatments, intended to modify and ameliorate behaviors based on inner conflicts (e.g., "Should I study for the test or cheat?") and/or interpersonal conflicts (difficulties with others). These techniques range from those intended primarily to support individuals, lending them the therapist's strength or understanding ("If you do that you'll get in trouble. Have you thought of handling it this way?"), to helping patients reach their own understanding of the origins and implications of their behaviors. The application of these techniques to the treatment of alcoholics and substance abusers is supported by the high incidence of co-occurrence of psychiatric illness—in several studies, 70 percent—some of which may play a role in initiating or maintaining the behavior. It has been suggested that for some substance abusers, the use of illicit compounds is a misguided attempt at self-medication. Often, psychotherapy must be provided in conjunction with other treatments—pharmacologic, such as disulfiram for alcoholics or methadone for heroin abusers; self-help groups, such as Alcoholics Anonymous; or family or group psychotherapy.

Psychotherapy is based on the assumption that the patient will think and talk about ideas and feelings rather than acting upon them. This may prove particularly difficult for substance abusers who often have little sense of what they feel, other than generalized pain, and who are used to action and immediate gratification. Therefore, treatment, particularly at the beginning, must take place within a structure that both supports and helps control impulsive behavior. Sometimes, treatment starts in a hospital or other residential setting; often, it is accompanied by regular drug testing. After the agreement to start therapy and setting goals, therapist and patient meet once to several times a week. As trust is developed between patient and therapist, the therapist can expect less lying and less denial of difficulties; treatment can, if indicated, begin to move from support toward expression of feelings—toward identification of conflicts and the understanding of their origins. Initially the therapist listens, struggling to understand the patient's inner experience and its meaning. The therapist then attempts to help patients to understand what they have presented, with appropriate changes and qualifications based on further information provided by the patient. Important issues to be explored in treatment include current relationships (with spouse, children, friends, coworkers), past relationships (with parents and other family), and the relationship within the treatment between the patient and the therapist. Often, the difficulties and distortions within this relationship mirror past and current relationships and may be used to help the patient see the nature and impact of the past on current behaviors.

Treating substance abusers can be frustrating for therapists; there are many slips with return to drug use, and patient behavior is often calculated to make the therapist angry and to give up. It is essential that therapists who make the attempt carefully monitor their own feelings so that they do not interfere with the treatment itself. It is also important to remember that when properly done, treatment can make the difference between suffering with chronic problems and successful adaptation. This is particularly true when substance abuse is accompanied by other psychiatric disease and/or disability.

See also **Epidemiology of Alcohol Use Disorders; Epidemiology of Drug Abuse; Models of Alcoholism and Drug Abuse.**

BIBLIOGRAPHY

American Psychiatric Association. (1989). *Treatments of psychiatric disorders: A task force report of the American Psychiatric Association*. Washington, D.C.: Author.

Hughes, P., & Riordan, D. (2006). *Dynamic psychotherapy explained*. Oxford, UK.: Radcliffe Publishing.

Kotin, J. (2004). *Getting started: An introduction to dynamic psychotherapy*. Lanham, MD: Jason Aronson.

WILLIAM A. FROSCH

TWELVE-STEP AND DISEASE MODEL APPROACHES

Twelve Step Facilitation, or TSF, is a manual-guided, twelve-step based treatment program that was developed for use in Project MATCH (Matching Alcoholism Treatments to Client Heterogeneity), a multicenter study examining patient-treatment matching for three different psychotherapies for alcohol dependence. TSF includes a range of interventions that are organized into a "core" program, an "elective" program, and a "conjoint" program. Thus, while the primary goal is facilitating the individual's relationship to self-help groups and fellowships such as Alcoholics Anonymous (AA), it is also an individual professional treatment and has no official relationship with AA or other such groups.

TSF is a structured intervention whose sessions follow a prescribed format. Each session begins with a review of the patient's recent efforts toward recovery, including any twelve-step meetings attended (and reactions to them), episodes of drinking or drug use versus sober days, urges to drink or use, reactions to any readings completed, and any journaling that the patient has done. The second part of each TSF session consists of presenting and discussing new material drawn from either the core, elective, or conjoint programs. Session guidelines and checklists are provided. These can be used by therapists to conduct TSF sessions, as well as by those who wish to monitor sessions to assess treatment fidelity. Each session ends with a wrap-up that includes the assignment of recovery tasks, which may include readings, meetings to be attended, and other behavioral work that the patient agrees to undertake between sessions. Most TSF topics include client handouts that are used either in-session or assigned as recovery tasks. The Twelve Step Facilitation Handbook (1998) includes troubleshooting guides for each topic that help practitioners anticipate and deal with potential issues that may arise in the course of treatment.

The TSF core program includes the following five topics: introduction and assessment; acceptance;

people, places, and routines; surrender; and getting active. The elective program is composed of the following five topics: genograms, enabling, emotions, moral inventories, and relationships. There is also a two-session conjoint program, consisting of the topics of enabling and detaching, which can be used if the client has a significant other who is willing to participate in treatment. Finally, TSF includes a termination session with its own format.

In implementing TSF, the therapist (or "facilitator") employs a variety of therapeutic techniques, including education and discussion, role-playing, confrontation, reinforcement, and coaching.

Patients need not necessarily be dependent on either alcohol or drugs to benefit from a twelve-step oriented treatment; rather, they must merely satisfy the basic criterion for becoming a member of a twelve-step fellowship, as set forth by Alcoholics Anonymous, namely, "a desire to stop drinking," or to stop using drugs (Alcoholics Anonymous, 1981, p. 139). Twelve-step fellowships advocate abstinence, as opposed to the controlled use of alcohol or drugs, as their goal. They do so, however, as a matter of practicality, as opposed to taking a moral stance on drinking per se. AA is for those who have already tried controlled drinking but have been unsuccessful in this effort. Bill Wilson, a cofounder of AA, put it this way: "We do not like to pronounce any individual as alcoholic, but you can quickly diagnose yourself. Step over to the nearest barroom and try some controlled drinking. Try to drink and stop abruptly. Try it more than once. It will not take long for you to decide, if you are honest with yourself about it" (Alcoholics Anonymous, 2001, pp. 31–32). Twelve-step fellowships exist to provide support and advice, and to facilitate the personal growth of individuals whose own efforts to control their use of alcohol and/or drugs have failed and whose lives have become increasingly "unmanageable" as a consequence of substance abuse.

In the years since the inception of AA, its twelve-step program and philosophy have been applied to a variety of addictive behaviors, such as smoking, gambling, and overeating. Mutual-support fellowships now exist for individuals seeking support in overcoming loss of control in each of these areas. AA conducts periodic surveys of its membership. As of 2006, AA estimated that there were 52,050 AA groups in the United States, with a membership totaling 1,069,000 people. Globally, it estimated

that there were 106,202 groups, with a total membership of 1,867,000 people (Alcoholics Anonymous, 2006). These are likely underestimates, however, given that AA is decentralized and has no formal membership requirements.

"EARLY" RECOVERY

Based on an assessment of a patient's lifestyle, prior treatment experiences, periods of sobriety, and circumstances surrounding relapse, an individual treatment plan is devised, typically including one or more elective topics plus the core TSF program. Broadly speaking, what could be called "early" recovery can be broken down into three components: acceptance, surrender, and getting active in a twelve-step fellowship.

"Acceptance" refers to the process in which the individual overcomes "denial"—the personal belief that one does not have a substance abuse problem, or that one can effectively and reliably control drinking or drug use. It is captured in the first step of AA: "We admitted we were powerless over alcohol—that our lives had become unmanageable" (Alcoholics Anonymous, 2001, p. 59). Recovery can therefore be thought of as beginning with an epiphany: The realization that one has in fact lost the ability to control his or her use of alcohol or drugs, and that as a consequence life has become progressively more unmanageable. This is a significant insight, given that previously the individual may have held onto the idea that he or she could effectively control use, and that the consequences of alcohol or drug use were not significant.

Acceptance leads to surrender, which has two components: (1) hope that one can in fact reverse the process of powerlessness and unmanageability, and (2) the belief that individual willpower alone is an insufficient force for creating sustained sobriety and restoring manageability to one's life. The concept of surrender is embodied in Steps 2 and 3: "Came to believe that a Power greater than ourselves could restore us to sanity;" and "Made a decision to turn our will and our lives over to the care of God as we understood Him" (Alcoholics Anonymous, 2001, p. 59).

Steps 2 and 3 have a spiritual aspect, to the extent that hope is arguably a spiritual concept, and also by virtue of the fact that the third step asks the individual to believe in a "higher power." Many people choose to think of this higher power as God, though even Bill Wilson consistently maintained that the higher power one chooses to believe in can just as well be AA itself and the power of fellowship. As Wilson put it, one key to recovery was to be found in humility: "This is the how and why of it. First of all, we had to quit playing God" (Alcoholics Anonymous, 2001, p. 62). Recovery, in other words, requires a willingness to place one's fate in the hands of something other than one's individual willpower.

Given the cognitive leap that acceptance and surrender represent, they lead in turn to the logical conclusion that the only sane alternative to continued chaos, loss, and accumulating negative consequences is to abandon willpower, turning instead to others—to become active in a twelve-step fellowship consisting of others who share the same goal of abstinence from alcohol or drugs.

As important as insight is, alone it is not sufficient for recovery, and that is where the concept of getting active comes in. Surrender implies not only a cognitive shift but a willingness to take action, and specifically to embrace the twelve steps as a guide for recovery and spiritual renewal. As much as they are programs of insight and spiritual renewal, AA and Narcotics Anonymous (NA) are also programs of action and lifestyle change.

Surrender and getting active follow acceptance and represent the individual's commitment to making whatever changes in lifestyle are necessary to sustain recovery. This requires action, including frequent attendance at AA or NA meetings, becoming active in meetings, reading AA or NA literature, getting a sponsor, making AA or NA friends, and replacing people, places, and routines that have become associated with substance abuse, and therefore represent a threat to recovery, with alternative relationships and habits of living. In TSF, the action and commitment that are the hallmarks of surrender are guided to some extent by the facilitator; but they are also heavily influenced by individuals the patient encounters and begins to form relationships with within twelve-step fellowships.

ADVANCED RECOVERY

Twelve-step fellowships regard spirituality as a force that provides direction and meaning to one's life, and they equate spiritual awakening with a realignment of personal goals, specifically a movement away from radical individualism and the pursuit of the material, and toward community and the pursuit of serenity as core values.

The twelfth step of AA states: "Having had a spiritual awakening as the result of these steps, we tried to carry this message to alcoholics, and to practice these principles in all our affairs" (Alcoholics Anonymous, 2001, p. 60). AA goes on to define what it means by spiritual awakening: "When a man or a woman has a spiritual awakening, the most important meaning of it is that he has now become able to do, feel, and believe that which he could not do before on his unaided strength and resources alone" (Alcoholics Anonymous, 1981, p. 106). This spiritual awakening comes, in time, as a result of involvement in the fellowship and "working" the twelve steps.

The process through which spiritual awakening is ultimately achieved is founded on a commitment to honesty and humility. This includes being honest with one's self and others, not only regarding alcohol and drug use, but also regarding such things as the harm that addiction has done (the "moral inventory"), plus ongoing vigilance regarding one's own character flaws. The individual in the advanced stages of recovery is someone who is always willing to acknowledge a fault and make amends for harm done, and who has discovered that giving to others—through sponsorship, for example—also supports one's own recovery. In this regard, twelve-step recovery has been likened to a form of spiritual conversion (Fowler, 1993).

Twelve-step fellowships are optimistic: "Rarely have we seen a person fail who has thoroughly followed our path" (Alcoholics Anonymous, 2001, p. 58). They believe that recovery leads to a profound reevaluation of how one relates to others, one's personal goals, and one's sense of purpose and meaning in life. They also accept the reality that abstinence is a goal that is rarely achieved without instances of either "slips" (single episodes of drinking or drug use) or "relapses" (a return to full-blown addiction). This attitude is reflected in the following statement, often quoted by AA members, from "the Big Book" (*Alcoholics Anonymous*): "The principles we have set down are guides to progress. We claim spiritual progress rather than spiritual perfection" (Alcoholics Anonymous, 2001, p. 60).

It is in this spirit that alcoholics and addicts are equally welcomed at meetings, whether they have one day or twenty years of sobriety.

THE EFFICACY OF TWELVE-STEP TREATMENT

TSF has been found to be effective in producing significant and sustained reductions in alcohol use lasting as long as 36 months after treatment (Project MATCH Research Group, 1997; Project MATCH Research Group, 1998). TSF has also been applied using a group format as an aftercare treatment with similar efficacy (Seraganian et al., 1998). In a study of depressed veterans with co-occurring substance use disorders and depression, TSF was correlated with improvement in substance use outcomes (Glassner-Edwards et al., 2007). When combined with the drug disulfiram, TSF was found to be effective in reducing cocaine and alcohol use (Carroll et al., 1998).

A significant finding from Project MATCH, which has been supported by other research, is a correlation between attendance at twelve-step meetings and abstinence from alcohol and drug use (Fiorentine, 1999). Greater involvement in twelve-step fellowships (e.g., getting a sponsor, taking on responsibilities) has also been found to correlate positively with recovery (Emrick, 1993). Finally, further analysis of Project MATCH data found that among patients whose social network (i.e., family and friends) supports drinking, TSF was associated with fewer drinking-associated consequences than two comparison treatments (Wu & Witkiewitz, 2008). Following a peer review, TSF was selected for inclusion in the National Registry of Evidence-Based Programs and Practices.

BIBLIOGRAPHY

Alcoholics Anonymous. (1981). *Twelve Steps and Twelve Traditions.* New York: Alcoholics Anonymous World Services.

Alcoholics Anonymous. (2001). *Alcoholics anonymous: The story of how many thousands of men and women have recovered from alcoholism* (4th ed.). New York: Alcoholics Anonymous World Services. Available from http://www.aa.org/bigbookonline.

Alcoholics Anonymous. (2006). Estimated AA Membership and Group Information. Available from http://www.alcoholics-anonymous.org/

Carroll, K. M., Nich, C., Ball, S. A., McCance, E., & Rounsaville, B. (1998). Treatment of cocaine and alcohol dependence with psychotherapy and disulfiram. *Addiction, 93*(5), 713–727.

Emrick, C. (1993). Efficacy of Alcoholics Anonymous: A meta-analysis of research. In B. S. McCrady & W. R. Miller (Eds.), *Research on Alcoholics Anonymous: Opportunities and alternatives.* New Brunswick, NJ: Rutgers Center of Alcohol Studies.

Fiorentine, R. (1999). After drug treatment: Are 12-step programs effective in maintaining abstinence? *American Journal of Drug and Alcohol Abuse, 25*(1), 93–116.

Fowler, J. (1993). Alcoholics Anonymous and faith development. In B. S. McCrady & W. R. Miller (Eds.), *Research on Alcoholics Anonymous: Opportunities and alternatives.* New Brunswick, NJ: Rutgers Center of Alcohol Studies.

Glassner-Edwards, S., Tate, S., McQuaid, J. R., Cumins, K., Granholm, E., & Brown, S. (2007). Mechanisms of action in integrated cognitive-behavioral treatment versus twelve-step facilitation for substance-dependent adults with comorbid major depression. *Journal of Studies on Alcohol and Drugs, 68*(5), 663–672.

National Registry of Evidence-Based Programs and Practices. Available from http://www. nrepp.samhsa.gov.

Nowinski, J. (2006). *The twelve step facilitation outpatient program.* Center City, MN: Hazelden.

Nowinski, J. & Baker, S. (2003). *The twelve step facilitation handbook: A systematic approach to early recovery from alcoholism and addiction.* Center City, MN: Hazelden.

Nowinski, J., Baker, S., & Carroll, K. (1992). *Twelve step facilitation therapy manual: A clinical research guide for therapists treating individuals with alcohol abuse and dependence.* DHHS Publication Mo. ADM 92-1893, Project MATCH Monograph Series, Vol. 1. Rockville, MD: National Institute on Alcohol Abuse and Alcoholism.

Project MATCH Research Group. (1997). Matching alcoholism treatments to client heterogeneity: Project MATCH Posttreatment drinking outcomes. *Journal of Studies on Alcoholism, 59*(1), 7–29.

Project MATCH Research Group. (1998). Matching alcoholism treatments to client heterogeneity: Project MATCH three year drinking outcomes. *Alcoholism: Clinical and Experimental Research, 22*(6), 1300–1311.

Seraganian, P., Brown, T. G., Tremblay, J., & Annies, H. M. (1998). *Experimental manipulation of treatment aftercare regimes for the substance abuser.* National Health Research and Development Program (Canada), Project #66O5-4392-404. Montreal: Concordia University.

Wu, J., & Witkiewitz, K. (2008). Network support for drinking: An application of multiple groups growth mixture modeling to examine client-treatment matching. *Journal of Studies on Alcohol and Drugs, 69*(1): 21–29.

JOSEPH NOWINSKI

TREATMENT, PHARMACOLOGICAL APPROACHES TO

This entry includes the following essays:

AN OVERVIEW

Pharmacological agents can be used for several purposes in the treatment of drug and alcohol addiction. These include the alleviation of acute withdrawal symptoms, the prevention of relapse to drug or alcohol use, and the blocking of the euphorigenic effects of drugs of abuse. Various medications are used in the treatment of addiction to alcohol, opiates, cocaine, tobacco, and sedatives.

ALCOHOLISM

Detoxification. Alcohol is currently one of the most widely used of the mood-altering substances. Habitual alcohol use is associated with the development of tolerance and physiological (physical) dependence. Tolerance refers to a decrease in susceptibility to the effects of alcohol following chronic alcohol use, which results in the user consuming increasing amounts of alcohol over time. Physical dependence can be conceptualized as a physiological state in which the recurrent administration of alcohol is required to prevent the onset of withdrawal symptoms. Symptoms of alcohol withdrawal include irritability, tremulousness, anxiety, sweating, chills, fluctuations in pulse and blood pressure, diarrhea, and, in severe cases, seizure. These symptoms generally begin within 24 hours following the last use of alcohol, peak within 48 hours, and subside over several days.

Pharmacotherapy for alcohol withdrawal includes the use of agents such as benzodiazepines and barbiturates, which are cross-tolerant with alcohol. These agents attenuate the symptoms of withdrawal and result in decreased arousal, agitation, and potential for seizure development. Medication is provided in doses that are sufficient to produce mild sedation and physiological stabilization early in the withdrawal period; this is followed by a gradual dose reduction and then discontinuation over the next one to two weeks. Currently, benzodiazepines are the agents of choice for the treatment of alcohol withdrawal because of the relatively high therapeutic safety index of these medications, their ability to be administered both orally and intravenously, and because of their anticonvulsant properties. Barbiturates can be used in a similar fashion but they have a lower therapeutic index of safety than do benzodiazepines.

Other medications used to treat alcohol withdrawal include clonidine and carbamazepine. Clonidine is an antihypertensive agent (i.e., it lowers blood pressure) that has been used in the treatment of drug withdrawal states and chronic pain. This medication decreases autonomic hyperactivity (i.e., it lowers an increased pulse and blood pressure) but it does not have the anticonvulsant properties of the benzodiazepines or barbiturates. Carbamazepine, an anticonvulsant, has also been employed in the treatment of alcohol withdrawal. Neither medication is habit-forming and thus may be of value in the treatment of alcohol withdrawal. Another anticonvulsant that may be useful in the treatment of alcohol withdrawal is valproic acid, though there is less evidence of its value for this indication than there is for carbamazepine.

Antidepressants. Depressive symptoms are noted in many alcoholics at the time that they enter treatment. Because of the frequent co-occurrence of depression and alcoholism, the use of antidepressants could be potentially useful in this population. Several studies have demonstrated the favorable effects of antidepressants on alcohol consumption, but several other studies have not. Tricyclic antidepressants such as imipramine and desipramine inhibit the reuptake of norepinephrine and serotonin in nerve terminals. The serotonin reuptake inhibitors (blockers) sertraline (Zoloft) and fluoxetine (Prozac) have shown a lack of efficacy in the treatment of major depression in alcoholics. Although antidepressants are not routinely administered to all recovering alcoholics, many physicians consider prescribing such medications to alcoholic patients if depressive symptoms do not resolve after several weeks of abstinence, or if a mood disorder was present prior to the onset of (alcohol) abuse.

Anxiolytics. Used to decrease anxiety, anxiolytics include benzodiazepines such as chlordiazepoxide (Librium) and diazepam (Valium), and azaspirodecadiones such as buspirone (BuSpar). Both classes of medication have been investigated for use in alcohol dependence. Early studies supported the use of benzodiazepines in recovering alcoholics with claims of decreased alcohol craving and consumption after chlordiazepoxide administration. Other controlled trials refuted this, however, and many physicians question the safety of using benzodiazepines in this population. The azaspirodecadiones such as buspirone are nonaddictive medications that have been marketed for the treatment of anxiety. Although few controlled trials have been conducted to evaluate the effect of buspirone on alcohol consumption in humans, there is some evidence of beneficial effects in anxious alcoholics. Animal studies have also demonstrated decreased alcohol consumption after treatment with this agent. Unlike benzodiazepines, buspirone is not known to be habit-forming and thus may be a promising agent for use in alcoholics.

Dopaminergic Agents. The effects of dopaminergic agents on the consumption of alcohol in animal studies have been conflicting because both agents that augment dopaminergic activity and those that diminish it have been noted to decrease alcohol consumption. In humans there are also conflicting findings, with some evidence that both dopamine agonists and antagonists reduce drinking behavior.

Opioid Antagonists. Opioid antagonists are competitive antagonists of opioids at opiate receptors. They include naloxone, which can be used intramuscularly or intravenously to rapidly reverse opiate intoxication and naltrexone, which is prescribed

orally to prevent or reverse intoxication from opioids and for the treatment of alcohol dependence. Unlike opioids these medications are not habit-forming and clearly have a place in the treatment of alcohol-dependent patients. A variety of studies have demonstrated a reduction of alcohol consumption or self-administration by animals treated with these agents. In human subjects naltrexone administered as an adjunct to substance-abuse treatment has resulted in a decreased rate of alcohol consumption. In addition, those patients who did experience a *slip* were less likely than those who were not treated with naltrexone to suffer a complete relapse to alcohol use. Like the oral medication, an extended release intramuscular injectable formulation of naltrexone is approved for treatment of alcohol dependence. The long-acting formulation may offer some advantages over oral administration. Keeping plasma levels relatively constant through slow release of naltrexone may keep therapeutic levels of the medication constant as well as reduce the occurrence of adverse effects such as nausea that occur following initial oral doses of naltrexone. In addition, depot naltrexone allows for less frequent dosing, which can contribute to better medication compliance.

Aversive Agents. Aversive agents are medications that are used to decrease alcohol consumption by creating an adverse reaction following alcohol use. They include disulfiram, calcium carbimide, and metronidazole (Flagyl). Levels of acetaldehyde, a toxic breakdown product of alcohol, accumulate when patients who are using disulfiram ingest alcohol. This results in symptoms of acetaldehyde toxicity including sweating, chest pain, palpitations, flushing, thirst, nausea, vomiting, headache, difficulty breathing, hypotension (low blood pressure), dizziness, weakness, blurred vision, and confusion. Symptoms may begin within minutes following alcohol ingestion and may last from thirty minutes to several hours. The use of disulfiram is based upon the premise that the fear or actual experience of this adverse event may serve as a deterrent to alcohol use. Despite its toxicity, disulfiram has been used safely by thousands of recovering alcoholics since its introduction in 1948. Supervised voluntary use of the medication as an adjunct to other rehabilitative therapy has resulted in reduced alcohol consumption and decreased alcohol-related criminal behavior among alcohol-dependent patients.

Compliance is the key to successful use of disulfiram in alcohol dependence, since patients need only discontinue using disulfiram if they wish to resume drinking. Indeed, in an unsupervised setting, disulfiram administration shows no superiority over placebo on outcome measures related to alcohol use. Methods that have been investigated to improve compliance include surgical implants of disulfiram, reinforcement by providing a reward for compliance, and contingency management techniques. Although surgical implants have met with little success, the other two methods have demonstrated various degrees of efficacy.

Reduction in alcohol use and an increase in alcohol-free days of alcohol-dependent individuals can be improved by treatment with topiramate, an anticonvulsant medication that stimulates the GABA pathway and blocks glutamate receptors. Topiramate may decrease the reinforcing effect of alcohol and other drugs such as cocaine and nicotine, based on its glutamate-mediated effects on the mesolimbic dopamine system. In addition it may contribute to abstinence by decreasing neuronal sensitivity. At a low dose, topiramate use may be effective in patients abusing alcohol while being maintained on therapy with buprenorphine or methadone and who do not need medical detoxification for alcohol. Topiramate is not approved by the U.S. Food and Drug Administration (FDA) for the treatment of alcohol dependence. Acamprosate is another medication that has shown efficacy in relapse prevention in alcohol dependence. Acamprosate attenuates alcohol desire or craving by normalizing the dysregulation of NMDA, glutamate-mediated excitation that occurs in alcohol withdrawal and the first 4 to 6 weeks of abstinence. Acamprosate is FDA approved for use in alcohol dependence and the side effects, primarily diarrhea, are generally well tolerated.

OPIOID DEPENDENCE

The opioids include opiates, which are drugs derived from the opium poppy (*Papaver somniferum*) as well as those synthesized to produce similar narcotic effects. Opium has been used as a medicinal substance for at least 6,000 years. Widespread abuse of opiates was noted by the eighteenth century with the smoking of opium in Asia; since the start of the twenty-first century in 2000 prescription opiates such as OxyContin and hydrocodone have surpassed heroin as the major opiates of abuse in the United States. Pharmacotherapy for opiate dependence may be employed both during the acute withdrawal syndrome and later to maintain abstinence from illicit opioids (e.g., heroin).

Acute Opioid Withdrawal. The syndrome of acute withdrawal from opiates varies in regard to the opiate of abuse. The time of onset, the intensity, and the duration of withdrawal symptoms depend on several factors including the half-life of the drug, the dose, and the chronicity of use. Heroin is a relatively short-acting agent; symptoms of withdrawal often begin within eight to twelve hours after the last use. Early symptoms include craving, anxiety, yawning, tearing, runny nose, restlessness, and poor sleep. Symptoms may progress to include pupil dilation, irritability, muscle and bone aches, piloerection (goose bumps—thus the term *cold turkey*), and hot and cold flashes. Peak severity occurs 48 hours to 72 hours after the last dose and includes nausea and vomiting; diarrhea; low-grade fever; increased blood pressure, pulse, and respiration; and muscle twitching. The opiate withdrawal syndrome following chronic heroin use can last seven to ten days. With longer-acting agents such as methadone, a similar constellation of symptoms can occur though they begin later, peak on the third to eighth day, and persist for several weeks.

A variety of medications can be used in the treatment of acute opiate withdrawal. The most common method is to use opiates alone. A dose high enough to stabilize the patient is administered on the first day and then gradually tapered over one to two weeks. Generally, long-acting opiates such as methadone are employed, but any opiate can be used.

Other medications used for opiate withdrawal are clonidine and buprenorphine. Clonidine is an alpha-2 adrenergic agonist that is commonly employed as an antihypertensive medication. It is active on central nervous system (CNS) locus coeruleus neurons in the same areas at which opiates exert their effects. Clonidine appears most effective in decreasing symptoms such as elevation of pulse and blood pressure and may be less effective in relieving other symptoms of withdrawal. The major side effects of clonidine are orthostatic hypotension (decreased blood pressure when rising from a sitting or lying position) and sedation. Rapid detoxification can occur through the combined use of clonidine with opiate antagonists such as naltrexone. This treatment can decrease the time required for the detoxification process to two to three days. Opiate addicts can be stabilized on buprenorphine, a mixed opioid agonist/antagonist with minimal discomfort and then withdrawn over five to seven days with less severe withdrawal symptoms than those associated with methadone withdrawal. Lofexidine and guanfacine are alternative alpha-2 adrenergic agonists that are under investigation for the management of opioid withdrawal. Lofexidine appears to be as effective as clonidine; however, it may be more suitable than clonidine for use in outpatient settings since some studies have shown fewer adverse effects, such as hypotension, with its use.

Antagonists. Opiate antagonists such as naloxone and naltrexone compete with opiates for CNS opioid receptors. Naloxone has a short half-life (two to three hours) and is generally employed on a short-term basis to reverse acute opiate intoxication. Naltrexone has a longer duration of action (approximately 24 hours) and is used as a long-term maintenance medication to inhibit euphoria in opioid addicts. Although not approved for use in the treatment of opioid dependence, long-acting naltrexone can be of use in this disorder. Oral opioid antagonist medications have been used with relative safety since 1975. Clinically, side effects of naltrexone may include mild dysphoria and elevation in cortisol and beta-endorphin levels; no withdrawal syndrome has been noted following its discontinuation. Oral naltrexone is generally administered three to four times a week at an average dose of 50 milligrams per day. The long-acting formulation is administered monthly. Despite its advantages, many opioid addicts resist therapy with naltrexone, and even in the most successful programs, six-month retention rates may range from only 20 to 30 percent. The addition of psychosocial interventions such as counseling and contingency-management programs is helpful. When these interventions are added, naltrexone has been noted to be particularly effective in selected groups including health care professionals, business people, and prisoners on work-release programs.

Methadone Maintenance. Methadone is a safe and effective treatment that has been used to treat opioid dependence since 1965. Heroin addicts easily adapt to using this long-acting opiate that possesses all of the physiological characteristics of heroin. When taken orally, methadone may have less abuse potential than heroin, but the onset of its CNS effects are slower and its tendency to induce euphoria is generally less than that of intravenous or inhaled heroin. In addition it has a longer half-life than heroin and if it is administered daily, tissue levels accumulate thereby decreasing withdrawal symptoms that occur between doses and that may lead to repeated opiate use. Methadone maintenance can be of benefit for addicts who have difficulty adjusting to a drug-free lifestyle or for those who have been unsuccessful with other forms of treatment. However, methadone maintenance is limited by the close regulation that it gets by the DEA and FDA. This regulation leads to the patient inconvenience of attending a dispensing facility 6 days per week for at least the first 3 to 6 months of treatment and to substantial administration costs from the nurses and pharmacists needed to provide this dispensing.

During maintenance therapy methadone is initiated at a low dose and then gradually increased to higher doses, which are associated with decreased opiate craving and secondary illicit opiate use. With methadone maintenance treatment many patients show significant decreases in illicit drug use, depression, and criminal activity, and they demonstrate increased employment. Therapy that is provided for extended periods of time and in the context of other psychosocial services has been associated with the highest success rates.

Buprenorphine. Buprenorphine is a mixed opioid agonist/antagonist that has been used experimentally since 1983 and clinically since 2001 as a maintenance medication for opioid dependence. As with methadone, maintenance treatment consists of daily administration of buprenorphine. At low doses, buprenorphine has agonist effects at opioid receptors and suppresses withdrawal symptoms. At higher doses antagonistic effects can occur, which act to block the reinforcing properties of the drug, thus lowering the potential for it to be abused. Buprenorphine maintenance has been associated with good treatment retention, decreased illicit opiate use, and a relatively mild withdrawal syndrome. Furthermore, a combination therapy of buprenorphine and naloxone is available as Suboxone. Suboxone has made office-based maintenance treatment of opiate dependence possible without the regulatory and administrative costs and complications of methadone maintenance. Any physician can prescribe Suboxone from his office after a relatively brief training from an approved source and an approval process by the Drug Enforcement Administration. This has led to a vast expansion of the treatments available with treatment access now possible in rural areas that had a great amount of prescription opiate abuse. It has also provided capacity expansion from about 220,000 methadone-treated patients to more than about 500,000 patients on either methadone or Suboxone in the United States. This expansion has benefited many who would not accept methadone maintenance or lived in areas that did not have methadone treatment. Overall this expansion has been essential with the growth in prescription opiate abuse since 2000.

COCAINE DEPENDENCE

Cocaine abuse increased markedly beginning in the 1970s, and by 1984 more than 20 million Americans reported that they had tried cocaine. In addition to psychotherapy and other traditional approaches to substance abuse treatment, a variety of medications may be of benefit to cocaine abusers. However, no medications have been approved by the FDA for this indication.

Pharmacotherapy for cocaine abuse can be employed to address specific symptoms that occur during the cocaine-withdrawal syndrome. Gawin and Kleber (1986) identified three phases in the cocaine abstinence syndrome. The crash phase generally begins soon after cocaine use ends and may last up to four days. Symptoms experienced at this time can include depression, suicidal ideation, irritability, anxiety, and intense cocaine craving. Sedatives such as alcohol and heroin can be used by addicts to alleviate these symptoms. The second, or withdrawal phase, can last two to ten weeks and is characterized by anxiety, depression, inability to experience pleasure, and increased cocaine craving. The third, or extinction phase, can last three to

twelve months; during this phase, cocaine craving may continue as well as increased susceptibility to relapse in response to environmental cues.

Pharmacotherapy for cocaine dependence can be used to alleviate symptoms experienced during the cocaine abstinence syndrome. During the crash period, early symptoms such as anxiety and insomnia may be relieved by benzodiazepines such as chlordiazepoxide. Antipsychotics can also be helpful during this period to alleviate psychotic symptoms such as paranoia.

Other agents that can be used on a short-term basis include dopaminergic agents such as bromocriptine and amantadine. Some investigators postulate that CNS dopamine can be depleted by chronic cocaine use. Dopaminergic agents can be used to augment CNS dopaminergic function and various dopaminergic agents such as amantadine, bromocriptine, and L-dopa have been employed for this purpose. Although few long-term, double-blind, placebo-controlled studies have been conducted, several studies have supported the use of dopaminergic agents, such as amantadine, as anti-craving medications during withdrawal.

Antidepressants can be helpful during the withdrawal and extinction stages of cocaine abstinence. One controlled and several uncontrolled studies in recovering cocaine addicts suggested that the tricyclic antidepressant desipramine might have decreased cocaine use and craving. Other antidepressants investigated in pilot studies included fluoxetine, imipramine, doxepin, and trazodone. Antidepressants can take several weeks to begin to alleviate symptoms of depression or craving, however, and some cocaine addicts may drop out of treatment during this period. These patients can benefit from initiation of treatment with a short-term medication (such as a dopaminergic agent) followed by long-term treatment with an antidepressant. As with every treatment, however, no firm conclusions are warranted about any agent until it has been tested in a controlled clinical trial that has been replicated at least once.

Pharmacotherapy can also be helpful for patients with psychiatric diagnoses other than cocaine dependence. In some patients cocaine abuse may be an attempt at self-medication to address the discomfort of depression or other psychiatric disorders. Patients with major depressive disorder or bipolar disorder may respond to therapy with antidepressants or lithium, respectively, and those with attention deficit disorder may benefit from the cautious use of low doses of a stimulant medication.

In summary, antipsychotics and benzodiazepines can be used to alleviate symptoms of acute cocaine withdrawal, whereas tricyclic antidepressants and dopaminergic agents can be helpful in the long-term treatment of cocaine withdrawal. Pharmacotherapy should be considered an adjunct to other forms of rehabilitative therapy during the long-term treatment of the cocaine-dependent patient.

TOBACCO DEPENDENCE

The main reason to quit smoking cigarettes is its powerful association with lung cancer, emphysema, and other medical problems. Yet nicotine, the active ingredient in cigarettes, is another drug that is associated with pleasant effects and with withdrawal discomfort, thereby making it an extremely addictive drug. Nicotine replacement therapy is a commonly used pharmacological treatment for tobacco dependence and is administered in the form of a gum, a patch, a lozenge, an inhaler, or a nasal spray. Providing cigarette smokers with nicotine replacement will help them avoid the health risks associated with smoking cigarettes. One problem with nicotine gum is that it is difficult to chew correctly and therefore people need to be trained to chew it correctly to derive the therapeutic effect and minimize adverse effects. The patch has been available since the early 1990s and was developed for placement on the skin, facilitating automatic release of nicotine. The nicotine inhaler and nicotine nasal spray are available by prescription and provide fast delivery of nicotine through the mouth and nose, respectively. Antidepressants like bupropion have also been quite successful in alleviating withdrawal symptoms from nicotine. Bupropion (Zyban) was approved by the FDA for this indication. Second-line medications for smoking cessation include antidepressants like nortriptyline. Detoxification from nicotine may also be facilitated with the medication clonidine, which is also used to help alleviate opiate withdrawal symptoms. Varenicline (Chantix), a *partial agonist* of the $\alpha_4\beta_2$ subtype of the *nicotinic cholinergic receptor*, is also FDA approved for smoking cessation based on evidence that it helps to reduce withdrawal symptoms and craving as well as reduce the level of smoking satisfaction.

SEDATIVE DEPENDENCE

Current treatments for sedative dependence include detoxification agents rather than anticraving agents. Detoxification is accomplished by tapering the dosage of benzodiazepines over two to three weeks. Carbamazepine, an antiseizure medication, has been shown to relieve alcohol and sedative withdrawal symptoms including delirium tremens. Agents that block the actions of benzodiazepines are promising as a maintenance or anticraving medication to help promote abstinence from sedative use.

PHARMACOTHERAPY

Medications must be accompanied by psychological and social treatments and support—they do not work on their own. Moreover, medications to block illicit drug effects in the brain are of little use if the patient does not take them. More research is needed to identify potential medications, but the clinical evaluation must recognize the need for psychosocial as well as neurobiological intervention. Without this integration the work to develop more effective treatments for the difficult problem of drug abuse and dependence cannot move forward.

BIBLIOGRAPHY

Centers for Disease Control and Prevention. (2006). Tobacco use among adults—United States, 2005. *MMWR Morbidity & Mortality Weekly Report, 55*(42), 1145–1148.

Fiore, M. C., Bailey, W. C., Cohen, S. J., Dorfman, S. F., Goldstein, M. G., Gritz, E. R., et al. (2000). Treating tobacco use and dependence: Quick reference guide for clinicians. U.S. Department of Health and Human Services, Public Health Service. Available from http://www.surgeongeneral.gov/.

Frances, R. J., & Franklin, J. E. (1990). Alcohol and other psychoactive substance use disorders. In J. A. Talbott, R. E. Hales, & S. C. Yudofsky (Eds.), *The American Psychiatric Press textbook of psychiatry.* Washington, DC: American Psychiatric Press.

Galanter, M., & Kleber H. D. (Eds). (2008). *Textbook of substance abuse treatment* (4th ed.). American Psychiatric Publishing.

Gawin, F. H., & Kleber, H. D. (1986). Abstinence symptomatology and psychiatric diagnosis in chronic cocaine abusers. *Archives of General Psychiatry, 43,* 107–113.

Jaffe, J. H. (1985). Drug addiction and drug abuse. In J. G. Hardman, L. E. Limbird, & A. G. Gilman (Eds.), *Goodman and Gilman's the pharmacological basis of therapeutics* (7th ed.). New York: Macmillan.

Jaffe, J. H. (1989). Drug dependence: Opioids, non-narcotics, nicotine (tobacco) and caffeine. In H. I. Kaplan & B. J. Sadock (Eds.), *Comprehensive textbook of psychiatry* (5th ed.). Baltimore: Williams & Wilkins.

Kleber, H. D., Weiss, R. D., Anton, R. F., George, T. P., Greenfield, S. H., Kosten, T. R., et. al. (2006). *Practice guidelines for the treatment of patients with substance use disorders* (2nd ed.). American Psychiatric Association Practice Guidelines for the Treatment of Psychiatric Disorders. Compendium. Arlington, VA. 291–563.

Kosten, T. R., & Kleber, H. D. (Eds.). (1992). *Clinician's guide to cocaine addiction.* New York: Guilford Press.

Lowinson, J. H., Ruiz, P., Millman, R. B., & Langrod, J. G. (Eds.). (2005). Substance abuse: A comprehensive textbook. Baltimore, MD: Williams & Wilkins.

Substance Abuse and Mental Health Services Administration. (2006). *National Survey on Drug Use and Health: National findings* (Office of Applied Studies, NSDUH Series H-30, DHHA Publication No. SMA 06-4194. Rockville, MD.

ELIZABETH WALLACE
THOMAS R. KOSTEN
REVISED BY TRACIE GARDNER (2009)
THOMAS R. KOSTEN (2009)

ANTICONVULSANTS

Anticonvulsants are medications approved to treat seizure disorders. Several anticonvulsants influence the reinforcing effects of psychoactive substances and have been used in the treatment of addictive disorder. These mechanisms appear to involve both gamma-amino butyric acid (GABA), the most abundant inhibitory neurotransmitter, and glutamate, the most abundant excitatory neurotransmitter in the brain. It has been hypothesized that anticonvulsants decrease the positive reinforcing effects of abused substances, such as reward and craving, by modulating dopamine neurotransmission through the facilitation of GABA neurotransmission. Perhaps more important, several anticonvulsants also appear to antagonize the glutamatergic activation and glutamate receptor upregulation associated with substance dependence and withdrawal. Thus, they influence the negative reinforcing effects associated with psychoactive substance withdrawal symptoms, especially that of ethanol and other depressants. Based on this general theoretical framework, there is a developing literature on the use of several anticonvulsants to treat alcoholism and other substance use disorders (SUDs). Here, the available evidence for the following anticonvulsants will be discussed: topiramate, carbamazepine, oxcarbazepine, divalproex, gabapentin, and lamotrigine.

Topiramate is thought to be a modulator of excitatory glutamatergic neurotransmission and a facilitator of the inhibitory GABA system. Strong evidence exists from two randomized, double-blind, placebo-controlled studies supporting the efficacy of topiramate for alcohol dependence: one single-site study with 150 patients (Johnson, Ait-Daoud, et al., 2003), and a more recent multisite, 14-week trial (Johnson, Rosenthal, et al., 2007). These studies reported a robust effect of topiramate compared to placebo in decreasing alcohol use, as indicated by multiple drinking outcomes such as percentage of heavy drinking days, secondary drinking outcomes, and a significant decrease in the liver enzyme, glutamyl transpeptidase (GGT), commonly elevated as a consequence of heavy alcohol use. In addition, these studies demonstrated that topiramate could be initiated safely and reliably in patients who are currently drinking heavily without the need to establish even a few days of abstinence before initiating treatment. Although some small-scale and open-label studies suggest that topiramate may promote abstinence from cocaine, nicotine, and MDMA, the evidence of its efficacy for these other addictions has yet to be established.

Carbamazepine has been tested for the treatment of alcohol withdrawal syndrome and for decreasing alcohol use in alcohol dependence. Carbamazepine suppresses withdrawal-induced kindling in limbic brain structures; it has reduced withdrawal symptoms and prevented alcohol withdrawal seizures in laboratory animals. Several studies, although not all, have documented its usefulness in the treatment of alcohol withdrawal. Available studies suggest that carbamazepine may have an advantage over benzodiazepines in the treatment of alcohol withdrawal because it decreases overall global distress. Preliminary indications also point to carbamazepine's usefulness in prolonging the time to relapse after detoxification (Malcolm, Myrick, et al., 2002). A small randomized trial evaluated the efficacy of carbamazepine for the treatment of alcohol dependence. Although this study indicated that carbamazepine did have some advantages over the placebo, in terms of the quantity of alcohol use, the time to next use, and a faster return to vocational functioning, definitive studies establishing the efficacy of carbamazepine in treating alcohol dependence are still to be conducted (Mueller, Stout, et al., 1997). A recent comprehensive review of the available clinical trials for carbamazepine in cocaine dependence concluded that no evidence existed to support the efficacy of carbamazepine in treating it (Minozzi, Amato, et al., 2008).

Divalproex is another GABAergic, anti-kindling agent that has been found helpful in treating alcohol withdrawal and in decreasing alcohol use among patients with alcohol dependence, and those with comorbid bipolar disorder (Salloum, Cornelius, et al., 2005). In addition, small-scale pilot studies have found divalproex helpful in treating cocaine use. However, no large-scale multi-site studies have tested the drug for these conditions, and although available data suggest its usefulness in this context, definitive studies are still to be conducted to establish its efficacy in treating addictive disorders.

In summary, certain anticonvulsants seem promising for the effective treatment of alcohol withdrawal and for the promotion of abstinence and relapse prevention in alcoholism. They may be helpful in treating other addictions as well. Other anticonvulsants, such as gabapentin, oxcarbazepine, and lamotrigine, have also been of interest. Of the medications reviewed above, only topiramate has been tested in a large multi-site clinical trial. As some of the mentioned medications are also effective mood stabilizers, they may be suitable for treating co-occurring bipolar disorder in patients with alcoholism.

See also **Gamma-Aminobutyric Acid (GABA); Glutamate; Neurotransmission; Neurotransmitters.**

BIBLIOGRAPHY

Johnson, B. A., Ait-Daoud, N., Bowden, C. L., DiClemente, C. C., Roache, J. D., Lawson, K., et al. (2003). Oral topiramate for treatment of alcohol dependence: A randomised controlled trial. *The Lancet* 361(9370): 1677–1685.

Johnson, B. A., Rosenthal, N., Capece, J. A., Wiegand, F., Mao, L., Beyers, K., et al. (2007). Topiramate for treating alcohol dependence: a randomized controlled trial. *Journal of the American Medical Association* 298(14), 1641–1651.

Malcolm, R., Myrick, H., Roberts, J., Wang, W., Anton, R. F., & Ballenger, J. C. (2002). The effects of carbamazepine and lorazepam on single versus multiple previous alcohol withdrawals in an outpatient randomized trial. *Journal of General Internal Medicine* 17(5): 349–355.

Minozzi, S., Amato, L., Davoli, M., Farrell, M., Lima Reisser, A. A., Pani, P. P., et al. (2008). Anticonvulsants for cocaine dependence. Cochrane Database of Systematic Reviews 2.

Mueller, T. I., Stout, R. L., Rudden, S., Brown, R. A., Gordon, A., Solomon, D. A., et al. (1997). A double-blind, placebo-controlled pilot study of carbamazepine for the treatment of alcohol dependence. *Alcoholism: Clinical & Experimental Research* 21(1): 86–92.

Salloum, I. M., Cornelius, J. R., Daley, D. C., Kirisci, L., Himmelhoch, J. M., & Thase, M. E. (2005). Efficacy of valproate maintenance in patients with bipolar disorder and alcoholism: A double-blind placebo-controlled study. *Archives of General Psychiatry* 62(1): 37–45.

IHSAN SALLOUM
ANTOINE DOUAIHY

ANTIDEPRESSANTS

Antidepressant drugs are a diverse group of medications that reduce the symptoms of clinical depression. The word *depression* is commonly used to describe a state of sadness, but health professionals describe illnesses very specifically in order to increase the precision of communication in research and clinical practice. For example, *major depression* is defined as a recurring problem characterized by severe and prolonged periods of depressed mood, often with other symptoms such as dejection, lack of energy, and inactivity. Major depression significantly interferes with everyday functioning in life. A similar illness, *dysthymia*, is a chronic mood state characterized by depression and irritability (dysthymia was once referred to as depressive neurosis). Depressive symptoms are also part of an important mood disorder called *bipolar disorder* (also known as *manic-depressive illness*), in which periods of depression alternate with periods of manic behavior. The signs and symptoms of depression or mood disorders may occur as part of other medical and psychiatric disorders. They may occur, for example, following stroke, as a result of endocrine disorders, or as a consequence of excessive drug use.

Antidepressants can also be useful in a number of medical and psychiatric disorders where depression is not the major feature. For example, some categories of antidepressants can be used to treat anxiety and panic disorders, and some are often useful as adjunctive medications for chronic pain. Antidepressant drugs are not generally helpful for short-term depressed moods that are part of everyday life, or for the normal period of grief that follows the loss of a loved one. One drawback of antidepressant drug treatment is that it takes weeks for the full therapeutic benefit to appear. In addition, patients should not stop taking the drugs abruptly, because symptoms of withdrawal may appear. Instead, the use of these drugs should be discontinued very gradually. Because of the complexity of their effects, antidepressants are prescription drugs that should be taken only under the care and guidance of a physician.

Various categories of antidepressants have been developed over the years, and they are still being developed and tested. These categories include tricyclic antidepressants, monoamine oxidase (MAO) inhibitors, atypical antidepressants, and selective serotonin-reuptake inhibitors (SSRIs). In addition, lithium and some antiepileptic drugs have mood-stabilizing effects and are used in bipolar disorder. The chemical structures of some of these are shown below.

The tricyclic antidepressants, which have been used for many years in the treatment of depression, include such compounds as imipramine (Tofranil), nortriptyline (Aventyl), and desipramine (Norpramin). Most of the tricyclics can be given in a single dose at bedtime. The tricyclics, like other antidepressants, require a period of two weeks or more before they are fully effective. The tricyclics also have many side effects and a relatively narrow margin of safety, which means that they have adverse effects (some of which can be fatal) that appear at a dosage that is not very much greater than the therapeutic dosage. As a rule, physicians are cautious about prescribing tricyclic antidepressants if the patient appears to be at risk for suicide.

The monoamine oxidase (MAO) inhibitors are not commonly used because of their side effects and because they require certain dietary restrictions (e.g., patients are not allowed to eat liver, aged meats, most cheeses, red wine, or soy sauce). They include phenelzine (Nardil), isocarboxazid (Marplan), and tranylcypromine (Parnate). These antidepressants may be given in either the morning or the evening, depending on their effect on the patient's sleep.

The selective serotonin-reuptake inhibitors (SSRIs) are a newer, major category of antidepressant medications, and they are currently among the first-line drugs used to treat depression. Fluoxetine (Prozac), which is now available in generic form, has been a best-selling antidepressant since the mid-1990s. Other SSRIs include paroxetine (Paxil), sertraline (Zoloft), and escitalopram (Lexapro, Cipralex). The SSRIs have several advantages. They have less toxicity than the tricyclics or the MAO inhibitors, which is a significant factor in their popularity. They can also be used to treat bulimia and obsessive-compulsive disorder. Since insomnia is a common side effect of SSRIs, they are usually given as a single dose in the morning. The SSRIs can have other side effects, including sexual dysfunction, and they can be expensive. A growing number of SSRIs are available as generics, which has reduced the cost of treatment with these medications.

Another antidepressant, bupropion (Wellbutrin, Zyban), is a member of the "atypical" class. It is often a choice if SSRIs fail to work or have intolerable side effects (such as weight gain, which has been observed commonly with the SSRIs, but not with bupropion). Although lithium (Eskalith, Lithonate) is useful in treating bipolar disorder, it is not generally used for other types of depression. Lithium may have serious side effects, and it may be toxic at high dosages. Patients taking lithium should have regular blood tests to be sure that lithium levels are acceptable. Exposure to lithium in early pregnancy is associated with an increased frequency of birth defects, and the long-term use of lithium can damage kidney function. Some antiepileptic drugs (e.g., carbamazepine, valproic acid) are effective mood stabilizers and are often prescribed for the treatment of bipolar disorder.

Antidepressants can be used to treat depression associated with drug dependence and withdrawal, and some studies suggest that they may reduce drug intake. Alcoholics, for example, are often depressed, and other drug abusers often have depression as a comorbid problem. Some antidepressants may reduce cocaine use, but there are no proven, highly effective drug treatments for psychostimulant abuse. Bupropion (Zyban) is approved and widely used to treat nicotine dependence. SSRIs have been studied extensively as treatments for alcohol dependence.

Overall, the literature indicates that these medications may be beneficial for the subgroup of individuals with late-onset (after age 25) alcoholism. In contrast, there is evidence that these medications are either ineffective or counterproductive in reducing drinking or promoting abstinence in early-onset alcoholics.

In summary, antidepressants are an effective and important class of drugs, partly because of the high prevalence of the illnesses for which they are effective treatments. Antidepressants also can have a role in treating some kinds of substance abuse or dependence, and they may be useful for treating the depression that can occur with various kinds of substance abuse.

BIBLIOGRAPHY

American Psychiatric Association. (1994). *Diagnostic and statistical manual of mental disorders* (4th ed.; *DSM-IV*). Washington, DC: Author.

Baldessarini, R. J. (2001). Drugs and the treatment of psychiatric disorders. In J. G. Hardman, L. E. Limbird, & A. G. Gilman (Eds.), *Goodman and Gilman's the pharmacological basis of therapeutics* (10th ed.). New York: Pergamon.

Graham, A. W., Schultz, T. K., Ries, R. K., & Mayo-Smith, M. (Eds.). (2003). *Principles of Addiction Medicine* (3rd ed.). Chevy Chase, MD: American Society for Addiction Medicine.

GEORGE R. UHL
VALINA DAWSON
REVISED BY REBECCA J. FREY (2001)
MICHAEL J. KUHAR (2009)

ANTIPSYCHOTICS

ANTIPSYCHOTIC MEDICATIONS

Antipsychotic medications are any of a group of drugs, sometimes termed neuroleptics, used in the therapy of schizophrenia, organic psychoses, manic-depressive illness, and other psychotic illnesses. The prototype (so-called *typical*) antipsychotics (Figure 1) are primarily phenothiazines such as chlorpromazine (Thorazine), and butyrophenones such as haloperidol (Haldol). These antipsychotics tend to be tricyclic compounds with chemical substitution at R1 and R2, which determine the side effects and the potency of the drug.

A group of newer *atypical* antipsychotics was introduced in the 1990s: clozapine (Clozaril) (Figure 2), risperidone (Risperdal), olanzapine (Zyprexa),

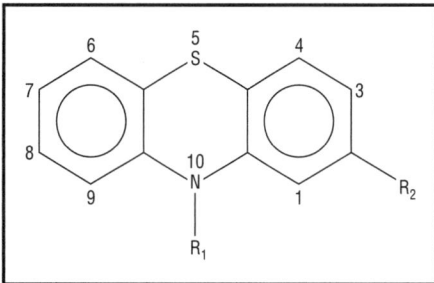

Figure 1. Chemical structure of an atypical antipsychotic.
ILLUSTRATION BY GGS INFORMATION SERVICES. GALE, CENGAGE LEARNING

quetiapine (Seroquel), aripiprazole (Abilify), ziprasidone (Geodon), and paliperidone (Invega).

The antipsychotics often effectively treat positive symptoms of the psychotic disorders, such as hallucinations; these drugs have a lesser effect in managing negative symptoms, such as social withdrawal. All of the antipsychotics are effective although clozapine seems to be the most effective in patients who do not have a good response to the other drugs.

The older typical antipsychotics tend to produce adverse effects on movements, which must be balanced against their beneficial effects. Many of the newer atypical antipsychotics also have adverse effects, particularly weight gain and metabolic side effects (such as elevated blood glucose and triglyceride concentrations), which must also be considered in their use. Clozapine, although very effective, produces the

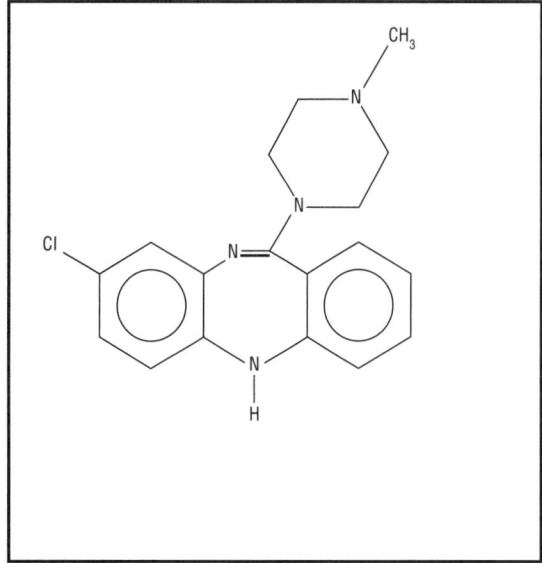

Figure 2. Clozapine—the first atypical antipsychotic.
ILLUSTRATION BY GGS INFORMATION SERVICES. GALE, CENGAGE LEARNING

most severe side effects, which can include a potentially life-threatening suppression of white blood cells.

See also Personality Disorders; Pharmacology; Research: Measuring Effects of Drugs on Behavior; Schizophrenia.

BIBLIOGRAPHY

Baldessarini, R. J. & Tarazi, F. I. (2006). Pharmacotherapy of psychosis and mania. In L. L. Brunton, J. S. Lazo, & K. Parker (Eds.), Goodman & Gilman's: The pharmacological basis of therapeutics, 11th ed. New York: McGraw Hill.

ALAN I. GREEN

AVERSION THERAPY

The method of treating alcoholics by pairing the consumption of alcohol with an aversive experience has been used since ancient times. In their review, Howard and co-workers (1991) cited several important examples from history and literature starting with the Romans, who used spiders or eels as an aversive effect in the bottom of wine cups to discourage the drinker. Benjamin Rush, one of the fathers of American psychiatry, reported a case of successful aversive treatment in 1815. In literature, Anton Chekhov in A Cure for Drinking and Anne Brontë in The Tenant of Wildfell Hall described individuals who experienced aversive treatment.

The first clinical use of aversion therapy in alcoholics was reported in 1930. The method was used in several countries over the subsequent decades. The method was first used in the United States in 1935 and became widely available in the subsequent decades.

The present entry concerns only chemical aversion therapy (CAT). The idea is that repeated pairing of alcohol and chemically induced nausea triggers a conditional response. The chemical agent commonly used is emetin.

Non-chemically induced nausea has been used with similar protocols. Electric aversion therapy has been applied in some studies with a similar outcome (Smith, Frawley, & Polisser, 1997). Another method is covert sensitization. In this form of treatment, imagined drinking episodes are repeatedly paired with nausea induced through noxious verbal suggestions (Miller & Dougher, 1984).

In the early days of disulfiram treatment, the drug was given in combination with alcohol. The aversive effect was regarded as beneficial for the long-term outcome of the patient. However, reports of severe or fatal disulfiram-ethanol reactions led to the abandonment of this procedure (Jabobsen, 1952). For the same reason, the use of disulfiram as an emetic agent in CAT was abandoned.

The protocol for CAT varies. A typical protocol, as described by Elkins (1991), consists of about five emetin sessions over an initial 10-day treatment phase. In addition, post-discharge reinforcement sessions are conducted, one after 30 and another after 90 days.

Many alcoholics display a conditioned response during CAT. This has been demonstrated using psychophysiological and behavioral indices (Elkins, 1991). Howard (2001) reported that positive alcohol-related outcome expectances were significantly reduced, whereas confidence that drinking could be avoided in various high-risk situations for alcohol consumption was increased following CAT. Patients prone to antisocial behavior appeared to be less susceptible to the CAT conditioning protocol.

As of 2008, the efficacy of CAT was not very well documented, with only two small, randomized studies available. Wallerstein (1957) evaluated the relative effectiveness of CAT, disulfiram, hypnotherapy, and milieu therapy. He found that 50 patients (80%) undergoing CAT completed treatment, compared to 47 (83%), 39 (64%), and 42 (62%) of disulfiram, hypnotherapy, and milieu therapy subjects, respectively. There were no significant differences between CAT and the other treatment options in retention or short-term outcome. Cannon and colleagues (1981) studied 20 patients who were randomized to CAT, shock aversion therapy, or a control group. At the six-month follow-up, CAT subjects had been abstinent for a mean of 170 days, while shock aversion therapy and control subjects were abstinent for 109 and 158 days, respectively. Group comparisons revealed that CAT subjects were abstinent for significantly more days than patients in the combined shock aversion and control groups. The significant differences disappeared at the one-year follow-up.

Among other studies, only one used a comparison group. Smith, Frawley, and Polisser (1991) compared 249 alcoholic inpatients that had undergone aversion therapy with patients from a national treatment registry who did not receive aversion therapy. The patients treated with aversion therapy had significantly higher abstinence rates at six and twelve months. Patients who accepted a booster dose after one and three months showed better outcome than the others. The patients receiving CAT had greater job stability, were more likely to live with a relative, and had no criminal records compared with the comparison group, all factors that can improve outcome, suggesting that the comparison was confounded by differences on background characteristics.

Several early studies lacked control and comparison groups. Lemere and Voegtin (1940) reported the results of a study based on the follow up 10 to 15 years after treatment of more than 34,000 patients who were conditioned to feel nauseated when exposed to alcohol. Sixty-six percent of these patients were abstinent, an impressive recovery rate compared to other forms of treatment. The patients who were most successful had undergone booster sessions; that is, they had returned to the clinic after the initial treatment to repeat the conditioning procedure. Of those who attended booster sessions, 90 percent were abstinent.

Frawley and Smith (1992) also reported remarkably high rates of abstinence from cocaine (current abstinence of at least six months, 68%) among a similar group of patients with good prognostic features, treated with aversion therapy. These patients were followed up for an average of 15 months after treatment. Again there was no control group.

From the 1950s to the 1970s, CAT was offered in a large variety of settings in the United States. After that, the use of CAT diminished considerably, and only the Schick Shadel Hospital still offered the therapy in 2008.

In conclusion, the efficacy of CAT is not well documented. There have only been a few randomized controlled trials, and these lacked sufficient statistical power and had other methodological limitations, yielding inconclusive results. Adequate evaluations of the efficacy of CAT will require that clinical trials evaluating its efficacy use more rigorous clinical trial methods.

See also **Calcium Carbimide; Treatment, Pharmacological Approaches to: Disulfiram.**

BIBLIOGRAPHY

Cannon, D. S., Baker, T. B., & Wehl, C. K. (1981). Emetic and electric shock alcohol aversion therapy: Six- and twelve-month follow-up. *Journal of Consulting Clinical Psychology* 49(3), 360–368.

Elkins, R. L. (1991). An appraisal of chemical aversion (emetic therapy) approaches to alcoholism treatment. *Behaviour Research Therapy, 29*(5), 387–413.

Frawley, P. J., & Smith, J. W. (1992). One-year follow-up after multimodal inpatient treatment for cocaine and methamphetamine dependencies. *Journal of Substance Abuse Treatment, 9,* 271–286.

Howard, M. O. (2001). Pharmacological aversion treatment of alcohol dependence. I. Production and prediction of conditioned alcohol aversion. *American Journal of Drug and Alcohol Abuse, 27*(3), 561–585.

Howard, M. O., Elkins, R. L., Rimmele, C., & Smith, J. W. (1991). Chemical aversion treatment of alcohol dependence. *Drug and Alcohol Dependence, 29*(2), 107–143.

Jacobsen, E. (1952). Deaths of alcoholic patients treated with disulfiram (tetraethylthiuram disulfide) in Denmark. *Quarterly Journal of Studies on Alcohol, 13*(1), 16–26.

Lemere, F., & Voegtin, W. L. (1940). Conditioned reflex therapy of alcoholic addiction: Specificity of conditioning against chronic alcoholism. *California and Western Medicine, 53*(6), 1–4.

Miller, W. R., & Dougher, M. J. (1984). Covert sensitization: Alternative treatment procedures for alcoholics. *Alcoholism: Clinical and Experimental Research, 8,* 108.

Smith, J. W., & Frawley, P. J. (1990). Long-term abstinence from alcohol in patients receiving aversion therapy as part of a multimodal inpatient program. *Journal of Substance Abuse Treatment, 7,* 77–82.

Smith, J. W., Frawley, P. J., & Polissar, N. L. (1991). Six- and twelve-month abstinence rates in inpatient alcoholics treated with aversion therapy compared with matched inpatients from a treatment registry. *Alcoholism: Clinical and Experimental Research, 5,* 862–870.

Smith, J. W., Frawley, P. J., & Polissar, N. L. (1997). Six- and twelve-month abstinence rates in inpatient alcoholics treated with either faradic aversion or chemical aversion compared with matched inpatients from a treatment registry. *Journal of Addictive Diseases, 16*(1), 5–24.

Wallerstein, R. S. (1957). Comparative study of treatment methods for chronic alcoholism: The alcoholism research at Winter V.A. Hospital. *American Journal of Psychiatry, 113,* 228–233.

MATS BERGLUND

ACAMPROSATE

Acamprosate (brand name Campral) is a synthetic compound with a structure similar to that of the neurotransmitter gamma-aminobutyric acid (GABA) and the neuromodulator taurine. Not completely understood as of 2008, the mechanism of action in this drug was thought to involve a functional antagonism of the glutamate n-methyl-d-aspartate (NMDA) receptor, including antagonism of the mGLu5 metabotropic glutamate receptor, to counteract the imbalance between the glutamate and GABA systems associated with chronic alcohol exposure and alcohol withdrawal. This effect may reduce craving and distress and may thus decrease the need to consume alcohol.

In double-blind, placebo-controlled trials, acamprosate effectively maintained complete abstinence in detoxified alcohol-dependent patients at a rate significantly higher than an inactive placebo. When used as an adjunct to psychosocial interventions, acamprosate also improves the length and rate of abstinence from alcohol. This effect is less likely if acamprosate is not initiated quickly after detoxification.

As of 2008, however, the success of acamprosate had only been demonstrated in trials conducted in Europe. In a meta-analysis of 17 randomized controlled trials conducted in Europe, which included 4,087 recently detoxified alcohol-dependent patients receiving psychosocial support, treatment with acamprosate for six months resulted in significantly higher rates of continuous abstinence than placebo. In contrast, acamprosate did not show efficacy in two U.S. studies.

The multicenter COMBINE study included 1,383 recently alcohol-abstinent patients with alcohol dependence and compared the efficacy of medical management plus oral naltrexone or acamprosate with placebo, combined with an intensive behavioral therapy or a less intensive medical management procedure. COMBINE found that acamprosate was no better than placebo, failing to produce either a greater decrease in the rate of heavy-drinking days or a greater increase in abstinent days from that seen with placebo treatment.

In the second U.S. clinical trial, there was an effect for acamprosate compared with placebo only in a subset of highly motivated patients. The reasons for the differences in effectiveness of acamprosate between European and U.S. studies were unknown as of 2008. It was hypothesized that differences in features that characterize patients (e.g., concurrent drug abuse, which is more common in the U.S. population) and greater severity of alcoholism and the use of inpatient detoxification in European populations may help to explain these findings.

Acamprosate has been approved for use in Europe since 1989 and was approved by the U.S. Food and Drug Administration (FDA) in July 2004 for abstinence maintenance in alcohol-dependent individuals who are abstinent at treatment initiation. Acamprosate is dispensed in 333 mg white and odorless tablets of acamprosate calcium, which is equivalent to 300 mg of acamprosate. The usual dose is 666 mg (i.e., two tablets) three times daily. Acamprosate is not well absorbed into the blood from the digestive tract, and it takes several days to achieve desired blood levels of the medication. The medication appears to be safe in alcoholics, with minimal side effects. It does not appear to produce sedation and does not cause drug dependence.

The most common adverse effects of acamprosate are headache and gastrointestinal effects, including nausea, diarrhea, and bloating. Because it only has these benign side effects, the drug can be started at full dosage without needing to be gradually increased. Acamprosate is not metabolized but is eliminated by renal excretion. It should therefore be given cautiously to patients with impaired kidney function (creatinine clearance = 30mL/min). The drug should be avoided in patients who previously exhibited hypersensitivity to acamprosate.

See also **Alcohol: Chemistry and Pharmacology; Alcoholism: Abstinence versus Controlled Drinking; Drug Interactions and Alcohol.**

BIBLIOGRAPHY

Anton, R. F., O'Malley, S. S., Ciraulo, D. A., Cisler, R. A., Couper, D., Donovan, D. M., et al. (2006). Combined pharmacotherapies and behavioral interventions for alcohol dependence: The COMBINE study, a randomized controlled trial. *Journal of the American Medical Association, 295,* 2003–2017.

Dahchour, A., & De Witte, P. (2003). Effects of acamprosate on excitatory amino acids during multiple ethanol withdrawal periods. *Alcoholism: Clinical and Experimental Research, 27,* 465–470.

Kranzler, H. R., & Gage, A. (2008). Acamprosate efficacy in alcohol-dependent patients: Summary of results from three pivotal trials. *American Journal of Addiction, 17,* 70–76.

Mann, K., & Morgan, M. Y. (2004). The efficacy of acamprosate in the maintenance of abstinence in alcohol-dependent individuals: Results of a meta-analysis. *Alcoholism: Clinical and Experimental Research, 28,* 51–63.

Mason, B. J., Goodman, A. M., Chabac, S., & Lehert, P. (2006). Effect of oral acamprosate on abstinence in patients with alcohol dependence in a double-blind, placebo-controlled trial: The role of patient motivation. *Journal of Psychiatric Research, 40,* 383–393.

Paille, F. C., Guelfi, J. D., Perkins, A. C., Royer, R. J., Steru, L., & Parot, P. (1995). Double-blind randomized multi-centre trial of acamprosate in maintaining abstinence from alcohol. *Alcohol and Alcoholism, 30*(2), 239–247.

LORENZO LEGGIO

BUPRENORPHINE

Buprenorphine is a semisynthetic opiate that is produced from thebaine, a naturally occurring alkaloid present in the ripe pods of the opium poppy (*Papaver somniferum*). Buprenorphine has an analgesic potency twenty-five to fifty times greater than morphine on a weight basis. However, after taking into consideration its greater potency, the analgesic actions of buprenorphine are quite similar to those of morphine and the other opiates, such as codeine, hydromorphone, oxymorphone, and fentanyl.

It is assumed that these effects are dependent upon its ability to act at *mu* (morphine) receptors in the brain. Once bound to the receptor, however, buprenorphine produces a limited effect, and thus it is termed a partial agonist. This ability to produce only a partial response may explain why buprenorphine has a lesser effect on reducing breathing (i.e., produces respiratory depression) than drugs such as morphine.

Because it is a partial agonist, buprenorphine administration to morphine-dependent patients does not elicit significant withdrawal symptoms and can therefore be used as a methadone-like opiate substitute in treatment programs. Another reason for the use of the agent in this respect is its particularly long duration of action. Single doses of buprenorphine can attenuate or prevent many of the actions of morphine for up to thirty hours. Thus, buprenorphine maintenance is used to treat opiate addiction.

The interactions of buprenorphine with opioid antagonists are interesting. Buprenorphine actions can be readily prevented by antagonists such as naloxone when the antagonist is administered prior to buprenorphine. However, antagonists given after buprenorphine do not readily reverse the opioid actions. This unique pharmacology distinguishes it from traditional opiates such as morphine. Many believe that this observation is due to the prolonged occupation of the receptor by buprenorphine. Once it is bound, other drugs can no longer effectively compete with buprenorphine to bind to the receptor.

Buprenorphine is available alone (Subutex) or in a 4:1 combination sublingual tablet with naloxone (Suboxone). A multi-center, randomized, placebo-controlled clinical experiment comparing buprenorphine tablets, Suboxone tablets, and placebos in opiate-dependent patients found that both buprenorphine alone and Suboxone reduced opiate use in the first month of the study compared to a placebo. Suboxone also appears to decrease the potential for abuse or diversion compared to methadone because injection of Suboxone can precipitate opioid withdrawal in an individual that is opiate dependent (due to the presence of naloxone, which is broken down before reaching the brain when taken orally). In 2002 the Food and Drug Administration (FDA) approved buprenorphine monotherapy (Subutex), as well as Suboxone, (the buprenorphine/naloxone combination product) for use in opioid addiction treatment. Subutex and Suboxone are currently the only Schedule III, IV, or V medications to have received FDA approval for this indication.

In addition, buprenorphine has been examined for use in HIV-infected patients with opioid dependence to improve treatment outcomes and to evaluate its role in HIV prevention. Following its initial approval, the drug has been made more widely accessible in healthcare settings by a law allowing individual physicians to treat up to 100 patients in private offices.

See also **Heroin; Treatment, Pharmacological Approaches to: An Overview.**

BIBLIOGRAPHY

Brunton, L., Lazo, J., & Parker, K. (2006). Opioid analgesics and antagonists. In J. G. Hardman, L. E. Limbird, & A. G. Gilman (Eds.), *Goodman and Gilman's the pharmacological basis of therapeutics* (11th ed.). New York: Pergamon.

Kosten, T. R., Kleber, H. D., & Morgan, C. (1989). Treatment of cocaine abuse with buprenorphine. *Biological Psychiatry, 26,* 637–639.

Kosten, T. R., Schottenfeld, R. S., Ziedonis, D., & Falcioni, J. (1993). Buprenorphine versus methadone maintenance for opioid dependence. *Journal of Nervous and Mental Disease, 181,* 358–364.

Substance Abuse and Mental Health Services Administration. (2004). Clinical guidelines for the use of buprenorphine in the treatment of opioid addiction. *Treatment Improvement Protocol Series 40,* (DHHS publication No. (SMA) 04-3939). Available from http://www.buprenorphine.samhsa.gov/.

GAVRIL PASTERNAK
REVISED BY THOMAS KOSTEN (2009)
TRACIE GARDNER (2009)

CLONIDINE

While not itself life threatening, the opioid withdrawal syndrome is extremely unpleasant and contributes to further opioid use and relapse. Heroin addicts report that the acute withdrawal syndrome begins approximately eight hours after their last injection and includes the following: craving for the drug, anxiety, perspiration with hot and cold flashes, tearing of the eyes and runny nose, restlessness, problems falling asleep and poor sleep quality, goose bumps, aching bones and muscles, loss of appetite, nausea, vomiting, diarrhea, abdominal cramps, spontaneous yawning, and a group of flu-like symptoms.

Opiate activation of mu opioid receptors in brainstem noradrenergic nuclei, including the locus coeruleus (LC), the major noradrenergic nucleus, suppresses neuronal activity, cyclic adenosine monophosphate (cAMP) signaling pathways, and norepinephrine (NE) release. In response to the chronic suppression induced by opiates, homeostatic mechanisms within these nuclei compensate by upregulating a number of molecules, including tyrosine hydroxylase (the rate-limiting enzyme for NE synthesis), cAMP response element binding protein (CREB), and adenylate cyclase. Upon opiate withdrawal and the absence of mu opioid activation, the noradrenergic system is disinhibited and, in fact, becomes overactive due to the persistence of the compensatory changes that took place during chronic opiate exposure. This noradrenergic hyperactivity significantly contributes to the opiate withdrawal syndrome described above. Some studies have implicated noradrenergic nuclei outside the LC, such as the nucleus tractus solitarius (NTS), in the opiate withdrawal syndrome.

CLINICAL CLONIDINE USE FOR OPIATE WITHDRAWAL

In the late 1970s, Gold and coworkers proposed that the alpha-2 adrenergic receptor agonist and hypertensive drug clonidine could be an effective treatment for opiate withdrawal distress. The alpha-2 adrenergic receptor is expressed by noradrenergic neurons, where it functions primarily as an inhibitory autoreceptor. Because activation of alpha-2 autoreceptors suppresses noradrenergic neuron firing and NE release, it dampens the hyperactivity of noradrenergic neurons that occurs during opiate withdrawal.

Clonidine has been tried in numerous inpatient and outpatient opioid addict populations worldwide and studied by researchers in numerous well-controlled studies. In virtually all studies, clonidine has been shown to be a safe and effective non-opioid treatment that ameliorates several aspects of opioid withdrawal. Clonidine has its most demonstrable effects on autonomic elements of opioid withdrawal: sweating, gastrointestinal complaints (cramps, diarrhea, nausea), and elevated blood pressure. Direct infusion of clonidine into the LC or brain areas innervated by the NTS noradrenergic cell group in animals can attenuate some aspects of opiate withdrawal, implicating both central and peripheral actions of clonidine.

Traditionally, clonidine has been used for the treatments of adult opiate addicts. However, its use as a detoxification treatment has been extended to neonates born to opiate-dependent mothers and to adolescent addicts. Clonidine has also been used successfully as an adjunctive therapy with the opiate receptor antagonist naltrexone or the partial opiate receptor agonist buprenorphine. In some cases, clonidine plus naltrexone shortened the detoxification period compared to naltrexone alone. Rapid opioid detoxification (ROD) with opioid antagonist induction using general anesthesia has emerged as an alternative approach to treat opioid dependence, but its safety and efficacy were the subject of debate as of 2008. In randomized trials, the success of clonidine-assisted detoxification has been comparable to that of ROD, but without the life-threatening risks of ROD. Using clonidine for withdrawal distress allows the brain to reestablish normal homeostatic patterns when given as part of a long-term recovery program. It allows patients sufficient motivation to achieve and sustain drug-free existence.

CLINICAL UTILITY OF CLONIDINE FOR OTHER ASPECTS OF DRUG ADDICTION

The noradrenergic system is involved in the processes underlying addiction to drug classes besides opiates, such as psychostimulants (e.g., cocaine, amphetamine), alcohol, and nicotine. Specifically, NE appears to be critical for the rewarding properties of morphine, ethanol, cocaine, and amphetamine. Although there are few clinical data to support it, clonidine may attenuate drug reward by acting on alpha-2 adrenergic autoreceptors and suppressing NE release.

It is widely agreed in the psychiatric community that stressful situations often precipitate relapse in abstinent drug-dependent individuals. Because the noradrenergic system is potently activated by stress, it has been hypothesized that blocking NE release (e.g., with clonidine) might attenuate stress-induced relapse. In the first decade of the twenty-first century, the stress-induced reinstatement paradigm gained popularity in rodents and nonhuman primates as a model for the stress-induced relapse observed in abstinent drug addicts. This paradigm consists of training animals to press a lever to obtain the drug, then extinguishing the lever pressing behavior by stopping drug delivery even upon correct lever presses. The lever pressing behavior can be reinstated by exposing the animal to various types of acute stress. Numerous studies have demonstrated that clonidine can block stress-induced reinstatement of heroin, cocaine, alcohol, and nicotine seeking in rats and monkeys. Its efficacy in preventing relapse in human addicts was unknown as of 2008.

CLINICAL UTILITY OF CLONIDINE FOR OTHER NEUROPSYCHIATRIC DISORDERS

Clonidine has been tried with varying success in the treatment of a number of medical problems in which the behaviors, signs, and/or symptoms resemble those seen in opiate withdrawal or following noradrenergic hyperactivity. Clonidine has also been tried in humans with generalized and panic anxiety, obsessive-compulsive symptomatology, Gilles de La Tourette's syndrome, mania, attention deficit and hyperactivity disorder, narcolepsy, neuroleptic-induced akathisia, and pheochromocytoma. Clonidine's analgesic effects have been rediscovered, and the drug has been given orally, transdermally (using skin patches), epidurally (into the area around the spinal canal), and parenterally (by injection) to decrease anesthetic requirements and to effect less respiratory depression than opioids alone.

Research and clinical experience since the original discoveries have (1) supported the notion of noradrenergic hyperactivity as one of the neural substrates for opioid withdrawal syndrome and led to considerable progress in the understanding of the critical cellular events causing noradrenergic hyperactivity in opioid withdrawal; (2) supported the efficacy of clonidine and established clonidine detoxification as one of the standard treatments for opioid addicts; (3) demonstrated that some individuals can receive further benefit from clonidine in combination with other drugs such as buprenorphine and naltrexone; and (4) suggested that clonidine may be useful for the treatment of other drug dependencies and neuropsychiatric diseases.

See also **Opioid Complications and Withdrawal.**

BIBLIOGRAPHY

Charney, D. S., Heninger, G. R., & Kleber, H. D. (1986). The combined use of clonidine and naltrexone as a rapid, safe and effective treatment of abrupt withdrawal from methadone. *American Journal of Psychiatry, 143,* 817–831.

Delfs, J. M., Zhu, Y., Druhan, J. P., & Aston-Jones, G. (2000). Noradrenaline in the ventral forebrain is critical for opiate withdrawal-induced aversion. *Nature, 403,* 430–434.

Erb, S., Hitchcott, P. K., Rajabi, H., Mueller, D., Shaham, Y., & Stewart, J. (2000). Alpha-2 adrenergic receptor agonists block stress-induced reinstatement of cocaine seeking. *Neuropsychopharmacology, 23,* 138–150.

Favrat, B., Zimmermann, G., Zullino, D., Krenz, S., Dorogy, F., Muller, J., et al. (2006). Opioid antagonist detoxification under anaesthesia versus traditional clonidine detoxification combined with an additional week of psychosocial support: A randomised clinical trial. *Drug and Alcohol Dependence, 8*(1),109–116.

Gold, M. S., Redmond, D. E., & Kleber, H. D. (1978). Clonidine blocks acute opiate symptoms. *Lancet, II,* 599–602.

Gold, M. S., Redmond, D. E., & Kleber, H. D. (1978). Clonidine in opiate withdrawal. *Lancet, I,* 929–930.

Jaffe, J. H. (1990). Drug addiction and drug abuse. In A. G. Gilman, et al. (Eds.), *Goodman and Gilman's the pharmacological basis of therapeutics* (8th ed., pp. 522–573). New York: Pergamon.

Lê, A. D., Harding, S., Juzytsch, W., Funk, D., & Shaham, Y. (2005). Role of alpha-2 adrenoceptors in stress-induced reinstatement of alcohol seeking and alcohol self-administration in rats. *Psychopharmacology (Berl), 179,* 366–373.

Maldonado, R. (1997). Participation of noradrenergic pathways in the expression of opiate withdrawal: Biochemical and pharmacological evidence. *Neuroscience & Biobehavioral Reviews, 21,* 91–104.

Nestler, E. J., & Aghajanian, G. K. (1997). Molecular and cellular basis of addiction. *Science, 278,* 58–63.

Olson, V. G., Heusner, C. L., Bland, R. J., During, M. J., Weinshenker, D., & Palmiter, R. D. (2006). Role of noradrenergic signaling by the nucleus tractus solitarius in mediating opiate reward. *Science, 311,* 1017–1020.

Platt, D. M., Rowlett, J. K., & Spealman, R. D. (2007). Noradrenergic mechanisms in cocaine-induced reinstatement of drug seeking in squirrel monkeys. *Journal of Pharmacology & Experimental Therapeutics, 322,* 894–902.

Shaham, Y., Highfield, D., Delfs, J., Leung, S., & Stewart, J. (2000). Clonidine blocks stress-induced reinstatement of heroin seeking in rats: An effect independent of locus coeruleus noradrenergic neurons. *European Journal of Neuroscience, 12,* 292–302.

Wallen, M. C., Lorman, W. J., & Gosciniak, J. L. (2006). Combined buprenorphine and clonidine for short-term opiate detoxification: Patient perspectives. *Journal of Addictive Disorders, 25,* 23–31.

Weinshenker, D., & Schroeder, J. P. (2007). There and back again: A tale of norepinephrine and drug addiction. *Neuropsychopharmacology, 32,* 1433–1451.

MARK S. GOLD
REVISED BY DAVID WEINSHENKER (2009)

DISULFIRAM

Disulfiram (Antabuse) was the first medication to be approved for alcoholism and for nearly fifty years was the only FDA-approved medication for alcoholism. Since 1994, three other medications were approved by the FDA for alcohol dependence treatment: oral naltrexone (ReVia), acamprosate (Campral), and long-acting intramuscular naltrexone (Vivitrol). The use of disulfiram has remained relatively constant and modest over the years. However, it may be anticipated that with the advent of subsequent medications that target the disease process of alcohol dependence more directly, the use of disulfiram may slowly wane. Disulfiram is not intended as a substitute for the counseling alcoholics receive while in treatment; it is meant to be an aid in keeping alcoholics sober, so that they may benefit from counseling. Although disulfiram has been in clinical use since the late 1940s, it is only since the 1980s that its efficacy has been studied using appropriate scientific methodology.

Disulfiram is used to deter drinking by causing an unpleasant reaction if a medicated person drinks alcohol (ethanol). This reaction is called the disulfiram-ethanol reaction (DER); the symptoms include flushing, dizziness, rapid heartbeat, nausea, vomiting, and headache. The DER can vary in severity, and the degree of severity often depends on the dose of disulfiram being taken plus the amount of alcohol that was consumed. A DER can cause hypotension (low blood pressure) and can be so severe that death occurs, although with adjusted dosage regimens this is very rare.

Disulfiram blocks the action of several of the body's enzymes, including aldehyde dehydrogenase (ALDH) and dopamine-β-hydroxylase. The inhibition of ALDH is responsible for the DER, which occurs because ethanol (drinking alcohol) is metabolized in the liver to acetaldehyde. Acetaldehyde, in turn, is converted to acetic acid, which is metabolized to water and carbon dioxide. Aldehyde dehydrogenase is the enzyme that facilitates the metabolism of acetaldehyde to acetic acid. When the action of ALDH is inhibited by disulfiram, acetaldehyde is not effectively converted to acetic acid but accumulates in the blood. Most of the symptoms of the DER are due to the increased circulating acetaldehyde. Since the inhibition of ALDH by disulfiram is irreversible, a person taking disulfiram cannot stop taking it one day and begin drinking the next: Several days (up to fourteen but usually fewer than seven) must go by because this amount of time is necessary for the body to produce new enzyme.

Attention has been drawn to positive findings with disulfiram in the management of cocaine dependence (Carroll et al., 2004). These effects are independent of an effect on alcohol consumption and have been hypothesized to relate to other biological actions of disulfiram such as its inhibition of dopamine-β-hydroxylase. This latter action likely affects the dopaminergic/noradrenergic transmission in the brain, which likely plays a role in cocaine addiction.

OTHER MEDICATIONS

Certain other medications cause a mild DER, including the antibiotic metronidazole (Flagyl). A medication available in Canada but not in the United States as of 2008 is citrated calcium carbimide (Temposil), which inhibits ALDH in a mixed reversible-irreversible fashion. When citrated calcium carbimide is discontinued, 80 percent of ALDH activity is restored within 24 hours. Hence, one can drink alcohol as soon as a day after stopping the use of citrated calcium carbimide without having a reaction.

In addition to disulfiram, there are medications with different mechanisms of action that are approved for use as of 2008 in helping recovering alcoholics maintain sobriety or reduce destructive drinking behavior. Oral naltrexone hydrochloride (ReVia) and long-acting intramuscular naltrexone (Vivitrol) are opioid antagonists that block the effects of endogenous opioids such as β-endorphin that are released by alcohol. The blockade of opioids counteracts the high feeling after alcohol consumption, and these medications have been found to reduce heavy drinking rates, to reduce relapse to heavy drinking, and, to some extent, enhance abstinence. Acamprosate (Campral), another medication approved for alcoholism, is thought to work by counteracting hyperglutamatergic activity that likely occurs in the recovery phase from alcohol dependence. This action may reduce the protracted withdrawal syndrome thereby decreasing one factor that contributes to relapse. Acamprosate has been shown to enhance the likelihood of abstinence and to reduce the number of drinking days in patients who are receiving alcoholism treatment.

ADMINISTRATION AND DOSAGE

Disulfiram should be administered only by a physician and is given by mouth in tablet form. It should never be given until the patient has abstained from alcohol for at least twelve hours and preferably for forty-eight hours. The FDA-approved dosage is 250 mg daily. Some patients report not experiencing a DER with smaller doses, so larger doses may be required. Clinical experience indicates, however, that doses larger than 500 mg are accompanied by a greater risk of serious side effects. A problem that limits the effectiveness of disulfiram is that patients frequently stop taking the medication. To enhance compliance, supervised administration by either a family member, treatment program, or even the legal system should be considered. Supervised administration has been shown to enhance outcomes in some trials (Chick et al., 1992; Martin et al., 2003). Given that compliance is perhaps the most significant impediment to the effective use of disulfiram, the development of a long-acting formulation of disulfiram has been a goal of research for many years. Unfortunately, no depot formulation of disulfiram has been developed, so clinicians and patients are left to use only oral disulfiram.

Patients should take disulfiram only under careful medical supervision. They should be warned that as long as they are taking the drug, ingesting alcohol in any form will make them sick and may be life-threatening. Patients should be taught to recognize and avoid disguised forms of alcohol such as cough syrups, mouthwashes, some sauces, fermented vinegar, and even aftershave lotion or rubbing alcohol. In addition, patients should be taught to recognize the signs of disturbed liver function (jaundiced eyeballs or skin, nausea or pain in the upper right quadrant of the abdomen, dark urine, clay-colored stool) and report them at once to their doctor. Patients should also be warned about signs of peripheral neuropathy, including sensory changes or weakness in the hands or feet.

SIDE EFFECTS

The use of disulfiram may be accompanied by side effects. The most common one is drowsiness; for this reason, the medication is usually taken at bedtime. Timing is usually sufficient to take care of this problem, but if not, the medication may have to be discontinued, especially for those who drive or work in hazardous environments. Idiosyncratic liver toxicity can occur from taking disulfiram. For this reason, liver function must be monitored closely during the first several months of treatment, and if blood tests indicate possible liver damage, disulfiram must be discontinued immediately.

A 1986 Swedish study found that disulfiram enhances the absorption and toxicity of lead in rats. Recovering alcoholics who must work in environments containing lead or lead products are advised not to use disulfiram to maintain sobriety.

In addition, serious psychotic reactions and depressive episodes have occurred in patients taking disulfiram. In a multisite study of 605 men, admissions for psychiatric problems were uncommon; as many admissions of this type occurred in men taking the placebo or not receiving disulfiram as in those receiving a 250-milligram dose (Branchey et al., 1987). The risk of serious psychoses or of major affective illnesses appears to be greater with higher doses.

Disulfiram has also been associated with cases of peripheral neuropathy. Patients should be cautioned to alert their physician if they note changes in sensation or weakness in the hands or feet.

INTERACTIONS WITH OTHER DRUGS
Disulfiram should not be given to patients who are taking metronidazole (Flagyl), which can also cause a reaction similar to disulfiram when combined with alcohol or paraldehyde (Paral). Doing so can produce a reaction similar to the DER. Amprenavir oral solution is contraindicated because it contains high levels of propylene glycol, which is also metabolized by aldehyde dehydrogenase, so that patients administered disulfiram could develop toxic levels of propylene glycol. Patients taking isoniazid (INH, Laniazid) may develop neurological symptoms if given disulfiram. Lastly, disulfiram may increase the blood levels and toxicity of warfarin (Coumadin), barbiturates, and phenytoin (Dilantin).

See also **Naltrexone; Relapse; Treatment: An Overview of Alcohol Abuse/Dependence.**

BIBLIOGRAPHY

Branchey, L., Davis, W., Lee, K. K., & Fuller, R. K. (1987). Psychiatric complications following disulfiram treatment. *American Journal of Psychiatry, 144,* 1310–1312.

Carroll, K. M., Fenton, L. R., Ball, S. A., Nich, C., Frankforter, T. L., Shi, J., et al. (2004). Efficacy of disulfiram and cognitive behavior therapy in cocaine-dependent outpatients: A randomized placebo-controlled trial. *Archives of General Psychiatry, 61*(3), 264–272.

Chick. J. (1999). Safety issues concerning the use of disulfiram in treating alcohol dependence. *Drug Safety, 20*(5), 427–435.

Chick, J., Gough, K., Falkowski, W., Kershaw, P., Hore, B., Mehta, B., et al. (1992). Disulfiram treatment of alcoholism. *British Journal of Psychiatry, 161,* 84–89.

Fuller, R. K., Branchey, L., Brightwell, D. R., Derman, R. M., Emrick, C. D., Iber, F. L., et al. (1986). Disulfiram treatment of alcoholism: A Veterans Administration cooperative study. *Journal of the American Medical Association, 256,* 1449–1455.

Fuller, R. K., Lee, K. K., & Gordis, E. (1988). Validity of self-report in alcoholism research: Results of a Veterans Administration cooperative study. *Alcoholism: Clinical and Experimental Research, 12,* 201–205.

Hardman, J. G., & Limbird, L. E. (Eds.). (1996). *Goodman and Gilman's the pharmacological basis of therapeutics* (9th ed.). New York: McGraw-Hill.

Martin, B., Clapp, L., Bialkowski, D., Bridgeford, D., Amponsah, A., Lyons, L., et al. (2003). Compliance to supervised disulfiram therapy: A comparison of voluntary and court-ordered patients. *The American Journal on Addictions, 12*(2), 137–143.

Wilson, B. A., Shannon, M. T., & Stang, C. L. (Eds.). (1995). *Nurses drug guide* (3rd ed.). Norwalk, CT: Appleton & Lange.

RICHARD K. FULLER
RAYE Z. LITTEN
REVISED BY REBECCA J. FREY (2001)
JAMES C. GARBUTT (2009)

LONG-ACTING PREPARATIONS
Poor medication compliance is a significant problem in clinical medicine (Osterberg & Blaschke, 2005), including adversely affecting the medical management of substance use disorders. One approach to dealing with compliance problems is to use long-acting preparations of medications. Early efforts to develop a long-acting formulation of disulfiram (Antabuse) for alcohol dependence were unsuccessful (Garbutt et al., 1999). However, subsequent efforts to develop a long-acting preparation of naltrexone were much more successful. Several clinical trials were completed as of 2008, demonstrating the efficacy and safety of long-acting naltrexone formulations (LA-NTX) for the treatment of alcohol dependence (Garbutt et al., 2005; Kranzler et al., 2004). In alcohol dependent patients, LA-NTX was effective in reducing rates of heavy drinking, and they

enhanced rates of total abstinence (Garbutt et al., 2005; Kranzler et al., 2004; O'Malley et al., 2007). Early evidence supported the efficacy of LA-NTX in opioid dependence as well (Comer et al., 2006), but additional work was required to verify this finding. As of 2008, LA-NTX was approved by the U.S. Food and Drug Administration (FDA) only for the treatment of alcohol dependence.

Naltrexone blocks endogenous opioid receptors thereby counteracting the effects of opioids released by alcohol. This action in turn counteracts the *high* experienced when alcohol is consumed and reduces the risk for relapse to heavy drinking. Naltrexone also blocks the effects of opioid drugs such as heroin or oxycodone. A patient taking oral or LA-NTX naltrexone will not experience the *high* from taking an opioid drug and, therefore, has a markedly reduced behavioral incentive to use opioid drugs.

Several LA-NTX formulations have been developed and studied in moderate-to-large clinical trials for alcohol dependence (Kranzler et al., 2004 [n=315]; Garbutt et al., 2005 [n=624]) and in a smaller trial in opioid dependence (Comer et al., 2006 [n=60]). These formulations use a polylactide polymer base, similar to that used in absorbable sutures, to provide a slow-dissolving matrix in which naltrexone is imbedded. This methodology has been shown to yield adequate levels of naltrexone for 28 days after injection (Johnson et al., 2004; Kranzler et al., 1998).

The one approved formulation of LA-NTX is for the treatment of alcohol dependence. It is given as a single, 380 mg, deep intramuscular injection in the buttock. It is recommended that the injection site be alternated from one buttock to the other. Injections are given once a month. The FDA label recommends that LA-NTX be started in patients who are able to abstain from alcohol in an outpatient setting prior to the initiation of treatment. The length of administration is not well defined. Most clinicians recommend that LA-NTX be used for 6 to 12 months together with counseling. Patients who have acute hepatitis or liver failure or who are abusing opiates or taking opiates for medical reasons should not receive LA-NTX.

LA-NTX has been associated with a number of side effects. Injection site reactions include tenderness, swelling, and pain and are common (69%), though usually well tolerated. Nausea is also common (33%) though generally short-lived. Other side effects include vomiting (14%), abdominal pain (11%), insomnia (12%), and anxiety (14%).

The primary drug-drug interaction with LA-NTX is with opiates such as oxycodone or morphine. Opiates will not have their expected pharmacological effect in the presence of naltrexone. Furthermore, opiate blockade can present a problem when a patient needs opiate treatment for acute pain. For acute pain conditions it is recommended that non-opiate interventions such as non-steroidal analgesics and regional analgesia be used. In cases in which opiates are necessary, high potency agents may be needed to override the blockade and, given the potential for adverse effects of such an override, should be monitored carefully. No other prominent drug interactions have been reported.

See also **Naltrexone.**

BIBLIOGRAPHY

Comer, S. D., Sullivan, M. A., Yu, E., Rothenberg, J. L., Kleber, H. D., Kampman, K. et al. (2006). Injectable, sustained-release naltrexone for the treatment of opioid dependence: A randomized, placebo-controlled trial. *Archives of General Psychiatry, 63*(2), 210–218.

Garbutt, J. C., Kranzler, H. R., O'Malley, S. S., Gastfriend, D. R., Pettinati H. M., Silverman, B. L., et al.; Vivitrex Study Group. (2005). Efficacy and tolerability of long-acting injectable naltrexone for alcohol dependence: A randomized controlled trial. *Journal of the American Medical Association, 293*(13), 1617–1625.

Garbutt, J. C., West, S. L., Carey, T. S., Lohr, K. N., & Crews, F. T. (1999). Pharmacological treatment of alcohol dependence: A review of the evidence. *Journal of the American Medical Association, 281*(14), 1318–1325.

Johnson, B. A., Ait-Daoud, N., Aubin, H. J., Van Den Brink, W., Guzzetta, R., Loewy, J. et al. (2004). A pilot evaluation of the safety and tolerability of repeat dose administration of long-acting injectable naltrexone (Vivitrex) in patients with alcohol dependence. *Alcoholism: Clinical and Experimental Research, 28*(9), 1356–1361.

Kranzler, H. R., Modesto-Lowe, V., & Nuwayser, E. S. (1998). Sustained-release naltrexone for alcoholism treatment: A preliminary study. *Alcoholism: Clinical and Experimental Research, 22,* 1074–1079.

Kranzler, H. R., Wesson, D. R., & Billot, L.; Drug Abuse Sciences Naltrexone Depot Study Group. (2004).

Naltrexone depot for treatment of alcohol dependence: A multicenter, randomized, placebo-controlled clinical trial. *Alcoholism: Clinical and Experimental Research, 28*(7), 1051–1059.

O'Malley, S. S., Garbutt, J. C., Gastfriend, D. R., Dong, Q., & Kranzler, H. R. (2007). Efficacy of extended-release naltrexone in alcohol-dependent patients who are abstinent before treatment. *Journal of Clinical Psychopharmacology, 27*(5), 507–512.

Osterberg, L., & Blaschke, T. (2005). Adherence to medication. *New England Journal of Medicine, 353,* 487–497.

JAMES C. GARBUTT

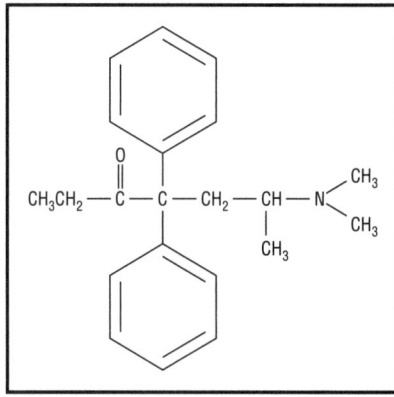

Figure 1. Chemical structure of methadone. ILLUSTRATION BY GGS INFORMATION SERVICES. GALE, CENGAGE LEARNING

METHADONE

Methadone (Dolophine) has pharmacological actions similar to those of the opioid drug, morphine. Methadone serves an important place in the history of opioid analgesics, since it is one of the first synthetic agents (having been synthesized in 1939). The ability to synthesize opioid analgesics from simple chemicals diminishes people's reliance on natural products (such as morphine, codeine, and thebaine) to provide the base for many opioid analgesics commonly used in the 2000s. Structurally, the drug does not look like morphine. Unlike the rigid fused ring structures of morphine, the structure of methadone is extremely flexible. It bends so that the key portions of the molecule can assume positions similar to those of morphine. The structure of methadone is similar to that of propoxyphene (Darvon), a weaker opiate widely used to treat mild-to-moderate pain. It has two stereoisomers, but the (-)isomer is far more active than the (+)isomer. Methadone can be administered orally, intramuscularly, or intravenously. It is well absorbed from the gastrointestinal tract making it useful orally. Its oral/parenteral ratio of potency is approximately two, far better than many other opioids. Methadone is threefold more potent than morphine orally, but about equipotent when given by injection. It is metabolized by the liver to a variety of inactive compounds, which then are eliminated by the kidneys.

Pharmacologically, methadone is used in the form of its hydrochloride salt. It has actions quite similar to morphine and works predominantly through mu opiate receptors. Like all mu opioid drugs, methadone elicits a variety of side effects, including respiratory depression, sedation, and constipation, in addition to pain relief. Although their potency is similar, the long half-life of methadone distinguishes it from morphine. For pain control, the drug is typically given to patients every six to eight hours. This long duration of action can be advantageous, particularly in patients who require the drug for long periods of time, such as cancer patients.

However, there are some disadvantages. With a half-life ranging from twenty to thirty hours, it may take many days of continued dosing to reach constant (or steady-state) levels of the drug in the body. Thus, the full effect of a change in drug dose may not be seen for three or four days. This factor may make it difficult to adjust the dose for an individual patient. Increasing the dose too rapidly may even lead to delayed increases in its concentration in the body, far beyond those anticipated and, in some situations, may actually lead to an overdose. Continued administration of methadone will produce tolerance and physical dependence. The actions of methadone, like those of morphine, are readily reversed by antagonists such as naloxone or naltrexone; however, these antagonists will also produce an immediate withdrawal syndrome in physically dependent people. Despite its clear utility in the control of pain, the major use of methadone in the United States is in the treatment of heroin addicts. Although methadone must be administered approximately every six to eight hours to maintain analgesia, its slow rate of elimination prevents the appearance of withdrawal signs and symptoms for over twenty-four hours. This slow appearance of withdrawal effects has made this agent useful in maintenance programs, since it permits once-a-day dosing. With chronic administration of high doses of methadone, addicts become tolerant, markedly limiting the euphoria an addict might obtain from illicit use of other opiates such as heroin. Thus, methadone minimizes occasional opiate use, is readily tolerated by the addicts, and can be administered once a day, which makes it easily dispensed. Methadone has been used clinically in maintenance programs and is one of the most effective treatment modalities as of 2008 available for opiate addicts.

See also **Addiction: Concepts and Definitions; Methadone Maintenance Programs; Pain, Drugs Used for; Treatment, Pharmacological Approaches to: An Overview.**

BIBLIOGRAPHY

O'Brien, C. P. (2006). Drug addiction and drug abuse. In L.L. Brunton, J. L. Lazo, K. L. Parker (Eds.). *Goodman and Gilman's the pharmacological basis of therapeutics* (11th ed., pp. 607–628). New York: McGraw-Hill.

Reisine, T., & Pasternak, G. (1996). Opioid analgesics and antagonists. In J. G. Hardman, L. E. Limbird, P. B. Molinoff, R. W. Ruddon, & A. G. Goodman (Eds.). *Goodman and Gilman's the pharmacological basis of therapeutics* (9th ed., pp. 521–555). New York: McGraw-Hill.

GAVRIL W. PASTERNAK

NALTREXONE

Naltrexone (Depade, Revia Vivitrol [U.S.]; Nalorex [France, U.K.]) is a synthetic antagonist of opioid (morphine-like) receptors, which blocks their actions without having any opioid effects itself. Naltrexone differs from most other pure opioid antagonists in having a relatively long duration of action (at least twenty-four hours) and being effective when taken by mouth or as a depot formulation (long-acting injection lasting thirty days). These characteristics have led to its clinical use as a long-term or maintenance treatment for alcohol and opioid dependence. As of 2008, Naltrexone was also being studied experimentally as a possible treatment for cigarette smoking.

OPIOID DEPENDENCE

The use of opioid antagonists as treatment for opioid dependence was first proposed by William Martin and Abraham Wikler and their colleagues at the U.S. Addiction Research Center in the early 1960s. These researchers hypothesized that chronic administration of an opioid antagonist, by blocking the pleasurable or rewarding effects of opioid drugs, would lead to the extinction of drug-seeking and drug-taking behavior—since the addict would no longer receive any pleasurable effects from taking an opioid. It was further suggested that antagonist treatment would have several advantages over treatment with an opioid such as methadone. Since antagonists do not produce any pleasurable effects, addicts have little incentive to misuse the medication or divert it to illegal channels. Chronic use of an antagonist would not produce physical dependence, and an overdose of antagonist would not cause life-threatening opioid effects such as suppression of breathing. Use of the antagonist in non-detoxified opioid addicts, however, would cause an acute but not life-threatening withdrawal reaction.

ALCOHOL DEPENDENCE

The efficacy of naltrexone for the treatment of alcohol dependence was established in at least twenty-three placebo-controlled randomized clinical trials, with many fewer trials failing to show a significant between-groups difference. The demonstration that naltrexone is effective in the treatment of alcohol dependence followed many years of human and animal research, which investigated the role of the opioid system in mediating the response to pain and pleasure. In December 1994, the FDA approved naltrexone, the first new medication for alcohol dependence in nearly 50 years, to be used in conjunction with psychosocial support to treat alcohol dependence. Research demonstrated that when used in conjunction with a psychosocial treatment program, naltrexone results in better treatment outcomes, particularly reducing the risk of relapse to heavy drinking. The mechanism of action is theorized to be a reduction in craving or alcohol stimulation effects such that when alcohol is consumed in the presence of naltrexone, the individual does not report as much reward and thus does not drink heavily.

TREATMENT

Opioid Dependence. Naltrexone is usually used in conjunction with counseling and other rehabilitation services, as part of a structured and monitored treatment program. The best treatment results tend to occur in highly motivated, psychologically healthy individuals who are employed and well-functioning socially, especially when they face severe economic or legal consequences for failing treatment. For example, addicted health professionals whose treatment is required by their professional licensing boards and monitored as a condition of continued licensure will regularly take naltrexone for several years and remain abstinent from opioids. Some programs have reported five-year success rates as high as 95 percent. Most street addicts (e.g., those with unstable living situations who support their drug use by criminal activity) refuse to take naltrexone or, if started in treatment, quickly drop out. This pattern is believed to be due to the lack of rewarding effects and the blockade of such effects when opioid drugs are self-administered. Many such addicts prefer maintenance treatment with the synthetic opioid methadone, and others find even methadone non-rewarding, so they relapse. Use of the depot formulation of naltrexone for opioid addiction was not FDA approved as of 2008 but may provide an alternative to methadone and assure treatment adherence for at least thirty days.

Fifty mg of naltrexone blocks the effects of 25 mg of heroin for twenty-four hours, so the typical weekly naltrexone dose for the treatment of opioid dependence is 350 mg. The actual medication schedule is adjusted to the individual patient and may range from 50 mg every day to 150 mg every third day. Patients are put on the least frequent medication schedule possible to enhance patient cooperation and reduce the number of clinic visits. The use of long-acting naltrexone in the treatment of opioid dependence, which can be injected once a month and which slowly releases the medication into the body, could substantially reduce the frequency of required visits but is not FDA approved for use in opioid addiction as of 2008.

Care must be taken to avoid administering naltrexone to individuals still physically dependent on opioids. In opioid-dependent individuals, an antagonist will precipitate an acute opioid withdrawal syndrome. While not life-threatening, this syndrome can be extremely uncomfortable, with symptoms such as abdominal cramps; diarrhea; muscle, joint, and bone pain; runny nose (rhinorrhea); and goose bumps (piloerection). To avoid this situation, naltrexone is not administered to

patients until they have been free of opioid drugs for at least seven to ten days to allow dependence to wear off. To confirm the absence of dependence, patients may be challenged with the short-acting antagonist naloxone before starting on naltrexone.

Alcohol Dependence. Again naltrexone or any other addiction pharmacotherapy should be given in conjunction with appropriate counseling or participation in an addiction treatment program. Ideally, naltrexone is started after two to three days of abstinence but can be used even when patients continue to drink. Abstinence may reduce the chance of side effects and establishes a level of motivation for treatment. Patients with severe liver disease should not take naltrexone unless under very close monitoring. The usual starting dose is 50 mg per day for the oral medication although a starting dosage of 25 mg may reduce the chances of side effects. Doses between 25 and 150 mg have been used in treatment, though generally 50 or 100 mg provides sufficient coverage. The depot formulation has been shown to be effective in reducing heavy drinking among alcohol dependent individuals and has the advantage of providing thirty days of treatment coverage. Some studies have suggested patients with a family history of addiction or possibly with a specific genotype may be the most responsive to treatment. As with the treatment of opioid addiction, care must be taken to avoid treatment in patients currently taking an opioid either abusively or by prescription. Most studies have found that reduction in heavy drinking (bingeing) is the major beneficial effect of naltrexone treatment though some research also shows that the medication improved the rate of abstinence.

See also **Treatment: An Overview.**

BIBLIOGRAPHY

Ginzburg, H. M., & Glass, W. J. (1984). The role of the National Institute on Drug Abuse in the development of naltrexone. *Journal of Clinical Psychiatry, 45*(9), 39–41.

Gonzalez, J. P., & Brogden, R. N. (1988). Naltrexone: A review of its pharmacodynamic and pharmacokinetic properties and therapeutic efficacy in the management of opioid dependence. *Drugs, 35,* 192–213.

O'Malley, S. S., Jaffe, A. J., Chang, G., Schottenfeld, R. S., Meyer, R. E., & Rounsaville, B. (1992). Naltrexone and coping skills therapy for alcohol dependence. *Archives of General Psychiatry, 49,* 881–887.

Oslin, D. W., Berrettini, W., Kranzler, H. R., Pettinati, H., Gelernter, J., Volpicelli, J. R., et al. (2003). A functional polymorphism of the mu-opioid receptor gene is associated with naltrexone response in alcohol-dependent patients. *Neuropsychopharmacology, 28*(8), 1546–1552.

Pettinati, H. M., O'Brien, C. P., Rabinowitz, A. R., Wortman, S. P., Oslin, D. W., Kampman, K. M., et al. (2006). The status of naltrexone in the treatment of alcohol dependence: Specific effects on heavy drinking. *Journal of Clinical Psychopharmacology, 26*(6), 610–625.

Volpicelli, J. R., Alterman, A. I., Hayashida, M., & O'Brien, C. P. (1992). Naltrexone in the treatment of alcohol dependence. *Archives of General Psychiatry, 49,* 876–880.

DAVID A. GORELICK
REVISED BY DAVID OSLIN (2009)

SEROTONIN-UPTAKE INHIBITORS

Successful pharmacotherapy of substance-related disorders requires an understanding of the factors that contribute to the development and maintenance of drug-seeking behaviors. Within this framework, insight into the neurochemical basis for drug addiction and the workings of the brain's reward circuit is key. Preclinical studies have demonstrated the importance of the neurotransmitters serotonin and dopamine in mediating the rewarding effect of substance use. Drugs that increase serotonergic neurotransmission have, therefore, been studied as treatments for abuse of a variety of substances. Serotonin uptake inhibitors, which are generally marketed as antidepressants, block the reabsorption of serotonin and increase its concentration in the nerve synapse. As of the first decade of the twenty-first century, they show some promise as effective treatments for the abuse of alcohol and other drugs.

Additionally, substance abuse or dependence often co-occurs with psychiatric disorders, including depression and anxiety, and patients who have both a substance use disorder and a psychiatric disorder are, in general, more difficult to treat successfully. The cause-and-effect relationships are unclear: Researchers seek to know if depressed and anxious patients self-medicate with drugs and alcohol or if anxiety and depression are consequences of addiction. In any given patient, both are likely true to some degree. As many serotonin uptake inhibitors are indicated for the treatment of anxiety and depression, it stands to reason that they may be especially useful in patients who have both addiction and anxiety or depression.

ALCOHOL

Clinical and preclinical research since the 1980s has demonstrated an inverse relationship between serotonergic activity and alcohol use. However, evidence available as of 2008 suggests that serotonin uptake inhibitors are not consistently effective as treatment for alcohol abuse or dependence in heterogeneous groups. They do show promise in specific groups of alcoholics, including specific genetic groups, early- or late-onset alcoholics, and alcoholics with comorbid anxiety or depression. Some evidence suggests that there may be distinct subtypes of alcoholism that may be distinguishable by the type and complexity of the serotonergic dysfunction. Response to serotonin uptake inhibitors varies greatly by individual, with drinking reductions from 10 to 70 percent in some studies. A major challenge is predicting which patients will respond to treatment.

A 2004 study showed that lower risk/lower severity alcoholics showed a better response to sertraline, as measured by time to relapse, days drinking, days drinking heavily, drinks per drinking day, and number of participants who were continually abstinent. These gains were consistent out to six months after treatment ended. Similar to findings of a previous study on citalopram, this study found that among these lower risk/lower severity alcoholics, men responded to sertraline better than women did, with women failing to show a difference from placebo on several measures. This difference was not found in the higher risk/higher severity alcoholics. This study, when analyzed using a different approach, showed that sertraline was superior to placebo in reducing drinking in alcohol dependent patients with no personal or family history of depression but was no better than placebo in patients with a personal history of depression—a somewhat counterintuitive result. A large study of sertraline for treatment of co-occurring alcohol dependence and major depression showed no advantage of the serotonin uptake inhibitor compared with placebo, either on measures of drinking or depressive symptoms. It seems clear that studies are needed to determine which subtypes of alcohol abuse and dependence are most responsive to treatment with serotonin uptake inhibitors.

COCAINE

Cocaine is a common drug of abuse and is used in a variety of ways—by smoking, snorting, or injection. As of 2008, there were no FDA-approved drugs for the treatment of cocaine addiction. Preclinical studies suggested that serotonin plays an important role in the dopamine reward pathway that is activated by cocaine use, suggesting a possible role for serotonin uptake inhibitors in the treatment of cocaine dependence. A randomized, double blind, placebo-controlled study done in 2007 showed that citalopram was more effective than placebo in reducing the number of cocaine-positive urines in patients also being treated with cognitive-behavioral therapy and contingency management. However, similar studies with sertraline, paroxetine, and venlafaxine failed to show an effect.

OPIATES

Opiate addiction is most commonly treated with opiate-agonist therapy, such as methadone; however, treatment response is often incomplete. As of 2008, few studies of serotonin uptake inhibitors as treatment for opiate dependence had been conducted in humans. A 2007 study failed to show an effect of citalopram as compared to placebo as adjunct for methadone maintenance therapy. A 2002 study showed that sertraline was not effective as an adjunct to naltrexone treatment. Fluoxetine was shown to decrease the dropout rate in a naltrexone treatment program for heroin dependence, but it did not show a specific effect on opiate use.

NICOTINE

Nicotine is an extremely common drug of abuse with multiple and severe negative health effects. Several therapies exist for treatment of nicotine dependence, including nicotine replacement therapy, bupropion, and varenicline. A 2004 study indicated that fluoxetine eases nicotine withdrawal symptoms, including weight gain, but did not reduce smoking. A 2007 study showed that paroxetine was effective, as compared to placebo, in reducing cigarette smoking in patients with major depression.

Serotonin uptake inhibitors show promise for some role in the treatment of substance use disorders. Evidence suggests that they are effective in particular subtypes of alcohol dependence, and studies with cocaine and nicotine, though few in number, show promise. As of 2008, there was little evidence that serotonin uptake inhibitors are an effective treatment for opiate dependence, although they may have a role in increasing treatment attendance.

BIBLIOGRAPHY

Farren, C. K., & O'Malley, S. (2002). A pilot double blind placebo controlled trial of sertraline with naltrexone in the treatment of opiate dependence. *The American Journal on Addictions, 11*(3), 228–234.

Johnson, B. A. (2004). Role of the serotonergic system in the neurobiology of alcoholism: Implications for treatment. *CNS Drugs, 18*(15), 1105–1118.

Kranzler, H. R., Mueller, T., Cornelius, J., Pettinati, H. M., Moak, D., Martin, P. R., et al. (2006). Sertraline treatment of co-occurring alcohol dependence and major depression. *Journal of Clinical Psychopharmacology, 26,* 13–20.

Landabaso, M. A., Iraurgi, I., Jimenez-Lerma, J. M., Sanz, J., Fernadez de Corres, B., Araluce, K., et al. (1998). A randomized trial of adding fluoxetine to a naltrexone treatment programme for heroin addicts. *Addiction, 93*(5), 739–744.

Miyamoto, K., Yoshimura, R., Ueda, N., Sugita, A., Umene, W., Hori, H., et al. (2007). Effects of acute paroxetine treatment on the consumption of cigarette smoking and caffeine in depressed patients. *Human Psychopharmacology, 22*(7), 483–490.

Moeller, F. G., Schmitz, J. M., Steinberg, J. L., Green, C. M., Reist, C., Lai, L. Y., et al. (2007). Citalopram combined with behavioral therapy reduces cocaine use: A double-blind, placebo-controlled trial. *The American Journal of Drug and Alcohol Abuse, 33*(3), 367–378.

Naranjo, C. A., & Knoke, D. M. (2001). The role of selective serotonin reuptake inhibitors in reducing alcohol consumption. *The Journal of Clinical Psychiatry, 62*(Suppl. 20), 18–25.

Naranjo, C. A., Knoke, D. M., & Bremner, K. E. (2000). Variations in response to citalopram in men and women with alcohol dependence. *Journal of Psychiatry and Neuroscience, 25*(3), 269–275.

Pettinati, H. M., Dundon, W. & Lipkin, C. (2004). Gender differences in response to sertraline pharmacotherapy in Type A alcohol dependence. *The American Journal on Addictions, 13*(3), 236–247.

Pettinati, H. M., Kranzler, H. R., & Madaras, J. (2003). The status of serotonin-selective pharmacotherapy in the treatment of alcohol dependence. *Recent Developments in Alcoholism, 16,* 247–262.

Pettinati, H. M., Volpicelli, J. R., Luck, G., Kranzler, H. R., Rukstalis, M.R., & Cnaan, A. (2001). Double-blind clinical trial of sertraline treatment for alcohol dependence. *Journal of Clinical Psychopharmacology, 21*(2), 143–153.

Poling, J., Pruzinsky, R., Kosten, T. R., Gonsai, K., Sofuoglu, M., Gonzalez, G., et al. (2007). Clinical efficacy of citalopram alone or augmented with bupropion in methadone-stabilized patients. *The American Journal on Addictions, 16*(3), 187–194.

Saules, K. K., Schuh, L. M., Arfken, C. L., Reed, K., Kilbey, M. M., & Schuster, C. R. (2004). Double-blind placebo-controlled trial of fluoxetine in smoking cessation treatment including nicotine patch and cognitive-behavioral group therapy. *The American Journal on Addictions, 13*(5), 438–446.

CLAUDIO A. NARANJO
KAREN E. BREMNER
REVISED BY THOMAS R. KOSTEN (2009)
DEIDRE E. DAVIS (2009)

VACCINES

Drug addiction, broadly defined as a chronic relapsing illness, is characterized by compulsive drug-taking behavior resulting in impairment in social and occupational functioning (Koob & Kreek, 2007; Le Moal & Koob, 2007). The search for effective treatments has intensified recently due to a better understanding of the underlying neurobiological mechanisms contributing to drug use and relapse (Koob & Kreek, 2007; Volman, 2007; George et al., 2007).

Immunologic therapies have emerged recently as possible treatment options for drug dependence. Immunopharmacotherapy is based on the generation or administration of antibodies that are capable of binding the targeted drug before it can reach the brain. Pharmacological strategies based on agonists or antagonists of these drugs generally cause many undesired side effects and have yielded only limited success (Karila et al., 2008; Elkashef et al., 2007). A large amount of data has been gathered in recent years on the effects of active and passive immunization against cocaine, nicotine, phencyclidine (PCP), and methamphetamine in animal models, suggesting potential efficacy of these treatments in humans (Morland, 2006; Roiko et al., 2008; Orson et al., 2007; Kosten & Owens, 2005). However, these vaccines may not provide adequate protection against drug abuse in all individuals. For example, in a Phase II study of a cocaine conjugate vaccine with cholera toxin B (CTB) as the carrier protein only 30 percent of the subjects produced enough antibody to block the drug (Kosten & Singh, unpublished work), therefore improving the quantity and quality of IgG (a type of antibody) response to such vaccines, which is critical for their future success.

Some reports suggest that the immune system in a drug abuser is defective, which may explain the limited success of some vaccines (Cabral, 2006; Kelschenbach et al., 2008). Therefore, it is logical to investigate immunoregulatory cells and pathways involved in inducing humoral immune responses (i.e., those involving antibodies) for possible defects and to maximize their potential in upregulating the humoral immune response. It remains to be investigated whether antigen-presenting cells such as dendritic cell (DCs) populations and their functions in terms of signaling pathways/molecules are intact or defective in drug abusers. If the hypothesized defects are borne out, then an important question surfaces about whether their activities could be restored or maximized by using appropriate stimulatory agents or genetic vaccines.

The activities of helper and regulatory T cells are crucial for antibody production. Investigation into the role of these cell types in antidrug vaccination strategies warrants serious consideration and they should be exploited to enhance antibody production. The central aspect in all these vaccination strategies is B cells. It would be beneficial to devise strategies to produce long-lived hapten-specific plasma B cells and memory B cells. Furthermore, longevity of the specific antibodies for the abused substance is critically important. The formed antibodies should have a maximal half life to block the pharmacological activity of the drug for prolonged periods.

See also **Research, Animal Model: An Overview.**

BIBLIOGRAPHY

Cabral, G. A. (2006). Drugs of abuse, immune modulation, and AIDS. *Journal of Neuroimmune Pharmacology, 1*(3), 280–295.

Elkashef, A., Biswas, J., Acri, J. B., & Vocci, F. (2007). Biotechnology and the treatment of addictive disorders: New opportunities. *BioDrugs, 21*(4), 259–267.

George, O., Ghozland, S., Azar, M. R., Cottone, P., Zorrilla, E. P., Parsons, L. H., et al. (2007). CRF-CRF1 system activation mediates withdrawal-induced increases in nicotine self-administration in nicotine-dependent rats. *Proceedings of the National Academy of Sciences, 104*(43), 17198–17203.

Karila, L., Gorelick, D., Weinstein, A., Noble, F., Benyamina, A., Coscas, S., et al. (2008). New treatments for cocaine dependence: A focused review. *International Journal of Neuropsychopharmacology, 11*(3), 425–438.

Kelschenbach, J., Ninkovic, J., Wang, J., Krishnan, A., Charboneau, R., Barke, R., et al. (2008). Morphine withdrawal inhibits IL-12 induction in a macrophage cell line through a mechanism that involves cAMP. *Journal of Immunology, 180*(6), 3670–3679.

Koob, G., & Kreek, M. J. (2007). Stress, dysregulation of drug reward pathways, and the transition to drug dependence. *American Journal of Psychiatry, 164*(8), 1149–1159.

Kosten, T., & Owens, S. M. (2005). Immunotherapy for the treatment of drug abuse. *Pharmacology & Therapeutics, 108*(1), 76–85.

Le Moal, M., & Koob, G. F. (2007). Drug addiction: Pathways to the disease and pathophysiological perspectives. *European Neuropsychopharmacology, 17*(6–7), 377–393.

Morland, J. (2006). *Tidsskr Nor Laegeforen* [Vaccines against substance abuse]. *126*(22), 2974–2976.

Orson, F. M., Kinsey, B. M., Singh, R. A., Wu, Y., Gardner, T., Kosten, T. R., et al. (2007). The future of vaccines in the management of addictive disorders. *Current Psychiatry Reports, 9*(5), 381–387.

Roiko, S. A., Harris, A. C., Keyler, D. E., LeSage, M. G., Zhang, Y., & Pentel, P. R. (2008). Combined active and passive immunization enhances the efficacy of immunotherapy against nicotine in rats. *Journal of Pharmacology and Experimental Therapeutics, 325*, 985–993.

Volman, S. F. (2007). Evaluating the functional importance of neuroadaptions in addiction. *Scientific World Journal, 7*, 4–8.

RANA SINGH
THOMAS KOSTEN

TREATMENT, SPECIALTY APPROACHES TO

This entry includes the following essays:

ACUPUNCTURE

The art of acupuncture is an ancient and integral part of the armamentarium that has been used in China for the treatment of medical problems for more than 2,000 years. Acupuncture consists of inserting very fine needles into the skin at specific points intended to, according to traditional Chinese medicine, influence specific bodily functions or body parts. In the traditional Chinese view of the body, life energy (chi) circulates through pathways; blockage of the pathways leads to a deficiency of chi, or disease. The goal of the traditional acupuncturist is to open up the pathways and stimulate the movement of chi. The specific points for needle insertion are based on traditional anatomical maps that depict which pathways affect which bodily functions.

HISTORY OF ACUPUNCTURE IN THE UNITED STATES

Following the historic trip to China in 1972 of U.S. president Richard M. Nixon, considerable public interest in acupuncture was generated when news coverage showed that acupuncture was effective not only in relieving pain, but also in substituting for general anesthesia. The following year, H. L. Wen, a neurosurgeon in Hong Kong, reported a serendipitous observation that acupuncture with electrical stimulation (AES) eliminated withdrawal symptoms in a narcotics addict for whom Wen had intended to perform brain surgery to treat drug addiction. Four needles were inserted into the right hand (at the defined points IL-4 and SI-3) and in the arm (EH-4 and TB-9), and another two needles were inserted into the right ear (brainstem and shen men). Fifteen minutes after AES began, the patient reported a significant reduction in drug withdrawal symptoms, which disappeared altogether 30 minutes after AES was started. Notably, Wen's initial observations occurred prior to the discovery in 1975 of endogenous opioid substances in the brain (also called endorphins).

In a 1977 study, Wen noted that AES increased endorphin levels and relieved abstinence syndromes while simultaneously inhibiting the autonomic nervous system, primarily the parasympathetic nervous system. The findings by Wen and several other scientific groups that peripheral stimulation could release endogenous opioids in the central nervous system gave scientific credibility to the possibility that this traditional Chinese therapy could help to ameliorate a contemporary problem. Chronic or repeated exposure to opioids leads to adaptive changes in the central nervous system. Withdrawal symptoms occur when these drugs are abruptly discontinued. Because the administration of opioid drugs alleviates withdrawal, a reasonable hypothesis was that one's own endogenous opioids might do the same.

In 1985, Michael O. Smith founded the National Acupuncture Detoxification Association (NADA). Smith was interested in alternatives to methadone for detoxification. Based on Wen's work, Smith first used electrical stimulation together with acupuncture, but he later discarded the use of electrical stimulation. Eventually, a standard protocol was developed that used four or five acupuncture points on each ear. The NADA protocol of five treatment points is still regarded as the standard approach for this application.

In the early 1990s, the use of acupuncture in addiction treatment became popular with many people working in the criminal justice system. Most funding for treatment programs using acupuncture at that time came initially from the criminal justice system, rather than from the federal and state agencies that usually fund drug treatment programs. Although it should be emphasized that the scientific community has been unable to show the efficacy of acupuncture in properly controlled clinical studies, this relatively inexpensive and easily expanded procedure became the mainstay for a number of *drug courts*, where judges involved themselves directly in managing the treatment of drug offenders. Thus, as of 2008, it remained a popular approach, although scientific support for its effectiveness as a treatment for substance use disorders was lacking.

TECHNICAL PROCEDURES AND REVIEWS

As practiced in the United States, several technical procedures broadly described as acupuncture have been used. Standard bilateral acupuncture is the application of five needles to the concha and cartilage ridge of each ear at defined points (shen men, lung, sympathetic, kidney, and liver) determined from traditional Chinese anatomy maps. With unilateral acupuncture, the needles are applied to one ear. Acupressure involves applying pressure by hand or by an object to the same areas. Electroacupuncture applies low-level electric current to needles placed at the traditional points. With moxibustion, herbs are burned near the needles to add heat. With neuroelectric stimulation, low-dose electrical current is passed through surface electrodes. Some practitioners advocate the use of surface electrodes and special currents, designating this approach neuroelectrical therapy.

Many acupuncture practitioners in the United States belong to and are accredited by the American Association of Acupuncture and Oriental Medicine (AAAOM), founded in 1981. Others may be accredited by the National Acupuncture and Oriental Medicine Alliance (NAOMA), founded in 1992, which accepts a broader range of training than AAAOM does for purposes of certification.

In 1991, the National Institute on Drug Abuse (NIDA) sponsored a technical review of the current state of knowledge about the use of acupuncture in the treatment of alcoholism and other drug-dependence problems. One of the participants, George Ulett, noted that although there is some evidence that electrical stimulation through needles or electrodes placed at certain points on the body can release endogenous opioids and other neuropeptides in the central nervous system, little evidence exists that such opioid release is caused by the needles alone. Ulett asserted that a critical factor is the frequency characteristic of the current, not the specific placement site of needles or electrodes. This group of researchers concluded that part of the difficulty in deciding whether acupuncture is effective is the lack of standard terminology and standard methods.

A number of procedures, all called acupuncture, were being applied to a variety of drug and alcohol problems, but in different ways, over varying periods of time, with results measured in different ways. One study of acupuncture for alcohol detoxification, by Bullock and coworkers (1989), which came closest to being scientifically valid, used appropriate controls (i.e., placement of needles in non-specific sites) and staff who were blinded to which group was control and which group received acupuncture at specific bodily sites. This study found a far better outcome for patients in the specific body-site group than for controls.

The study also found that the difference persisted even when measured six months later. However, another research group using similar methodology could not replicate the findings and reported no difference between point-specific acupuncture, sham transdermal stimulation, or standard care (no acupuncture control) (Margolin et al., 2002). Further, Bullock and coworkers (2002) were unable to replicate their positive findings in a subsequent multi-center trial.

Many practitioners who have used acupuncture, even those who are convinced of its efficacy, report that only a small proportion of people who start treatment actually complete the typical series of ten to twenty treatments. Those who have used the technique believe that the minimal amount of treatment required for benefit is at least one twenty-minute session per day of bilateral acupuncture for at least ten days. In general, among both opioid-dependent and cocaine-dependent patients, those who have less severe dependence seem to fare the best.

The NIDA technical review panel concluded at the time of review in 1991 that no compelling evidence existed that acupuncture is an effective treatment for opiate or cocaine dependence. Nevertheless, they found no evidence that acupuncture is harmful. A major multi-site trial of acupuncture treatment for cocaine dependence found no evidence to support its effectiveness (Margolin et al., 2002).

See also **Cocaine; Drug Courts; Opiates/Opioids; Treatment, Stages/Phases of: Non-Medical Detoxification; U.S. Government Agencies: National Institute on Drug Abuse (NIDA).**

BIBLIOGRAPHY

Avants, S. K., Margolin, A., Holford, T. R., & Kosten, T. R. (2000). A randomized controlled trial of auricular acupuncture for cocaine dependence. *Archives of Internal Medicine, 160,* 2305–2312.

Brumbaugh, A. G. (1993). Acupuncture: New perspectives in chemical dependency treatment. *Journal of Substance Abuse Treatment, 10,* 35–43.

Bullock, M. L., Culliton, P. D., & Olander, R. T. (1989). Controlled trial of acupuncture for severe recidivist alcoholism. *Lancet, 1*(8652), 1435–1439.

Bullock, M. L., Kiresuk, T. J., Sherman, R. E., Lenz, S. K., Culliton, P. D., Boucher, T. A., et al. (2002). A large randomized placebo controlled study of auricular acupuncture for alcohol dependence. *Journal of Substance Abuse Treatment, 22,* 71–77.

Han, J. S. (2003). Acupuncture: Neuropeptide release produced by electrical stimulation of different frequencies. *Trends in Neurosciences, 26,* 17–22.

Han, J. S. (2004). Acupuncture and endorphins. *Neuroscience Letters, 361,* 258–261.

Margolin, A., Kleber, H. D., Avants, S. K., Konefal, J., Gawin, F. H., Stark, E., et al. (2002). Acupuncture for the treatment of cocaine addiction: A randomized controlled trial. *Journal of American Medical Association, 287*(1), 55–63.

McLellan, A. T., Grossman, J. B., & Haverkos, H. W. (1993). Acupuncture treatment for drug abuse: A technical review. *Journal of Substance Abuse Treatment, 10,* 569–576.

FRANCES R. LEVIN
HERBERT D. KLEBER
REVISED BY ANNE DAVIDSON (2001)
WEI-LI ZHU (2009)
LIN LU (2009)

HYPNOSIS

Hypnosis is a normal state of attentive, focused concentration with a relative suspension of peripheral awareness, a shift in attention mechanisms in the direction of focus at the expense of the periphery. Being hypnotized is something like looking through a telephoto lens. What is seen, is seen in great detail, but at the expense of context. The use of hypnosis has been associated with inducing a state of relaxation and comfort, with enhanced ability to attend to a therapeutic task, with the capacity to reduce pain and anxiety, and with heightened control over somatic function. For these reasons, hypnosis has been used with some benefit as an adjunct to the treatment of certain kinds of drug and alcohol abuse and addiction.

Therapeutic approaches involving hypnosis include using it as a substitute for the pleasure-inducing substance, taking a few minutes to induce a self-hypnotic state of relaxation (for example, by imaging oneself floating in a bathtub or a lake, or visualizing pleasant surroundings on an imaginary screen). In this strategy the hypnosis is a safe substitute for the pleasure-inducing effects of the drug. A second approach involves ego-enhancing techniques, providing the subject with encouragement, picturing himself or herself living well without the substance, and able to control the desire for it. A third approach involves instructing subjects to reduce or eliminate their craving for the drug. A fourth involves cognitive restructuring, diminishing the importance of the craving for the drug by focusing instead on a commitment to respect and protect the body by eliminating the damaging drug. One widely used technique for smoking control, for example, has people in hypnosis repeat to themselves three points: (1) For my body, smoking is a poison; (2) I need my body to live; (3) I owe my body respect and protection. This approach places an emphasis on a positive commitment to what the person is for, rather than paying attention to being against the drug, thereby keeping attention on protection rather than on abstinence.

Hypnosis has been most widely used in the treatment of nicotine dependence, and although the results vary, a number of large-scale studies indicate that even a single session of training in self-hypnosis can result in complete abstinence of six months or more by approximately one out of four smokers.

There are fewer systematic data regarding use of hypnosis with cocaine, opiate, or alcohol addiction. The success of the approach is complicated by the fact that the acute effects of substance intoxication and/or the chronic effects on cognitive function of alcohol and other drug abuse hampers hypnotic responsiveness, thereby diminishing the potential of addicted individuals to enter this state and benefit from it. Nonetheless, there may be occasional individuals who are sufficiently hypnotizable and motivated to use this approach as an adjunct to other treatment, diminishing the dysphoria and discomfort that can accompany withdrawal and abstinence while enhancing and supporting their commitment to a behavior change. Hypnosis can be used by licensed and trained physicians, psychologists, dentists, and other health-care professionals who have special training in its use. The treatment is employed in offices and clinics as well as in hospital settings. It should always be used as an adjunct to a broader treatment strategy.

Hypnosis is a naturally occurring mental state that can be tapped in a matter of seconds and mobilized as a means of enhancing control over

behavior, as well as the effects of withdrawal and abstinence, in motivated patients supervised by appropriately trained professionals.

See also **Nicotine; Withdrawal.**

BIBLIOGRAPHY

Botsford, D. (2007). *Hypnosis for smoking cessation: An NLP and hypnotherapy practitioner's manual.* Bethel, CT: Crown House Publishing.

Childress, A. R., et al. (1994). Can induced moods trigger drug-related responses in opiate abuse patients? *Journal of Substance Abuse Treatment, 11,* 17–23.

Haxby, D. G. (1995). Treatment of nicotine dependence. *American Journal of Health Systems Pharmacists, 52,* 265–281.

Orman, D. J. (1991). Reframing of an addiction via hypnotherapy: A case presentation. *American Journal of Clinical Hypnosis, 33,* 263–271.

Page, R. A., & Handley, G. W. (1993). The use of hypnosis in cocaine addiction. *American Journal of Clinical Hypnosis, 36,* 120–123.

Spiegel, H., & Spiegel, D. (2004). *Trance & treatment: Clinical uses of hypnosis* (2nd ed.). Washington, D.C.: American Psychiatric Publishing.

Stoil, M. J. (1989). Problems in the evaluation of hypnosis in the treatment of alcoholism. *Journal of Substance Abuse Treatment, 6,* 31–35.

Valbo, A., & Eide, T. (1996). Smoking cessation in pregnancy: The effect of hypnosis in a randomized study. *Addictive Behavior, 21,* 29–35.

DAVID SPIEGEL

ADOLESCENTS

Adolescent substance use is a significant public health problem in the United States. Data from the national *Youth Risk Behavior Survey* indicate that between 2004 and 2006, 43 percent of high school students reported having at least one drink of alcohol and 26 percent acknowledged one or more instances of heavy drinking (defined as consuming five or more drinks in a row) during the previous thirty days (Centers for Disease Control and Prevention, 2006). Similarly, among a large national sample of twelfth graders participating in the *2007 Monitoring the Future* study, 36 percent reported using an illicit drug during the past year (Johnston, O'Malley, Bachman, & Schulenberg, 2008). The most commonly used drugs were marijuana (32%), amphetamines (8%), sedatives (6%), hallucinogens (5%), cocaine (5%), and heroin (1%).

RISK FACTORS

Risk factors for adolescent substance use are well documented and involve influences at multiple individual and environmental levels (Schinke, Brounstein, & Gardner, 2002). At the individual level, adolescent substance use is associated with delinquent behavior, emotional problems such as anxiety or depression, and social skill deficits. Environmental influences are present in the contexts of the family, peer network, school, and neighborhood. For example, high levels of parental substance use, low parental supervision, and inconsistent family discipline are linked with elevated risk for using alcohol and illicit drugs. Association with deviant peers and peer substance use are consistently strong predictors of adolescent substance use. School-level influences include low academic achievement and low commitment to education. Neighborhoods characterized by high levels of poverty, crime, and drug availability are also associated with elevated rates of substance use among youth. The multi-determined nature of adolescent substance use suggests the need for comprehensive services that can address the various factors associated with this problem behavior.

LONG-TERM DELETERIOUS EFFECTS

Adolescent substance use is linked with a range of negative outcomes (Biglan, Brennan, Foster, & Holder, 2004). For example, adolescents who use alcohol and/or drugs are more likely than their non-substance-using peers to drop out of school early, which limits their opportunities to obtain employment later in life. Adolescents who use substances are also more likely to report earlier initiation of sexual activity, engagement in sexual activity with multiple partners, and inconsistent condom use, placing them at elevated risk for unplanned pregnancy and for contracting sexually transmitted diseases. Substance use also plays a role in other serious adolescent problem behaviors, such as motor vehicle accidents and suicide. Such findings highlight the need for effective interventions.

EVIDENCE-BASED INTERVENTIONS

Until the mid-1980s, relatively few interventions for adolescent substance abuse had received empirical support. After that time, however, several treatment approaches were developed and validated in randomized clinical trials. These include four family therapy models and cognitive behavioral therapy (CBT) delivered in individual and group formats.

Family Therapy. Although a wide and highly diverse range of family therapy models have been developed, four have emerged as having the most empirical support (Waldron & Turner, 2008): multisystemic therapy, functional family therapy, multidimensional family therapy, and brief strategic family therapy. These treatments share several important features. They each (a) are comprehensive and address known risk factors for substance use, (b) view the family as the primary vehicle for achieving favorable outcomes, (c) provide services in community-based settings, (d) use behavioral treatment principles, and (e) rely on strong quality assurance procedures to support therapist adherence to the treatment models.

Multisystemic Therapy. Multisystemic therapy (MST; Henggeler et al., 1998) is a comprehensive family- and community-based treatment for youth with serious substance use and delinquent behavior problems and who are at imminent risk of out-of-home placement. Treatment is provided by therapists using a home-based model of service delivery. Drawing upon evidence-based intervention strategies (e.g., CBT, pragmatic family therapy approaches), MST therapists individualize interventions to address the individual, family, peer, school, and neighborhood factors that are linked with the youth's behavioral and substance use problems, with caregivers viewed as the keys to achieving positive outcomes. For example, parent training techniques are often used to improve caregivers' ability to monitor their youth's whereabouts and provide consistent discipline. Similarly, with guidance from the therapist, caregivers also develop strategies to improve their youth's school performance, decrease his or her involvement with delinquent peers, and increase his or her participation in positive social activities (e.g., sports, church youth groups). Contingency management (CM), a widely supported substance abuse intervention with adults (Higgins, Silverman, & Heil, 2007), has been effectively integrated with MST to accelerate abstinence (Henggeler et al., 2006). Sheidow and Henggeler (2008) provide a detailed summary of MST substance-related outcomes with serious juvenile offenders and substance abusing juvenile offenders.

Functional Family Therapy. Functional Family Therapy (FFT; Alexander et al., 1998) includes three phases of intervention: (1) engagement and motivation, (2) behavior change, and (3) generalization. During the engagement and motivation phase, therapists work to create a positive therapist-family relationship and to increase motivation for change by behaving respectfully toward family members and working to reduce anger and other negative emotions among family members. During the behavior change phase, therapists use parent training, family communication training, problem-solving skills training, and behavioral contracting to improve family relations in ways that lead to positive changes in youths' behavior, including substance use. During the generalization phase, therapists work to maintain clinical improvements by linking families with longer-term support services in the community (e.g., mental health, social service agencies).

Multidimensional Family Therapy. Multidimensional Family Therapy (MDFT; Liddle, Dakof, & Diamond, 1991) is a multi-component intervention that aims to reduce adolescent substance use by intervening directly with the adolescent and with the multiple systems that influence his or her behavior (e.g., family, peer network, school). During the initial stages of treatment, therapists try to develop a strong working relationship with the family and conduct a comprehensive assessment of the adolescent's substance use and other problem behaviors. Therapists subsequently work to bring about positive changes through the use of individual- and systems-level interventions. For example, individual therapy is conducted with the adolescents to improve their emotional and behavioral functioning and drug refusal skills. In addition, individual sessions are conducted with caregivers to improve their own emotional well-being, access to social support, and family management practices. Family sessions focus on improving the caregiver-adolescent relationship, and community-level advocacy is conducted to enhance family members' interactions with external sources of influence (e.g., school staff, peers, juvenile justice system personnel).

Brief Strategic Family Therapy. The underlying principle of brief strategic family therapy (BSFT; Szapocznik & Kurtines, 1989) is that adolescent substance use results from maladaptive interactions within the family. BSFT includes three primary intervention components: joining, diagnosis, and restructuring. In the early phases of treatment, the BSFT therapist works to join with the family by establishing a close therapeutic relationship with each participating family member. Over time, the therapist develops hypotheses about the family's diagnosis, which refers to those interactional patterns that encourage adolescent problem behavior. For example, the therapist might determine that adolescent substance use is influenced, in part, by inconsistent discipline and poor communication between the adolescent and his or her caregivers. Once identified, the BSFT therapist works to restructure these maladaptive family interactions using various techniques such as reframing, boundary setting, and communication skills training.

Individual- and Group-Based Cognitive Behavioral Therapy. Individual- and group-based CBT interventions are based on principles of social learning theory. According to this theory, adolescents may begin using alcohol or illicit drugs because this behavior is modeled by others in their home, school, or community. Once initiated, substance use can be maintained by a variety of factors. For instance, adolescents might continue to use substances because they produce pleasant feelings, help relieve anxiety or stress, or help the youth gain acceptance from peers.

Whether delivered in an individual or group setting, CBT interventions are designed to teach adolescents how to identify internal (e.g., stress) and environmental (e.g., parties) triggers for substance use and to develop strategies for avoiding those triggers. Adolescents are also taught various drug refusal and problem-solving skills as well as more positive strategies for coping with stress and anxiety. In some CBT interventions, motivational techniques are used during the initial sessions to help motivate adolescents to change their behavior. Unfortunately, and in contrast with the aforementioned family therapy models, many of the family, peer, and community-level risk factors for adolescent substance use are rarely addressed directly in the context of CBT. Nevertheless, several individual- and group-based CBT interventions have received empirical support (Waldron & Turner, 2008).

It should be noted, however, that there is debate in the field regarding the use of group treatment for adolescents with substance use and other externalizing behavior problems. A few early studies found that the aggregation of antisocial adolescents in groups can actually intensify their problem behavior (Dishion, McCord, & Poulin, 1999). Other investigators, however, have reported positive effects of group treatment for substance-abusing adolescents (Burleson, Kaminer, & Dennis, 2006; Waldron et al., 2001). Some theorists have hypothesized that the likelihood of negative effects of group treatment probably depends on the level of structure of the group and the skill level of the group leader (Dishion & Dodge, 2005). Nonetheless, more research is needed to help reconcile these discrepant findings.

FREQUENTLY USED TREATMENTS WITH LITTLE EMPIRICAL SUPPORT

Despite the frequent use of residential, inpatient, and twelve-step (i.e., Alcoholics or Narcotics Anonymous) programs in the adolescent substance-use treatment field, their effectiveness has not been established in rigorous research (Brown & Abrantes, 2006). Residential and inpatient interventions might be indicated if the adolescent poses significant safety concerns and his or her needs cannot be addressed in a less restrictive environment. Reviewers have noted, however, that the long-term effects of these restrictive interventions may be limited (American Academy of Child and Adolescent Psychiatry, 2005). For example, in light of the multiple family- and community-level risk factors for adolescent substance use, removing youth from their natural environment (sending them to residential treatment) without altering that environment will likely result in only temporary reductions in substance use. Once youth are discharged from these programs, they often resume their substance use because the factors that support such use (i.e., family, peer, school, and neighborhood influences) have not been addressed. Finally, some data suggest that twelve-step programs can be helpful

when used as an adjunct to more formal treatment (Williams & Chang, 2000), although these programs have not been evaluated in controlled studies.

Extensive research has documented the prevalence and correlates of alcohol and drug use among youth, and this body of work strongly supports the view that substance use is multi-determined, involving influences at multiple environmental levels. Based largely on this research, several family-based treatments were developed, and these proved effective in reducing adolescent substance use. Individual- and group-based CBT interventions also emerged as having some empirical support. Although widely used, scant evidence supports the effectiveness of residential, inpatient, and twelve-step programs, and additional research was needed as of 2008 to determine the short- and long-term effects of these approaches.

See also **Adolescents and Drug Use.**

BIBLIOGRAPHY

Alexander, J., Barton, C., Gordon, D., Grotpeter, J., Hansson, K., Harrison, R., et al. (1998). *Blueprints for violence prevention, Vol. 3: Functional family therapy.* Boulder, CO: Center for the Study and Prevention of Violence.

American Academy of Child and Adolescent Psychiatry. (2005). Practice parameters for the assessment and treatment of children and adolescents with substance use disorders. *Journal of the American Academy of Child and Adolescent Psychiatry, 44,* 609–621.

Biglan, A., Brennan, P. A., Foster, S. L., & Holder, H. D. (2004). *Helping adolescents at risk: Prevention of multiple problem behaviors.* New York: Guilford Press.

Brown, S. A., & Abrantes, A. M. (2006). Substance use disorders. In D. A. Wolfe & E. J. Mash (Eds.), *Behavioral and emotional disorders in adolescents: Nature, assessment, and treatment* (pp. 226–256). New York: Guildford Press.

Burleson, J. A., Kaminer, Y., & Dennis, M. L. (2006). Absence of iatrogenic or contagion effects in adolescent group therapy: Findings from the cannabis youth treatment study. *American Journal of Addictions, 15,* 4–15.

Centers for Disease Control and Prevention. (2006). Youth risk behavior surveillance, 2005. *Morbidity and Mortality Weekly Report, 55*(SS–5), 1–108.

Dishion, T. J., & Dodge, K. A. (2005). Peer contagion in interventions for children and adolescents: Moving toward an understanding of the ecology and dynamics of change. *Journal of Abnormal Child Psychology, 33,* 395–400.

Dishion, T. J., McCord, J., & Poulin, F. (1999). When interventions harm: Peer groups and problem behavior. *American Psychologist, 54,* 755–764.

Henggeler, S. W., Halliday-Boykins, C. A., Cunningham, P. B., Randall, J., Shapiro, S. B., & Chapman, J. E. (2006). Juvenile drug court: Enhancing outcomes by integrating evidence-based treatments. *Journal of Consulting and Clinical Psychology, 74,* 42–54.

Henggeler, S. W., Schoenwald, S. K., Borduin, C. M., Rowland, M. D., & Cunningham, P. B. (1998). *Multisystemic treatment of antisocial behavior in children and adolescents.* New York: Guilford Press.

Higgins, S. T., Silverman, K., & Heil, S. H. (2007). *Contingency management in substance abuse treatment.* New York: Guildford Press.

Johnston, L. D., O'Malley, P. M., Bachman, J. G., & Schulenberg, J. E. (2008). *Monitoring the Future national results on adolescent drug use: Overview of key findings, 2007* (NIH Publication No. 08–6418). Bethesda, MD: National Institute on Drug Abuse.

Liddle, H. A., Dakof, G. A., & Diamond, G. (1991). Adolescent substance abuse: Multidimensional family therapy in action. In E. Kaufman & P. Kaufman (Eds.), *Family therapy with drug and alcohol abuse* (pp. 120–171). Boston, MA: Allyn & Bacon.

Schinke, S., Brounstein, P., & Gardner, S. (2002). *Science-based prevention programs and principles* (DHHS Publication SMA 03–3764). Rockville, MD: Center for Substance Abuse Prevention, Substance Abuse, and Mental Health Services Administration.

Sheidow, A. J., & Henggeler, S. W. (2008). Multisystemic therapy with substance using adolescents: A synthesis of the research. In A. Stevens (Ed.), *Crossing frontiers: International developments in the treatment of drug dependence,* (pp. 11–33). Brighton, England: Pavilion Publishing.

Szapocznik, J., & Kurtines, W. M. (1989). *Breakthroughs in family therapy with drug-abusing and problem youth.* New York: Springer.

Waldron, H. B., Slesnick, N., Brody, J. L., Turner, C. W., & Peterson, T. R. (2001). Treatment outcomes for adolescent substance abuse at 4- and 7-month assessments. *Journal of Consulting and Clinical Psychology, 69,* 802–813.

Waldron, H. B., & Turner, C. W. (2008). Evidence-based psychosocial treatments for adolescent substance abuse. *Journal of Clinical Child and Adolescent Psychology, 37,* 238–261.

Williams, R. J., & Chang, S. Y. (2000). A comprehensive and comparative review of adolescent substance abuse

treatment outcome. *Clinical Psychology: Science and Practice, 7,* 138–166.

SCOTT W. HENGGELER
MICHAEL R. MCCART

OLDER ADULTS

In the United States and many other nations, older adult populations are growing rapidly. "Older adults" have been variously defined in the literature, ranging from age 50 and over to age 65 and over. According to the U.S. Census Bureau (2003), by the year 2030, approximately 69 million Americans will be age 65 or older. Along with a growing demand for other health-care services, the substance abuse treatment needs of older adults are also increasing. For example, a 2003 study analyzed the growth in the size of the older population, taking into consideration the levels of alcohol and drug consumption among baby boomers (which are higher than those of the current elderly cohort), and projected that the number of adults age 50 and over in need of drug and alcohol abuse treatment will double by 2023 (Gfroerer et al., 2003).

RISKS FOR OLDER ADULTS

Researchers and clinicians are becoming more aware of the specific alcohol and drug problems experienced by older adults, and they have begun to develop strategies to address the specific treatment needs of this population, particularly in regard to the substantial medical, social, and personal costs associated with alcohol and drug problems in older adults, which include gastrointestinal, cardiovascular, endocrine, and neurological disorders (Gambert & Katsoyannis, 1995). Because alcohol sensitivity increases with age, older adults are more vulnerable than younger adults are to these problems. Further, the risks of delirium, adverse medication interactions, and falls are also increased in this age group. Finally, as is true for the population in general, a substantial number of older adults who commit suicide have a history of alcohol dependence (Waern, 2003).

Alcohol remains the most common substance of abuse among older adults. In community samples, the prevalence of alcohol abuse or dependence is approximately 1 percent to 3 percent for men over age 65, and .5 percent to 1 percent for women over

65 (Bucholz, Sheline, & Helzer, 1995). Due to the medical and psychiatric disorders associated with heavy alcohol use, clinical samples have consistently shown an even higher prevalence. Prescription drug misuse by older adults is also a significant concern, because older adults are more likely than younger adults to take several medications concurrently. Older adults are among the patient groups at highest risk for the misuse of medications resulting in dependence (Simoni-Wastila & Strickler, 2004). When using multiple medications, adverse drug interactions (or interactions between drugs and alcohol) are also potential problems, due to the greater number of medications taken by this population, as well as their greater vulnerability to adverse drug reactions.

SCREENING AND TREATMENT REFERRAL

The identification of alcohol or drug abuse can be more challenging in older adults than it is in younger populations. Older adults tend to drink at home and are less likely than younger adults to draw the attention of law enforcement, the courts, and the other agencies that often refer younger people to alcohol and drug treatment services. Older people are also less likely to have noticeable problems at work, school, or childrearing, mainly because they are less likely to have these types of responsibilities. As a result, there is a reduced visibility of addiction among older adults, and thus fewer opportunities to identify older patients in need of treatment.

Medical and social service appointments are important screening opportunities. A study of adults in a managed care outpatient program found that older patients were more likely than younger patients to report that a physician encouraged them to enter the program (Satre, Mertens, Areán & Weisner, 2003). In contrast, younger adults were more likely to report that an employer had recommended treatment. This suggests that health providers play an especially important role in helping to motivate older adults to seek treatment.

The Center for Substance Abuse Treatment has recommended that all older adults be screened for alcohol misuse during routine medical appointments. This provides an opportunity to identify those in need of specialized services. When screening, providers should ask older adults how much

they typically drink, keeping in mind that no more than one standard drink per day is recommended for men and women over age 65. In addition to questions regarding quantity and frequency of alcohol consumption, screening instruments may be helpful in determining the severity of any problems (Fink et al., 2002). Where significant misuse of alcohol or a dependence on prescription or illegal drugs is present, referral to an outpatient or residential treatment program may be appropriate.

STUDIES OF OLDER ADULTS IN TREATMENT

There is, however, comparatively little research on treatment outcomes among older populations. Studies conducted in mixed-age settings have found that older adults stay in treatment longer and have post-treatment abstinence outcomes as good as or better than those of younger adults. In a study conducted in a large managed care outpatient program that included 12-step and relapse-prevention components, older patients had several clinical characteristics associated with good outcomes (Satre, Mertens, Areán & Weisner, 2003). Older adults (age 55 and over) had lower rates of drug dependence (versus dependence only on alcohol), scored lower on a hostility measure, and were more likely to state that total abstinence (versus controlled use) was their goal of treatment, compared with adults aged 18 to 39. These factors were associated with abstinence six months post-treatment. Thus, the study helped to demonstrate some of the strengths that older adults may bring to treatment.

Even though older adults appear to succeed reasonably well in mixed-age settings, limited research suggests that they may do even better in treatment settings where only older adults are present (Blow, 1998; Kofoed et al., 1987). For one thing, age-specific groups may facilitate sharing between patients with similar life experiences and treatment issues. However, funding constraints may limit many service agencies from providing a wholly separate treatment program for older adults. Within mixed-age chemical dependency programs, therefore, it may be beneficial (and more feasible) to provide a weekly group session for older patients as a supplement to other clinic services.

The lack of women in studies of treatment for older adults creates a significant gap in the literature (Blow, 2000). Because much of the treatment outcome research has been conducted in Veteran's Administration programs, women have generally not been included. However, some studies have examined gender differences among older adults in treatment. One study looked at gender differences among alcohol-dependent adults aged 55 and over in outpatient treatment at Kaiser Permanente (Satre, Mertens & Weisner, 2004). Both clinical characteristics and abstinence outcomes were examined in this study. At the point of treatment entry, women and men had comparable drinking levels, although the women reported a later onset of heavy drinking. Women, however, stayed in treatment longer and had significantly higher rates of abstinence six months following treatment than men. While further research is needed, these findings show that clinically important gender differences may exist among older adults in treatment.

TREATMENT STRATEGIES
Service providers addressing alcohol and drug problems in older adults should take into account the specific needs of the individual, such as severity of addiction and overall level of functioning. Not all patients may need formal substance abuse treatment. Older adults considered "at risk" of developing alcohol-related health problems because they drink above recommended limits but do not meet criteria for substance abuse or dependence appear to benefit from brief interventions to reduce drinking (Fleming et al., 1999). Such individuals are not likely to seek out formal treatment, but they may come to the attention of health and social service agencies, especially if providers conduct regular screening. For these older adults, brief interventions (usually one to five sessions) are designed to motivate individuals to limit the amount of alcohol they consume. The interventions focus on health effects and other problems associated with alcohol misuse, and they are effective in reducing drinking to safer levels (Blow and Barry, 2000). These sessions may be conducted in primary care or other settings where adults receive services.

In traditional outpatient alcohol and drug treatment settings, relatively straightforward adaptations that consider patient age can substantially increase treatment effectiveness. For example, to accommodate possible hearing loss and cognitive changes (if these are present), it may be helpful to speak slowly and more loudly, use simpler language, and present information at a slower pace, with frequent repetition of material to assist in learning (Satre, Knight & David, 2006). Assistive listening devices such as earphones and an amplifier may be useful with hearing-impaired patients. In a group context, it may be necessary for leaders to be more active and provide more structure than they would with younger patients. This could include taking the lead in introducing topics for discussion or encouraging relatively quiet group members to participate more fully.

Confrontational tactics do not generally work well with older patients. A better approach is to increase motivation by focusing on the reasons for older people to maintain sobriety. These include maintaining independence and good health, improving financial security, avoiding depression, and repairing relationships with family members who may have become estranged in the course of addiction. These concerns are generally applicable in treatment.

Topics that should be addressed in the treatment of older adults may be somewhat different than those that are important in working with younger patients. For example, the loss of a spouse or partner may lead to increased drinking among individuals who may already have been heavy consumers of alcohol. Such patients are likely to be struggling with grief, and they may therefore need to use some of their session time to explore their feelings of loss. In addition, an important treatment task for these patients is to identify new sources of social support. A development of more effective coping strategies will help to reduce their reliance on alcohol or drugs in coping with feelings of sadness. Retirement is another potentially stressful late-life transition, and some retirees may cope with the end of a career by increasing their drinking. Other issues to address in treatment may include housing problems, decreased physical mobility, and comorbid depression and anxiety. To help address these challenges, the coordination of substance abuse treatment with medical and social services is highly desirable.

CONCLUSION

Drug and alcohol abuse pose a significant threat to the health and well-being of older adults, and prevalence is likely to increase with the aging of the baby boom generation. For these reasons, health and social service providers should be attentive to the potential for substance misuse among older adults. Fortunately, there is evidence that older adults benefit from interventions to reduce harmful drinking or drug use. Studies in this area strongly support screening for substance problems among older adults, particularly in medical and social service contexts. For those with an alcohol or drug problem, brief interventions or referral to formal substance abuse treatment programs may be effective.

Clinicians working in the alcohol and drug abuse treatment field have a responsibility to understand the specific treatment needs of older patients. Adaptations of existing treatment strategies to suit the special needs of older patients are likely to be useful in providing services to this important and rapidly growing population.

See also **Aging, Drugs, and Alcohol; Alcohol; Complications: Cognition; Prescription Drug Abuse; Risk Factors for Substance Use, Abuse, and Dependence: An Overview; Treatment: An Overview of Alcohol Abuse/Dependence; Treatment: An Overview of Drug Abuse/Dependence; Treatment, Stages/Phases of: Screening and Brief Intervention.**

BIBLIOGRAPHY

Blow, F. C. (1998). *Substance abuse among older adults.* Treatment Improvement Protocol (TIP) Series 26. DHHS Publication (SMA) 98-3179. Rockville, MD: U.S. Department of Health and Human Services, Center for Substance Abuse Treatment.

Blow, F. C. (2000). Treatment of older women with alcohol problems: Meeting the challenge for a special population. *Alcoholism: Clinical and Experimental Research, 24*(8), 1257–1266.

Blow, F. C., & Barry, K. L. (2000). Older patients with at-risk and problem drinking patterns: New developments in brief interventions. *Journal of Geriatric Psychiatry and Neurology, 13*(3), 115–123.

Bucholz, K. K., Sheline, Y. & Helzer, J. E. (1995). The epidemiology of alcohol use, problems, and dependence in elders: A review. In T. P. Beresford & E. S. Gomberg (Eds.), *Alcohol and aging* (pp. 3–18). New York: Oxford University Press.

Fink, A., Morton, S. C., Beck, J. C., Hays, R. D., Spritzer, A., Oishi, S. & Moore, A. A. (2002). The alcohol-related problems survey: Identifying hazardous and harmful drinking in older primary care patients. *Journal of the American Geriatrics Society, 50*(10), 1717–1722.

Fleming, M. F., Manwell, L. B., Barry, K. L., Adams, W., & Stuffacher, E. A. (1999). Brief physician advice for alcohol problems in older adults: A randomized community-based trial. *Journal of Family Practice, 48*(5), 378–384.

Gambert, S. R., & Katsoyannis, K. K. (1995). Alcohol-related medical disorders of older heavy drinkers. In T. P. Beresford & E. S. Gomberg (Eds.), *Alcohol and aging* (pp. 70–81). New York: Oxford University Press.

Gfroerer, J., Penne, M., Pemberton, M., & Folsom, M. (2003). Substance abuse treatment need among older adults in 2020: The impact of the aging baby-boom cohort. *Drug and Alcohol Dependence, 69*(2), 127–135.

Kofoed, L. L., Tolson, R. L., Atkinson, R. M., Toth, R. L., & Turner, J. A. (1987). Treatment compliance of older alcoholics: An elder-specific approach is superior to "mainstreaming." *Journal of Studies on Alcohol, 48*(1), 47–51.

Satre, D. D., Mertens, J. R., Areán, P. A., & Weisner, C. (2003). Contrasting outcomes of older versus middle-aged and younger adult chemical dependency patients in a managed care program. *Journal of Studies on Alcohol, 64*(4), 520–530.

Satre, D. D., Mertens, J. R., & Weisner, C. (2004). Gender differences in older adult treatment outcomes for alcohol dependence. *Journal of Studies on Alcohol, 65,* 638–642.

Satre, D. D., Knight, B. G., & David, S. (2006). Cognitive behavioral interventions with older adults: Integrating clinical and gerontological research. *Professional Psychology: Research and Practice, 37*(5), 489–498.

Simoni-Wastila, L., & Strickler, G. (2004). Risk factors associated with problem use of prescription drugs. *American Journal of Public Health, 94*(2), 266–268.

U.S. Bureau of the Census (2003). *Aging in the United States: Past, present, and future.* Washington, DC: Department of Commerce. http://www.census.gov/.

Waern, M. (2003). Alcohol dependence and misuse in elderly suicides. *Alcohol and Alcoholism, 38*(3), 249–254.

DEREK D. SATRE
SARAH S. OLSON

THERAPEUTIC COMMUNITIES

Therapeutic communities (TCs) are drug-free residential treatment facilities for drug and/or alcohol addiction. TCs emerged in the 1960s as a self-help alternative to the conventional medical and psychiatric approaches being used at that time.

Most traditional TCs have similar features, including their organizational structure, staffing patterns, perspectives, rehabilitative regimes, and a twelve- to eighteen-month duration of stay. They differ greatly, however, in size (30–600 beds) and client demography. Most people entering TCs have used multiple drugs—including tobacco, marijuana, alcohol, opiods, pills, and, recently, cocaine and crack-cocaine. In addition to their substance abuse, most TC clients also have a considerable degree of psychosocial dysfunction (Jainchill, 1994). In traditional TCs, 70 to 75 percent of clients are men, but admission for women is increasing. Most community-based TCs are integrated across gender, race/ethnicity, and age. Primary clinical staff are usually former substance abusers who were rehabilitated and trained. Other staff are the professionals who provide medical, mental health, vocational, educational, family-counseling, fiscal, administrative, and legal services.

Traditional TCs share a defining view of substance abuse as a deviant behavior, which may be attributed to psychological factors, poor family effectiveness, and, frequently, to socioeconomic disadvantage. Drug abuse is thus seen as a disorder of the whole person and recovery as a change in lifestyle and personal identity. As part of the recovery process, TCs seek to eliminate antisocial attitudes and activity, develop employable skills, and inculcate prosocial attitudes and values. This TC view of recovery is based upon several broad assumptions: the client's motivation to change, the client's main contribution to the change process (*self-help*), the mediation of this recovery through peer confrontation and sharing in groups (*mutual self-help*), the affirmation of socially responsible roles through a positive social network, and the understanding that treatment is a necessarily intense "episode" in a drug user's life.

Diverse elements and activities within the TC foster rehabilitative change. Junior, intermediate, and senior peer levels stratify the *community*, or the family. The TC's basic program elements, consisting of individual counseling and various group processes, make up the therapeutic and educative elements of the change process. The daily activities, including morning meetings, seminars, house meetings, and general meetings facilitate assimilation into the community as a *context for social learning*. Clients are oriented into the program during the *orientation-induction* stage. They progress through the *primary treatment* stage of the program by achieving plateaus of stable behavioral change. Client development reflects their changing relationship with the community, characterized as *compliance*, *conformity*, and *commitment*. Finally, *reentry* represents the final program stage where the skills needed in the greater social environment are fostered through increased self-management and decision making.

The effectiveness of the traditional long-term residential TC, as described here, has been well-documented (De Leon, 1997, 2000). Today, TCs include a wide range of programs serving diverse clients who use a variety of drugs and present complex social/psychological problems. Client differences, clinical requirements, and funding realities have all encouraged the development of modified residential TCs with shorter stays (3, 6 and 12 months) as well as TC-oriented day treatment and outpatient models. Most traditional TCs have expanded their social services or incorporated new interventions to address the needs of special populations such as adolescents, mothers and children, homeless, mentally ill chemical abusers, and prison inmates. In these modifications the cross-fertilization of personnel and methods from the traditional TC, mental health, and human services portends the evolution of a new therapeutic community.

See also **Sobriety.**

BIBLIOGRAPHY

De Leon, G. (Ed.). (1997). *Community as method: Therapeutic communities for special populations and special settings.* Westport, CT: Greenwood Publishing Group, Inc.

De Leon, G. (2000). *The therapeutic community: Theory, model, and method.* New York: Springer Publishing Company.

Inciardi, J. A., Martin, S. S., & Butzin, C. A. (2004). Five-year outcomes of therapeutic community treatment of drug-involved offenders after release. *Crime & Delinquency, 50,* (1) 88–107.

Jainchill, N. (1994). Comorbidity and therapeutic community treatment. In F. M. Tims, G. De Leon, & N. Jainchill (Eds.), *Therapeutic community: Advances in research and application.* National Institute on Drug Abuse Research Monograph 144. Publication no. 94-3633 (pp. 209–231). Rockville, MD: National Institute on Drug Abuse.

Rawlings, B. (2001). *Therapeutic communities for the treatment of drug users.* London: Jessica Kingsley Publishers.

GEORGE DE LEON

TREATMENT, STAGES/ PHASES OF

This entry includes the following essays:
INITIATION OF ABSTINENCE
MEDICAL DETOXIFICATION
NON-MEDICAL DETOXIFICATION
SCREENING AND BRIEF INTERVENTION
RELAPSE PREVENTION
STABILIZATION
AFTERCARE

INITIATION OF ABSTINENCE

Individuals recovering from substance-use disorders (SUD), irrespective of treatment type (e.g., 12-step or cognitive behavioral) or modality (e.g., outpatient, inpatient, detoxification, or residential), achieve significant improvement in their substance-use behavior, including becoming abstinent, via various pathways. For example, it is not uncommon for individuals to significantly reduce their substance use prior to initiating treatment, as reported by Elizabeth E. Epstein and coworkers (2005), and Jon Morgenstern and colleagues (2007). Alternatively, some individuals do not significantly improve their substance-use behavior until after extensive treatment and/or participation in self-help groups (e.g., Alcoholics Anonymous or Narcotics Anonymous). In addition, many people substantially improve their substance-use behavior in response to undergoing assessment for their substance use, which contributes to both clinical improvements (e.g., reduced substance use; Clifford et al., 2007) and enhanced treatment participation (Maisto et al., 2007a).

Although it is likely that significant differences exist between early and late treatment responders, as well as differences between those substance users who modify their behavior with and without professional assistance, relatively little is known about the factors that differentiate these groups. Likely factors in this distinction include biological susceptibility; environmental factors such as unemployment, homelessness, and social support; clinical factors such as comorbidity and SUD severity; and personal factors such as the motivation to change and self-efficacy.

Individuals receiving treatment for SUD often achieve significant but varying periods of abstinence interspersed with periods of problematic substance use and psychological and/or social distress. It is not clear to what extent changes in substance use are associated with changes in other areas of functioning (e.g., employment) or how these distinct domains of functioning are related temporally. A major challenge facing clinicians who treat substance users is the maintenance of behavioral change, particularly a reduction in substance use. In this regard, it appears that the first year following treatment initiation is a critical period. For example, Stephen A. Maisto and colleagues (2007b) investigated the stability of alcohol-use patterns across Project Match's three-year follow-up period and found that 71 percent of subjects who abstained during the first year reported still being abstinent at three years, 69 percent of the heavy drinkers continued to drink heavily, and 50 percent of the moderate drinkers reported either continued moderate alcohol use or abstinence.

James R. McKay and Richard V. Weiss (2001) reported that SUD treatment outcomes were associated with client treatment performance and pro-recovery behaviors (e.g., coping or self-help participation). As with alcohol treatment outcomes, the first year following drug treatment may be especially important with respect to longer-term substance use. D. Dwayne Simpson and colleagues (2002), for example, reported that among a national cocaine treatment sample, the large decreases in cocaine use observed one year post-treatment were sustained at the year five follow-up.

Thus, it appears that no specific treatment stage or phase may be associated with the onset of abstinence; rather, abstinence can, and does, occur at any point. What appears to be important for better longer-term functioning is a period of sustained abstinence, or at least the avoidance of frequent heavy substance use, particularly during the initial one-year post-treatment period.

See also **Alcoholism: Abstinence versus Controlled Drinking.**

BIBLIOGRAPHY

Clifford, P. R., Maisto, S. A., & Davis, C. M. (2007). Alcohol treatment research assessment exposure subject reactivity effects: Part I—alcohol use and related consequences. *Journal of Studies on Alcohol and Drugs, 68*, 519–528.

Epstein, E. E., Drapkin, M. L., Yusko, D. A., Cook, S. M., McCrady, B. S., & Jensen, N. K. (2005). Is alcohol assessment therapeutic? Pretreatment change in drinking among alcohol-dependent women. *Journal of Studies on Alcohol, 6*, 369–378.

Maisto, S. A., Clifford, P. R., & Davis, C. M. (2007a). Alcohol treatment research assessment exposure subject reactivity effects: Part II—treatment engagement and involvement. *Journal of Studies on Alcohol and Drugs, 68*, 529–533.

Maisto, S. A., Clifford, P. R., Stout, R. L., & Davis, C. M. (2007b). Moderate drinking in the first year after treatment as a predictor of three-year outcomes. *Journal of Studies on Alcohol and Drugs, 68*, 419–427.

McKay, J. R., & Weiss, R. V. (2001). A review of temporal effects and outcome predictors in substance abuse treatment studies with long-term follow-ups: Preliminary results and methodological issues. *Evaluation Review, 25*(2), 113–161.

Morgenstern, J., Irwin, T. W., Wainberg, M. L., Parsons, J. T., Muench, F., Bux, D., et al. (2007). A randomized controlled trial of goal choice interventions for alcohol use disorders among men-who-have-sex-with-men. *Journal of Consulting and Clinical Psychology, 75*, 72–84.

Simpson, D. D., Joe, G. W., & Broome, K. M. (2002). A national 5-year follow-up of treatment outcomes for cocaine dependence. *Archives of General Psychiatry, 59*, 538–544.

PATRICK R. CLIFFORD

MEDICAL DETOXIFICATION

Medical detoxification can be defined as the use of medical interventions to facilitate safe withdrawal from psychoactive substances. Implicit in the term is the assumption that alcohol and drugs are toxic and the process of recovery must involve the removal of these toxins and their effects from the system. Besides its role in individuals addicted to a substance, detoxification may also be necessary in some patients who may not be addicted in the behavioral sense but have developed physiological dependence due to extended treatment with certain medications, such as opioid pain medications or sedative-hypnotic medications for anxiety or insomnia.

NEUROBIOLOGICAL BASIS

When a person consumes a psychoactive substance, it induces changes in brain neurotransmitter systems. After repeated use of the substance, adaptive mechanisms come into play in an effort to restore the balance. This can manifest clinically as tolerance (the need to use increasing amounts of the substance to achieve the same effect). A related, but different, phenomenon is seen when the individual tries to stop using the substance. In this case the adaptive mechanisms operate unchecked, causing a withdrawal syndrome, which generally involves symptoms that are opposite those of the major effects of the substance. These symptoms emerge and peak over a period of several hours to days, depending on the half-life of the substance, and then gradually diminish as balance is reestablished. All symptoms may not resolve at the same rate, and some individuals may have a prolonged period of discomfort, sometimes referred to as protracted withdrawal.

PROCESS OF MEDICAL DETOXIFICATION

The primary goal of detoxification is to safely and effectively manage the withdrawal symptoms that can emerge upon cessation or reduction of the use of a psychoactive substance. Individuals with lesser degrees of physiological dependence may stop using a substance on their own with no adverse effects. In a treatment setting, detoxification should be preceded by a careful evaluation of the patient, including the substance(s) used; the duration, quantity, and frequency of use; the time of last use; and any medical and psychiatric risk factors.

The process of medical detoxification varies depending on the substance and involves three major components: monitoring, supportive measures, and medication. It may take place in outpatient or inpatient settings, based on the substance(s) involved, the anticipated severity of withdrawal, the availability of support and monitoring in the patient's home environment, the patient's general physical condition, and the presence of associated medical and psychiatric disorders. Rating scales to assess severity of withdrawal from specific substances, such as the Clinical

Institute Withdrawal Assessment for Alcohol Scale-Revised (CIWA-Ar; Sullivan et al., 1989) and the Clinical Opiate Withdrawal Scale (COWS; Wesson & Ling, 2003), may be used to guide the detoxification process.

DETOXIFICATION FROM SPECIFIC SUBSTANCES

Alcohol. Withdrawal from alcohol and sedative-hypnotics (substances that depress the functioning of the central nervous system) can be serious, and even life-threatening in a small proportion of patients. The symptoms and signs of withdrawal may range from more minor—including tremor ("shakes"), anxiety, and elevated pulse and blood pressure—to more severe—such as auditory, visual, or tactile hallucinations; seizures; and delirium tremens (a combination of delirium and confusion, agitation, disorientation, and tremor). Delirium tremens is a serious condition with an associated mortality of approximately 1 percent (Mayo-Smith et al., 2004). Patients at the highest risk of severe withdrawal are those with a history of prolonged heavy drinking, those in poor physical condition with associated medical problems, and those with a history of prior severe withdrawal episodes. The symptoms usually emerge within a few hours (but may not emerge until three to four days after the last drink), peak over the next two to three days, and then resolve over four or five days.

Patients at risk of severe withdrawal may require management in an inpatient unit under medical supervision. Supportive measures such as the monitoring of vital signs and level of consciousness, the maintenance of fluid and electrolyte balance, and precautions against falls, together with other protective measures, may be needed. Medication management typically includes benzodiazepines such as diazepam (Valium), chlordiazepoxide (Librium), or lorazepam (Ativan). These are tapered off as the patient's condition improves. Many patients who drink heavily are nutritionally deficient, and some may develop complications such as Wernicke's encephalopathy, a condition caused by a thiamine (Vitamin B1) deficiency. If untreated, it may result in Korsakoff syndrome, which is a highly disabling, often irreversible, disorder of memory. Giving thiamine supplements routinely to all patients with a history of heavy alcohol consumption can effectively prevent this complication.

Sedatives and Hypnotics. The features of sedative-hypnotic withdrawal are similar to those of alcohol withdrawal, but with some noteworthy differences: Onset may be within hours of the last use of a short-acting drug such as alprazolam (Xanax), or delayed for several days for long-acting drugs such as diazepam or phenobarbital. There is also a greater risk of withdrawal seizures, particularly from the shorter-acting substances; the withdrawal symptoms often intensify during the later part of the detoxification process; and the process may need to be extended over weeks, or even months in some patients. Two main approaches are utilized for detoxification: (1) tapering down the dose of the substance being abused, or (2) switching to an equivalent dose of a long-acting benzodiazepine or barbiturate (such as diazepam or phenobarbital, respectively), which is then slowly tapered off (Center for Substance Abuse Treatment, 2006, pp. 75–78). Because of the risk involved in sedative-hypnotic detoxification, it is generally better done under the supervision of a specialist, particularly when the patient has been abusing large amounts of the substance over a long period.

Opioids. Withdrawal from opioids (such as heroin, methadone, and narcotic pain medications) can be painful and distressing, but is rarely life-threatening except in debilitated individuals. It somewhat resembles a severe case of influenza, with body ache, back pain, watering of the eyes, runny nose, sneezing, yawning, diarrhea, abdominal cramps, nausea, vomiting, elevated blood pressure and pulse, dilated pupils, gooseflesh (hence the term *cold turkey*), and jerky movements of the legs (giving rise to the expression *kicking the habit*). The time of onset with a short-acting opioid such as heroin is six to eight hours after the last use, with a peak on the second or third day; withdrawal symptoms diminish by the fourth or fifth day. Withdrawal from a longer-acting opioid such as methadone may be delayed for up to two or three days and may last two or three weeks.

Several approaches are used to minimize the symptoms and shorten the duration of withdrawal. Most commonly, a full or partial opioid agonist medication (such as methadone or buprenorphine, respectively) is started and slowly tapered off over five to seven days. Another approach utilizes clonidine, which helps to reduce anxiety, blood pressure, and pulse rate, along with adjunctive medications for other withdrawal symptoms. Sometimes, an opioid antagonist (such as naltrexone) is utilized with clonidine to shorten the detoxification process (this is known as rapid opioid detoxification). A more aggressive, and potentially more risky, approach involves administering an opioid antagonist to precipitate acute withdrawal after placing the patient under general anesthesia; its practitioners claim that it shortens the withdrawal duration to just a few hours (called ultra-rapid opioid detoxification). Whatever the approach used for detoxification, there is a high risk of relapse without extended aftercare engagement. There is also a greater risk of accidental overdose, and possible mortality, after voluntary or involuntary detoxification (such as during a hospitalization or incarceration) as the patient's tolerance to opioids is diminished. For these reasons, long-term maintenance on methadone or buprenorphine may be preferred for patients willing to engage in it.

Stimulants. Cocaine and amphetamine withdrawal consists of prominent symptoms such as mood, sleep, and appetite disturbances; psychomotor agitation or retardation; fatigue; and intense cravings. Detoxification primarily involves supportive measures. Suicidal behavior can occur during this period and may last several days, occasionally necessitating a brief inpatient stay.

Other Drugs. The American Psychiatric Association's *Diagnostic and Statistical Manual, Text Revision* (2000) does not recognize clinically significant withdrawal syndromes for cannabis, hallucinogens, phencyclidine, or inhalants. However, there is growing evidence that a cannabis withdrawal does occur, with anxiety, restlessness, irritability, anger, strange dreams, decreased appetite, and weight loss as its main symptoms. Most symptoms begin within 24 hours of abstinence, peak within the first week, and last approximately one to two weeks. Little research has been done on the management of these symptoms.

It is a common misconception that detoxification constitutes a stand-alone treatment for drug addiction. Although it is often a necessary first step in the recovery process, detoxification by itself is nearly always insufficient to achieve long-term abstinence and recovery from addiction. Medical detoxification reduces the discomfort experienced by the patient and the risk of more serious adverse consequences. It also provides an opportunity to establish a therapeutic alliance and engage the patient in long-term, recovery-oriented treatment.

See also **Addiction: Concepts and Definitions; Treatment: An Overview; Treatment, Pharmacological Approaches to: Clonidine; Treatment, Stages/ Phases of: Non-Medical Detoxification; Withdrawal: Alcohol.**

BIBLIOGRAPHY

American Psychiatric Association. (2000). *Diagnostic and statistical manual of mental disorders* (text rev.). Washington, DC: Author.

Center for Substance Abuse Treatment. (2006). *Detoxification and substance abuse treatment.* Treatment Improvement Protocol (TIP) Series 45 (DHHS Publication No. [SMA] 06-4131). Rockville, MD: Substance Abuse and Mental Health Services Administration.

Mayo-Smith, M. F., Beecher, L. H., Fischer, T. L., Gorelick, D. A., Guillaume, J. L., Hill, A., et al. (2004). (Working Group on the Management of Alcohol Withdrawal Delirium, Practice Guidelines Committee, American Society of Addiction Medicine). Management of alcohol withdrawal delirium: An evidence-based practice guideline. *Archives of Internal Medicine, 164,* 1405–1412.

Sullivan, J. T., Sykora, K., Schneiderman, J., Naranjo, C. A., & Sellers, E. M. (1989). Assessment of alcohol withdrawal: The revised Clinical Institute Withdrawal Assessment for Alcohol Scale (CIWA-Ar). *British Journal of Addiction, 84,* 1353–1357.

Wesson, D. R., & Ling, W. (2003). The Clinical Opiate Withdrawal Scale (COWS). *Journal of Psychoactive Drugs, 35,* 253–259.

DEVANG H. GANDHI

NON-MEDICAL DETOXIFICATION

The term *detoxification* can refer to the management of two distinct types of problems resulting from excessive alcohol or other drug use. These are the physical and behavioral symptoms of intoxication on the one hand or of withdrawal following a prolonged period of substance use on the other. Although both involve recovering from the toxic effects of a drug while refraining from further use, the problems associated are dissimilar and require different management approaches. Non-medical approaches have been developed for the management of both intoxication and withdrawal that for most people are equally as safe and effective as more expensive medical approaches.

In most countries alcohol and other drug problems are so widespread that cost containment in healthcare becomes a priority. This requirement rules out an exclusive reliance on expensive medical settings, medical personnel, and medication. A number of relatively safe and cost-effective alternatives to inpatient hospital care have been devised that are frequently preferred by clients and also have other advantages. Despite research evidence for equivalent effectiveness and some tangible advantages, non-medical detoxification remains unavailable in some healthcare systems because only hospital-based medical detoxification is eligible for payment from state or private health funds.

MANAGING PUBLIC DRUNKENNESS

The most visible problems associated with extreme intoxication concern public order, particularly in relation to the use of alcohol. Drunkenness is associated with violence both to the self and to others as well as with public nuisance offenses. The habitual drunken offender and the potentially dangerous disorderly drunk present themselves in large numbers to police forces the world over, placing a substantial burden on criminal justice systems. For this reason a number of countries have experimented with decriminalizing public drunkenness. There is also a growing awareness that locking intoxicated people in police cells puts them at risk of serious harm. In Australia, for example, the tragic deaths of many Aboriginal people while in police custody are thought to have been caused by the combined effects of alcohol and confinement.

Setting up non-medical detoxification services has sometimes occurred hand-in-hand with decriminalization of drunkenness. Early pioneers in the 1970s were the Addiction Research Foundation in the Canadian province of Ontario and St. Vincent's Hospital in New South Wales, Australia. In both cases services were set up with the principal aim of diverting drunkenness offenders from the criminal justice system to a more humane setting where they might receive counseling and support. Both utilized a residential social setting staffed by non-medical personnel and provided no medical care or medication. When fully functioning, these services successfully supervised thousands of problem drinkers, mainly self-referred, through

sobering-up and/or alcohol withdrawal with an impressive record of safety. In its first ten years of operation, the New South Wales facility dealt with nearly 14,000 admissions and recorded only two fatalities among this high risk population (Pedersen, 1986). Only 1 percent of admissions required transfer to a nearby hospital for specialized medical care, often for reasons unrelated to alcohol withdrawal. Sandra C. Lapham et al. (1996) describe a model of drug-free management of alcohol withdrawal in a sample of 160 homeless men and women with alcohol withdrawal signs who were admitted to a non-medical residential setting in New Mexico. Most experienced minor symptoms and only two required referral to a medical facility. The rest were managed safely without medication and without serious complications.

SOBERING-UP AND WET SHELTERS

In designing detoxification services, intoxication and withdrawal should not be confused. While highly successful and cost-effective alternatives to hospital care for alcohol withdrawal exist, they are not the panacea for problems posed by habitual drunken offenders. Australia's continuing concern to prevent Aboriginal deaths in custody has also prompted an increasing use of what have come to be called *sobering-up shelters*. These are supportive non-medical settings where people can stay a few hours or, if necessary, overnight until they are sober. They provide an inexpensive alternative to prison and have gained the necessary support of the local police (Drug and Alcohol Office, 2007). Sobering-up shelters need access to specialist treatment facilities, so they can refer people requiring urgent medical attention or longer-term help with a drinking problem.

There are potentially serious medical emergencies associated with extreme levels of drug intoxication. Poisoning through overdose, accidental or otherwise, is a common cause of admission to hospital emergency rooms the world over and all too frequently this results in death. Overdosing on heroin can also be quite common where that drug is widely used, especially if users have lost tolerance to the drug's effects after a period of abstinence, if it is used with other CNS depressant drugs such as alcohol or benzodiazepines, and/or if the heroin is unusually pure. For this reason staff of sobering-up shelters, or of any facility that also caters to drug users, should be trained to identify warning signs of overdose so that the sufferer may be taken to a hospital with as little delay as possible. In some countries the opiate-antagonist drug naloxone is used in a variety of non-medical settings, including by drug-using peers at the scene of an overdose (Baca and Grant, 2005). Similarly, there is a great educational need among the general drug-using and drinking public who may abandon their friends to "sleep it off" only later to find them asphyxiated.

A relatively recent approach to the management of homeless, habitual drunken offenders in Canada and the United Kingdom is the establishment of *wet shelters*, where alcohol is provided freely in regular, measured doses throughout the day for residents with established levels of alcohol dependence. This stabilizes clients and reduces the risk both of intoxication and withdrawal with all their attendant complications (Podymow, 2006). Similar programs have been developed in the state of Washington that allow residents to continue their drinking and have alcohol on the premises, although it is not directly provided to them. This *harm reduction* approach to the management of serious alcohol-related problems mirrors that used in *safe consumption* or *safe injection* sites for injecting drug users in a number of European cities as well as Canada. These can reduce the risk of fatal drug overdoses as well as the transmission of blood-borne viruses (Health Canada, 2008).

MANAGING ALCOHOL AND OTHER DRUG WITHDRAWAL

Detoxification services exist on a continuum ranging from supervision by an informed lay person (a relative, a recovered problem drinker or user, or non-medical professionals) all the way to 24-hour nursing and medical care in a specialist hospital unit. Even in the latter case, substantial variations exist regarding the amount of medication used during withdrawal, or even whether any medication is used at all. Detoxification services designed to minimize discomfort and the possibility of actual harm occurring during withdrawal may be non-medical in several senses, either by using non-medical settings (e.g., hostels, the client's home), non-medical personnel (e.g., relatives, ex-problem drinkers), or non-medical procedures (e.g., alternative medicine approaches). There is wide consensus that medical assistance needs to be available if required, but the responsibility for providing this need not be left only with medical personnel.

An influential early North American study showed that in the relative safety of an alcoholism treatment unit only five percent of admissions required any form of medical assistance. In addition to the residential, *social-setting* model of detoxification, *ambulatory* or outpatient detoxification procedures that relied on the drinker calling in daily to a clinic to collect his or her medication and receive a brief check-up were developed. Evaluations of these types of service conducted in several countries have demonstrated that their success rate in terms of both safety and effectiveness is at least the equal of inpatient care and is considerably less expensive.

A variation of this approach, *home detoxification*, is an approach developed initially in the United Kingdom with problem drinkers and is now widely used in many other countries. This usually involves a community alcohol worker (e.g., nurse, counselor, or psychologist) assisting a family practitioner to assess a drinker who wishes to stop drinking alcohol but who may experience severe withdrawal symptoms in the process. Providing that the home environment is deemed supportive and the client is sufficiently motivated to stop drinking, the detoxification then occurs in the patient's home with visits from the alcohol worker. The family doctor's telephone number is provided to the client and any close relative or partner in case of emergency. A particular effort is made to screen out drinkers with a history of withdrawal seizures, delirium tremens, or Korsakoff's Psychosis. To reduce the risk of overdose with some types of medication (notably chlormethiazole), either the alcohol worker or a relative holds the medication. In the United Kingdom many family doctors were already prescribing chlormethiazole to cover alcohol withdrawal but without accompanying supervision and often longer than the recommended maximum period. This was the single most common method of managing alcohol withdrawal among a group of individuals who were loathe to enter a psychiatric hospital or specialized treatment unit. Later studies showed that home detoxification is more acceptable to groups that are frequently underrepresented in traditional treatment settings such as the young, the elderly, and women. Home detoxification therefore offers a safe alternative to completely unsupervised withdrawal on the one hand and a cost-effective alternative to inpatient hospital care on the other. The cost of home detoxification per client has been estimated to be approximately one-quarter that of inpatient hospital care. Formal evaluations of the U.K. service suggest that not only is there no loss in terms of either safety or efficacy but that the clients prefer to be treated at home and that many would refuse admission to a hospital.

A consistent finding regarding nonmedical or social approaches to detoxification across several countries has been that they are not only equally safe but have the advantage of being more likely to result in clients being successfully referred for further treatment, whether residential or nonresidential. One U.S.-based review comparing traditional and nonmedical approaches to detoxification (Beshai, 1990) strongly recommended that both types of service were necessary and that screening should be conducted so that more severely dependent cases and those with a history of delirium tremens or withdrawal seizures can be referred on to specialist medical service providers.

CONCLUSIONS

Cost-effective, nonmedical approaches have been developed to manage both problems of intoxication and alcohol or other drug withdrawal. It is very important to be clear about the different objectives and issues to be managed in relation to these two core elements involved in detoxification. Both intoxication and alcohol withdrawal are so common in Western society that, although they carry a small but significant risk of serious injury or death, it is too costly to provide specialist medical care in every instance. Safe and inexpensive alternatives have been developed in a number of countries that are to be recommended over a laissez-faire or punitive approach to these major social problems. Encouraging evidence suggests that community-based detoxification services attract problem drinkers who are usually underrepresented in treatment services, such as women, young people, and the elderly. Furthermore, social or nonmedical detoxification has been found to be consistently superior to traditional medical inpatient care in terms of facilitating referral to ongoing support and follow-up services. It is important, however, to screen out individuals with a history of severe complications from alcohol withdrawal such as delirium tremens or seizures, who will normally require specialized medical care to safely manage the withdrawal process. There is only limited published research concerning the efficacy of such approaches for the management of problems with drugs other than alcohol.

See also **Antagonist; Australia; Britain; Britain: Alcohol Use and Policy; Canada; Delirium Tremens (DTs); Funding and Service Delivery of Treatment; Harm Reduction; Naloxone; Overdose, Drug (OD); Prevention, Education and; Treatment: Outpatient Versus Inpatient Setting; Withdrawal: Alcohol.**

BIBLIOGRAPHY

Annis, H. (1985). Is inpatient rehabilitation of the alcoholic cost effective? *Advances in Alcohol and Substance Abuse, 5*, 175–190.

Baca, C. T., & Grant, K. J. (2005) Take-home naloxone to reduce heroin death. *Addiction, 100*(12):1823–1831.

Bennie, C. (1998). A comparison of home detoxification and minimal intervention strategies for problem drinkers. *Alcohol and Alcoholism, 33*(2), 157–163.

Beshai, N. N. (1990). Providing cost efficient detoxification services to alcoholic patients. *Public Health Reports, 105*(5), 475–481.

Cooper, D. (1994). *Home detoxification and assessment.* Oxford, UK: Radcliffe Medical Press.

Drug and Alcohol Office. (2007). Utilisation of sobering up centres, 1990–2005. *Statistical Bulletin, 36*, 1–12.

Fleman, N. (1997). Alcohol home detoxification: A literature review. *Alcohol and Alcoholism, 32*(6), 649–656.

Health Canada. (2008, March 31). Vancouver's INSITE service and other supervised injection sites: What has been learned from research? Final report of the Expert Advisory Committee on Supervised Injection Site Research. Available from http://www.hc-sc.gc.ca/.

Lapham, S. C., Hall, M., Snyder, J., Skipper, B., McMurray-Avila, M., Pulvino, S., & Kozeny, T. (1996). Demonstration of a mixed social/medical model detoxification program for homeless alcohol abusers. *Contemporary Drug Problems, 23*, 331–345.

McGovern, M. P. (1983). Comparative evaluation of medical vs. social treatment of alcohol withdrawal syndrome. *Journal of Clinical Psychology, 39*(5), 791–803.

Midford, R., Daly, A., & Holmes, M. (1994). The care of public drunks in Halls Creek: A model for community involvement. *Health Promotion Journal of Australia, 4*(19), 5–8.

Pederson, C. (1986). Hospital admissions from a non-medical alcohol detoxification unit. *Drug and Alcohol Review, 5*, 133–137.

Podymow, T., Turnbull, J., Coyle, D., Yetisir, E., & Wells, G. (2006). Shelter-based managed alcohol administration to chronically homeless people addicted to alcohol. *Canadian Medical Association Journal, 174*(1), 45–49.

Stockwell, T., Bolt, E., & Hooper, J. (1986). Detoxification from alcohol at home managed by general practitioners. *British Medical Journal, 292*, 733–735.

Stockwell, T., Bolt, E., Milner, I., Russell, G., Bolderston, H., & Pugh, P. (1991). Home detoxification for problem drinkers: Its safety and efficacy in comparison with inpatient care. *Alcohol and Alcoholism, 26*(2), 207–214.

TIM STOCKWELL

SCREENING AND BRIEF INTERVENTION

Screening and Brief Intervention (SBI) is an integrated approach to early intervention for individuals with substance-abuse disorders, as well as those who are at risk of developing them. SBI is sometimes included in a more comprehensive approach that adds referral to treatment (called SBIRT). SBI is based on public health procedures, as described by Thomas Babor and colleagues in 2007, designed to reduce the burden of injury, disease, and disability associated with the misuse of psychoactive substances, particularly alcohol, illicit drugs, tobacco products, and prescription medications with high abuse potential. SBI begins with the introduction of systematic screening in medical facilities and other community settings where people engaged in substance misuse are likely to be encountered (e.g., emergency rooms, community health clinics, social service settings). Screening is a preliminary procedure to evaluate the likelihood that an individual has a substance-abuse disorder or is at risk of negative consequences from the use of alcohol, tobacco, or other drugs. It may be conducted by means of interviews, questionnaires, or biological tests based on samples of blood, urine, hair, or saliva. Screening can also be conducted on a routine basis for all patients, or opportunistically with those who offer evidence of substance use because of their presenting symptoms or problems (e.g., high blood pressure or an injury resulting from a fight or motor vehicle accident).

Typically, SBI programs provide a brief intervention to individuals considered to be at elevated risk, and referral to further evaluation and treatment for those identified at high risk. The term *brief intervention* refers to any time-limited effort to change health behavior or attitudes in relation to substance misuse. When conducted in a medical setting, it usually consists of one to two visits or consultations lasting from 5 to 20 minutes. It generally takes the form of a short conversation between a substance user and a concerned physician, nurse, physician assistant, or social worker. The aim is to provide objective feedback about the results of the screening test, to give information about the health risks associated with continued substance use, to establish a goal for the patient to either stop or cut down use (depending on the substance), and to motivate the patient to work toward that goal through encouragement and support. Screening often identifies those who already have a substance-related health condition or a suspected substance-abuse disorder that warrants a formal diagnosis and possible referral to treatment. In these cases the brief intervention may take the form of referral advice and encouragement to seek treatment.

BIBLIOGRAPHY

Babor, T. F., & Higgins-Biddle, J. C. (2001a). *AUDIT—The Alcohol Use Disorder Identification Test: Guidelines for use in primary care* (2nd ed.). Geneva, Switzerland: World Health Organization.

Babor, T. F., & Higgins-Biddle, J. C. (2001b). *Brief intervention for hazardous and harmful drinking. A manual for primary care* (2nd ed.). Geneva, Switzerland: World Health Organization.

Babor, T. F., McRee, B., Kassebaum, P., Grimaldi, P., Ahmed, K., & Bray, J. (2007). Screening, brief intervention, and referral to treatment (SBIRT): Toward a public health approach to the management of substance abuse. *Substance Abuse, 28*, 7–30.

THOMAS BABOR

RELAPSE PREVENTION

After an individual successfully decreases or abstains from a problematic behavior (e.g., drinking excessively, drug use, binge eating, pathological gambling), the risk of returning to a pre-change level of behavior remains. Relapse prevention (RP) is therefore an important component in maintaining the positive behavior change. The primary goals of RP are to: (1) provide the skills needed to anticipate risks and prevent an initial lapse, and (2) keep a lapse from becoming a full relapse. RP is based on research showing that there is an increased risk of relapse following behavior change. Theories of relapse initially assumed a linear "if …then" relationship between risks and relapse, but more recent research has supported a dynamic model of relapse. This model includes the consideration that many factors interact with one another during high-risk situations. For example, cognitive processes (e.g., self-efficacy, expectations, motivation, and craving) interact with coping behaviors (e.g., cognitive-behavioral, approach-avoidance, self-regulation), affective states, and maladaptive behaviors. Identifying these interactions allows for more specificity in tailoring self-management skills to the needs of the individual.

There are many important components in RP, including recognizing high-risk situations, self-efficacy, motivation, coping skills, and social support. Assessing high-risk situations, including cues, triggers, and cravings, allows the development of individual-oriented plans to help avoid particular situations or implement other coping strategies. High-risk situations can include both external events (e.g., parties or celebrations) and internal states (e.g., anxiety or depression). Along with identifying these risky situations, identifying positive coping skills is necessary to change the problematic behavior. Coping skills involve both cognitive (i.e., related to motivation and self-efficacy) and behavioral (i.e., action-oriented) strategies. For example, "urge surfing" involves noticing but not resisting urges to engage in pre-change behavior, as these urges will wax and wane (like an ocean wave). By not resisting the urge this does not mean giving in to the urge and engaging in pre-change behavior. Often times attempts to resist the urge will make the client feel the urge more intensely for a longer period of time. Mindfulness meditation also identifies a coping strategy of "staying in the moment" and becoming thoughtfully aware of urges and cravings without reacting to them.

Increasing self-efficacy (i.e., beliefs about one's ability to influence the events that affect one's life) is associated with a person's ability to cope in high-risk situations. Low self-efficacy may be a mediating factor in lapse or relapse. Following the identification of high-risk situations and successful implementation of coping strategies, self-efficacy may increase regarding one's ability to maintain the positive behavioral change. For example, after becoming anxious (a high-risk situation), an individual may employ a new coping strategy by applying relaxation techniques; the person may then notice a decrease in anxiety without substance use. The person's self-confidence in applying new techniques and avoiding problematic behaviors is thereby increased.

RP also addresses ambivalence, which can undermine behavior change and maintenance. RP attempts to shift the focus from immediate desires (e.g. "drinking with my friends will be fun tonight") to long-term goals and values (e.g., "although I may have fun tonight, having a hangover would get in the way of studying, and my grades are starting to slip"). Finally, RP considers the importance that social support has in the long-term maintenance of behavior change. RP seeks to integrate additional interventions, including marital counseling, involvement in social organizations, and enhancement of existing supportive relationships.

The process of changing one's habits is not always a binary condition (use/don't use, drink/don't drink), and RP cannot be considered in simplistic terms either. When a commitment for change has been achieved, it is critical to address all the conditions that may result in relapse and undermine success. The dynamic model of RP provides a foundation for supporting these positive changes.

See also **Relapse; Treatment, Behavioral Approaches to: Overview; Treatment, Stages/Phases of: Aftercare.**

BIBLIOGRAPHY

Larimer, M. E., Palmer, R. S., & Marlatt, G. A. (1999). Relapse prevention: An overview of Marlatt's cognitive-behavioral model. *Alcohol Research and Health, 23*(2), 151–160.

Marlatt, G. A., & Donovan, D. M. (Eds.). (2005). *Relapse prevention: Maintenance strategies in the treatment of addictive behaviors* (2nd ed.). New York: Guilford Press.

Witkiewitz, K., & Marlatt, G. A. (2004). Relapse prevention for alcohol and drug problems: That was zen, this is tao. *American Psychologist, 59*(4), 224–235.

Witkiewitz, K., van der Maas, H. L. J., Hufford, M. R., & Marlatt, G. A. (2007). Nonnormality and divergence in posttreatment alcohol use: Reexamining the Project MATCH data "another way." *Journal of Abnormal Psychology, 116*(2), 378–394.

LISA ANDREWS-MACHOTKA
DIANE E. LOGAN

STABILIZATION

Various evidence-based pharmacological and psychosocial interventions are relevant to different stages in the addiction career and treatment process (UNODC, 2008). Stabilization is a fundamental concept woven into these programs and can refer to several processes. A stabilizing period is generally meant to provide a safe, secure environment in which to engage the patient and develop a treatment plan that he or she will follow after discharge.

The first step in treatment is often detoxifying the patient. This phase includes a brief stabilization period designed to detoxify the patient from addictive drugs, to assess his or her psychosocial stability, and to begin to establish basic recovery supports. This process might include medical detoxification, in which the client is systematically withdrawn from drugs that produce physical dependence, typically under the care of a physician and through the use of medications that reduce the risks to the patient and/or increase the patient's comfort. The primary goals of this phase include stabilizing the acute symptoms of the drug use disorder, helping the patient establish abstinence, and motivating the patient to continue in treatment once the acute crisis has subsided or the involuntary period of commitment expires. This phase can last as long as two weeks, after which patients usually start individual or group treatment and move toward a period of more stable abstinence. Stabilization is usually indicated by a significant period of abstinence, a safe and consistent housing situation, adequate levels of social support, and the absence of acute or unstable medical or legal problems.

For patients with opioid dependence, maintenance medications such as methadone or buprenorphine have proven efficacy in stabilization and relapse prevention. Although these drugs themselves can produce physical dependence, they serve to stabilize and reduce illicit opioid abuse by these patients, making them more receptive to other forms of intervention.

Social assistance and support are often also needed. To achieve sustainable livelihoods, addicted patients who are unemployed, homeless, and/or rejected by their families benefit from programs such as dormitories, vouchers, and temporary job opportunities. These support the patients' stabilization when offered in combination with social services and treatment services.

For many people, alcohol and drug abuse have characteristics of chronic disorders, with recurring cycles of cessation and relapse. Similarly, many drug users go through cycles of treatment, abstinence, and relapse (Hser et al., 1997). McKay (2005) emphasized this cyclic nature of treatment and the importance of establishing stabilization each time. He writes that methods need to be developed to increase patients' willingness to return to more intensive forms of treatment as needed until stabilization is achieved once again.

See also **Treatment, Stages/Phases of: Initiation of Abstinence; Treatment, Stages/Phases of: Relapse Prevention.**

BIBLIOGRAPHY

Daley, D. C. *Dual disorders recovery counseling.* Available from http://www.drugabuse.gov/.

Hser, Y.I., Anglin, M.D., Grella, C., Longshore, D., & Prendergast, M.L. (1997). Drug treatment careers: A conceptual framework and existing research findings. *Journal of Substance Abuse Treatment, 14*(6), 543–558.

McKay, J. R. (2005). Is there a case for extended interventions for alcohol and drug use disorders? *Addiction, 100,* 1594–1610.

United Nations Office on Drugs and Crime (UNODC). *Principles of drug dependence treatment.* Available from http://www.unodc.org/.

JOEL GROW
G. ALAN MARLATT

AFTERCARE

The recovery process does not end when an individual completes a detoxification, rehabilitation, or stabilization program. Due to the relapsing nature of substance abuse, individuals receiving treatment for the disorder are generally urged to participate in some form of continuing care after their initial phase of treatment has ended (McKay et al., 2004). In the realm of substance abuse treatment, the terms *continuing care* and *aftercare* have similar, yet distinct, meanings.

Substance abuse treatment used to be delivered primarily in inpatient or residential settings, and patients would participate in aftercare group therapy sessions near the end of their treatment stay. These aftercare sessions were intended to maintain the progress achieved in the inpatient/residential program by easing the transition from the controlled therapeutic environment to one in which alcohol and drugs are readily available.

As of 2008, in the United States, most substance abuse treatment is provided in outpatient settings, with residential or inpatient treatment restricted to those with severe comorbid medical or psychiatric problems (McKay, 2005). The continuing care phase in the outpatient model is typically delivered in group sessions, focuses on substance use, and is often structured like twelve-steps mutual/self-help programs.

Differences exist between the role of continuing care in outpatient programs and aftercare programs from the old residential service delivery model. In contrast with the inpatient model, most graduates of an outpatient treatment program have already demonstrated some ability to achieve and maintain abstinence outside a controlled environment (McKay et al., 2004). While maintaining abstinence is paramount for these individuals, some researchers argue that continuing care should also include other components of recovery, such as focus on improving the individual's social support system and making use of recovery houses. These researchers assert the need for vocationally- and activities-focused skills-training programs (Donovan, 1998).

Aftercare also plays an important role in drug treatment programs within U.S. prisons, although the evidence for its effectiveness continued to be evaluated in the early twenty-first century. In awarding residential substance abuse treatment grants for state prisoners, the Bureau of Justice Assistance requires states to give preference to programs that provide aftercare services. Also, the standard of care established by the Office of National Drug Control Policy specifies that community-based aftercare must continue for at least six months. In addition to this emphasis on aftercare, researchers emphasize the need to understand better how different criminal justice systems conceptualize and implement these programs. Standard definitions and procedures are needed to determine the level and intensity of services required for different types of offenders in various types of settings (Pelissiera et al., 2007).

Given that long-term programs are expensive, it makes sense to select candidates who will be best served by them. Research shows that some individuals with substance use disorders recover without formal treatment (Sobell et al., 1993) and that others experience durable improvements following such brief interventions as motivational interviewing. Individuals who are unable to achieve sustained reductions in alcohol or drug use either on their own or following brief interventions may be the best candidates for extended interventions (McKay, 2005).

See also **Methadone Maintenance Programs; Relapse.**

BIBLIOGRAPHY

Donovan, D. (1998). Continuing care: Promoting the maintenance of change. In W. Miller, & N. Heather, (Eds.), *Treating addictive behaviors* (2nd ed., pp. 317–336). New York: Plenum.

McKay, J. (2005). Is there a case for extended interventions for alcohol and drug use disorders? *Addiction, 100*, 1594–1610.

McKay, J., Foltz, C., Leahy, P., Stephens, R., Orwin, R., & Crowley, E. (2004). Step down continuing care in the treatment of substance abuse: Correlates of participation and outcome effects. *Evaluation and Program Planning, 27*(3), 321–331.

Pelissiera, B., Jones, N., & Cadigan, T. (2007). Drug treatment aftercare in the criminal justice system: A systematic review. *Journal of Substance Abuse Treatment, 32*(3), 311–320.

Sobell, L., Sobell, M., Toneatto, T., & Leo, G. (1993). What triggers the resolution of alcohol problems without treatment? *Alcoholism: Clinical and Experimental Research, 17*, 217–224.

JOEL GROW
G. ALAN MARLATT

TREATMENT: OUTPATIENT VERSUS INPATIENT SETTING.

The marketplace for treatment for substance use disorders (often referred to as SUDs) offers a range of options from which to choose. These options are commonly classified as either *inpatient* or *outpatient* treatment. Selecting treatment is based on matching an individual's care needs with the necessary supports and an appropriate level of treatment intensity. Although many frameworks exist for describing the variety of treatment options along a continuum of care, the levels of care framework provided by the American Society of Addiction Medicine (ASAM) is one of the most widely used; it is helpful for describing and differentiating between inpatient and outpatient treatments, as reported by the Center for Substance Abuse Treatment (1994).

INPATIENT TREATMENT

Inpatient treatment generally refers to treatment that is provided in a controlled environment, such as a residential center or hospital. Patients remain in these settings until they are deemed to be ready for treatment in an outpatient setting. Patients with significant withdrawal symptoms, serious medical conditions, suicidal or homicidal ideation, and an inability to function in the community, or those who reside in highly disruptive and unsupportive environments, may benefit most from inpatient treatment (Fuller & Hiller-Sturmhofel, 1999).

The ASAM distinguishes two types of inpatient treatment: medically *managed* and medically *monitored* treatment. Medically managed is the most intensive form of treatment. Because of its high costs, it is typically reserved for persons with acute care needs and severe comorbid conditions (McKay, 2001). Services include ongoing primary care to manage withdrawal symptoms and other psychiatric, medical, and emotional problems associated with substance dependence. This treatment creates a safe environment for detoxification, while allowing clinicians to make differential diagnoses, stabilize symptoms, and develop care management plans.

Medically monitored treatment is also provided in a residential setting but does not include primary medical services. Medically monitored treatments may be provided in private or public treatment centers, as well as state and local psychiatric hospitals. Treatment may last from several days to several weeks. Depending on the specific care needs of the patient, treatment may focus on managing symptoms, developing coping skills, reducing risk of self-harm, improving independent living skills, and establishing supportive social networks (see Daley & Salloum, 2001).

OUTPATIENT TREATMENT

Outpatient treatment involves nonresidential services and does not include an overnight stay in a hospital or treatment center. This type of treatment allows an individual to receive treatment services while maintaining normal daily activities. Outpatient treatments rely heavily on individual- or group-based psychosocial

interventions including (but not limited to) cognitive-behavioral therapy (CBT), motivational enhancement therapy (MET), and psychoeducation. A meta-analysis conducted by Dutra and colleagues (2008) showed that psychosocial interventions for substance use disorders exhibited effect sizes that were comparable to other efficacious treatments in psychiatry. Pharmacological treatment is also considered an important treatment component for many patients in outpatient treatment. Such therapies may be agonist medications (e.g., methadone and buprenorphine for opioid dependence), antagonist medications (e.g., naltrexone for opioid dependence), abstinence- and relapse-preventing medications (e.g., disulfiram, naltrexone, and acamprosate for alcohol dependence; bupropion and varenicline for tobacco dependence), or those used for the treatment of comorbid psychiatric conditions (e.g., antidepressants, antipsychotics, and mood stabilizers) (Work Group on Substance Use Disorders et al. & American Psychiatric Association Steering Committee on Practice Guidelines et al., 2006).

The ASAM recognizes two levels of outpatient treatment: intensive outpatient and standard outpatient. Intensive outpatient treatment is the highest and most comprehensive level of outpatient treatment. Also referred to as partial hospitalization, it is considered a *step-down* from inpatient services. This treatment option bridges inpatient and outpatient services, offering daily treatment groups and professional contacts while allowing patients to return to their primary residence rather than stay overnight in a hospital. Intensive outpatient treatment may last a few days to a few weeks. Standard outpatient treatment differs in intensity and duration from intensive inpatient treatment and is offered in a variety of settings that range from community mental health centers to patient-driven support groups. Depending on the care needs of the patient, standard outpatient treatment may involve a few treatment sessions a month or multiple sessions each week.

Other outpatient treatment options exist, although they do not fall within the ASAM level of care taxonomy. For example, self-help groups, such as Alcoholics Anonymous (AA), Narcotics Anonymous (NA), and other 12-step models, are outpatient treatments that may constitute a person's primary form of treatment, may be an adjunct to existing professional services, or may be a way of providing additional support following intensive treatment, also referred to as aftercare. For example, Gossop and coworkers (2008) reported that attending AA or NA meetings after receiving inpatient services was associated with higher levels of abstinence for opioids and alcohol at one, two, and five years follow-up compared to those who did not attend AA or NA, or who attended infrequently.

Brief interventions delivered by health service providers from numerous disciplines are another type of treatment. These are structured interventions of short duration—typically 5 to 30 minutes—designed to help people think differently about their level of substance use. They have been shown to reduce substance misuse, particularly alcohol consumption, and are cost-effective. Brief interventions can also serve to enhance a person's motivation to participate in formal treatment services. In addition to reducing substance use, brief interventions have also been found to reduce utilization of health-care services (e.g., Fleming, Barry, Manwell, et al., 1997).

Case management is another form of treatment for substance use disorders. This type of treatment does not directly target the substance use disorder. Instead, it helps address many of the commonly co-occurring psychosocial, psychiatric, and medical problems associated with substance use disorders that interfere with treatment. For example, case management for a patient with limited resources and lacking health insurance may seek to connect this individual with existing public support programs, as suggested by the Center for Substance Abuse Treatment (1998). There is growing evidence of the utility of case management. A series of randomized, controlled trials demonstrated the significant positive effects of case management on measures of substance use, employment, quality of life, psychological functioning, and service utilization (Vanderplasschen, Wolf, Rapp, et al., 2007; see also Saleh et al., 2002).

CONCLUSIONS

Although various frameworks exist to describe the continuum of care options for treating substance use disorders, no framework fully captures the significant heterogeneity that exists within the various types of inpatient and outpatient treatment options. For example, these different types of services may have differing theoretical orientations, terms of attendance, completion requirements, physical settings, and staff training requirements. Moreover, although the framework can help guide the selection of treatments, other factors also determine where an individual receives treatment. This includes, but is not limited to, the availability of services, connection with the criminal justice or psychiatric system of care, cultural compatibility of services, and funding.

It is also important to consider how these service types will continue to change in the future. In the early twenty-first century inpatient services remain the treatment of choice for severe and acute conditions; however, to reduce cost and increase access for underserved populations, many efforts are being made to adapt inpatient services to outpatient settings. Across all types of treatment options, additional research is needed to identify the key ingredients of treatment and determine how treatments can be better tailored for comorbid conditions. Research is also needed to understand better how treatments can be adapted for at-risk populations, such as minorities, women, and adolescents, as advanced by Ashley, Marsden, and Brady (2003).

BIBLIOGRAPHY

Ashley, O. S., Marsden, M. E., & Brady, T. M. (2003). Effectiveness of substance abuse treatment programming for women: A review. *The American Journal of Drug and Alcohol Abuse*, 29(1), 19–53.

Center for Substance Abuse Treatment. (1994). *Intensive outpatient treatment for alcohol and other drugs.* Treatment Improvement Protocol (TIP) Series, No. 8. DHHS Pub. No. (SMA) 94-2077. Rockville, MD: Author.

Center for Substance Abuse Treatment. (1998). *Comprehensive case management for substance abuse treatment.* Treatment Improvement Protocol (TIP) Series, No. 27. DHHS Pub. No. (SMA) 98-3222. Rockville, MD: Author.

Daley, D. C., & Salloum, I. M. (Eds.). (2001). *A clinician's guide to mental illness.* New York: McGraw-Hill.

Dutra, L., Stathopoulou, G., Basden, S. L., Leyro, T. M., Powers, M. B., & Otto, M. W. (2008). A meta-analytic review of psychosocial interventions for substance use disorders. *The American Journal of Psychiatry, 165*(2), 179–188.

Fleming, M. E., Barry, K. L., Manwell, L. B., Johnson, K., & London, R. (1997). Brief physician advice for problem alcohol drinker: A randomized controlled trial in community-based primary care practices. *Journal of the American Medical Association, 277*(13), 1039–1045.

Fuller, R. K., & Hiller-Sturmhofel, S. (1999). Alcoholism treatment in the United States: An overview. *Alcohol Research and Health, 23*(2), 69–77.

Gossop, M., Stewart, D., & Marsden, J. (2008). Attendance at Narcotics Anonymous and Alcoholics Anonymous meetings, frequency of attendance and substance use outcomes after residential treatment for drug dependence: A 5-year follow-up study. *Addiction, 103*(1), 119–125.

McKay, J. R. (2001). The role of continuing care in outpatient alcohol treatment programs. *Recent Developments in Alcoholism, 15*, 357–372.

Saleh, S. S., Vaughn, T., Hall, J., Levey, S., Fuortes, L., & Uden-Holmen, T. (2002). Effectiveness of case management in substance abuse treatment. *Care Management Journals, 3*(4), 172–177.

Vanderplasschen, W., Wolf, J., Rapp, R. C., & Broekaert, E. (2007). Effectiveness of different models of case management for substance-abusing populations. *Journal of Psychoactive Drugs, 39*(1), 81–95.

Work Group on Substance Use Disorders, Kleber, H. D., Weiss, R. D., Anton, R. F., Rounsaville, B. J., George, T. P., Strain, E. C., et al.; American Psychiatric Association Steering Committee on Practice Guidelines, McIntyre, J. S., Charles, S. C., Anzia, D. J., Nininger, J. E., Cook, I. A., Summergrad, P., et al. (2006). Treatment of patients with substance use disorders (2nd ed.). *American Journal of Psychiatry, 163*(8 Suppl), 5–82.

JENNA K. NIENHUIS
BRIAN E. PERRON

TREATMENT ACCOUNTABILITY FOR SAFER COMMUNITIES (TASC).

Developed in 1972, the Treatment Accountability for Safer Communities (TASC) was created by President Richard M. Nixon's Special Action Office for Drug Abuse Prevention (SAODAP) and funded by the Law Enforcement Assistance Administration (LEAA) and the National Institute of Mental Health (NIMH). The acronym originally stood for "Treatment Alternatives to Street Crime," reflecting the original emphasis of the program. Since its inception, TASC has provided leadership and advocacy to foster and improve the integrated delivery of substance abuse treatment to non-

violent offenders. The first TASC programs under SAODAP were operational in Wilmington, Delaware, and Philadelphia, Pennsylvania.

In the mid-1990s, TASC programs received support from the U.S. Department of Justice through the Bureau of Justice Assistance (BJA) Criminal Justice Block Grants, which are given to state and local governments. (LEAA was discontinued in 1982.) Many TASC programs have expanded their base of support so that state and federal funding is supplemented by private donations and grants or client fees. In 2008 TASC was operating in more than 100 jurisdictions in 28 of the U.S. states and territories. National TASC provides membership association and represents over 220 programs across the United States. The programs supported by National TASC are dedicated to the professional delivery of assessment and case management services to substance-involved individuals in the criminal justice and court systems. TASC has a large presence in some states, such as Florida, New York, North Carolina, Ohio, Pennsylvania, Illinois, Arizona, and Colorado.

Since the 1970s, TASC has evolved from providing the infrastructure to manage clients throughout the criminal justice system and supporting both justice and treatment independently to working in conjunction with drug courts, reentry management programs, and other efforts. The idea for the initial TASC programs derived from an analysis of the criminal justice system that indicated that many drug-addicted arrestees were released on bail while awaiting trial, and that these individuals were likely to continue to commit crimes. Although there were provisions for supervision of drug-dependent offenders after conviction (through probation) or after release from prison (through parole), no such mechanisms were in place to provide supervision of those awaiting trial. It was felt that if these arrestees could be directed to treatment, any success in treatment could be taken into consideration at the time of trial.

In addition to being an effective program model, TASC has also brought together the critical elements fundamental to integrating the criminal justice and substance abuse treatment systems. Both of these systems, as well as the offenders, are held accountable through the implementation of client-specific case management. TASC methods can be utilized by programs or systems attempting to manage drug-involved offenders. Because it is a methodology as well as a program model, TASC methods are applicable for moving offenders through a range of sentencing options—from deferred prosecution or pretrial release through incarceration and probation or parole, as well as residential and nonresidential treatment programs and aftercare. TASC methodology is essential to developing the partnerships between the justice system and the treatment delivery system that characterize many successful offender management programs, including drug courts and Breaking the Cycle programs. Between 1997 and 2001, Breaking the Cycle demonstration programs tested the feasibility and impact of system-wide intervention to reduce drug use among offenders by identifying and intervening with drug-involved felony defendants.

The TASC approach is to engage addicted offenders referred by criminal justice officials in substance abuse treatment and other ancillary services that address the needs of this population. The goal of TASC programs is to provide a treatment intervention that can stop the cycle of addiction, arrest, incarceration, and release. This is achieved through a specialized system of clinical case management that encourages positive behavior change and long-term recovery for individuals in criminal justice, corrections, juvenile justice, child welfare, and public aid settings. The purpose of the TASC program is to ensure that underserved populations gain access to the services they need for health and self-sufficiency, while also ensuring that public and private resources are used most efficiently.

In addition, TASC seeks to:

1. Serve as a vehicle for coordinating decision making and programming related to substance involved justice populations.

2. Offer information and education to both treatment providers and the justice system.

3. Provide practitioners with effective strategies for managing this population.

4. Participate and serve on boards and other entities that determine policies and procedures regarding the delivery of services.

5. Facilitate activities and events that encourage collaboration.

To standardize TASC as an effective national model for dealing with substance-abusing offenders, the U.S. Department of Health and Human Services developed guidelines for jurisdictions to operate an effective TASC program. The guidelines developed reflect those methods that can best identify eligible candidates, address critical service gaps, improve program management, and enhance service delivery standards. The guidelines incorporate 13 elements that are divided into three sections: (1) systems coordination, (2) organization, and (3) operation. The two systems coordination elements help provide the overarching support from the criminal justice, treatment, and other social services systems needed to manage addicted offenders effectively. The five organizational elements attempt to build the structural foundation necessary for TASC programs to provide client services that support the larger systems. The six operational elements delineate the minimum set of client activities that are performed by the TASC organization on an ongoing basis.

TASC procedures determine a drug-dependent offender's eligibility for intervention. These include an assessment of the offender's risk to the community, severity of drug dependence, and appropriateness for treatment placement. After an individual is referred to a treatment program, TASC case-management services monitor that individual's compliance with the conditions of the treatment and rehabilitation regime, including expectations for abstinence, employment, and improved personal and social functioning. Progress is reported to the referring justice-system agency. Clients who violate the conditions of their justice mandate—the TASC "contract," or treatment agreement—are usually returned to the justice system, where the legal process interrupted by the TASC diversion goes forward.

TASC programs play an important role in reducing the growing rates of drug-related street crime and alleviating court backlogs. They have been effective in identifying drug-involved offenders in need of treatment, assessing the nature and extent of their drug use and their specific treatment needs, and referring them to treatment. TASC clients have been found to remain in treatment longer and have better posttreatment success than those offenders who do not participate in the program. In addition, as an adjunct to parole and work release, TASC programs have the potential to help ease prison overcrowding. TASC also effectively fulfills its original purpose of linking the criminal justice system and the treatment system by providing client identification and monitoring services for the courts, probation departments, and other segments of the criminal justice system.

See also **Civil Commitment; Civil Remedies; Coerced Treatment for Substance Offenders; Crime and Drugs; Criminal Justice System, Treatment in the; Narcotic Addict Rehabilitation Act (NARA); U.S. Government Agencies: National Institute on Drug Abuse (NIDA).**

BIBLIOGRAPHY

Inciardi, J. A., & McBride, D. C. (1991). *Treatment alternatives to street crime: History, experiences, and issues* (DHHS Publication no. ADM 91–1749). Rockville, MD: U.S. Department of Health and Human Services, National Institute on Drug Abuse.

Morgan, J. (1992). *Treatment alternatives to street crime.* (State ADM Report no. 15). Washington, DC: George Washington University, Intergovernmental Health Policy Project.

National TASC. *About National TASC.* Washington, DC. Available from http://www.nationaltasc.org/.

New York State Division of Probation and Correctional Alternatives. (2008). *Treatment Accountability for Safer Communities (TASC) standards.* Albany, NY. Available from http://dpca.state.ny.us/.

Peyton, E. TASC in the 21st Century: A Guide for Practitioners and Policymakers (NCJ 193695). Washington, DC: National TASC; U.S. Department of Health and Human Services. Available from http://www.nationaltasc.org/.

JEROME H. JAFFE
FAITH K. JAFFE
REVISED BY JAYME DELANO (2009)

TREATMENT OUTCOME PROSPECTIVE STUDY (TOPS). This entry reports
the results of a clinical, epidemiological study of clients who entered drug-abuse treatment programs from 1979 to 1981. During the course of the Treatment Outcome Prospective Study (TOPS), 11,182 clients were interviewed at admission to drug-abuse treatment by program researchers hired to work in assigned clinics and professionally trained, and supervised by Research Triangle Institute (RTI) field staff. The interviews at admission covered demographics; history of drug use, treatment, arrest, and employment in the year prior to treatment; and status upon admission to treatment. The National Institute on Drug Abuse (NIDA) and RTI cosponsored the study. The population under study included 4,184 clients from 12 outpatient methadone programs, 2,891 clients from 14 residential programs, and 2,914 clients from 11 outpatient drug-free programs in 10 cities. Program researchers collected the responses to questions on behavior, services received, and satisfaction posed during interviews conducted every three months while clients remained in treatment. The self-report data were supplemented with data abstracted from the clinical and medical records of all clients selected for follow-up, and counselors and program directors completed questionnaires describing the treatment philosophy, structure, practice, and process.

The follow-up data included interviews 1 and 2 years after treatment with 1,130 clients who had been admitted in 1979; follow-ups 90 days and 1 year after treatment of 2,300 clients who had entered treatment in 1980; and follow-ups 3 to 5 years after treatment of 1,000 clients who had entered programs in 1981. Professional field interviewers hired, trained, and supervised by RTI field staff were able to locate and interview between 70 and 80 percent of the clients selected for these interviews.

TOPS resulted in a substantial body of important knowledge about drug-abuse treatment and its effectiveness. The client populations of outpatient methadone programs, long-term residential programs, and outpatient drug-free programs who participated in TOPS differed on many sociodemographic and background characteristics. Residential clients were significantly more likely to report the multiple use of drugs, drug-related problems, suicidal thoughts and attempts, heavy drinking, predatory crimes, and less full-time employment compared to methadone clients. Outpatient drug-free clients were more likely than methadone clients to report drug-related problems, suicidal thoughts or attempts, predatory crimes, and heavy drinking, but were less likely than residential clients to use multiple drugs. These results demonstrated that each type of program served very different, important segments of the drug-abusing population. The high rates of self-referrals to methadone treatment (48%) and criminal justice referrals to residential and outpatient drug-free treatment (31%) suggest differences in clients' motivations for seeking treatment and, consequently, differences in retention, services received, and outcomes.

The drug-abuse patterns reveal the differential concentration of types of drug abusers across major categories. Clients on methadone were primarily (52%) traditional heroin users who used only cocaine, marijuana, and alcohol in addition to heroin. One in five of these clients, however, used heroin and other narcotics, as well as a variety of non-narcotic drugs. The remaining twenty-five percent of clients on methadone were classified as former daily users who had a history of regular use but did not use heroin on a weekly or daily basis in the year prior to treatment. Residential clients had diverse patterns of use, and the majority of outpatient drug-free clients were users of alcohol and marijuana (36%) or single non-narcotics users (22%).

Symptoms of depression are very commonly reported by clients entering drug-abuse treatment programs. Overall, about 60 percent of TOPS clients reported at least one of three symptoms of depression at intake. Nearly 75 percent of the women under 21 years of age reported one or more symptoms of depression. Other results suggest that the duration of regular drug use and the number of prior treatment episodes are important indicators of the effectiveness of any single treatment episode; clients with lengthy drug-abuse or drug-treatment histories have poorer prognoses.

Clients who have come into treatment by way of the criminal justice system do as well or better than other clients in drug-abuse treatment. Formal or informal mechanisms of the criminal justice system appear to refer individuals who had not been treated previously and many who were not yet heavily involved in drug use. Involvement with the criminal justice system also helps retain clients in treatment up to an estimated six to seven additional weeks. Drug-abuse treatment programs vary in the nature and intensity of the treatment services provided, the types of therapists and therapies provided, the average length of stay, and the inclusion or exclusion of aftercare.

The study of the treatment process in TOPS programs focused on many important aspects of the structure, nature, duration, and intensity of drug-abuse treatment. Descriptions of aspects of the treatment process were developed from clients' self-reports of the need for treatment services, services received, and satisfaction, combined with abstractions of clinical and medical records and descriptions of programs by counselors and directors. The outpatient methadone and outpatient drug-free treatment programs had budgets per slot of approximately $2,000. U.S. therapeutic communities expended an average of $6,135 per bed.

The number of available services (medical, psychological, family, legal, educational, vocational, and financial services) varied during the years 1979 to 1981. Fewer services appeared to be available in the later years of the study. The proportion of clients in residential treatment programs who received family, educational, and vocational services decreased noticeably during the three-year period. During this same period, the clients' demands for services increased. Programs in TOPS appeared to focus on a client's primary drug of abuse rather than addressing his or her multiple drug use, drug-related problems, and social and economic functioning. Low-dose methadone (69% of the clients admitted were initially treated with less than 30 milligrams of oral methadone daily) was the most common pattern of methadone treatment in the programs participating in TOPS.

In TOPS multiple measures of treatment outcome were necessary to describe changes in the client's ability to function in society after treatment. In general, clients who remained in treatment at least 3 months had more positive post-treatment outcomes, but the major changes in behavior were seen only in those who remained in treatment for more than 12 months. Analyses of the TOPS data show that the posttreatment rate of daily heroin, cocaine, and psychotherapeutic-agent use among clients who spent at least 3 months in treatment was half that of the pretreatment rate. The posttreatment rates of weekly or more frequent use for clients who stayed in treatment at least 3 months were 10 to 15 percent lower than the rates for shorter-term clients. The results showed that time spent in treatment was among the most important predictors of positive treatment outcomes. Stays of one year or more in residential or methadone treatment, or continuing maintenance with methadone, produced significant decreases in the odds of a client using heroin in the follow-up period. Clients in TOPS also reported a substantial decrease in the symptoms of depression during the years after treatment.

Analyses of the effects of treatment on behavior have focused on reductions in predatory crime and the costs associated with crime. The assessment of the cost-benefit ratio indicates that substantial benefits are obtained in reductions of crime-related costs regardless of the measures used within the year after treatment. Reducing transmission of the acquired immunodeficiency syndrome (AIDS) virus would increase the benefit portion of the cost-benefit ratio even further.

See also **Drug Abuse Treatment Outcome Studies (DATOS); Treatment Accountability for Safer Communities (TASC).**

BIBLIOGRAPHY

Adair, E. B., Craddock, S. G., Miller, H. G., & Turner, C. F. (1996). Quality of treatment data: Reliability over time of self-reports given by clients in treatment for substance abuse. *Journal of Substance Abuse Treatment, 13*, 145–149.

Flynn, P. M., Simpson, D. D., Anglin, M. D., & Hubbard, R. L. (2001). Comment on nonresponse and selection bias in treatment follow-up studies [Letter to the editor]. *Substance Use & Misuse, 36*(12), 1749–1751.

Hser, Y., Grella, C. E., Hubbard, R. L., Hsieh, S. C., Fletcher, B. W., Brown, B. S., & Anglin, M. D. (2001). An evaluation of drug treatment for adolescents in four U.S. cities. *Archives of General Psychiatry, 58*(7), 689–695.

Hubbard, R. L., Craddock, S. G., & Anderson, J. (2003). Overview of 5-year follow-up outcomes in the Drug Abuse Treatment Outcome Studies (DATOS). *Journal of Substance Abuse Treatment, 25*(3), 125–134.

Hubbard, R. L., Craddock, S. G., Flynn, P. M., Anderson, J., & Etheridge, R. M. (1997). Overview of 1-year follow-up outcomes in the Drug Abuse Treatment Outcome Study (DATOS). *Psychology of Addictive Behaviors, 11*(4), 261–278.

Hubbard, R. L., Flynn, P. M., Craddock, S. G., & Fletcher, B. W. (2001). Relapse after drug abuse treatment. In F. M. Tims, C. G. Leukefeld, & J. J. Platt (Eds.), *Relapse and recovery in addictions* (pp. 109–121). New Haven, CT: Yale University Press.

Hubbard, R. L., Marsden, M. E., Rachal, J. V., Harwood, H. J., Cavenaugh, E. R., & Ginzburg, H. M. (Eds.). (1989). *Drug abuse treatment: A national study of effectiveness.* Chapel Hill, NC: University of North Carolina Press.

Kristiansen, P. L., & Hubbard, R. L. (2001). Methodological overview and research design for adolescents in the Drug Abuse Treatment Outcomes Studies (DATOS-A). *Journal of Adolescent Research, 16*(6), 545–562.

Simpson, D. D. (2003). Introduction to 5-year follow-up treatment outcome studies. *Journal of Substance Abuse Treatment, 25*(3), 123–124.

Simpson, D. D., Joe, G. W., & Broome, K. M. (2002). A national 5-year follow-up of treatment outcomes for cocaine dependence. *Archives of General Psychiatry, 59*, 538–544.

Simpson, D. D., Joe, G. W., Fletcher, B. W., Hubbard, R. L., & Anglin, M. D. (1999). A national evaluation of treatment outcomes for cocaine dependence. *Archives of General Psychiatry, 56*, 507–514.

ROBERT HUBBARD
REVISED BY PAMELA V. MICHAELS (2009)

U

UNITED KINGDOM: ALCOHOL AND TOBACCO USE AND POLICY. *See* **Britain; Britain: Alcohol Use and Policy; Britain: Tobacco Use and Policy.**

U.S. GOVERNMENT

This entry includes the following essays:
THE ORGANIZATION OF U.S. DRUG POLICY
AGENCIES IN DRUG LAW ENFORCEMENT AND SUPPLY CONTROL
AGENCIES SUPPORTING SUBSTANCE ABUSE PREVENTION AND TREATMENT
AGENCIES SUPPORTING SUBSTANCE ABUSE RESEARCH

THE ORGANIZATION OF U.S. DRUG POLICY

Reducing drug abuse became a priority for the U.S. government in the late 1960s, with continuing expansion of management attention and federal budgets thereafter. In 1969, eight agencies and four cabinet departments received drug-program funding; in 1975, seven cabinet departments were included; the federal drug control program for 2008 involved eleven cabinet departments. In 1969, the total budget for federal drug-abuse programs was $81 million; for 2008, the president's requested budget was approximately $14.1 billion (National Drug Control Strategy, 2008).

Illegal drug trafficking and use present complicated social and law enforcement challenges. The federal government has responded to these challenges in the four decades since the 1960s with increasing governmental agencies and laws. Executive and legislative response has varied over several administrations as the national problems presented by illegal drugs have developed. Drug prevention policy issues are as complex as the illegal drugs they aim to control. This entry explains the development of federal response to the complicated social and legal issues associated with illegal drug trafficking and use.

DIFFICULTIES IN ORGANIZING DRUG POLICY

Illegal drugs come from both international and domestic sources; they include a wide variety of substances; they involve many different forms of transportation, geographical areas, criminal activities, use patterns, and social effects. All these elements are dynamic and constantly adjust to changes in availability of substances and the demand for them. Drug traffickers and active drug users react quickly to drug law enforcement pressures by shifting to areas or techniques that have less risk.

Positive social and legal responses to the illegal drug activity includes all efforts to increase public understanding about the effects of illegal drugs; to develop and increase community-, school-, and family-based programs to reduce drug use; and to promote effective treatment, rehabilitation, and counseling methods. These efforts often require the development and dissemination of new knowledge. They also require evolution of effective laws, development of official roles, and the creation of agencies and other institutions with diverse agendas and sometimes conflicting interests.

The challenge to federal managers and policy-makers is to understand the complex and ever-changing factors that define illegal trafficking and drug use in the United States, and to adjust and adapt the federal response in a timely and effective manner. The executive and legislative branches of government, along with cabinet departments and other governmental agencies, attempt to handle the illegal drug problems at the same time that they work to resolve interdepartmental differences of opinion.

The organization of the federal government is not designed to respond specifically or exclusively to criminal drug activity. There is no cabinet department with line authority over all drug-program resources, and as of 2008 only a few federal agencies are organized around a single drug-related function (e.g., the Drug Enforcement Administration, National Institute on Drug Abuse, and the Substance Abuse and Mental Health Services Administration). All departments have other, often overarching, roles, so they must balance their drug and non-drug responsibilities. Indeed, every step in the policy-determination and -implementation process is subject to bureaucratic, political, and technical differences of opinion. Two challenges in addressing the drug problem are: (1) reaching agreement on the extent and nature of the problem, and (2) assessing the impact of the federal effort on the ever changing nexus of factors. To overcome these and other difficulties, between the early 1970s and the early 2000s, the federal organization for determining drug policy and implementing drug programs expanded in both scope and effort. As of 2008, eleven federal departments were involved in drug prevention efforts (*2008 National Drug Control Strategy*).

HISTORY

A chronological summary of drug-policy coordinating mechanisms is presented below, beginning with 1971, first from the perspective of the Executive Branch and then from the perspective of the Legislative Branch.

Executive Drug Policy (1971–1976). President Richard M. Nixon created the Special Action Office for Drug Abuse Prevention (SAODAP) in the Executive Office of the President (EOP) in June 1971, which was designed to lead and coordinate all federal drug-abuse prevention activities. The first director, Jerome H. Jaffe, also served as consultant to the president for narcotics and dangerous drugs. SAODAP monitored the annual budget and prepared budget analyses of all federal drug-abuse programs, by agency and by activity.

After the 1971 creation of SAODAP, there was a continuous presence in the White House structure of a federal drug coordinating and management effort. Thus, the federal responders to criminal drug activity had a special pleading office for these social issues with a consistent presence in the White House, which is most unusual.

Also in 1971, President Nixon called for "an all out global war on the international drug traffic" (*1973 Federal Strategy*, p. 112). His organization for policy incorporated an international perspective. International efforts were coordinated by the Cabinet Committee on International Narcotics Control (CCINC), chaired by the secretary of state. Established in August 1971, CCINC was responsible for developing a strategy to stop the flow of illegal narcotics into the United States and for coordinating federal efforts to implement that strategy. Domestic drug-law enforcement had a high priority within the normal cabinet-management system.

In January 1972, President Nixon created the Office of Drug Abuse Law Enforcement (ODALE) in the Department of Justice (DOJ) and gave the ODALE director, Myles J. Ambrose, the added title of consultant to the president for drug abuse law enforcement. The directors of both SAODAP and ODALE had a policy oversight role in advising the president.

The 1972 legislation authorizing SAODAP also created the Strategy Council on Drug Abuse (known as the Strategy Council) and directed the "development and promulgation of a comprehensive, coordinated, long-term Federal strategy for all drug abuse prevention and drug traffic functions conducted, sponsored, or supported by the Federal government." The cabinet-level Strategy Council, with the directors of SAODAP and ODALE as co-chairmen, prepared the *1973 Federal Strategy for Prevention of Drug Abuse and Drug Trafficking*, the first explicit drug-prevention strategy document.

Additional federal strategies were published in 1974 and 1975 during the directorship of Robert L. DuPont, establishing the precedent for the over 25 similar strategies that were subsequently published, and as of 2008 remained an important product of the federal drug-prevention policy effort.

In 1975, SAODAP was phased out under a sunset provision in its enabling legislation. Program initiatives in research, prevention, treatment, and rehabilitation were transferred to the newly established national Institute on Drug Abuse (NIDA), and SAODAP director DuPont became the founding director of NIDA. Responsibility for federal drug prevention coordination fell to the office of Federal Drug Management (FDM), within the Office of Management and Budget (OMB), which supported senior officials of OMB, the CCINC, and the White House Domestic Council.

In early 1975, President Gerald R. Ford directed the White House Domestic Council to review the federal drug effort. Vice President Nelson A. Rockefeller chaired the interagency Domestic Council Drug Abuse Task Force, with the chief of FDM as study director. The task force, with advice from community organizations, prepared the comprehensive *1975 White Paper on Drug Abuse*. This report recommended assigning responsibility for overall policy guidance to the Strategy Council on Drug Abuse; creating an EOP Cabinet Committee to coordinate prevention and treatment activities; and continuing a small staff in OMB to assist the Strategy Council and the EOP. In April 1976, President Ford announced two new cabinet committees, the Cabinet Committee on Drug Law Enforcement and the Cabinet Committee on Drug Abuse Prevention "to ensure the coordination of all government resources which bear on the problem of drug abuse" (*Federal strategy: Drug abuse prevention*, 1976, p. 26). The cabinet committee structure, supported by the FDM staff, worked to the satisfaction of President Ford but did not satisfy Congress.

Congress enacted legislation establishing an Office of Drug Abuse Policy (ODAP) in March 1976, seeking a single individual in the EOP with responsibility for the overall drug program. President Ford did not activate the new agency, however, but chose to continue with the three cabinet committees, supported by the FDM staff.

Executive Drug Policy (1977–1980). In March 1977, President Jimmy Carter revised the drug-policy structure, activating ODAP and abolishing the three drug-related cabinet committees. He also revitalized the Strategy Council, with the director of ODAP as executive director, to serve as the government-wide advisory committee for all drug-abuse matters. ODAP worked particularly well with the White House staff, partially because Director Peter Bourne was also special assistant to the president for health issues and had an excellent relationship with President Carter and the White House staff. ODAP aggressively pursued a wide range of policy and coordination activities, including a major review of all federal drug programs.

The President's Reorganization Project reviewed the organization of the Executive Branch and recommended abolishing ODAP in mid-1977. Within the EOP, ODAP was an unusual federal agency, with a strong presence and authority for a single issue, somewhat atypical in the EOP structure. Thus, ODAP was a logical target in efforts to streamline the EOP. Congress disagreed strongly with the elimination of ODAP, however. After congressional hearings and negotiations, the Carter administration compromised by continuing part of the ODAP staff and all the ODAP functions as part of the White House Domestic Policy Staff (DPS).

In March 1978, six members of the ODAP staff were transferred to DPS and became the Drug Policy Office (DPO). The DPO continued to perform ODAP functions, including responding to congressional interests and reporting directly to Peter Bourne. After Bourne departed the White House staff in 1978, the drug staff worked through the DPS director. In May 1979, the president affirmed the head of DPO, Lee Dogoloff, as the individual primarily responsible for federal drug-abuse prevention and control programs. DPO published the *1979 Federal Strategy* and the *1980 Annual Report*. A major policy-coordinating mechanism was the monthly meetings held by DPO with the heads of the major operating agencies (called the Principals Group). DPO also supported the National Narcotics Intelligence Consumers Committee, another policy-coordinating mechanism, which was established in April 1978, and it initiated efforts to increase military support for drug-interdiction activities.

Executive Drug Policy (1981–1988). In 1981, President Ronald Reagan's Office of Policy Development (OPD) included a Drug Abuse Policy Office (DAPO) similar in organization and role to the preceding DPO. President Reagan charged DAPO with (1) a full range of policy-development and coordination activities, (2) international negotiations, and (3) assisting the drug-abuse prevention efforts of First Lady Nancy Reagan. In addition to overseeing the efforts of the federal drug agencies, DAPO emphasized the use of all opportunities for the federal government to encourage a wide range of non-government anti-drug activities. DAPO was directed by Carleton Turner, a pharmacologist, who was succeeded in 1987 by Donald Ian MacDonald, a pediatrician. DAPO published the *1982 Federal Strategy*, and reflecting the subsequent broader policy direction, in 1984 it published the *National Strategy for Prevention of Drug Abuse and Drug Trafficking*.

DAPO continued the coordination meetings with the agency heads (the previous Principals Group, renamed the Oversight Working Group) and assisted in the design and implementation of the National Narcotics Border Interdiction System (NNBIS), headed by Vice President George H. Bush. DPO assisted the Cabinet Council on Legal Policy and the Cabinet Council on Human Resources with drug matters until the cabinet councils were replaced by the Domestic Policy Council in April 1985. The Domestic Policy Council Working Group on Drug Abuse Policy prepared a major presidential drug initiative in 1986, with assistance from DAPO.

During the 1980s, the oversight of drug law enforcement moved away from the White House. In 1984, Congress had established a federal drug law-enforcement czar to "facilitate coordination of U.S. operations and policy on illegal drug law enforcement." The attorney general was chairman of the new cabinet-level National Drug Enforcement Policy Board (NDEPB) with staff offices in the Department of Justice. DAPO was charged with ensuring "coordination between the NDEPB and the health issues associated with drug abuse," in addition to supporting the president and the White House staff. In January 1987, the NDEPB published the *National and International Drug Law Enforcement Strategy*, which expanded on the

sections of the *1984 National Strategy* pertaining to drug law enforcement and international controls. DAPO continued to provide Executive Office oversight of the entire drug program.

In 1987, President Reagan replaced the NDEPB by creating the National Drug Policy Board (NDPB) to coordinate all drug-abuse policy functions. The director of the White House DAPO was a member and assisted the NDPB in developing health-related drug policy. The NDPB published *Toward a Drug-Free America—The National Drug Strategy and Implementation Plans* in 1988.

In late 1988, Congress again passed drug czar legislation, authorizing a new agency named the Office of National Drug Control Policy (ONDCP) in the EOP.

Executive Drug Policy (1989–2000). ONDCP began operation in the EOP in early 1989, absorbing the NDPB and terminating the two existing White House drug activities, DAPO and NNBIS. Although never actually a member of the cabinet, the first two cabinet-level directors were given broad responsibilities for developing and guiding the National Drug Control Program, including developing an annual strategy and overseeing its implementation. The first director, William Bennett, had been secretary of education in the Reagan administration; he was succeeded by Robert Martinez, a former governor of Florida. ONDCP had oversight of organization, management, budget, and personnel allocations of all departments and agencies engaged in drug control activities. ONDCP used a complex set of interagency coordinating committees under a Supply Reduction Working Group, a Demand Reduction Working Group, and a Research and Development Committee. The director chaired the NSC Policy Coordinating Committee for Narcotics, which ensured coordination between drug law enforcement and national security activities. The director also provided administrative support to the President's Drug Advisory Council, which in turn assisted ONDCP in supporting national drug-control objectives through private sector initiatives. ONDCP was required to establish realistic and attainable goals for the following two years and the following ten years and to monitor progress toward the goals. Following the election of President Bill Clinton, Lee Brown, a criminologist and former New York police commissioner, was appointed director of ONDCP and was also given membership in the cabinet. The fourth director, retired U.S. Army General Barry R. McCaffrey, was appointed in 1996 and served until 2001.

Executive Drug Policy (2001–2008). Strong drug policy national leadership characterized the Bush White House in the years from 2001 through 2008. During this period, while law enforcement efforts remained robust, more White House attention was given to primary prevention issues, especially school-based drug prevention efforts that included random drug testing. In addition, ONDCP increasingly reached out to state and local stakeholders. John Walters served as drug czar from 2001 into 2008, a period of unprecedented stability and consistent policy leadership.

Beginning in 2002, the National Drug Control Strategy included specific goals. That year, it was announced that the strategy would pursue ambitious goals: a 10 percent reduction in youth drug use in two years, and a 25 percent reduction in youth drug use over five years. This action constituted one of the first instances in which specific goals were established for the reduction of drug use in the United States. Each successive strategy tracked these goals. The 2005 and 2008 strategies cited other surveys and other data that indicated decreases consistent with these goals. The goals were restated in 2008 for an additional 10 percent reduction in youth drug use in 2008, using 2006 as the baseline.

The *2008 Strategy* had three main initiatives. The first initiative was aimed at preventing drug use through the development and implementation of community efforts designed to change attitudes. These efforts included school-based random testing, combating doping in sports, promoting drug-free programs, and developing community-based programs to support a drug-free society. A national antidrug media campaign supported efforts to educate youth about the dangers of drug use and encourages states to use federal block grant money to promote local efforts.

The second initiative was designed to improve nationwide efforts to effectively identify and treat people who have drug problems, including between screening to detect drug use, effective measures of intervention, medical education initiatives, and advances in treatment regimens. These efforts were supported by the continued promotion of drug courts, which serve as important referral sources, and of family drug treatment courts. Also promoted were new approaches to treating co-occurring disorders because many people entering drug treatment programs have other medical or psychological problems such as schizophrenia and depression. These efforts represented a clear departure from strategy focus at the end of the twentieth century.

The third initiative was to continue a robust effort designed to disrupt the market for illegal drugs at home and abroad. Efforts included increasing the viability and effectiveness of local and state law enforcement in recognition of their growing role in fighting pharmaceutical diversion, closing open-air drug markets, and tackling domestic marijuana cultivation. Border security remained a high priority for reducing the flow of drugs coming into the United States from Mexico, the Caribbean, and South America, and for attacking trafficker finances by improving intelligence and assisting other governments developing their capabilities to interdict couriers through training and technical assistance programs funded by the U.S. Department of State.

BUDGET INDICATORS

The budget is divided into two broad components aimed at reducing the demand for drugs and disrupting their supply. The budgets span five years of the Clinton administration and five years (including one projected based on the 2005 request) of the George W. Bush administration. One administration was Democrat, the other Republican, yet the allocation of funding was similar. Both the highest and lowest percentage of funds allocated to the response side took place during the Clinton administration, the highest in FY 1998 when 50.1 percent of the budget went to treatment and prevention, the lowest in FY 2000, when only 43.2 percent of funds went to stem demand. FY 2000, conversely, also saw the highest allocation of funds to disrupting the supply of drugs, 56.7 percent of the budget. The Bush administration's request for FY 2008 divided funding: 35 percent for demand reduction and 65 percent for disrupting supplies (*2008 National Drug Control Strategy,* p. 4). In the ten years since FY 1998, funds for law enforcement, interdiction, and international programs were higher than funds allocated to treatment, prevention, and research to support these efforts.

A study of the budget allocations between 1996 and 2005 indicated that funds were divided (unequally) between drug abuse treatment and programs of prevention (*The National Drug Control Strategy—The Federal Drug Budget*). Treatment received 24.5 percent of the total budget during the FY 1996–2005 period, prevention 14.4 percent. In the requested budget for FY 2005, treatment made up 24.4 percent and prevention 12.4 percent, both increases over the previous few years, but still below historic averages over the previous decade.

The study also noted that when the research funding to support these two activities was added, treatment for 29.2 percent of the total budget over the period and 29.4 percent in the 2005 budget request (28.1% enacted in 2004); prevention, with research, averaged 17.6 percent over the ten-year period and received 15.6 percent in the 2005 budget request (16.4% enacted by Congress in FY 2004) (*2008 National Drug Control Strategy*, p. 4). On average, over the ten-year period shown, treatment (with research) received 62.5 percent and prevention (with research) 37.1 percent of the demand-reduction component of the budget. Treatment funds went into actual treatment of individuals, typically through grant programs to states.

During the entire ten-year period supply distribution consumed 53.2 percent of the total federal drug control budget, slightly less than the percentage that it was allocated in the FY 2005 budget request. Within this component, domestic law enforcement was the largest piece (46.6% over the ten-year period). Interdiction came next (36.9%), and international programs were last (16.5%).

As of 2008, most domestic law enforcement funds were spent by the DOJ (or on its behalf) and underwrote the operations of the Drug Enforcement Administration, the chief domestic drug control agency. Interdiction funds were managed by the U.S. Department of Homeland Security (DHS), which as of 2008 oversaw all border control functions and the U.S. Coast Guard. International funds were divided roughly equally between the U.S. State Department and the U.S. Department of Defense. The Department of State's Bureau of International Narcotics and Law Enforcement Affairs was the lead agency managing international programs. The Department of Defense was involved in supporting anti-insurgency programs in the Andean region and elsewhere.

As of 2008, the most budgetary fluctuation over time was associated with international programs. Significant portions of this budget were expended on supporting international eradication efforts that, in turn, depend on the cooperation of other countries and on the U.S. drug certification program, which was able to temporarily deny funding to certain regimes. Funds ranged from 3.9 percent of the total budget (FY 1996) to 15.9 percent (FY 2000); in 2001 funding dropped again to 6.3 percent. The 2008 president's budget request of approximately $1.610 billion comprised just over 11 percent of the president's requested budget.

CONGRESSIONAL DRUG-POLICY OVERSIGHT

Between 1971 and the early 2000s, Congress had a strong and continuing interest in establishing an effective drug-policy oversight mechanism, which would respond to the difficulties of the various committees in attempting to address the drug activities of a single agency within the context of the overall federal effort. Congress was frustrated by repeated failed efforts to establish a drug czar in the EOP to oversee federal drug policy and to advise both the president and Congress.

For example, the Senate Committee on Government Operations had a long-term interest in drug-program oversight and reiterated the programmatic needs for a single, high-level coordinating body with broad statutory authority over federal drug-abuse policy and its implementation. In the House of Representatives, the Select Committee on Narcotics Abuse and Control, headed by Representative Charles Rangel, played an important role in congressional oversight of drug programs and policy. The select committee was formed in July 1976 "to oversee all facets of the Federal narcotics effort and coordinate the response of the seven legislative committees in the House which have jurisdiction over some aspect of the narcotics problem." Without legislative jurisdiction, the select committee was primarily a fact-finding activity to support the seven standing committees in the House of Representatives. The select committee was also a focal point for congressional pressure for a legislatively based drug czar. In early 1993, Select Committee on Narcotics Abuse and Control was discontinued.

DRUG-POLICY LEGISLATION

In 1972, Congress passed legislation authorizing the Special Action Office for Drug Abuse Prevention, as requested by President Nixon. After SAODAP expired in 1975, Congress authorized a replacement drug-policy agency (ODAP) in early 1976 and was critical of President Ford's decision not to open the new agency.

When President Carter decided to activate ODAP in early 1977, Congress applauded the decision and confirmed the director and deputy director; but ODAP was abolished in early 1978 despite congressional objections, ending the successful relationship between ODAP and Congress. The resulting executive/congressional negotiations required the Drug Policy Office of the DPS to carry out the functions previously assigned to ODAP and to allow congressional access to the drug-policy staff.

In late 1979, Congress followed up with legislation requiring the president to establish a drug-abuse policy coordination system and to designate a single officer to direct the activities (21 USC 1111 & 1112). A system was established by President Carter (Executive Order 12133, 1979, Drug Policy Office) and by President Reagan (Executive Order 12368, 1982, Drug Abuse Policy Office).

In late 1982, Congress enacted a strong drug czar in an Office of National and International Drug Operations and Policy, with a cabinet-level director. The director was granted broad powers to develop, review, implement, and enforce government policy and to direct departments and agencies involved. The explicit power to direct other departments and agencies was seen as too strong and in conflict with the principles of cabinet government. President Reagan did not accept the legislation.

In 1984, the Congress and the administration agreed to establish a cabinet-level NDEPB with a limited charter to coordinate drug law enforcement. The legislation designated the attorney general as chairman and primary adviser to the president and to Congress, on both national and international law enforcement.

In 1987, President Reagan signed Executive Order 12590, broadened the charter of the attorney general and the NDEPB to include the entire federal drug program, and named the new activity the National Drug Policy Board.

In late 1988, Congress passed new drug czar legislation, creating the Office of National Drug Control Policy in the EOP, with a cabinet-level director and funding provisions for both operating expenses and program activities. President George H. W. Bush accepted the new agency and appointed a cabinet-level director, but he did not include the first director or his successor in his immediate cabinet.

Thus, Congress achieved the drug czar objectives that it pursued for two decades: a cabinet-level drug-policy manager with broad oversight of policy and budgets, responsible both to Congress and the president.

WHITE HOUSE DRUG CZARS BY PRESIDENT

Nixon: Jerome H. Jaffe, Robert L. DuPont

Ford: Robert L. DuPont, Edward Johnson (OMB)

Carter: Peter Bourne, Lee I. Dogoloff

Reagan: Ian MacDonald, Carleton Turner

G. H. W. Bush: William J. Bennett, Robert Martinez

Clinton: Lee Brown, Barry McCaffrey

G. W. Bush: John Walters

See also **Anslinger, Harry Jacob, and U.S. Drug Policy; International Drug Supply Systems; Treatment: A History of Treatment in the United States.**

BIBLIOGRAPHY

Hogan, H.; Congressional Research Service, the Library of Congress. (1989). *Drug control at the federal level: Coordination and direction* (Report 87–780 GOV).

National drug control strategy: The federal drug budget. Available from http://www.libraryindex.com/.

Office of National Drug Control Policy. (2008). *National drug control strategy.* Washington, DC: Government Printing Office.

U.S. Congress, House. Select Committee on Narcotics Abuse and Control. (1978). *Congressional resource guide to the federal effort on narcotics abuse and control, 1969–76: Part 1. A report of the Select Committee on Narcotics Abuse and Control,* 95th Congress, 2nd sess. Washington, DC: Government Printing Office.

U.S. Congress, House. Select Committee on Narcotics Abuse and Control. (1980). *Recommendation for continued house oversight of drug abuse problems: A report of the Select Committee on Narcotics Abuse and Control* (Report No. 96–1380). 96th Congress, 2nd sess. Washington, DC: Government Printing Office.

U.S. Executive Office of the President. Domestic Council Drug Abuse Task Force. (1975, September). *White paper on drug abuse.* Washington, DC: Government Printing Office.

U.S. Executive Office of the President. Domestic Policy Staff. (1980). *Annual report on the federal drug program.* Washington, DC: Government Printing Office.

U.S. Executive Office of the President. Drug Abuse Policy Office, Office of Policy Development, The White House. (1984). *1984 national strategy for prevention of drug abuse and drug trafficking.* Washington, DC: Government Printing Office.

U.S. Executive Office of the President. Office of Drug Abuse Policy. (1978). 1978 annual report. Washington, DC: Government Printing Office.

U.S. Executive Office of the President. Office of National Drug Control Policy. (1990, January). *National drug control strategy.* Washington, DC: Government Printing Office.

U.S. Executive Office of the President. Office of National Drug Control Policy. (1991, January). *National drug control strategy.* Washington, DC: Government Printing Office.

U.S. Executive Office of the President. Office of National Drug Control Policy. (1992, January). *National drug control strategy.* Washington, DC: Government Printing Office.

U.S. Executive Office of the President. President's Advisory Commission on Narcotic and Drug Abuse. (1963). *Final report.* Washington, DC: Government Printing Office.

U.S. Executive Office of the President. Strategy Council on Drug Abuse. (1973). *Federal strategy for drug abuse and drug traffic prevention.* Washington, DC: Government Printing Office.

U.S. Executive Office of the President. Strategy Council on Drug Abuse. (1976). *Federal strategy for drug abuse prevention.* Washington, DC: Government Printing Office.

U.S. Executive Office of the President. Strategy Council on Drug Abuse. (1979). *Federal strategy for drug abuse and drug traffic prevention.* Washington, DC: Government Printing Office.

RICHARD L. WILLIAMS
REVISED BY RICHARD H. BUCHER (2009)

AGENCIES IN DRUG LAW ENFORCEMENT AND SUPPLY CONTROL

This entry provides an overview of the many federal agencies involved in drug law enforcement and supply control. The Department of Justice serves as the hub for research, crime and law enforcement data, funding for law enforcement efforts, and a significant portion of the law enforcement programs. Other federal agencies playing vital roles in law enforcement efforts are the Office of National Drug Control Strategy, the Department of Homeland Security, the Department of Transportation, the Department of State, the Department of Defense, and the U.S. Postal Service.

DEPARTMENT OF JUSTICE

The Department of Justice (DOJ) was established by the U.S. Congress in 1870 as a part of the Act to Establish the Department of Justice (chap. 150, 16 Stat. 162). The mission of the department is to "enforce the law and defend the interests of the United States according to the law; to ensure public safety against threats foreign and domestic; to provide federal leadership in preventing and controlling crime; to seek just punishment for those guilty of unlawful behavior; and to ensure fair and impartial administration of justice for all Americans." As of 2008, DOJ included fifty-nine executive offices, divisions, bureaus, commissions, and other offices. Approximately sixteen of these offices were actively involved in drug law enforcement and supply control. The Drug Enforcement Administration (DEA); Federal Bureau of Investigation (FBI); Bureau of Alcohol, Tobacco, Firearms, and Explosives (ATF); and Office of Justice Programs (OJP) are discussed below.

Drug Enforcement Administration (DEA).

The DEA was created in 1973 to consolidate and coordinate the government's drug control activities by combining the efforts and personnel of four federal drug law enforcement programs. Its legal authority stems primarily from the Controlled Substance Act and other laws directed at control of essential chemicals and precursors. The DEA operates domestically and in foreign countries with the agreement of the government in each country to enforce regulations concerning importation, manufacture, storage, and dispensing of all drugs scheduled under the Controlled Substances Act.

In 2008, DEA employed nearly 11,000 special agents and support staff. Its enforcement programs include asset forfeiture, aviation, computer forensics, demand reduction, diversion control, marijuana eradication, money laundering, and organized crime. Each program was designed to focus on a specific drug threat or facet of the illicit drug trade. Other efforts, such as the Southwest Border Initiative, focused on specific regions of the country identified as primary distribution or manufacturing areas.

In addition to the enforcement efforts described above, the DEA supports intelligence efforts such as the El Paso Intelligence Center (EPIC), a fully coordinated, tactical intelligence center supported by databases and resources from twelve member agencies. EPIC was designed to enable agents to target, track, and interdict drugs, aliens, and weapons moving across U.S. borders.

Federal Bureau of Investigation (FBI). In 1982, FBI resources were significantly expanded and it was given concurrent jurisdiction with the DEA to investigate drug offenses. The FBI concentrates primarily on drug trafficking by organized crime and violent gangs and drug-related financial activities such as international money laundering. Investigations are conducted using electronic surveillance techniques and other law enforcement techniques. In 2007, the FBI had more than 30,000 employees, including more than 12,000 special agents and nearly 18,000 support professionals.

Bureau of Alcohol, Tobacco, Firearms and Explosives (ATF). In 2003, the ATF was transferred from the Department of Treasury to the Department of Justice. In the process the function of ATF shifted from tax and trade functions to an expanded law enforcement focus. The mission subsequently involved both enforcing federal criminal laws and regulating the firearms and explosives industries. ATF is committed to working directly, and through partnerships, to investigate and reduce crime involving firearms and explosives, acts of arson, and illegal trafficking of alcohol and tobacco products. The combined efforts of special agents and industry operations investigators allow ATF to effectively identify, investigate, and recommend for prosecution violators of the federal firearms, explosives, arson, and tobacco and alcohol diversion laws.

As of 2008, ATF was the lead agency in the DOJ Project Safe Neighborhoods, which focuses on reducing gun violence. In addition, ATF worked to prevent terrorism and monitor firearm licensees and provide a variety of resources to other law enforcement agencies, including the National Integrated Ballistic Information Network, gun tracing, national response teams, and national laboratory services.

Office of Justice Programs (OJP). After 1984, OJP developed the capacity to prevent and control crime by generating statistics on law enforcement and crime, supporting research, and funding criminal justice programs. As of 2008, OJP maintained seven bureaus and offices, including the Bureau of Justice Assistance (BJA), the Bureau of Justice Statistics (BJS), and the National Institute of Justice (NIJ). BJA provides technical and financial assistance to state and local governments through formula grants designed to support the enforcement of local and state laws, including drug laws, and to provide resources and intelligence to the law enforcement agencies enforcing these laws. BJS collects, analyzes, and disseminates information on crime, its victims, and its perpetrators. NIJ is the major research and development entity within the DOJ. Its activities include evaluating the effectiveness of programs supported by BJA.

In addition, DEA, FBI, and ATF participate in joint operations run by DOJ, such as the Asset Forfeiture Program, and other agencies, such as the Office of National Drug Control Policy's High Intensity Drug Trafficking Areas Program described below. These efforts are designed to focus on specific drug threats, drug trafficking organizations, or regions of the country.

OFFICE OF NATIONAL DRUG CONTROL POLICY (ONDCP)

The White House Office of National Drug Control Policy (ONDCP) is a part of the Executive Office of the President. It was established by the Anti-Drug Abuse Act of 1988. The principal purpose of ONDCP is to establish policies, priorities, and objectives for U.S. drug control programs. The goals of the program are to reduce illicit drug use, manufacturing, and trafficking; drug-related crime and violence; and drug-related health consequences. ONDCP works with the National Drug Intelligence Center to prepare annual drug threat assessments and reports on U.S. drug

	FY 2007 final	FY 2008 enacted	FY 2009 request
	Budget authority in millions		
Department of Defense	1,329.8	1,177.4	1,060.5
Department of Education	495.0	431.6	218.1
Department of Health and Human Services			
Centers for Medicare & Medicaid Services	—	45.0	265.0
Indian Health Service	148.2	173.2	162.0
National Institute on Drug Abuse	1,000.0	1,000.7	1,001.7
Substance Abuse and Mental Health Services Administration	2,443.2	2,445.8	2,370.6
Total HHS	**3,591.4**	**3,664.8**	**3,799.3**
Department of Homeland Security			
Office of Counternarcotics Enforcement	2.5	2.7	4.0
Customs and Border Protection	1,968.5	2,130.9	2,191.9
Immigration and Customs Enforcement	422.8	412.3	428.9
U.S. Coast Guard	1,080.9	1,004.3	1,071.0
Total DHS	**3,474.8**	**3,550.1**	**3,695.8**
Department of the Interior			
Bureau of Indian Affairs	2.6	6.3	6.3
Total DOI	**2.6**	**6.3**	**6.3**
Department of Justice			
Bureau of Prisons	65.1	67.2	69.2
Drug Enforcement Administration	1,969.1	2,105.3	2,181.0
Interagency Crime and Drug Enforcement	497.9	497.9	531.6
Office of Justice Programs	245.5	222.8	114.2
Total DOJ	**2,777.7**	**2,893.2**	**2,896.0**
ONDCP			
Counterdrug Technology Assessment Center	20.0	1.0	5.0
High Intensity Drug Trafficking Area Program	224.7	230.0	200.0
Other Federal Drug Control Programs	193.0	164.3	189.7
Drug-Free Communities (non-add)	*79.2*	*90.0*	*80.0*
National Youth Anti-Drug Media Campaign (non-add)	*99.0*	*60.0*	*100.0*
Salaries and Expenses	26.8	26.4	26.8
Total ONDCP	**464.4**	**421.7**	**421.5**
Small Business Administration	1.0	1.0	1.0
Department of State			
Bureau of International Narcotics and Law Enforcement Affairs	1,055.7	640.8	1,173.2
United States Agency International Development	239.0	361.4	315.3
Total State	**1,294.7**	**1,002.2**	**1,489.0**
Department of Transportation			
National Highway Traffic Safety Administration	2.9	2.7	2.7
Department of Treasury			
Internal Revenue Service	55.6	57.3	59.2
Department of Veterans Affairs			
Veterans Health Administration	354.1	447.2	465.0
Total	**$13,844.0**	**$13,655.4**	**$14,114.4**

NOTE: Detail may not add due to rounding.
In addition to the resources displayed in the table above, the Administration requests $385.1 million in FY 2008 supplemental funding for counternarcotics support to Mexico and Central America.

Table 1. Drug control funding by agency, FY 2007–FY 2009. (Source: National Drug Control Strategy, 2008 Annual Report. Office of National Drug Control Policy.) ILLUSTRATION BY GGS INFORMATION SERVICES. GALE, CENGAGE LEARNING

control strategy. ONDCP's key drug law enforcement and supply control initiative is the High Intensity Drug Trafficking Areas Program. Other initiatives focus on prevention, treatment, and recovery.

HIGH INTENSITY DRUG TRAFFICKING AREAS (HIDTA) PROGRAM

The purpose of the High Intensity Drug Trafficking Areas (HIDTA) Program is to provide resources to federal, state, and local agencies to coordinate and carry out activities that address drug trafficking activities in specially designated regions of the United States. The HIDTA Program was first authorized in the Anti-Drug Abuse Act of 1988, the same statute that created the Office of National Drug Control Policy (ONDCP), and it has been reauthorized on three occasions, for example, in the ONDCP Reauthorization Act of 2006. That statute authorized the director of ONDCP to designate an area as a HIDTA only if the following apply:

the area is a significant center of illegal drug production, manufacturing, importation, or distribution

state, local, and tribal law enforcement agencies have committed resources to respond to the drug trafficking problem in the area, thereby indicating a determination to respond aggressively to the problem

drug-related activities in the area are having a significant harmful impact in the area and in other areas of the country

a significant increase in allocation of federal resources is necessary to respond adequately to drug-related activities in the area.

In 1990, the director of ONDCP designated the first five HIDTAs in Los Angeles, Houston, Miami, New York, and along the entire length of the southwest U.S.-Mexico border. These five regions were considered to be gateways for the entry of illegal drugs into the United States. As the advantages of the HIDTA Program became apparent, the program was expanded to include other areas in which drug trafficking problems met the statutory requirements. As of 2008, there were twenty-eight HIDTAs located in forty-three states plus Puerto Rico, the U.S. Virgin Islands, and the District of Columbia. These HIDTAs include more than 13 percent of all counties in the United States and approximately 60 percent of the U.S. population. In 2006, more than 20,000 federal, state, and local law enforcement officers and other staff participated in the HIDTA Program.

The mission of the HIDTA Program is to disrupt the market for illegal drugs in the United States by assisting federal, state, and local law enforcement HIDTA participants in dismantling and disrupting drug trafficking organizations. Simply put, the mission is to take traffickers and drugs off the streets of the United States. To accomplish this mission, the HIDTA Program provides an infrastructure and coordinated umbrella for participating law enforcement agencies to enable it to combine and leverage resources and capabilities and expand the scope of its investigations.

To monitor the effectiveness and efficiency of this approach, the HIDTA directors developed the Performance Management Process (PMP). The PMP involves six key phases that are completed annually: identifying threats and needs, setting performance targets and implementing a strategy for achieving them, identifying a measurement protocol, budgeting for results, monitoring and managing results, and reporting on the outcomes. In 2006, the operations of 2,522 drug trafficking organizations and money laundering organizations were either completely dismantled or disrupted to the point where their ability to operate was severely diminished. More than $16 billion worth of illegal drugs, more than $834 million in illegally gained assets, and 1,522 clandestine labs capable of producing a minimum of $12 million worth of methamphetamine per year were seized. For every dollar invested in HIDTA enforcement and intelligence initiatives, the HIDTA Program took $92 in illegal drugs off the streets and seized nearly $5 in cash and other assets.

DEPARTMENT OF HOMELAND SECURITY

The Department of Homeland Security (DHS) was established as a part of the Homeland Security Act of 2002 to provide the unifying core for the vast national network of organizations and institutions involved in efforts to secure the United States. As of 2008, the four entities housed in DHS that touch on drug law enforcement and supply control were the U.S. Citizenship and Immigration Services (USCIS), Bureau of Customs and Border Protection (BCBP), Bureau of Immigration and Custom's Enforcement (ICE), and the Office of Immigration Statistics (OIS). Each of these entities is actively involved in protecting U.S. borders and disrupting smuggling activities. ICE was established in March 2003 as the largest investigative arm of the DHS. It works with U.S. and foreign authorities to locate and apprehend dangerous individuals running or involved in drug trafficking organizations. Through

Operation Community Shield, ICE agents partner with federal, state, and local law enforcement to target violent transnational street gangs through the use of ICE's broad law enforcement powers, including the unique and powerful authority to remove (deport) criminal aliens, including illegal aliens and legal permanent resident aliens. ICE agents also participated in HIDTA initiative investigations of drug trafficking organizations across the country.

OTHER FEDERAL DEPARTMENTS

Other federal departments involved in drug law enforcement and supply control include the Department of Transportation, the Department of Defense, the U.S. Postal Service, and the Department of State. The Federal Aviation Administration and U.S. Coast Guard in the Department of Transportation and the Department of Defense use radar systems and other technology to detect and interdict drug smuggling by air and water. The U.S. Postal Service investigates smuggling efforts using mail services. The Department of State establishes international antidrug policies and coordinates drug control efforts with foreign governments.

See also **Controlled Substances Act of 1970; Crime and Drugs; Drug Interdiction; International Drug Supply Systems; Terrorism and Drugs.**

BIBLIOGRAPHY

Department of Homeland Security (DHS). Available from www.dhs.gov.

Federal Bureau of Investigation (FBI). Available from www.fbi.gov.

Office of National Drug Control Policy (ONDCP). Available from www.whitehousedrugpolicy.gov.

Office of National Drug Control Policy. (2008). *2006 National HIDTA Program Annual Report.* Washington, DC: Author.

United States Department of Justice (DOJ). Available from www.usdoj.gov.

United States Department of Justice, Bureau of Alcohol, Tobacco, Firearms, and Explosives (ATF). ATF snapshot 2007. Available from http://www.atf.gov.

United States Drug Enforcement Administration (DEA). Available from www.usdoj.gov/dea/.

United States Immigration and Customs Enforcement (ICE). Available from www.ice.gov.

ERIN ARTIGIANI

AGENCIES SUPPORTING SUBSTANCE ABUSE PREVENTION AND TREATMENT

Within the U.S. Department of Health and Human Services (DHHS), originally established in 1953 as the Department of Health, Education, and Welfare (DHEW), a number of Public Health Service (PHS) agencies have been involved in reducing drug abuse. From 1974 to 1992 many demand-reduction activities were related to increasing, through research, the scientific foundations for a better understanding of how drugs of abuse interact with individuals, so as to prevent drug abuse and effectively treat those who do abuse drugs. Included among these agencies are the National Institute on Drug Abuse (NIDA) and the National Institute on Alcohol Abuse and Alcoholism (NIAAA), both components of the National Institutes of Health (NIH), as well as the Center for Substance Abuse Prevention (CSAP) and the Center for Substance Abuse Treatment (CSAT), components of the Substance Abuse and Mental Health Services Administration (SAMHSA). In addition, the Health Resources and Services Administration (HRSA) and the National Institute of Child Health and Human Development (NICHD), another NIH component, play a role in the department's anti-drug abuse mission.

From its creation in 1974 by statute, the National Institute on Drug Abuse has conducted research on drugs of abuse and their effects on individuals. In its early days, NIDA supported prevention and treatment programs and conducted clinical training programs for professional healthcare workers (particularly in schools of medicine, nursing, and social work), counselors and other paraprofessionals. With the advent of the Alcohol and Drug Abuse and Mental Health Services block grant, enacted into statute in 1981, the direct provision of treatment and prevention services became a state responsibility. Enactment of the block grant that is currently administered within SAMHSA refocused the NIDA role on the generation of knowledge through scientific research so that more could be learned about strategies and programs to prevent and treat drug abuse.

The National Institute on Alcohol Abuse and Alcoholism (NIAAA) conducts research on alcohol abuse and alcoholism. Because a comprehensive approach to prevention and treatment of drug abuse requires attention to alcohol as well as to illicit drugs, and because individuals who abuse illicit drugs often abuse alcohol as well, the research programs of NIDA and NIAAA are symbiotic. Furthermore, the genetic, environmental, and social influences important to the initiation of drug and alcohol use are similar, and research in one area suggests researchable hypotheses in the other.

The Center for Substance Abuse Prevention (CSAP), established in 1986 as the Office for Substance Abuse Prevention (OSAP), has led national efforts to prevent alcohol and other drug use, with a special emphasis on youth and families at particularly high risk for drug abuse. Youth considered to be at high risk include school dropouts, economically disadvantaged youth, or children of parents who abuse drugs or alcohol or who are at high risk of becoming drug or alcohol abusers. CSAP administers a variety of programs, including prevention demonstration grants targeting youth at high risk and pregnant and postpartum women and their infants.

The Center for Substance Abuse Treatment (CSAT), formerly the Office of Treatment Improvement (OTI), was established administratively in 1990 to improve treatment services and expand the capacity for delivering treatment services. CSAT administers the State Substance Abuse Prevention and Treatment block grant and undertakes knowledge development, education, and communications initiatives that promote best practices in substance use/abuse treatment and intervention. The CSAT Targeted Capacity Expansion Program—and its specialized program focused on HIV/AIDS services—help communities respond rapidly to emerging local drug use trends.

Drug and alcohol abuse are complex behaviors that often result in a multitude of adverse consequences. Thus, to understand them necessitates multifaceted, often crosscutting, areas of research. Because many individuals who suffer from alcohol or drug abuse also suffer from mental illness (called *co-occurring disorders*), NIAAA and NIDA, as well as the National Institute of Mental Health (NIMH) of the NIH, are engaged in initiatives to learn more about individuals who have co-occurring disorders.

Acquired immunodeficiency syndrome (AIDS) has become a chronic health concern among intravenous drug users, and an increased risk of human immunodeficiency virus (HIV) infection in those who share drug paraphernalia with other drug users has been clearly demonstrated. Accordingly, NIDA collaborates with the Centers for Disease Control (CDC) on AIDS prevention programs and with the National Institute of Allergy and Infectious Diseases (NIAID) to provide HIV therapeutics to intravenous drug abusers with HIV.

The study of maternal and fetal effects of drug abuse is another high-priority focus within the department. Research and demonstration programs have been undertaken by NIDA and CSAP, and the NICHD is also conducting studies in this area.

Recent research has shown that the most effective treatment for drug abusers is a comprehensive array of services that address not only their drug-abuse problems but also other health problems and their potential need for education and vocational rehabilitation as well as a host of ancillary services. Accordingly, NIDA, the centers within SAMHSA, and HRSA are exploring the effectiveness of providing a comprehensive range of services in drug-abuse and primary-care settings.

In addition to the DHHS, many other agencies are involved in prevention and treatment efforts. For example, the Food and Drug Administration (FDA) plays a determining role in deciding when new pharmacological treatment agents can be marketed for clinical use, and it is one of the key agencies setting policies and standards for the use of opioid drugs in the treatment of opioid dependence. Both the Department of Education and the Department of Justice (through the Drug Enforcement Administration [DEA]) have significant programs aimed at prevention; the Department of Veterans Affairs and the Department of Defense (U.S. military) have also made major commitments to treatment.

See also **Prevention, Education and; Substance Abuse and AIDS.**

BIBLIOGRAPHY

Anderson, P. (1990). Controlled drinking and a public health approach to alcohol. *Addiction, 90,* 1162–1164.

Burman, S. (1994). The disease concept of alcoholism: Its impact on women's treatment. *Journal of Substance Abuse Treatment, 11*(2), 121–126.

Henderson, E. C. (2000). *Understanding addiction.* Jackson: University Press of Mississippi.

Hughes, A., Sathe, N., & Spagnola, K. (2008). *State Estimates of Substance Use from the 2005–2006 National Surveys on Drug Use and Health* (DHHS Publication No. SMA 08-4311, NSDUH Series H-33). Rockville, MD: Substance Abuse and Mental Health Services Administration, Office of Applied Studies.

Meyer, R. E. (1996). The disease called addiction: Emerging evidence in a 200-year debate. *The Lancet, 347*, 162–166.

Straussner, L. L. A., & Brown, S. (2002*). The handbook of addiction treatment for women.* San Francisco, CA: Jossey-Bass.

Substance Abuse and Mental Health Services Administration, Office of Applied Studies. (2007). *SAMHSA: Building resilience…facilitating recovery…life in the community for everyone.* Rockville, MD: Author.

Substance Abuse and Mental Health Services Administration, Office of Applied Studies. (2007). *National Survey of Substance Abuse Treatment Services (N-SSATS): 2006. Data on substance abuse treatment facilities,* DASIS Series: S-39, DHHS Publication No. (SMA) 07-4296. Rockville, MD: Author.

Substance Abuse and Mental Health Services Administration, Office of Applied Studies. (2007). *Treatment Episode Data Set (TEDS): 1995–2005. National Admissions to Substance Abuse Treatment Services,* DASIS Series: S-37, DHHS Publication No. (SMA) 07-4234. Rockville, MD: Author.

Substance Abuse and Mental Health Services Administration, Office of Applied Studies. (2007). *Treatment Episode Data Set (TEDS) highlights—2006 National Admissions to Substance Abuse Treatment Services.* OAS Series #S-40, DHHS Publication No. (SMA) 08-4313. Rockville, MD: Author.

Tracy, S. W., & Acker, C. J. (Eds.). (2004). *Altering American consciousness: The history of alcohol and drug use in the United States, 1800–2000.* Amherst: University of Massachusetts Press.

Walters, G. D. (1999). *The addiction concept: Working hypothesis or self-fulfilling prophecy?* Boston: Allyn & Bacon.

Weisner, C. (1995). Controlled drinking issues in the 1990s: The public health model and specialty treatment. *Addiction, 90,* 1164–1166.

RICHARD A. MILLSTEIN
REVISED BY PAMELA V. MICHAELS (2009)

AGENCIES SUPPORTING SUBSTANCE ABUSE RESEARCH

In the United States, federal support of drug-abuse research began in the 1920s with the work of Lawrence Kolb. It became more formalized with the establishment of the Addiction Research Center in 1935. By 1944 a small research unit was formed with only 15 employees in a U.S. Public Health Service Hospital in Lexington, Kentucky. The Addiction Research Center was designed for federal prisoners who were narcotics addicts. This research group became part of the National Institute of Mental Health (NIMH) in 1948, the year the institute was established. In 1979 the Addiction Research Center moved to Baltimore, Maryland, and became the in-house (intramural) research program of the National Institute on Drug Abuse (NIDA), which had been established by Congress in 1974.

For fiscal year 2009 (FY 2009), NIDA's budget was estimated at more than one billion dollars. The research thus funded included studies in practically every basic and clinical science, both biomedical and social. The National Institute on Alcohol Abuse and Alcoholism (NIAAA), established in 1970, conducts parallel efforts in the area of alcohol-abuse research. In FY 2009, NIAAA funded more than 200 grants, with a budget of nearly $437,000,000.

Both NIDA and NIAAA became part of the National Institutes of Health (NIH) in October 1992. They had previously been part of the Alcohol, Drug Abuse, and Mental Health Administration (ADAMHA), which included both research and services components. By separating these two components, Congress indicated its intention to give proper emphasis to both. Treatment and prevention services for alcohol and drug abuse are under the direction of the Substance Abuse and Mental Health Services Administration (SAMHSA).

NIDA and NIAAA are the two largest federal research institutes dedicated to drug abuse and alcohol research, but many other agencies have a stake in these areas. They include other institutes in the NIH; for example, the Eunice Kennedy Shriver National Institute of Child Health and Human Development focuses a significant portion of its research on the effects of drugs and alcohol on fetal development and on the consequences for the neonate of exposure to drugs and alcohol during pregnancy. The NIMH conducts research on the high coincidence of mental illness and substance-abuse disorders. Some of the other institutes have similarly targeted interests as, for example, the National Cancer Institute, which played an important role in support of research on tobacco dependence and the adverse health effects of tobacco. The Centers for Disease Control (CDC) use their epidemiological expertise to resolve certain questions about the nature and extent of the abuse of drugs and alcohol.

Beyond the Public Health Service and the Department of Health and Human Services, many other federal agencies and departments are concerned with and conduct research on the social problems caused by drug and alcohol abuse: the Departments of Education, Labor, Transportation, Treasury, Justice, State, Veterans Affairs, and even Defense—each has a stake in drug-abuse research. The Department of Education is concerned primarily with drug and alcohol prevention; the Departments of Labor and Transportation, with workplace performance impaired by drugs and alcohol.

The Department of Veterans Affairs has played an important role in both basic and clinical research. Some of the most important work on the treatment of opioid dependence as well as on alcoholism and the toxic effects of alcohol has been conducted by researchers based at Veterans Administration (VA) hospitals and funded in part by the Department of Veterans Affairs. Other federal agencies have a regulatory role in drug-abuse research. Many of the drugs that are studied in animals and volunteer human subjects are included under the Controlled Substances Act of 1970. In order to obtain and store the drugs, researchers must be properly registered with the Drug Enforcement Administration (DEA). The DEA is also responsible for ensuring that the drugs are properly stored and that researchers keep records of their use. In addition, researchers who are interested in studying any drug not yet approved for clinical use or in studying an approved drug for a new use (such as using the analgesic drug buprenorphine to combat opiate addiction) must obtain an Investigational New Drug (IND) authorization from the Food and Drug Administration (FDA). Further, when a new agent seems promising, a sponsor (usually a pharmaceutical company) must submit the data supporting its safety and effectiveness to the FDA before it can be approved for marketing and general use.

Both the Department of Justice and the Department of the Treasury are concerned with law enforcement issues surrounding drug and alcohol use, and they have funded research on detection of clandestine laboratories and the nature of club and designer drugs. In 2008 the Department of Homeland Security spent $4 million on counternarcotics enforcement, and the Department of the Treasury, via the IRS, targeted $59.2 million toward drug control efforts.

The Department of State and the Department of Defense are also involved in matters relating to international narcotics control. The 2009 National Drug Control Strategy earmarked one billion dollars of the Department of Defense's funding for drug control spending. Department of Justice's FY 2009 DEA spending was estimated at around $2.2 billion.

Congress in 1988 mandated the Office of National Drug Control Policy (ONDCP) to coordinate the federal antidrug-abuse effort. The Office of the President develops the annual National Drug Control Strategy with its accompanying budget summary. It contains three areas of emphasis: (1) stopping use before it starts; (2) intervening and healing America's drug users; and (3) disrupting the market. For FY 2009, the drug budget totaled $14.1 billion, an increase of 3.4 percent or $459 million from the previous budget. The Administration also requested $385.1 million for counternarcotics support to Central America and Mexico under the Merida Initiative. Fostering improved security cooperation between the United States, Mexico, and Central America is the focus of the Merida Initiative, a multi-year $1.4 billion program aimed at decreasing cross-national crime. In FY 2008, ONDCP requested a budget supplement of $385.1 million to launch the program. The supplemental request for Merida in FY 2009 was $432.2 million. All of these policy-related organizations rely on facts based on the biomedical, epidemiological, and behavioral research funded by NIDA, NIAAA, and NIMH.

See also **Prevention, Education and; Wikler's Conditioning Theory of Drug Addiction.**

BIBLIOGRAPHY

Center for Substance Abuse Treatment. (2007). *Addressing co-occurring disorders in non-traditional service settings. COCE overview paper 4.* (DHHS Publication No. SMA 07-4277). Rockville, MD: Substance Abuse and Mental Health Services Administration and Center for Mental Health Services.

Center for Substance Abuse Treatment. (2007). *The epidemiology of co-occurring substance use and mental disorders. COCE overview paper 8.* (DHHS Publication No. SMA 07-4308). Rockville, MD: Substance Abuse and Mental Health Services Administration and Center for Mental Health Services.

Department of Health and Human Services. (2008). *Treatment episode data set (TEDS). Highlights–2006. National admissions to substance abuse treatment services.* (DASIS Series: S-40, DHHS Publication No. SMA 08-4313). Rockville, MD: Author.

Executive Office of the President. (2008). *National drug control strategy: 2008 annual report.* Washington, DC: U.S. Government Printing Office.

Executive Office of the President of the United States. (2007, February). *National drug control strategy: 2008 annual report.* Washington, DC: The White House.

Executive Office of the President of the United States. (2008, February). *National drug control strategy: FY 2009 budget summary.* Washington, DC: The White House.

Henderson, E. C. (2000). *Understanding addiction.* Jackson: University Press of Mississippi.

Hughes, A., Sathe, N., & Spagnola, K. (2008). *State estimates of substance use from the 2005–2006 National Surveys on Drug Use and Health.* (DHHS Publication No. SMA 08-4311, NSDUH Series H-33). Rockville, MD: Substance Abuse and Mental Health Services Administration, Office of Applied Studies.

Office of National Drug Control Policy, Executive Office of the President. (2008, March). *What works: Effective public health response to drug use.* Washington, DC: Author.

Office of National Drug Control Policy, Executive Office of the President. (2007, August). *Cocaine smuggling in 2006.* Washington, DC: Author.

Tracy, S. W., & Acker, C. J. (Eds.). (2004). *Altering American consciousness: The history of alcohol and drug use in the United States, 1800-2000.* Amherst: University of Massachusetts Press.

CHRISTINE R. HARTEL
REVISED BY PAMELA V. MICHAELS (2009)

U.S. GOVERNMENT AGENCIES

This entry includes the following essays:

BUREAU OF NARCOTICS AND DANGEROUS DRUGS (BNDD);
CENTER FOR SUBSTANCE ABUSE PREVENTION (CSAP);
CENTER FOR SUBSTANCE ABUSE TREATMENT (CSAT);
NATIONAL INSTITUTE ON ALCOHOLISM AND ALCOHOL ABUSE (NIAAA);
NATIONAL INSTITUTE ON DRUG ABUSE (NIDA);
OFFICE OF DRUG ABUSE LAW ENFORCEMENT (ODALE);
OFFICE OF DRUG ABUSE POLICY (ODAP);
OFFICE OF NATIONAL DRUG CONTROL POLICY (ONDCP);
SPECIAL ACTION OFFICE FOR DRUG ABUSE PREVENTION (SAODAP);
SUBSTANCE ABUSE AND MENTAL HEALTH SERVICES ADMINISTRATION (SAMHSA);
U.S. CUSTOMS AND BORDER PROTECTION (CBP)
U.S. PUBLIC HEALTH SERVICE HOSPITALS

BUREAU OF NARCOTICS AND DANGEROUS DRUGS (BNDD)

Presidential Reorganization Plan No. 1 of 1968 created the Bureau of Narcotics and Dangerous Drugs (BNDD) in the U.S. Department of Justice. The new agency combined the drug law enforcement functions of two predecessor organizations—the Federal Bureau of Narcotics (FBN) in the Department of the Treasury and the Bureau of Drug Abuse Control in the Food and Drug Administration, Department of Health and Human Services. Long-standing conflicts between two Department of the Treasury agencies that shared drug-enforcement responsibilities—the Federal Bureau of Narcotics and the Bureau of Customs—led to the decision to move the FBN functions into a new agency (BNDD) in a different cabinet department (Justice).

MISSION AND EXPERIENCE

BNDD's role was to suppress illicit narcotics trafficking and to control the diversion of legally manufactured drugs. BNDD was responsible for working with foreign governments to halt international drug traffic, immobilizing domestic illegal drug-distribution networks, providing a wide range of technical assistance and training to state and local officers, and preparing drug cases for prosecution.

BNDD emphasized investigations of high-level drug trafficking to identify and target major national and international violators. Director John E. Ingersoll described the success of BNDD as being "able to apprehend scores of illicit drug traffickers who were previously immune to the feeble efforts which law enforcement was formerly able to mount." In 1968 and 1969, BNDD contributed to major international success in stopping heroin traffic originating in Turkey.

The Bureau of Customs continued interdiction of drug smuggling at the borders and ports of entry. Customs special agents investigated drug cases based on seizures made by Customs inspectors and on antismuggling intelligence. Conflict between BNDD and Customs continued, with allegations of lack of cooperation and failure to share intelligence with each other.

The White House and Office of Management and Budget (OMB) tried to resolve the conflict and, in early 1970, President Richard M. Nixon directed BNDD and Customs to work out a set of operating guidelines. After considerable interagency discussion, formal guidelines were prepared to give to BNDD full jurisdiction over drug-enforcement operations both within the United States and overseas. Customs was to be limited to border operations. The president approved the guidelines, but the conflicts continued. Neither Congress nor the White House was satisfied. Senator Abraham Ribicoff described the detailed guidelines as "more reminiscent of a cease-fire agreement between combatants than a working agreement between supposedly cooperative agencies."

ADDITIONAL DRUG ENFORCEMENT COMPLICATIONS

The "war against drugs" continued to expand. In 1972, President Nixon established two new drug agencies in the Department of Justice—the Office of Drug Abuse Law Enforcement (ODALE) and the Office of National Narcotics Intelligence (ONNI). ODALE's operational involvement with state and local law enforcement against local drug dealers was intended to complement BNDD's focus on high level traffickers. ODALE, however, depended on existing federal agencies for agents and attorneys, and BNDD was required to lend over 200 narcotics agents to ODALE. The additional antidrug agencies, combined with sensational reporting of conflicts between special agents from BNDD and Customs, added to the public perception of fragmentation and disorder in federal drug law enforcement.

In early 1973, another presidential reorganization plan was designed to eliminate the overlap and duplication of effort in drug enforcement. A factual assessment of the BNDD/Customs situation, provided to the Congress by the chief of OMB's Federal Drug Management Division, Walter C. Minnick, reported "Having attempted formal guidelines, informal cooperation and specific Cabinet-level mediation, all without success, the President concluded in March of 1972 that merging the drug investigative and intelligence responsibilities of Customs and BNDD into a single new agency was the only way to put a permanent end to the problem." Under Reorganization Plan No. 2 of 1973, BNDD, ODALE, and ONNI were eliminated; their functions and resources, along with 500 Customs special agents (those previously involved in drug investigations), were consolidated in the new Drug Enforcement Administration (DEA) in the Department of Justice.

See also **Anslinger, Harry Jacob, and U.S. Drug Policy.**

BIBLIOGRAPHY

Bonafede, D. (1970). Nixon approves drug guidelines, gives role to Narcotic Bureau. *National Journal, 2* (29), 1532–1534.

Bonafede, D. (1970). Nixon seeks to heal top-level feud between customs, narcotics units. *National Journal, 2* (15), 750–751.

Finlator, J. (1973). *The drugged nation.* New York: Simon & Schuster.

Moore, M. H. (1978). Reorganization Plan #2 reviewed: Problems in implementing a strategy to reduce the supply of drugs to illicit markets in the United States. *Public Policy, 26* (2), 229–262.

Musto, D. F., & Korsmeyer, P. (2002). *The quest for drug control: Politics and Federal policy in a period of increasing substance abuse, 1963–1981.* New Haven, CT: Yale University Press.

Rachal, P. (1982). *Federal narcotics enforcement.* Boston: Auburn House.

United States Drug Enforcement Administration (2008). *DEA History.* Available from http://www.usdoj.gov/.

United States Senate Committee on Government Operations (1973). *Reorganization Plan No. 2 of 1973, Hearings before the Subcommittee on Reorganization, Research, and International Organizations.* 93rd Congress, 1st sess., Part 1. April 12, 13, and 26, 1973. Washington, DC.

RICHARD L. WILLIAMS

CENTER FOR SUBSTANCE ABUSE PREVENTION (CSAP)

The Center for Substance Abuse Prevention (CSAP) was originally established as the Office for Substance Abuse Prevention (OSAP). It was created by the Anti-Drug Abuse Act of 1986 for the prevention of alcohol and other drug problems among U.S. citizens, with special emphasis on youth and families living in high-risk environments. From 1986 to 1992, OSAP operated as a unit of the Alcohol, Drug Abuse, and Mental Health Administration (ADAMHA), one of the eight Public Health Service agencies within the U.S. Department of Health and Human Services. In 1992, Public Law 102–321 reorganized ADAMHA and renamed it the Substance Abuse and Mental Health Services Administration (SAMHSA); it also created CSAP to replace OSAP.

The stated mission of CSAP is to bring effective substance abuse prevention to every community. On the federal level, CSAP is tasked with leading the nation's efforts to eliminate alcohol, tobacco, and drug use problems. To improve the health and quality of life for people across the nation, CSAP employs a community-based, structured prevention approach through its Strategic Planning Framework (SPF). The SPF is designed to provide education, tools, and techniques for the creation of a broad-based prevention framework that can be easily employed and replicated by the states, regions, and local communities. The goal of the SPF is to target youth: to provide education about risk reduction (offering healthier alternatives to risk-taking behaviors) and to build on existing strengths, skills, and resiliency as a means of preventing youth from making negative choices. By fostering greater strengths in young people, the SPF intends to promote healthier choices throughout life.

The primary goal of CSAP is to promote choosing not to use illicit drugs and refraining from illegal or high-risk use of alcohol or other legal drugs. High-risk alcohol use includes drinking and driving, drinking while pregnant, drinking while recovering from alcoholism and/or when using certain medications, having more than two drinks a day for men and more than one for women, and drinking to intoxication.

These are the principles that guide the prevention work of CSAP:

1. The earlier prevention is started in a person's life, the more likely it is to succeed.

2. Prevention programs should be knowledge-based and should incorporate state-of-the-art findings and practices drawn from scientific research and field expertise.

3. Prevention programs should be comprehensive and take a strengths-based approach.

4. Programs should include both process and outcome evaluations.

5. The most successful programs are those initiated and conducted at the community level.

To utilize these principles and achieve its goals, CSAP performs the following functions:

1. Carries out demonstration projects targeting specific groups and individuals in high-risk environments.

2. Assists communities in developing long-term, comprehensive alcohol and other drug use prevention and early intervention programs.

3. Operates a national clearinghouse for publications on prevention and treatment and other materials and services.

4. Supports the National Training System, which develops new drug use prevention materials and delivers training.

5. Supports field development.

6. Utilizes numerous assessment tools: the prevention platform, state prevention profiles, national outcome measures, state juvenile justice profiles, and the Helping America's Youth Program Tool Database.

7. Conducts an evaluation strategy consisting of individual grantee evaluations, contractual program-wide evaluations, and the National Evaluation Project.

8. Provides technical assistance for capacity building and promotes collaborations to help states, communities, and organizations develop and implement communications, drug use prevention, and early intervention efforts.

9. Develops and implements public information and educational media campaigns and other

special-outreach and knowledge-transfer prevention programs.

10. Maintains a national drug use prevention database to provide information on substance-abuse prevention programs.

11. Provides technical assistance and materials to small businesses for the development of employee-assistance programs.

12. Operates the SAMHSA's Prevention Platform, which is targeted to ensure that local community prevention programs achieve successful outcomes. The program is Web-based and user-friendly.

To promote interagency cooperation and facilitate jointly sponsored prevention activities, CSAP's staff meets routinely with various federal organizations, including the departments of Defense, Justice, Education, Transportation, Labor, and Housing and Urban Development; the Bureau of Indian Affairs; and others.

CSAP also develops partnerships with the research community, parent groups, foundations, policymakers, health-care practitioners, faith-based community programs, state and community leaders, educators, law enforcement officials, and others to enhance opportunities for comprehensive approaches to prevention and early intervention.

See also **Parent Movement, The; Prevention, Education and.**

BIBLIOGRAPHY

Hughes, A., Sathe, N., & Spagnola, K. (2008). *State estimates of substance use from the 2005–2006 national surveys on drug use and health.* NSDUH Series H-33 (DHHS Publication No. SMA 08-4311). Rockville, MD: Substance Abuse and Mental Health Services Administration, Office of Applied Studies.

U.S. Department of Health and Human Services. (2008). Treatment episode data set (TEDS). *Highlights 2006: National admissions to substance abuse treatment services.* DASIS Series: S-40 (DHHS Publication No. SMA 08-4313), Rockville, MD: Author.

ELAINE JOHNSON
REVISED BY PAMELA V. MICHAELS (2009)

CENTER FOR SUBSTANCE ABUSE TREATMENT (CSAT)

The Center for Substance Abuse Treatment (CSAT) was established in January 1990 as the Office for Treatment Improvement (OTI) of the Alcohol, Drug Abuse, and Mental Health Administration (ADAMHA) within the Department of Health and Human Services (DHHS). Dr. Beny J. Primm, a physician who had spent more than 20 years developing a major treatment program in New York City, was appointed as its first director. Following the reorganization of ADAMHA in 1992, the agency was renamed and is now part of the Substance Abuse and Mental Health Services Administration (SAMHSA), which replaced ADAMHA.

The congressional mandate of CSAT is to expand the availability of effective treatment and recovery services for people with drug and alcohol problems. One of its goals is to ensure that new treatment technology is absorbed by the addiction-treatment infrastructure, the system of state and local government agencies and public and private treatment programs providing addiction-treatment services. In carrying out this responsibility, CSAT collaborates with states, communities, and treatment providers to upgrade the quality and effectiveness of treatment and enhance coordination among drug-treatment providers; human services, educational, and vocational services; the criminal justice system; and a variety of related services. CSAT provides financial and technical assistance to targeted geographic areas and patient populations, with an emphasis on assistance to minority racial and ethnic groups, youth and adolescents, homeless and displaced persons, women of childbearing age, and people living in frontier or in rural areas.

CSAT also collaborates with other government agencies, such as the National Institute on Drug Abuse (NIDA), the National Institute on Alcohol Abuse and Alcoholism (NIAAA), the National Institute of Mental Health (NIMH), and the Center for Substance Abuse Prevention (CSAP), as well as state and local governments, to promote the utilization of effective means of treatment and develop treatment standards. In addition, CSAT has interagency agreements with the Department of Labor and the Department of Education that are designed to improve the coordination of health and human services, education, and vocational training. CSAT also promotes the mainstreaming of alcohol, drug abuse, and mental health treatment into the primary health-care system, and is responsible for administering the Substance Abuse

Prevention and Treatment (SAPT) Block Grant program, which provides federal support to state substance-abuse prevention and treatment programs (the total appropriation for 2007 was $1,758,591,000).

Research has generated a vast body of knowledge regarding the nature of chemical dependency and about what works in the treatment of addiction and addiction-related health and mental health disorders. From this research, three key observations formed the basis for CSAT's initial treatment philosophy. First, addiction is a complex phenomenon and cannot be treated in isolation from addressing the primary health, mental health, or socioeconomic deficits of addicted persons. Second, addiction is frequently a chronic, relapsing disorder, and the gains made during treatment are often lost following a person's return to the community. CSAT therefore tried to foster programs that provided those treated for chemical dependency with a series of interventions along a sustained continuum. These two observations constituted the basis for CSAT's Comprehensive Treatment Model, which was a central principle in all of its demonstration grant programs and technical-assistance initiatives.

During its first few years of existence, CSAT targeted resources to the people it perceived as most adversely affected by extreme socioeconomic problems and at highest risk for addiction because of exposure to crime, abuse, poverty, and homelessness, or because of a lack of access to primary health and mental health care, social services, and vocational training and education. For this reason, the early Comprehensive Treatment Model demonstration grants fostered a wide array of primary interventions geared to addressing each patient's health and human service needs, coupled with a readily accessible, intensive aftercare component.

At the core of CSAT's overall approach is the conviction that treatment works, the third key observation. Treatment has proved effective in reducing the use of illicit drugs and alcohol, improving rates of employment, reducing rates of human immunodeficiency virus (HIV) seroconversion, reducing criminal activity, and reducing overall patient morbidity.

In addition to the SAPT Block Grant, CSAT awarded grants for a variety of demonstration and service programs. Access to Recovery (ATR) is a three-year SAMHSA-funded grant. ATR provides consumers with vouchers that can be used to purchase clinical treatment and recovery support services for substance abuse disorders. ATR is designed to expand the capacity of funded service providers, thereby increasing consumer choice. Partners for Recovery (PFR) provides support and technical assistance to providers of substance abuse prevention and treatment services. The Knowledge Application Program (KAP) produces written and electronic media for substance abuse consumers and treatment providers. The Treatment Improvement Protocol (TIP) series and Technical Assistance Publications (TAPs), under the auspices of KAP, create and distribute consumer-targeted literature as well and technical and training manuals and guides for providers.

The National Center on Substance Abuse and Child Welfare (NCSACW) seeks to improve outcomes for families involved in the child welfare and judicial systems by partnering with local, state, and tribal judiciaries. Medication-Assisted Treatment (MAT) augments traditional behavioral substance abuse treatment models with the judicious use of medications in order to facilitate recovery. The Recovery Community Services Program (RCSP) utilizes a peer-to-peer recovery support model as a means of aiding individuals in recovering (and maintaining recovery) from substance abuse disorders. The Screening, Brief Intervention, and Referral to Treatment (SBIRT) program is a comprehensive, integrated, multidisciplinary public health model for delivery of early intervention and treatment services for persons with substance abuse disorders (SUDs), coupled with a prevention program aimed at reducing the incidence of SUDs.

Since the mid-1990s, CSAT's demonstration grant program has broadened to encompass not only the improvement of services for those populations in greatest need, but also to develop a knowledge base about the effectiveness of treatment for different subgroups of the drug-using population.

See also **Treatment: An Overview.**

BIBLIOGRAPHY

Center for Substance Abuse Treatment. (2007). *Addressing co-occurring disorders in non-traditional service settings.*

COCE Overview Paper 4, DHHS Publication No. (SMA) 07-4277. Rockville, MD: Substance Abuse and Mental Health Services Administration, and Center for Mental Health Services.

Center for Substance Abuse Treatment (2007). *The epidemiology of co-occurring substance use and mental disorders.* COCE Overview Paper 8, DHHS Publication No. (SMA) 07-4308. Rockville, MD: Substance Abuse and Mental Health Services Administration, and Center for Mental Health Services.

Department of Health and Human Services. (2008). *Treatment episode data set (TEDS) Highlights—2006 national admissions to substance abuse treatment services.* OAS Series S-40, DHHS Publication No. (SMA) 08-4313. Rockville, MD: Substance Abuse and Mental Health Services Administration, Office of Applied Studies.

Hughes, A., Sathe, N., & Spagnola, K. (2008). *State estimates of substance use from the 2005–2006 national surveys on drug use and health.* OAS Series H-33, DHHS Publication No. (SMA) 08-4311. Rockville, MD: Substance Abuse and Mental Health Services Administration, Office of Applied Studies.

SAMHSA. (2008). Center for Substance Abuse Treatment. Available from http://csat.samhsa.gov.

BENY J. PRIMM
REVISED BY PAMELA V. MICHAELS (2009)

NATIONAL INSTITUTE ON ALCOHOL ABUSE AND ALCOHOLISM (NIAAA)

The National Institute on Alcohol Abuse and Alcoholism (NIAAA) is the principal federal agency for research on the causes, consequences, treatment, and prevention of alcohol-related problems. NIAAA supports studies in both biological and behavioral research, research training and health professions development programs, and research on alcohol-related public policies. The FY2008 budget for the NIAAA was in excess of $436.5 million.

ORGANIZATION

NIAAA is one of 27 research institutes and centers of the prestigious National Institutes of Health (NIH), a component of the U.S. Department of Health and Human Services. The mission of the NIAAA is to lead the nation in the efforts to reduce alcohol-related problems. This is accomplished by managing a large-scale scientific research program encompassing genetics, neuroscience, epidemiology, health risk management, treatment, and prevention:

- By collaboration and coordination with other private, state, and federal research, treatment and prevention programs;
- By working in collaboration with alcohol-related facilities, organizations, programs, and agencies—both within the United States and abroad;
- By communication of the research results and outcome findings to the general public, the scientific and research communities, and to policymakers and legislators

The goals of the work of the NIAAA are threefold: (1) to increase the understanding of normal and abnormal behavior and biology in the context of alcohol use; (2) to facilitate effective diagnosis, treatment, prevention, and early intervention of alcohol abuse and dependence; and (3) to improve continual health care quality.

Under the auspices of the Office of the Director, there are three principal offices and five divisions that manage and coordinate NIAAA activities.

Office of Extramural Activities
Office of Science Policy and Communications
Office of Resource Management and the Division of Intramural Clinical and Biological Research
——Division of Epidemiology and Prevention Research
——Division of Metabolism and Health Effects
——Division of Neuroscience and Behavior
——Division of Treatment and Recovery Research

NIAAA supports research principally through extramural grants awarded to scientists at leading U.S. research institutions and through research conducted by NIAAA's own intramural staff scientists. Findings from these research areas are made available and accessible through a wide variety of research dissemination activities.

INTRAMURAL RESEARCH

Intramural research is carried out under the auspices of the Division of Intramural Clinical and Biological Research. Scientists in the NIAAA Intramural Research Program (IRP) focus on research opportunities that allow intensive, long-term commitment as well as the flexibility to adjust research priorities in response to new findings. Because clinical and laboratory studies occur side by side, new findings from basic research may be readily transferred for appropriate testing and application, and clinical hypotheses may be in turn posited to lab scientists. Areas of study include (a) identification and assessment of genetic and environmental risk factors for the development of alcoholism; (b) effects of alcohol on the central nervous system including how alcohol modifies brain activity and behavior; (c) metabolic and biochemical effects of alcohol on various organs and systems of the body; (d) noninvasive imaging of the brain structure and activity related to alcohol use; (e) development of animal models of alcoholism; and (f) diagnosis, prevention, and treatment of alcoholism and associated disorders. NIAAA uses a combination of clinical and basic research facilities that enable a coordinated interaction between basic research findings and clinical applications in pursuit of these goals. A 12-bed inpatient unit and a large outpatient program are located in the NIH Clinical Center in Bethesda, Maryland.

The primary goal for the intramural research program is to clearly define and understand the means by which alcohol intoxication, dependence and subsequent physiological damage to vital organs occurs, and to develop effective behavioral and biological intervention and prevention strategies. Some of the current areas of focus for intramural research involve (a) genetic studies designed to identify and describe the genes involved in alcohol use disorders by increasing genetic vulnerability to alcohol abuse and dependence; (b) determination of the foundations of alcohol-related liver disease; (c) epidemiological studies on prevalence of alcohol-related use, abuse, and dependence; (d) research on the neurophysiology and behavioral mechanisms stimulating the desire to consume alcohol; (e) identification of environmental risk factors acting as a precursor to alcohol abuse or dependence; (f) central nervous system effects of alcohol use; (g) brain imaging of the effects of alcohol use; (h) animal models predictive of human alcohol use disorders; and (i) research on the neurobiology of alcohol dependence, aimed at the creation of improved prevention and early intervention strategies.

EXTRAMURAL RESEARCH

Division of Epidemiology and Prevention Research. External research is supported by four extramural divisions that provide grant dollars and support to cutting-edge research facilities across the United States. The Division of Epidemiology and Prevention Research (DEPR) focuses on the reduction of alcohol-related disorders, mortality, and morbidity through the use of epidemiological and prevention studies—funding and supporting research and scholarly publications, training, and professional and scientific workforce development, involvement in alcohol use surveillance, and communication of research results to the general public. This research program provides the foundation for monitoring the health of the population, developing and evaluating prevention and treatment services for alcohol problems, and establishing alcohol-related social policies. NIAAA-supported epidemiology research examines the context, volume, and specific drinking patterns that lead to particular alcohol-related problems. It also studies the impact of age, gender, race or ethnicity, and other sociodemographic factors as well as genetic, environmental, and other factors that influence injury or disease occurrence.

The two overarching areas of interest for DEPR are epidemiology and prevention. The epidemiology research arm seeks to understand the (a) etiology and progression of alcohol use disorders (AUDs); (b) co-occurrence of AUDs and disorders of physical or mental health; (c) AUDs and behavioral outcomes or consequences such as motor vehicle accidents, negative impact on job performance or stability, decreased academic performance, sexual risk-taking, interpersonal violence, and illness or death; (d) biopsychosocial, socioeconomic, and social-cultural impacts of drinking behaviors; and (e) prevention and early intervention with AUDs; and methodological considerations.

The prevention section conducts research on the efficiency and effectiveness of screening, brief intervention and referral to treatment protocols (SBIRT grants) including comprehensive community prevention programs, total community approach programs, anti-drinking and driving programs, as well as on the impact of the media, alcohol promotion and marketing efforts, and public policy on alcohol-related behaviors.

Division of Metabolism and Health Effects. Chronic consumption of large amounts of alcohol has profound physiological impacts over time.

AUDs during pregnancy can result in one of the fetal alcohol spectrum disorders (FASDs). Across a life span, chronic alcohol use can lead to liver diseases, pancreatitis, cardiomyopathy, and impaired immune and metabolic system functioning. Co-occurring disorders associated with AUDs are type 2 diabetes, hepatitis C, obesity, osteoporosis, degenerative neurological syndromes or dementias, and several types of cancer. The research supported by the Division of Metabolism and Health Effects (DMHE) examines the genetics, metabolism, and immunology contributing to and resulting from AUDs that both cause and advance the above listed disorders. A central goal of DMHE research is to uncover mechanisms for developing medications targeted at treatment and prevention of AUDs. Genetic research is aimed at creation of mechanisms for repair of tissue and organ damage caused by chronic AUDs; both pharmaceutical, such as the use of medications; and physiological, such as stem cell transplants, metabolic manipulations, or gene targeting. In addition to studying the negative effects of alcohol use, DMHE supports research on the potential positive impacts of alcohol consumption on diabetes, some inflammatory processes, and cardiovascular disease.

Division of Neuroscience and Behavior.

Many of the behaviors associated with alcohol use problems are the result of alcohol's effects in the brain. NIAAA research is designed to learn how these effects influence the development of alcohol abuse and alcoholism. Molecular biology and genetic techniques, including the use of transgenic animals, are becoming an integral part of this research. In addition noninvasive, functional imaging techniques are used in animal and human studies to identify neural circuits influenced by alcohol. The Division of Neuroscience and Behavior is particularly focused on research concerned with alcohol use during pregnancy resulting in the development of a fetal alcohol spectrum disorder and the long-term effects of alcohol use on the rapidly developing adolescent brain.

Division of Treatment and Recovery Research.

The Division of Treatment and Recovery Research studies the progression of alcohol use from heavy drinking through the spectrum of AUDs as well as factors that influence positive changes in alcohol use behavior, whether they are such natural consequences associated with drinking as compromised physical health, job or academic failure, motor vehicle accidents; or within such self- or mutual-help groups as twelve-step programs or community treatment centers; or in professional settings such as hospitals or rehabilitation facilities. There is also ongoing research focused on the treatment of AUDs from a disease prevention and medical management model. Some of this work is aimed at developing medications that decrease the craving for alcohol and thereby decrease recidivism during recovery efforts.

NIAAA continues to emphasize research to improving treatment of alcohol abuse and alcoholism and supports a range of treatment or clinical studies including clinical trials of treatment therapies, patient-treatment matching studies, and behavioral or pharmacological treatment approaches. Prevention research is also aimed at developing effective measures to reduce alcohol-related problems These include the study of alcohol-related intentional and unintentional injury, alcohol-related violence, alcohol in the workplace, drinking and driving deterrence, and the relationship between alcohol availability and alcohol-related problems. New methodologies permit prevention researchers to target high-risk neighborhoods within larger cities.

Cross-Institute and Transdisciplinary Programs.

There are several multi-disciplinary programs supported by NIAAA. One of the pivotal activities involves a study of the ways in which alcohol use during pregnancy affects the developing fetus, potentially leading to one of the fetal alcohol spectrum disorders. The Interagency Coordinating Committee on Fetal Alcohol Syndrome (ICCFAS), created in response to an Institute of Medicine report in 1996, is chaired by the NIAAA. The Collaborative Institute on Fetal Alcohol Spectrum Disorders (CIFASD), launched by NIAAA in 2003, is a cooperative agreement program aimed at refining both diagnostic accuracy and developing improved treatment protocols across the entire FASD spectrum. CIFASD research occurs internationally as well as within multidisciplinary sites across the United States.

The NIAAA partnered with the National Institute on Child Health and Human Development in

2003 to create the longitudinal Prenatal Alcohol in Sudden Infant Death Syndrome (SIDS), and Stillbirth (PASS) Network, whose mission is to discern the causes of SIDS and stillbirth and to ascertain the role played by prenatal alcohol use in both syndromes. Twelve thousand pregnant women from South Africa and the Northern Plains and their babies will be studied until the children complete one year of life, in an effort to discern interactions between alcohol use and specific maternal and fetal factors.

Binge drinking, alcohol abuse, and alcoholism are global problems and the NIAAA is involved in a variety of collaborative and cooperative international research programs in these areas. Transdisciplinary programs involve Intramural and Extramural Research Emphasis and Resource Development Teams. The major areas of current interest for the transdisciplinary teams are the genetic and environmental etiology of risk, mechanisms of alcohol action and injury, mechanisms of behavior change, medications development, and research on the causes, consequences, and prevention of underage drinking, particularly adolescent binge drinking.

RESEARCH RESULTS DISSEMINATION
NIAAA shares relevant findings from alcohol research with health care practitioners, policymakers and others involved in managing alcohol-related programs, and the general public through publications in scientific and clinical journals, general and specialized brochures, pamphlets, manuals, clinical bulletins, and several online database services supported by the institute and the NIH:

- Alcohol and Alcohol Problems Science Database. http://etoh.niaaa.nih.gov/
- Alcohol Policy Information System. http://alcoholpolicy.niaaa.nih.gov/
- NESARC: National Epidemiologic Survey on Alcohol and Related Conditions. http://www.nesarc.niaaa.nih.gov/
- NIAAA Data and Statistical Tables. http://www.niaaa.nih.gov/Resources/Database Resources/QuickFacts/
- National Library of Medicine: MEDLINE. http://www.nlm.nih.gov/databases/index.html

See also **Accidents and Injuries from Alcohol; Alcohol: An Overview; Epidemiology of Alcohol Use Disorders; Fetal Alcohol Syndrome; Models of Alcoholism and Drug Abuse; National Council on Alcoholism and Drug Dependence (NCADD); Prevention; Prohibition of Alcohol; Temperance Movement; Treatment: An Overview of Alcohol Abuse/Dependence.**

BIBLIOGRAPHY

Centers for Disease Control and Prevention. (2002). Fetal alcohol syndrome—Alaska, Arizona, Colorado and New York, 1995–1997. *Morbidity and Mortality Weekly Report 51,* 433–435.

Hingson, R., Heeren, T., & Winter, M. (2000). Effects of recent 0.08% legal blood alcohol limits on fatal crash involvement. *Injury Prevention 6,* 109–114.

Holder, H., Gruenewald, P. J., Ponicki, W. R., Treno, A. J., Grube, J. W., & Saltz, R. F., et al. (2000). Effect of community-based interventions on high-risk drinking and alcohol-related injuries. *Journal of the American Medical Association 284,* 2341–2347.

Le Fauve, C. E., Lowman, C., Litten, R. Z., & Mattson, M. E. (2003). National Institute on Alcohol Abuse and Alcoholism Workshop on Treatment Research Priorities and Health Disparities. (Introduction). *Alcoholism: Clinical and Experimental Research* 27(8),1318–1320.

Lowman C., & Le Fauve, C. E. (2003). Health disparities and the relationship between race, ethnicity and substance abuse treatment outcomes. *Alcoholism: Clinical and Experimental Research* 27(8), 1324–1326.

Marlatt, G. A., Baer, J. S., & Larimer, M. (1995). In Boyd, G., Howard, J., & Zucker, R. A. (Eds.) *Alcohol problems among adolescents: Current directions in prevention research* (pp.147–172). Hillsdale, NJ: Erlbaum Associates.

National Institute on Alcohol Abuse and Alcoholism. (1996). State trends in alcohol-related mortality, 1979–1992. *U.S. Alcohol Epidemiologic Data Reference Manual,* (1st ed., Vol. 5). Bethesda, MD: National Institute on Alcohol Abuse and Alcoholism. (NIH Publication No. 96-4174).

National Institute on Alcohol Abuse and Alcoholism. (2001). Alcohol-related birth defects: An update. *Alcohol Research and Health* 25,149–210.

Perry, C. L., Williams, C. L., Veblen-Mortenson, S., Toomey, T. L., Komro, K. A., Anstine, P. S., et al. (1996). Project Northland: Outcomes of a communitywide alcohol use prevention program during early adolescence. *American Journal of Public Health 86,* 956–965.

Stratton, K., Howe, C., & Battaglia, F. (Eds.) (1996). *Fetal alcohol syndrome: Diagnosis, epidemiology, prevention, and treatment.* Washington, DC: National Academy Press.

U.S. Department of Health and Human Services. (2000). Objectives for Improving Health. *Healthy people 2010: Volume II.* Washington, DC: U.S. Government Printing Office.

ENOCH GORDIS
REVISED BY PAMELA V. MICHAELS (2009)

NATIONAL INSTITUTE ON DRUG ABUSE (NIDA)

As of 2008 the National Institute on Drug Abuse was a premier research institute supporting research on the health aspects of drug abuse and addiction. The vast NIDA portfolio supports research on all drugs of abuse from opiates and cocaine to more recent and emerging drugs such as methamphetamine and Ecstasy. In addition to research on illegal drugs, NIDA supports an extensive research portfolio to combat what may be the most critical and costly U.S. public health problem—tobacco use. NIDA nicotine research continues to increase knowledge about the social, economic, cultural, and biological factors that influence smoking initiation and vulnerability to nicotine addiction, and it continues to bring effective prevention and treatment approaches to the U.S. public attention. Additionally, NIDA supports research on the health consequences of nicotine as well as on the medical consequences of all illicit drugs.

Given that as of 2008 drug abuse was the greatest vector for the spread of HIV, a significant portion of NIDA research investment was spent on researching effective prevention and treatment strategies to combat HIV/AIDS and other infectious diseases. NIDA comprehensive research portfolio included studies on the causes and consequences; the prevention and treatment; and the biological, social, behavioral, and neuroscientific bases of drug abuse and addiction. NIDA was also charged with the development of medications to treat drug addiction. Additionally, NIDA supported research training and career development, science and public education, and research dissemination.

NIDA is the largest institution devoted to drug-abuse research in the world, supporting drug-abuse research through grants to scientists, primarily at major research facilities in the United States, abroad, and at NIDA Intramural Research Program (IRP).

HISTORY

Drug-abuse research and treatment was a concern of the U.S. Public Health Service from the early 1930s into the twenty-first century. The Public Health Service Hospitals at Lexington, Kentucky, and at Fort Worth, Texas, were established in 1929, and the research laboratories were established at Lexington in 1935.

NIDA was formally established in 1974 as one of three applied and basic research institutes within the Alcohol, Drug Abuse, and Mental Health Administration (ADAMHA), a Public Health Service agency within the Department of Health and Human Services. The NIDA mandate was to collect information on the incidence, prevalence, and consequences of drug abuse; to improve the understanding of drugs of abuse and their effects on individuals; and to expand the ability to prevent and treat drug abuse. During this time, NIDA supported model and demonstration programs in prevention, treatment, and rehabilitation as well as basic research.

In October 1992, the drug, alcohol, and mental-health activities within the Department of Health and Human Services (NIDA, along with the National Institute on Alcohol Abuse and Alcoholism and National Institute on Mental Health), were transferred from ADAMHA to the National Institutes of Health.

FUNCTIONS

Through scientific research, NIDA built a base of information on how drugs affect people: what they do to the human body; to human behavior, thoughts, and emotions; to social relationships; and to society in general. This understanding of the biological, social, behavioral, and environmental influences that place individuals at risk for drug abuse is of great importance to prevention and treatment practitioners, to educators, and to policymakers.

NIDA has two principal goals. The first is the strategic support and conduct of research across a broad range of disciplines. The second is ensuring the rapid and effective dissemination and use of the results of that research to significantly improve prevention, treatment, and policy as it relates to drug abuse and addiction.

To improve the ability to prevent drug abuse, NIDA concentrates on the variety of biological, behavioral, social, and environmental factors involved in vulnerability to drug abuse. This information enables NIDA to improve both prevention and treatment approaches—which are essential for overcoming the demand for drugs—and to inform effective U.S. demand-reduction policies.

Since research has shown that treatment can be an effective tool in helping some to break the addiction cycle, NIDA researches ways to improve the effectiveness of treatment and works to increase retention rates and reduce relapse rates. Through an understanding of the effects of drugs on the brain, NIDA develops more effective treatments, including medications, for specific drugs of abuse, such as cocaine and heroin, and for the toxic effects on the brain and other organs that drugs of abuse produce. NIDA has engaged in a major effort to improve research on, and its application to, services for drug-abusing pregnant and postpartum women. NIDA also seeks to develop strategies to prevent or ameliorate the consequences of drugs of abuse on the children of drug-abusing parents and continues to study the links between addiction and other diseases, including HIV/AIDS and mental disorders.

To support this array of research programs, NIDA sponsors drug-abuse research programs in the biomedical and behavioral sciences. These programs include support of pre- and postdoctoral training in medical schools, universities, and other institutions of higher education in basic, clinical, behavioral, and epidemiological research, to assure the steady supply of trained scientists. These findings are disseminated to the widest audience possible. NIDA has an extensive outreach and public education program to rapidly provide research-based information to scientists, practitioners, policy makers, and the general public. NIDA staff works closely with local community-based networks to hold town meetings at various locations across the country, as well as other major conferences, to ensure that the latest scientific information is disseminated to those working to prevent and treat drug abuse and addiction. NIDA also develops written and electronic materials for researchers,

prevention practitioners, treatment practitioners, young people, parents, policy-makers, and others. Additionally, NIDA develops materials for K-12 students and teachers, as well as the general public, and funds grants with educators and scientists for the development of programs, materials, and museum exhibits. Through NIDA research dissemination programs, science-based information can then be used to educate, prevent, treat, and rehabilitate.

NIDA conducts and supports research that has as its underlying principles the goals of eliminating drug abuse, treating those whom prevention fails, increasing retention and decreasing relapse, and improving the health and well-being of all Americans, their families and their communities. Current and future directions in NIDA research can be found at http://www.nida.nih.gov/.

NIDA collaborates with other research institutes, and with other agencies and departments of the U.S. government. More information is available at the NIDA website at http://www.nida.nih.gov.

See also **U.S. Government Agencies: U.S. Public Health Service Hospitals.**

RICHARD A. MILLSTEIN
REVISED BY ALAN I. LESHNER (2001)
RICHARD H. BUCHER (2009)

OFFICE OF DRUG ABUSE LAW ENFORCEMENT (ODALE)

Located within the U.S. Department of Justice, the Office of Drug Abuse Law Enforcement (ODALE) was established by President Richard M. Nixon with Executive Order 11641 in January 1972. Myles J. Ambrose was appointed director of ODALE and held two other concurrent titles: special consultant to the president for drug abuse law enforcement and special assistant attorney general.

FEDERAL, STATE, AND LOCAL TEAMWORK

Complementing federal efforts directed at "high-level drug traffickers," ODALE was charged with attacking the heroin-distribution system at the street level to reduce the drug's availability there. Patterned after the Justice Department's Organized Crime Strike Forces, the ODALE program included task forces of federal, state, and local law-enforcement officers and attorneys. The full use of federal, state, and local narcotics laws, the availability of assigned attorneys, and the use of the investigative grand jury made possible a wide range of approaches in pursuing violators.

ODALE established task forces in thirty-four cities in 1972 and encouraged citizens to "report information regarding alleged narcotics law violators in strict confidence." The federal government paid for task force equipment and operational expenses, including payments for a portion of the salaries and overtime of state and local officers. ODALE was credited with more than 8,000 narcotics arrests with a conviction rate of more than 90 percent during its 17 months of operation. Nevertheless, ODALE agents were widely criticized for conducting several drug raids involving unauthorized forcible entries into private homes and failures in identifying themselves as law officers during drug raids.

REORGANIZATION
ODALE was abolished on July 1, 1973, by Presidential Reorganization Plan No. 2 of 1973 and "those Federal operations designed to attack narcotics traffic at the street level in cooperation with local authorities" were transferred to the newly established Drug Enforcement Administration (DEA). The ODALE program was redesignated as DEA's State and Local Task Force program. ODALE's Deputy Director John R. Bartels, Jr., became the first administrator of the DEA.

See also **Anslinger, Harry Jacob, and U.S. Drug Policy.**

BIBLIOGRAPHY

Erlen, J., & Spillane, J. F. (2004). *Federal drug control: The evolution of policy and practice.* New York: Haworth Press.

Rachal, P. (1982). *Federal narcotics enforcement.* Boston: Auburn House.

U.S. Congress, Senate, Committee on Government Operations. (1973). *Reorganization Plan No. 2 of 1973, Establishing a Drug Enforcement Administration in the Department of Justice. Report of the Subcommittee on Reorganization, Research, and International Organizations,* 93rd Congress. 1st sess., Report No. 93–469. Washington, D.C.

United States Drug Enforcement Administration (2008). *DEA history.* Available from http://www.usdoj.gov/dea/history.

United States General Accounting Office. (1975). *Federal drug enforcement: Strong guidance needed.* Report No. GGD-76-32. Washington, D.C.

RICHARD L. WILLIAMS

OFFICE OF DRUG ABUSE POLICY

In March 1976, Congress authorized the creation of the Office of Drug Abuse Policy (ODAP) in the Executive Office of the President, with an annual budget of $1.2 million. President Jimmy Carter opened the office in March 1977 and appointed Dr. Peter G. Bourne as director.

The director of ODAP was given wide responsibilities in assisting the president with all federal drug-abuse matters, including providing "policy direction and coordination among the law enforcement, international and treatment/prevention programs to assure a cohesive and effective strategy that both responds to immediate issues and provides a framework for longer-term resolution of problems." The statutory authority included setting objectives, establishing priorities, coordinating performance, and recommending changes in organization.

During the first year of operation, ODAP conducted several international missions and worked closely with United Nations narcotics organizations. In coordinating federal drug activities, ODAP relied on biweekly discussion meetings with the heads of the principal drug agencies. Policy determination was executed through cooperative interagency study efforts. ODAP completed six comprehensive interagency policy reviews: border management, drug law enforcement, international narcotics control, narcotics intelligence, demand reduction, and drug abuse in the armed forces.

The ODAP staff coordinated preparation of President Carter's August 1977 Message to the Congress on Drug Abuse and initiated the planning for a comprehensive federal strategy to be published by the revitalized Strategy Council.

REORGANIZATION
After one year of successful operation, ODAP was abolished by Reorganization Plan No. 1 of 1977, effective March 31, 1978. Six ODAP staff members were transferred to a special drug-policy unit (Drug Policy Office) within the White House Domestic Policy Staff. The drug-policy staff continued to report to Dr. Bourne who became special assistant to the president for health issues.

See also **Anslinger, Harry Jacob, and U.S. Drug Policy.**

BIBLIOGRAPHY

Erlen, J., & Spillane, J. F. (2004). *Federal drug control: The evolution of policy and practice.* New York: Haworth Press.

Executive Office of the President of the United States. Office of Drug Abuse Policy. (1978). *1978 Annual Report.* Washington, D.C.: Government Printing Office.

Havemann, J. (1978). Carter's reorganization plans—Scrambling for turf. *National Journal, 10,* 20, 788–794.

Musto, D. F., & Korsmeyer, P. (2002). *The quest for drug control: Politics and Federal policy in a period of increasing substance abuse, 1963–1981.* New Haven, CT: Yale University Press.

RICHARD L. WILLIAMS

OFFICE OF NATIONAL DRUG CONTROL POLICY

The Office of National Drug Control Policy (ONDCP) was established on January 29, 1989, by Public Law 100-690 (21 USC 1504) as the drug-coordination agency for the Executive Office of the President (EOP) under President George H. W. Bush. It resulted from the Anti-Drug Abuse Act of 1988. ONDCP is responsible for coordinating federal efforts to control illegal drug abuse. It is the product of almost two decades of congressional efforts to mandate a so-called drug czar—the law providing for cabinet-level status and congressional involvement in drug-control policy. ONDCP oversees the international and domestic antidrug functions of all executive agencies and ensures that such functions sustain and complement the government's overall antidrug efforts.

ONDCP's overarching purpose is to set the objectives, priorities, and policies for drug control in the United States. Its stated mission is to decrease the manufacture, distribution, and use of illegal drugs; to combat the violence and illegal activities associated with illicit drugs; and to ameliorate or mediate drug-related health problems.

THE DIRECTOR

ONDCP is led by a director (commonly referred to as the drug czar) with cabinet-level rank (executive level 1), two component deputies (supply reduction and demand reduction), and one associate director (state and local affairs), all appointed by the president with the advice and consent of the Senate. The director has a broad mandate for establishing policies, objectives, and priorities for the National Drug Control Program. Serving as the president's drug-control adviser and as a principal adviser to the National Security Council (NSC), the director has extraordinary management tools available to influence national drug-control efforts.

ONDCP is required to produce an annual National Drug Control Strategy for the president and Congress, and is responsible for overseeing its implementation by the federal departments and agencies. Included are an annual consolidated National Drug Control Program budget and the director's certification that the budget is adequate to implement the strategy's objectives. In addition to the strategy and program oversight, the director has two other legislated management tools: (1) approval of reprogramming of each agency's drug funds and (2) formal notification to the involved agency and the president when a drug-program agency's policy does not comply with the mandated strategy. The director also recommends changes in the organization, management, and budgets of departments and agencies engaged in the drug effort, including personnel allocations.

Reflecting congressional desire to participate in drug policy, the director must represent the administration's drug policies and proposals before Congress. Additionally, the authorizing legislation specifically allows Congress access to "information, documents, and studies in the possession of, or conducted by or at the direction of the Director" and to personnel of the office.

ORGANIZATION AND AUTHORITY

ONDCP's authority to provide direction to diverse federal departments and agencies is based on a program-management structure known as the National Drug Control Program. The ONDCP program and budget authority coexist with the line authority of the cabinet departments and with the president's annual budget process (directed by the Office of Management and Budget). The structure for the parallel drug-control system is created by designating National Drug Control Program agencies, defined as "any department or agency and all dedicated units thereof, with responsibilities under the National Drug Control Strategy." The designated federal departments and agencies have special program and budget responsibilities to the director of ONDCP. ONDCP's broad coordination authority over budgets and program activity also presents extraordinary opportunities for conflict with the existing line of authority in the departments and agencies. Simultaneously, ONDCP receives congressional and press criticism regarding lack of influence over operating activities.

POLICY DEVELOPMENT AND COORDINATION

The continued success of the complex drug-policy system depends on the continuing high priority of drug programs and seeking of widespread understanding and endorsement of the goals and objectives for the national program. An element essential to effective communication is a public document that explains the program's strategy, goals, and responsibilities—including a dynamic process of evaluating results and updating U.S. strategy.

The annual National Drug Control Strategy and accompanying budget summary are developed annually by the Office of the President. It contains three areas of emphasis: (1) stopping use before it starts, (2) intervening and healing America's drug users, and (3) disrupting the market. For fiscal year (FY) 2009 the drug budget totals $14.1 billion, representing an increase of 3.4 percent or $459 million from the previous budget. The administration also has a pending request for $2385.1 million for counternarcotics support to Central America and Mexico as a result of the Merida Initiative. Fostering improved security cooperation between the United States, Mexico, and Central America is the focus of the Merida Initiative, which is a multiyear $1.4 billion program aimed at decreasing cross-national crime. In FY 2008 ONDCP requested a budget supplement of $385.1 million to launch the program. The supplemental request for Merida in FY 2009 is $432.2 million.

Twelve agencies work together under the budget auspices of ONDCP. The drug-control programs funded and supported through the Departments of Education, Health and Human Services, Interior, Small Business Administration, and Veterans Affairs are dedicated to demand reduction activities, whereas the Departments of Defense, Homeland Security, Justice, State, Transportation, and Treasury focus on supply reduction activities. The ONDCP is involved in both demand and supply reduction.

The National Drug Control Strategy acknowledges that no single tactic will solve the drug problem. Therefore, the annual strategies call for improved and expanded treatment, prevention, and education; increased international cooperation; aggressive law enforcement and interdiction; expanded use of the military; expanded drug intelligence; and more research.

ORGANIZATION FOR COORDINATION

ONDCP has established a drug-control management agenda, including federal coordinating mechanisms and senior-level management committees and working groups. The organization of ONDCP includes staff for supply reduction, demand reduction, and state and local affairs. ONDCP working groups and committees coordinate the implementation of the policies, objectives, and priorities established in the National Drug Control Strategy.

PROGRAMS

Stopping Use Before It Starts. The $1.6 billion budget is dedicated to prevention, education, and outreach efforts designed to deter American youth from initiating drug use. Some of the pivotal programs are Safe and Drug-Free Schools and Communities, the National Youth Anti-Drug Media Campaign, Drug-Free Communities, and Student Drug Testing.

Intervening and Healing America's Drug Users. More than $3 billion of the drug budget is earmarked for drug-abuse interventions and treatment programs. Screening, Brief Intervention, Referral, and Treatment (SBIRT) activities are local (state, territory, and tribe) grant programs located within medical settings (such as community health centers and emergency rooms) where health providers screen and assess persons for substance-abuse-related problems. Those who are positively identified are afforded brief interventions and referred, as necessary, for higher levels of care. The Healthcare Common Procedure Coding System (HCPCS) has instituted two codes specific to alcohol and drug screening and brief intervention (SBI). SBI has demonstrated efficacy for reducing substance use, and approval of the HCPCS codes will allow state Medicaid dollars to pay for SBI programs. Access to Recovery (ATR) vastly expands access to treatment through the use of smaller community-run or faith-based programs. ATR programs use voucher systems to create a means of payment for persons who would not otherwise be able to afford help. Family, adult, and juvenile drug courts offer grant-based programs that provide participants with the ability to participate in treatment programs as an alternative to incarceration when possible.

Disrupting the Market. These funds, totaling over $8 billion, are used for emergency designations such as the operations occurring in Afghanistan, and for numerous other programs designed to disrupt the illegal drug trade worldwide. The funds are used for interdiction operations at national borders, and for improving mechanisms for detecting, tracking, and interrupting drug manufacture and trafficking.

The federal drug-control agencies and departments are represented on the various working groups and committees, along with ONDCP staff. The organizational structure includes the following coordinating mechanism.

ONDCP Supply Reduction Working Group. Chaired by the ONDCP deputy director for supply reduction, this working group includes three committees:

- The Border Interdiction Committee. Coordinates strategies and operations aimed at interdicting drugs between source and transit countries and at U.S. borders.
- The Public Land Drug Control Committee. Coordinates federal, state, and local drug-control programs (primarily marijuana eradication efforts) on federal lands.
- High-Intensity Drug Trafficking Area Program (HIDTA). Coordinates drug law enforcement activities in designated areas, including federal, state, and local enforcement task forces and intelligence activities, which have particularly significant drug trafficking problems that transcend their geographic areas and impact other parts of the nation. HIDTA directs additional federal resources to those areas with the goals of reducing, and eventually eliminating, trafficking and its attendant problems. HIDTA partners with local and regional law enforcement agencies in order to design and implement programs

specifically tailored to the needs of the area, using a multimodal approach to eliminate the sources of manufacture, distribution, and transport and other criminal activities while also addressing issues of treatment and prevention.

ONDCP Demand Reduction Working Group. Chaired by the ONDCP deputy director for demand reduction, this working group coordinates policies, objectives, and outreach activities for treatment, education and prevention, workplace, and international demand reduction.

Research and Development Committee. Chaired by the director of ONDCP, this committee provides policy guidance for the research and development (R&D) activities of all federal drug-control agencies, including the following R&D working committees:

- The Data Committee. Improves the relevance, timeliness, and usefulness of drug-related data collection, research studies, and evaluations of both demand-related and supply-related activities.
- The Medical Research Committee. Coordinates policy and general objectives on medical research by federal drug-control agencies and promotes the dissemination of research findings.
- The ONDCP Science and Technology Committee. Chaired by the ONDCP chief scientist, the committee is responsible for the oversight of counterdrug research and development throughout the federal government.

RELATED POLICY ACTIVITIES

The Counterdrug Technology Assessment Center, established by Public Law 101-509 in 1991, provides oversight of the federal government's counternarcotics R&D activities. ONDCP's chief scientist is responsible for defining scientific and technological needs for federal, state, and local law enforcement agencies, and for determining feasibility and priorities. The chief scientist also coordinates the technology initiatives of federal civilian and military departments, including research on substance abuse addiction and rehabilitation.

ONDCP works with the NSC, chairing the Policy Coordinating Committee for Narcotics to oversee coordination among agencies with law enforcement and national security responsibilities. The director also participates in meetings of the Domestic Policy Council, which reviews the annual drug control strategy before it goes to the president.

ONDCP's state and local affairs staff have traditionally sought wide public involvement in developing and implementing drug policy at all levels of government. The ONDCP sponsored several national conferences on state and local drug policy during 1990 and 1991 to highlight successful state and local programs, seek input on the national strategy, and inform participants of funding and initiatives available to them. ONDCP staff coordinated with both the White House Office of National Service and the president's Drug Advisory Council in encouraging private-sector and state and local initiatives for drug prevention and control.

ONDCP also provides administrative support to the president's Drug Advisory Council. With 32 private citizens as members, the Drug Advisory Council focuses on private-sector initiatives to support national drug-control objectives, and it assists the ONDCP. The advisory council is financed by private gifts.

See also **Anslinger, Harry Jacob, and U.S. Drug Policy; U.S. Government: The Organization of U.S. Drug Prevention Policy.**

BIBLIOGRAPHY

Advocates say ONDCP strategy offers few solutions. (1999). *Alcoholism & Drug Abuse Weekly, 11*(7), 3–4.

Anti-drug czar Gen. McCaffrey: Make treatment key weapon. (1996). *American Media News, 39*(26), 27–28.

Dettmer, J., & Linebaugh, S. (1997). McCaffrey's no-win war on drugs. *Insight on the News, 13*(7), 8–12.

Executive Office of the President of the United States. (Feb. 2007). *National drug control strategy: 2008 annual report.* Washington, DC: U.S. Government Printing Offices.

Executive Office of the President of the United States. (Feb. 2008). *National drug control strategy: FY 2009 budget summary.* Washington, DC: U.S. Government Printing Offices.

A general focuses on community leaders in the drug war. (1996). *The Addiction Letter, 4*(4), 4–5.

Office of National Drug Control Policy. (March 2000). *McCaffrey commends House on passage of Columbia/Andrean drug emergency assistance package, urges Senate to act swiftly.* Washington, DC: Author.

Office of National Drug Control Policy. (2007). *National Southwest border counternarcotics strategy: Unclassified summary.* Washington, DC: Author.

Office of National Drug Control Policy. (Updated May 7, 2007). *National leadership conference on medical education and substance abuse.* Washington, DC: Author.

Office of National Drug Control Policy. (August 2007). *Cocaine smuggling in 2006.* Washington, DC: Author.

Office of National Drug Control Policy. (March 2008). *What works: Effective public health response to drug use.* Washington, DC: Author.

ONDCP match information now available online. (2000). *Insight on the News, 12*(19), 6.

Report on McCaffrey departure adds grist to D.C. rumor mill. (1999). *Alcoholism & Drug Abuse Weekly, 13*(8), 5–6.

Report to question strength of ONDCP after McCaffrey. (2000). *Alcoholism & Drug Abuse Weekly, 12*(27), 5.

RICHARD L. WILLIAMS
REVISED BY PAMELA V. MICHAELS (2009)

SPECIAL ACTION OFFICE FOR DRUG ABUSE PREVENTION (SAODAP)

The Special Action Office for Drug Abuse Prevention (SAODAP) was created by Executive Order of President Richard M. Nixon on June 17, 1971, as a response to public concern about drug abuse, particularly heroin addiction. SAODAP was given legislative authority by the Drug Abuse Office and Treatment Act on March 21, 1972. The formation of SAODAP represented the first attempt to establish a stable focus within the federal government for the coordination of the many facets of U.S. drug policy, including law enforcement, border control, control of selected medicines, treatment, prevention, education, and research.

More than twenty agencies, offices, and bureaus within the U.S. government were responsible for activities relating to drug problems. Yet there was no evident central authority other than the president. Congress and the public seemed eager to be able to hold accountable the head of one agency who, unlike the president, could be asked to testify before Congress—a "drug czar." Although the term "drug czar" was popularly used, and it was expected that the person holding the office would exert power over the various agencies dealing with both law enforcement (supply side) and treatment and prevention (demand side) aspects of the problem, neither the president nor the Congress were entirely comfortable with delegating such broad authority to only one individual.

The legislation submitted to Congress by the White House, which finally emerged from debate, gave SAODAP unprecedented authority over demand side activity—treatment, prevention, education, research—wherever these were carried out within the federal government. However, its mandate with respect to drug-control agencies such as the U.S. Customs Bureau, which reported to the Secretary of the Treasury, and the Bureau of Narcotics and Dangerous Drugs, which reported to the Attorney General, was limited to coordination. SAODAP was also charged with developing a formal, written, national strategy for drug-abuse prevention. To head the new office, President Nixon appointed Dr. Jerome H. Jaffe, then a professor of psychiatry at the University of Chicago and director of the Illinois Drug Abuse Programs. Dr. Jaffe, who had helped the White House develop its response to heroin use in Vietnam, was also appointed special consultant to the president on narcotics and dangerous drugs.

A primary goal of SAODAP, stated at the press conference that announced the new office, was to make treatment so available that no addicts could say they committed crimes because they could not get treatment. Although the Bureau of Narcotics and Dangerous Drugs (BNDD) had estimated that there were about a half million heroin users in the United States, in mid-1971 the true extent of the drug-abuse problem was unknown. The estimating techniques that were developed in the 1970s—the National Household Survey on Drug Abuse, the DAWN system (or Drug Abuse Warning Network), and the High School Senior Survey—did not yet exist, but the rising rate of heroin-related deaths in several major cities and the thousands of addicts waiting for treatment because there was not enough treatment capacity gave stark evidence for the growing size of the heroin problem. There were drug overdose (OD) deaths among U.S. troops in Vietnam also. Surveys generally indicated widespread drug use among U.S. servicemen in Vietnam, with the extent of the problem estimated at 15 to 30 percent, but it was not known if these estimates were of drug users or of addicts.

In addition to the mandate to coordinate all the demand side drug-abuse activities of the federal bureaucracy so as to reduce overlap and redundancy and to expand treatment capacity, some of the additional tasks of the office included overseeing and coordinating the Vietnam drug-abuse intervention; creating a new federal agency with competence to develop national policy; creating the data systems by which the effectiveness of national policy could be evaluated; creating a science base so that research might lead to better ways to treat and prevent addiction; and developing a formal, written National Strategy for drug-abuse treatment and prevention.

Four major policy changes helped the agency achieve its objectives. The first was made by the president when the Vietnam testing and treatment program was initiated: Drug use was no longer a court-martial offense. The second was having the federal government take responsibility for developing and funding treatment. The third made methadone-maintenance treatment, already being used for 20,000 people, an established and acceptable treatment method rather than an experiment. The fourth had to do with changes that were made in the thinking, language, and means by which treatment was supported.

A central effort for SAODAP was the expansion of treatment capacity, increasing not only the number of programs, but also their actual capacity and geographic distribution. In addition, recipients of funding for treatment programs became accountable for what they provided, such as the number of treatment slots and the type of treatment. While legitimizing methadone-maintenance treatment and developing regulations for its use were highly visible and highly controversial activities, they were only incidental to the overall mission of making effective treatment central to the nation's response to the drug problem. Within the first 18 months of SAODAP's efforts, the number of communities with federally supported drug-treatment programs increased from 54 to 214, and the number of programs grew to almost 400. More federally supported treatment capacity was developed within two years than over the previous fifty years.

Some of the other projects SAODAP initiated, funded, or grappled with were the Vietnam drug intervention and the Vietnam drug intervention follow-up study; the development of confidentiality regulations to protect the medical records of people seeking treatment; funding clinical research on new pharmacological treatments for drug dependence; initiating with other agencies projects such as treatment alternatives to street crime (TASC), research centers for clinical and basic research on drug abuse and addiction, the Career Teachers program that incorporated drug abuse into medical school curricula, and a National Training Center. SAODAP introduced formula or block grants that gave money through the National Institutes on Mental Health (NIMH) to the states for treatment and prevention programs; it also introduced management concepts and language into treatment systems. SAODAP played a major role in improving drug-abuse treatment in the Veterans Administration; establishing laboratory standards for urine-testing facilities; and initiating several of the epidemiological tools that continue to shape policy, such as the National Household Survey of Drug Abuse and the Drug Abuse Warning Network (DAWN) system. Many of the programs and activities developed with interagency cooperation were implemented by the agencies involved in the collaboration. Many of the activities are ongoing in the mid-1990s. SAODAP also produced the first written national strategy, entitled "Federal Strategy for Drug Abuse and Drug Traffic Prevention."

Since the baseline funding for drug-abuse treatment, prevention, and research was so low in 1971, the new resources given to SAODAP for the task represented a manyfold increase—and in some instances were the very first resources available for the purpose. The same legislation that authorized SAODAP provided for the establishment of the National Institutes on Drug Abuse (NIDA); in addition, the resources and policies for an invigorated research effort were put into place over the three budgetary cycles that preceded NIDA's creation. Dr. Robert Dupont, who succeeded Dr. Jaffe as director of SAODAP, became the first director of NIDA. Dr. Peter Bourne and Mr. Lee Dogoloff, both of whom worked at SAODAP during the first two years, later became key advisors on drug policy to President Jimmy Carter.

A noted researcher, Dr. Solomon Snyder, credits the SAODAP support he received with enabling him to discover the opiate receptor a year or two later. This discovery forms the basis for much of the neuroscience research into understanding the biology of drug dependence.

SAODAP was able to change the national response to illicit drug use by developing an infrastructure for treatment that is largely still in place, one that recognizes the heterogeneity of the drug-using population, their need for several different types of treatment, and the need for research on the efficacy of treatment. For a brief period after SAODAP's mandate expired in 1975, drug-abuse policy was coordinated by a smaller office within the Office of Management and Budget (OMB) under President Gerald R. Ford, and then by the Drug Abuse Policy Office within the White House under presidents Jimmy Carter and Ronald W. Reagan. However, until President George H. Bush established the Office of National Drug Control Policy (ONDCP), there was no formal agency with substantial authority for coordinating federal drug policy.

See also **Industry and Workplace, Drug Use in.**

BIBLIOGRAPHY

Caulkins, J. P. (2005). *How goes the war on drugs?: An assessment of U.S. drug problems and policy.* Santa Monica, CA: Rand Corporation.

Erlen, J., & Spillane, J. F. (2004). *Federal drug control: The evolution of policy and practice.* New York: Haworth Press.

Musto, D. F., & Korsmeyer, P. (2002). *The quest for drug control: Politics and Federal policy in a period of increasing substance abuse, 1963–1981.* New Haven, CT: Yale University Press.

FAITH K. JAFFE
JEROME H. JAFFE

SUBSTANCE ABUSE AND MENTAL HEALTH SERVICES ADMINISTRATION (SAMHSA)

The Substance Abuse and Mental Health Services Administration (SAMHSA), established by Congress on October 1, 1992 (Public Law 102-321), works with states, communities, and organizations to strengthen the national capacity to provide substance abuse prevention, addiction treatment, and mental health services for people experiencing or at risk for mental health and substance abuse disorders. The SAMHSA fiscal year 2009 budget was approximately $3.2 billion; it employed a staff of approximately 550. In 2008 the SAMHSA Administrator was Dr. Terry Cline, and the Deputy Administrator was Dr. Eric Broderick. The Agency houses three Offices: Office of Applied Studies, Office of Policy, and Office of Program Services; and three program Centers: Center for Mental Health Services (CMHS), Center for Substance Abuse Prevention (CSAP), and Center for Substance Abuse Treatment (CSAT). (More specific information can be found at the respective Web sites for each center.)

Because the main objective of SAMHSA is to continually expand and improve the quality and availability of mental health, substance abuse prevention and treatment, and behavioral health (combined mental health and substance abuse) services throughout the United States, the organization developed grant funding programs. Grant portfolios include both block and discretionary grants. Block grants enable states to maintain and enhance their substance abuse and mental health services. Targeted Capacity Expansion grants provide resources to communities to identify and address emerging substance abuse and mental health service needs at their earliest stages. The SAMHSA Knowledge Application Program grants implement and assess new community-based prevention and treatment methods. Grant funds are awarded through CMHS, CSAP, and CSAT.

The SAMHSA Center for Mental Health Services (CMHS) works to improve the availability and accessibility of high-quality care for people with or at risk for mental illnesses as well as for their families by creating a nationwide community-based mental health service infrastructure. CMHS education programs are helping to end the stigma associated with these illnesses. While the largest portion of the Center's annual budget supports the Community Mental Health Services Block Grant Program to states, CMHS also supports grant programs to develop and apply knowledge about best community-based practices designed to serve adults with serious mental illnesses and children with serious emotional disturbances. The Center also collects and analyzes national mental health services data to help inform future services decision-making.

The Center for Substance Abuse Prevention (CSAP) is the national focal point for the identification, promotion, and dissemination of effective strategies to prevent drug and alcohol abuse and tobacco use. CSAP programs identify prevention strategies—such as targeted family and community strengthening—that work best for specific populations at risk of substance abuse. Program approaches emphasize both cultural relevance and competence. The Center oversees federal workplace drug-testing programs as well as state implementation of the Synar Amendment, which prohibits youths under age 18 from purchasing tobacco. In addition CSAP supports the National Clearinghouse for Alcohol and Drug Information (NCADI), the largest information source on substance abuse research, treatment, and prevention in the nation. CSAP also oversees four grant programs (State Incentive, Drug-Free Community, HIV, and Methamphetamine).

The Center for Substance Abuse Treatment (CSAT) works to enhance the quality of substance abuse treatment services and to ensure that services are available to all who need them. It supports the identification, evaluation, and dissemination of proven effective treatment services. CSAT administers the state Substance Abuse Prevention and Treatment block grant and undertakes knowledge development, education, and communications initiatives that promote best practices in substance use/abuse treatment and intervention. The CSAT Targeted Capacity Expansion Program—and its specialized program focused on HIV/AIDS services—helps communities respond rapidly to emerging local drug use trends. In addition to the Co-Occurring Center for Excellence, CSAP oversees many programs including Access to Recovery (ATR), Partners for Recovery (PFR), the Knowledge Application Program (KAP), the National Center on Substance Abuse and Child Welfare (NCSACW), National Alcohol and Drug Addiction Recovery Month, the Substance Abuse Treatment Facility Locator, Medication Assisted Treatment (MAT), the Recovery Community Services Program, Addiction Technology Transfer Centers, Practice/Improvement Collaboratives Program, Persistent Effects of Treatment Studies, CMHS/CSAT Spending, Organization, and Financing Treatment Services, the Treatment Improvement Exchange Forum, As You Age, the Do the Right Dose program for discouraging elders from abusing prescription pain medications, and the *SBIRT* programs. CSAP also funds programs at the state and local levels to improve and expand substance abuse treatment services via Substance Abuse Treatment and Prevention (SAPT) block grants.

While SAMHSA's Office of the Administrator and Office of Program Services are primarily administrative in nature, the Office of Applied Studies (OAS) has program authority to gather, analyze, and disseminate data on substance abuse practices in the United States. It collects data on alcohol, tobacco, marijuana, and other drug abuse; drug-related emergency department episodes; medical examiner cases; and the national substance abuse treatment system. OAS directs the annual National Survey on Drug Use and Health (NSDUH), the Drug Abuse Warning Network (DAWN), and the Drug and Alcohol Services Information System (DASIS), among others. Through these studies, SAMHSA identifies trends in substance abuse and mental health care. OAS also coordinates evaluation of models developed through SAMHSA knowledge development and application programs.

Other SAMHSA initiatives include the 15+ Make Time To Listen...Take Time to Talk program, the As You Age public education campaign, the Building Blocks for a Healthy Future early prevention program, the Fetal Alcohol Spectrum Disorders (FASD) Center, the nationwide Helping America's Youth effort led by First Lady Laura Bush, the Mental Health Services Locator searchable online directory, the National Strategy for Suicide Prevention (NSSP), the Older Americans Technical Assistance Center, Partners for Recovery (PFR) support and technical resource system, Projects for Assistance in Transition from Homelessness (PATH) formula grants, the Recovery Community Services Program (RCSP) peer-to-peer recovery support services, Recovery Month programs, Safe Schools/Healthy Students (SS/HS) Initiative, Systems of Care grants and community/local programs, and the Knowledge Application Program (KAP) initiative, among many others. (A more complete listing of initiatives and more information about those listed can be found at the SAMHSA Web site.)

SAMHSA comes up with new program ideas in varying ways. Some are developed by SAMHSA leadership and staff; others result from congressional mandate. Still other grow from Center-sponsored meetings that highlight empirically validated intervention models ripe for replication. Some new program directions originate at the state and local levels, some from SAMHSA and Center National Advisory Councils, and some from the research community.

SAMHSA programs bring new science-based knowledge to community-based prevention, identification, and treatment programs for mental and substance abuse disorders. Results are evident in improved approaches to addiction treatment, substance abuse prevention, and mental health services at the federal, state, and community levels. Equally important, the results are obvious in the improved quality of people's lives.

See also **Treatment: An Overview; Treatment, Behavioral Approaches to: An Overview.**

BIBLIOGRAPHY

Department of Health and Human Services. (2008). *Fiscal year 2009 Substance Abuse and Mental Health Services Administration: Justification of estimates for appropriations committees.* Rockville, MD.

Hughes, A., Sathe, N., & Spagnola, K. (2008). *State estimates of substance use from the 2005–2006 National Surveys on Drug Use and Health* (DHHS Publication No. SMA 08-4311, NSDUH Series H-33). Rockville, MD: Substance Abuse and Mental Health Services Administration, Office of Applied Studies.

Substance Abuse and Mental Health Services Administration, Office of Applied Studies. (2007). *SAMHSA: Building resilience...facilitating recovery...life in the community for everyone.* Rockville, MD.

Substance Abuse and Mental Health Services Administration, Office of Applied Studies. (2007). *Treatment Episode Data Set (TEDS) Highlights—2006 National Admissions to Substance Abuse Treatment Services.* (OAS Series #S-40, DHHS Publication No. (SMA) 08-4313). Rockville, MD.

Substance Abuse and Mental Health Services Administration, Office of Applied Studies. (2007). *Treatment Episode Data Set (TEDS): 1995–2005. National Admissions to Substance Abuse Treatment Services.* (DASIS Series: S-37, DHHS Publication No. (SMA) 07-4234). Rockville, MD.

Substance Abuse and Mental Health Services Administration, Office of Applied Studies. (2007). *National Survey of Substance Abuse Treatment Services (N-SSATS): 2006. Data on Substance Abuse Treatment Facilities.* (DASIS Series: S-39, DHHS Publication No. (SMA) 07-4296). Rockville, MD.

United States Department of Health and Human Services: Substance Abuse and Mental Health Services Administration. (2008). *Center for Substance Abuse Treatment.* Available from http://csat.samhsa.gov/.

United States Department of Health and Human Services: Substance Abuse and Mental Health Services Administration. (2008). *Office of Applied Studies.* Available from http://www.oas.samhsa.gov/.

United States Department of Health and Human Services: Substance Abuse and Mental Health Services Administration. (2008). *SAMHSA's Center for Substance Abuse Prevention.* Available from http://prevention.samhsa.gov/.

United States Department of Health and Human Services: Substance Abuse and Mental Health Services Administration. (2008). *SAMHSA's National Mental Health Information Center.* Available from http://mental-health.samhsa.gov/cmhs/.

United States Department of Health and Human Services: (2008). *Substance Abuse and Mental Health Services Administration: SAMHSA.* Available from http://www.samhsa.gov/.

ELAINE JOHNSON
REVISED BY THEODORA FINE (2001)
PAMELA V. MICHAELS (2009)

U.S. CUSTOMS AND BORDER PROTECTION (CBP)

Housed within the Department of Homeland Security, the U.S. Customs and Border Protection (CBP) is tasked with securing the entirety of the U.S. border from human and drug smuggling, terrorism, and illegal migration (both immigration and emigration), as well as overseeing international trade and travel. The CBP guards the 7,000 miles of border between the United States and Canada and Mexico, in addition to the California coastline and the waters surrounding Florida. The U.S. Coast Guard works with the CBP in patrolling the 95,000 miles of maritime border surrounding the United States.

Of CBP's more than 44,000 staff, over 13,000 are Border Patrol or CBP Air and Marine agents, while some 20,000 are CBP officers and agriculture specialists. In addition, CBP employs the largest number of canine patrol teams in the United States. CBP Officers are stationed at official points of entry into the country (also called CBP Stations), and Border Patrol agents are tasked with the prevention of illegal entry of contraband and persons between these official border-crossing locations. CBP also conducts a wide range of statutory and regulatory activities, ranging from interdicting and seizing contraband entering the United States to intercepting illegal exports of high-technology items. Put simply, U.S. Customs and Border Protection serves as the single unified agency responsible for protecting the country's borders.

CBP'S ROLE IN DRUG ENFORCEMENT

CBP is both a leader and a major player in stopping drug contraband from entering the United States. CBP's inspection and control function is directed at stopping illegal entry of drugs and other contraband, while also accommodating the normal flow of persons and cargo entering the United States and enforcing export laws. More than $9.2 billion of the annual federal budget is allocated to interrupting illegal drug trade, and the Department of Homeland Security, the U. S. Coast Guard, and CBP play major roles in the interdiction of contraband substances along the borders of the country. The Merida Initiative, which was established in February 2008, is a $1.4 billion multiyear program designed to expand the cooperative relationship between Central America, Mexico, and the United States. The intention of this program is to dramatically decrease the incidence of cross-border drug trafficking and other international crimes. In fiscal year 2008, $385.1 million will specifically target drug-related activities; in fiscal year 2009, the budget will be increased to $550 million, with $432.2 million targeted specifically toward work with Mexico and Central America. Approximately $570 million of the 1993 CBP budget was related to antidrug operations.

As the lead federal agency at U.S. ports of entry, CBP inspects individuals, conveyances, mail, and cargo entering the United States by land, sea, and air. It has broad search and seizure authority at the U.S. borders and handles enormous workloads. On a typical day, for example (using 2006 data), CBP processes roughly one million passengers and pedestrians, 327,000 privately owned vehicles, 71,000 containers, and 85,000 shipments of goods and cargo. CBP operates a comprehensive computerized border information system and uses other domestic and international drug-intelligence networks. The agency's efforts are prioritized to target the illegal traffic in precursor chemicals, to improve interdiction intelligence, and to engage in special high-intensity enforcement operations, particularly along the southwest border. More than 60 people are arrested at points of entry every day, and nearly 3,000 are caught attempting to enter the country illegally. In addition, on an average day CBP seizes 1,800 pounds of narcotics at border crossings, nearly 4,000 pounds of narcotics between legal border crossing areas, more than $150,000 in illicit or undeclared currency, and about $650,000 in fraudulent commercial merchandise at border entry points. In order to achieve this mission, approximately 1,250 human-canine pairs, 6,000 vehicles, 260 aircraft, 200 watercraft, and 200 equestrian patrols are utilized.

APPROACHES TO INTERDICTION

As a large, multipurpose border-control agency, CBP has considerable flexibility in determining the most effective means to meet its responsibilities. The traditional approach involves the physical presence of uniformed officers at the border to detect and seize violators and contraband. CBP emphasizes the development of the best possible detection capabilities and information systems to facilitate identification of persons who might pose a terrorist threat. These include the Advance Passenger Information System (APIS), the Student and Exchange Visitor System (SEVIS), and U.S. Visitor and Immigrant Status Indication Technology (US-VISIT). The Automated Targeting System (ATS) and the Automated Export System (AES), along with the Advance Electronic Information regulations that were part of the Trade Act of 2002, facilitate the identification of cargo or goods that could pose a threat.

The CBP became part of the Department of Homeland Security following the terrorist attacks on September 11, 2001. Since then, it has utilized its Office of Intelligence and the National Targeting Center (NTC) to increase its capabilities for processing and synthesizing information and improve its tactical accuracy in identifying suspicious cargo prior to its arrival at a U.S. border. CBP also works closely with the U.S. Coast Guard and U.S. military forces in providing surveillance, interception, and deterrence against drug smuggling by air and sea. CBP is working actively with Mexico and Canada to facilitate the smooth flow of legal travel and trade activities across these borders, while also intensifying cooperative efforts aimed at preventing the smuggling of contraband, weapons, drugs, and humans.

See also **Anslinger, Harry Jacob, and U.S. Drug Policy; Border Management; Drug Interdiction; International Drug Supply Systems; Operation Intercept; Zero Tolerance.**

BIBLIOGRAPHY

Prince, C. E., & Keller, M. (1989). *The U.S. Customs Service, a bicentennial history.* Washington, DC: U.S. Government Printing Office.

U.S. Executive Office of the President, Office of Drug Abuse Policy. (1977). *Border management and interdiction: An interagency review.* Washington, DC: Author.

U.S. Executive Office of the President, Office of National Drug Control Policy. (2001). *Measuring the deterrent effect of enforcement operations on drug smuggling, 1991–1999.* Washington, DC: Author. Available from http://www.whitehousedrugpolicy.gov/.

U.S. Executive Office of the President, Office of National Drug Control Policy. (2007). *National southwest border counternarcotics strategy: Unclassified summary, October 2007.* Washington, DC: Author. Available from http://www.whitehousedrugpolicy.gov/.

U.S. Executive Office of the President, Office of National Drug Control Policy. (2008). *Cocaine smuggling in 2006.* Washington, DC: Author. Available from http://www.whitehousedrugpolicy.gov/.

U.S. Executive Office of the President, Office of National Drug Control Policy. (2008). *National drug control strategy.* Washington, DC: Author. Available from http://www.whitehousedrugpolicy.gov/.

U.S. Executive Office of the President, Office of National Drug Control Policy. (2008). *National drug control strategy: FY 2009 budget summary.* Washington, DC: Author. Available from http://www.whitehousedrug policy.gov/.

U.S. Executive Office of the President, Office of National Drug Control Policy. (2008). *U.S. cocaine data, 2007.* Washington, DC: Author. Available from http://www.whitehousedrugpolicy.gov/.

RICHARD L. WILLIAMS
REVISED BY PAMELA V. MICHAELS (2009)

U.S. PUBLIC HEALTH SERVICE HOSPITALS

In 1929, President Herbert C. Hoover signed a law enacted by the U.S. Congress to establish two federal institutions for treatment of narcotic addiction. The principal purpose of the institutions was to confine and treat persons addicted to narcotic drugs who had been convicted of offenses against the United States. However, the law also provided for voluntary admission and treatment of addicts who were not convicted of any offense. The two institutions were named U.S. public health service hospitals. One was opened in 1935 at Lexington, Kentucky, and the other in 1938 at Fort Worth, Texas. The Lexington hospital had a capacity of 1,200 patients; the Fort Worth hospital could accommodate 1,000 patients. From opening to closure in 1974, the hospitals admitted over 60,000 narcotic addicts; because of readmissions, the total admissions exceeded 100,000. Most of the admissions were voluntary. The term *narcotic addiction* has been replaced in modern diagnostic terminology by the term *opioid dependence*, but in this discussion the older term is retained because it was regularly used during the era reviewed here. The history of the hospitals is divided into three periods.

FIRST PERIOD, 1935–1949

From the start, the hospitals were designed to treat not only the physical dependence but also the mental and emotional problems thought to be related to addiction. This was an advanced conception, for treatment of narcotic addiction until then had been focused almost exclusively on the physical dependence. The initial treatment programs at both hospitals emphasized residence in a drug-free environment for at least six months, during which time the patient could not only recover from the physical dependence but perhaps also overcome the mental difficulties or learn to adapt to them without using drugs. While all patients received psychological help in the form of encouragement and persuasion, only small numbers received formal psychotherapy. That was because few of the staff were trained in psychotherapy. All patients considered physically able had work assignments, and all had access to educational and vocational services, recreation, and religious activities. Treatment of voluntary patients was hindered because most left during or shortly after withdrawal treatment (often to return to lower doses of their drug—before readmission). In 1948, the research division of the Lexington hospital reported that a new synthesized narcotic drug called methadone was effective in the treatment of opiate withdrawal. Methadone substitution followed by a gradual decrease of its

dose subsequently became the standard treatment for morphine and heroin withdrawal in the United States. Also in 1948 the research division of the Lexington hospital was administratively separated from the hospital, renamed the Addiction Research Center (ARC) and made a part of the National Institute of Mental Health (NIMH).

SECOND PERIOD, 1950–1966

After World War II, the prevalence of heroin addiction in the United States markedly increased. Heroin replaced morphine as the primary narcotic used. Annual admissions to the two hospitals doubled from the 1940s to the 1950s. The prewar addicts differed from their postwar counterparts. More of the postwar addicts came from large cities, and more came from minority groups (mainly black and Hispanic).

While residence in a drug-free environment continued as a major feature, new psychosocial treatments were made a part of the program. Psychoanalytically oriented psychotherapy was offered, but few patients seemed willing or able to engage in this form of therapy. Group therapy, however, seemed more acceptable, and most patients participated in it to some extent. Influenced by new concepts of the therapeutic community, staff members tried to improve the quality of the patients' psychosocial experience in the hospital.

THIRD PERIOD, 1967–1974

In 1967, a research mission was assigned to the two hospitals, and each was renamed a National Institute of Mental Health Clinical Research Center. Before the research mission could be developed, however, a new clinical mission was assigned to the two institutions. The Narcotic Addict Rehabilitation Act (NARA), enacted in 1966, provided for the civil commitment of addicts instead of prosecution on a criminal charge, or sentence after conviction, or by petition with no criminal charge. The law authorized the Public Health Service to enter into contracts with any public or private agencies to provide examination or treatment of addicts committed under the NARA, but it was decided to use the two clinical research centers to implement the act quickly. Admission of prisoners and voluntary patients was phased out, and the centers concentrated on service to the NARA patients.

From 1967 through 1973, over 10,000 NARA patients were admitted to the two centers. Nearly all were admitted under the provision of the law that permitted commitment with no federal criminal charge.

The NARA civil commitment seemed a promising way to eliminate the problem of voluntary patients who signed out prematurely. In practice, it only reduced the problem. Patients learned that commitment could be avoided or terminated if they refused to participate in treatment activities or engaged in disruptive or antagonistic behavior. Only about one-third of the NARA patients completed a six-month period of institutional treatment.

The NARA program led to the closure of the two centers. As more contracts were made with local facilities for examination and treatment of NARA patients, admissions to the two centers decreased. In addition, a new federal program, started in the late 1960s, of grants to states and communities for drug-abuse treatment programs made the centers less needed. The Fort Worth Center was closed in 1971 and the Lexington Center in 1974. The facilities were transferred to the Federal Bureau of Prisons and were converted into correctional institutions.

HISTORIC ROLES OF THE HOSPITALS

For approximately three decades, from the 1930s into the 1960s, the two Public Health Service hospitals were almost the only institutions in the United States engaged in the study and treatment of narcotic addiction. They became international centers of expertise. Staff members published many reports on the psychosocial characteristics of the addicts, the treatment programs, treatment outcomes, and related topics. Many clinicians and investigators who worked at Lexington and Fort Worth left these institutions to become leaders in treatment of or research on narcotic addiction at other locations. Despite great efforts, however, the hospitals failed to develop an enduring cure for narcotic addiction. Hospital treatment often produced a temporary remission in the addiction, but relapse within a year was the typical outcome.

See also **Opioid Dependence: Course of the Disorder Over Time; Wikler's Conditioning Theory of Drug Addiction.**

BIBLIOGRAPHY

Acker, C. J. (2005). *Creating the American junkie: Addiction research in the classic era of narcotic control*. Baltimore, MD: The Johns Hopkins University Press.

Erlen, J., & Spillane, J. F. (2004). *Federal drug control: The evolution of policy and practice*. New York: Haworth Press.

Leukefeld, C. G., & Tims, F. M. (Eds). (1988). *Compulsory treatment of drug abuse: Research and clinical practice*. National Institute on Drug Abuse Research Monograph 86. DHHS Publication no. (ADM) 88–1578. Rockville, MD: U.S. Department of Health and Human Services.

Martin, W. R., & Isbell, H. (Eds). (1978). *Drug addiction and the U.S. Public Health Service*. DHEW Publication no. (ADM) 77-434. Rockville, MD: U.S. Department of Health, Education, and Welfare.

Musto, D. F., & Korsmeyer, P. (2002). *The quest for drug control: Politics and Federal policy in a period of increasing substance abuse, 1963–1981*. New Haven, CT: Yale University Press.

JAMES F. MADDUX

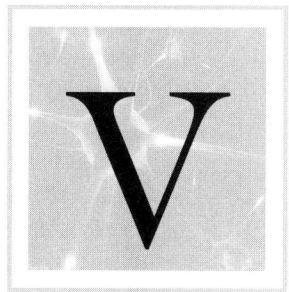

VALUES AND BELIEFS: EXISTENTIAL MODELS OF ADDICTION.

Existential models of addiction focus on the sense of self of drug users, and the meanings the experience of drug use has for the individual. According to one existential theory of drug dependence certain individuals are "addiction prone" because of a disordered emotional state and pathological personality factors (Greaves, 1980). Other accounts focus on the values, attitudes, and beliefs of drug users. For example, psychologists have found that problem drinkers and alcoholics anticipate greater benefits and more powerful effects from drinking than do other drinkers. These beliefs precede actual drinking experiences (Miller et al., 1990). Khantzian has proposed that some users are predisposed to addiction because they take drugs to self-medicate emotional distress and psychiatric problems such as depression (1985). According to Peele, the individual becomes addicted to a substance because it fulfills essential intrapsychic, interpersonal, and environmental needs (1985).

CULTURAL BELIEFS IN ADDICTION

Cultural beliefs, norms, and values are intimately connected with existential experiences. They are among the most powerful determinants of the patterns of alcohol and drug use (Heath, 2000). Early work on cultural variations in drinking behavior in the United States found that moderation was inculcated as an early and firm cultural style among Mediterranean ethnic groups, Jews, and the Chinese (Barnett, 1955; Hanson, 1995). Such cultural socialization incorporates beliefs about the power of alcohol and the nature of those who overindulge or misbehave when drinking. Groups such as the Irish that invest alcohol with the power to control and corrupt their behavior were found to have high levels of alcoholism. In contrast, Jews, Italians, and Chinese believed that those who drink to excess are displaying poor self-control and/or psychological dependence, rather than responding to the power of the alcohol itself (Vaillant, 1983; Glassner & Berg, 1984; Bales, 1946). MacAndrew and Edgerton's influential book *Drunken Comportment* (1969) emphasized cross-cultural variation in intoxicated behavior, observing that in some cultures drunkenness operated as an accepted excuse for bad behavior whereas in others behavioral norms for sober and drunken states were similar.

Other work has stressed the need to recognize the multiple effects of socioeconomic status, gender, education, generation, age, and occupation rather than treating ethnicity or cultural background as simple determinants of views about alcohol and drinking behavior (Ames & Rebhun, 1996; Dawson, 1998). Ethnic categories need to be carefully employed; for example, while it is possible to generalize that Asian Americans generally drink less than white Americans and that there are relatively few alcohol problems among Asian Americans, Japanese Americans appear to have relatively high rates of heavy drinking (O'Hare, 1995). Dwight Heath, one of the key scholars of alcohol and culture, has observed that ethnicity has been used too loosely in alcohol studies, in ways that overlap with nationality, religion, race, and cultural background (1998). Cultural identities should not be regarded as uniform and static entities; their content and salience change over time, location, and social context (Heath, 2000).

The existential and cultural approaches to addiction, along with other social constructionist frameworks, are often assumed to be alternatives to biological models and incompatible with explanations that draw on the neuropharmacology of different drugs. However, the integration of the cultural and the biological is a key issue in addiction and drug research (Kushner, 2006). The question of how cultural beliefs interact with pharmacology requires further research. Steele and Joseph's notion of "alcohol myopia" provides one starting point as it attempts to explain how a single drug can have diverse behavioral effects (1990; Room, 2001). It proposes that alcohol intoxication restricts attention to the most immediate cues in a setting, a cognitive short-sightedness that can produce a range of effects from altruism and conviviality to violence. Thus, the effects of alcohol vary from person to person, occasion to occasion, and culture to culture, depending on the cues that are relevant.

Another pressing question is how to conceptualize the interaction of cultural and biological factors in the influential "dependence syndrome" model of addiction developed by Griffith Edwards. Edwards argues that as a syndrome, rather than a disease, alcohol dependence should be thought of as something that is not all or nothing, but something that can be experienced in varied degrees, with a collection of signs and symptoms that are not definitive but may vary over time and cultural location (2003). Syndromes of dependence thus have multiple triggers and pathways informed by what Kushner has called "cultural biology" (2006).

VALUES

In general, scientific and scholarly accounts of addiction have distanced themselves from claims about the relationship between values, morals, and excessive drug and alcohol use. Indeed, such perspectives are seen as impeding the development of an objective science of addiction. Because pharmacologically-based theories often emphasize the potency of the drug and the altered physiology and neurology of the addict as the basis of compulsion,

they tend to exclude the role of values in influencing people's choices about drugs.

Peele has challenged this approach, claiming that people become addicted due to a failure of other values that maintain ordinary life involvements (1987). In Peele's view, personal values influence whether people use drugs, whether they use them regularly, whether they become addicted, and whether they remain addicted. These values include prosocial behavior (including achievement, concern for others, and community involvement), self-awareness and intellectual activity, moderation and healthfulness, and self-respect. According to Peele, the explicit values people cite as reasons for giving up addictions to cocaine, alcohol, and nicotine are evidence of the importance of values in drug use (Reinarman et al., 1991). However, the protective values Peele cites such as achievement, self-awareness, and self-respect are themselves culturally-specific ideals of individual virtue. The relationship between these values and different cultural beliefs about alcohol is not clear.

See also **Alcoholism: Origin of the Term; Chinese Americans, Alcohol and Drug Use among; Jews and Alcohol.**

BIBLIOGRAPHY

Ames, G., & Rebhun, L. (1996). Women, alcohol and work: Interactions of gender, ethnicity and occupational culture. *Social Science & Medicine, 43,* 1649–1663.

Bales, R. (1946). Cultural differences in rates of alcoholism. *Quarterly Journal of Studies on Alcoholism, 6,* 480–499.

Barnett, M. (1955). Alcoholism in the Cantonese of New York City: An anthropological study. In O. Diethelm (Ed.), *Etiology of chronic alcoholism* (pp. 179–227). Springfield, IL: Charles C. Thomas.

Dawson, D. (1998). Beyond black, white, and hispanic: Race, ethnic origin and drinking patterns in the United States. *Journal of Substance Abuse, 10,* 321–339.

Edwards, G., Marshall, E. J., & Cook, C. (2003). The alcohol dependence syndrome. In G. Edwards, E. J. Marshall, & C. Cook (Eds.), *The treatment of drinking problems* (4th ed., pp. 47–69). Cambridge, England: Cambridge University Press.

Glassner, B., & Berg, B. (1984). Social locations and interpretations: How Jews define alcoholism. *Journal of Studies on Alcohol, 45,* 16–25.

Greaves, G. B. (1980). An existential theory of drug dependence. In D. J. Lettieri, M. Sayers, & H. W. Pearson (Eds.), *Theories on drug abuse* (pp. 24–28).

Washington, DC: U.S. Government Printing Office (DHHS Pub. No. ADM 80–967)

Hanson, D. (1995). The United States of America. In D. Heath (Ed.), *International handbook on alcohol and culture* (pp. 300–315). Westport, CT: Greenwood Press.

Heath, D. (1998). Cultural variations among drinking patterns. In M. Grant & J. Litvak (Eds.), *Drinking patterns and their consequences* (pp. 103–128). Washington DC: Taylor & Francis.

Heath, D. (2000). *Drinking occasions: Comparative perspectives on alcohol and culture.* Ann Arbor, MI: Sheridan Books.

Khantzian, E. J. (1985). The self-medication hypothesis of addictive disorders: Focus on heroin and cocaine dependence. *American Journal of Psychiatry, 142,* 1259–1264.

Kushner, H. (2006). Taking biology seriously: The next task for historians of addiction? *Bulletin of the History of Medicine, 80,* 115–143.

Macandrew, C., & Edgerton, B. (1969). *Drunken comportment: A social explanation.* Chicago: Aldine.

Miller, P. M., Smith, G. T., & Goldman, M. S. (1990). Emergence of alcohol expectancies in childhood. *Journal of Studies on Alcohol, 51,* 343–349.

O'Hare, T. (1995). Differences in Asian and White drinking: Consumption level, drinking contexts and expectances. *Addictive Behaviors, 20,* 261–266.

Peele, S. (1985). *The meaning of addiction: Compulsive experience and its interpretation.* Lexington, MA: Lexington Books/Heath.

Peele, S. (1987). A moral vision of addiction: How people's values determine whether they become and remain addicts. In S. Peele (Ed.), *Visions of addiction* (pp. 201–233). Lexington, MA: Lexington Books/Heath.

Reinarman, C., Waldorf, D., & Murphy, S. (1991). *Cocaine changes: The experience of using and quitting.* Philadelphia: Temple University Press.

Room, R. (2001). Intoxication and bad behavior: Understanding cultural differences in the link. *Social Science & Medicine, 53,* 189–198.

Steele, C., & Josephs, R. (1990). Alcohol myopia: Its prized and dangerous effects. *American Psychologist, 45,* 921–33.

Vaillant, G. E. (1983). *The natural history of alcoholism.* Cambridge, MA: Harvard University Press.

STANTON PEELE
REVISED BY HELEN KEANE (2009)

VENTRAL TEGMENTAL AREA.

The ventral tegmental area, (VTA), is a very important brain area in the field of drug abuse. It is one of only two main areas that contain dopamine cell bodies. The mesolimbic dopamine pathway originates in the VTA. Dopamine neurons in the VTA project to areas of the brain associated with emotion and motivation, the so-called limbic areas. However, the projection to the nucleus accumbens is the most important in understanding the action of drugs of abuse, especially psychostimulants. In addition, neurons in the nucleus accumbens and other limbic areas project to the VTA, providing the substrate for many neurochemicals to modulate the dopamine cells in the VTA.

There are two main experimental paradigms used in animals to assess the effects of drugs and endogenous neurotransmitters, such as dynorphin, on these dopaminergic cells at the level of the VTA. Chemicals can be injected directly into the VTA in order to study their effects. Conditioned place preference is a method that allows the animal to be tested for the reinforcing properties of a chemical in a drug-free state. Also, increases in locomotor activity can be measured, psychomotor stimulants in addition to being rewarding increase locomotor activity, and one substrate underlying this increase is the VTA.

The most extensively studied drugs of abuse, psychostimulants and opiates, both interact with the mesolimbic dopamine system. Future studies fully elucidating the modulation of VTA dopamine neurons will greatly contribute to the understanding of the mechanism of action of drugs of abuse, and may lead to the development of medications to treat drug abusers.

See also **Dopamine; Dynorphin; Limbic System; Neurotransmitters; Nucleus Accumbens.**

BIBLIOGRAPHY

Davis, K. L., et al (2002). *Neuropsychopharmacology: The fifth generation of progress.* Philadelphia: Lippincott Williams & Wilkins.

Erickson, C. K. (2007). *The science of addiction: From neurobiology to treatment.* New York: W. W. Norton.

STEPHANIE DALL VECCHIA-ADAMS

VIETNAM ERA STUDY (VES), WASHINGTON UNIVERSITY.

Opiates were used extensively by American servicemen deployed to Southeast Asia during the latter part of the Vietnam War. The availability of high-potency heroin increased suddenly in the spring of 1970. Drug-related hospitalizations and deaths among servicemen in Vietnam sharply increased in the following months. A concurrent U.S. drug epidemic accelerated in the late 1960s and continued through the mid-1970s, with heroin use incidence peaking in 1971. The dire prospect of large numbers of returning servicemen addicted to opiates spurred the fear that the heroin epidemic would further spread in the United States.

In June 1971 President Nixon declared the War on Drugs. *Operation Golden Flow*, as facetiously termed by soldiers, commenced at departure locations in Vietnam where soldiers were tested for drugs by urinalysis through the Date Eligible for Return from Overseas (DEROS) program. Soldiers whose urine was positive for narcotics (opiates, amphetamines, or barbiturates) were provided five to seven days of detoxification and treatment prior to their return to the United States. The Special Action Office for Drug Abuse Prevention (SAODAP)—what is now considered the first Drug Czar office—launched a follow-up survey in the United States with the collaboration of the Department of Defense, the Veterans Administration (VA), the National Institute of Mental Health (NIMH), and the Department of Labor. The study was conducted by Washington University School of Medicine in St. Louis, with Lee N. Robins, Ph.D., as principal investigator. The study examined how many men had actually been addicted in Vietnam, and whether those addicted would continue to use heroin or become re-addicted after their return to the United States (Robins, 1974; Robins & Helzer, 1975a).

ORIGINAL STUDY

Two groups of 500 army enlisted men were selected for the first in-person survey, a random sample of veterans returning in September 1971 (general-sample), and another random sample of men whose urines had been positive when tested at DEROS (D+ sample). A total of 898 men were interviewed in 1972 within 12 months of their return from Vietnam. The servicemen were extremely frank: 97 percent of men whose military record showed drug use reported it to the interviewer. Subsequently, a total of 571 veterans were reinterviewed in person in 1974, three years after returning home. A total of 284 nonveterans were also interviewed in 1974 to take into account the natural remission pattern from drug use of men in that age group who were eligible for draft but never served. They were selected from Selective Service registrations and individually matched to the general-sample veterans with respect to draft eligibility, draft board location, age, and education completed by the time of the veteran's entry into service (Robins & Helzer, 1975a).

FOLLOW-UP STUDIES

After two decades of hiatus, Washington University began third and fourth surveys (VES-III & IV) in 1994, with Rumi Kato Price, Ph.D., as principal investigator (Price et al., 2001a, 2001b). The surveys were conducted in collaboration with the VA and with funding from the National Institute of Drug Abuse (NIDA) and later funding from NIMH. Of the total 1,226 veterans and nonveterans whose location information was stored from earlier surveys, 10.5 percent died by the end of 1996, when they would have been 47.5 years old on average if they had been alive (Price et al., 2001b, p. 311). The location rate was more than 93 percent for the surviving members, and 841 men were reinterviewed in 1996–1997. The main purpose of the third study, a 25-year follow-up, was to examine long-term mortality and morbidity consequences of the Vietnam War and drug abuse in middle age. The fourth follow-up, completed in 2006, focused on coping with mental health consequences of war experiences, such as post-traumatic stress disorder (PTSD) and suicidality.

The findings from the earlier 1972 and 1974 follow-ups surprised the scientific community. First, opiate use in Vietnam was much more common than the military had estimated: Almost half (43%) of the army enlisted men had used heroin or opium in Vietnam. Second, 20 percent of the general sample reported being addicted to narcotics (mostly opiates) in Vietnam, but only 12 percent of those addicted in Vietnam became re-addicted in the year after return (Robins et al., 1975b, pp. 957–959). Follow-up interviews two years later showed that this low rate of readdiction continued. During their second and third years home, addiction rates among drafted men were not significantly greater than among men who qualified for the draft but did not serve. Those who relapsed to narcotics were predominantly men who had used drugs before they entered the service (Robins & Helzer, 1975a). Noteworthy are other reports of this study group and other veterans, which show an excess of alcohol abuse (O'Brien et al., 1980) and poor social adjustment among those with a history of opiate use in Vietnam, as well as the appearance of depressive syndrome associated with combat experience (Helzer et al., 1976).

The third follow-up in 1996–1997 showed that the 25-year cumulative mortality rate since 1971 was 17.4 percent among drug-positive (D+) veterans and 7.4 percent among the remaining general-sample veterans; the nonveteran sample experienced a 2.8 percent mortality rate (Price et al., 2001b, pp. 311–313). Both in-Vietnam and post-Vietnam drug use factors were large and significant independent predictors of mortality, controlling for preservice drug use, continuity to later drug use, and demographic and other behavioral measures (Price et al., 2001b). Among the surviving members, the study found relatively stable patterns of frequent use of sedatives, stimulants, marijuana, cocaine, and opiates over the 25-year period. New relapse to opiates was extremely rare. The mean duration from initiation to the last remission ranged from 9 to 14 years. A majority intentionally attempted to quit illicit drugs; however, most did not use traditional drug treatment in their last attempts. Continued drug dependence often occurred with psychiatric disorders. Whereas 17.2 percent met the criteria for a drug dependence diagnosis since 1972, 20.7 percent met criteria for a lifetime post-traumatic stress disorder (PTSD) diagnosis, according to the *Diagnostic and Statistical Manual of Mental Disorder, Fourth Edition* (*DSM-IV*). The drug dependence rate decreased over time from 45.1 percent in 1971 to 5.9 percent in 1996; on the other hand, PTSD was stable and chronic. The rate of suicidality increased until around 1985, then hovered between seven to eight percent each year after that. Drug dependence increased the likelihood of having PTSD and suicidality during young adulthood. In later years those who were suffering from PTSD or suicidality may have used illicit drugs in part to self-medicate psychiatric symptoms (Price et al., 2004).

Less than nine percent of the then-current drug users in 1996 had been treated for their drug problems in a hospital setting during the previous five-year period. This rate was considerably lower than alcohol abuse treatment and psychiatric treatment among those with PTSD. A selected sample of veterans answered open-ended questions about their health care problems at the fourth follow-up (VES-IV) when they reached their mid-50s. The group at higher risk of suicidality in mid-life was significantly more likely to report both individually-based (such as belief in self-healing and not wanting care) and system-based (such as lack of insurance and bad experience) barriers to care and also more likely to experience negative effects of seeking care (Price et al., 2001a; Virgo et al., 2007). Thirty years after Vietnam, veterans' health care needs still appeared undermet.

See also **Addiction: Concepts and Definitions; Drug Testing Methods and Clinical Interpretations of Test Results; Opioid Dependence: Course of the Disorder Over Time; Vietnam War: Drug Use in U.S. Military.**

BIBLIOGRAPHY

Helzer, J. E., Robins, L. N., & Davis, D. H. (1976). Depressive disorders in Vietnam returnees. *The Journal of Nervous and Mental Disease, 163,* 177–185.

O'Brien, C. P., Nace, E. P., Mintz, J., Meyers, A. L., & Ream, N. (1980). Follow-up of Vietnam veterans. I. Relapse to drug use after Vietnam service. *Drug and Alcohol Dependence, 5,* 333–340.

Price, R. K., Risk, N. K., Haden, A. H., Lewis, C. E., Spitznagel, E. L. (2004, December 7). Post-traumatic stress disorder, drug, and suicidal ideation among male Vietnam veterans with a history of heavy drug use. *Drug and Alcohol Dependence, 76,* S31–S43.

Price, R. K., Risk, N. K., & Spitznagel, E. L. (2001a). Remission from illicit drug use over a 25-year period. Patterns of remission and treatment use. *American Journal of Public Health, 91,* 1107–1113.

Price, R. K., Risk, N. K., Murray, K. S., Virgo, K. S., & Spitznagel, E. L. (2001b). Twenty-five year mortality of U.S. servicemen deployed in Vietnam. Predictive utility of early drug use. *Drug and Alcohol Dependence, 64,* 309–318.

Robins, L. N. (1974). *The Vietnam drug user returns: Special Action Office Monograph,* (Series A, No. 2). Washington, DC: U.S. Government Printing Office.

Robins, L. N., & Helzer, J. E. (1975a). Drug use among Vietnam veterans—Three years later. *Medical World News Psychiatry, 16*, 44–49.

Robins, L. N., Helzer, J. E., & Davis, D. H. (1975b). Narcotic use in Southeast Asia and afterward: An interview study of 898 Vietnam returnees. *Archives of General Psychiatry, 32*(8), 955–961.

Virgo, K. S., Piry, J. R., Valentine, M. P., Denner, D. R., Ryan, G., Risk, N. K., et al. (2007). Access, quality, and satisfaction with care: Concerns of Vietnam veterans. *Research in the Sociology of Health Care, 24*, 17–40.

LEE N. ROBINS
REVISED BY RUMI KATO PRICE (2009)

VIETNAM WAR: DRUG USE IN U.S. MILITARY.

In the spring of 1971, two members of Congress (John Murphy and Robert Steele) released an alarming report alleging that 15 percent of U.S. servicemen in Vietnam were addicted to heroin. The armed forces were attempting to cope with the drug problem by combining military discipline with "amnesty." Anyone found using or possessing illicit drugs was subject to court martial and dishonorable discharge from the service; but drug users who voluntarily sought help might be offered "amnesty" and brief treatment. This policy apparently was having little impact, as heroin use had increased dramatically over the preceding year and a half.

Because the United States was trying to negotiate settlement of the war, military forces in Vietnam were being rapidly reduced. About 1,000 men were being sent back to the United States each day, many of them to be discharged shortly thereafter to civilian life. If the reported rate of heroin addiction among servicemen were accurate, this rapid reduction in force meant that hundreds of active heroin addicts were being sent home each week. Concerned about the social problems that could ensue from such an influx of addicts, President Richard M. Nixon charged his staff with seeking an effective response. Domestic Council staff members Jeffrey Donfeld and Egil Krogh, Jr., sought advice from Dr. Jerome H. Jaffe, then on the faculty of the University of Chicago, who had previously prepared a report for the president on the development of a national strategy for the treatment of drug dependence. Dr. Jaffe recommended a radical change in the policy for responding to the problem of drug use in the military. The suggested plan included urine testing, to detect heroin use, and treatment rather than court martial when drug use was detected. President Nixon endorsed the plan and the military responded with such remarkable rapidity that, on June 17, 1971, less than six weeks from the time it was proposed, the plan was initiated in Vietnam.

In fact, there was no way to know whether the new approach would be better than the old one, no reliable information on the actual extent of drug use and addiction, and no solid information on which to base estimates of how many servicemen would require additional treatment after discharge. To obtain information on the extent of drug use, the effectiveness of treatment, and the relapse rates it would be necessary to find and interview the servicemen at time of discharge and at various intervals after discharge.

In June 1971, President Nixon also announced the formation of the Special Action Office for Drug Abuse Prevention (SAODAP) charged with coordinating the many facets of the growing drug problem and named Dr. Jaffe as its first director. One of the first tasks of the office was to evaluate the results of the new drug policy for the military, especially as it was implemented in Vietnam. SAODAP arranged for Dr. Lee Robins, of Washington University in St. Louis, to obtain records from the Department of Defense and the Veterans Administration to conduct the study. The findings on drug use prior to and during service are summarized here.

Around 1970, before going overseas, about half the army's enlisted men had had some experience with illicit drugs. However, only 30 percent had tried any drug other than marijuana. At that time, the most common civilian drugs other than marijuana were barbiturates and amphetamines. Before going to Vietnam, only 11 percent of soldiers had tried an opiate, and those who did so generally took cough syrups containing codeine, not heroin or opium.

The men sent to Vietnam had either been drafted or had enlisted. Toward the end of the war, when drug use in the United States was highest, draftees were chosen by a lottery designed to make selection less susceptible to social-class biases. This produced draftees who were a reasonably representative sample of young American men. Those who enlisted voluntarily, however, who made up about 40 percent of the armed forces, were disproportionately school dropouts. Many of them enlisted before reaching draftable age because of their limited occupational opportunities. They also arrived in Vietnam with considerably more drug experience than the draftees.

Men who were sent to Vietnam before 1969 found marijuana plentiful but little else in the way of illicit drugs (Stanton, 1976). Some amphetamines were available—in part, because the military issued them to help men stay alert on reconnaissance missions. In 1969, heroin and opium began to arrive on the scene, and by 1970–1971 these opiates were very widely available. Marijuana was still the most commonly used illicit drug, but opiates outstripped amphetamines and barbiturates in availability. Heroin and opium were relatively cheap and very pure, so pure that the soldiers could get ample effect by smoking heroin in combination with tobacco or marijuana. This made opiates appealing to men who would have been reluctant to inject them.

At the height of the use of opiates, in 1971, almost half the army's enlisted men had tried them; of those who tried them, about half used enough to develop the hallmarks of addiction—tolerance and withdrawal symptoms (Robins et al., 1975). Marijuana use was even more common; about two-thirds of these soldiers used it. The estimates come from an independent survey of a random sample of army enlisted men eight to twelve months after their return from Vietnam, after the great majority had been discharged (Robins et al., 1975). Previous studies in Vietnam (Stanton, 1972; Roffman & Sapol, 1970; Char, 1972) or among men still in service after return (Rohrbaugh et al., 1974) were less reliable, because of difficulties in collecting a random sample, use of questionnaires rather than interviews (which can lead to careless responses or failure to answer completely), and because the surveys were being done by the army itself, while the men were still subject to possible disciplinary action.

The standard tour of duty for Vietnam soldiers was twelve months. Drug use typically began soon after arrival in Vietnam, showing that it was not at all difficult to find a supplier. Older men used less

than younger soldiers, career soldiers less than those serving their first term. Drug experience before induction was a powerful predictor of use in Vietnam (Robins et al., 1980). Essentially all those with drug experience before enlistment used drugs in Vietnam. Of course, there were also some soldiers who used drugs there for the first time.

One interesting observation was that men who drank alcohol in Vietnam tended not to use opiates, and opiate users tended not to drink (Wish et al., 1979). This is a very different pattern from the one seen in the same men both before and after Vietnam, when drinkers were much more likely to use illicit drugs than abstainers.

Soldiers who used drugs had more disciplinary problems, on average, than those who abstained. However, the great majority of drug users received little or no disciplinary action and were honorably discharged. Although there were instances in which drug use impaired a soldier's combat readiness, evidence is lacking that it had much impact on soldiers' ability to carry out orders or wage war.

See also **Addiction: Concepts and Definitions; Drug Testing Methods and Clinical Interpretations of Test Results; Military, Drug and Alcohol Abuse in the United States.**

BIBLIOGRAPHY

Char, J. (1972). Drug abuse in Vietnam. *American Journal of Psychiatry, 129*, 4, 123–125.

Gossop. M. (2007). *Living with drugs*, 6th ed. Burlington, VT: Ashgate Publishing.

Price, R. K., et al. (2004). Post-traumatic stress disorder, drug dependence, and suicidality among male Vietnam veterans with a history of heavy drug use. *Drug and Alcohol Dependence, 76*, S31–S43.

Robins, L. N., Helzer, J. E., & Davis, D. H. (1975). Narcotic use in Southeast Asia and afterward: An interview study of 898 Vietnam returnees. *Archives of General Psychiatry, 32*, 8, 955–961.

Robins, L. N., Helzer, J. E., Hesselbrock, M., & Wish, E. (1980). Vietnam veterans three years after Vietnam: How our study changed our view of heroin. In L. Brill and C. Winick (Eds.), *Yearbook of substance use and abuse.* New York: Human Science Press.

Roffman, R. A., & Sapol, E. (1970). Marijuana in Vietnam: A survey of use among Army enlisted men in the two southern corps. *International Journal of the Addictions, 5*, 1, 1–42.

Rohrbaugh, M., Eads, G., & Press, S. (1974). Effects of the Vietnam experience on subsequent drug use among servicemen. *International Journal of the Addictions, 9,* 1, 25–40.

Stanton, M. D. (1976). Drugs, Vietnam, and the Vietnam veteran: An overview. *American Journal of Drug & Alcohol Abuse, 3,* 4, 557–570.

Stanton, M. D. (1972). Drug use in Vietnam: A survey among Army personnel in the two Northern corps. *Archives of General Psychiatry, 26,* 3, 279–286.

Tegan, K., et al. (2004). Postservice mortality in Vietnam veterans: 30-year follow-up. *Archives of internal medicine, 164,* 1908–1916.

Wish, E. D., Robins, L. N., Hesselbrock, M., & Helzer, J. E. (1979). The course of alcohol problems in Vietnam veterans. In M. Galanter (Ed.), *Currents in alcoholism.* New York: Grune & Stratton.

LEE N. ROBINS

VIOLENCE AND DRUGS. *See* **Aggression and Drugs: Research Issues.**

VITAMINS. Vitamins are organic substances that are required in small amounts for normal functioning of the body. Lack of adequate quantities of vitamins results in well-known deficiency diseases, such as scurvy from Vitamin C deficiency and rickets from Vitamin D deficiency in childhood. For the most part, vitamins are not synthesized by the body but are found in a variety of foods, hence the need for a well-balanced diet or supplementation by taking the vitamins separately.

In the United States, daily minimum requirements for vitamins are recommended and periodically reassessed by the Food and Nutrition Board of the National Academy of Science, National Research Council. Some professionals advocate taking larger amounts of certain vitamins is for better health or for disease prevention or therapy. The question of whether vitamins are drugs is, in one sense, a semantic issue. Sometimes very high doses of a vitamin can actually be used as a medication. For example, in very high doses—twenty or more times higher than needed to prevent the vitamin deficiency disease pellagra—niacin, a member of the B vitamin complex, lowers blood levels of cholesterol and triglycerides, and niacin is commonly prescribed for this purpose.

It is possible to overdose and have serious side effects from large quantities of certain vitamins, such as Vitamins A and D. Therefore, taking larger than needed amounts of vitamins should be done only with the advice of a physician. Deficiencies in vitamin intake can occur under a variety of situations including poverty, dieting, or certain disease states where antibiotics or other factors reduce vitamin absorption. Individuals who drink large quantities of alcohol, for example, without adequate attention to diet often become deficient in some vitamins, such as B_1 (thiamine), and may require their administration to avoid serious and permanent toxicity. Prolonged serious shortages of Vitamin B_1 can cause the death of certain neurons in the brain, a situation that leads to confusion and severe impairment of short-term memory (Wernicke-Korsakoff syndrome).

BIBLIOGRAPHY

Combs, Jr., G. F. (2007). *The vitamins,* 3rd ed. San Diego, CA: Academic Press.

Marcus, R., & Coulston, A. M. (1990). The vitamins. In A. G. Gilman et al. (Eds.), *Goodman and Gilman's the pharmacological basis of therapeutics,* 8th ed. New York: Pergamon. (2005, 11th ed. New York: McGraw-Hill Medical.)

Whitney, E. N., & Rolfes, S. R. (2005). *Understanding nutrition,* 11th ed. Belmont, CA: Wadsworth Press.

MICHAEL J. KUHAR

VULNERABILITY AS A CAUSE OF SUBSTANCE ABUSE. *See* **Risk Factors for Substance Use, Abuse, and Dependence.**

WASHINGTON UNIVERSITY VIET-NAM ERA STUDY (VES). *See* **Vietnam Era Study (VES), Washington University.**

WELFARE POLICY AND SUB-STANCE ABUSE IN THE UNITED STATES.

Typical of income maintenance schemes in liberal welfare states, the U.S. system emphasizes economic returns to work. Thus, the U.S. income maintenance system is divided into two tracks, based on the relationship of beneficiaries to the labor force. For the insurance-like programs, notably Old Age and Survivors Insurance (what Americans refer to colloquially as *Social Security*), Social Security Disability Insurance, and Unemployment Compensation; eligibility is linked to an applicant's history of payroll deductions—contributions from wages to the public fund that supports the program. The welfare programs, on the other hand, are means-tested. That is, eligibility depends on meeting strict limits on current earnings and accumulated wealth. Welfare programs are for very poor people, and benefits are substantially less than those paid by the insurance-like programs.

The U.S. system is categorical. For the most part, eligibility is based on membership in a particular category defined by administrative rules: Old age benefits are for those who meet the administrative definition of aged status; disability benefits are for those who meet the medical and vocational standards defining that category, and so forth. Except as discussed below in connection with General Assistance, there are no welfare programs for healthy, non-elderly adults without children.

Finally, the income maintenance system in the United States is funded and administered by federal, state, and local (primarily county) governments. Insurance-like programs are usually funded and administered by the federal government, thus creating a significant degree of uniformity in benefits and eligibility rules. Welfare programs, however, usually are funded and administered by two or more levels of government, so benefit levels and eligibility rules vary considerably among political jurisdictions.

This entry concerns the intersection of substance abuse and initial and continuing eligibility for welfare programs in the context of important policy changes made during the 1990s. It focuses on Temporary Assistance for Needy Families (TANF); Supplemental Security Income (SSI), a federally funded and administered welfare program for the elderly, blind, and disabled; and, to a lesser extent, General Assistance (GA), a state and local form of assistance.

TEMPORARY ASSISTANCE FOR NEEDY FAMILIES

For 60 years after enactment of the Social Security Act of 1935, the United States' cash assistance program for impoverished families was Aid to Families with Dependent Children (AFDC; Aid to Dependent Children until 1961). As the result of liberal court rulings in the 1960s and the separation of casework from the financial administration of recipients' grants in 1972, AFDC became substantially free of the restraints that characterized an earlier era when social workers raided the houses of welfare mothers to search closets for evidence of a man in the house, who might be made to support the women and their children. Although various work incentives were tried over the years, particularly during the 1980s, they had indifferent results and affected relatively few recipients. Even so, only a small percentage of AFDC families remained on the rolls for years at a time, and most AFDC heads of household, the great majority of them women between 18 and 35 years old, worked part-time or intermittently while raising their children.

However, the ascendancy of the Republican Party following the November 1994 elections yielded the Personal Responsibility and Work Opportunity Reconciliation Act (PRWORA) of 1996 (P.L. 104–193). The PRWORA was based on premises laid out succinctly in *Contract with America*, the 1994 campaign manifesto drafted by Republican leaders in the House of Representatives. *Contract* opined that the liberal welfare regime dating from the 1960s "had the unintended consequence of making welfare more attractive than work" (p. 67). Moreover: "Government programs designed to give a helping hand to the neediest of Americans have instead bred illegitimacy, crime, illiteracy, and more poverty." Welfare reform should thus "change this destructive social behavior by requiring welfare recipients to take personal responsibility for decisions they make" (p. 65).

Reauthorized in 2006, the PRWORA's countermeasures are a complicated combination of incentives and punishments directed at both welfare recipients and the states. The act creates a lifetime limit of 5 years of welfare receipt for TANF families. Further, its funding mechanism requires that each year the states move progressively greater numbers of TANF parents into jobs or face cuts in the overall federal grant to the state (known as a *block grant*). Each state may exempt a small percentage of its caseload from job placement, but in the long run the states are faced with the formidable task of making work-ready and placing in employment thousands of mothers with little work experience and few marketable skills. At the same time, the PRWORA permits the states a great deal of flexibility in using various funds to create training programs, support childcare, and even fund alcohol and other drug treatment.

The PRWORA also requires or permits the states to enforce a variety of behavioral requirements for continuing eligibility for full TANF benefits. Among these, the PRWORA permits states to mandate treatment for alcohol and other drug abusers as well as to require random drug testing under the threat of forfeited benefits. (A failed provision of the original legislation would have forced the states to implement these provisions.) Research on TANF parents has found that the prevalence of substance-use disorder in the adult TANF population, as measured by a rigorous standard, is very similar to that in the population at large: about 8 to 10 percent. Except in connection with the drug felon ban discussed below, few states have expressed serious interest in drug testing or mechanisms for mandatory treatment that are not triggered by new criminal behavior or the abuse or neglect of children. In these cases, the mandate for treatment arises outside of the welfare system itself.

A further drug-related provision of the PRWORA is both more stringent and more common. The act provides that unless a state passes contrary legislation, any person with a felony drug conviction after August 22, 1996 (the date PRWORA was signed into law), will be banned for life from TANF (among other federal benefits). This provision reflected a negotiated compromise on the House of Representatives version of the act that would have extended the ban to those convicted of misdemeanors. The drug ban has proved extremely unpopular in the states. By 2006, 32 states had opted out of the ban or dramatically modified it, and others were in the process of doing so. One modification applied in a few states is a requirement for treatment and sometimes subsequent urine testing of TANF-eligible drug felons.

SUPPLEMENTAL SECURITY INCOME

Since 1950 the federal government has provided income support from welfare or social insurance to individuals with work disabilities unrelated to military service. In 1972 welfare programs for the disabled, blind, and impoverished elderly that had been administered and funded in collaboration with the states came under the federal administration and financial support of Supplemental Security Income (SSI).

From the first SSI payments in January 1974 until March 1996, drug addiction and alcoholism (DA&A) were treated as potentially disabling impairments, but until about 1990 relatively few applicants qualified on this basis. Indeed, there were fewer than 10,000 DA&A cases on SSI as late as the end of 1986. By mid-1996, however, there were almost 166,000. Most of this growth seems to have resulted from four factors. First, federal circuit court decisions during the mid-1980s removed substantial technical obstacles to claimants seeking benefits on the grounds of addiction. Second, in the wake of these decisions many state and county governments set out to transfer recipients of General Assistance, a welfare program supported entirely with state and local funds, to SSI (a federally-funded program). To promote this process, some states or counties contracted with private non-profit legal advocates to support applications and appeals. When the DA&A SSI population is disaggregated by state, it is clear that California, Michigan, Illinois, and a few others made much higher per capita use of the DA&A category than did other states. For example, by 1996 Oregon had as many DA&As on SSI as Texas, a state with several times the adult population of Oregon.

The last two contributors to the growth in the DA&A rolls are related to a famous Reagan-era controversy concerning Social Security disability programs. During the early 1980s, responding in part to a Carter administration initiative and also drawing on a similar tactic applied during his governorship of California between 1967 and 1974, President Reagan's Social Security administrators launched a roll-cutting campaign that relied on continuing disability reviews (CDRs). As a result, more than 500,000 people lost federal disability benefits, a large percentage of them people with mental illness. Subsequent backlash from the courts and Congress restored many to the rolls, further liberalized eligibility criteria, and all but paralyzed the CDR process for years to come. As a result of perennially backlogged CDRs, many DA&As who regained their ability to work remained on the rolls, particularly as the economic conditions of the late 1980s and early 1990s provided few opportunities for poor, unskilled, ill-educated people. In

part as the result of this episode and in part due to the dramatic rise in homelessness during the 1980s, the Social Security Administration was charged with increasing its outreach efforts, especially among homeless people. This brought more DA&As into the application process.

Throughout the history of SSI, the Social Security Administration saw the operation of its program for DA&A cases as low-priority. With no specific appropriations from Congress to ensure that DA&As received treatment or were separated from the rolls for failing to participate and with no resources to thoroughly investigate the relationship of beneficiaries to representative payees (those who receive their checks and supervise their expenditures), the agency allowed the program to drift. However, it attracted a great deal of critical and unwanted attention as it grew rapidly. Beginning in 1991, the program was the subject of unflattering reports from federal watchdog agencies and a mounting number of highly publicized incidents involving DA&A recipients using benefits to purchase drugs and signing up representative payees (like bartenders) with little fiduciary interest in them. The more scandalous claims about the program were largely unfounded, but many legislators and representatives of the alcohol and drug treatment community saw the DA&A program as enabling addiction. Moreover, the program's rapid growth, and the Social Security Administration's apparent inability to curb it, lent credence to the claim that it was an entitlement program "out of control" in an era of bipartisan fiscal retrenchment.

In August 1994, after Congressional hearings and national media coverage (almost exclusively negative), Congress limited DA&A benefits to three years and reiterated the necessity to participate in treatment. Although the Social Security Administration made no effort to defend the DA&A program, it worked very hard to implement treatment referral and monitoring arrangements in all of the states. But as it did so, the November 1994 elections shifted control of the House of Representatives to conservative Republicans who were against the program.

On March 29, 1996, Congress eliminated the DA&A category in SSI and Social Security Disability Insurance (DI), the first time any qualifying impairment had been legislated out of existence.

The benefits of 209,000 recipients of SSI and DI ceased after 1996 unless they applied for redetermination and were reclassified based on other impairments (mental illness, for example). Only 34 percent were restored to the rolls.

In retrospect, the demise of the DA&A program seems to have been over-determined. It was at once culturally problematic and, thus deprived of a unified constituency, extremely difficult to administer (and thus disliked by the Social Security Administration). As a result of its administrative problems, the program was susceptible to discrediting. The program left behind a legacy of mandatory treatment and representative payee provisions that seem to have become more common features of state and local welfare reform measures, but no observers see any chance of its resurrection at the federal level in the foreseeable future.

GENERAL ASSISTANCE

General Assistance (known in some places as General Relief) is a form of welfare financed and operated entirely by state, county, or municipal governments. Many states do not have GA programs, or GA exists only in some local jurisdictions. GA benefit levels and eligibility rules also vary from state to state, and in some states, notably California and Wisconsin, from county to county. Some states (or smaller jurisdictions) provide GA benefits merely on the basis of need, but most GA programs are categorical (e.g., Oregon and Washington), restricting eligibility to older people not yet eligible for Social Security or Supplemental Security Income (SSI), to parents waiting for TANF benefits or temporarily suspended from that program, to those with an SSI application pending, or to those who are realistically unemployable by some criteria of age and infirmity, but who do not meet the stringent disability criteria of SSI. GA programs also vary in the way that benefits are paid: by cash, by rent and food vouchers, or some combination. Some GA programs are time-limited (in Pennsylvania, e.g.). All GA programs have extremely low benefits in the range of $200–$250 per month.

Probably due to the overrepresentation of single men among GA beneficiaries, many jurisdictions estimate that the prevalence of alcohol and drug problems among GA recipients is several times that of the general population. Historically, GA has been the welfare program most accessible to people with alcohol and other drug problems. After World War II, many large cities used some combination of cash, hotel vouchers, and restaurant chits to keep single, addicted men (mainly) housed and fed without giving them much money to handle. This system was largely abandoned as the cost of its administration rose. However, with the elimination of addiction as a qualifying impairment in the SSI program, some cities and counties have revived such arrangements. In San Francisco this system is called "Care Not Cash."

CONCLUSION

The thrust of recent federal welfare reform has been to rely on fiscal incentives and penalties to encourage welfare recipients to work and state governments to see that they do. As a corollary, welfare eligibility is once again being used as leverage on the behavior of poor people, and drinking and drug use have been salient targets of this effort—whose complete effects remain to be seen. Given the resources (no small caveat), many state and local General Assistance programs seem inclined to follow suit.

See also **Economic Costs of Alcohol and Drug Abuse; Funding and Service Delivery of Treatment; Homelessness, History of Association with Alcohol and Drugs.**

BIBLIOGRAPHY

Baumohl, J., et al. (Spring and Summer, 2003). Results of the multi-site study of the termination of SSI benefits for drug addicts and alcoholics. *Contemporary Drug Problems*, whole issue.

Danziger, S. K., Corcoran, M. E., Danziger, S. H., Heflin, C. M., Kalil, A., Levine, J. A., et al. (1999). *Barriers to the employment of welfare recipients*. Ann Arbor: Poverty Research and Training Center, University of Michigan.

Gillespie, E., & Schellhas, B. (Eds.). (1994). *Contract with America*. New York: New York Times Books.

United States Government Accountability Office. (September 2005). *Drug offenders: Various factors may limit the impacts of federal laws that provide for denial of selected benefits.* Available from http://www.gao.gov/.

JIM BAUMOHL

WIKLER'S CONDITIONING THEORY OF DRUG ADDICTION.

Abraham Wikler (1910–1980) was one of the founding researchers of the United States Public Health Service Addiction Research Center, in Lexington, Kentucky. (It is now the Intramural Program of the National Institute on Drug Abuse in Baltimore, Maryland.) Wikler, a psychiatrist, was particularly interested in understanding why the heroin addicts he interviewed at Lexington so frequently relapsed after treatment, long after any signs of acute opiate withdrawal had subsided. He was intrigued by their reports that upon returning to their old neighborhoods, they felt as if they were experiencing withdrawal symptoms. In 1948 he began to develop his theory about the role of conditioning in addiction, and over the next 30 years he continued to elaborate on this theory and its implications for understanding and treating addictions.

Within Wikler's model, opioids such as heroin or morphine are viewed as having pharmacological effects that reduce certain *needs,* thereby reinforcing the behavior that leads to their repeated use (operant reinforcement). He proposed that the behavioral chain leading to addiction often begins when a young person with prevailing moods of hypophoria (feeling unliked or unappreciated) and anxiety, frequently combined with a strong need to belong to some identifiable group, uses heroin in response to peer pressure. The drug reduces hypophoria and anxiety, and the drug-using behavior is reinforced both by those effects and by increased peer group acceptance. With repeated drug use, especially of opioids, tolerance and physical dependence develop.

Wikler recognized that the small degree of physical dependence that develops after only a few doses of an opioid drug, and the aversive quality of withdrawal, create a new *need state,* the need to alleviate the withdrawal syndrome. For short-acting opioids such as heroin, withdrawal begins a few hours after the last dose, so the user self-administers the drug several times a day. Because a heroin user who is physically dependent frequently experiences some degree of withdrawal between doses, recurring environmental stimuli (street associates, neighborhood surroundings, drug paraphernalia, drug dealers) prompt feelings of withdrawal, which become

classically conditioned to these stimuli. Furthermore, internal stimuli—such as anxiety, stress, or depression—that are experienced when withdrawal occurs may also become linked to withdrawal, and these emotional states can trigger conditioned withdrawal and craving in former addicts who have been free from drugs for many months. If someone who was formerly addicted responds to the conditioned withdrawal by using drugs, the cycle is initiated anew.

Even in his earliest writings Wikler noted that the acute opioid withdrawal syndrome, which typically lasts for one to four weeks, is followed by a more protracted state of physiological abnormality that often lasts several months; and during this period the impact of conditioned withdrawal and associated craving may be of considerable importance in leading to relapse. Subsequent work by William Martin and colleagues clearly demonstrated the existence of such a protracted opioid withdrawal syndrome.

Wikler also saw a role for the *hustling* behavior required to obtain illicit drugs (earning or stealing enough to get drugs, seeking *connections, scoring,* and avoiding arrest). Hustling is at first maintained by getting and using heroin; but with time, Wikler postulated, it becomes a self-reinforcing behavior as a result of the sense of achievement felt for having successfully survived another day on the street.

Wikler argued that conditioned responses did not simply decay with the passage of time, but required some form of active extinction. Thus, the practice of treating addicts in a drug-free environment, even for several months, left them vulnerable to relapse when they returned to an environment where drugs were available. The former stresses were likely to occur again, and the previous drug use had become conditioned to external and emotional stimuli. Wikler proposed that one way to extinguish the linkage between operantly reinforced drug use and conditioned withdrawal would be for the addict to engage in the usual rituals of working to get and use drugs but to experience no reinforcement from the drug's actions. He suggested that the use of long-acting opioid antagonist drugs such as cyclazocine and naltrexone, developed by Martin and colleagues in the late 1960s, might permit a test of this approach.

Subsequent research found that even when opioid addicts volunteered to take these antagonists, they were rarely willing to continue taking them, and so antagonist treatment did little to alter the likelihood of relapse. Martin suggested that because opioid antagonists did not alleviate hypophoria, the addicts' lack of enthusiasm for them was understandable. But since the development and approval, in the early twenty-first century, of long-acting (depot) forms of naltrexone that make compliance with taking the drug less problematic, new efforts are underway to determine if such opioid antagonists can play the useful role in the treatment of opioid addiction that Wikler foresaw for them.

Wikler's ideas about the operant reinforcement of drug-taking and development of conditioned withdrawal in response to external and emotional stimuli are generally accepted by most experts in the field of addiction treatment. However, very few programs attempt to treat addictions by seeking to extinguish the learned behavior by means of extinction. For example, although the theoretical concepts underlying the present-day widespread use of relapse prevention and cognitive-behavioral therapy (CBT) seem at first to be closely related to Wikler's ideas about the role of learning and conditioning, this treatment approach emerged from different clinical observations and led to very different treatment procedures. Like Wikler, the developers of CBT emphasized the role of learning—both operant and classical (conditioned)—in the genesis of addiction, but combined this understanding with cognitive psychology, behavior modification, social skills training, and efforts to help patients recognize that a single episode of alcohol or drug intake need not lead to a full relapse. Rather than aiming for extinction of drug use, CBT tries to teach the patient how to avoid the situations and emotions that are likely to trigger a relapse and to develop nondrug techniques for controlling aversive emotional states (coping skills).

Because of his own observations of addicts maintained on opiates, Wikler was skeptical about the theory underlying Vincent Dole's and Marie Nyswander's work with methadone. Dole and Nyswander saw opiate addiction as a persistent metabolic disorder (*drug hunger*) induced by opiate use. They argued that this drug hunger could be corrected by maintaining addicts on appropriate doses of methadone which, they believed, would allow former addicts to be essentially normal and to exhibit little or no psychopathology. Like Dole and Nyswander, Wikler recognized that protracted withdrawal and its associated craving could contribute to relapse, but he did not assign it so central a role in relapse. Wikler's perspective was that whatever form of psychopathology may have contributed to the initial use of a drug, the repeated reinforcement of the drug-using behavior, and the linkage of withdrawal symptoms through conditioning to environmental stimuli and to internal states such as anxiety and stress created a new disorder—a disease *sui generis*.

In short, Wikler, as well as Dole and Nyswander, viewed opioid addiction not as a character defect or hedonistic pursuit of euphoria, but as a distinct disorder that arose as a result of repeated use of opioid drugs.

See also **Opioid Complications and Withdrawal; Treatment, Behavioral Approaches to: Cognitive-Behavioral Therapy.**

BIBLIOGRAPHY

Dole. V., & Nyswander, M. (1968). Methadone maintenance and its implications for theories of narcotic addiction. In A. Wikler (Ed.), *The addictive states* (pp. 359–366). Baltimore: Williams & Wilkins.

Jaffe, J. H. (1981). Abraham Wikler: A scholar *sui generis*. (Obituary). *British Journal of Addiction, 76,* 431–432.

Martin, W. R. (1980). Emerging concepts concerning drug abuse. In D. Letteiri, M. Sayers, & H. W. Pearson (Eds.), *Theories on drug abuse: Selected contemporary perspectives.* NIDA Research Monograph 30. Washington, DC: Department of Health and Human Services.

Wikler, A. (November 1948). Recent progress in research on the neurophysiological basis of morphine addiction. *American Journal of Psychiatry, 105,* 329–338.

Wikler, A. (1965). Conditioning factors in opiate addiction and relapse. In D. I. Wilner, & G. G. Kassebaum (Eds.), *Narcotics.* New York: McGraw-Hill.

Wikler, A. (1968). Interaction of physical dependence and classical and operant conditioning in the genesis of relapse. In A. Wikler (Ed.), *The addictive states* (pp. 280–287). Baltimore: Williams & Wilkins.

Wikler, A. (1980). A theory of opioid dependence. In D. Letteiri, M. Sayers, & H. W. Pearson (Eds.), *Theories on drug abuse: Selected contemporary perspectives.* NIDA Research Monograph 30. Washington, DC: Department of Health and Human Services.

Witkiewitz, K., & Marlatt, G. (2004). Relapse prevention for alcohol and drug problems. That was Zen, this is Tao. *American Psychologist*, 59, 224–235.

JEROME H. JAFFE

WITHDRAWAL

This entry includes the following essays:

ALCOHOL

BENZODIAZEPINES

COCAINE

NICOTINE (TOBACCO)

NONABUSED DRUGS

ALCOHOL

The human nervous system undergoes an adaptation in response to the chronic consumption of alcohol (ethanol). If the consumption is heavy enough (adequate dose) and occurs for a long enough time period (adequate duration), a rapid decrease or sudden cessation of drinking will result in a withdrawal syndrome. This syndrome occurs in association with re-adaptation of the nervous system to a drug-free state. The dose and duration of alcohol consumption required to produce a withdrawal syndrome in a given population, or even a given individual, are difficult to predict, because no well-controlled studies have been conducted (or are likely to be, for ethical reasons). Such studies have been done in animals, however.

In the nondrinker or social drinker who consumes alcohol to the point of intoxication, symptoms of a "hangover" (e.g., insomnia, headache, and nausea) may ensue. It has been suggested that these are symptoms of acute alcohol withdrawal, but that interpretation is controversial, and other explanations (e.g., dehydration) have also been proposed to explain hangover symptoms. Usually, no treatment is required, and there are no serious consequences from a hangover.

ALCOHOL DEPENDENCE AND WITHDRAWAL

The natural progression of alcohol dependence leading to the point of requiring detoxification usually takes 15 to 20 years. The average age of persons admitted to detoxification units in the United States is around 42 years, although detoxification services may be required at almost any age. The withdrawal syndrome seen in persons requiring detoxification ranges from a mild degree of discomfort to a potentially life-threatening disorder.

The severity of the withdrawal syndrome is dependent on both the dose and duration of alcohol exposure. In studies conducted on rats, a severe withdrawal syndrome has been seen following high-level exposure to alcohol in a vapor chamber in as short as a week. The administration of alcohol directly into the rat's stomach is associated with a longer time period for the acquisition of physical dependence. In humans, the severity of withdrawal depends also on the amount of alcohol consumed and the time period over which it has been consumed. For practical purposes, this can be measured in terms of the amount ingested on a daily basis for the weeks and months preceding detoxification. One study of inpatients (federal prisoners and narcotic users) demonstrated that the consumption of 442 grams of alcohol, or 32 standard drinks per day for about two months (a standard drink being 13.6 grams, or 0.6 fluid ounces, of alcohol, the amount in 12 oz. of beer, 5 oz. of wine, or 1.5 oz. of liquor) results in a major withdrawal syndrome in all subjects, whereas the consumption of 280 to 377 grams (21 to 28 standard drinks) per day results in a mild syndrome of anxiety and tremor (Isbell et al., 1955).

Studies that involve patients (as opposed to research subjects) have not been able to demonstrate a consistent relationship between recent alcohol consumption and the severity of the withdrawal syndrome (Shaw et al., 1981). This in part relates to the lack of accurate recall of exact quantities consumed within a given time period. Furthermore, in the real world there are different patterns of consumption (e.g., some drinkers consume alcohol in a binge pattern, whereas others drink in a more regular pattern), and different drinkers have varying durations of lifetime exposure to alcohol. One drinker may take two or three years to become dependent, another may take 15 years, and yet another 40 years. In addition, a person who has previously experienced significant alcohol withdrawal may be at higher risk for developing a repeat withdrawal, both in terms of the severity of the syndrome and the rate of reacquisition of physical dependence. In these individuals, it takes a shorter time to become re-addicted, a situation that has been attributed to sensitization (or "kindling") of the central nervous system (Bayard et al., 2004). Other factors that may be implicated in the severity of the withdrawal syndrome include age, nutritional status, and the presence of concurrent physical disorders or illness such as pancreatitis or pneumonia (Sullivan & Sellers, 1986). Alcoholics are at increased risk for these and other medical disorders.

WITHDRAWAL SYMPTOMS

The symptoms of alcohol withdrawal appear in inverse relation to the elimination of alcohol from the body, which can be measured via the blood alcohol concentration (BAC). Many alcoholics note this phenomenon on a daily basis; that is, they require a drink in the morning to suppress tremor and anxiety, or to "steady the nerves." Some of the more common symptoms of alcohol withdrawal are: anxiety, agitation, restlessness, insomnia, a "shaky" feeling, anorexia (loss of appetite), nausea, changes in sensory perception (e.g., itchy skin, sounds seem louder, lights look brighter), headache, and palpitations. These are often accompanied by vomiting, sweating, an increased heart rate, an increase in blood pressure, tremor (shakiness of hands, and sometimes of the face, eyelids, and tongue), and seizures.

More severe withdrawal is associated with an intensification of the above symptoms and signs, together with a progression to tactile, auditory, and visual hallucinations (e.g., feeling, hearing, and seeing things that are not there), disorientation, and confusion (delirium tremens, or the "DTs") (Bayard et al., 2004). After stopping alcohol consumption, the more common and milder symptoms usually reach a peak after 12 to 24 hours, and they have mostly subsided by 48 hours after consumption has ceased (Sellers & Kalant, 1976). More severe, or late, withdrawal symptoms usually reach a peak at around 72 to 96 hours, and these are potentially life threatening. Less than 5 percent of persons withdrawing from alcohol (depending on how they are selected) are estimated to develop a severe reaction. With appropriate drug treatment, an even lower percentage is estimated to develop a major withdrawal reaction. Under ideal circumstances, there should be almost no mortality from this disorder on its own, so overall mortality ought to be similar to that of any concurrent medical disorder.

An assessment of the severity of withdrawal can be accomplished on the basis of clinical experience or with the assistance of various rating instruments. One of the simplest and easiest to administer is the Clinical Institute Withdrawal Assessment for Alcohol, Revised (CIWA-Ar). This assessment tool consists of 10 items that can be scored at frequent intervals, and a health-care provider can administer it in less than a minute (see Figure 1).

TREATMENT

The goals of treatment for alcohol withdrawal syndrome are to relieve discomfort and to prevent complications. Kasser et al. (1997) identify some immediate goals in detoxifying patients of alcohol and other abused substances: (1) "to provide a safe withdrawal from the drug(s) of dependence and enable the patient to become drug-free," (2) "to provide a withdrawal that is humane and thus protects the patient's dignity" and (3) "to prepare the patient for ongoing treatment of his or her dependence on alcohol or other drugs." Treatment consists of supportive care, general drug treatment, and specific drug treatments.

Supportive care consists of reassurance; reality orientation; reduced sensory stimuli (e.g., a dark, quiet room); attention to fluid and electrolyte balance, nutrition, physical comforts, and body temperature; sleep and rest; and positive encouragement toward long-term rehabilitation. Most patients can be treated with supportive care alone, but it is impossible to predict which patients will require more intensive care.

General drug treatment includes the B vitamin thiamine, which should be given to all patients to prevent the brain damage that commonly occurs in alcoholics who are thiamine deficient. In varying degrees, thiamine deficiency occurs commonly in alcoholics, and it is thought to result from several factors, including poor diet, malabsorption of the vitamin, excess excretion of the vitamin, and altered metabolism and physiologic trafficking of the vitamin within the body. Thiamine deficiency contributes to neuronal damage and cell death through four main effects caused by changes in intracellular metabolism: (1) a disruption in the production of key molecules required for cell structure and function, such as the myelin sheath on

Addiction Research Foundation Clinical Institute Withdrawal Assessment for Alcohol (CIWA-Ar)

Patient _____   Date |___|___|___| Time _____ : _____
                                  y   m   d   (24-hour clock, midnight = 00:00)

Pulse or heart rate, taken for one minute: _____   Blood pressure: _____ / _____

NAUSEA AND VOMITING—Ask "Do you feel sick to your stomach? Have you vomited?" Observation.
0 no nausea and no vomiting
1 mild nausea with no vomiting   .
2
3
4 intermittent nausea with dry heaves
5
6
7 constant nausea, frequent dry heaves and vomiting

TREMOR—Arms extended and fingers spread apart. Observation.
0 no tremor
1 not visible, but can be felt fingertip to fingertip
2
3
4 moderate, with patient's arms extended
5
6
7 severe, even with arms not extended

PAROXYSMAL SWEATS—Observation.
0 no sweat visible
1 barely perceptible sweating, palms moist
2
3
4 beads of sweat obvious on forehead
5
6
7 drenching sweats

ANXIETY—Ask "Do you feel nervous?" Observation.
0 no anxiety, at ease
1 mildly anxious
2
3
4 moderately anxious, or guarded, so anxiety is inferred
5
6
7 equivalent to acute panic states as seen in severe delirium
   or acute schizophrenic reactions

AGITATION-Observation.
0 normal activity
1 Somewhat more than normal activity
2
3
4 moderately fidgety and restless
5
6
7 paces back and forth during most of the interview, or
   constantly thrashes about

VISUAL DISTURBANCES—Ask "Does the light appear to be too bright? Is its color different? Does it hurt your eyes? Are you seeing anything that is disturbing to you? Are you seeing things you know are not there? Observation.
0 not present
1 very mild sensitivity
2 mild sensitivity
3 moderate sensitivity
4 moderately severe hallucinations
5 severe hallucinations
6 extremely severe hallucinations
7 continuous hallucinations

TACTILE DISTURBANCES—Ask "Have you any itching. pins and needles sensations, any burning, any numbness or do you feel bugs crawling on or under your skin?" Observation
0 none
1 very mild itching, pins and needles, burning or numbness
2 mild itching, pins and needles, burning or numbness
3 moderate itching, pins and needles, burning or numbness
4 moderately severe hallucinations
5 severe hallucinations
6 extremely severe hallucinations
7 continuous hallucinations

AUDITORY DISTURBANCES—Ask "Are you more aware of sounds around you? Are they harsh? Do they frighten you? Are you hearing anything that is disturbing to you? Are you hearing things you know are not there?" Observation.
0 not present
1 very mild harshness or ability to frighten
2 mild harshness or ability to frighten
3 moderate harshness or ability to frighten
4 moderately severe hallucinations
5 severe hallucinations
6 extremely severe hallucinations
7 continuous hallucinations

HEADACHE, FULLNESS IN HEAD—Ask "Does your head feel different? Does it feel like there is a band around your head?" Do not rate for dizziness or lightheadedness. Otherwise, rate severity.
0 not present
1 very mild
2 mild
3 moderate
4 moderately severe
5 severe
6 very severe
7 extremely severe

ORIENTATION AND CLOUDING OF SENSORIUM-Ask "What day is this? Where are you? Who am I?"
0 oriented and can do serial additions
1 cannot do serial additions or is uncertain about date
2 disoriented for date by no more than 2 calendar days
3 disoriented for date by more than 2 calendar days
4 disoriented for place and/or person

Total CIWA-A Score _____
   Rater's Initials _____
   Maximum Possible Score 67
   This scale is not copyrighted and may be used freely.

Figure 1. Addiction Research Foundation Clinical Institute Withdrawal Assessment for Alcohol (CIWA-Ar). ILLUSTRATION BY GGS INFORMATION SERVICES. GALE, CENGAGE LEARNING

neurons; (2) lactate accumulation; (3) glutamate accumulation and subsequent excitotoxicity, overstimulation of neurons by excitatory neurotransmitters leading ultimately to neuronal death; and (4) cellular energy deficits.

The prompt replacement of thiamine (and to some degree the other B vitamins) is essential in preventing and treating the neuronal damage that occurs from its depletion. The most severe form of thiamine deficiency, Wernicke-Korsakoff syndrome, can also be abruptly induced by glucose infusion prior to vitamin replacement in an alcoholic who has low blood sugar. Occasionally, magnesium may be given if there is a severe deficiency and there are potential cardiac problems. Intravenous fluids may be required in uncommon circumstances.

Specific drug treatments may also be given to suppress the signs and symptoms of withdrawal. While more than 100 drug treatments have been suggested for the treatment of alcohol withdrawal, very few adequate scientific studies have been conducted, primarily because appropriate studies are difficult to conduct. In addition, many patients do very well with placebo or supportive care alone. Nevertheless, appropriate and effective specific treatments are available. These consist of drugs belonging to the same general class as alcohol (central nervous system depressants). The drugs of choice are the longer-acting benzodiazepines (usually diazepam [Valium] or chlordiazepoxide [Librium]), but shorter-acting benzodiazepines (such as lorazepam [Ativan], and oxazepam [Serax]) are often used to avoid the cumulative effects of repeated doses.

The specific drug treatment is usually given either before most withdrawal has occurred (substitution or prophylactic treatment) or after significant symptoms and signs manifest themselves (suppressive treatment). The advantages of substitution treatment include the prevention of discomfort and the more severe withdrawal symptoms. The disadvantages include unnecessary treatment for some patients. The advantages of suppression treatment include more appropriate titration, or determination, of the dose of medication for a given patient's needs. The disadvantages include unnecessary patient discomfort, at least initially; the potential for development of more severe withdrawal; and drug-seeking behavior by patients. Benzodiazepines have been demonstrated to prevent complications of serious withdrawal, such as

seizures, hallucinations, and cardiac arrhythmias (Sellers et al., 1983). In general, high doses of these benzodiazepines (with medium-to-long half-lives) are provided early in treatment to cover the patient for the time period of acute withdrawal (usually between 24 to 48 hours after cessation of alcohol consumption). Rarely do patients require very large doses of these drugs (e.g., several hundred milligrams of diazepam) to suppress symptoms and signs. Patients with histories of withdrawal seizures (convulsions), or those that have epilepsy, are always treated prophylactically, usually with benzodiazepines and any other anticonvulsant medication that they are prescribed on a regular basis. Patients who develop hallucinations are often given (in addition to benzodiazepines) haloperidol (Haldol) or another antipsychotic medication. These drugs are effective in the treatment of hallucinations.

Since the late 1990s, there has been some enthusiasm for the use of anticonvulsants as a primary treatment for alcohol withdrawal, and also as adjunctive treatments to the benzodiazepines. These drugs may indeed be effective, particularly in milder cases of withdrawal. Beta-blockers such as atenolol can be used to reduce cardiovascular strain and regulate the heart rate, but caution must be used in this approach because it does not treat the underlying withdrawal syndrome and could mask worsening withdrawal symptoms, thereby preventing adequate treatment with benzodiazepines.

In summary, alcohol withdrawal syndrome is a constellation of symptoms and signs that accompany the detoxification and re-adaptation of the nervous system to a drug-free state in chronic users. In most cases, these signs and symptoms are a source of mild discomfort and run a self-limited course. Occasionally, more severe withdrawal occurs or patients have concurrent complications (e.g., seizures). Under these circumstances appropriate drug treatment is mandatory to relieve symptoms and prevent complications.

BIBLIOGRAPHY

Bayard, M., McIntyre, J., Hill, Keith R., & Woodside, J., Jr. (2004). Alcohol withdrawal syndrome. *American Family Physician 69*(6), 144–1450.

Isbell, H., Fraser, H. F., Wikler, A., Bellevilla, R. E., & Eisenman, A. J. (1955). An experimental study of "rum fits" and delirium tremens. *Quarterly Journal of Studies on Alcohol, 16,* 1–33.

Kasser, C., Geller, A., Howell, E., & Wartenberg, A. (1997). Detoxification: Principles and protocols. In B. B. Wilford (Ed.), *Topics in addiction medicine.* Chevy Chase, MD: American Society of Addiction Medicine.

Krishel, S., SaFranek, D., & Clark, R. F. (1998). Intravenous vitamins for alcoholics in the emergency department: A review. *Journal of Emergency Medicine 16*(3), 419–424.

Linnoila, M., Mefford, I., Nutt, D., Adinoff, B. (1987). Alcohol withdrawal and noradrenergic function. *Annals of Internal Medicine, 107*, 875–889.

Sellers, E. M., & Kalant, H. (1976). Alcohol intoxication and withdrawal. *New England Journal of Medicine, 294*, 757–762.

Sellers, E. M., Nranjo, C. A., Harrison, M., Devenyi, P., Roach, C., & Sykora, K. (1983)."Oral diazepam loading: Simplified treatment of alcohol withdrawal. *Clinical Pharmacology and Therapeutics, 34*, 822–826.

Shaw, J. M., Kolesar, G. S., Sellers, E. M., Kaplan, H. L., & Sandor, P. (1981). Development of optimal tactics for alcohol withdrawal: 1. Assessment and effectiveness of supportive care. *Journal of Clinical Psychopharmacology, 1*, 382–389.

Sullivan, J. T., & Sellers, E. M. (1986). Treating alcohol, barbiturate, and benzodiazepine withdrawal. *Rational Drug Therapy, 20*, 1–8.

Sullivan, J. T., Sykora, K., Schneiderman, J., Naranjo, C. A., & Sellers, E. M. (1989). Assessment of alcohol withdrawal: The revised Clinical Institute Withdrawal Assessment Scale for Alcohol (CIWA-Ar). *British Journal of Addiction, 84*, 1353–1357. Scale. Available from http://images2.clinicaltools.com/.

Thomson, A. D., Cook, C. C., Touquet, R., Henry, J. A., & Royal College of Physicians, London. (2002). The Royal College of Physicians report on alcohol: Guidelines for managing Wernicke's encephalopathy in the accident and emergency department. *Alcohol and Alcoholism, 37(6)*, 513–521. Erratum in: *Alcohol and Alcoholism, 38(3)*, 291.

JOHN T. SULLIVAN
REVISED BY JAMES T. MCDONOUGH JR. (2001)
ALBERT J. ARIAS (2009)

BENZODIAZEPINES

Like many other drugs that alter central nervous system (CNS) neurotransmission, benzodiazepines may produce a withdrawal syndrome when the drugs are abruptly discontinued. These withdrawal symptoms, including increased anxiety and insomnia, are often the mirror image of the therapeutic effects of the drug. Since the term *withdrawal* is usually applied to drugs of abuse, these symptoms are sometimes called *abstinence syndrome* or *discontinuance syndrome* when associated with benzodiazepines when used as prescribed, thereby distinguishing these substances from abused drugs such as alcohol and cocaine or the non-therapeutic use of opioids or barbiturates.

ETIOLOGY

Not all patients who take benzodiazepines experience a discontinuance syndrome when the drug is stopped. Several conditions must be present before the discontinuance syndrome is likely:

Duration of treatment. The benzodiazepine must be taken for long enough to produce alterations in the CNS that predispose individuals to a discontinuance syndrome. When benzodiazepines are taken at a therapeutic dosage, the range of time that usually produces a discontinuance syndrome is from several weeks to several months. Taking benzodiazepines once or twice during a crisis, or even for several weeks during a prolonged period of stress, ordinarily does not set the stage for discontinuance symptoms.

Dose. The amount of drug taken on a daily or nightly basis is also a critical factor. When higher-than-therapeutic doses are taken—for example, for treatment of panic disorder—then the period required before a discontinuance syndrome may develop is shortened.

Abrupt discontinuance of the benzodiazepine. Discontinuance symptoms arise because the level of drug at the CNS receptor sites is suddenly diminished. Since drug level in the CNS is proportional to the amount circulating throughout the body, an abrupt decline in CNS drug levels occurs when the blood level abruptly drops. Gradual tapering of benzodiazepines usually prevents the appearance or reduces the intensity of discontinuance symptoms.

Type of benzodiazepine. Benzodiazepines are classified into short and long half-life compounds (see Table 1). These terms refer to the time it takes for the body to remove (clear) the benzodiazepine. Short half-life benzodiazepines are cleared very rapidly, usually from four to about 16 hours, depending on the drug. In contrast, long half-life

Generic name	U.S. Brand name	Half-life	Commonly used dose range	Duration of therapeutic action	Common therapeutic Indications
Alprazolam	Xanax	11.2 hours	0.5–4.0 mg/day	3–4 hours	Anxiety
Lorazepam	Ativan	12 hours	2–6 mg/day	4–6 hours	Anxiety
Temazepam	Restoril	3.5–18.4 hours	7.5–30 mg/day	4–8 hours	Insomnia
Clonazepam	Klonopin	30–40 hours	0.5–4 mg/day	6–8 hours	Anxiety
Diazepam	Valium	20–54 hours	5–40 mg/day	varies	Anxiety, Insomnia

SOURCE: Adapted from Thomson Micromeded, 2008.

Table 1. Characteristics of different benzodiazepines' withdrawal symptoms. ILLUSTRATION BY GGS INFORMATION SERVICES. GALE, CENGAGE LEARNING

benzodiazepines may take anywhere from 24 to 100 or more hours to be cleared. Since the appearance of discontinuance symptoms depends, in part, on the rapidly diminishing blood level of the drug, abrupt cessation of the short half-life benzodiazepines is more likely to produce discontinuance symptoms. Controversy existed as of 2008 about whether other factors that distinguish one benzodiazepine from another are associated with the appearance of a discontinuance syndrome.

MANIFESTATIONS

Virtually all who experience discontinuance symptoms from benzodiazepines describe increased anxiety, restlessness, and difficulty falling asleep. These symptoms may be mild, little more than an annoyance for a few days, or they may be quite severe and even more intense than the symptoms of anxiety or insomnia for which the drugs were initially prescribed. The reappearance of the initial symptom, such as anxiety or insomnia, only in greater severity, is known as a *rebound symptom*. Rebound symptoms usually occur within hours to days of benzodiazepine discontinuance and then gradually fade. In some cases, however, they may be so intense that the patient resumes taking the benzodiazepine to avoid the discontinuance symptoms themselves. Thus, a cycle of benzodiazepine dependence may begin: The patient takes the drug primarily to treat or prevent rebound discontinuance symptoms from appearing, rather than treating an underlying anxiety or sleep disorder.

Benzodiazepines that are given to induce sleep may also be associated with the development of discontinuance symptoms. Rebound insomnia, the most common discontinuance symptom, typically occurs on the first night and sometimes the second night after discontinuance of short half-life benzodiazepines. Rebound insomnia may be so intense during these nights that the patient may be unwilling to risk another sleepless night and so returns to taking the benzodiazepine hypnotic. Rebound insomnia is less common with long half-life benzodiazepines, though this benefit comes with the possible disadvantage of daytime sedation that is more commonly associated with long half-life benzodiazepines.

If untreated, rebound symptoms may sometimes persist for many months. When this situation occurs it is difficult to determine whether the symptoms are still manifestations of discontinuance or are the result of the return of the problems (anxiety, insomnia) for which the drug was originally prescribed. Sometimes new symptoms that did not exist before the patient took the benzodiazepine appear after discontinuance; these are termed *true withdrawal symptoms*, indicating a change in CNS functioning. Usual withdrawal symptoms include headache, anxiety, insomnia, restlessness, depression, irritability, nausea, decreased appetite, gastrointestinal upset, and unsteadiness. Patients may also experience increased sensitivity for sound and smell, difficulty concentrating, and a sense that events are unreal (derealization) or feeling detached from oneself (depersonalization). Unusual withdrawal symptoms include psychosis and seizures.

OCCURRENCE OF SEIZURES

From a medical perspective, the most serious of all discontinuation symptoms is the development of withdrawal seizures. Seizures are generally grand mal in type (tonic-clonic; epileptic) and may threaten the life of the patient. They tend to occur only when higher-than-therapeutic doses are abruptly discontinued.

Withdrawal seizures almost always occur when the patient has been taking other drugs, such as antidepressants or antipsychotic agents, which can reduce the threshold for seizures, together with a benzodiazepine.

COEXISTING PSYCHOPATHOLOGY

Apparently some people are more predisposed to develop the discontinuation syndrome than others. Those who have been previously dependent on benzodiazepines, alcohol, or other sedative-hypnotic drugs, such as barbiturates, are more likely to experience discontinuance symptoms after the termination of benzodiazepine therapy. It is especially important, therefore, that such patients never stop taking their benzodiazepines abruptly.

TREATMENT

Although a variety of treatments have been proposed for the discontinuance syndrome, the best approach is to prevent its occurrence. Logically, prevention consists of a very gradual tapering of the benzodiazepine dose, with a firm rule never to discontinue these medications abruptly if they have been taken for more than a few weeks on a regular basis.

Even with gradual tapering, however, some patients may continue to experience rebound or withdrawal symptoms that are sufficiently disturbing to require treatment. Drugs that tend to reduce CNS hyperarousal states, such as anticonvulsants, have sometimes been employed to treat benzodiazepine discontinuance, though their effectiveness in this situation had not been well documented as of 2008. Alternatively, benzodiazepine treatment is restarted using a long half-life compound that is then very gradually tapered.

WITHDRAWAL

For the great majority of patients, benzodiazepine discontinuance is a relatively benign and short-lived syndrome; many, if not most, patients have no difficulty. It is generally agreed that the therapeutic benefits of taking benzodiazepines far outweigh any problems with discontinuance when drug treatment is no longer necessary.

BIBLIOGRAPHY

Charney D. S., Mihic, J., & Harris, R. (2006). Hypnotics and sedatives. In L. Brunton, J. Lazo, K. Parker, I. Buxton, & D. Blumenthal (Eds.), *The pharmacological basis of therapeutics* (pp. 401–428). New York: McGraw-Hill.

Rickels, K., Schweizer, E., Weiss, S., & Zavodnick, S. (1993). Maintenance drug treatment for panic disorders. *Archives of General Psychiatry, 50,* 61.

Salzman, C. (1991). The APA Benzodiazepine Task Force Report on dependency, toxicity, and abuse. *American Journal of Psychiatry, 148,* 151–152.

Salzman, C., ed. (1990). *American Psychiatric Association Task Force on benzodiazepine dependency, toxicity, and abuse.* Washington, DC: American Psychiatric Press.

CARL SALZMAN
REVISED BY ALBERT J. ARIAS (2009)

COCAINE

H. W. Maier first mentioned cocaine withdrawal in his 1928 book *Der Kokainismus,* and early descriptions were provided in the 1980s during an epidemic of cocaine use in the United States. These descriptions emphasized subjective states rather than the physiological symptoms typically observed in sedative, alcohol, and opiate withdrawal (Satel et al., 1991; Weddington et al., 1990). The symptoms are listed in the *DSM-IV* diagnostic criteria for cocaine dependence and include depressive symptoms, poor sleep, lack of energy, agitation, and craving for cocaine. The duration of these withdrawal symptoms is typically a few days but might extend for as long as three to four weeks in some patients. Subjects particularly suffer from difficulty with sleeping. An early stage of withdrawal lasting several hours to a day and often called a crash has been described. During this period patients may appear quite agitated, paranoid, and suicidal. This crash appears to be related to sleep deprivation, which complicates the typical effects of stimulants on cognition and is terminated by the patient sleeping for 10 to 15 hours. Benzodiazepines are often given in emergency settings in order to induce this sleep and end this early period of withdrawal symptoms, when they occur.

The evidence for brain abnormalities associated with chronic cocaine dependence and possibly related to withdrawal symptoms includes electroencephalogram (EEG) and functional magnetic resonance imaging (fMRI) abnormalities (Kosten et al., 2007). More fundamental abnormalities in brain structure (e.g., size to anterior cingulate cortex) and neuronal receptors (e.g., reduced number of dopamine D2 type receptors on caudate neurons) are evident in these patients but are unlikely to be related to the pathophysiology of any acute withdrawal syndrome. Instead, these abnormalities reflect either inherited traits or damage induced by long-term high dose cocaine use, which would not change quickly during the relatively brief period of cocaine withdrawal.

Protracted withdrawal lasting for several months after acute withdrawal has subsided has been considered for many abused substances with the best evidence for alcohol and opiates (Satel et al., 1993). Little data support such phenomena with stimulants such as cocaine. While many patients relapse weeks and months after stopping cocaine and when the symptoms of acute withdrawal are long gone, these relapses are related to complex psychological processes of cue-induced craving, drug priming, and stressful events that have a neurobiology probably related to general aspects of learning and memory rather than to a withdrawal syndrome from stimulants.

BIBLIOGRAPHY

Kosten, T. R., Sofuoglu, M., & Gardner, T. J. (2008). Clinical management: Cocaine. In M. Galanter & H. Kleber (Eds.), *American Psychiatric Publishing textbook of substance abuse treatment* (4th ed.). Washington, DC: American Psychiatric Publishing.

Maier, H. W. (1987). *Maier's cocaine addiction/Der kokainismus* (O. J. Kalant, Trans.). Toronto: Addiction Research Foundation. (Original work published in 1928).

Satel, S. L., Kosten, T. R., Schuckit, M. A., & Fischman, M. W. (1993). Should protracted withdrawal from drugs be included in *DSM-IV*? *American Journal of Psychiatry, 150*, 695–701.

Satel, S. L., Price, L. H., Palumbo, J. M., McDougle, C. J., Krystal, J. H., Gawin, F., et al. (1991). Clinical phenomenology and neurobiology of cocaine abstinence: A prospective inpatient study. *American Journal of Psychiatry, 148*, 1712–1716.

Schuckit, M. A., Kosten T. R., & Fischman, M. W. (1940) *American Psychiatric Association's diagnostic and statistical manual of mental disorders (DSM-IV). Substance related disorders. Protracted abstinence syndromes in alcohol, opioids, and stimulants.* Arlington, VA: American Psychiatric Association.

Weddington, W. W., Brown, B. S., Cone, E. J., Haertzen, C. A., Dax, E. M., Herning, R. I., et al. (1990). Changes in mood, craving, and sleep during short-term abstinence reported by male cocaine addicts: A controlled residential study. *Archives of General Psychiatry, 47*, 861–868.

THOMAS R. KOSTEN
SALLY L. SATEL
REVISED BY TRACIE J. GARDNER (2009)
THERESE R. KOSTEN (2009)

NICOTINE (TOBACCO)

Nicotine is one of the most addicting substances known. Indeed, the risk of becoming dependent on nicotine following any tobacco use is higher than the risk of becoming dependent on alcohol, cocaine, or marijuana following the use of those substances. Among multiple drug users, quitting tobacco use is often cited as more difficult than giving up alcohol or cocaine. Most current views of tobacco use include physiological addiction to nicotine as a factor in the difficult course of achieving smoking cessation.

Nicotine, the active ingredient in tobacco, shares characteristics with other addictive drugs. First, these drugs alter central nervous system function at specific receptors, and they often change the structure of these receptors. In addition, increases (up regulation) or decreases (down regulation) in receptor numbers occur. Second, repeated exposure to addictive drugs results in "tolerance," which means that the individual must progressively self-administer higher drug doses to obtain the same effects that initially occurred at lower doses. Third, as cellular and neurological functioning adapt to the continuous presence of these drugs, a state of physical or physiological dependence is produced. As a result of this dependence, the removal of any of these drugs is accompanied by feelings of emotional and physical discomfort and an inability to function normally. Finally, a hallmark of dependence-producing drugs is that they serve as biological reinforcers (rewards) for animals, including humans.

NICOTINE TOLERANCE AND DEPENDENCE
Nicotine is a pharmacologic agent that acts on the central nervous system. Specifically, it acts on cholinergic receptors in the brain. The cigarette is a very fast and effective delivery system for nicotine,

and effects occur rapidly after a single inhalation of tobacco smoke. Nicotine quickly crosses the blood-brain barrier and interacts with brain receptors. Nicotine alters moods and acts on pleasure-seeking receptors in the brain, including dopamine and serotonin. The nicotine alkaloid affects numerous body systems. It raises blood pressure and heart rate, for example, and it also affects the peripheral nervous system. Both stimulant and depressive effects are observed in cardiovascular, endocrine, gastrointestinal, and skeletal systems.

A person's initial exposure to nicotine may be an unpleasant experience, for it often causes sickness, intoxication, and disruptions in physiologic functioning. Among individuals presumed to be at greatest risk of becoming regular users of tobacco, the body quickly adapts to nicotine and the initial unpleasant effects become less pronounced. Thus, tolerance develops and physical dependence occurs. Smokers are free to self-administer the dose of nicotine they desire, and as their tolerance increases, they often increase tobacco use accordingly. The level of dependence is strongly related to the dose of nicotine.

As an individual becomes addicted to smoking, the smoker feels normal, comfortable, and effective when taking nicotine, but physically and emotionally uncomfortable and ineffective when deprived of nicotine. The development of dependence weakens the ability of the person to achieve and sustain even short-term abstinence. Thus, in the nicotine-dependent person, "normal" function depends on nicotine, and the removal of nicotine results in impairment.

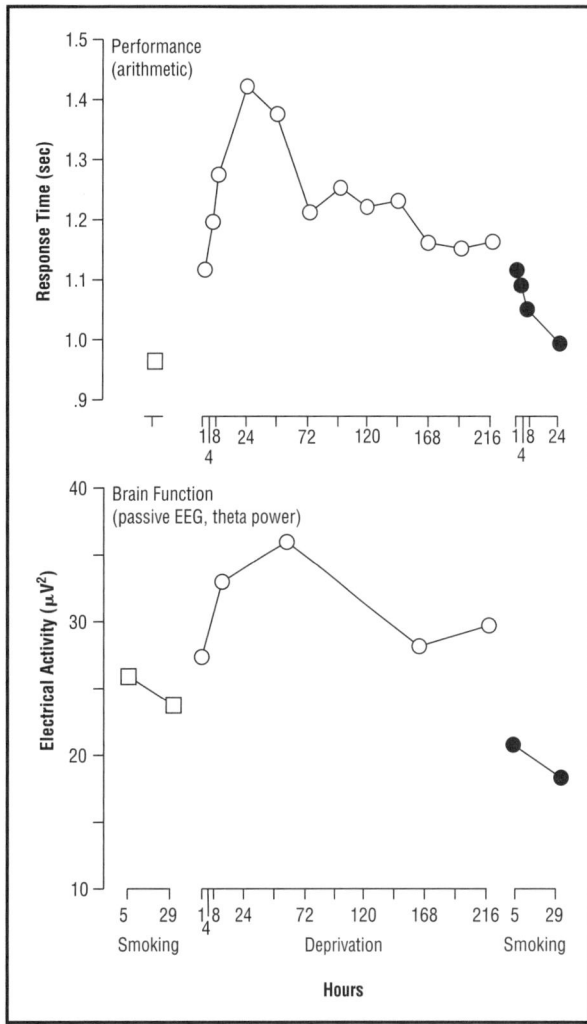

Figure 1. Cognitive performance and an electrophysiological measure of brain function during smoking and abstinence. ILLUSTRATION BY GGS INFORMATION SERVICES. GALE, CENGAGE LEARNING

NICOTINE WITHDRAWAL SYMPTOMS

The *Diagnostic and Statistical Manual of Mental Disorders, Fourth Edition (DSM-IV)*, recognizes nicotine dependence as a substance-related disorder, with a well-defined withdrawal syndrome (*DSM-IV-TR*, p. 265). The potential withdrawal symptoms include depressed mood, insomnia, irritability, frustration or anger, anxiety, difficulty concentrating, restlessness, decreased heart rate, and increased appetite or weight gain. These symptoms must cause significant distress or impairment in order to be diagnosable as withdrawal. The severity of the symptoms will depend on the severity of nicotine dependence. Evidence suggests that withdrawal may begin earlier than previously appreciated, with many

symptoms emerging within one to three hours of nicotine abstinence. Withdrawal symptoms are strongest in the first few days after smoking cessation and usually diminish within a month, although some smokers may continue to experience withdrawal symptoms for many months.

There are a number of other effects of smoking cessation. There is evidence, for example, that cognitive ability is impaired when smoking cessation is attempted. The cognitive deficits are correlated with disruptions in brain electrophysiologic function. Figure 1 shows that deficits in an arithmetic task follow a similar time course as changes in the brain's electrical activity. These effects begin a few hours after the last dose of nicotine, peak during the first few days of abstinence (when smokers trying to quit are most likely to relapse), and mostly subside within a few weeks. An impairment of sustained attention may set in even more quickly, with one study showing significant impairment after 30 minutes of abstinence. Another study of cognitive impairment, using four complex cognitive tasks during withdrawal from smoking in heavy smokers, ex-smokers, and those who had never smoked, assessed ability to perform those tasks; smokers with 12 hours of abstinence had the worst scores on the tasks.

Another symptom associated with withdrawal is a craving for cigarettes. This craving is strongly related to the degree of nicotine dependence. Frequent craving may last for six months, with some smokers reporting occasional episodes of craving even years after cessation, which is far longer than most of the other symptoms associated with tobacco withdrawal. Craving is a major obstacle to cessation and, together with other indicators of nicotine dependence, it is strongly related to relapse, with the majority of smokers who attempt to quit relapsing within the first week of cessation.

Although the foregoing symptoms are universal (albeit with some variation among individuals), some withdrawal symptoms are unique to individuals with specific characteristics. Smokers with a history of major depression, for example, are at some risk of having another depressive episode during the course of stopping smoking. Smokers with various forms of preexisting cognitive dysfunction (e.g., attention-deficit disorder, schizophrenia) may experience a resurgence of their cognitive deficits during nicotine withdrawal. Smokers with comorbid substance-use disorders such as alcohol dependence or illicit substance dependence are likely to have more severe withdrawal symptoms as they attempt to address more than one dependency.

While the withdrawal syndrome is undoubtedly biologically based, behavioral factors have a strong influence on smoking cessation. Cigarette smoking involves a number of rituals that become an integral part of the smoker's daily life, resulting in numerous individual, social, and environmental prompts to smoke. At the individual level, the smoker may associate a cup of coffee, the end of a meal, or watching television as a prompt to light a cigarette. Socially, being with friends or family members who smoke may represent other cues to smoke. Environmental stimuli, such as being in bars or other places where many people smoke, are also likely to reinforce the smoker's desire to smoke. Exposure to any of these cues to smoke may result in relapse.

MEASUREMENT AND TREATMENT OF NICOTINE WITHDRAWAL

Several scales are commonly used to measure withdrawal symptoms, including the Shiffman-Jarvik Withdrawal Scale, the Minnesota Withdrawal Scale, and the Wisconsin Smoking Withdrawal Scale. Each scale consists of a list of various withdrawal symptoms, along with instructions to rate the severity of each symptom. Of these scales, however, only the Wisconsin Smoking Withdrawal Scale utilizes the most recent diagnostic criteria for withdrawal symptoms included in the DSM-IV-TR.

Two pharmacologic approaches—nicotine replacement therapy and non-nicotine drugs—have been shown to reduce nicotine withdrawal symptoms. In addition, behavioral approaches have proven useful for managing symptoms associated with withdrawal.

Nicotine Replacement Therapy (NRT). The purpose of nicotine replacement is to substitute a safer and more controllable form of nicotine to the smoker to aid in cessation. Although nicotine replacement delivery systems vary, all attempt to reduce the amount of nicotine available during cessation, so that an individual is weaned from nicotine addiction more slowly. Three nicotine replacement therapies are available over-the-counter: nicotine polacrilex gum (Nicoderm, Nicorette DS, Nicotinell), nicotine lozenges (Commit) and the transdermal nicotine patch (Nicoderm CQ, Nicotrol, Habitrol). Two other delivery systems are available by prescription: an oral nicotine inhalation system (Nicotrol Inhaler, Nicorette Inhaler) and a nasal nicotine spray (Nicotrol NS). The effectiveness of each of the systems has been well established in randomized, controlled trials. The limited evidence comparing different forms of NRT shows them all to be equally efficacious. However, combining the patch with rapid delivery forms of NRT (i.e., gum, lozenge, nasal spray, or inhaler) has been shown to be more effective than a single type of NRT.

Non-nicotine Pharmacotherapy. A number of drug therapies have been approved to alleviate or reduce some of the discomfort that accompanies smoking cessation. The newest of these, varenicline (Chantix) was approved by the U.S. Food and Drug Administration in May 2006. This drug binds to the same brain receptors as nicotine, so that it blocks nicotine from having reinforcing effects, while simultaneously providing some stimulation to curb withdrawal symptoms. Its efficacy is well established, and early research has shown it to be more effective than bupropion (Zyban), another smoking cessation drug. Bupropion acts as an antidepressant, and it is often used for this purpose. However, it is effective in smokers who have no history of depression. Thus, other factors appear to be involved in the success of this drug in smoking cessation.

Another antidepressant, nortriptyline (Aventyl, Pamelor, Nortrilen) has also been shown to be useful for smoking cessation. Clonidine (Catapres), originally used to treat hypertension, appears to be modestly effective in blocking the cravings for nicotine, especially in women. Other pharmacologic therapies are being tested for their value in ameliorating the withdrawal symptoms associated with smoking cessation. These include mecamylamine (Inversine), which is thought to block the reinforcing action of nicotine, and anti-anxiety medications (such as benzodiazepines), which generally lower stress and decrease anxiety.

Behavioral Approaches. Behavioral approaches for preventing relapse have a long history of use in smoking cessation. Behavioral strategies generally focus on the social reinforcers of smoking. The most effective behavioral programs are those that have multiple components. Strategies for mitigating withdrawal include relaxation exercises (e.g., deep breathing), coping tactics (e.g., distracting oneself during periods of high craving), formation of social support networks (e.g., telling family and friends of your plans to quit), anticipation and avoidance of tempting situations (e.g., avoiding bars immediately after quitting if one associates drinking with smoking), simple messages to deal with withdrawal symptoms (e.g., reminding oneself that they are only temporary), and stimulus control (e.g., getting rid of ashtrays, having a smoke-free home). Multiple-component behavioral programs have been successful in helping smokers achieve cessation, and research suggests that nicotine replacement or pharmacologic approaches without a behavioral component have significantly lower success rates than those with a behavioral component. However, the addition of medications to behavioral treatment substantially increases quit rates compared with behavioral treatment alone.

WITHDRAWAL: NICOTINE (TOBACCO): SUMMARY

Nicotine is a very addictive drug that affects the central nervous system. Its use results in tolerance and dependence, so that the user feels most normal when using tobacco. A clear nicotine withdrawal syndrome is recognized; smokers attempting cessation may experience unpleasant or uncomfortable mood, insomnia, irritability, anxiety, difficulty concentrating, restlessness, decreased heart rate, and increased appetite. Further, cognitive ability is somewhat impaired during cessation, strong craving for the drug is present, and powerful behavioral cues make cessation difficult. New approaches to the withdrawal syndrome include the administration of nicotine in a safer delivery system that can be tapered over time, and drugs to counter the unpleasant symptoms of withdrawal. Along with behavioral treatment, such pharmacologic tools may assist the smoker in achieving cessation.

BIBLIOGRAPHY

American Psychiatric Association. (2000). *Diagnostic and statistical manual of mental disorders* (4th ed., text revision, *DSM-IV-TR*). Washington, DC: Author.

Balfour, D. J., & Ridley, D. L. (2000). The effects of nicotine on neural pathways implicated in depression: A factor in nicotine addiction? *Pharmacology, Biochemistry, & Behavior, 66*(1), 79–85.

Benowitz, N. L. (1999). Nicotine addiction. *Primary Care: Clinics in Office Practice, 26*(3), 611–631.

Fletcher, C., & Doll, R. (1969). A survey of doctors' attitudes to smoking. *British Journal of Preventive and Social Medicine, 23*(3), 145–153.

Ghatan, P. H., Ingvar, M., Eriksson, L., Stone-Elander, S., Serrander, M., Ekberg, K., & Wahren, J. (1998). Cerebral effects of nicotine during cognition in smokers and non-smokers. *Psychopharmacology, 136*(2), 179–189.

Gonzales, D., Rennard, S. I., Nides, M., Oncken, C., Azoulay, S., Billing, C. B., et al. (2006). Varenicline, an α4β2 nicotinic acetylcholine receptor partial agonist, vs sustained-release bupropion and placebo for smoking cessation. *Journal of the American Medical Association,* *296*(1), 47–55.

Hall, S. M., Reus, V. I., Muñoz, R. F., Sees, K. L., Humfleet, G., Hartz, D. T., et al. (1998). Nortriptyline and cognitive-behavioral therapy in the treatment of cigarette smoking. *Archives of General Psychiatry, 55*(8), 683–690.

Hendricks, P. J., Ditre, J. W., Drobes, D. J., & Brandon, T. H. (2006). The early time course of smoking withdrawal effects. *Psychopharmacology, 187*(3), 385–396.

Henningfield, J. E. (1995). Nicotine medications for smoking cessation. *New England Journal of Medicine, 333*(18), 1196–1203.

Hughes, J. R., Goldstein, M. G., Hurt, R. D., & Shiffman, S. (1999). Recent advances in the pharmacotherapy of smoking. *Journal of the American Medical Association, 281*(1), 72–76.

Hughes, J. R., & Hatsukami, D. (1986). Signs and symptoms of tobacco withdrawal. *Archives of General Psychiatry, 43*(3), 289–294.

Shiffman, S. M., & Jarvik, M. E. (1976). Smoking withdrawal symptoms in two weeks of abstinence. *Psychopharmacology, 50*(1), 35–39.

Snyder, F. R., Davis, F. C., & Henningfield, J. E. (1989). The tobacco withdrawal syndrome: Performance assessed on a computerized test battery. *Drug and Alcohol Dependence, 23,* 259–266.

Stead, L. F., Petera, R., Bullen, C., Mant, D., & Lancaster, T. (1996). Nicotine replacement therapy for smoking cessation. *Cochrane Database of Systematic Reviews 1996, 3*(CD000146).

Sziraki, I., Sershen, H., Benuck, M., Lipovac, M., Hashim, A., Cooper, T. B., & Lajtha, A. (1999). The effect of cotinine on nicotine- and cocaine-induced dopamine release in the nucleus accumbens. *Neurochemical Research, 24*(11), 1471–1478.

U.S. Department of Health and Human Services (DHHS). (1988). *The health consequences of smoking: Nicotine addiction. A report of the surgeon general.* Washington, DC: DHHS, Office on Smoking and Health. DHHS Publication No. (CDC) 88-8406.

U.S. Department of Health and Human Services (DHHS). (1989). *Reducing the health consequences of smoking: 25 years of progress: A report of the surgeon general.* Washington, DC: DHHS, Office on Smoking and Health. DHHS Publication No. (CDC) 89-8411.

U.S. Department of Health and Human Services (DHHS). (1990). *The health benefits of smoking cessation: A report of the surgeon general.* Washington, DC: DHHS, Office on Smoking and Health. DHHS Publication No. (CDC) 90-8416.

Welsch, S. K., Smith, S. S., Wetter, D. W., Jorenby, D. E., Fiore, M. C., & Baker, T. B. (1999). Development and validation of the Wisconsin Smoking Withdrawal Scale. *Experimental and Clinical Psychopharmacology, 7*(4), 354–361.

Jack E. Henningfield
Leslie M. Schutt
Revised by Beti Thompson (2001)
Jason A. Oliver (2009)
David J. Drobes (2009)

NONABUSED DRUGS

Although drug withdrawal is often considered synonymous with matters relating to drug abuse, a number of drugs that have no abuse potential and are prescribed for medical illness are associated with clear symptoms of withdrawal when their use is abruptly discontinued. The symptoms do not necessarily indicate drug dependence, a syndrome that has several features, including tolerance, inability to control drug use, and continued drug use despite deleterious effects.

CARDIOVASCULAR DRUGS

Beta-adrenergic blockers are taken by many people to treat hypertension (high blood pressure), angina pectoris (chest pain that occurs when the heart muscle is deprived of oxygen), heart arrhythmias following heart attack, and for migraine headache. The mechanism for each of these effects is related to the drug occupying the beta-adrenergic receptors in the blood vessels and the heart. When a patient abruptly stops taking a beta blocker, particularly when angina pectoris is the symptom being treated, a marked increase in the frequency and/or severity of angina pectoris may occur. This response occurs within the first few days of discontinuing the beta blocker; it may be prevented by slowly decreasing the drug dose over several days before completely stopping the drug. The discontinuation symptom is probably related to an increased sensitivity of the beta receptor to the body's own hormones norepinephrine and epinephrine, when its antagonist, the beta blocker, is suddenly removed. The withdrawal syndrome disappears in a few days.

Clonidine is used for hypertension and to treat withdrawal from opiate narcotics. Its mechanism of effect is stimulation of alpha (type 2)-adrenergic receptors in the central nervous system, which results in decreased stimulation of nerves that release norepinephrine and epinephrine in blood vessels. When clonidine is abruptly stopped, blood pressure increases to well above baseline levels and may become dangerously high. This response occurs within one to two days after stopping the drug and is prevented by slowly (over several days) decreasing the drug dose before stopping it completely. The symptom may be due to a rebound over-stimulation of norepinephrine and epinephrine releasing nerves in blood vessels. This rebound hypertension disappears within a few days, again consistent with the time required for alpha-adrenergic receptor re-regulation.

Nitroglycerin and other nitrates are taken to treat angina pectoris. They cause the relaxation of blood vessels by the activation of an intracellular enzyme, guanylyl cyclase, which catalyzes formation of cyclic GMP (guanosine monophosphate). The coronary arteries (blood vessels that supply heart muscles) relax when exposed to nitrates. If the coronary arteries are blocked by atherosclerosis, causing insufficient blood supply to the heart, angina pectoris can occur. Relaxation of these arteries improves blood supply to the heart, and the chest pain rapidly disappears. When nitrates are taken continuously for relief of chest pain and then abruptly discontinued, rebound angina pectoris that is more frequent or more severe than the angina experienced prior to treatment may occur. This symptom begins within a few hours of the last nitrate dose and in a time course consistent with the metabolism and removal of the nitrate drug from the body. If the nitrate dose is slowly decreased before discontinuation, the rebound angina may be prevented. The mechanism for this withdrawal syndrome is not known.

NEUROPSYCHOPHARMACOLOGICAL DRUGS

Abrupt discontinuation of any of the major classes of antidepressants may result in discontinuation reactions. Antidepressants vary in their ability to cause reactions, and reactions are more common after abrupt discontinuation and longer courses of treatment. Common symptoms include gastrointestinal problems such as nausea, abdominal pain, and diarrhea. In addition, some patients complain of a flu-like illness consisting of weakness, chills, fatigue, headaches, and muscle aches. Central nervous system dysfunction characterized by difficulty falling asleep, anxiety, vivid dreams or nightmares, or jitteriness can also occur, as can such affective symptoms such as irritability and low mood. Symptoms usually start a few days after termination of the antidepressant and continue for between one day and three weeks. Selective serotonin reuptake inhibitors (SSRIs), a class of antidepressants, have several distinct discontinuation symptoms, including dizziness and such sensory abnormalities as electric shock-like sensations, numbness, and paresthesia. The symptoms typically go away the day after antidepressant treatment has resumed. To reduce the risk of withdrawal symptoms, some physicians have recommended that antidepressants be gradually reduced over a four-week period rather than abruptly discontinued.

Monoamine oxidase inhibitor (MAOI) antidepressant drugs interfere with the enzymatic breakdown of neurotransmitters (such as norepinephrine) in the brain. Sudden discontinuation after high chronic dosing has been associated with psychosis (including visual hallucinations) and delirium (with agitation and mental confusion). Milder symptoms consisting of anxiety, vivid dreaming, or nightmares may also occur. The exact mechanism of withdrawal had not been well studied as of 2008, but it was suspected to relate to the way nerve cells regulate the release of neurotransmitters in the brain.

Antipsychotic agents are commonly used in psychiatric practice for the treatment of psychotic disorders such as schizophrenia. These agents all block brain dopaminergic receptors—the basis for their effectiveness in treating psychotic illness. These agents also inhibit emesis (vomiting) by blocking dopamine in the brain. Chronic dopamine blockade results in increased numbers of these receptors. The abrupt discontinuation of this class of drugs results in nausea, vomiting, and headaches. The antipsychotic and antiparkinsonian effects of neuroleptics are also still present for a prolonged period. According to some research, it is not known whether the prolonged effects of neuroleptic drugs in humans are due to the continued presence of drug in brain tissue or to long-lasting, drug-induced physiologic changes.

Clozapine is in a class of atypical antipsychotic drugs associated with discontinuation symptoms. Although atypical antipsychotics may be different from other drugs used to treat psychosis, there are also significant differences among these drugs in their effects on the receptors of the central nervous system. Clozapine interacts with a wide range of neurotransmitter receptors, especially serotonin receptors. Common discontinuation symptoms of clozapine include delusions, hallucinations, hostility, and paranoia. The underlying mechanism of these symptoms is thought to be supersensitivity of the cholinergic receptor (i.e., the muscarinic acetylcholine receptor, one of the main receptors for cholinergic neurotransmission in the central nervous system).

OTHER DRUGS

Baclofen, a muscle relaxant, is used to treat muscle spasticity associated with certain paralytic states. It acts as an agonist (mimic) of the inhibitory neurotransmitter, gamma-aminobutyric acid (GABA). Therefore, baclofen inhibits excitatory neural pathways, which are modulated by GABA. This is a rather selective effect as there are two types of GABA receptors and pathways, GABA-A and GABA-B, and baclofen only acts on GABA-B receptors. The symptoms experienced by a person suddenly discontinuing baclofen may include auditory and visual hallucinations, severe anxiety, increased heart rate and blood pressure, delirium, and generalized seizures. Such clinical symptoms are consistent with the impaired modulation of neural-excitatory pathways. When the dosage of baclofen is gradually reduced before discontinuation, these symptoms either do not occur or are attenuated.

In mimicking the endogenous corticosteroid cortisol, corticosteroids signal the pituitary gland to stop the synthesis and release of the adrenocorticotrophic hormone (ACTH) and, perhaps, the hypothalamus to stop the release of the corticotropin-releasing hormone (CRH). ACTH release from the pituitary, which normally stimulates the adrenal glands to produce corticosteroids and which is modulated by the hypothalamic CRH, is blocked by exogenous corticosteroids. Adrenal production of cortisol decreases and the adrenal glands atrophy. When corticosteroid therapy is abruptly discontinued, the atrophic adrenal glands no longer respond to ACTH stimulation, so the patient has symptoms of adrenal insufficiency. Clinically, this condition is manifested by fatigue, weakness, electrolyte imbalance, and the lack of many bodily responses to stress. If an individual remains in this state for more than a few hours, severe illness and death can be expected. When the adrenal glands become atrophic during long-term corticosteroid treatment, discontinuation must be done slowly, with the dose decreased gradually over many weeks to permit the adrenal glands sufficient time to be restored to their normal size under the influence of ACTH stimulation and to have sufficient stores of the body's own cortisol to respond to stress in a physiologically appropriate manner.

Human physiology is characterized by the coordinated and finely tuned operation of multiple messaging systems, exhibiting both positive and negative feedback regulation, with multiple levels of control. All the drugs mentioned exert both their desired and undesired effects by interfering with these systems. In the drug-treated individual, homeostasis is maintained by counteracting some of the drug effects at the cellular level. However, such adaptation is not without cost. Sudden discontinuation of a drug to which the nervous system has adapted can produce a period of disequilibrium between the affected messaging systems. The disturbed physiology is expressed by withdrawal symptoms that are specific to the systems involved.

BIBLIOGRAPHY

Berecz, R., Glaub, T., Kellermann, M., De La Rubia, A., Llerena, A., & Degrell, I. (2000). Clozapine withdrawal symptoms after change to sertindole in a schizophrenic patient. *Pharmacopsychiatry, 33,* 42–44.

Byyny, R. L. (1976). Withdrawal from glucocorticoid therapy. *New England Journal of Medicine, 295,* 30–32.

Cederbaum, J. M., & Schleifer, L. S. (1990). Drugs for Parkinson's disease, spasticity, and acute muscle spasms. In A. G. Goodman, T. W. Rall, A. S. Nies, & P. Taylors (Eds.), *Goodman & Gilman's the pharmacological basis of therapeutics* (8th ed., pp. 463–484). New York: Pergamon.

Durst, R., Teitelbaum, A., Katz, G., & Knobler, H. Y. (1999). Withdrawal from clozapine: The "rebound phenomenon." *Israel Journal of Psychiatry and Related Sciences, 36,* 122–128.

Goldstein, J. M. (1999). Quetiapine fumarate (Seroquel): A new atypical antipsychotic. *Drugs of Today, 35,* 193–210.

Goudie, A. J., Smith, J. A., Robertson, A., & Cavanagh, C. (1999). Clozapine as a drug of dependence. *Psychopharmacology, 142,* 369–374.

Haddad, P. (1999). Do antidepressants have any potential to cause addiction? *Journal of Psychopharmacology, 13,* 300–307.

Haddad, P., LeJoyeux, M., & Young, A. (1998) Antidepressant discontinuation reactions are preventable and simple to treat. *British Medical Journal, 316,* 1105.

Houston, M. C., & Hodge, R. (1988). Beta-adrenergic blocker withdrawal syndromes in hypertension and other cardiovascular diseases. *American Heart Journal, 116,* 515–523.

Kotlyar, M., Golding, M., Brewer, E. R., & Carson, S. W. (1999). Possible nefazodone withdrawal syndrome. *American Journal of Psychiatry, 156,* 1117.

Levin, A. A. (1998). Antidepressant dependency. *Healthfacts, 23,* 2.

Parker, M., & Atkinson, J. (1982). Withdrawal syndromes following cessation of treatment with antihypertensive drugs. *General Pharmacology, 13,* 79–85.

Shatan, C. (1966). Withdrawal symptoms after abrupt termination of imipramine. *Canadian Psychiatric Association Journal, 2,* 150–157.

Tollefson, G. D., Dellva, M. A., Mattler, C. A., Kane, J. M., Wirshing, D. A., & Kinon, B. J. (1999). Controlled, double-blind investigation of the clozapine discontinuation symptoms with conversion to either olanzapine or placebo. *Journal of Clinical Psychopharmacology, 19,* 435–443.

Young, A., & Haddad, P. (2000). Discontinuation symptoms and psychotropic drugs: Letter to the editor. *The Lancet, 355,* 1184.

Darrell R. Abernethy
Paolo DePetrillo
Revised by Patricia Ohlenroth (2001)
Albert J. Arias (2009)

WOMAN'S CHRISTIAN TEMPERANCE UNION.

The nineteenth century was a time of drastic changes in the way many Americans viewed alcohol. Early in the century, on average, U.S. citizens each consumed approximately 7 gallons of alcohol annually, the equivalent of about 2.5 ounces of pure alcohol daily. Concern that the United States would turn into a "nation of drunkards" sparked the temperance movement of the early nineteenth century. This movement was loosely organized, consisting of diverse factions: (a) neorepublicans, who were concerned with a host of problems that threatened the nation's security; (b) temperance societies, such as the Washingtonians, which served as the forerunners of modern-day self-help groups; (c) local women's groups that organized spontaneous protests against saloonkeepers from the 1830s on; and (d) physicians, who came to view habitual drunkenness as a disease called "inebriety." The goals of these groups varied; they ranged from helping habitual drunkards, to discouraging the use of alcoholic beverages, to advocating prohibition of alcoholic beverages, to signing pledges to abstain from drink, and to closure of saloons.

This first wave of temperance activists met with some success: 13 states passed prohibition laws by 1855, and average alcohol consumption rates dropped to less than 3 gallons per person annually. Momentum slowed during the Civil War, but the early movement set the stage for the post-Civil War temperance movement. Physicians formed the American Association for the Cure of Inebriety in 1870, an organization advocating medical treatment for "inebriety" in asylums specifically built for that purpose, according to William L. White (1998).

Many Americans experienced the years following the Civil War as a chaotic time of rapid social and technological change during which many sought what Mark E. Lender and James K. Martin (1982, p. 92) term "a search for order." Broad-based social reform movements attacked a number of issues. Paul Aaron and David Musto (1981) refer to this period as the second great prohibition wave. Although the Washingtonians were in decline by 1845, evangelical Christians formed fraternal societies based on "gospel temperance" (Chavigny, 2004, p. 113). Many local temperance societies survived the Civil War, as did the American Temperance Union. In 1869 the National Prohibition party formed to support the abolition of alcohol. The National Prohibition party recruited women into the organized fight against liquor and advocated complete and unrestricted suffrage for women.

The post–Civil War Progressive movement also influenced the issue of temperance. The Progressives believed that alcohol was "the enemy of industrial efficiency, a threat to the working of democratic government, the abettor of poverty and disease" (Bordin, 1981, p. xvi). To the Progressives, temperance reform was a means for confronting genuine social problems. Business leaders increasingly came to view the use of alcohol as incongruous with the new technological society that America was becoming. Alcohol symbolized wastefulness, rampant pluralism, individualism, and potential social disorder.

At the same time, a growing number of physicians and temperance workers began to regard habitual drunkenness as an inherently progressive disease. According to their "stepping stone" theory, even moderate drinking inevitably led to addiction. As long as liquor was available, people would be enticed to drink. As long as moderate drinkers were around to act as models, then there would be drunkards. Increasingly, the blame for addiction to alcohol was placed less on the individual and more on the society that permitted the sale of liquor, tolerated saloons, and condoned drinking.

The women's temperance movement developed in a context that included better education for women, a declining birth rate, and growing urbanization. Women were portrayed as the moral guardians of society and protectors of the home, and increasingly, alcohol was seen as a threat to moral values and to the security of the home. These factors, combined with a larger middle class and better communications, set the stage for the first mass movement of women into U.S. politics.

THE WOMEN'S CRUSADE

Ironically, the direct origins of the movement through which women gained entry into the political arena can be traced back to a man, Dio Lewis. As a child, Lewis witnessed his mother organize a protest against a saloonkeeper in Clarkesville, New York. This protest was similar to the many confrontations between groups of women and saloonkeepers across New England and the Midwest. In the 1850s and 1860s, lectures by Dio Lewis persuaded women to organize similar campaigns, according to Barbara L. Epstein (1981, pp. 93–95). By the 1870s Lewis, a trained homeopathic physician, had given up his medical practice and embarked full-time on the lecture circuit. In December 1873 Lewis's lecture in Hillsboro, Ohio, instigated a grass-roots movement that came to be known as the Women's Crusade.

The Women's Crusade quickly moved through Ohio and into neighboring states. Typically, the women of a community called a meeting eliciting support from other women. After praying over their cause, they organized their efforts, which included asking local ministers to preach on the topic of temperance and seeking pledges of support from local political leaders. Finally, they took to the streets, marching on distributors of liquor, in an attempt to persuade them to cease their sales of alcohol.

HISTORY OF THE WCTU

By November 1874 the Women's Crusade had grown to the point that they called a national convention. Sixteen states were represented at this convention, out of which the Woman's Christian Temperance Union (WCTU) emerged. Annie Wittenmyer was named the first president of the WCTU. Wittenmyer gained leadership experience in the Sanitary Commission during the Civil War, an organization that was the forerunner of the American Red Cross. The WCTU platform of action included the principle of total abstinence for members and a commitment (a) to introduce temperance education in both Sunday schools and public schools; (b) to continue to use the evangelical methods, mass meetings, and prayer services that had been successful during the Women's Crusades; (c) to urge newspapers to report on their activities; and (d) to distribute literature informing people of their cause.

1874–1879. Under the leadership of Annie Wittenmyer, the primary commitment of the WCTU was to gospel temperance. Wittenmyer contended that the WCTU program should stress personal reform and religious conversion of the drunkard and of the whole liquor industry by moral suasion. Under her leadership the WCTU committed to a "singleness of purpose" that shied away from seeking legislative mandates as the solution to intemperance (Wittenmyer, 1877). This commitment also led Wittenmyer to distance herself and the organization from the women's suffrage movement; she feared possible repercussions for women *in the home*, should they campaign for the right to vote. In 1876 Frances Willard introduced the concept of "home protection" to the WCTU, building on notions of women's traditional roles within the home and the need to defend and protect those roles,

Although Wittenmyer's single-minded goal of abstinence was instrumental in the WCTU's early success, the movement soon widened to embrace a broader set of goals and objectives under the leadership of Willard, chosen as the national secretary at the first convention. Succeeding Wittenmyer as president in 1879, Willard served in that role until her death in 1898 and is recognized as the most influential leader of the women's temperance movement. Some observers of the women's temperance movement may be more familiar with the name of Carrie Nation, who was known for raiding saloons armed with axes and hatchets; however, militant individuals such as Nation constituted a small fringe element of the WCTU. During the latter part of the nineteenth century, the true spirit of the WCTU was embodied in the person of Frances Willard.

1879–1898. While Wittenmyer's primary commitment was to moral suasion, Willard held more radical views on women's rights and industrial practice. Willard pushed the WCTU into broader commitments to other social reforms. Taking up Wittenmyer's narrower concept of "home protection," Willard proposed extending women the right to vote on prohibition issues as a means of further protecting women. The idea of granting women the right to vote based on their natural or political right to do so was *not* palatable to many people, women and men alike. By introducing the suffrage issue under the guise of home protection, Willard introduced the right-to-vote issue within the WCTU with less opposition than if she had sought solely to address women's suffrage.

As president, Willard emphasized organization at the local level, establishing the mass base necessary for effective action. By 1880 the WCTU easily outstripped other women's organizations in both size and importance. Ruth Bordin (1981) estimates that there were 1,200 local unions with 27,000 WCTU members by the time Willard became president. From 1882 to 1902 the WCTU was able to establish laws in every state compelling temperance education in schools, according to Joseph R. Gusfield (1986, p. 86).

Under Willard's leadership, the WCTU continued many of the programs that Wittenmyer had begun. The push for abstinence from alcoholic beverages typified the movement's goals. The WCTU of the 1880s, however, also departed from its roots, evolving from a temperance praying society to an activist organization. Whereas Wittenmyer sought change through moral suasion, Willard saw the advantages of political solutions to the problems caused by intemperance as well as the problems facing women. She supported federal constitutional prohibition as the most effective way to deal with alcohol abuse, endorsing the temperance ballot for women as the surest way to achieve prohibition.

By the mid-1880s the WCTU had expanded to every U.S. state and territory, and its platform had undergone similar expansion. Willard adopted the slogan "Do Everything" to describe the expanded activities of the WCTU under her guidance; initially, she had coined this phrase to depict the lengths to which she was willing to go to support the prohibition cause. The WCTU was internally organized into departments that illustrate the scope of activities: the Department of Scientific Temperance Instruction provided the first antidrug education and prevention programs in schools; the Department for Temperance Work among Negroes and Foreigners connected temperance to immigration, labor, and civil rights issues; and the Department of Health and Hygiene educated women about the need for exercise, comfortable dress, and proper diet (Epstein, 1981, p. 124).

The membership of the WCTU in the early 1890s grew to an estimated 150,000 dues-paying members, with an additional 150,000 in affiliated groups. From its original base among white, middle-class women, the WCTU reached out to women of all social classes and minority groups. The growing influence of the WCTU was evident in the passage of several state prohibition laws in the 1880s as well as in the growing support for a federal constitutional prohibition of liquor.

Although the number of women involved in the WCTU numbered approximately 1.5 million in the early twentieth century, the organization had begun to lose its power and importance. Most notably, Willard became less visible in the years preceding her death, and conflicts arose among other leaders as to the organization's proper direction. When older leaders withdrew from active participation, fewer young women replaced them. However, the WCTU remained dominant in the content of school-based anti-alcohol education programs and textbooks well into the twentieth century (Gusfield, 1986, p. 86, n. 44).

1898–2000s. Other prominent organizations endorsed women's rights and/or prohibition in the early twentieth century as membership in the WCTU slowly dwindled. Following Willard's death in 1898, the WCTU returned to a single-issue approach, focusing solely on prohibition. However, it was not until the growth of the Anti-Saloon League (established 1896) that national prohibition was realized. The Eighteenth Amendment to the U.S. Constitution was proposed and sent to the states on December 18, 1917, and was ratified by three-quarters of the states by January 16, 1919; it became effective January 16, 1920, prohibiting the manufacture, sale, or transportation of intoxicating liquors, for beverage purposes. During the 1920s the enforcement of prohibition was almost impossible in the face of pressure from the alcohol-beverage industry and because Americans would not easily give up drinking. The Repeal of Prohibition culminated in the Twenty-first Amendment to the U.S. Constitution; it was proposed and sent to the states February 20, 1933, and was ratified December 5, 1933.

Small groups of WCTU members can still be found in, for the most part, rural areas of the United States. Based in Evanston, Illinois, the organization can be considered among the forerunners of the "abstinence-only" movement, the "Just Say No" campaigns of the Reagan era, and other attempts to persuade more Americans to pledge abstinence.

BIBLIOGRAPHY

Aaron, P., & Musto, D. (1981). Temperance and prohibition in America: A historical overview. In M. H. Moore & D. R. Gerstein (Eds.), *Alcohol and public policy*. Washington, DC: National Academy Press.

Blocker, J. S. (1985). *"Give to the winds thy fears": The women's temperance crusade, 1873–1874*. Westport, CT: Greenwood Press.

Bordin, R. (1986). *Frances Willard: A biography*. Chapel Hill: University of North Carolina Press.

Bordin, R. (1981). *Woman and temperance: The quest for power and liberty, 1873–1900*. Philadelphia: Temple University Press.

Chavigny, K. A. (2004). Reforming drunkards in nineteenth-century America. In S. W. Tracy & C. J. Acker (Eds.), *Altering American consciousness: The history of alcohol and drug use in the United States, 1800–2000*. Amherst and Boston: University of Massachusetts Press.

Epstein, B. L. (1981). *The politics of domesticity: Women, evangelism, and temperance in nineteenth-century America*. Middletown, CT: Wesleyan University Press.

Gusfield, J. R. (1986). *Symbolic crusade: Status politics and the American temperance movement*. (2nd ed.). Urbana and Chicago: University of Illinois Press.

Lender, M. E., & Martin, J. K. (1982). *Drinking in America: A history*. New York: Free Press.

Levine, H. G. (1984). The alcohol problem in America: From temperance to alcoholism. *British Journal of Addiction, 79*, 109–119.

Murdock, C.G. (1998). *Domesticating drink: Women, men, and alcohol in America, 1870–1940*. Baltimore and London: Johns Hopkins University Press.

White, W. L. (1998). *Slaying the dragon: The history of addiction treatment and recovery in America*. Bloomington, IL: Chestnut Hill Health Systems/Lighthouse Institute.

Wittenmyer, A. (1877). Presidential address. *Annual Report of the National Woman's Christian Temperance Union*, 12–13.

GARY BENNETT
REVISED BY NANCY D. CAMPBELL (2009)

WOMEN AND SUBSTANCE ABUSE.

Each year 9 million women in the United States use illicit drugs. Another 3.7 million women use prescription drugs in non-prescribed ways. Gender differences in the prevalence of substance abuse reflect a combination of social, cultural, economic, and neurobiological differences. Women use the same psychoactive substances as men, but women use drugs in ways that lead them to experience different neurochemical and physiological effects than do their male counterparts. Unlike men, women's perceptions of well-being increase after they ingest alcohol, nicotine or tobacco, and cocaine, according to James A. Fallon et al. (2005) and Elinore McCance-Katz et al. (2005).

Historically, women have been differentially involved with alcohol, tobacco, illegal drugs, and prescription drugs. Before the Harrison Narcotic Act of 1914, the typical opiate addict in the United States was a white, middle-aged, middle- or upper-class woman addicted to medically prescribed drugs or nonprescription patent medicines. As changes in medical practice led physicians to cease overprescribing narcotics, David T. Courtwright (2001) notes that this pattern began to decline even before the Harrison Act. Overall levels of opiate use declined dramatically in the early twentieth century, and women were not recruited into the ranks of heroin users at the same rates as men.

Systematic studies of gender-specific differences in the causes and consequences of substance abuse emerged only after the mid-1970s. In the latter decades of the twentieth century, drug use by pregnant and parenting women attracted increasing concern, despite this population comprising but a small part of the overall drug-using population. In the early twenty-first century overall rates of substance abuse remained about twice as high for men (12.3%) as for women (6.3%). However, the rates are similar (8%) in boys and girls ages 12 to 17 years of age (all statistics are from the National Household Survey on Drug Abuse 2006 unless otherwise indicated).

ALCOHOL AND TOBACCO USE

Although surveys of the U.S. population indicate that fewer women drink than men and women who do drink consume less alcohol than men, the gender gap narrowed during the twentieth century. Drinking rates rose slowly after the repeal of Prohibition. By 1940 only 38 percent of adult women drank compared to 64 percent of men; by 1965 consumption rates had increased, with 60 percent of adult women and 77 percent of men drinking (Golden, 2005, p. 44). However, consumption rates say little about problem drinking. Until recently little was known about women's alcoholism, but national surveys under way since the 1970s show that women comprise less than one-third of the estimated 17 million alcohol-abusing or alcohol-dependent individuals in the United States. The 2006 National Household Survey on Drug Abuse (NHSDA) showed 57 percent of men reporting drinking alcoholic beverages in the previous month,

Although some have suggested that social norms regarding male and female drinking may converge, there is little evidence of increased female alcoholism or problem drinking. AP IMAGES

compared with 45 percent of women. The NHSDA defines heavy alcohol use as five or more drinks per day on five or more days in the past month. By this definition men are much more likely than women to be heavy drinkers (approximately 10% and 2%, respectively).

Although some have suggested that social norms regarding male and female drinking may converge, there is little epidemiological evidence of increased female alcoholism or problem drinking. Changing female drinking patterns have resulted more in a reduction in female abstainers than an increase in problem drinkers. The smallest sex differences are found among the youngest cohorts (with 7.9% of boys and 4.3% of girls aged 12 to 20 drinking heavily in 2006). Among adults aged 35 and older, men are eight times as likely as women to be heavy drinkers (8% compared with 1%).

There is evidence of sex-role convergence in tobacco use. In 1955, 52 percent of adult men smoked, compared with 25 percent of adult women. Since then, the proportion of men who smoke has decreased markedly while rates among women have held fairly steady. Among those aged 12 or older in 2006, 27 percent of men and 22 percent of women were current smokers. Among youths aged 12 to 17, girls and boys differ little in rates of current cigarette use (10% of girls and boys). Overall adolescent smoking has declined due to increased perceptions of health risks associated with smoking (NHSDA, 2006).

Tobacco companies have targeted advertising to make smoking attractive to young women. Once they begin smoking, women typically have a harder time quitting. Smoking-related health problems such as lung cancer have increased among women since the 1970s. Lung cancer now surpasses breast cancer as the leading cause of cancer deaths among women.

ILLICIT DRUG USE

Approximately 40 percent of women report using an illicit drug at some point in their lives and, in 2006, 6.2 percent of women aged 12 and older reported using one in the past month. In 2004 approximately 14 percent of those arrested for drug-abuse violations were female. Males, however, are more likely than females to be arrested for possessing or selling illicit drugs. From 2001 to 2005 women's arrest rates for drug abuse violations increased dramatically despite the fact that males are more likely than females to use illicit drugs. Gender differences are smallest among adolescents aged 12 to 17 and among adults aged 35 and older and largest among young adults aged 18 to 34, the age range in which illicit-drug use is most prevalent. Among both men and women, marijuana is the most frequently used illicit substance, with more than 35 percent of high school females reporting use in 2005.

Early research on illicit drug-using women tended to focus on sexuality, pregnancy, or fetal and neonatal development. This trend was pronounced in the 1980s when women's use of cocaine and crack-cocaine was on the rise (Murphy & Rosenbaum, 1999, p. 7). Since then cocaine use has decreased, and sex differences in regular cocaine use are small even in young adults, among whom cocaine use is most common. Crack-cocaine posed a specific problem for women, bringing them into the criminal justice system in ever-greater numbers. Between 1980 and 1992 the number of women in prison tripled due largely to patterns of drug arrests and sentencing (Kandall, 1996, p. 252).

Although heroin use became quite rare in the United States in the last three decades of the twentieth century, media attention to the problems of women and crack-cocaine overshadowed the fact that women continued to struggle with opiates. By the early 1990s women comprised nearly one-third of patients in methadone clinics in New York state (Kandall, 1996).

PRESCRIPTION DRUG ABUSE

In the 1970s feminist scholars drew attention to the overmedication of women with psychoactive drugs. These early critiques derived from content analyses of sex-stereotyped advertisements in medical publications. Most ads for prescription psychoactives depicted woman patients, and survey research on representative populations confirmed that women were using more of these drugs than were men. Concerned that psychoactive drugs were being used as a subtle form of social control, critics charged that physicians were prescribing tranquilizers and antidepressants to alleviate women's normal life transitions, such as menopause, college attendance, or empty-nest syndrome, as well as women's discontent with limiting and inequitable sex roles.

Some prescription psychoactives have dangerous long-term side effects and a high potential for producing dependency. Further, since women also use more over-the-counter medications and women's alcohol problems often go undetected by physicians, women who use prescription psychoactive drugs are vulnerable to adverse drug interactions. Alcohol in combination with other substances is the most frequent cause of emergency-room episodes in the Drug Abuse Warning Network (DAWN) system. Although women drink less and are less likely to use illicit drugs, they have equaled or exceeded men in drug-related emergency room episodes since the mid-1980s due to tranquilizer, sedative, and analgesic use.

Abuse of prescription painkillers such as Vicodin and OxyContin and stimulants such as Ritalin increased in the 1990s as these drugs became more available through Internet sales and diversion to the illegal market. Although men and women use prescription drugs nonmedically at similar rates, women are more likely than men to suffer from co-morbidities that accompany substance abuse such as depression, anxiety, and trauma. Girls and women report using drugs to cope with stressful life events, and doctors are more likely to prescribe narcotics and anti-anxiety medications for females than males in conjunction with these events. In the youngest study group, girls ages 12 to 17 are more likely than boys to abuse psychotherapeutic drugs, including stimulants (NSDUH, 2006).

GENDER DIFFERENCES IN SUBSTANCE ABUSE

Studies of adolescents generally find similar correlates of substance abuse among both boys and girls. The strongest predictor of adolescent alcohol, tobacco, and illicit-drug use is having friends who use alcohol, tobacco, and drugs. Other factors that predict substance abuse by peers include parental substance abuse, poor academic performance, and low commitment to educational pursuits.

Researchers have identified some gender differences in the development of alcohol and drug problems. Relationship issues are salient in the etiology of female substance abuse. Alcoholism in women is more strongly correlated with family history than is alcoholism in men. Girls and women are likely to be introduced to alcohol or illicit drugs by a boyfriend or spouse, and female alcohol or drug dependence may develop in the context of such relationships.

Alcohol and drug abuse are more often associated with depression in girls and women than in males. It is unclear whether depression is a cause or a consequence of substance abuse among girls and women. Women in treatment for substance abuse are more likely than men to say their problem with drinking or drug abuse developed after a life crisis, trauma, or tragedy such as the death of a family member. A sizable proportion of women in treatment report histories of sexual abuse.

Some believe these different attributions and recollections reflect genuine sex differences in the etiology or causation of substance abuse. Others caution that the greater stigma attached to female substance abuse may motivate women to develop socially acceptable explanations, such as personal crises and emotional difficulties, for their problem drinking or drug use. The course of problem drinking and drug addiction varies by gender. Women entering treatment for alcoholism or drug abuse tend to have begun heavy drinking or drug use at a later age, on average, compared with men entering treatment. The term *telescoping* has been used to describe women's rapid progression from controlled alcohol or drug use to alcohol and drug dependency.

EFFECT OF SUBSTANCE ABUSE BY GENDER

For many reasons alcohol and drug abuse produce more deleterious social, economic, and health consequences among women than among men. Women metabolize alcohol and drugs differently due to their lower ratio of water to total body weight. When equivalent alcohol is consumed, more alcohol passes into a woman's bloodstream, so women reach higher peak blood alcohol concentrations than men. Liver disease progresses more rapidly in women, and they are more prone to alcohol-related brain damage, exhibiting physical brain abnormalities and cognitive deficits after a shorter drinking history as compared to men. Drugs such as marijuana that are deposited in body fat may have slower clearance rates in women, creating potential cumulative toxicity and adverse drug and alcohol interactions. Such physiological differences are compounded by social settings in which women drink or use drugs that render them vulnerable to violence and/or sexual abuse and hasten the onset of physical health consequences.

Women diagnosed as alcoholic have very high mortality rates relative to both the general population of women and to alcoholic men. Although deaths due to drugs other than alcohol and tobacco are relatively uncommon among women, overdose death rates among women began to climb from 1999 to 2004. Nevertheless, men remain twice as likely to die from overdoses of sedatives, prescription painkillers, and illicit narcotics such as heroin. According to the Centers for Disease Control, accidental drug overdose ranks just below traffic fatalities as the leading cause of preventable deaths in the United States

Social and biological factors place women at risk for contracting HIV, the virus that causes AIDS via infected blood and semen. Social practices like sharing needles or having sexual relations with intravenous (IV) drug users places both men and women at risk, although there is some evidence for women's greater biological vulnerability for contracting AIDS during any given sexual encounter. Most AIDS cases have resulted from transmission of HIV during intimate sexual contact between men who have sex with men; between 2001 and 2004 only 17 percent of all AIDS cases involved IV drug use as a route of transmission. When women contract AIDS, the most common route of transmission is through their own IV drug use or sexual contact with an IV-drug-using partner. Racial and ethnic minorities have been disproportionately affected by HIV/AIDS. In 2004 AIDS case rates were seven times higher among African American men than among white men and 21 times higher among African American women than among white women (Centers for Disease Control and Prevention, 2007).

Women's social roles as mothers and their reproductive functions increase alcohol- and drug-related health risks to children and fetuses. Alcohol, tobacco smoking, and drug abuse are associated with female reproductive disorders including breast cancer, amenorrhea, failure to ovulate, atrophy of the ovaries, miscarriage, low birth weight, and early menopause. Although men also experience reproductive and sexual difficulties as a result of alcohol and drug abuse, including erectile dysfunction, low testosterone levels, testicular atrophy, and diminished sexual interest; little attention has been focused on these problems. Surveys in 2002 and 2004 revealed that 109,000 pregnant women abused pain relievers in the past year. Past-year abuse of legal and illegal stimulants and sedatives/tranquilizers was reported by 32,000 and 56,000 pregnant women, respectively (NSDUH, 2006).

Infants born to women who used alcohol, tobacco, or other drugs during pregnancy can experience numerous health problems, including low birth weight, major congenital malformations, neurological problems, and withdrawal symptoms. Although substance abuse at any time during pregnancy can cause birth defects, rapid cell division in the first weeks of embryonic development means the teratogenic (capable of interfering with fetal development) effects of alcohol and drugs are generally greatest early in pregnancy, before women even realize they are pregnant. Despite the difficulty of establishing criminal intent if substance abuse occurred early in an unintended or unrecognized pregnancy, some state legislatures and courts have tried to terminate women's parental rights when newborns tested positive for drug or alcohol exposure. Beginning in the 1980s some jurisdictions charged mothers who used alcohol or drugs during pregnancy with child abuse, neglect, or delivery of a controlled substance to a minor. Critics charge that such policies deter women from prenatal care and drug treatment. Disentangling alcohol or drug effects from other adverse conditions such as poverty, poor nutrition, acute or chronic illness, and inadequate prenatal care is difficult. Prenatal drug-use screening raises important questions of fairness because hospitals and clinics serving poor and minority patient populations are more likely to detect prenatal substance abuse despite evidence that substance abuse occurs in all socioeconomic categories.

Gender differences in the effects of substance abuse are the combined product of different social expectations and norms that govern drinking and drug use. Male substance use is less socially controlled—occurring more often in recreational contexts, public places, and all-male settings—whereas female substance use more likely occurs in the home, with a male partner, or under medical auspices. Despite women's greater biological vulnerability and the social stigma associated with female alcohol and drug abuse, men are still more likely to experience problems with social functioning related to heavy drinking and illicit drug use. Women's substance abuse is more strongly associated with intrapsychic problems. Advocates have sought to expand drug treatment for women and create programs that address gender-specific needs.

GENDER AND SUBSTANCE ABUSE TREATMENT

Despite recognition that women alcoholics and drug abusers have gender-specific treatment needs, men outnumber women in drug and alcoholism treatment units. According to the 2006 National Survey on Drug Use and Health, approximately 4 million people (representing 1.6% of the population) in the United States received substance abuse or alcoholism treatment. Women account for approximately 30 percent of treatment admissions; and repeated surveys since the 1970s have demonstrated that women's need for treatment outstrips the quantity of treatment slots available (NSDUH, 2006).

Historically, substance abuse treatment programs have been geared more to the problems and needs of male clients. Recent attention to the history of trauma, including sexual abuse and domestic violence, has emerged in treatment contexts with findings that many women substance abusers have been diagnosed with posttraumatic stress disorder (PTSD). Advocates urge treatment programs to address women's histories of physical and sexual abuse, domestic violence, and relationships with substance-abusing partners.

Among alcoholics and addicts, a greater percentage of women are parents; and among substance-abusing parents, more mothers have child custody than fathers. Concern that they will lose custody remains a major barrier to women seeking substance-abuse treatment. Few residential treatment programs make provisions for child care. Many women are unable to find caregivers for their children if they enter residential treatment and fear permanent loss of custody of their children to foster care. Incarcerated women, who retain custody at much higher levels than their male counterparts, face the dearth of drug treatment in prison as well as social intolerance and stigma.

BIBLIOGRAPHY

Campbell, N. D. (2000). *Using women: Gender, drug policy, and social justice.* New York: Routledge.

Centers for Disease Control and Prevention. (2007). Heightened national response to the AIDs crisis among African-Americans. Atlanta: Center for Disease Control and Prevention.

Courwright, D. T. (2001). *Dark paradise: A history of opiate addiction in America.* Cambridge, MA: Harvard University Press.

Ettorre, E. (1992). *Women and substance use.* New Brunswick, NJ: Rutgers University Press.

Ettorre, E., & Riska, E. (1995). *Gendered moods: Psychotropics and society.* New York: Routledge.

Fallon, J. H., Keator, D. B., Mbogori, J., Taylor, D., & Potkin, S. G. (2005). Gender: A major determinant of brain response to nicotine. *International Journal of Neuropsychopharmacology, 8*(1),17–26.

Golden, J. (2005). *Message in a bottle: The making of fetal alcohol syndrome.* Cambridge, MA: Harvard University Press.

Kandall, S. R. (1996). *Substance and shadow: Women and addiction in the United States.* Cambridge, MA: Harvard University Press.

Mccance-Katz, E. F., Hart, C., Boyarsky, B., Kosten, T., & Jatlow, P. (2005). Gender effects following repeated administration of cocaine and alcohol in humans. *Substance Use & Misuse, 40*(4), 511–528.

Murphy, S., & Rosenbaum, M. (1999). *Pregnant women on drugs: Combating stereotypes and stigma.* New Brunswick, NJ: Rutgers University Press.

National Survey on Drug Use and Health. Available from https://nsduhweb.rti.org/.

Rosenbaum, M. (1981). *Women on heroin.* New Brunswick, NJ: Rutgers University Press.

Smith, W. B., & Weisner, C. (2000). Women and alcohol problems: A critical analysis of the literature and unanswered questions. *Alcohol in Clinical Experimental Research, 24*, 1320–1321.

U.S. Department of Health and Human Services. Substance Abuse and Mental Health Services Administration (SAMHSA). (2008). Drug Abuse Warning Network. Available from http://dawninfo.samhsa.gov/.

U.S. Department of Health and Human Services. Substance Abuse and Mental Health Services Administration

(SAMHSA). (2006). *National Survey on Drug Use and Health.* Available from http://www.oas.samhsa.gov/.

CYNTHIA ROBBINS
REVISED BY REBECCA J. FREY (2001)
NANCY D. CAMPBELL (2009)

WOOD ALCOHOL. *See* **Methanol.**

WORLD HEALTH ORGANIZATION EXPERT COMMITTEE ON DRUG DEPENDENCE.

The World Health Organization (WHO) originated from a proposal at the first United Nations (UN) conference held in San Francisco in 1945 that "a specialized agency be created to deal with all matters related to health." This proposal resulted in a draft WHO constitution signed by sixty-one governments at an international health conference held in New York City in 1946. The constitution was subsequently ratified by the twenty-six member states of the UN and came into force on April 7, 1948. The enormous proposed scope of WHO led to the early concept of Expert Committees, and they have become an essential part of the machinery of the organization. Their function is to give technical advice to WHO. Members of these committees are "appointed by the Director-General, in accordance with regulations established by the Executive Board." The members are chosen for their "abilities and technical experience" with "due regard being paid to adequate geographical distribution." Reports of expert committees can only be published with the authorization of the World Health Assembly or the WHO executive board.

One of the first tasks of the UN and WHO was to take over the regulatory work on addiction-producing drugs that had been initiated and carried out by the League of Nations. Thus, the Expert Committee on Habit-Forming Drugs was established in 1948 to provide expert technical advice to the UN Permanent Central Opium Board and Drug Supervisory Body and the Division of Narcotic Drugs. The first meeting of the expert committee was held January 24–29, 1949, at the Palais des Nations in Geneva, Switzerland, where it continued to meet until the WHO building opened in 1961. The expert committee, in its report on the second session, felt that the expression *habit forming* was no longer appropriate and recommended that the designation of the committee be changed to Expert Committee on Drugs Liable to Produce Addiction. This change was adopted by the WHO executive board at its fifth session and remained until 1964, when it was altered to Expert Committee on Dependence Producing Drugs and finally in 1968 to its present designation, Expert Committee on Drug Dependence.

In its early years, the expert committee reported directly to the director-general of WHO through its own secretary. In 1965 it became part of the Division of Pharmacology and Toxicology. From its inception to 1972, the Secretariat was mainly in the hands of Dr. Hans Halbach. In 1977 the expert committee became part of the Division of Mental Health, under the direction of Dr. Inayat Khan, where it remained until 1990 when a new Programme on Substance Abuse was created.

The early meetings of the expert committee were mainly devoted to the opioids—including the natural products, semisynthetics, and synthetics. The committee responded to notifications on specific compounds by individual nations and made recommendations as to international control, which they communicated to the secretary-general of the UN. Often-recurring discussions began concerning definitions, methods for evaluating dependence liability in animals and humans, the need for accurate epidemiological data concerning the extent of abuse, and public health problems associated with drugs in general and of specific compounds in particular. During this period, the expert committee had an important consultative role in developing a new international drug-control treaty, the result of an international conference held in New York City in January 1961. From this Conference emerged the Single Convention on Narcotic Drugs, 1961. This convention was amended in 1972, again with strong input from the expert committee, and remains the early twenty-first century instrument for international control of opioids, cocaine, and cannabis (marijuana).

The committee's concern for the potential abuse of the newly emerging ataractics (tranquilizing drugs)

Meeting	Considerations
19th meeting, 1972	• Discussed the current status of the epidemiological study of drug dependence
20th meeting, 1973	• Primarily concerned with the topic of prevention • Reviewed the literature
21st meeting, 1977	• Mainly a convention on psychotropic substances • Considered appropriate pharmacological studies in animals and humans • Assessed public health and social problems • Assessed therapeutic usefulness, the problem of chemically generic extensions to the list of scheduled substances and the decision-making process • Recommendations made on international cooperation • Collection of data deemed necessary to make decisions on controlling substances
22nd meeting, 1985	• Implemented new procedures for review of substances approved by the WHO Executive Board • Considered twenty-eight phenethylamines for control • Requested more and better epidemiological data and more consideration of structure-activity relationships, isomeric state and drug metabolism
23rd meeting, 1986	• Reviewed thirty-one barbiturates
24th meeting, 1987	• Rejected control of seven nonbarbiturate sedative hypnotics • Considered the marked increase in the illicit trafficking of secobarbital • Recommended control of a number of fentanyl and meperidine analogs
25th meeting, 1988	• Recommended control of four additional nonbarbiturate sedative hypnotics including methaqualone • Revisited the opioid agonist-antagonist analgesics and recommended that buprenorphine and pentazocine be controlled under Schedule III of the Psychotropic Convention
26th meeting, 1989	• Considered four additional uncontrolled benzodiazepines and recommended control for one
27th meeting, 1990	• Devoted to the scheduling of the benzodiazepines as a class • Recommended that WHO keep diazepam and flunitrazepam under surveillance
28th meeting, 1992	• Recommended requesting the integration of substance misuse treatment services with mental, primary and general health services • Recommended the use of oral methadone • Highlighted the social and financial cost of incarcerating substance users when appropriate treatment services are available
29th meeting, 1994	• Requested that comprehensive guidelines be drawn up by the WHO, detailing the procedures and policies for treating and rehabilitating people with substance abuse issues • Called for a more careful analysis of how governments can reduce demand for drugs
30th meeting, 1996	• Focused on treatment effectiveness • Aimed to gain a greater understanding of the effectiveness of compulsory treatment in comparison to voluntary treatment • Highlighted the need to target resources to fight the spread of Hepatitis B and C through sexual activity and the sharing of needles • Considered classifying benzodiazepines in terms of their misuse potential • Decided to critically review dihydroetorphine, ephedrine, remifentanil and sumatriptan • Noted the marketing of different nicotine preparations such as gum and patches to people who are involved in cessation programs
31st meeting, 1998	• Concerned with the critical review of a number of substances following the thirtieth report of 1998, including dihydroetorphine and remifentanil • Undertook a preliminary review of gamma hydroxybutyric acid (GHB), dimethoxyphenethylammine (2C-B), zolpidem and methylenedioxyphenyl 2 butanamine (MBDB) • Although there was no significant reported abuse of MBDB and zolpidem, the other substances were sent for critical review
32nd meeting, 2000	• Reviewed dimethoxyphenethylammine (2C-B), methylthioampetamine (4MTA), gamma hydroxybutyric acid (GHB), methylenedioxyphenyl 2 butanamine (MBDB), diazepam and zolpidem • Sent amfepramone, amineptine, buprenorphine, carisoprodol, dronabinol, pentazocine, poppy straw and tramadol for preliminary review
33rd meeting, 2002	• Critical review of amfepramone, amineptine, buprenorphine, delta 9 tetrahydrocannabinol (THC) and tramadol • Dronabinol was perceived as having therapeutic uses for people suffering from weight loss due to the effect of the HIV virus and was therefore moved to schedule IV of the1971 Convention
34th meeting, 2006	• Reviewed ketamine, zalepion, zoplicone, butorphanol, oripavine and khat • Requested an educational campaign on the appropriate use of SRIs (serotonin re-uptake inhibitors)

For detailed information, see http://www.who.int/substance_abuse/right_committee/en/index.html

Table 1. Considerations by the World Health Organization Expert Committee on Drug Dependence. ILLUSTRATION BY GGS INFORMATION SERVICES. GALE, CENGAGE LEARNING

began in the mid-1950s. Discussions of the problems created by amphetamines, amphetamine-like drugs, and hallucinogens followed in the 1960s. The difficulties associated with controlling these new heterogeneous groups of drugs under the Single Convention of 1961 became apparent. At its seventeenth meeting in 1969, the committee discussed a draft Protocol on Psychotropic Substances, developed by the UN Commission on Narcotic Drugs, which formalized a classification of psychotropic drugs developed by the expert committee at its sixteenth meeting in 1968. The increasingly serious international public-health problems created by these drugs led the United Nations to hold a conference for the Adoption of a Protocol on Psychotropic Substances in Vienna in February 1971; this resulted in the Convention on Psychotropic Substances, 1971, that the United Nations finally ratified in 1976. One important feature of this convention is that it mandates a WHO assessment of a substance prior to control and states that the WHO "assessments shall be determinative as to medical and scientific matters." This mandate added great responsibility to the functional role of the expert committee.

The expert committee did not meet formally again until 1985. In the interim, however, a number of WHO ad-hoc committees met to consider various aspects of implementing the treaty. In 1980 an extensive review of the Assessment of Public Health and Social Problems Associated with the Use of Psychotropic Drugs was carried out. To assist WHO, the U.S. National Institute on Drug Abuse, in collaboration with the Committee on Problems of Drug Dependence, published a monograph on "Testing Drugs for Physical Dependence Potential and Abuse Liability," which updated a similar WHO report published a decade earlier. A particularly difficult section of the psychotropic convention concerns exempt preparations. This involves thousands of pharmaceutical products and their handling, and had still not been resolved as of 2008, despite three meetings of WHO advisory groups in 1977, 1982, and 1984.

Initially, to handle the necessary WHO functions under the conventions, ad-hoc advisory groups met rather than call formal meetings of the expert committee. The first of these was held in 1978. In 1979 specific compounds were considered under both conventions and the recommendation was made that, in the future, compounds proposed for control under the psychotropic convention be considered by class. In 1980 nine anorectic substances (drugs that cause loss of appetite) were reviewed and recommendations as to control were forwarded. Discussions concerning khat and its active principals—cathine and cathinone—began, and a widespread group of laboratories initiated research. In 1981 the mixed opioid agonist-antagonist drugs were reviewed, and in 1981 and 1982 the benzodiazepines as a class were reviewed, and recommendations for control were sent to the UN. Also during this period a more formal method for review emerged from discussions with the UN Commission on Narcotic Drugs and the WHO executive board. Detailed critical reviews of substances to be considered for control were developed, and the Programme Planning Working Group formed to review these and suggest future classes of compounds for review by the expert committee. Two additional ad hoc advisory committee meetings were held in 1983 and 1984 to consider a variety of individual compounds and exempt preparations.

As a result of structural changes within WHO and the creation of the new Programme on Substance Abuse, in the future the expert committee will change its focus from reviewing substances for control under the international conventions to a broader consideration of the issues of prevention and reduction of demand.

See also **Abuse Liability of Drugs: Testing in Humans.**

BIBLIOGRAPHY

World Health Organization. (1985). *Handbook of resolutions and decisions of the World Health Organization Assembly and the executive board.* (Vols. I and II). Geneva: Author.

World Health Organization. (1988). *W.H.O.: What it is, what it does.* Geneva: Author.

World Health Organization. (2008). *About WHO.* Available from http://www.who.int/.

LOUIS HARRIS
REVISED BY DEAN WHITTINGTON (2009)

Z

ZERO TOLERANCE. The phrase *zero tolerance* has come to be associated with government and private employer policies that mandate predetermined consequences or punishments for specific offenses. However, the phrase first became associated with U.S. drug interdiction during the 1980s and 1990s. Most public schools now have zero tolerance policies for firearms and other weapons as well as alcohol, drugs, and tobacco. Zero tolerance policies generally are rigid and can produce results out of proportion to the improper behavior. Nevertheless, the courts have endorsed drug-testing programs that allow employers to enforce zero tolerance policies.

U.S. DRUG CONTROL POLICY

Zero tolerance was a federal drug policy initiated during the War on Drugs campaign of the Reagan and George H. W. Bush administrations (1981–1993). Under this policy, designed to prohibit the transfer of illicit drugs across U.S. borders, no possession, importation, or exportation of illicit drugs was tolerable, and possession of any amount of illicit drugs was subject to civil and criminal sanctions. Zero tolerance was an example of a criminal justice approach to drug control. Under such an approach, drug control is the responsibility of the criminal justice system, and the use of drugs is a criminal act, with legal sanction as the consequence.

Zero tolerance is a *user-focused* strategy of drug control in which law-enforcement agents target illicit drug users rather than dealers or transporters.

The rationale is that users of illicit substances create the demand for drugs and constitute the root cause of the problem. If, therefore, demand for drugs can be curbed by imposing harsh penalties on users, the supply of drugs into the country will slow.

The U.S. Customs Service initiated the zero-tolerance policy in conjunction with the U.S. Attorney's office in San Diego, California, as part of an effort to stop drug trafficking across the U.S.-Mexican border. Individuals in possession of illicit drugs were arrested and charged with both a misdemeanor and a felony offense. Customs Service officials believed the policy to be successful in reducing the flow of drugs across the border and recommended that it be implemented nationwide. Subsequently the National Drug Policy Board, in conjunction with the White House Conference on a Drug-Free America, had all federal drug-enforcement agencies implement zero tolerance in 1988 at all U.S. points of entry.

The policy did not involve enacting new laws or regulations; it only entailed instituting strict interpretation and enforcement of existing laws. In practice it meant that any vehicle—including bicycles, transfer trucks, and yachts—would be confiscated and drivers and passengers arrested if any amount of illicit drugs was discovered. The U.S. Coast Guard and the U.S. Customs Service cracked down on all cases of drug possession on the water and at all borders. If, during the course of their regular patrols and inspections, Coast Guard personnel boarded a vessel and found one marijuana cigarette or even the remnants of a marijuana cigarette, they arrested the individual and seized the boat. Before this policy was instituted, the Coast Guard had either ignored it or issued fines when personal-use quantities of illicit substances were discovered.

Zero tolerance was criticized because federal agencies expended substantial resources to identify individual drug users instead of concentrating those resources on halting the influx of major quantities of drugs into the country for street sale. The policy of seizing boats upon the discovery of trace amounts of drugs was also controversial. Some believed the policy to be an unfair and unusually harsh punishment; seizing a commercial boat that was the sole source of income for an individual or family was denounced as being too severe a penalty for possession of one marijuana cigarette. There were some highly publicized cases of commercial fishing boats being seized on scant evidence that the boat owner was responsible for the illicit drugs found.

GENERAL POLICY

The term *zero tolerance* has a broader application than the Reagan-Bush drug interdiction approach. Zero tolerance is a perspective that maintains that any amount of illicit drugs is harmful to the individual and society and that the drug policy should prohibit any and all illicit drug use. According to the contrasting viewpoint, the simple use of drugs is distinguishable from problem drug use and, although absence of all drug use is desirable, government resources would be used more efficiently if they targeted problem users or addressed problems related to or caused by illicit drug use.

Drug testing in the workplace typically uses a zero tolerance approach. In the late 1970s employees challenged these policies in the courts. However, the U.S. Supreme Court, in *New York City Transit Authority v. Beazer*, 440 U.S. 568, 99 S.Ct. 1355, 59 L.Ed.2d 587 (1979), ruled that a city agency blanket exclusion of persons who regularly use narcotic drugs does not violate the Equal Protection Clause of the Fourteenth Amendment. This zero-tolerance decision subsequently was extended to various employment situations. By 2000 many employers routinely required a drug test as part of the employee hiring process. Applicants who fail the test usually are not hired because employers use a zero-tolerance drug policy.

Zero-tolerance policies have become a standard part of U.S. public schools. With the increase in serious and fatal school violence since the 1990s, zero tolerance weapons policies have dominated the media coverage, yet zero tolerance drug polices are also part of school rules. Zero tolerance has widespread public support, as it mandates high standards and signifies a tough stance toward drugs and school violence.

Nevertheless, there are many critics of zero-tolerance polices. Critics liken zero tolerance to mandatory minimum sentencing in the criminal justice system. Under both systems there are no exceptions made for individual circumstances; this policy results in punishments that appear excessive, such as a student suspension for bringing aspirin to school without permission.

RANDOM STUDENT DRUG TESTING

Decades of research on substance abuse and dependence have shown that prevention through education and other means is the most effective method of decreasing/eliminating the use of illicit drugs and the misuse of prescription medications. In September 2007 President George W. Bush reiterated his belief that substance abuse among the American youth can be halted through a comprehensive community approach. He stated that programs such as random student drug testing work "to help our Nation's young people make healthy choices throughout their lives and to encourage community- and family-based approaches to the challenges and risks facing today's youth."

Under the auspices of the Office of National Drug Control Policy's *Stopping Drug Use Before It Starts* initiatives, random student drug testing is considered a powerful motivator for students to abstain from drug use. Research has shown that adolescents are at their most vulnerable both to peer pressure and to the long-term damaging effects of drugs. If they can be encouraged to avoid experimenting with drugs, the health benefits are thought to be lifelong. Currently, the most highly abused drug among students is marijuana, closely followed by prescription painkillers (such as OxyContin).

To help schools combat this problem, federal funding is available for random drug testing. Currently, more than 80 school districts across the nation have received grants from the United States

Department of Education to develop, implement, or expand random drug-testing programs in more than 400 schools. Of the roughly one-quarter school districts with random drug testing programs, nearly one-third also had voluntary drug-testing programs available to all students. Nearly three-quarters of the school districts that conduct drug testing also offer substance-abuse treatment programs, either within the school physical or mental health system or by referral to allied community providers.

The U.S. Department of Education has a three-fold goal: to prevent substance use and abuse entirely; to identify students who are at an early stage in their substance abuse and to provide them with resources to stop further use; and to identify students who are either at risk for or who are already substance-dependent and to refer them for appropriate treatment services and programs. In contrast to the traditional zero tolerance programs, the philosophy of the random student drug-testing programs, as administered through the U.S. Department of Education grant funding system, is nonpunitive—its focus is on prevention, early intervention, and appropriate treatment and support.

See also **Drug Interdiction; Operation Intercept; U.S. Government: The Organization of U.S. Drug Policy.**

BIBLIOGRAPHY

Curwin, R. L. & Mendler, A. N. (1999). Zero tolerance for zero tolerance. *Phi Delta Kappan, 81*, 119.

Executive Office of the President of the United States. (2007, February). *National drug control strategy: 2008 annual report.* Washington, DC: The White House.

Executive Office of the President of the United States. (2008, February). *National drug control strategy: FY 2009 budget summary.* Washington, DC: The White House.

Office of National Drug Control Policy, Executive Office of the President. (2008, March). *What works: Effective public health response to drug use.* Washington, DC: Author.

United States Congress. House Committee on Merchant Marine and Fisheries. Subcommittee on Coast Guard and Navigation. (1988). *"Zero Tolerance" drug policy and confiscation of property: Hearing before the Subcommittee on Coast Guard and Navigation of the Committee on Merchant Marine and Fisheries* (House of Representatives, 100th Congress, 2nd session). Washington, DC: U.S. Government Printing Office.

AMY WINDHAM
REVISED BY FREDERICK K. GRITTNER (2001)
PAMELA V. MICHAELS (2009)

INDEX

This index is sorted word-by-word. Boldface page locators refer to the main entry on the subject. Italicized page locators refer to illustrations, figures, and tables.

Index created by Laurie Andriot

G

H

O

Oxycontin, **3:193**
Canada, 1:269
pain relief, 3:200
pharmacokinetics, 3:225–226
prescription drug abuse, 3:265
Oxymorphone, **3:193–194**, *194*, 226

P

Package warnings, 2:357
PAGAD (People Against Gangsterism
and Drugs), 4:50
Pain, chronic, **1:304–306**
Pain perception research, 3:351
Pain relief drugs, **3:195–196,
196–201**, *199*
prescription drug abuse, 3:265
women, 4:311
Pakistan, 1:446, **2:269–274**
Pamelor. *See* Nortriptyline
PAMs (pulmonary alveolar macro-
phages), 1:372–373
Panama, 2:167
Pancreas, 1:353, 401
Panic disorders, 1:219, 390–391
Papaver somniferum, 1:331,
3:201–202, 3:255
Paracelsus, 2:352
Paracrine communication, 3:128
Paradoxical responses, 1:224
Paramilitary groups, 1:343
Paranoia
alcohol abuse and alcoholism, 1:363
amphetamines, 1:150
freebasing, 2:177
Paraphernalia laws, 2:357, **3:202–204,**
203, 205, 206
Paraquat, 3:205
Parcelsus, 3:179
Paregoric, 2:353, **3:204**, 255
The Parent Movement, **3:205–207**
Parental educational attainment, 3:76
Parenting
adolescent drug use, 1:35
alcohol use disorders risk factor,
2:118–119
conduct disorder, 1:415
drug abusing parents, 1:289
drug dependent parents, 3:263
prevention programs, 3:273–274,
276
Toughlove, 4:133–134
Parents
child abuse and substance abuse,
1:286–291
religion and drug use, 3:331
rights, 4:312

Parents, Peers and Pot (Manatt), 3:205,
206
Parents' Resource Institute for Drug
Education (PRIDE), 3:206
Parke-Davis Company, 1:319
Parker, Charlie, 2:153, 3:89
Parkinson's disease, 2:30, 3:87–88
Paroxetine, 4:137, 204
Partial agonists, 1:177, 219, 3:162
Partners for Recovery (PFR) program,
4:256
Passive smoke. *See* Secondhand smoke
Pastrana, Andrés, 1:343
Pataki, George, 3:434
Patches, nicotine, 3:137, 140,
4:114–115, 185
Patent medicine, 1:319, 416
Pathological gambling. *See* Gambling;
Gambling addiction: assessment
Pathological Gambling Modification:
Yale-Brown Obsessive Compulsive
Scale (PG-YBOCS), 2:189
Pathological intoxication, 2:293
Pathophysiology
cocaine withdrawal, 4:297–298
gambling, 2:184–185
Patient controlled analgesia (PCA),
3:200
Patient Placement Criteria for the
Treatment of Substance-Related
Disorders, 1:145
Patients, physicians as, 3:246
Paul, St.
Pavlov, Ivan, 2:27, 3:352
Pavlovian conditioning model,
1:412–413
Paz Zamora, Jaime, 1:236
PCA (patient controlled analgesia),
3:200
PCP. *See* Phencyclidine (PCP)
Peace pills. *See* Meprobamate
Pedestrian accidents, 1:10
Peer cluster theory, 2:40
Peer groups
adolescent drug use, 1:33
alcohol- and drug-free housing
certification, 1:116, 118–119
childhood behavior and later
substance use, 1:293
influence on substance use, 3:381
religion and drug use, 3:331–332
Students Against Destructive
Decisions (SADD), 4:66–67
Pegylated interferon, 1:382
Pellens, Margaret, 3:187
Pemoline, *3:207*, **207–208**
Penalties. *See* Punishment and penalties
Pentobarbital, 3:234

People Against Gangsterism and Drugs
(PAGAD), 4:50
People's Temple, *1:453*, 454
Pep pills. *See* Amphetamines
Perception, 2:375–376, **4:13–14**
Perceptual release theory of
hallucinations, 2:221
Perchloroethylene, 2:284
Performance effects
amphetamines, 1:152
anabolic steroids, 1:163–168
caffeine, 1:259–260
cocaine, 1:329
Performance Management Process,
4:247
Performance tests, 1:4
Perfusion MRI, 2:262
Peripheral neuropathy, 3:197, 4:197,
198
Perpetuation of drug abuse, 3:341
Perry, Matthew, 2:331
Persia, 3:40–41
Personal development, 3:7
Personal responsibility, 4:4
Personal Responsibility and Work
Opportunity Reconciliation Act,
3:196
Personality
Al-Anon, 1:83
childhood behavior and later
substance use, 1:293, 294
health professionals, drug use among,
3:245
Minnesota Multiphasic Personality
Inventory, 3:59
Personality disorders, **3:208–210**, *209*
codependence, 1:332
comorbidity, 3:411–412
substance use disorders with,
1:391–392
Personality risk factors, **3:407–413**
alcohol use disorders risk factor,
2:119
genetics, 3:399–400
influence on substance use, 3:381
Personality tests, **1:30–32**
Peru, 2:304, **3:210–214**
PET (positron emission tomography),
2:259, 263–264
Peyote, *3:214*, **214–215**, 256
Pfizer, 1:184–185
PFR (Partners for Recovery) program,
4:256
PG-YBOCS (Pathological Gambling
Modification: Yale-Brown
Obsessive Compulsive Scale), 2:189
Pharmaceutical companies,
1:198–200, 3:337

World Health Organization (WHO) *(continued)*
  Framework Convention on Tobacco Control, 2:298
  recreational drug use, 1:19
  smokeless tobacco, 4:108, 127
  tobacco, 4:105, 109
  violence definition, 2:311
  See also International Classification of Diseases
World War I
  Britain, 1:245, 249
  temperance movement, 4:88
World War II
  amphetamine use, 1:148
  amphetamines, 1:154–155
  coca, 1:320
  Japanese opium monopoly, 2:333

Writers, 1:429, 2:153
Wynder, Ernst, 4:104

Y

Yaa-baa, 2:301
Yale Center of Alcohol Studies, 1:138
Yemen, 2:345
YES project, 2:289
York, Phyllis an David, 4:133
Young adults, 3:330–331
Youth. *See* Adolescents
Youth culture, 1:279, 280, 452
Youth League, 4:50

Youth-only prevention programs, 3:274–275
Youth Risk Behavior Surveillance System, 3:419–420

Z

Zeese, Kevin B., 2:76
Zero-order kinetics, 3:228
Zero tolerance, **4:317–319**
  Internet as tool for, 2:308
  Japan, 2:333
  legal regulation, 2:361–362
Zolpidem, 1:219
Zoning laws, 2:72–73
Zyban. *See* Bupropion